Canadian and International Law

Lead Authors

Annice Blair
Kathleen Ryan Elliott

Bonnie Manning
Marcus Mossuto

OXFORD

UNIVERSITY PRESS

1904 ❦ 2004

100 YEARS OF
CANADIAN PUBLISHING

OXFORD
UNIVERSITY PRESS

8 Sampson Mews, Suite 204, Don Mills, Ontario M3C 0H5
www.oupcanada.com

Oxford University Press is a department of the University of Oxford.
It furthers the University's objective of excellence in research, scholarship,
and education by publishing worldwide in

Oxford New York

Auckland Cape Town Dar es Salaam Hong Kong Karachi
Kuala Lumpur Madrid Melbourne Mexico City Nairobi
New Delhi Shanghai Taipei Toronto

With offices in

Argentina Austria Brazil Chile Czech Republic France Greece
Guatemala Hungary Italy Japan Poland Portugal Singapore
South Korea Switzerland Thailand Turkey Ukraine Vietnam

Oxford is a registered trademark of Oxford University Press
in the UK and in certain other countries

Published in Canada by Oxford University Press

Copyright © Oxford University Press Canada 2004

The moral rights of the author have been asserted

Database right Oxford University Press (maker)

First published 2004

National Library of Canada Cataloguing in Publication Data

Blair, Annice, 1948-
    Canadian and International Law / Annice Blair, Kathleen Ryan Elliott.

Includes bibliographical references and index.
ISBN-13: 978-0-19-5420470   ISBN-10: 0-19-542047-0

    1. Law—Canada. 2. International law. I. Elliott, Kathleen Ryan
II. Title.

KE444.B43 2004   349.71   C2004-901738-1

Printed and bound in the United States
This book is printed on permanent (acid-free) paper. ∞

6 7 8 - 16 15 14

Publisher: Janice Schoening
Managing editor: Monica Schwalbe
Lead developmental and coordinating editor: Tracey MacDonald
Developmental editors: Evelyn Maksimovich, Irene Cox, Jessica Pegis
Copy editors: Karen Kligman, Niki Walker
Production editor: Niki Walker
Photo research and permissions: Maria DeCambra
Cover design: Brett Miller
Text design: VISU TronX

Acknowledgements

Oxford University Press would like to thank the
following dedicated group of reviewers for their valued
contributions to the development of this text:

David B. Buchanan, BA, LLB, Partner, Miller Thomson
LLP

Michael Butler, Northern Secondary School, Toronto
District School Board

James (Sa'ke'j) Youngblood Henderson, Director, Native
Law Centre of Canada, College of Law, University of
Saskatchewan

Marc Keirstead, Secondary Consultant for the York
Catholic District School Board

Mary Jo Morrison, R. S. McLaughlin Collegiate and
Vocational Institute, Durham District School Board

Catherine Nealon, Dr. G. W. Williams Secondary School,
York Region District School Board

Elizabeth Parchment, Principal, Brandon Gate Public
School, Peel District School Board

Cheryl A. Rosenthal, Newtonbrook Secondary School,
Toronto District School Board

Lisa Stalteri, Harold M. Brathwaite Secondary School,
Peel District School Board

John Tidball LLB, of Miller Thomson LLP

Doris M. Townsend, Brookfield High School, Ottawa-
Carleton District School Board

Christine Banjac, student

Rena Parsons, student

David Stewart, student

■ CONTENTS ■

Unit 4 Regulations and Dispute Resolution

◼ F E A T U R E S ◼

Landmark Cases

Asking Key Questions

Shifting Perspectives

Connections

Viewpoints

About this Textbook

> *Education's purpose is to replace an empty mind with an open one.*
>
> –Malcolm Forbes, (1919-1990)
> American publisher and editor

The central theme of this text is the quest to find a balance between the competing concepts of law and justice. There is a constant tension in law between equality and predictability on one hand, and equity and fairness on the other. You will be asked to explore these issues and to develop your own understanding of law and justice in the twenty-first century. You will be given the opportunity to read cases, develop opinions, debate issues, make informed judgments, and challenge your personal views about key areas of Canadian and international law.

This book goes beyond examining the laws themselves and delves into the question of why the laws are as they are. What purposes are laws designed to achieve? How are laws properly enforced? Are the laws just or unjust?

In a democratic society we each accept a certain amount of responsibility for the laws by which we live in our community. We cannot blame the tyrant or the dictator for putting in place laws that are ultimately harmful to certain members of our society. The harmful effects of an unjust law are far-reaching. We continue to deal with the ramifications of the government's treatment of Aboriginal peoples, Japanese Canadians during WWII, and other minority groups. We will in turn be judged by future generations for the laws we permit our legislatures to make on our behalf today. For that reason, as Canadian citizens in a democratic society, and as members of a global community, it is important to know more than *what* the law is; we must also ask,

Why?

Political philosopher Thomas Aquinas (1225-1274) argued that the first precept of law is that good be done and evil avoided. You are tasked with continually developing your critical thinking skills in order to make informed judgements. This text will be your first step in becoming a properly informed citizen who can examine, investigate, research, and challenge assumptions regarding what is "good" and what is "evil," and evaluate how we treat each other in a legal context.

In order to develop your ability to make informed judgments, your critical analysis will be expanded to include such questions as: *What conclusions can you draw from the data?* and *What different viewpoints exist?* You will be asked to speculate on changes in the law, analyze case decisions, and apply a decision to a new set of facts. The text will provide you with many opportunities to develop your critical thinking skills through the use of five distinct text features. These features are summarized below.

Landmark Cases

This feature will give you the opportunity to analyze precedent-setting rulings or other high-profile or Supreme Court cases. You will be asked to use your understanding of the legal issues involved either to apply the precedent to another set of facts or to develop your legal reasoning skills by writing a concurring or dissenting opinion.

Asking Key Questions

All quests for knowledge and understanding begin with a question. Therefore knowing which questions to ask and how to ask them in such a way as to best extend your learning is a valuable skill. In the context of law, the answers may not be as important as your ability to identify the key legal issues in a case.

This feature will provide you with an analysis or particular point of view on an aspect of law. You will then be asked to formulate three meaningful questions that would enable you to clarify the issue and help you make informed judgments.

Shifting Perspectives

Theories of law and justice are often considered from different perspectives. Changing public opinion or societal values on a particular issue related to law may result in changes in the law. In this feature, you will be asked to document changes chronologically, analyze the changes from various perspectives, or speculate as to possible future changes in the law.

Connections

Law influences every aspect of life. This feature will ask you to analyze connections and perceive relationships between law and other areas of study such as genetics, the media, and literature. Questions at the end of these features will help you to examine the connection and comment on its significance to your life.

Viewpoints

This feature will help you develop your debating skills by asking you to challenge the various viewpoints presented. The level of skill required for this feature will increase throughout the text, beginning with mini-debates requiring little research, and moving to formal debates requiring fully prepared and well-researched arguments on differing sides of the issue.

Legal Handbook

In addition to these special features, the text also provides you with a Legal Handbook to help you further develop your skill set. Some of the skills included are specific to the field of law, such as reading case law and preparing case briefs. Other skills can be more broadly applied, such as writing argumentative essays, making oral presentations, and conducting Internet research. The Legal Handbook may be used on its own or in conjunction with the activities in each chapter to help guide your skill development.

A Legal Handbook— Methods of Legal Inquiry

LEARNING EXPECTATIONS

After reading this chapter, you will be able to:

- use research methods appropriately to gather, organize, and synthesize information
- evaluate the credibility of sources
- explain, discuss, and interpret legal issues orally and in writing

FIGURE 1.1   When she was appointed to the Ontario Court of Justice in 1993, Maryka Omatsu became Canada's first woman of Asian heritage to become a judge. Before her appointment to the bench, Omatsu was the Chair of the Ontario Human Rights Board of Inquiry and was counsel and a negotiator for the National Association of Japanese Canadians in their successful claim for compensation from the Canadian government for their internment during World War II. Omatsu has been quoted reciting a judge's saying: "I can't promise you an empty mind, just a fair one."

In your opinion, what are the most important skills and personality traits for a legal professional to have? Explain.

2

CHAPTER CONTENTS

The law requires not only knowledge and the ability to reason or argue vigorously. It demands those other capacities—not so easily categorized or taught—as insight, intuition, wisdom, and courage. In short it is intensely human, touching on everything that is essential in our lives, and quintessential to the liberal arts.

—Neil L. Rudenstine, President, Harvard University

■ INTRODUCTION ■

Studying the law means more than learning a set of rules or legal terms; it includes learning how to use your critical thinking skills to make informed judgments and solve problems. Throughout your law course, you will be asked to think about and analyze the law. You may even be asked to try to "think like a lawyer." What does this mean? Some would say thinking like a lawyer involves using the law to arrive at a logical solution to a problem. You will sometimes be asked to read complex and dense material, but you will be expected to write with clarity and simplicity. You will be required not only to know the law, but also to be able to apply it to a new set of facts. You will be expected to learn a new vocabulary and be able to argue an opponent's view as well as your own. You will be asked to find the right answer but will discover there may not be a "right" answer, only an answer that merely asserts an opinion without support or thoughtfulness or an answer that reflects considered analysis and research and is well argued.

Throughout this course, you will discover that the law deals primarily with people, and one of the interesting aspects of law is the conflict between abstract principles and the very human problems of everyday life. The cases that come before the courts represent the most difficult of these problems to resolve. If they were simple, they would have been settled much sooner. Each side brings to court an equally valid point of view, as you will discover when you begin to analyze legal cases. The law is often imprecise, and sometimes there are no definitive answers. To get the most from the study of law, you should have an open mind, be willing to struggle with legal principles, and provide sound, substantial reasons for your decisions.

This chapter focuses on five areas to provide you with the necessary skills for legal inquiry: (1) Legal Literacy, (2) Understanding Case Law, (3) Legal Research, (4) Detecting Bias, and (5) Communication. This Legal Handbook is provided as a reference guide for you to use as you begin to make informed judgments about the law and its effects on society. Whether you formulate meaningful questions, analyze a case, prepare and present legal arguments, conduct a debate, or engage in legal research, the handbook will enable you to pursue your legal studies with greater confidence and skill. You will also find exemplars relating to many of the research assignments you will be asked to complete during your course.

Legal Literacy

Many disciplines have their own codes, terms, acronyms, and peculiarities. Law is no exception. For most of us, the language of law is both familiar and foreign. It is familiar because it is part of our popular culture—we read books and newspapers and watch television shows and movies based on law and the justice system. On the other hand, law often seems mysterious and complex—Canadian lawyers and judges wear unique gowns that distinguish them from the public, and the courtrooms they occupy are often grandiose and awe-inspiring. In addition, the specialized language they use can seem indecipherable to the unaccustomed ear.

In all aspects of your study of law, you will be asked to use correct legal terminology as much as possible. The study of law is very particular, and the words used are precise. Small variations in interpretations of the words can lead to major differences in legal decisions. You will see that, because of the precision of legal terminology, it

requires skill to summarize legal cases and issues and to identify legal concepts.

All questions and activities in this textbook are designed to help you develop your legal literacy skills. You will be asked to justify and support your opinions using correct legal terminology and informed research and to make inferences based on facts. Many opportunities will be provided for you to extend your legal knowledge, think and communicate about the law, and apply the principles of law to other cases.

Discovering Legal Vocabulary

The study of law can be intimidating because it seems to revolve around the learning of a whole new language. Some legal words may look and sound unfamiliar, for example, *audi alterum partem*, *mens rea*, and *stare decisis*. You will recognize other words, such as "judgment," "intent," and "consideration," but may not be familiar with their specific meaning in a legal context. Often

Legal Word or Phrase	Origin	Legal Meaning	Example
actus reus	Latin (means "guilty act")	guilty or criminal act; one of two components needed for a conviction (the other component is *mens rea*—meaning "guilty mind")	Assault is committed when a person intentionally touches another without consent. Proof of physical contact without consent is the *actus reus* of the offence; whether or not it was done "intentionally" is the *mens rea* component.
voir dire	French (means "truth say")	trial within a trial	A *voir dire* is held to determine whether evidence, for example, the testimony of a certain witness, should or should not be admissible in court.

FIGURE 1.2 Sample Legal Dictionary

the meaning of legal terms is critical to your understanding of a case or a statute.

Legal words and phrases are often derived from Latin or French, a fact that can sometimes help you decode their meanings if you are familiar with either language. For example: *rigor mortis* is a Latin term meaning "stiffening of death"; *venue* is a French word meaning "place"—in a legal context, it means "place of holding a trial." Note that legal terms or terms that have a particular legal meaning are in **boldface** throughout your text and are defined in the Glossary at the back of the book.

You may be tempted to gloss over unfamiliar words, but part of your daily class preparation should include looking up and striving to understand the definitions for unfamiliar vocabulary.

Create your own dictionary of legal terms, as in Figure 1.2, and soon you will find it much easier to read and understand legal cases.

Reading Law

You will find the style of writing and the content of law cases, statutes, and reports quite different from most works of fiction. Court opinions are not descriptive text; rather they are factual and can be loaded with legal jargon. It is therefore important that you read efficiently and with concentration. You will soon become more familiar with reading law and be able to develop your own methods of quickly absorbing the information, but the following suggestions will provide you with some initial strategies.

Legal writing is one of those rare creatures, like the rat and the cockroach, that would attract little sympathy even as an endangered species.

—Richard Hyland, in
A Defense of Legal Writing, 1986

Strategies for Reading Law

1. Preview

Skim over the piece to familiarize yourself with its subject. If you are reading a case, look for clues to identify the most important pieces of information. For example, the word "Held" usually precedes the decision, and phrases such as "It is important..." often signal the most relevant facts.

Read the **dissent** (opposing opinion) if there is one. Cases often begin with a short synopsis of the situation and conclude with a summary of the reasons for the court's decision. Read those first.

2. Formulate Questions

Formulate your own questions about the case or report based on your preview.

3. Take Notes

Read the case or report more thoroughly this time. Take notes and try to find answers to the questions you raised earlier.

4. Review

Review your notes and reread the case carefully looking for common threads. For example, in the *Murdock v. Richards* case on page 14, you would note consistent references to the words "reasonable" and "excessive." By using these particular words, the judge is making it clear that parents or those who stand in the place of a parent are limited in the punishment they can give to children. Lawyers either defending or prosecuting similar cases will look carefully at the judge's definitions of "reasonable" or "excessive" to try to argue their case.

As you read, jot down any questions that remain unresolved in your mind. Also note the broader issues raised within the reading.

5. Practise

Without reading your notes or referring to the case or report, explain the key issues of the case or report in your own words.

FIGURE 1.3 Lawyers and judges spend a great deal of their time reading cases and other types of documents. Legal writings have a unique style that you will become accustomed to with practice.

CONFIRM YOUR UNDERSTANDING

1. Using a legal dictionary or the Glossary at the back of your text, research and explain the meaning of the following legal terms in your own words:
   a) objective foreseeability
   b) subjective foreseeability
   c) judgment
   d) *obiter dictum*
   e) specific intent
   f) respondent
   g) style of cause
   h) sovereignty
   i) appellant
   j) statute

2. In a local or national newspaper, find three law-related articles. Highlight unfamiliar terms, look up and record their meanings, and then read the articles again.

3. Read the synopsis of the following case using the Strategies for Reading Law provided on pages 5–6 as your guide.
   a) Briefly describe the facts of the case in your own words.
   b) Identify the crucial question raised in this case.
   c) What other questions would you anticipate in deciding this case?
   d) How would you have decided this case?

CONFIRM YOUR UNDERSTANDING (continued)

e) Was Green guilty of murder? Explain.

R. v. Green & Harrison, [1988] 43 C.C.C. (3d) (B.C.S.C.)

Mr. Green is appealing his conviction of first-degree murder on the grounds that the deceased was already dead when Mr. Green fired two gunshots into the victim, Roche Charles Frie. The evidence shows that three bullets were fired into the head of Mr. Frie. According to medical evidence, any one of the three bullets could, by itself, have killed Mr. Frie. Mr. Harrison fired the first shot, and, sometime later, Mr. Green fired two more shots at Mr. Frie. If Mr. Frie was already dead when the first of these two shots was fired, then Green cannot be convicted of murder. Thus it becomes crucial for the jury to know, as a matter of law, when death can be said to occur.

The definition of "death" is not clear. The Crown argues that the traditional view should be used, namely, that life continues until all vital functions of the human body cease to operate. The medical profession considers a person to be brain-dead when 24 hours of continuous EEG monitoring produces no sign of any brain activity. If the onus were on the Crown to satisfy the jury beyond a reasonable doubt that Mr. Frie was still alive when the accused shot him, such an onus would be impossible to satisfy. Criminal law should, when possible, strive for certainty and simplicity, so if we accept the traditional view of "death," Mr. Frie was alive so long as any of his vital organs continued to operate.

Understanding Case Law

Reading cases will allow you to expand your legal vocabulary and develop your analytical skills. Not only will you be asked to explain what happened in a particular case, but you will also be asked to consider how the law is applied.

As you read in the *R. v. Green & Harrison* case above, Mr. Green was convicted under statute law, namely, the Canadian *Criminal Code*. However, when Mr. Green's lawyer decided to appeal Mr. Green's conviction by challenging the traditional view of "when death occurs," he was instrumental in establishing new case law. The judges in the Green case will likely establish a precedent by their interpretation of this phrase or section of the *Criminal Code*. Subsequently, lawyers either defending or prosecuting a similar case will spend a lot of time comparing or contrasting it to *R. v. Green & Harrison* with a

view to bringing about a favourable decision. Learning how to study cases is one of the most important and interesting legal skills. This part of your Legal Handbook will introduce you to case law.

A **case** is simply the written record of a legal dispute that has proceeded through the courts. The full proceedings of a case are released to the public and recorded in various legal reports, such as *Canadian Criminal Cases* or *Dominion Law Reports*. (See the section on Conducting Law Research on the Internet, p. 23, for further information on case publications.) Criminal cases begin when the **Crown attorney**, on behalf of the Queen (state), files charges against someone who has allegedly committed a crime. The case ends when the accused is either found guilty and sentenced or found innocent and released. If a guilty verdict is reached and the person decides to appeal that decision, then the case ends when the highest court of appeal to which the case is brought either confirms or rejects the original trial decision. **Civil actions** begin when the **plaintiff** files a lawsuit against a **defendant** and end when the court rules either in favour of the plaintiff or the defendant and both parties accept that decision. If one party decides to appeal, then the case ends when the Court of Appeal affirms or rejects the original decision.

Precedent-setting Cases

Cases are important to the study of law because of the doctrine of **stare decisis**, or the rule of precedent. The full legal phrase is *"stare decisis et no quiesta movere,"* which means to stand by precedents and not to disturb settled points. Precedents form the basis of all Canadian court decisions, and once the disputed legal issue has been settled, the precedent must be followed in all subsequent cases that deal with the same issue. Lawyers and other interested parties read cases in order to apply the principle of the law in those cases to a new set of facts. The following hypothetical case illustrates what is meant by the rule of precedent, or *stare decisis*.

> The defendant, M, appealed his conviction of assault with a dangerous weapon. The evidence showed that M was riding his horse on a well-marked trail. B was riding his bike along the same trail in the opposite direction. As B rounded the bend in the trail, he startled M's horse, causing the horse to throw M to the ground. B immediately went to help M, but M, who was very angry, thrashed him with his riding crop, causing B serious injury. A riding crop, which is about 45 cm in length and made of braided leather, is used by a rider to control a horse. M was convicted at trial of assault with a dangerous weapon. The defendant appealed the conviction, arguing that the riding crop should not have been considered a "dangerous weapon," as stipulated in the *Criminal Code,* since that is not its main

purpose. The defendant argued that only instruments specifically designed and constructed to cause injury, such as guns or knives, are dangerous weapons under the statute. The defendant contended that the trial judge had erred in refusing to direct the jury on this issue.

The judges of the Court of Appeal decided there was no error:

The conviction is appropriate because although the Code does not specifically refer to a riding crop as "dangerous," the intent of the law is to assume that all instruments used to cause serious harm may be construed as dangerous weapons. Although the defendant's position may have merit, we do not believe it is what the legislation intended. We believe that any independent instrument used that enhances a person's ability to cause serious injury or increases the likelihood that the injury inflicted will be more serious than if inflicted without a weapon can be considered a dangerous weapon.

FIGURE 1.4   These items were confiscated from passengers by the airport authority in Toronto. What criteria do you think the courts should use to determine what constitutes a "dangerous weapon"?

The trial judge did not make a mistake in law. The responsibility was correctly left to the jury to decide, according to the circumstances, whether the riding crop was used as a weapon.

In the case you just read about, the Court of Appeal has to consider a number of issues, such as M's rights under the *Charter of Rights* not to have his liberty removed except in accordance with the **principles of fundamental justice**. Convicting M of assault with a dangerous weapon is a serious charge and carries a more severe penalty than other assault offences. At the same time, the Court of Appeal must try to inter-

pret the meaning of the *Criminal Code*. For this example, the court might ask: Is it the intent of the *Code* that an item must have been created for a specifically dangerous purpose (e.g., a knife or brass knuckles) in order to be designated as "dangerous"? Or is it how the item is used that renders it dangerous?

The court's statement (shown in italics in the sample case) then becomes a precedent and will be cited by lawyers who represent clients with similar situations. Thus a person who injured another using a golf club or garden spade may, therefore, be convicted of assault with a dangerous weapon.

Confirm Your Understanding

1. Answer the following questions about the case on page 8.
   a) Summarize the key facts of the case.
   b) What is the issue that is being decided upon? Write this issue in question form.
   c) What was the decision at trial?
   d) What was the decision on appeal? Was that the final decision in the case?

2. If a person injured another using his/her teeth or a skilled boxer seriously injured another using his/her bare hands, would the precedent still apply? What points would the courts consider in rendering their decision?

Case Citations

The series of names, numbers, and letters that make up a **case citation** conform to a very specific style so that students of law and those in the legal profession can use it to find the case they are looking for quickly and easily.

A citation begins by indicating the parties involved in the action. These names are referred to as the "**style of cause**." For example, a lawsuit in which Lee sues Selvadurai for negligence would be written as *Lee v. Selvadurai*. If the case involved a criminal charge, the government would be represented by the Crown and would be given the designated letter "R.," which stands for *Rex* or *Regina* depending on whether a king or queen is head of state for Canada at that time.

The style of cause is usually followed by a year date. If the date is shown in square brackets, it indicates the year the case was published.

Rounded parentheses indicate the year in which the case was decided.

The citation then includes a set of numbers and abbreviations to indicate where the published decision can be found. Usually, case decisions are included in a case-reporting series, although they can sometimes also be found on the Internet (see Conducting Law Research on the Internet, p. 23, for more information). The style of this portion of the citation varies according to the case-reporting series or the on-line source. Usually, the particular case report volume is indicated, as well as the series edition number. The citation always indicates the page on which the decision can be found in the reporting series and then gives the name of the court where the decision was rendered.

FIGURE 1.5 Citation styles—these examples show several different citations.

The Appeal Process

When analyzing a case, it is important to be able to determine the verdict at various levels of the trial process, which can be confusing when cases are appealed. The appeal process begins with the **appellant**, the person who is seeking an appeal. In some cases he or she must obtain permission or "leave to appeal" in order to have the case heard at a higher-level court. The **respondent** is the person (or the Crown in a criminal case) against whom the appeal is being launched.

An appeal could be heard if the trial judge made an error on a question of law (i.e., an error was made in excluding evidence) or on a question of fact (i.e., the error was made in analyzing relevant information). The defence and Crown can appeal a trial court decision without having to obtain leave or permission to appeal if the error was made on a question of law. The defence must seek leave to appeal if the error was made on a question of fact or involved both law and fact. The Supreme Court of Canada requires leave to appeal. The reasons for the appeal are often identified in the case as **grounds for appeal**.

There are several options open to the Court of Appeal when deciding upon a request for appeal:

- **Leave to appeal denied**: The Court of Appeal will not hear the case, and the original trial court decision will stand or the decision of the most recent verdict in a court level will stand.
- **Leave to appeal granted**: The Court of Appeal will hear the case, and a new decision will be rendered.

- **New trial ordered**: The Court of Appeal orders that an entirely new trial occur.

When a court decides to hear an appeal, it relies heavily on reviewing the original court transcript. The judge must decide whether he or she agrees with the original trial decision or believes an error was made. The courts use very specific language at the appeal level to indicate whether they agreed with the original trial judge's decision. The two options available to the appeal judges are (1) **appeal dismissed**—the decision of the most recent court that heard the case will stand; or (2) **appeal allowed**—the decision of the previous court is overturned and a new decision is rendered.

Use the following three-step plan when analyzing a case for decisions that have gone through the appeal process to the Supreme Court level.

Step 1: What was the decision at the *original trial*?
Example: The accused was acquitted at trial because his *Charter* rights were violated.
Step 2: What was the decision on *appeal*?
Example: The appeal was dismissed whereby the acquittal at trial stands, or the appeal was allowed and a conviction entered.
Step 3: What was the decision of the *Supreme Court of Canada*?
Example: The appeal was dismissed whereby the most recent verdict from the previous court stands; or the appeal was allowed, the decision of the court of appeal was overturned, and the original trial verdict was upheld.

CONFIRM YOUR UNDERSTANDING

1. Analyze the following case using the three-step appeal process analysis.
   a) What was the decision at trial?
   b) What was the decision on appeal?
   c) What was decision of the Supreme Court of Canada?
   ***R. v. Askov,* [1990] 2 S.C.R. 1199**
   The appellants, Askov, Hussey, Gugliotta, and Melo, were charged with conspiracy to commit extortion in November 1983. Due to adjournments, the preliminary hearing was not held until September 1984. Further delays ensued, and the trial did not take place until September 1986. When the trial did take place, the lawyers for the appellants moved to **stay**, or stop, the proceedings on the grounds that there was a violation of the *Charter*.

Section 11(b) of the *Charter* provides that any person has the right to be tried within a reasonable period of time after being charged with an offence. The trial judge agreed with the motion to stay the proceedings and cited institutional problems for the delay.

The Crown appealed and the Court of Appeal allowed the appeal and directed that the trial proceed. The court considered that there had been no Crown misconduct, that the appellants had not objected to previous adjournments, and that the appellants had not provided any evidence of being prejudiced. The case was appealed to the Supreme Court of Canada, where the appeal was allowed and a stay was directed. The Supreme Court ruled that it is in the interest of fundamental justice to have a trial within a reasonable time. This provision protects the interests of the accused and society. The court indicated that factors such as the length of the delay, the explanation for the delay, waiver, and prejudice to the accused must be taken into consideration in assessing whether the trial has taken place within a reasonable time.

Methods for Conducting Legal Research

When conducting legal research, you will need to organize your material coherently and logically in order to understand information, discover relationships, and ultimately make informed judgments. While you may have been given opportunities in school to create organizers, charts, Venn diagrams, and graphs, there are additional tools that can help you process information. Two research strategies specific to legal inquiry—the Case Study Method and the Legal Quest Research Model—are outlined below.

The Case Study Method

One of the key learning tools in law is the use of the Case Study Method. This method involves reading judgments in decided cases and extracting a principle of law crucial to the court's decision, which can then be applied to other situations.

The Case Study Method consists of three main skills, the first of which is learning how to brief cases. In creating a case brief, you will become familiar with the facts of the case and the legal process the case passed through before the final

FIGURE 1.6   Why do you think it is so important for legal professionals to have top-notch research skills?

verdict was reached. The second skill in the Case Study Method is the ability to analyze a court decision and come to understand the reasons for that decision. Once you have a firm understanding of the facts of the case and the reasons for the verdict, you are ready to begin comparing and contrasting the case to other similar cases, which is the third skill in this research method. These three skills are outlined in the following pages with examples and practice questions to help you master each one.

Creating Case Briefs

Briefing a case is writing a short summary, or **abstract**, of the case in your own words. In a **brief**, the case is broken down into its most basic parts so that it can be more easily compared and contrasted to other situations. This allows the court's reasoning to be exposed for critical analysis. The process of briefing a case is important because, first, it forces you to read the case more carefully in an effort to dig out the essential components. Second, summarizing the case in your own words ensures that you understand and are not merely copying material. Third, and most importantly, making a summary of the significant facts of a case requires skill and judgment. The ability to distinguish pertinent facts from less important information is a good skill for all subjects, but especially for law.

Most case briefs follow a particular format and contain certain key components. (*Note:* Not all briefs have a dissenting opinion, and some include other components such as additional comments by the judge that may not have a direct bearing on the case but are noteworthy nevertheless. Such comments are referred to as *obiter dictum.*)

The following examples illustrate the basic format and main components of a case brief:

Citation

Identify the names of the parties, the place in which the case was heard, and the year. For example: *Murdock v. Richards et al.,* [1954] 1 D.L.R. 766 (N.S.S.C.)

Facts

Decide what is significant in the case, and briefly explain the facts. Present a clear understanding of the flow of events that gave rise to **litigation**, that is, legal action. This would seem the easiest part of the brief to write, but, in fact, it is one of the most difficult. The cases that you will read throughout this textbook have already been edited down from their original length. In actuality, most cases deal with many issues and include many insignificant facts.

Legal Issue(s)

What question(s) must the court answer in order to arrive at its decision? Frame the issue in the form of a question that can be answered yes or no. The question may be framed narrowly or widely, and a case may contain more than one issue. For example, in the *Murdock v. Richards* case (see p. 14), the narrow issue might be: Was the punishment administered to the student reasonable under the circumstances? The wider issue that could be applied to other cases might be: Can parents or teachers apply strictly limited corrective force to children under their care?

Decision

Indicate the decision reached by the majority of the court. The decision is usually easy to find since it follows the word "Held."

Ratio Decidendi

Identify the rule of law used to support or rationalize the judge's argument, that is, the reasoning behind the court's decision. In some instances, the ruling has a significant impact on case law and will be used to guide decisions in future cases. In other instances, the ruling applies to only a specific case.

This section usually begins by naming the judge who read the decision. The judge's last name is given, followed by the abbreviation "J."

Dissent

Identify the arguments of the judge(s) who did not agree with the majority opinion if applicable.

Although the dissenting opinion has no bearing on the actual case, it is important nevertheless to add it to the case brief. The dissenting opinion is often well reasoned because it is a harder task to justify a view that runs contrary to the majority opinion. The dissenting opinion is therefore examined carefully by lawyers because it offers another possible argument. If a decision is close (e.g., 5 to 4), the dissenting judges' opinions will most certainly carry weight in future similar cases.

The following is an example of a case brief. Note that because it is a *civil* case, the plaintiffs are seeking damages.

Landmark CASE

Murdock v. Richards et al., (1954) 1 D.L.R. 766 (N.S.S.C.)

Facts: The defendant teacher had some difficulty in class with one of her pupils, the infant plaintiff. (In civil law, the term "infant" is used to describe anyone under the age of 18.) The defendant caught the plaintiff by her arm or collar and pulled her from her seat. The plaintiff resisted and had to be pulled or pushed toward the front of the room. The plaintiff struck her head against a desk by accident or as a result of the plaintiff's own resistance and not as a result of the act of the defendant. It was alleged that the defendant struck the plaintiff on the palm of the hand with a strap. The defendant agrees that the plaintiff was struck by the defendant but disputes the number of times the plaintiff was struck. There was no conclusive evidence from the witnesses present on the number of strappings. The plaintiff suffered no permanent or serious injuries as a result of being pulled from her seat or from the strappings to the hand.

Section 43 of the *Criminal Code of Canada* allows parents and schoolteachers to use force by way of correction as long as the force does not exceed what is reasonable under the circumstances.

Relief Sought: Damages for assault.

Issue: Was the punishment carried out reasonable or excessive?

Held: For the defendant. Action dismissed with costs.

Ratio Decidendi: (Doull J.) A schoolteacher is entitled to administer reasonable chastisement, including reasonable corporal punishment, to a pupil for breach of regulations. The punishment must not be of a kind likely to injure the child seriously or permanently. Punishment, however, may be excessive and unreasonable even though no serious or permanent injury results. There is a sense in which parents, in sending their children to school, delegate to teachers their authority as far as is necessary for the welfare of the child (known as the delegation theory). Therefore, teachers are entitled to administer reasonable punishment to children. A parent or one who stands in place of a parent may use reasonable force, including corporal punishment, for discipline and control. A schoolteacher has the same authority. Although the delegation theory provides justification for this, it is also the right of the teacher to use reasonable corporal discipline to maintain order in the school.

The following is an example of a criminal case brief and an important precedent-setting case. The decision in R. v. Vaillancourt (1987), 60 C.R. (3d) 298 (S.C.C.) is referred to in many of the cases you will read throughout this text. This case deals with the issue of objective and subjective foreseeability. The following chart will assist you in understanding the difference in these two legal standards (they are also explained in more detail in Chapter 9, p. 279).

Distinguishing Between Objective and Subjective Forseeability

Objective Forseeability	Subjective Forseeability
In cases where more than one person commits an indictable offence, such as a robbery, the courts have always relied on the principle of joint liability. This principle also applies in a case where a murder occurs during an indictable offence. The courts have assumed that even if one person actually commits the murder, the other parties involved *ought to have known* that someone might get hurt. Because of this ruling, many people have been convicted of murder even if they did not actually kill anyone.	In order to convict someone of murder, the Crown must prove that the accused *knew* that harm was going to come to the victim. It is not sufficient to prove that the accused *ought to have known*.

Landmark CASE

R. v. Vaillancourt (1987), 60 C.R. (3d) 298 (S.C.C.)

Facts: The appellant was convicted of murder under s. 230 of the *Criminal Code*, which states:

Culpable homicide is murder where a person causes the death of a human being while committing or attempting to commit... (343) robbery, whether or not the person means to cause death to any human being and whether or not he knows that death is likely to be caused to any human being, if (d) he uses a weapon or has it upon his person (i) during or at the time he commits or attempts to commit the offence, or (ii) during or at the time of his flight after committing or attempting to commit the offence, and the death ensues as a consequence.

The appellant and an accomplice committed an armed robbery in a pool hall.

The appellant was armed with a knife and his accomplice with a gun. During the robbery, the appellant remained near the front of the hall while the accomplice went to the back. The accomplice got into an altercation and shot and killed one of the pool hall's clients. The accomplice managed to escape and has never been found. The appellant was arrested at the scene.

In the course of his testimony, the appellant said that he and his accomplice had agreed to commit this robbery armed only with knives. On the night of the robbery, however, the accomplice arrived with a gun. The appellant said that he insisted that the gun be unloaded. The accomplice removed three bullets from the gun and gave them to the appellant. The appellant placed the bullets in his glove, where they were later found by police. The appellant testified that, at the time of the robbery, he was certain that the gun was unloaded.

Issue: Does s. 230 of the *Criminal Code* violate ss. 7 or 11(d) of the *Canadian Charter* *of Rights and Freedoms*, and should it, therefore, be struck down?

7. Everyone has the right to life, liberty and security of the person and the right not to be deprived thereof except in accordance with the principles of fundamental justice.

11. Any person charged with an offence has the right

d) to be presumed innocent until proven guilty according to law in a fair and public hearing by an independent and impartial tribunal.

Held: The appellant was convicted under s. 230 of the *Criminal Code*. This section is inconsistent with sections 7 and 11(d) of the *Charter* and therefore is of no force or effect. The appellant is entitled to a new trial.

Ratio Decidendi: (Lamer J.) Section 230 of the *Criminal Code* determines that an accused who is an accomplice to a crime in which there is a homicide is guilty of murder whether the accused killed the victim or not. The punishment for murder is the most severe in our society. Since murder is distinguished from manslaughter by only the mental element with respect to death, it is clear that there must be some special mental element with respect to the death before a culpable homicide can be treated as a murder. It is a principle of fundamental justice that a conviction for murder cannot rest

on anything less than proof beyond a reasonable doubt of subjective foresight. The presumption of innocence in s. 11(d) of the *Charter* requires that an accused be presumed innocent until proven guilty beyond a reasonable doubt. Section 230 requires the accused to disprove on a balance of probabilities an essential element of the offence. In the case of a homicide where the penalty is life, an accused must not be deprived of his liberty without adequate proof of intent. It is not enough that the accused ought to have known harm might ensue; the Crown must prove that the accused knew harm would ensue.

Dissent: (McIntyre J.) "There was, in this case, evidence of active participation in the commission of the robbery, the underlying offence. It must be accepted that there is a principle long accepted of joint criminal liability." No principle of fundamental justice is offended if parliament classifies as murder serious criminal conduct involving the commission of a crime of violence that results in the killing of a human being. One who joins a common purpose to commit a serious offence and who knows or ought to know that his accomplice has upon his person a weapon must bear the risk of death. Section 230 of the *Criminal Code* does not violate the principles of fundamental justice and should not be struck down.

CONFIRM YOUR UNDERSTANDING

1. For the *Murdock v. Richards* case:
   a) Identify the parts of the citation in the case.
   b) Identify the precedent.
   c) Write a brief *ratio decidendi* of this case in your own words.
2. What is a dissent and why is it important in law?
3. "It is a principle of fundamental justice that a conviction for murder cannot rest on anything

less than proof beyond a reasonable doubt of subjective foresight." Explain Justice Lamer's meaning in your own words.

4. Compare the reasons behind the *ratio decidendi* and the dissent in *R. v. Vaillancourt*. Briefly sum up the key points in each position. Would you concur or disagree with the majority opinion in this case? Explain.

Analyzing Court Decisions

The judge's job is not an easy one. He or she must always arrive at a well-reasoned decision, no matter how difficult the case. Judges cannot simply say they can't make up their mind, since the appellant, respondents, and society as a whole require a verdict.

In addition, our courts have made it clear that not only is a trial judge expected to make a decision, but he or she must also provide reasons for the decision. In *R. v. Sheppard*, [2002] 1 S.C.R. 869, the case was straightforward. The accused, Mr. Sheppard, had allegedly stolen two windows from a builder to use in the renovation of his own home. He got into some difficulty with his partner, and she informed police of the theft. Mr. Sheppard was convicted at trial. The trial judge did not give any reasons for his decisions and said only, "Having considered all the testimony in this case and reminding myself of the burden on the Crown and the credibility of witnesses, I find the defendant guilty as charged."

The lawyer for the accused appealed, and the Court of Appeal set aside the conviction based on the absence of adequate reasons given by the judge. The appeal judge said, "The delivery of a reasoned decision is inherent in the judge's role.

FIGURE 1.7   Justice Claire L'Heureux-Dubé stands next to a photo of her and her colleagues in the lobby of the Supreme Court of Canada in 2002. She is one of three women on the Supreme Court. Do you feel it is important that women and visible minorities, both men and women, are represented in the legal professions? Why?

It is part of his or her accountability for the discharge of the responsibilities of the office. In its most general sense, the obligation to provide reasons for the decision is owed to the public at large."

There is also an obligation on you, the law student, to provide reasons for your decisions. The following tips will help you accomplish this.

Formulate Your Understanding of a Court Decision

State and Support Your Opinion

Clearly and concisely state which viewpoint you support. If you support the decision of the concurring judges, explain the arguments that informed your opinion. If you agreed with the dissenting judge or judges, indicate the specific reasoning that swayed your decision. Acknowledge arguments of the opposing view that you found particularly strong, and outline the counter-arguments to these to support your view.

Do Not Rush Difficult Decisions

Most cases are difficult. Trial judges could come to one decision on a case, while courts of lower appeal agree to the opposite. Supreme Court justices, in turn, may offer an entirely new interpretation on that same case. When you come across a case that you find particularly difficult to decide, do not rush to judgment.

1. Read the case several times, making sure you completely understand the flow of events and the terminology used. Rewrite the judges' statements in your own words and find explanations for any points you are not sure about.
2. Let the facts of the case rest in your mind for a day or two, if time permits. Mull over each side without drawing any conclusions.
3. Think the case through point by point, and articulate all sides of the argument. You might consider making a chart to list the arguments that you agree and disagree with, as well as those that you are undecided about.
4. Choose the side you believe *best* represents your view. Often you will be faced with making a decision that you do not completely agree with but is still preferable to the alternative view.

CONFIRM YOUR UNDERSTANDING

1. In the *R. v. Sheppard* case you read about on p. 17, the Court of Appeal argued that a judge has an obligation not only to provide a decision, but also to include reasons for his or her decision. However, not all the judges in *R. v. Sheppard* agreed. The dissenting judge said, "It is not an error in law to not give reasons if a case is not complicated or confusing and there is no uncertainty in law. There is no general duty to give reasons." Should there be a legal obligation to provide reasons for the decisions in all cases before the courts? Explain your answer.

2. Analyze the following case and the relevant sections of the *Criminal Code*. Would you allow the appeal? Indicate what factors you would consider in making your decision.

R. v. McGowan (2001), ONSC

Facts: The accused was observed by other motorists operating his snowplow in a dangerous manner. The other motorists also noticed that there was the odour of alcohol on the accused's breath. Police were called, but before they arrived, the accused managed to drive his snowplow home. As the accused was about to enter the house, the police arrived and told the accused to stop. The accused ignored the officers and went inside. An officer knocked on the door, which was opened by the accused's mother. The officer asked the accused to come outside. He refused. The police officer went into the house uninvited for the purpose of continuing his investigation into the possible impaired driving charge. The officer determined that the accused was impaired and placed him under arrest. He was taken to the police station, where he refused to provide a breath sample for analysis. At trial, the accused testified that he had consumed alcohol after he went into his house, just before his arrest, and this was why he appeared intoxicated at the station. He was convicted of impaired driving and refusal to

CONFIRM YOUR UNDERSTANDING (continued)

provide a sample. He appealed on the grounds that the police had no authority to arrest him.

The relevant sections of the *Criminal Code*:

529.3 (1) Without limiting or restricting any power a peace officer may have to enter a dwelling-house under this or any other Act or law, the peace officer may enter the dwelling-house for the purpose of arresting or apprehending a person, without a warrant referred to in section 529 or 529.1 authorizing the entry, if the peace officer has reasonable grounds to believe that the person is present in the dwelling-house, and the conditions for obtaining a warrant under section 529.1 exist but by reason of exigent circumstances it would be impractical to obtain a warrant.

529.4 (3) A peace officer who enters a dwelling-house without a warrant under section 529.3 may not enter the dwelling-house without prior announcement unless the peace officer has, immediately before entering the dwelling-house,

(a) reasonable grounds to suspect that prior announcement of the entry would expose the peace officer or any other person to imminent bodily harm or death; or

(b) reasonable grounds to believe that prior announcement of the entry would result in the imminent loss or imminent destruction of evidence relating to the commission of an indictable offence.

3. Examine the case of *R. v. Proulx* below, and consider the arguments made by the trial judge, the Court of Appeal, and the Supreme Court of Canada. Which of the three decisions would you be most likely to support? What objections would you raise to the arguments you did not support?

In the case of *R. v. Proulx*, [2000] 1 S.C.R. 61, the accused, a newly licensed driver, had been drinking at a party. He drove home on slippery roads weaving in and out of traffic and passing cars without signalling. In attempting to pass a car, he swerved, lost control, side-swiped one vehicle, and crashed into another. The passenger in his car was killed; the driver in the other car was seriously injured. The accused pleaded guilty to one count of dangerous driving causing death and one count of dangerous driving causing bodily harm.

At trial, Proulx was sentenced to 18 months in jail. The judge reasoned that although Proulx was not a danger to the community and didn't need to be deterred from similar future conduct or need rehabilitation, a jail sentence should be imposed to condemn his conduct to the community and to deter others. Proulx appealed the sentence, and the Court of Appeal allowed the appeal and substituted a conditional sentence. The Court of Appeal argued that a conditional sentence would better achieve the restorative objectives of rehabilitation and reparations to the victim and the community. The Crown appealed, and the Supreme Court of Canada reinstated the term of incarceration, arguing that the original trial judge's decision was correct because a trial judge is closer to his or her community and would know better what is or is not acceptable. The judges also argued that where objectives such as condemnation and deterrence are particularly pressing, jail time would generally be the preferred sanction.

Comparing and Contrasting Cases

As mentioned earlier, your goal as a student of law is not just to learn rules, but to understand them and apply them to other problems. One of the principles of law is that like cases should be decided alike. However, no two cases are alike in all respects. It is crucial to be able to recognize what is similar and what is different between cases, as well as which facts are most relevant to a decision. A useful method to help you do this is to create a comparative chart in which you generalize the facts of a couple of similar cases broadly or narrowly to fit your case.

For example, assume that you have a client, Elliott, who is suing Manning to recover damages that resulted when her stereo was stolen by Morrison and sold to Manning. You have found two cases that might be used as precedents. As you read the cases, you will:

- choose facts that are important to the outcome,
- compare the facts of those cases to the facts of your case, and
- explain why the similarities or differences you have identified are important.

Use the following comparison chart as a model.

Comparison Chart

	Client's Situation *Elliott v. Manning*	Case 1 *Smith v. Thomson*	Case 2 *Jones v. Williams*
Fact	Morrison took Elliott's stereo and sold it to Manning.	James took Smith's watch and sold it to Thomson.	Gill took Jones's fur coat and sold it to Williams.
Fact	Morrison took Elliott's stereo as part of a break-in. Manning purchased stereo for fair value and in good faith.	James gave Smith a cheque for watch. Cheque was declared NSF. Thomson purchased watch for fair value and in good faith.	Gill fraudulently misrepresented himself to Jones as Mr. McQuaid, a respectable businessman. Gill (McQuaid) wrote Jones a phony cheque. Williams purchased coat for fair value and in good faith.
Fact	Manning was not aware that stereo was stolen.	Thomson was not aware watch was stolen.	Williams was not aware coat was stolen.
Decision	?	Smith did not recover cost because his intention was to make a contract with James. The watch still belonged to Thomson.	Jones did recover because he did not contract with McQuaid, so goods still belonged to him.

FIGURE 1.8   By looking closely at the decisions the court made in Case 1 and Case 2, you may be able to argue that your case is the same as the one with the favourable outcome, or you may distinguish the difference between your case and the one with the unfavourable outcome.

CONFIRM YOUR UNDERSTANDING

1. Consider the arguments made in Case 1 and Case 2 in the chart above. You are the lawyer acting on behalf of Manning. Based on the decisions made in Case 1 and Case 2, how would you argue that your client should keep the stereo originally owned by Elliott?

The Legal Quest Research Model

In Canada, new laws are created and old ones are modified in response to public opinion, events, and evolving societal values and environmental factors. Therefore, it is important that students of law be able to research current controversial issues and questions *outside* of case law in order to form educated opinions about potential future changes to laws and other legal matters. The mass media, for example, books, magazines and journals, newspapers, the Internet, and broadcast news, are some of the best places to conduct such research. Read the following newspaper article entitled "Polluter must pay, top court agrees." The content of this article is used to show the steps of the Legal Quest Research Model that follows it.

Polluter must pay, top court agrees

Ruling endorses key legal principle
Oil firm ordered to clean depot site

TONDA MACCHARLES
OTTAWA BUREAU

OTTAWA—The country's top court gave strong backing yesterday to the "polluter pays" principle found in almost every environmental law across Canada, saying a healthy environment must be preserved now and for future generations.

The Supreme Court of Canada found Québec's former environment minister Paul Bégin had the power to order Imperial Oil to pay for the cleanup of a fuel depot it had owned near Québec City for more than 50 years—even years after the land had been sold, and later flipped to developers. The unanimous ruling is being hailed as a huge victory by environmentalists.

"The Québec legislation reflects the growing concern on the part of legislatures and of society about the safeguarding of the environment...and the living species inhabiting it," wrote Justice Louis LeBel.

The Québec law and others like it signal an emerging sense "of an environmental debt to humanity and to the world of tomorrow," and give ministers broad powers to act in the public interest, the court found.

The high court rejected arguments by Imperial Oil that governments are in a potential conflict where cleanup orders shield their own treasuries from costs.

The ruling has implications across Canada, environmental advocates said yesterday.

"This decision gives the clear message that ministers of the environment have all the tools they need to aggressively proceed with cleanup orders for some 30,000 contaminated sites in Canada," said Beatrice Olivastri, of Friends of the Earth Canada, which intervened in the appeal through the Sierra Legal Defence Fund.

"This is a ringing endorsement of the polluter-pays principle," said Sierra Legal managing lawyer Jerry DeMarco.

"This is for years to come going to be considered the leading case on pollution law in Canada."

DeMarco pointed to a clear explanation in the judgment of the duty on polluters.

The court said polluters bear "the responsibility for remedying contamination for which they are responsible" and must assume the direct and immediate costs of pollution. They must also "pay more attention to the need to protect ecosystems in the course of their economic activities."

FIGURE 1.9   Was environmental activist Beatrice Olivastri pleased or displeased with the ruling outlined in the article "Polluter must pay, top court agrees"? Explain her take on the judge's decision.

continued

Olivastri said that means commercial and industrial polluters, and governments as well, must heed their duties to safeguard the environment.

Imperial Oil spokesperson Richard O'Farrell said the company is disappointed with the decision but will comply with the cleanup order.

"We believed in our case. We feel we had a view that had merit and it got heard and a decision was made. We will comply."

O'Farrell said he did not think the decision would have far-reaching implications. He said Imperial has a policy for dealing with contaminated sites and has always respected government regulations, but expectations have changed over the years.

The national roundtable on the environment last year estimated there are as many as 30,000 contaminated sites in Canada—often called "brownfields."

With files from Canadian Press, 2003.

Key Components of the Legal Quest Research Model

Resource Selection and Documentation: Select a news article concerning a current legal issue from a newspaper, magazine, or Internet news source. Check the credibility of your source (see "Detecting Bias," p. 25, for more information on this). Reference the article using proper documentation style (see "Citing Sources," p. 31, for more information on how to do this). For example:

The newspaper article was selected from the *Toronto Star* and is titled "Polluter must pay, top court agrees." It is written by Tonda MacCharles of the Ottawa Bureau with additional files from the Canadian Press. The correct citation is as follows:

MacCharles, Tonda. "Polluter Must Pay, Top Court Agrees." *Toronto Star* 31 Oct. 2003: A4.

Summary of the Legal Issue: Identify the area of law you are studying. Summarize the key facts and legal information in the source using your own words. (Use a maximum of two paragraphs.) For example:

Environmental law is the focus area for the research.

Summary: In October 2003, the Supreme Court of Canada held Imperial Oil responsible for the cleanup of a fuel depot it had owned for more than 50 years. Imperial Oil had argued that the former environment minister of Québec, Paul Bégin, did not have the authority to order Imperial Oil to pay for the cleanup and cited conflict of interest as cleanup orders would help to reduce the government's own potential liability costs. The court rejected this argument. In the interest of safeguarding the environment, Imperial was held accountable for its actions.

Identification of Questions and Legal Concepts: Identify three questions you can ask about the legal issues raised in the article, and categorize these questions according to the concepts of law (which are explained in greater detail in Chapter 2):

For example:

Authority: Did the former Québec environment minister have the power to order the fuel depot cleanup?

Justice: Does the principle of "polluter pays" require those who caused the harm to right the wrong?

Ownership: Should the original owner be responsible for an environmental cleanup despite the fact that the land had been sold many times since?

Preparation of a Supported Legal Argument: Develop a one- to two-page informed argument on the legal issues and concepts identified in the original article. Support your argument by finding and documenting other sources, making sure you have assessed their credibility by checking for errors in logic, accuracy, and underlying assumptions.

For the sample article above, you could develop your argument by searching for other articles on the same topic and by reading the original court transcripts of the case. Reviewing the relevant laws and acts concerning environmental cleanup would also inform your argument, as would literature from the environmental organizations mentioned—Friends of the Earth Canada and the Sierra Legal Defence Fund.

Legal Conclusion: Prepare a brief summary of your opinion and the key legal arguments presented in your analysis.

For the sample article provided, you might conclude your argument by speculating on the potential for future lawsuits as a result of the precedent.

Conducting Law Research on the Internet

The Internet can be an extremely useful tool for law-related research. Not only are there sites dedicated to case law, there is also a seemingly endless supply of news articles, scholarly papers, informational sites, and opinion pieces. There is so much information, in fact, that a person could quickly become overwhelmed and end up lost in a maze of connecting links or wading through hundreds of useless document pages for hours. It is also easy, given the wealth of interesting material on the Web, to become sidetracked from the original research topic.

The skills involved with conducting Internet research are learning how to locate what you are looking for as quickly and efficiently as possible and being able to judge the trustworthiness of information you find.

Using Search Engines

Search engines are tools that collect and organize lists of Web sites according to the criteria outlined by the user. Some well-known search engines include <www.google.com>, <www.altavista.com>, and <www.yahoo.com>. Most search engines offer instruction to users on the best methods of filling in their search criteria fields. However, the following tips may help you produce a quality list of results no matter which search engine you use.

• Carefully choose the key words for your search. This can make all the difference

FIGURE 1.10 Why is it important to carefully select and document your sources of information?

Choosing and Bookmarking Sites

Once your search engine presents you with a narrowed-down list of Web sites that match your search criteria, it is time to start sifting through the sites to find the ones best suited to your needs. When choosing the sites to explore, keep in mind that some types of sites are more reliable than others. Anyone with the technical know-how can create and list a personal or commercial Web site; that person need not be an expert in the field he or she is writing about, nor must the person be factually accurate or unbiased in the presentation of information. Official Web sites that are maintained by recognized organizations, governments, or educational institutions are usually more reliable. You can tell which type a Web site is by noting the suffix used in its address:

> **.com** = a commercial site
> **.ca** = a Canadian site
> **.edu** = a site run by an educational institution
> **.gov** = a government site
> **.org** = a site run by a recognized organization

between getting back a very specialized list of quality links and getting a huge list of mostly useless sources. If, after trying several key terms, you are still unsuccessful in finding the information you need, do not give up. Think of words or terms with similar meanings (e.g., decision/verdict), and try again.

- If you end up with a huge list of potential sites, try narrowing your topic by using more detailed key words to limit the number of hits you will receive. Another option is to use the "advanced search," which is available on many search engines.
- Be aware of the fact that you could enter your key word in singular or plural form, or use the singular form followed by an asterisk (which should give you both singular and plural hits).
- Whether you are searching for a person, place, or thing, make sure you spell it correctly.
- Use Boolean search words (AND/OR/NOT) very carefully to get more focused results.
- Some sites contain lists of hotlink connections to other related sites, which you may find very useful.

Even after weeding out the types of sites you are not interested in visiting, you may still have a long list of potentially good addresses to explore. One method of doing this efficiently is to visit a number of promising sites and quickly skim their contents. Then bookmark the best ones in a labelled file. Once you have bookmarked about a half-dozen good sites, go back and explore each one in greater detail until you find the information you want. You can keep the rest of the bookmarks for future reference.

The following is a list of case law sites that you may want to bookmark. Note that because of the fluctuating nature of the Internet, some of these sites may have moved to new addresses. If this is the case, use the name of the organization in a search engine to try to find its new address.

- **www.canlii.org** Canadian Legal Information Institute: This is the main on-line source in Canada for free access to case decisions from each jurisdiction in Canada. It also provides links to statutes and regulations for each jurisdiction.
- **http://canada.justice.gc.ca** Department of Justice Canada: This federal government Web site provides detailed information on justice issues in Canada.
- **www.e-laws.gov.on.ca/** Ontario government: On-line source for Ontario statutes and regulations.
- **www.chrc-ccdp.ca** Canadian Human Rights Commission: This Web site contains information about the commission and human rights issues.
- **www.statcan.ca** Statistics Canada: This Web site provides current statistical data pertaining to justice and crime.

FIGURE 1.11   Due to the proliferation of case law sites on the Internet, much legal research can be conducted from the nearest computer. However, students of law at the university level and professionals working in the field still require the services of law libraries such as the Bora Laskin Library at the University of Toronto for more detailed information and for older cases.

CONFIRM YOUR UNDERSTANDING

1. Select a newspaper article that deals with a law-related issue.
   a) Identify the area of law, and summarize the main facts in one or two paragraphs.
   b) For the article selected, identify three questions you could ask about the legal issues raised.
   c) What is your opinion on the issues outlined above? Generate a thesis statement that could be used as a basis for further research.

2. Why is it important to develop effective Internet legal research skills?
3. Why are government Web sites particularly effective for Internet research?
4. Visit the Canadian Legal Information Institute's Web site at <www.canlii.org>. How would information provided on this Web site assist you with your legal research?

Detecting Bias

"All people are equal before the law." What does this statement mean to you? In an ideal legal system, bias of any sort would not exist, and, therefore, justice would serve everyone equally well. However, we do not live in an ideal world. We are human, and, as such, we have biases. What is important for you, as a student of law, is to not let your biases cloud your thinking and critical reasoning on cases and controversial issues. You must strive to see all sides of an issue to the best of your ability and only then make your choice based on an impartial assessment of the available evidence.

What Is Bias?

> *Men who travel much—commercial salesmen, say—make fine jurors. They're not set in their ways, they're tolerant. Some big businessmen make acceptable jurors; some, especially those with close-set eyes, tight lips and square jaws, don't. They have a pompous disdain for the underdog.*
>
> —Samuel S. Leibowitz, New York trial lawyer (1893–1978)

Bias is demonstrated when a person forms an opinion about something or someone without examining the facts thoroughly and fairly. In law, for example, some people may already be biased toward the guilt of an accused just by seeing that person in the prisoner's box.

Bias usually develops out of our frame of reference—our family, friends, religion, occupation, or experiences. It is for this reason that lawyers are interested in the occupation of potential jury members, for instance, sometimes assuming that members of a particular occupation will be more, or less, favourable to their client. American legal analyst and prosecution lawyer Jeffrey Toobin says that when he first came to the bar, he was told to avoid teachers and social workers because they were too sympathetic. In some American states, citizens ordered to show up for jury duty must fill out forms containing questions dealing with personal matters such as religious beliefs and occupation before they reach the courtroom. In Canada, the questions are first put forward by the prosecution and defence and then approved by the trial judge. Both sides get copies of the written answers (Corelli 1995).

When bias occurs in the justice system, its negative impact affects the whole society. Maryka Omatsu, the first female judge of Japanese descent in Canada, who was profiled at the beginning of this chapter, has discussed racism that existed in the Canadian legal system: "Japanese Canadians came here 115 years ago. For 71 years we were subject to legal

FIGURE 1.12 The role of judge is challenging and demanding in many ways, but it has also been described as edifying. Pictured here is Toronto lawyer Rosalie Abella, who was appointed to the Ontario Family Court Bench in 1976 at the age of 29, making her Canada's youngest (and first Jewish female) judge. In 1992, she was promoted to the Court of Appeal. Is the role of judge a career you might be interested in pursuing someday?

discrimination, denied the right to vote, paid half the hourly wages of whites, and until 1949 were barred from the professions of law, pharmacy, teaching, etc." (Clemens 1994).

Omatsu has also commented on the bias and discrimination faced by women in the legal profession. She believes that female lawyers, for example, have difficulty climbing to positions of power because they come up against a biased attitude that assumes they cannot handle the high-profile, or most serious, cases. Omatsu stated: "The top women in criminal law, like Marlys Edwardh [a Toronto lawyer], all talk about the glass ceiling. The better you are, the more serious cases you do, but the more serious cases don't want women lawyers. Most women leave criminal law after five years" (Clemens 1994).

Bias in Legal Research

When conducting legal research, it is important to recognize and restrain our biases, otherwise we may limit our research to information that reinforces our opinions and ignore research that may provide another view. For example, if you are researching a controversial topic such as gun control, you may already believe that controlling or restricting guns will reduce crime, and you may, unintentionally, seek out information that reinforces your view. The following Bias Analysis Guide will help you recognize and avoid bias in sources of information:

Bias Analysis Guide

Consider the Background

- Who is the author? Is he or she associated with a particular organization that may hold and have expressed a particular view?
- When was the information created? Is the information still relevant? This is especially crucial in legal research because the law can change quickly.
- Is the author writing from personal experience or original documents? Are you provided with actual statistics or the author's interpretation of those statistics?
- Who is the intended audience? Is the information presented intended to shape opinion?

Assess the Information

- Are the words used emotional rather than factual?
- Are facts used to support opinions?
- Has the issue been oversimplified, and have certain facts been left out?

Find Supporting Evidence

- Are proper documentation and footnotes provided?
- Examine the "facts" used in support of the opinion expressed. Can these be corroborated; that is, can the facts be confirmed in more than one source?
- Do the words and arguments seem more subjective than objective? (Objective writing is fact-based, whereas subjective writing is based more on emotions and is influenced by the author's personal views and biases.) If the arguments seem more subjective, it is important to find other sources on the topic to acquire a more balanced perspective.

CONFIRM YOUR UNDERSTANDING

1. Using the Bias Analysis Guide above, complete a bias analysis on the column published in the *Toronto Star* in 2000 on the following page.

2. Choose an editorial or an article from a newspaper or magazine on a legal issue.

Complete a bias analysis using the questions provided in the Bias Analysis Guide above.

3. The use of statistics in an article tends to make the article seem more trustworthy. What questions would you ask to determine the validity of statistics in a legal article?

You don't fight with the police...

ROSIE DIMANNO

The next time I see Constable Mike Hoskin, I'm going to break his...legs.

Is that a threat?

Will the York Region police officer show up on my doorstep eight days from now, after the Christmas weekend has passed, of course, because he's such a nice guy and wouldn't want to cause unnecessary distress over the holiday?

And how many other cops will he have in tow this time? And will he tape our conversation on a micro-cassette recorder whirring silently, surreptitiously, inside his jacket pocket?

Perhaps—if I refuse to step outside my home—he will issue a stern warning, suggest he might come by my workplace instead and arrest me there, this by way of intimidation. Of course, he will need a warrant for that, and never before has Hoskin applied for an arrest warrant, despite 10 years on the job as an officer, just as he'd never before conducted an investigation beyond the requirements of his routine traffic cop duties.

And if my father happened to be visiting (an Italian man of a certain volatile nature; I'm sure a top-drawer legal team could find a few people who've witnessed his temper in the past) and stepped between myself and whichever officer should attempt to put his hand on my arm whilst making that arrest (a symbolic gesture, signifying control)—as my father would undoubtedly do, instinctively, never imagining this would be perceived as a hostile gesture, would somehow provoke a battle royale—would then my father be...shot dead?...

See, I know—from two decades as a reporter—as apparently the Romagnuolo family of Sunderland did not, that in Hoskin's own words: "You don't fight with the police!"

Not under any circumstances. Not even when severely provoked or suckered into it. Which is not a description of what happened once upon a winter's night dreary, at an isolated house northeast of Toronto. Because, in fact, we

will never know what truly transpired on Dec. 28, 1998, between members of the Romagnuolo family and three police officers. Their narratives, delivered over a five-week period in a Whitby courtroom, were so wildly in conflict. And the accused, the officers, they stuck to their guns—you should forgive the expression—at least insofar as they described their own circumstances. Each said they could not relate what was happening with their colleagues at the same time.

Given what boiled down to two general versions of events, however—that of the Romagnuolos (didn't start it) and that of the cops (reacted in self-defence)—the jury opted for the latter.

In the vernacular of the court, Constables Hoskin, Randy Martin and Al Robins walked.

I say they waltzed....

SOURCE: Dimanno, Rosie. "You Don't Fight with the Police...." *Toronto Star* 20 Dec. 2000.

The Importance of Communication in Law

> *There is no display of human ingenuity, wit, and power so fascinating as that made by trained lawyers in the trial of an important case; nowhere else is exhibited such subtlety, acumen, address, eloquence.*
>
> —Mark Twain, in *The Gilded Age* (1873)

As this quotation suggests, one of the most important skills a lawyer can possess is the ability to communicate effectively. Every task that the lawyer performs requires the use of language. A lawyer must be able to argue logically and persuasively in court, write extensively on complex matters, and offer clear advice both orally and in writing. A good lawyer should have the ability to convey his or her meaning in words that reach audiences and sway them to the preferred point of view.

You will be given extensive opportunities to present your ideas, opinions, and arguments orally and in writing throughout this text. In many instances, you will be asked to justify and support those opinions and to think critically about issues. The following sections will offer you guidelines and tips for writing argumentative essays, giving oral presentations, and debating.

Tips for Writing an Argumentative Essay

An argumentative essay requires you to write an answer to a question on a controversial issue. Whatever the topic of your argumentative essay, make sure you focus on the legalities of the issue and not the sociological, economic, or psychological issues. You may have strong views on the issue, but you will be expected to present both sides of the argument equally well. It is a good idea to start by forming the argument against your own views as strongly as possible, and only then construct the other side. It is important that

you express your own view, but your essay must show that you appreciate the strength of the opposing view as well.

One of the criticisms of the language of law is that it has become a form of **legalese**, a language understood only by lawyers but incomprehensible to the rest of us, as the following anecdote on legalese illustrates:

The lawyer thus illustrates the language of his craft: If a man were to give another an orange he would simply say: "Have an orange." But when the transaction is entrusted to a lawyer to be put in writing he writes: "I hereby give and convey to you all and singular, my estate and interests, rights, title, claim and advantages of and in said orange, together with all its rind, juice, pulp and pips. And all rights and advantages therein, to bite, cut, suck and otherwise eat the same or give the same away with or without the rind, skin, juice, pulp or pips, anything hereinbefore or hereinafter or in any other deed or deeds, instrument of whatever nature whatsoever to the contrary in any ways notwithstanding." (Mellinkoff 1973)

When you are analyzing a case, preparing for a mock trial, or writing an argumentative essay for your law teacher, keep in mind that the best legal writing is the simplest. The following checkpoints will help you keep your writing simple but clear.

Make things as simple as possible—but no simpler!
—Albert Einstein, scientist (1879–1955)

1. Choose Your Thesis Carefully

A thesis statement is a clearly worded sentence that expresses the essential idea or viewpoint of your essay. Choose a thesis that you feel can be well argued with sufficient supporting evidence. Thesis statements should be short, concise, and positioned in the opening paragraph of your paper. The following are some examples of good thesis statements:

– Compassionate homicide is not and should not be a legal defence.

– The United Nations is a toothless tiger that has failed in its mandate to save the world from war.

– The *Charter* has been a boon for criminals and a disaster for ordinary citizens.

– All inmates should serve their full sentences; statutory release and parole should be abolished.

– There is no such thing as "victims' rights."

– The jury should be abolished, since it has outlived its usefulness and should go the way of trial by ordeal and trial by combat.

2. Get to Your Point

You should introduce the key points of your thesis early in your essay. Do not leave your reader guessing until the last page what you are arguing. Remind the reader of your thesis throughout the essay. In the summation to a jury, a lawyer consistently reminds the jury of the key reasons why the client is guilty or not guilty.

3. Adopt a Tone

Your intent is to persuade your reader to agree with your thesis. Your tone should be measured and professional. Do not use colloquial language or an emotional style. Foresee and address arguments that might be made in opposition to your thesis.

4. Respect Your Reader

Assume your reader is a reasonably knowledgeable individual who may have some reservations concerning your argument but who has not yet made up his or her mind.

5. Formulate an Outline and Structure

Make an outline of the paper by organizing your various arguments into separate paragraphs. Assign each piece of your research material to its appropriate argument. These paragraphs will form the body of your essay. It is often suggested that the most convincing method is to arrange the body of an essay so that you begin with your strongest argument and end with your second strongest, while the weaker arguments fill out the middle.

6. Revise Your Essay

When you have finished writing the first draft, reread it using the following checklist:

• Is your thesis statement clearly worded, and does it carry through the entire paper including the conclusion?

• Is each of the arguments in the body of the essay fully supported by fact-based evidence?

• Are there any holes in your logic or arguments? That is, are there counter-arguments to your thesis that you failed to address?

• Have you acknowledged all your sources and properly credited them in your bibliography or footnotes?

• Did you proofread your essay to ensure it is grammatically correct and free of spelling errors?

CONFIRM YOUR UNDERSTANDING

1. Thesis statements should reflect a particular point of view. The topics chosen should be controversial; that is, arguments could be made for either side of the issue. The following topics deal with controversial issues. Create two possible thesis statements for each.

a) Euthanasia
b) Victims' rights
c) Drunkenness as a defence for murder
d) Decriminalization of marijuana

2. Write an introductory paragraph for the following thesis statements. You can choose to argue in favour of or against the statements.

a) It is essential that we allow cameras in Canadian courtrooms since all Canadians should be able to see the justice system at work.
b) Lawyers are now so expensive that the average citizen can no longer afford one.
c) The age of criminal responsibility should be returned to seven years as it was under the old *Juvenile Delinquents Act.*
d) Boot camps for young offenders violate their rights under the *Charter.*

Citing Sources

No matter where information comes from, if someone else wrote it and you want to use it, you must credit the original author by citing the source. The two main styles for documenting sources are the Modern Language Association (MLA) and the American Psychological Association (APA). The chart below exemplifies these two styles with some of the different types of sources you might use.

Citation Styles

	MLA	**APA**
In-text Citation	Author's surname and page number in parentheses at the end of the sentence, e.g., (Singh 135)	Author's surname, year of publication, page number in parentheses at the end of the sentence, e.g., (Singh 2001, 135)
Books	Simpson, Jeffrey. *Faultlines: Struggling for a Canadian Vision.* Toronto: HarperCollins, 1993.	Simpson, J. (1993). *Faultlines: Struggling for a Canadian vision.* Toronto: HarperCollins.
Newspapers	Freeze, Colin. "One Year After Bloody Sunday." *The Globe and Mail* 25 October 2003: M5.	Freeze, C. (2003, October 25). One year after bloody Sunday. *The Globe and Mail*, p. M5.
Periodical or Magazine	Gillmor, Don. "The Book Thief." *Toronto Life.* Nov. 2003: 89–98.	Gillmor, D. (2003, November). The book thief. *Toronto Life*, 89–98.
Interview	Chong, Wei, Personal Interview. 31 October 2003.	Chong, Wei. (2003, October 31). Personal Interview.
Internet	*CBC News Online.* Home Page. Updated 1 Nov. 2003. Accessed 1 Nov. 2003 <http://www.cbc.ca>.	*CBC News Online.* Home Page. Updated Nov. 1, 2003. Retrieved Nov. 1, 2003, from http://www.cbc.ca.

FIGURE 1.13 For more detailed information on the MLA and APA styles, see the following: Gibaldi, Joseph. *MLA Handbook for Writers of Research Papers*, 5th ed. New York: Modern Language Association, 1999.
Publication Manual of the American Psychological Association, 4th ed. Washington, DC: APA, 1994.

Delivering an Oral Presentation

Expressing ideas in oral form is likely one of the most useful communication skills that you can develop. In current and future life experiences, you may want to pass on valuable information, answer questions, relate an encounter, or entertain listeners; you might want to honour, persuade, or instruct.

Many people feel nervous about speaking in front of groups. However, the more prepared you are for an oral presentation, the more confident you will likely feel. Preparation involves knowing your topic and becoming familiar with the issues surrounding it.

Whether you are leading a seminar, delivering a lecture, or participating in a group effort, preparation for oral presentations entails the same basic steps: researching the topic, organizing the material logically, rehearsing, and, following the presentation, answering questions and resolving any confusion. The guidelines below will help you with these tasks.

Research Your Topic
As with any research or position paper, you must decide on a topic for your oral presentation and find appropriate sources to gather the facts you need to make your case.

Write Your Script
The structure of your script should be the same as that of an argumentative essay; your thesis should be stated in your opening, followed by a body of supporting evidence, and concluding with a summary of your argument and main points. However, with an oral presentation, you have leeway to be more creative in how you set up these elements. For example, you could begin with a dramatic quotation or a statistic, or by "hooking" your audience with an interesting excerpt from a magazine or newspaper article related to your topic.

After writing your script, transfer its outline, in detailed form with key points, onto cue cards. Ideally you will have most of your presentation committed to memory and should need to refer to these cue cards only occasionally, if at all. However, if you are nervous, you may find reassurance in having them in hand.

Rehearse and Present
Rehearse your script using the technology that you will use for your actual presentation. If you need an overhead projector or PowerPoint equipment, make sure you know how to operate the equipment and practise speaking with it. This will lessen your anxiety about the flow of your presentation. If you have photographs to show, ensure they are big enough and clear enough for the audience to see. If you have handouts for your audience, make sure you have more than enough copies.

Rehearse several times until you feel completely comfortable with the material. Practising in front of a mirror or family or friends may help you to recognize and correct any weak aspects of your presentation style. Time your presentation, and revise it as required to keep within the limits set by your teacher.

Arrive early for your presentation so that you can set up any equipment you plan to use. When it is your turn to present:
- Make sure you stand in a position where everyone can see you.

- Face your audience when you speak, and project clearly and loudly so that even the people at the back can hear.
- Make eye contact with the audience members to engage them in the presentation.
- Smile and show enthusiasm for your topic.

Honing Your Debating Skills

Simply put, a debate is a formal discussion during which two individuals or groups present arguments for and against a particular issue. In this sense, the courtroom is the ultimate theatre of debate. Lawyers for the defence and Crown attorneys put forth their opposing views in hopes of convincing either the judge, the jury, or both to rule in their favour. Having excellent debating skills, therefore, is extremely important for students of law and those in the legal profession.

There are numerous debating opportunities placed throughout this textbook. For example, "Viewpoints"—an issues-based feature found within each unit—presents one or more views on a particular question and then poses a "Be it resolved that" statement to initiate a classroom debate.

The Ontario Student Debating Union describes three types of debating styles on its Web site as follows:

Parliamentary Style Debating: This is a more formal style of debating, similar to that used in the House of Commons. There is a prime minister and second government member on one side and a leader of the opposition and first opposition member on the other. Points of order, personal privilege, and heckling are allowed.

Cross-Examination Style Debating: This type of debating is rather like what happens in a courtroom when each person has had a chance to speak and then each is cross-examined by a lawyer from the other side.

FIGURE 1.14 The courtroom casts lawyers, judges, and juries in the roles of the participants in a cross-examination style debate. In order to convince the judge and/or jury to rule in their favour, lawyers and Crown prosecutors must be able to compose strong logical arguments and be able to communicate those arguments in a confident and convincing manner.

Discussion Style Debating: This style of debating is one of the easier styles to master. It is much like cross-examination style debating, but rather than individual question-and-answer periods, there is one discussion period during which debaters can ask one another questions and get replies. This discussion period is regulated by a moderator.

Once the topic and style of the debate has been decided upon, you may want to use the following generalized steps as a guideline for developing your debating skills.

FIGURE 1.15   Debating skills are useful for a wide range of professions. Politicians such as Prime Minister Paul Martin use their analytical abilities and rhetorical skills on a daily basis to contend in the parliamentary style debates of the House of Commons. What makes this style of debate different from the style used in a court of law? Which style would you prefer? Why?

Debating Guidelines

Roles

The Affirmative and Negative Teams: There are two sides in a debate, the affirmative (or government) and the negative (or opposition). The affirmative team supports the resolution while the negative team opposes it. Each side consists of three speakers. The affirmative team speaks first in the debate, and the negative team has the last say.

Chairperson: You may want to assign one member of the class to be the chairperson. The chairperson sits between the two teams with the aim of controlling the debate and helping the process run smoothly. He or she is responsible for announcing the topic of the debate and introducing each debater before he or she begins to speak.

Timekeeper: The role of the timekeeper is to monitor how long each debater speaks to make sure he or she keeps within the minimum and maximum time allotted.

Judge: There may be one or several judges, but if there is more than one, there should be an odd number. Their role is to decide which team wins the debate. Since your debate will likely take place during class time, you may want to assign the role of judge to all students who are not part of either debating team.

Procedures

The speakers for the two teams take turns presenting their arguments:
The first member of the affirmative team begins by presenting the team's stance. Then he or she briefly outlines what each of the other members will talk about and then presents arguments to support the team's position.

Then the first member of the negative team begins by presenting his or her team's stance. He or she continues by briefly outlining what each of the negative speakers will say and then rebutting a few of the main points of the first affirmative member. The member should end by presenting arguments to support his or her team's position.

When it is your turn to argue a point, keep in mind that you will not win the support of the judge(s) by stating simply that the other side is wrong. You must convincingly explain why the other team is wrong using well-researched arguments supported by facts.

This back-and-forth procedure will continue until all members of each team have spoken or until the chairperson calls the end of the debate. This is the point at which the adjudicator(s) decide(s) the outcome of the debate.

Points to Remember

- Debates can be exciting events, but do not let your emotions get in the way of presenting logical arguments to the best of your skills and knowledge. Whether or not you strongly agree or disagree with the position you are arguing, you should not lose sight of your role in the debate.
- It is also important to make sure your arguments and criticisms are directed toward the other team's arguments and not toward the team members themselves. Debaters should never call names or launch personal attacks.
- Unless it is a parliamentary style debate, do not interrupt or heckle the person speaking.
- When the debate is over and the judge(s) has (have) made a decision, do not argue with the decision. It is more constructive to discuss the debate as a class, particularly why certain arguments were or were not successful. Class members may suggest arguments that were left out during the debate or refute points raised by either team.

CONFIRM YOUR UNDERSTANDING

1. In your own words, explain the importance of communication skills in the practice of law.

2. Choose a newspaper or magazine article that concerns some aspect of Canadian or international law, and give your views on the topic to the class in an oral presentation.

3. Skim through a couple of chapters in this textbook, and choose three topics that you feel would make good issues for debate. Write out the debate topics using "Be it resolved that…" statements.

In Closing

The activities and special features within this text, and within the study of law in general, will require you to engage in the legal inquiry process. For this, you need to be open-minded. You will be asked to consider viewpoints and perspectives that may differ from your own. Be respectful of the opinions and perspectives of others. Tolerance is a valued life skill. When you are developing arguments, work to defend your position strongly and support your view, but also recognize contrary views. Question at all times. Use research methodology and models to produce clear and coherent research, and be sure to document your sources.

The classic image of the isolated thinker is a misleading one; we should not expect to be able to think through all of our 'problems' by ourselves. Rather we should actively develop, supplement and test our ideas in conjunction with others—to put our heads together. (Case and Wright 1997)

Referring frequently to the Legal Handbook of your text will help you strengthen and improve your legal skills. By engaging in the legal inquiry process, you will soon be able to test your ideas against those of your classmates and teacher and further your quest for a better understanding of law and justice.

CHAPTER ACTIVITIES

Extend Your Legal Knowledge

1. Explain the meaning of the following terms associated with a case brief:
   a) *ratio decidendi*
   b) *obiter dictum*
   c) dissent
   d) citation

2. "The rule of law can be wiped out in one misguided, however well-intentioned, generation"—Wm. T. Gossett, President of American Bar Association, 1988.
   What did Gossett mean by this statement? Provide historical examples that support his statement.

3. Read the following brief quote from *R. v. Jobidon* (1991) 66 C.C.C. (3d) 457 (S.C.C.).

   > The Attorney General's reference makes it clear that a conviction of assault will not be barred if "bodily harm is intended and/or caused." Since this test is framed in the alternative, consent could be nullified even in situations where the assailant did not intend to cause the injured person bodily harm but did so inadvertently. In Canada, however, this very broad formulation cannot strictly apply.

   a) Rewrite this statement in your own words.
   b) Why do you think legal judgments are worded so carefully?

Think About the Law

4. Research three different cases, and record the proper citation for each. Select one of the cases, and briefly outline the facts and decision in the case.

5. Using the steps provided in the Legal Quest Research Model, research a current legal issue in the news and prepare a two-page analysis of the news item.

6. Select a specific legal topic or issue, and formulate three meaningful questions that could help to guide your research in learning more about it.

7. As you have observed throughout this chapter, the kinds of cases that come before the courts are difficult. Even judges have difficulty agreeing with one another. In the case that follows, five judges agreed, but four disagreed with the majority. A brief summary of the judges' decision follows this case. You are to assume the role of a tenth judge. Examine the circumstances of the case, the relevant sections of the *Criminal Code,* and the comments from Justice Steele. Summarize the position for the original conviction and the position of the Manitoba Court of Appeal. What arguments would you consider in coming to your own decision in this case? Review the guidelines on case analysis on pages 17–18.

R. v. Fontaine, [2002] MBCA 29

Facts: Darrell Fontaine, 21, deliberately crashed his car into a semi-trailer while being pursued by police on the highway. A female passenger in his car was killed and another passenger was injured. At trial, Fontaine claimed that he had crashed his car because he wanted to attempt suicide. He agreed that he was indifferent as to the probable death of his two female passengers. He claimed he did not think about them at all.

Fontaine was convicted at trial of first-degree murder, two counts of attempted murder, one count of criminal negligence causing death, and one count of criminal negligence causing bodily harm. The trial judge explained to the jury the concept of "transferred malice," which is defined in s. 229(b). This rule holds that a person commits murder if the person intended to kill someone but accidentally killed the wrong person. For example, if J decides to kill A but misses and kills C, the intent to kill someone is there. Such a mistake would not negate the **mens rea**, or the criminal intent. The defence argued there was no transferred intent because the accused intended to kill only himself, and there is no crime of suicide in the *Criminal Code*. Fontaine appealed his conviction based on the *Criminal Code* definition of murder.

229. Culpable homicide is murder
   (a) where the person who causes the death of a human being
      (i) means to cause his death, or
      (ii) means to cause him bodily harm that he knows is likely to cause his death, and is reckless whether death ensues or not;
   (b) where a person, meaning to cause death to a human being or meaning to cause him bodily harm that he knows is likely to cause his death, and being reckless whether death ensues or not, by accident or mistake causes death to another human being; or
   (c) where a person, for an unlawful object, does anything that he knows or ought to know is likely to cause death, and thereby causes death to a human being, notwithstanding that he desires to effect his object without causing death or bodily harm to any human being.

Issue: As suicide is not a criminal offence, can the *mens rea* of suicide be transferred to the crime of murder?

Held: The appeal should be allowed; a new trial ordered.

Ratio Decidendi: (Steele J.) Whereas suicide is legal and murder is illegal, the transfer of intent from one to the other should not necessarily follow. When the *Code* is ambiguous, as s. 229(b) is, on whether it is intended to be limited to killing of another or to include the killing of oneself, the statutory interpretation rule of strict construction must weigh heavily in favour of the accused, which would result in a conclusion that s. 299(b) refers to the killing of another and not the killing of oneself.

Communicate About the Law

8. Prepare a debate on the following issue: Be it resolved that lawyers should no longer be required to wear legal gowns.

9. Choose one of the following topics, and prepare a short oral presentation to the class. Be creative. You may choose to perform a dramatic skit, create a PowerPoint presentation, film a video, or use any other method of presenting your viewpoint.
   a) The use of "legalese"
   b) The skills and qualities that make a good lawyer
   c) TV law versus reality
   d) The impact of women on the legal profession
   e) The use of TV cameras in the courtroom

10. Assume you were one of the judges on the case briefed below. Write a dissenting opinion on this case.

***Campbell v. Acuff-Rose Music,* (1994) 510 US 569**

Facts: In 1964, Roy Orbison and William Dees wrote the song "Oh, Pretty Woman" and sold their rights to it to Acuff-Rose Music, Inc. Acuff-Rose registered the song for copyright protection. On July 5, 1989, the manager of the rap group 2 Live Crew, Luther Campbell, informed Acuff-Rose that the group had written a parody of "Oh, Pretty Woman"; that they would afford all credit for ownership and authorship of the original song to Acuff-Rose, Dees, and Orbison; and that they were willing to pay a fee for the use they wished to make of it. Acuff-Rose refused permission.

In June or July 1989, 2 Live Crew released records, cassette tapes, and compact discs containing the song "Pretty Woman." Almost a year later, after nearly a quarter of a million copies of the recording had been sold, Acuff-Rose sued 2 Live Crew and its record company for copyright infringement.

At the trial, it was held that 2 Live Crew's song made fair use of Dees' and Orbison's original song. Acuff-Rose appealed, and the appellate court reversed the original decision. 2 Live Crew appealed.

Issue(s): Was 2 Live Crew's parody of the original song "fair use"?

Held: Decision for appellant.

Ratio Decidendi: The court outlined four factors under section 107 of the *Copyright Act of 1976*: the purpose and character of the use—whether it was commercial or non-commercial, the nature of the copyright work, the amount and substantiality of the work copied, and the effect of its use on the potential market.

The court reasoned that 2 Live Crew's use of the song for commercial purposes did not deny them the right to claim "fair use." And "parody," like other comments or criticism, may claim fair use. The court also held that the original song did fall within the "protective purpose" of the act. In examining how much of the original song was used, the court held that the parts that 2 Live Crew copied, the opening riff of the original and the first line of the Orbison lyrics, were no more than was necessary. Regarding the effect the new work would have on the potential market of the original, the court said, "It is

more likely that the new work will not affect the market for the original. This is so because the parody and the original usually serve different market functions."

Apply the Law

11. The following case, *Canadian Foundation for Children, Youth, and the Law v. Canada (Attorney General)*, (2002) Docket C34749 ONCA, challenged s. 43 of the *Criminal Code*, which reads:

> 43. Every schoolteacher, parent or person standing in the place of a parent is justified in using force by way of correction toward a pupil, or child, as the case may be, who is under his care, if the force does not exceed what is reasonable under the circumstances.

This is a defence for any parent, surrogate parent, or teacher who may correct a child by using force, which might otherwise be considered a criminal assault. The Canadian Foundation for Children, Youth, and the Law challenged s. 43 of the *Criminal Code,* arguing that it violated a child's constitutional rights to security of person, to be protected against cruel and unusual punishment, and to equality. The Ontario Court of Appeal heard the case.

a) The case of *Murdock v. Richards* (p. 14) deals with a similar issue, although the intent was different. Using the Murdock case as your guide, what do you think the issue would be in this more recent case?

b) After examining the decision and *ratio decidendi* in the Murdock case, do you think the Court of Appeal will strike down s. 43? Explain.

c) If you were one of the judges on the Ontario Court of Appeal, would you strike down s. 43? Explain your decision in the form of a *ratio*.

12. Select a case from an on-line source, a case digest, or a reporting series in a law library, or use a case provided by your teacher. Using the case brief examples on pages 14–16 as a model, prepare the citation, the facts of the case, and the decision.

13. Read the following edited case carefully. The case challenged the validity of s. 213(a) and (d) of the *Criminal Code* and cited the precedent established in *R. v Vaillancourt*.

   a) Using the Comparison Chart on page 20 as your model, prepare a similar chart for the Vaillancourt (see pp. 15–16) and Martineau (see below) cases.

   b) Using *R. v. Vaillancourt* as your model, prepare a case brief for *R. v. Martineau*. Include citation, facts, decision, issue, and *ratio*. (You may wish to read the complete transcripts of both these cases, which are available at www.canlii.org.)

R. v. Martineau (1991), 58 C.C.C. (3d) 353 (S.C.C.)

(Lamer C.J.) This appeal arises as a result of the application to s. 213(a) by the Alberta Court of Appeal of this court's decision in *R. v. Vaillancourt* (1987), 39 C.C.C. (3d) 118 in which s. 213(d) of the *Criminal Code* was declared of no force or effect because it infringed ss. 7 and 11(d) of the *Canadian Charter of Rights and Freedoms* and could not be saved by s. 1 of the *Charter*.

The facts of this case may be briefly summarized as follows: On February 7, 1985, the bodies of James McLean and Ann McLean were found in the bathroom of their home, a trailer, in Valleyview, Alberta. A police investigation led to Martineau and one Patrick Tremblay. Martineau, who was 15 at the time, was charged with both murders and was transferred to adult court. Martineau was tried by a judge and jury starting on September 12, 1985. Thirty witnesses gave evidence, including the accused. The evidence revealed that Martineau and his friend, Tremblay, had set out one evening armed with a pellet pistol and a rifle. Martineau testified that he knew that they were going to commit a crime, but he thought it would be a

"B and E." After robbing the trailer and its occupants, Martineau's friend shot and killed the McLeans. The evidence showed Mr. McLean was shot after having received a protracted beating prior to death. Mrs. McLean returned home during the robbery, and Tremblay told Martineau to put a blanket over Mrs. McLean's head. There was evidence that Martineau said, "Lady, say your prayers," before Mrs. McLean was shot. Martineau and Tremblay were both wearing stocking masks, and Martineau asked Tremblay why he had shot them. Tremblay answered, "They saw our faces." They drove James McLean's car to Grand Prairie, where they abandoned it.

The respondent was convicted of second-degree murder. The trial judge charged the jury on s. 213(a) and (d) of the *Criminal Code*: "Section 213(a) of the *Code* defines culpable homicide as murder where a person causes the death of a human being while committing or attempting to commit a range of listed offences, whether or not the person means to cause death or whether or not he or she knows that death is likely to ensue. The introductory paragraph of the section, therefore, expressly removes from the Crown the burden of proving beyond a reasonable doubt that the accused had subjective foresight of death. I am of the view that a special mental element with respect to death is necessary before a culpable homicide can be treated as murder. The special mental element gives rise to moral blameworthiness that justifies the stigma and punishment attaching to a murder conviction. For all the foregoing reasons, and for the reasons stated in Vaillancourt, I conclude that it is a principle of fundamental justice that a conviction for murder cannot rest on anything less than proof beyond a reasonable doubt of subjective foresight of death. Therefore, since s. 213 of the *Criminal Code* expressly eliminates the requirement for proof of subjective foresight, it infringes ss. 7 and 11(d) of the *Charter*."

BIBLIOGRAPHY

Canadian Legal Information Institute. Accessed Nov. 2003 <www.canlii.org>.

Case, Roland, and Ian Wright. "Taking Seriously the Teaching of Critical Thinking." *Canadian Social Studies* 32.1 (Fall 1997): 12–19.

Clemens, Micki. "Becoming a Judge Vindicates Her Father." *Justice.* The Issues Collection. Ed. Judy Steed. Toronto: McGraw-Hill Ryerson Ltd, 1994: 35.

Corelli, Rae. "North Versus South: Two Trials Show the Difference Between Canadian and US Criminal Law." *Maclean's.* 29 May 1995: 19.

Dimanno, Rosie. "You Don't Fight with the Police." *Toronto Star* 20 Dec. 2000.

Fines, Barbara. *Critical Writing Skills: An Introduction to Briefing.* University of Missouri-Kansas City Law School. Accessed Nov. 2003 <www.law.umkc.edu/faculty/profiles/glesnerfines/Success2.html>.

"How to Write a Brief." Accessed Nov. 2003 <www.cjed.com/write brief.pdf>.

MacCharles, Tonda. "Polluter Must Pay, Top Court Agrees." *Toronto Star* 31 Oct. 2003.

Mellinkoff, David. *The Language of the Law.* Frederick, VA: Aspen Publishers, Inc., 1973.

Ontario Student Debating Union. Accessed 18 Nov. 2003 <http://www.osdu.on.ca/>.

Waddams, S.M. *Introduction to the Study of Law.* 5th ed. Toronto: Carswell, 1997.

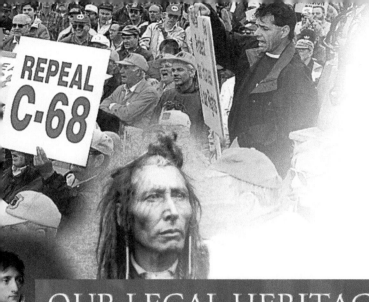

UNIT 1

OUR LEGAL HERITAGE

OVERALL LEARNING EXPECTATIONS

By the end of this unit, you will be able to:

- demonstrate an understanding of the historical and philosophical origins of law and their connection and relevance to contemporary society
- evaluate different concepts, principles, philosophies, and theories of law
- demonstrate an understanding of the relationship between law and societal values
- assess the influence of individual and collective action on the evolution of law

TABLE OF CONTENTS

ORIGINS OF LAW

LEARNING EXPECTATIONS

After reading this chapter, you will be able to:

- trace the development of law from its primary sources in religion, customs, and social and political philosophy

- distinguish between primary and secondary sources of law, including customs, religious influences, constitutions, and judicial decisions

- compare various historical methods and systems of adjudication

- distinguish between the different types of law, including common and civil, substantive and procedural, and private and public

FIGURE 2.1 A duke has been accused of conspiring with the English against France and is being tried for treason before the court of Charles VII (the king of France 1422–61). What influence have early French and English court systems and Aboriginal cultures had on the Canadian judicial system?

> *There is hardly an absurdity of the past that cannot be found flourishing somewhere in the present.*
>
> —Will Durant (1885–1981), US philosopher and historian

■ INTRODUCTION ■

Famed British scientist Sir Isaac Newton (1643–1727) once said, "If I have seen further, it is only because I have stood on the shoulders of giants." This quotation may hold great significance for people who have made modern scientific discoveries or technological breakthroughs. It means that without the body of knowledge created by the inventors and theorists of the past, the innovations of the present would be impossible to achieve. The complex, sophisticated, and sometimes chaotic Canadian system of law also rests on the pillars of the past. Our understanding of such concepts as justice, fairness, and equity; our acceptance of such principles as the presumption of innocence; and our methods of judging have evolved slowly and cumulatively from the ideas of past legal experts and from the influence of citizens. In this chapter, you will examine the origins of law in Canada and see that the process of discovery and change in law continues.

The Nature of Law

Law plays an important role in our everyday lives. Laws written by the Canadian government regulate who and when we can marry, what will happen if we fail to pay our debts, and who may be financially liable if there is an act of negligence that causes us harm. We can turn to the law for **redress**, or remedy, if we have been wrongfully dismissed from our job, discriminated against in renting an apartment, or cheated out of an expected inheritance. If someone steals from us or injures a member of our family, we would not retaliate personally, but rather look to the law for justice and fairness. But the law encompasses much more than the rules that regulate our everyday lives.

In 1885, Plains Cree Chief Pitikwahapiwiyin (known in English as Poundmaker) was sentenced to felony-treason for his part in the Siege of Battleford, despite the fact that he tried to prevent the armed confrontation that broke out between his people and the government troops. Chief Pitikwahapiwiyin's objective at Battleford was to try to convince the government to uphold the "Famine Clause" of Treaty No. Six peaceably, by giving food and supplies to his band. He reflected at his trial in Regina, Saskatchewan, in 1885: "The law is a hard, queer thing. I do not understand it." Many Canadians may identify and agree with the chief's words today, given the complexity and often contradictory nature of Canadian law. For example, our laws protect our liberty through the *Charter of Rights and Freedoms* yet can take away our liberty through the use of the relatively new *Anti-Terrorism Act*. Our laws have changed dramatically over the decades. At one time, there were no laws preventing the possession and consumption of illegal narcotics, and suicide was a crime. Now the law prohibits the use of illegal drugs, while suicide is no longer mentioned in our _Criminal Code_. Although people's perceptions of law are often based on _personal_ philosophical and cultural references, the law reflects the values that _society_ holds in common.

To gain a better understanding of the law, you will examine both its practical and theoretical roots. This will involve asking questions about the nature of law in our society. What is the origin of our laws dealing with contracts, negligence, and crime? Why does Canada consider certain acts criminal, while other nations do not? Who decided what our laws should be? How do the economic, political, religious, and cultural characteristics of a country affect its laws? Thinking and asking questions about the law is part of the study of jurisprudence.

Jurisprudence

Jurisprudence means the philosophy or science of law. The word is derived from Latin and has two parts—_juris_, meaning "of right" or "of law," and _prudens_, which refers to being skilled or learned in law. Today, jurisprudence embraces all aspects of legal thought and is used in the study of the legal theories, principles, concepts, institutions, and the historical development upon which our law is based.

The law has sometimes been compared to one of the great pyramids of Egypt. Created by humans, a pyramid is imposing and awe-inspiring from the outside. There is uncertainty and speculation regarding the process of its creation. It appears impenetrable and complex, yet as you move inside the structure, it reveals more and more of the secrets of the history, society, and beliefs of the people responsible for it.

It might be useful to visualize jurisprudence as though you were looking down on a pyramid

FIGURE 2.2 Cree Chief Pitikwahapiwiyin (Poundmaker) was frustrated by the seemingly contradictory and unjust nature of early Canadian law. In your opinion, would his characterization of the judicial system apply today?

and viewing all the different aspects that make up the law (see Figure 2.3). By studying these different but integrated parts, it is possible to better understand the law. Jurisprudence ensures that changes to our laws are made with careful consideration and are informed by the insights of the legal writers, law-makers, and scholars of the past.

Sources of Law

How did the complex legal system we have in Canada develop? Canadian law is derived from many sources. For example, the influence of the British can be seen in the photographs of the Queen of England that hang in courtrooms

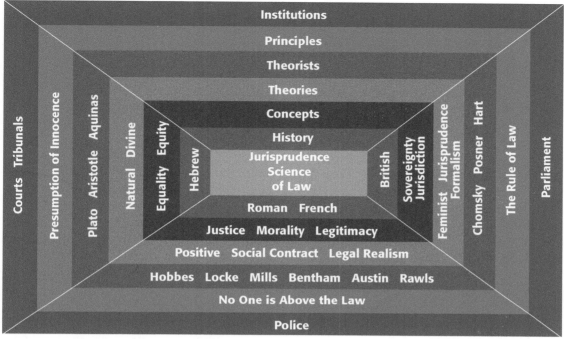

FIGURE 2.3   To understand our present legal system we need to study how the concepts, principles, and institutions are integrated.

across the country and in the English-style robes worn by our lawyers and judges. Many of the prohibitions in our *Criminal Code*, such as murder and theft, are also found in many different religious codes. Social and moral values are reflected in our laws that restrict gambling and prohibit prostitution.

To gain a better understanding of the origins of our law and their influence on our present legal system, it is useful to differentiate two main sources of law—primary sources and secondary sources. **Primary sources** are those that have influenced our ideas and values about law over hundreds and even thousands of years. They include customs and conventions, religious doctrines, and social and philosophical views. **Secondary sources** include the laws and cases that were codified, that is, written down in response to these cultural, religious, and philosophical values. Our Constitution, legal statutes, and judicial writings and decisions are examples of secondary sources of law.

Primary Sources

Customs and Conventions

Many ancient societies had prohibitions on certain kinds of behaviours. **Customs**, or practices, and general rules were created to deal with situations that arose from everyday living. These were likely passed on instinctively, meaning they came to people naturally or innately, or orally from one generation to the next. Some of these customs continued to survive even though the original reason for them no longer existed or had been forgotten, and some of them eventually developed into formal, or written, laws. For example, some provinces in Canada have **adverse possession** laws, which stem from the old English custom of "squatters' rights." These laws state that if a person who has no legal title to land remains on that land without permission for a certain period of time (assuming the legal owner of the land has knowledge of the occupant), the occupant may be entitled to acquire title or ownership of the property by virtue of his or her having remained on the land.

Conventions refer to agreements or arrangements that are not necessarily part of a formal contract but nevertheless impose an obligation on the parties involved. An example is the *Geneva Conventions*—an international agreement that sets out standards for the treatment of prisoners of war.

Another meaning of a convention in law refers to a way of doing something because that is the way it has always been done. In constitutional law, for example, some of the rules are written down, but others are not. Because the unwritten rules have existed for so long, they are considered binding conventions. For instance, in Canada, the party with the majority of seats in Parliament forms the government; however, this is not actually written down. Nor is it written down that the leader of the party with the majority of seats becomes the prime minister. However, because that is the way it has always been done, the rule has become a binding convention.

When a convention becomes accepted practice, law-makers consider it in determining the law. For example, in 1980, the Supreme Court of Canada was asked by three provincial governments whether it was a constitutional convention for the federal government to **patriate**, that is, bring to Canada, the Constitution of Canada from Britain without first obtaining the agreement of the provinces. The Supreme Court determined that, although in theory the federal government could patriate our Constitution without agreement from the provinces, there was a constitutional convention that gave the provincial governments a degree of participation in the amendment of the Canadian Constitution.

Religion

"Thou shalt not" is the beginning of all Law.
—Henry Adams (1838–1918), American writer and historian

The *Canadian Charter of Rights and Freedoms* begins with these words: "Whereas Canada is founded upon principles that recognize the supremacy of God and the rule of law…." Although the Church has no official position in the Canadian legal system, the inclusion of the words "supremacy of God" in our *Charter* supports the notion that religion has helped shape our law.

The influence of religion on our justice system can be traced back to the *Mosaic Law* of 1200 BCE. According to the Bible, God gave Moses laws to be followed by the Hebrew people. These laws, commonly called the Ten Commandments, can be found in the Book of Exodus in the Old Testament. The *Mosaic Law*, although written thousands of years ago, is the foundation of Judeo-Christian moral teachings and is one of the bases of our legal system. Prohibitions against murder, theft, and **perjury**, or lying under oath, found in the Ten Commandments, remain in our present *Criminal Code*.

Although many of the moral and religious restrictions found in the Ten Commandments are still with us today, some of them have much less influence in our contemporary society. For example, prior to the introduction of the *Charter*

The Law of God

1. Thou shalt not have other gods before Me.
2. Thou shalt not make for yourself a carved image—any likeness of anything that is in heaven above or that is in the earth beneath or that is in the water under the earth.
3. Thou shalt not take the name of the Lord your God in vain.
4. Remember the Sabbath day, to keep it holy.
5. Honour your father and your mother.
6. Thou shalt not murder.
7. Thou shalt not commit adultery.
8. Thou shalt not steal.
9. Thou shalt not bear false witness against your neighbour.
10. Thou shalt not covet your neighbour's house; you shall not covet your neighbour's wife nor his male servant nor his female servant nor his ox nor his donkey nor anything that is your neighbour's.

FIGURE 2.4   The Ten Commandments are declared in Exodus 20 of the ancient Jewish Scriptures. They are said to have been delivered by God nearly 3500 years ago. For each of the commandments, give a present-day Canadian law that seems to correspond.

of Rights and Freedoms in 1982 and a successful *Charter* challenge, every student across the country recited the Lord's Prayer at the beginning of each school day. In accordance with the *Lord's Day Act*, it was illegal to shop on a Sunday in Ontario, and it was against the law for children to play in the park on that day. The influence of religion on Canadian law may be waning, since few of these obligations and restrictions remain in effect today. Nevertheless, the inclusion of the "supremacy of God" in our *Charter of Rights and Freedoms* remains.

Social and Political Influences

Law cannot be separated from the social, political, economic, and cultural characteristics of a country. Some people would argue that, in Canada, our laws are the written expression of what most citizens feel is right and proper. Our laws, such as the *Charter of Rights and Freedoms*, reflect the value that the majority of Canadians place on individual rights and freedoms. Our *Criminal Code* suggests we place a high value on the protection of people and property. Our tax and social welfare laws indicate that we have some acceptance of the idea that wealth and privilege should be more evenly distributed.

However, those who support other social, economic, and political structures may view Canadian law in a different light. People who support a Marxist or Communist political structure might argue that Canadian law represents the interests of the ruling class and serves to further the interests of businesses. People who are to the right of the political spectrum and who support a more conservative, capitalist political structure may believe Canadian laws unfairly limit the potential and power of the most wealthy and influential people in our society.

As well, law cannot be divorced from the social, political, economic, and cultural beliefs of the time. Laws dealing with women's rights, for example, have been modified over time to reflect more enlightened attitudes and socio-economic changes. In 1983, Canada officially **repealed**, or withdrew, the offence of rape. Previously, a husband could not be charged with raping his wife as you can see from this earlier version of our *Criminal Code*.

> 143. A male person commits rape when he has sexual intercourse with a female person who is not his wife
> a. without her consent.

Our sexual assault laws today have been altered considerably from those that existed pre-1980, with the clause "who is not his wife" being eliminated completely. Currently, either a husband or a wife may be charged with sexual assault with respect to his or her spouse.

Our laws will continue to be influenced by the social, political, economic, and cultural forces of the day, but they must strike a fine balance: laws that are too far behind or too far ahead of the attitudes of society may not be obeyed by the majority of people. In the case of *R. v. Lavallee*, cited on the next page, the court set a precedent when it upheld the acquittal of a woman who killed her common-law spouse. Angelique Lavallee argued she killed her partner in self-defence although at the time of the shooting her partner had turned away and was shot in the back of the head. Judge Sopinka, writing for the majority, upheld the acquittal. In his argument he said:

> Far from protecting women from spousal abuse the law historically sanctioned the abuse of women within marriage as an aspect of the husband's ownership of his wife, and his right to chastise her. One need only recall the centuries old law that a man is entitled to beat his wife with a stick "no thicker than his thumb." Laws do not spring out of a social vacuum. The notion that a man has the right to discipline his wife is deeply rooted in the history of our society. One consequence of this was that "wife battering" was rarely spoken of, rarely reported, rarely prosecuted, and even more rarely punished.

Judge Sopinka went on to point out that there had been a change in public attitude in recent years that no man has the right to abuse any woman under any circumstances. The Lavallee case below not only set a precedent in that it allowed a battered woman to use self-defence even though the threat was not immediate, but also demonstrated a shift in attitude toward the battered spouse. In previous cases involving women who had killed their spouse while he was asleep or drunk, the courts had denied the claim of self-defence. Some law experts argue that the courts had begun admitting this controversial defence due to the influence of changing societal attitudes and the lobbying of women's groups.

Landmark CASE

R. v. Lavallee, [1990] 1 S.C.R. 852

Read the following case analysis and then answer the following questions. The facts, issue, and *ratio* have been provided for you.

1. Should judges consider shifting public opinion when making their judgments? Explain.
2. Assume you are making an appeal on behalf of the Crown in this case to the Supreme Court of Canada. What arguments would you make that the defence of "battered woman syndrome" should not be permitted?

Facts: The appellant, who was in an abusive relationship, killed her partner one night by shooting him in the back of the head as he left her room. The shooting occurred after an argument during which the appellant had been beaten and was fearful for her life after being taunted with the threat either she kill him or he would get her. She had frequently been a victim of his physical abuse and had concocted excuses to explain her injuries to medical staff on those occasions. A psychiatrist explained her ongoing terror, her inability to escape the relationship despite the violence, and the continuing pattern of abuse that put her life in danger. He testified that, in his opinion, the appellant's shooting of the deceased was the final desperate act of a woman who sincerely believed she would be killed some time that night. The jury acquitted the appellant but its verdict was overturned by a majority of the Manitoba Court of Appeal. Lavallee appealed to the Supreme Court of Canada.

Criminal Code: 34 (2) Everyone who is unlawfully assaulted and who caused death or grievous harm in repelling the assault is justified if:

a) he causes it under reasonable apprehension of death or grievous bodily harm from the violence with which the assault was originally made or with which the assailant pursued his purpose and

b) he believes on reasonable and probable grounds that he cannot otherwise preserve himself from death or grievous bodily harm

Issue: Should the psychiatric evidence have been before the court, and were the trial judge's instructions to the jury with respect to psychiatric evidence adequate?

Held: The appeal is allowed and the original acquittal restored.

Ratio Decidendi: (Sopinka J.) "Expert testimony is admissible to assist the fact-finder in drawing inferences in areas where the expert has knowledge beyond that of a lay person. It is difficult for the lay person to understand the battered woman syndrome. It is commonly thought that battered women are not really beaten as badly as they claim, otherwise they would have left the relationship. Alternatively, some believe that women enjoy being beaten. Each of these stereotypes may adversely affect consideration of a battered woman's claim to have acted in self-defence. Expert evidence can assist the jury in dispelling these myths.

"This testimony relates to the ability of an accused to perceive danger and goes to the issue of whether she 'reasonably apprehended' death or grievous bodily harm. There was ample evidence on which the trial judge could conclude that the appellant was battered repeatedly and brutally by the deceased over the course of their relationship. The trial judge properly admitted the evidence and adequately charged the jury.

"Greater media attention to this phenomenon in recent years has revealed both its prevalence and horrible impact on women from all walks of life. Far from protecting women from it, the law historically sanctioned the abuse of women within marriage as an aspect of the husband's ownership of his wife and his right to chastise her.

"Subsection (2) s. 34 of the Criminal Code stipulates the accused's apprehension must be a reasonable one based on reasonable and probable grounds. However, it strains credulity to imagine what a 'reasonable man' would do in the position of a battered woman as men do not typically find themselves in that situation. Some women do, however. The definition of 'reasonable' must be adapted to circumstances that are by and large foreign to the world inhabited by the hypothetical 'reasonable man.' I would allow the appeal and restore the original acquittal."

CONFIRM YOUR UNDERSTANDING

1. Explain the meaning of "jurisprudence." Why is it important?
2. Local customs are often the source of many municipal bylaws. Try to imagine the circumstances that led to the following old, rather strange bylaws.
   a) A lady's bathing suit must cover her from neck to knee (early twentieth-century Toronto bylaw).
   b) Homeowners must sweep and wash sidewalks by 8 a.m. (Toronto bylaw).
   c) Expectoration on sidewalks, streetcars, and other public places is prohibited (Toronto bylaw).
   d) It is illegal to drive a pig through the streets, unless the animal is in a vehicle (Louisville, Kentucky, bylaw).
   e) It is against the law to give a moose a beer (Fairbanks, Alaska, bylaw).
   f) It is illegal for street vendors to sell flowers (Chicago bylaw). (Condon 1992)
3. Read the following prayer recited by members of Parliament at the opening of the Canadian legislature. What does the prayer tell you about the social, religious, and cultural values of Canada?

A Prayer for MPs

Almighty God, we give thanks for the great blessings which have been bestowed on Canada and its citizens, including the gifts of freedom, opportunity, and peace that we enjoy.

We pray for our sovereign, Queen Elizabeth, and the Governor General.

CONFIRM YOUR UNDERSTANDING (continued)

Guide us in our deliberations as members of Parliament, and strengthen us in our awareness of our duties and responsibilities as members.

Grant us wisdom, knowledge, and understanding to preserve the blessings of this country for the benefit of all and to make good laws and wise decisions.

4. a) What laws can you think of that support the idea that there is a religious foundation to our legal system?

b) What evidence can you provide that religious influences on our law are weakening?

5. Social attitudes toward women have changed over the years, and these changes have been reflected in our laws. You read earlier how laws dealing with sexual assault have changed. Identify three other areas of Canadian law that have changed regarding women as a result of changing social views.

Secondary Sources of Law

Constitutions

The Canadian Constitution, enacted in 1867 and amended in 1982, is the highest level of law in Canada, taking precedence over all other laws. The Constitution is the basic blueprint for the governance of our country. This document gives authority to the various levels of government to make laws. For example, the federal government has the authority to enact legislation dealing with criminal law. When there is disagreement about which level of government has jurisdiction over a certain area of law, it is up to the Supreme Court of Canada to make the decision. The Ontario government, for example, passed a law called the *Safe Streets Act* in 1999. This law was challenged by lawyers who argued that the *Safe Streets Act* dealt with criminal behaviour, and if the Supreme Court agrees that the law is criminal in scope, they may rule that the provincial governments do not have the authority to make criminal law and strike down the act. If a government does not have the authority to make a law because the law is outside its jurisdiction, it is said to be *ultra vires*, or outside its power. If the courts determine that the legislation does fall within the authority of the government, it is referred to as *intra vires*.

Since the *Charter of Rights and Freedoms* was added to our Constitution in 1982, all laws must conform to the *Charter*, and any law that violates a right under the *Charter* can be struck down by the Supreme Court of Canada.

Statute Law

The *Criminal Code*, *Highway Traffic Act*, and *Canada Evidence Act* are all examples of statutes. A **statute** refers to a law passed by our elected representatives at either the federal or provincial level. Some statutes, such as the *Criminal Code* or the *Anti-Terrorism Act* are very lengthy, detailed documents. Others, such as the *Education Act*, are broader in scope, and their details are written in separate legal documents. These documents are known as regulations or **orders-in-council**, and they have the same authority as statutes.

The process of turning a proposed piece of legislation into a law begins when the proposed legislation is introduced into the federal or provincial legislature in the form of a draft **bill**. The bill must undergo examination by a legislative committee and three readings in the House of Commons, and must then receive a majority vote in both Parliament and the Senate before becoming law. Once the Governor General (the

Queen's representative in Canada) or the Lieutenant-Governor (the representative of the monarchy at the provincial level) signs the bill, giving it royal assent, it becomes law and is renamed a statute or an act. (This process is described in greater detail in Chapter 5.)

Our federal and provincial governments were given the power to enact statutes according to the *British North America Act* of 1867. The *BNA Act* outlines the responsibilities and division of power at each level of government (in ss. 91 and 92).

Judicial Decisions (Case Law)

In some countries, the law is based only on statutes and legal codes. Canada, along with other countries such as Britain, the United States, Australia, and New Zealand, has a dual system of law in that it has statutes and codes but also looks to the recorded decisions of judges for guidance in the law. This latter system is referred to as **common law**, a legal term that, in this context, means law that is based on judicial decisions, as opposed to areas of law governed mostly by statutes.

The common law of England began when King Henry II directed English judges, who decided local cases, to record their decisions. The judges were then required to read their decisions to other judges and, through a process of debate and discussion, decide which were the best-reasoned verdicts. The best judgments were written down, shared, and thus became "common" laws throughout England. This collection of judgments became known as **case law**, and it continues to form a major part of Canadian law today. **Tort law** (law dealing with negligence), for example, is almost entirely based on case law. Since the introduction of the *Charter of Rights and Freedoms*, we rely on judicial decisions to interpret all laws in light of the *Charter*.

The use of case law involves extracting legal principles from past judgments and applying them to new situations. This principal that prior judgments are to be followed is called the **rule of precedent** or *stare decisis*, which is an abbreviation of the Latin phrase *stare decisis et non quieta*

movere and translates as "to stand by what has been decided and not to disturb settled matters." The rule of precedent assumes that cases should be decided in the same way if the very important facts, or **material facts**, are the same. The advantage of such a system is that it provides predictability and uniformity. Consider the following hypothetical situation: Horse breeder Judy Tran notices that part of her fence is broken, and she is concerned that one of her horses will get out and be injured. Her friend Bill Wyles tells her he will, as a favour, come over that afternoon and repair the fence. Wyles forgets to come and mend the fence, and, as a result, Tran's horse does leave the field, wanders onto the road, and is injured when it is struck by an oncoming car. Tran sues Wyles for the resulting damages.

The judge who decides the case sympathizes with Tran's loss but determines that Tran cannot collect damages. He reasons that since Wyles received no payment for the repair of the fence, there was no valid contract, and therefore Tran cannot sue. The judge argues that a contract is an agreement between parties whereby each gets something in return for his or her promise. The "something" that the person receives in return for his or her promise is called "consideration." The decision in the *Tran v. Wyles* case sets a precedent that a legally binding contract must include consideration; that is, something of value must be exchanged. In other words, the court recognizes that in contract law no one does anything for nothing.

In a later case, Betsy Toulis has a leak in her basement. She is afraid that if it rains heavily, her basement will flood. Her friend Ronald Fulford agrees to fix it for free. He fails to show up, it rains, and Toulis's basement is flooded. Toulis sues Fulford for damages. Although the material facts of the case are different from those of *Tran v. Wyles* (it is a leaky basement, not an injured horse), the principle that a contract must have consideration is still applicable. Toulis's and Ronald's lawyers will examine the precedent set in *Tran v. Wyles* and advise their clients that Toulis would be unlikely to win against Fulford because

Fulford received no payment or promise of payment, and therefore there was no legally binding contract.

If a similar case were before the courts today, the judge would likely rely on the earlier decision providing there was **uniformity** (like cases must be decided alike) and **impartiality** (judges cannot permit their feelings for those involved in the case to enter into their judgments). The rule of precedent thus allows judges to decide present disputes by examining the decisions made by judges in previous cases.

But does this mean that judges will always be bound by decisions of the past and will never be free to make their own decisions? The answer is no. Although the rule of precedent applies in theory, in practice very few cases are so similar. What is binding is the general rule that explains the reason for the verdict and could be applicable to at least some other cases. This rule is called the ***ratio decidendi***, or reason for deciding. Lawyers compare and contrast the *ratio decidendi* of cases and try to find similarities or differences that will support their argument. For example, consider a situation similar to the *Tran v. Wyles* case discussed earlier. In this instance, Rafi Syed agrees to mend David Brooke's fence, and, in return, Brooke says that when Syed's daughter turns 9 years old in a few months, she can have a free horseback-riding lesson. Syed fails to mend the fence, and Brooke's horse is injured when it gets out. Brooke sues Syed. The lawyers for Brooke and Syed will examine the decision made in *Tran v. Wyles*. Syed's lawyer will argue that there was no consideration. Although Brooke offered to give a free riding lesson to Syed's daughter, the daughter did not make the contract to fix the fence, and therefore the precedent set in *Tran v. Wyles* still applies. Brooke's lawyer may argue that although the judge in *Tran v. Wyles* ruled that a contract was not binding unless there was consideration, the Brooke situation is different. Brooke's lawyer might suggest that Syed was receiving consideration because he agreed that the payment was to be in the form of his daughter's riding lesson. The judge deciding *Brooke v. Syed* would have to make

his or her own assessment of the precedent in *Tran v. Wyles* and perhaps modify the rule or even introduce a new precedent.

In this way, although case law does lend predictability and uniformity to our law, it also allows for a certain amount of flexibility and an ability to evolve with changing times and circumstances. If there is no precedent, that is, if there is no previous case that is similar to the one being heard, the judge must rely on his or her own sense of fairness and justice, and create a new precedent. As well, a precedent can be overturned: lower-court decisions can be overturned by the Court of Appeal, and the Supreme Court of Canada can overturn any lower-court decision. However, the Supreme Court of Canada is not bound by its own previous decisions. It recognizes that decisions made in the past may not be appropriate today because societal values and laws are always changing. In *Minister of Indian Affairs and Northern Development v. Ranville*, [1982] 2 S.C.R. 518, Justice Dickson said:

> The traditional justification for the *stare decisis* principle is certainty in the law. This of course remains an important consideration even though this court has announced its willingness, for compelling reasons, to overturn a prior decision. In this instance, adherence to the *stare decisis* principle would generate more uncertainty than certainty.

 That case law is predictable yet flexible, uniform yet changing with the times, is what makes our law so compelling, challenging, and interesting. Keep in mind that statute law always overrides case law and that judicial decisions from the highest court are binding on all lower courts, but judicial decisions can be overturned if the government decides to make new laws. As a student of law, you should try to grasp the legal reasoning the judge applied to the cases provided throughout this text to see if you can apply the same principle to other similar, but more recent, cases. (See Analyzing Court Decisions in the Legal Handbook.)

LEGAL HANDBOOK p. 17

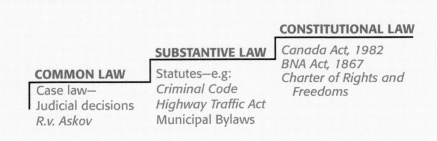

FIGURE 2.5   This diagram illustrates the legal hierarchy in Canada. Why is constitutional law at the top of the hierarchy?

CONFIRM YOUR UNDERSTANDING

1. Explain what is meant by the term *"ultra vires."* Provide an example to illustrate your meaning.

2. Identify the following examples as either a primary or secondary source of law:
   a) the Ten Commandments
   b) the presumption of innocence until proven guilty
   c) the *British North America Act, 1867*
   d) the *Consumer Protection Act*

3. Provide an example of statute law at the federal, provincial, and municipal levels.

4. In Canada, where does the authority to make laws reside?

5. Create an example to explain how a lawyer might use case law and the rule of precedent to defend a client.

6. Some critics argue that case law gives judges the role of making the law when that is supposed to be the responsibility of the elected legislature.
   a) Make an argument against this position.
   b) Explain how a precedent made in a lower court can be overturned.

7. Our legal system assumes that once a judge reaches a decision, that decision is final. For example, if a judge at a final appeal determines that an accused is properly convicted of possession of marijuana and a week later the Supreme Court in another similar case decides there should be no conviction, there is no remedy for the person whose case was decided first. This is known as **res judicata**, or matter adjudicated.
   a) What reasons are there for the ruling of *res judicata*?
   b) Do you agree or disagree with this principle? Explain your answer.

8. Read the following case and the view of the dissenting judge.
   a) How does Justice Goudge's decision apply to the principle of *res judicata*?
   b) Consider what Justice Dickson argued with regard to *stare decisis* on page 52. Which legal opinion would you support if you were a judge on this case? Explain your answer.

R. v. Burke (2001), 153 C.C.C. (3d) 97 (Ont. C.A.)

Facts: Mr. Burke was charged with attempted murder. When the jury foreperson declared the verdict, the trial judge mistakenly heard "not guilty" when, in fact, the jury foreperson had said "guilty." The judge recorded a verdict of not guilty, and the accused was released. Later that day, the judge realized his mistake, overturned the earlier verdict, entered a conviction, and sentenced Burke to $12\frac{1}{2}$ years' imprisonment. Burke's lawyer appealed the conviction to the Ontario Court of Appeal.

Ratio Decidendi: The majority of the court rejected the appeal, arguing that the original verdict was clearly a mistake due to a clerical error and could be easily corrected.

Dissent: (Goudge J.) Justice Goudge argued that the trial judge should have brought back the jury and questioned them on whether the verdict recorded by the judge was a mistake. Justice Goudge pointed out that the importance of finality in cases should be respected and a person's liberty should not be left hanging under a cloud.

Historical Perspectives on Law

Our legal system has its origins in earlier surviving legal codes and legal writings. Many of these early legal writings codified the rules and customs of everyday living, but they also demonstrated that from very early times, humans have been struggling to find the meaning of justice.

Early Legal Codes

One of the earliest surviving legal codes was written by Hammurabi (1792–1750 BCE). Hammurabi was a king in Babylon who had a code of laws engraved in columns in the town square. The *Code of Hammurabi* provides insight into the beliefs and social structure of ancient Babylon. Punishments for offences were severe and were based primarily on the principle of an eye for an eye and a tooth for a tooth. The society was hierarchical, that is, based on levels of authority, and patriarchal in that the key authority figure was the father of the household. Therefore, the severity of the punishment depended on the individual's status within the community. For example, if an enslaved

FIGURE 2.6 The *Code of Hammurabi* was engraved on black basalt stone about 3800 years ago. What is the significance of the fact that these laws were written down and displayed in a public space?

person committed an assault, he or she would be put to death, but a free man might lose a hand or have to pay a fine for the same crime.

The ancient laws of Athens, Greece, were inscribed on large marble slabs and placed in the centre of town, where any citizen could consult them. This allowed the people of Athens to have access to the law and to ensure the law was applied impartially.

We can find the origins of our own jury system and many of our modern principles of democracy in these early Greek laws. Around 400 BCE, Athenians introduced the idea of randomly chosen citizens to serve on large, impartial juries. They also established principles such as equality before the law, meaning that no man, woman, or ruler was exempt from following the law.

Like the *Code of Hammurabi* and *Mosaic Law*, Roman laws also regulated all aspects of daily life, from trial proceedings to parental rights and obligations, contracts, property rights, and torts. Roman laws were originally engraved on bronze plaques called the *Twelve Tables* (451–450 BCE). Although these tables were lost, records of sections of them have survived. It is believed that these ancient laws were commissioned by the lower classes (plebeians), because they believed that the unwritten laws of the day were arbitrary and gave too much power to the ruling or wealthy classes (patricians).

Roman law continued to develop as the Roman Empire grew. In 529 CE, Roman Emperor Justinian created a code that later became the basis of the legal systems in most European countries. Justinian's code, for example, made slavery against the law. Some 1200 years later, French Emperor Napoleon Bonaparte commissioned a new code of laws called the *Napoleonic Code*, or the *French Civil Code*, which also forms the basis of the *Civil Code of Québec*.

Other ancient civilizations also recorded laws. For example, the *Laws of Manu* were recorded in India between 1280–880 BCE, and in China the *Code of Li k'vei*, written in approximately 350 BCE, included laws dealing with many of the same issues found in other ancient legal codes, such as property rights, marriage laws, and laws prohibiting murder and theft.

If we view these early legal codes from our twenty-first–century perspective, we may conclude that they reflect harsh, unjust societies. However, many of these codes reveal a desire to use law not only as a source of rules and regulations, but also as the basis for fairness and justice. They also indicate that ancient civilizations had the capacity to reason about the function of law and how best to make it achieve its purpose. Before the *Code of Hammurabi*, for example, people had to find their own means of justice if a loved one was killed or property stolen. The *Code of Hammurabi* established the concept that the state could intervene as arbiter of disputes. Only the state could punish, and people could no longer be punished without first being proven guilty. Hebrew law took these concepts a step further and imposed moral values we would support today, such as "Thou shall take no bribe, for a bribe blinds the officials and subverts the cause of those who are in the

FIGURE 2.7 Byzantine Emperor Justinian is seen here surrounded by his court in a painting from a 14th century Latin manuscript of *The Institutions of Justinian*. What evidence of the influence of early Roman law can you see in the current Canadian judicial system?

right." Justinian's code, the *Corpus Juris Civilis*, was important not just because of its content, but also because it established the idea that laws were applicable to all and that all citizens were equal in the eyes of the law.

Code of Hammurabi	Twelve Tables: Table VIII, Torts or Delicts
"If a man wish to separate from a woman who has borne him children, or from his wife who has borne him children: then he shall give that wife her dowry and a part of the usufruct of field, garden, and property, so that she can rear her children. When she has brought up her children, a portion of all that is given to the children, equal as that of one son, shall be given to her. She may then marry the man of her heart."	"Whoever destroys by burning a building or a stack of grain placed beside a house…, shall be bound, scourged, burned to death, provided that knowingly and consciously he has committed this crime; but if this deed is by accident, that is, by negligence, either he shall repair the damage or if he is unable he shall be corporally punished more lightly."

SOURCE: *The Avalon Project @ Yale Law School*. "Code of Hammurabi" and "Twelve Tables." Accessed 5 Oct. 2003 <http://yale.edu/lawweb/avalon>.

FIGURE 2.8   These examples of laws from the *Code of Hammurabi* and the *Twelve Tables* suggest an understanding of fairness with respect to a deserted wife and an acknowledgment of the difference between a deliberate act and an accident (similar to our present-day understanding).

CONFIRM YOUR UNDERSTANDING

1. Why is it important to preserve and learn about earlier legal codes and systems of law?

2. One conclusion that could be drawn after reading the *Code of Hammurabi* is that the key political and social structure of that time was hierarchical and patriarchal. What two key descriptors, in your opinion, would future historians use to describe our social and political structure if they were to examine our legal system?

3. Which ideas from the various historical roots of law (such as the use of a jury to determine guilt or innocence) had the most signifi-cant impact on the evolution of law and justice in Canada?

4. What evidence do you see in early legal codes that reflect a concern for justice and fairness?

5. Criminal acts or civil disputes were at one time viewed as personal wrongdoings. Compensation was paid to the victims, and if compensation was not paid, the victim's family would attempt to collect damages formally or exact revenge. What advantages and disadvantages do you see in this more personal type of adjudication?

Historical Influences on Canadian Law: Aboriginal, French, and British

Aboriginal Influences

When the earliest British and European settlers arrived in North America, they did not find an empty land. From the Haida in the West to the Mi'kmaq of the East Coast, the Aboriginal communities of North America had established legal systems and religious and social structures. The rules governing the various Aboriginal groups were based on an oral tradition. For examples, around 1450, the Aboriginal nations of the Mohawk, Onondaga, Seneca, Oneida, and Cayuga joined together to form a league of nations, known as the Iroquois (Haudenosaunee) Confederacy. In 1714, the Tuscarora also joined the Iroquois Confederacy, and it became known as the Six Nations. The influence of the Six Nations extended from Québec in the east to the western United States. The constitution of the Iroquois Confederacy was eventually recorded in the *Great Binding Law*, or *Gayanashagowa*.

This law covered many of the same areas as other legal codes, including emigration, treason, and secession. The *Gayanashagowa* also outlined many of the principles of justice and fairness that are found in modern civil rights documents. Its underlying principle was that since hierarchy breeds conflict, the confederacy must organize in a way that prevents the internal rise of hierarchy. In this early document, the Six Nations outlined historical reasons for conflict and addressed them. Noting, for example, that territorial hunting grounds were often the source of conflict, they abolished the importance of territories, welcomed those who entered their territory, and guaranteed the visitors' safety. When the founding fathers of the United States of America were writing the constitution of their newly established country, they borrowed from the *Great Binding Law*.

Few early settlers in Canada gave Aboriginal law and customs the respect they deserved. The settlers brought with them their own social struc-

FIGURE 2.9   This carving, called *Turtle Island*, by Mohawk artist Stanley R. Hill illustrates the creation of the world and the founding of the Six Nations. The Tree of Peace is the central symbol representing the Confederacy and the eagle is considered a very wise creature that represents strength, power and clearness of vision.

tures and legal systems, and it was these systems—civil law from the French and common law from the British—that ultimately became the foundation of Canadian law. Over the centuries, Aboriginal laws have been having a greater influence on Canadian law with the recognition of early land claims and treaty rights (as you will learn in Chapter 8). Also, Aboriginal ideas of **restorative justice**—a legal system that requires an offender to "restore" justice by recognizing, accepting, and taking real responsibility for his or her actions—and community involvement in legal disputes are finding their way into our present legal system.

The French Influence: Civil Law

Civil law is a legal term that can mean different things depending on its context. In a discussion on systems of law, civil law refers to the type in which all laws are codified in statutes. This system is based on the *French Civil Code* enacted

Aboriginal Perspectives on Justice

The Canadian criminal justice system is based primarily on the concept of using coercive force, that is, fear of punishment such as prison, to ensure compliance with the law. However, Aboriginal concepts are very different. The Aboriginal community is more interested in the involvement of the community and the restoration of respect between the perpetrator and the victim. European legal systems view crime as a violation of the laws of the state, but in Aboriginal law, all matters are private. Aboriginal societies do not make a distinction between criminal and civil law. In an Aboriginal society, when a crime is committed, the debt that is created is owed to the victim, not to the state. The victimizer is required to restore the victim to the situation he or she enjoyed prior to the commission of the offence. The community works to help facilitate the resolution of disputes, and the community sees the justice process as a teaching/learning experience for the whole community. The process is somewhat more interconnected and fluid than the judgmental, hierarchical approach of European legal systems.

The members of the Aboriginal community do not view the wrongdoer as bad; rather they believe the wrongdoing reflects misbehaviour and is a result of a lack of harmony between the wrongdoer and the community.

This very different view results in an equally different approach to sentencing. In Canadian and European law, the victim is usually not addressed. The victim of a robbery, for example, is not compensated for his or her loss. To receive compensation, the victim must enact proceedings in civil court and may or may not receive compensation. In an Aboriginal justice system, there is recognition of the victim and an understanding that the negative experience of the victim can be felt throughout the community. For example, a victim of sexual abuse may abuse others. Aboriginal communities therefore focus on connecting the offender to the community and helping the offender to see and empathize with the victim. When conflicts arise, the Aboriginal community has the responsibility of ensuring there is a speedy and peaceful resolution.

The Canadian justice system is slowly borrowing some of the principles of Aboriginal justice. For example, the new Canadian *Youth Criminal Justice Act* has put more emphasis on community justice for young offenders. In addition, sentencing circles have been introduced in small communities. In 2000, a program called PACT Youth Crime Reduction Program was set up in Scarborough, Ontario. This program applies a restorative justice approach and attempts to offer young people who have committed less

FIGURE 2.10 Aboriginal Ganootamaage Justice Services of Winnipeg volunteers take part in a healing circle for a 20-year-old shoplifter (not shown in photo) at the Aboriginal Center in 1998. It was the first sentence handed down by a healing circle under a new provincial program for Aboriginal offenders.

serious offences an alternative to custody. The premise is that for the 100 000 children and young people charged each year, shame and restitution will be much more effective than punishment such as imprisonment.

SOURCES: Guest, James. "Aboriginal Legal Theory and Restorative Justice." Native Law Centre of Canada, 1999. (Mr. Guest is the Law Clerk of the Mashantucket Pequot Tribal Nation) Accessed 20 Dec. 2003 <www.usask.ca/nativelaw>;

Lockett, David. "Coming to Grips with Youth Crime." *Toronto Star* 21 Dec. 2003: A19.

Form Your Questions

Assume the role of a reporter interviewing either James Guest or David Lockett (see Sources above) regarding his views on how the Aboriginal justice system differs from Western European justice systems and how it is influencing the Canadian system. Create three key questions you would ask to gain a better understanding of these issues.

by Napoleon Bonaparte of France in 1804. In the civil law system, the inquisitorial, rather than **adversarial trial system** is used in court. In general, the **inquisitorial trial system** permits the judge to ask questions and to take a more active role in the process than the adversarial system.

Legal systems in countries such as France, South Africa, and in the Canadian province of Québec still follow this code. Although the French colonists in Québec were defeated by the English settlers in 1759, an agreement was reached that guaranteed the French the right, under the *Québec Act of 1774*, to use civil law for all non-criminal and non-constitutional matters in that province.

The British Influence: Common Law

The present legal system in Canada has been influenced by many legal systems, writings, and legal codes, but perhaps the most significant influence comes from British law. When William of Normandy conquered England in 1066, he inherited a kingdom with an already developed system of law. However, it was a decentralized system, with each county following its own set of customs and rules. William set about centralizing

FIGURE 2.11 Napoleon Bonaparte was responsible for developing the *French Civil Code*, which is still used in the province of Québec today. Why do you think its use was limited to non-criminal and non-constitutional matters in that province?

and creating a system of law that applied to all of England. Slowly, a system of common law developed that helped standardize law and justice.

The current English system of law came into existence during the reign of Henry II (1154–1189). King Henry set up a system of travelling judges, known as circuit judges. These judges travelled a specific route, visiting villages and hearing cases. At first, it was difficult for King Henry's judges to overcome local traditions and customs in deciding cases, but as new situations arose, the judges were able to create new laws. At formal and informal gatherings with other judges, they likely discussed the cases they decided upon.

Eventually, the decisions made by the judges in the cases they heard were written down, forming what is called "common law." The foundation of Canadian law is English common law.

Common law therefore has three meanings. It refers to the law that comes from Britain. It means law that is common to all, that is, law that applies to all subjects in the land. It also means law that is based on the past decisions of judges, that is, judge-made or case law.

Adversarial Versus Inquisitorial Trial Systems

One of the key differences between civil and common law is the trial system used for each. In 1995, Paul Bernardo was tried in an Ontario courtroom, under the adversarial trial system of common law, for the murders of Leslie Mahaffy and Kristen French. Both girls, who were teenagers at the time, were kidnapped, sexually assaulted, and murdered by Bernardo and his then wife, Karla Homolka. At no time during his trial did Paul Bernardo have to explain his actions to the court. Although he pleaded not guilty, Bernardo did not have to enter the witness box to defend himself, nor was he subjected to cross-examination by the Crown. Paul Bernardo was able to remain silent throughout his trial because of our adversarial system of justice. The burden of proof rested entirely on the Crown to prove Bernardo's guilt beyond a reasonable doubt. The role of the defence under this system is to ensure

that the Crown meets that standard. The judge makes sure that both sides abide by the rules. Under our system of justice, although the judge plays an important role, it is limited. The judge cannot call witnesses, though he or she can ask questions for clarification. The judge determines the admissibility of evidence, decides procedural issues, and instructs the jury. If there is no jury, it is the judge who determines guilt or innocence and decides the appropriate sentence.

Many European countries, such as France, Italy, and Scotland, and the Canadian province of Québec (for civil law only) follow the principles of Roman law. Most countries that follow Roman law support the inquisitorial system. Under this system, the accused is obligated to answer questions from the prosecutor, from his or her own lawyer, and, most important, from the presiding judge. Unlike their adversarial system counterparts, judges under the inquisitorial system take the lead in questioning the accused. They can insist that the accused explain anything that may touch on the crime before the court. The emotions, thoughts, and actions of the accused are all subject to questioning that would likely not be permitted under the rules of evidence in Canadian courts outside Québec.

There are advantages and disadvantages to both systems. Under the adversarial system, the assumption is that when opponents equally motivated to win present strong arguments, the truth will emerge. However, it is a more antagonistic approach, in which one side wins and the other loses, compared to the inquisitorial system, in which impartial judges actively seek out the truth by asking questions. The adversarial system also assumes that both sides will be equally represented, which may not always be the case. In addition, the process of cross-examination may distort rather than reveal truth. Litigants, the parties involved in the dispute, may construct their case mainly by selecting evidence that is advantageous to them rather than evidence that might point to the truth. On the other hand, in an inquisitorial system, the defendant has few rights and is not necessarily presumed innocent. The trial usually takes place behind closed doors, and the fact that the judge directs the investigation may lead to an unfair verdict if the judge is biased against one of the parties.

No system is perfect, and, in fact, both adversarial and inquisitorial systems have borrowed from each other. Many countries have modified versions of either inquisitorial or adversarial systems.

Methods of Adjudication

It is also from British law that we trace the origins of our trial procedures and methods of determining guilt or innocence. Determination of guilt or innocence was decided by divine intervention during the Middle Ages. People believed that God would judge the guilt or innocence of the accused. Various means were devised to reveal God's judgment, such as trial by ordeal and trial by combat (judicial duel).

Trial by Ordeal

One of the ways to determine guilt or innocence was to make the accused undergo some kind of ordeal. For example, the accused would be forced to hold his or her hand in scalding water or be made to grip a red-hot iron bar. The wound would then be bandaged and re-opened after a predetermined number of days. If the wound was healing, it was seen as a sign that God had judged the person innocent; if it was infected, the person was found guilty. It was possible to dispute guilt by having a number of people swear an oath (oath-helpers) as to the innocence of the accused.

Trial by Combat (Judicial Duel)

Another way to determine innocence was for the accused to challenge the accuser to a duel. It was assumed that God would be on the side of the righteous party, and therefore the victor was presumed innocent.

Trial by combat is said to be the forerunner of our own adversarial system. Instead of a physical battle between two supposedly evenly matched adversaries, we now have a mental battle of wits between two parties headed by legal professionals.

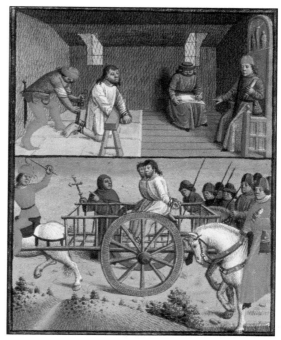

Figure 2.12   In medieval Europe, the accused were often subjected to tortures or other physical tests to determine their guilt or innocence.

As religious devoutness decreased and more and more members of the clergy spoke out against such methods of adjudication, trial by ordeal and trial by combat eventually disappeared.

Early Court Systems

Once it was determined that a crime was not merely an offence against an individual but an offence against society or the state, it was necessary to create a new form of trial and a method for determining the guilt or innocence of the accused. Our modern court system finds its roots in three court systems. The first was a **communal court** located within a small community and usually administered by local inhabitants. The second court system consisted of the feudal or **manorial tribunals**, common during the period when the feudal system was used in England. The last development was the royal court system.

Initially, the **royal court system** was set up to administer the collection of taxes through the

Court of the Exchequer. Another type of court was the Court of Chancery, where **writs,** or commands in the name of the sovereign, and **summonses,** or calls to appear in court, were obtained. Other courts, such as the **Court of Common Pleas**, were created to handle civil matters. The grandest and most expensive court was the **Court of King's Bench**. This court dealt with serious criminal cases and was made up of various nobles appointed by the king. In Canada today, the equivalent court is referred to as the Court of Queen's Bench, since our head of state is currently a queen.

By the thirteenth century, judicial authority came from the Crown. Today, in all Commonwealth countries including Canada, judicial authority lies with the Crown. An offender commits an offence not only against a victim but also against the Crown (*Rex* or *Regina*). To be compensated for damages, the victim must go to the civil court system (in the past, the Court of Common Pleas). The emergence of our modern court system owes much to sheer necessity, changes in authority, and, in some cases, historical chance.

The Origins of the Jury

Our modern jury system also has its roots in British jurisprudence. Initially, the jury was made up of local landlords, who listened to cases involving primarily land disputes. By 1219, the jury (from the Latin term *jurati*, meaning "to be sworn") began to hear criminal cases as well. At first, jurors acted as witnesses, telling the judge what they knew about the case, but by the fourteenth century, jurors had become the triers of fact. Over time, the jury came to be seen as an independent check on the government. A jury was free to reach a verdict based on the evidence rather than on fear of punishment or obtaining favour from those in authority.

CONFIRM YOUR UNDERSTANDING

1. The terms "civil law" and "common law" have a number of different meanings. Identify the various meanings of each, and provide an example to illustrate each definition.

2. What would be the present-day equivalent of the following courts:
   a) Court of the Exchequer
   b) Court of Common Pleas
   c) Court of King's Bench

3. a) What evidence supports the idea that judicial authority in Canada lies with the Crown?
   b) If Canada abolished all ties to the British monarchy, where, in your opinion, would judicial authority lie?

4. Why is it important that the jury be independent of the state?

5. Create a Venn diagram showing the similarities and differences between the adversarial and inquisitorial legal systems.

6. Trial by ordeal and trial by combat may seem strange to us today. What, if any, was the logic or justification for these two methods of adjudication?

7. Provincial court Judge Jim Igloliorte is an Inuk, the first and only Aboriginal judge in Newfoundland and Labrador. He travels to such places as Davis Inlet, Sheshatshiu, and Nain, listening to cases involving, for example, the shooting of polar bears after dark or someone throwing a stereo at his or her spouse. Inuit concepts of justice are very different from European concepts of justice. Judge Igloliorte says that the words "guilty" and "innocent" do not even exist in Inuktitut. The emphasis in Inuit culture is on solving the problem, not punishing the victim (Toughill 2001).
   a) What similarities do you see between Judge Igloliorte's Aboriginal system of justice and early communal courts?
   b) Judge Igloliorte does not believe in harsh sentences; rather he promotes sentencing circles and allows the community to

decide what to do with most offenders. Should a judge consider the cultural values of a community in making decisions about offenders, or should justice be uniform for all people across Canada? Discuss the advantages and disadvantages of both views.

Classifying the Law

Although laws can be divided according to their purpose, form, or historical development, unlike many other disciplines, law does not always lend itself to neat categorization. Laws are always changing. As well, the development of law has been a messy process, and there is a great deal of overlap among categories, types of law, and even terms we associate with the law. The classification chart in Figure 2.13 provides you with one way to categorize law. You may find other ways that better suit your understanding of the law.

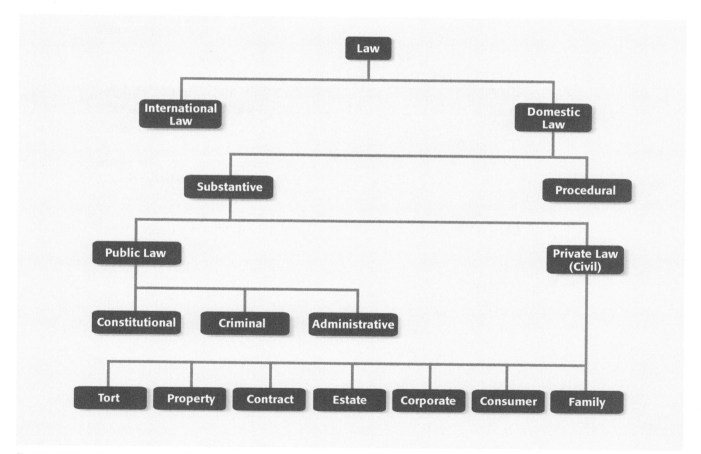

FIGURE 2.13 There are many different ways laws can be classified and divided into categories. This flow diagram illustrates one way.

Substantive and Procedural Law

Substantive law refers to the body of laws described in our various statutes, codes, and judicial decisions. For example, if a police officer stops a motorist and charges that person with drinking and driving, the officer must refer specifically to the section in the _Highway Traffic Act_ or _Criminal Code_ that describes the motorist's illegal action. The situation is similar for non-criminal matters. For example, if the brakes in a person's car fail because of his or her mechanic's negligence, the car owner would have to demonstrate that the mechanic's actions were negligent according to the law dealing with negligence.

Procedural law refers to the proper steps that must be applied and the rules that must be followed in any legal action. In the case of the charge for drinking and driving, the police officer who makes the arrest must follow proper arrest procedure, administer a Breathalyzer test using proper procedure, and follow all the rules pertaining to the collection of evidence. At trial, all the proper procedures must be followed, including those for the admission of evidence and the examination of witnesses, before a conviction can be registered against an accused. Similarly, in the civil case discussed in the previous paragraph, the **plaintiff** (the person bringing the case against another before the court) must gather evidence of negligence, file a statement of claim, and proceed according to the rules of the court.

Private Law

Private law, sometimes referred to as "civil law," simply means the law that involves disputes between individual citizens and/or private entities such as corporations. Usually, the state does not interfere with civil disputes other than to provide a court or other agency to hear the dispute.

The plaintiff in a civil case must bring the case before the courts and prove his or her case based on a civil standard, that is, a balance of probabilities. This means that the plaintiff must present evidence showing that his or her story is more likely to be true than the story of the person he

FIGURE 2.14 An RCMP forensic team member looks for more evidence along a fence after finding and bagging a purse at a farm in Port Coquitlam, B.C., in February 2002. Police were scouring a house and surrounding property as part of their investigation into the disappearance of up to 50 women. The collection of evidence must be done according to procedural law in order to be admissible in court.

or she is suing, called the **defendant**. This is a less strict standard of proof than in a criminal case. If the plaintiff succeeds in demonstrating that his or her story is more probable than the defendant's, the defendant will be found liable. The remedy is a private one: the defendant owes the plaintiff damages, generally in the form of monetary compensation.

Civil law areas include tort, property, contract, estate, corporate, consumer, and family law.

Tort Law

Tort law is a branch of law that determines compensation if someone is injured as the result of another's unlawful action or negligence. You may have read about tort cases under headlines similar to "Man Seeks $2 Million in Damages

After Slipping on an Icy Sidewalk." Generally, the plaintiff in tort actions seeks money to compensate for the harm, pain, suffering, or financial loss caused by the careless actions of others.

Property Law

Property law refers to the rights and obligations associated with ownership of property, such as a car, cottage, or home. Laws dealing with property rights were originally found in British case law; however, today most laws dealing with property in Canada can be found in statutes.

Contract Law

Contract law is the law that upholds legal agreements to exchange or sell goods or services. Whether you purchase a chocolate bar at your local store, get your hair cut, or buy a new car, you are entering into a contractual agreement. If everyone is satisfied with the service or sale, the law is not involved. However, if one party fails to uphold the terms of the agreement, the other may seek a remedy in court.

Estate Law

Estate law or succession law involves the making of a will and inheritance rights. Estate lawyers ensure that wills are legally binding and properly reflect how their clients wish their estate or property to be divided. Estate law is also involved when there is a dispute or if a challenge is made on the terms of a will after the person is dead. Estate law also determines property division if a person dies without a will.

Corporate Law

Corporate law covers everything associated with public and private corporations, including the rules and regulations that govern the buying and selling of stocks on the stock market. The takeover of one company by another and rulings on corporate liability all fall under the category of corporate law.

Consumer Law

Consumer law provides protection for consumers regarding the purchase and safety of the products and services they buy. For example, if a company misrepresents its product by making false or unfair statements about its goods or services, its owners may be charged under the *Consumer Protection Act*.

Family Law

Family law governs legal relations between family members, including marriage, support and custody of children, separation, and divorce.

Public Law

Public law deals with the relationship between the state and the individual. Because issues involving public law are seen as affecting everyone, the state assumes responsibility for handling these matters. Constitutional law, administrative law, and criminal law are all branches of public law.

Constitutional Law

Constitutional law refers to the principles or rules that define the elements of the government of a country. Our Constitution outlines the function of different levels of government and indicates the limitations on the governments' power. For example, since the responsibility for education was given to the provinces under the *British North America Act*, the federal government could not make a ruling on what courses should be taught in high schools. Similarly, the federal government was given sole responsibility for criminal law under the *BNA Act*, making our criminal laws uniform across Canada.

Administrative Law

Administrative law involves government agencies that are set up by the legislature to make decisions on certain matters. Administrative law affects many aspects of everyday life. For example, immigration and refugee tribunals determine who can or cannot be admitted to Canada. The Workers' Compensation Board decides if workers injured on the job are entitled to compensation. There are a number of labour relations tribunals that make decisions about disputes between parties, such as unions and companies. Disputes involving immigration or labour relations are not resolved in the court system. The agencies regulated to hear these disputes serve a valuable function: they provide the authority of the law and free the courts for other issues.

Criminal Law

Criminal law deals with relations between the state and individuals. You will read more about criminal law in Chapter 9, but generally, criminal law is involved when someone commits an offence contrary to the *Criminal Code,* the *Youth Criminal Justice Act*, the *Controlled Drugs and Substances Act*, or a few other federal statutes. Some of these offences are murder, theft, fraud, and sexual assault. In criminal law, it is the state that brings the accused to trial, and the case is cited as *Regina* versus the accused. *Regina* is the Latin term for "Queen," the head of state in Canada, and all actions in court are taken on her behalf. (When the head of state is a king, the term "*Rex*" is used instead of "*Regina*.") In criminal cases, the burden of proof on the Crown is more stringent than in civil cases. The Crown must prove its case beyond a reasonable doubt. A person who is found guilty or convicted of the crime can be fined or imprisoned.

Domestic and International Law

A few years ago, William Sampson, a Canadian citizen, was arrested in Saudi Arabia and charged with conspiracy. Even though he was a Canadian citizen, Sampson was subject to the domestic laws of the sovereign state of Saudi Arabia. Officials from the Canadian Embassy in Saudi Arabia and the Canadian government could do nothing more than ensure that Sampson was afforded the same treatment as any Saudi citizen would be given.

Domestic law refers to the laws a sovereign (independent) state can make within its own defined territory or boundaries. Although Canada and the United States are not separated geographically, there is a political boundary between the two countries. Laws in the United States are different from our own. For example, some American states can impose a death penalty on individuals who have committed crimes in the United States, but Canada does not allow capital punishment within its borders. Similarly, if Canada chooses to decriminalize marijuana or approve same-sex marriage, the United States may express disapproval and try to exert political pressure, but it cannot directly affect changes to our laws.

International law refers to agreements between sovereign states. Sometimes these laws involve a small number of countries that agree to act for mutual benefit. Extradition acts and laws dealing with free trade may fall into this category. Other international laws, which are signed by many countries, have a broader scope, with such aims as safeguarding human rights, preventing terrorism, and protecting the environment. The *Universal Declaration of Human Rights* and the *Kyoto Protocol* are examples of these types of international agreements.

CONNECTIONS: Law and Diplomacy

by Miro Cernetig

Call it the *Midnight Express* moment. Like the traveler in that cautionary film, you are arrested in [a foreign country], stuck into a dank prison cell, terrorized and left to wonder who might come to rescue you and when. When I began an assignment as a foreign correspondent in 1998, before I joined the *Star*, I knew precisely who I wanted making the rescue calls if it ever happened to me: Canada.

A few months before heading to Beijing, I took out my Canadian citizenship, believing our diplomats would be my best guardians.

Now, sad to say, I'm no longer sure. I had my first doubts during my first week in China. I was grabbed out of a crowd of about 300 000 people in Tiananmen Square by the Secret Police and marched into a room inside the Forbidden City. For hours, the police questioned me about how I happened to be there for that rare anti-Mao outbreak. Then they took my camera, took the film and sent me home.

Nguyen Thi Hiep, a Vietnamese Canadian wasn't so lucky. She was picked up by Vietnamese police in 1996 at Hanoi's airport and charged with smuggling $5 million worth of heroin that was stuffed into a painting she was bringing back to Toronto. Even though many believed she was set up, she was

FIGURE 2.15 Tran Thi Cam (centre), a Brampton, Ont., woman returned to Canada by plane in 2000 after serving four years in a Vietnamese prison for an alleged drug run. Cam's grandson, Tu Le (right), holds a photo of his mother, Nguyen Thi Hiep, who was executed in Vietnam earlier that year.

executed at dawn on April 25, 2000. Her husband, Tran Hieu, said that the Canadian embassy had told him to be patient as they negotiated out of the spotlight.

Similar details have emerged about the alleged torture of William Sampson in a Saudi Arabian jail and the year-long imprisonment of Maher Arar in Syria. In many of these countries our diplomats are supposedly trying to teach the local justice minister about the rule of law. Surely they then have an obligation to fight to free a Canadian wrongly jailed.

And if you find yourself or a loved one stuck in one of those terrifying *Midnight Express* moments, make sure more than just our diplomats know about it.

SOURCE: Adapted from Cernetig, Miro. "Diplomatic Voices Fail." *Toronto Star* 11 Oct. 2003: A31.

Questions

1. Should Canada have a responsibility or duty to help Canadian citizens who get in trouble with the law in a foreign country? Explain.
2. Do some research to find out if there are international laws that protect Canadian citizens abroad.
3. Should Canadian citizens who commit a crime in another country be returned to Canada to serve their sentence? Discuss.
4. If you are travelling abroad as a Canadian citizen and you commit a crime that would not be considered criminal in Canada, should you be convicted under foreign law? Discuss.

CONFIRM YOUR UNDERSTANDING

1. Explain the difference between substantive and procedural law. Provide an example of each to illustrate your meaning.
2. Create your own classification chart to help you differentiate and easily identify the categories of law.
3. What is the difference between a criminal and a civil case regarding the burden of proof?
4. Provide three examples of legal situations that might involve administrative law.
5. In a courtroom in Paris, France, a French citizen was accused of committing a crime while on holiday in Thailand. The convicted man, Amnon Chemouil, was sentenced to seven years in prison for raping a 12-year-old Thai girl while on a "sex holiday" in Thailand. This was the first attempt on the part of prosecutors to convict French travellers who go overseas to sexually exploit children (*Toronto Star* 21 Oct. 2000: A23).

a) Do you agree that the French authorities should have convicted this man, even though he committed no crime according to Thai law?
b) What problems could arise when a country prosecutes a citizen who violates its laws outside its borders, when the offense is not illegal in the country he or she is visiting?
c) Canada has a law similar to that of France, but it stipulates that such cases cannot proceed unless the country where the offence occurred formally requests the intervention of Canada's Minister of Justice. Are you in favour of this law? Explain.
d) Canadians may go to another country and engage in gambling, drug use, sexual activities, money laundering, or business practices that are not permitted under Canadian law. Should Canada be able to prosecute such offenders if they return to Canadian jurisdiction? Explain your answer.

In Closing

That the past informs the present state of the Canadian legal system is evident. In this chapter, you have learned that our law has borrowed heavily from the customs, traditions, and ideas of centuries ago. We can trace the origins of our jury system to the Athenian witnesses or jurors who participated in trials in ancient Greece. Our court system owes much to King Henry II and his ideas of a royal court system. Our renewed interest in the principles of restorative justice can be found in early Aboriginal codes of law.

When you examine the roots of Canadian law, you see that there has been a continual move-

ment to wrest power from the elite and place it in the hands of the people. Western law has slowly evolved from the idea of the supremacy of God, to the supremacy of the monarchy, to a recognition of the importance of citizen participation in the making and administering of laws.

Law in a democracy is under continual pressure to change to meet the needs of the people. By examining how law worked in the past and how different societies viewed and applied the law, you are better able to understand the evolution of our own legal system.

CHAPTER ACTIVITIES

Extend Your Legal Knowledge

1. Jurisprudence has been compared to a pyramid in this text. Create your own analogy to explain the concept of jurisprudence and all its parts.

2. Critics of the *Canada Evidence Act* argue that the act is too complex, and even judges do not fully understand it. Is this a criticism of substantive or procedural law? Explain your answer.

3. Using any legal search tool, find a case that represents a category of civil or private law, for example, a tort or family-law case. Cite the case, and write a brief summary of the facts and the *ratio decidendi*.

4. The following selection is from *Martin's Annual Canadian Criminal Code 2003*:

   Section 231
   (1) Murder is first degree murder or second degree murder.
   (2) Murder is first degree murder when it is planned and deliberate....
   (4) Irrespective of whether a murder is planned and deliberate on the part of any person, murder is first degree murder when the victim is

   > a police officer, police constable, constable, sheriff, deputy sheriff, sheriff's officer or other person employed for the preservation and maintenance of the public peace, acting in the course of his duties;

   > a warden, deputy warden, instructor, keeper, jailer, guard or other officer or a permanent employee of a prison, acting in the course of his duties; or

   > a person working in a prison with the permission of the prison authorities and acting in the course of his work therein.

   What evidence is there in the following selections to indicate that our law in regard to murder is made up of statute law and case law?

   a) ***R. v. Shand* (1971), 3 C.C.C. (2d) 8, [1971] 3 W.W.R. 573 (Man. C.A.)**

   Mens rea: It was held that knowledge by the accused that the person killed was a police officer or other person employed for the preservation and maintenance of public peace is requisite for a conviction under that section.

   b) ***R. v. Fitzgerald and Schoenberger* (1982), 70 C.C.C. (2d) 87, 37 O.R. (2d) 750 (C.A.)**

   Acting in the course of his duties: Evidence that the victim was a member of a police detachment, was performing regular police duties, was assigned to a police cruiser, was in uniform when his body was discovered, and had made a radio transmission shortly before his death was, in the absence of evidence to the contrary, sufficient to discharge the evidentiary burden on the Crown to prove that the deceased was acting in the course of his duties, notwithstanding the lack of any evidence as to exactly what the officer was doing at the time of his death.

Think About the Law

5. You have read about the advantages and disadvantages of the inquisitorial and adversarial systems of justice. Assume you have been assigned the task of creating a new system that uses the best of both systems. What aspects of each system would you apply to your new system of justice? What would you call this new system?

6. In this chapter, you have read about the historical origins of our law. Many of our laws are based on the laws of the past. The following case questions the *Act of Settlement, 1701*, a British statute that is still part of Canada's constitutional arrangement. The *Act of Settlement* limits succession to the British throne to Protestants. Tony O'Donohue said that he thought some provisions of the act were

medieval laws based on discrimination of religion and should be removed. Read the facts of the case and the decision made by Justice Paul S. Rouleau of the Ontario Superior Court.

a) Do you think that laws enacted in Britain in 1701 should have any influence on Canadian law today? Explain your answer.

b) Why do you think that Justice Rouleau decided against declaring the *Act of Settlement* in violation of the *Charter of Rights and Freedoms*?

O'Donohue v. Canada, (2003-06-26) ONSC 01-CV-217147CM

Facts: Mr. O'Donohue is a Canadian citizen and a Roman Catholic. He believes that certain provisions of the *Act of Settlement* are clearly discriminatory against Roman Catholic people and offensive to the Roman Catholic faith. The *Act of Settlement* is a statute that was adopted by the United Kingdom in 1701. It is an act "established and declared in the Kingdoms of England, France and Ireland, and the dominions thereunto belonging." As a result, it became and remains part of the laws of Canada. The provision disputed by Mr. O'Donohue states that succession to the British throne is limited to the "Protestant line, for the happiness of the nation." The act excludes Catholics or anyone who marries a Catholic from inheriting, possessing, or enjoying the Crown of England. Mr. O'Donohue brings the present application to have those parts of the *Act of Settlement* that refer to Roman Catholics and limit their rights declared to be in breach of s. 15 (1) of the *Canadian Charter of Rights and Freedoms*.

Held: Case dismissed.

Ratio Decidendi: (Rouleau J.) "If the courts were free to review and declare inoperative certain parts of the rules of succession, Canada could break symmetry with Great Britain, and could conceivably recognize a different monarch than does Great Britain. This would be contrary to settled intention, as demonstrated by our written Constitution, and would see the courts changing rather than protecting our fundamental constitutional structure. A constitutional monarchy where the monarch is shared with the United Kingdom and other Commonwealth countries, is, in my view, at the root of our constitutional structure. One cannot accept the monarch but reject the legitimacy or legality of the rules by which this monarch is selected."

Communicate About the Law

7. To paraphrase Canadian political economist Harold Innis from his book *The Fur Trade in Canada*, Aboriginal peoples and their culture were fundamental to the growth of Canadian institutions. Research and prepare a report using this statement as your thesis.

8. Create a timeline showing the evolution of the justice system from the *Code of Hammurabi* to the Court of King's Bench.

9. The role of religion in law is often controversial, and critics continue to object to the inclusion of the word "God" in Canada's Constitution. The European community is drafting a new constitution for Europe. The framers of this new constitution are debating whether it should have a religious or spiritual clause. Read the following draft of the preamble to the new constitution for Europe dated 18 July 2003.

Our Constitution...is called a democracy because power is in the hands not of a minority but of the greatest number.

—Thucydides II, 37

Conscious that Europe is a continent that has brought forth civilization; that its inhabitants, arriving in successive waves from earliest times, have gradually developed the values underlying humanism: equality of persons, freedom, respect for reason,

Drawing inspiration from the cultural, religious and humanist inheritance of Europe, the values of which, still present in its heritage, have embedded within the life of society the central role of the human person and his or her inviolable and inalienable rights, and respect for law,

Believing that reunited Europe intends to continue along the path of civilization, progress and prosperity, for the good of all its inhabitants, including the weakest and most deprived; that it wishes to remain a continent open to culture, learning and social progress; and that it wishes to deepen the democratic and transparent nature of its public life, and to strive for peace, justice and solidarity throughout the world,

Convinced that, while remaining proud of their own national identities and history, the peoples of Europe are determined to transcend their ancient divisions and, united ever more closely, to forge a common destiny.

a) Do you think the framers of this possible new constitution should include a statement referring to the "supremacy of God" as is included in our own Constitution? Explain why or why not.

b) What does this draft constitution tell you about the political, social, economic, and legal values of this new Europe?

c) What differences do you see between the values expressed in this proposed European constitution and our own or that of the United States?

Apply the Law

10. Read the following case, and apply your knowledge of domestic and international law to explain whether you think the *Charter* rights of the accused applied in Michigan. Write a brief *ratio decidendi* for this case.

R. v. Harrer (1994-04-25), B.C.C.A. CA016710

The accused was arrested in Michigan for immigration offences. The police were aware that the accused was also wanted in Canada for her involvement in assisting in a prison escape. The Michigan police advised the accused of her rights, called "Miranda rights" in American law. They also asked her about her role in assisting a prisoner to escape from a Canadian jail. Without a lawyer being present, the accused made three incriminating statements, which were recorded by Michigan police. These statements were subsequently provided to the RCMP and were to be used by the Crown as evidence at her trial. The lawyer of the accused challenged the admissibility of the statements, arguing that the accused should have had a Canadian lawyer present when the Michigan police were questioning her. At trial, the judge determined that the failure to have a lawyer present violated the *Charter* rights of the accused and therefore excluded the statements. The Crown appealed.

11. Read the *Kindler v. Canada* case involving Canada's *Extradition Act*. Then read and compare the UN ruling on Canada's extradition policies in the *Judge v. Canada* case following. The government of Canada must contact the UN committee to explain its policy.

a) What arguments would you make to justify Canada's position in returning fugitives to the United States even if it means they will face the death penalty?

b) Should Canada abide by the United Nations' ruling and refuse to return escaped fugitives to countries where they may face the death penalty? Discuss.

Kindler v. Canada (Minister of Justice), [1991] 2 S.C.R. 779

The appellant was found guilty of first-degree murder, conspiracy to commit murder, and kidnapping in the United States. The jury imposed the death penalty, but before the sentence could be carried out, the accused escaped from prison and fled to Canada where he was arrested. The United States applied to have Kindler extradited. The Minister of Justice of Canada, after reviewing the material supplied by the appellant, ordered his extradition pursuant to s. 25 of the *Extradition Act* without seeking assurances from the United States, under Article 6 of the treaty, that the death penalty would not be carried out. The Court of Appeal of the Federal Court dismissed the appellant's application to review the minister's decision. The appellant's lawyer appealed the case to the Supreme Court of Canada, arguing that the minister's decision to extradite the appellant without seeking assurances that he would not face the death penalty violated the appellant's rights under s. 7 and s. 12 of the *Canadian Charter of Rights and Freedoms*.

The court determined that the appellant's rights had not been violated since the execution, if it ultimately took place, would be in the United States under American law against an American citizen for an offence that had taken place in the United States, and not from any initiative taken by the Canadian government.

Judge v. Canada, Communication No. 829/1998, (U.N.H.R.C.), August 5, 2002

Roger Judge was sent to death row in Pennsylvania after being convicted of a pair of drive-by murders in 1984. He escaped and resurfaced in Vancouver, where he was sentenced to 10 years in jail for a series of armed robberies and assaults. Judge served his sentence in Québec. At the end of his sentence, he argued before the Québec Superior Court that he should not be deported to the United States to face the death penalty. His arguments were rejected, and he was deported. His lawyer then took his case before the United Nations.

In September 2003, the United Nations agreed that Canada had violated Mr. Judge's rights under Article 6 of the *Universal Declaration of Human Rights* and ruled in his favour. Their argument was as follows:

The committee considered the question of whether Canada, having abolished the death penalty, had violated Roger Judge's right to life guaranteed in Article 6 by sending him to the United States without seeking assurance that it would not carry out the death penalty. This matter was considered earlier in the *Kindler v. Canada* case when it was determined that countries who have not abolished the death penalty may impose it for serious crimes. But in light of the growing consensus in favour of abolishing the death penalty and Canada's own domestic policy on this issue, the committee concluded that for countries that have abolished the death penalty, there is an obligation not to expose a person to the real risk of its application. Thus by deporting Mr. Judge to the United States where he was under sentence of death, Canada established the crucial link in the causal chain that would make possible the execution of Mr. Judge. This deportation therefore violated Article 6 of the *Universal Declaration of Human Rights*. The Canadian government was required to contact the committee within 90 days to inform the committee what action it had taken.

SOURCE: Office of the High Commissioner of Human Rights.

BIBLIOGRAPHY

The Avalon Project @ Yale Law School. Accessed 5 Oct. 2003 <http://yale.edu/lawweb/avalon>.

Bennet, Paul. *Canada: A North American Nation.* Whitby, ON: McGraw-Hill Ryerson Ltd., 1995.

Canadian Legal Information Institute. Accessed 20 Oct. 2003 <www.canlii.org>.

Cernetig, Miro. Adapted from "Diplomatic Voices Fail." *Toronto Star.* 11 Oct. 2003: A31.

Condon, Anne, and Tom Condon. *Legal Lunacy.* Los Angeles: Price Stern Sloan, 1992.

Dickason, Olive P. *Canada's First Nations.* Toronto: Oxford University Press, 1997.

Duhaime and Company. Accessed 17 Oct. 2003 <www.duhaime.org>.

"French Court Convicts 'Sex Tourist' for Rape." *Toronto Star.* 21 Oct. 2000: A23.

Guest, James. "Aboriginal Legal Theory and Restorative Justice." Native Law Centre of Canada, 1999. Accessed 20 Dec. 2003 <www.usask.ca/nativelaw>.

Lockett, David. "Coming to Grips with Youth Crime." *Toronto Star* 21 Dec. 2003.

Office of the High Commissioner of Human Rights. Accessed 21 Dec. 2003 <www.unhchr.ch/hurricane/huricane.nsf/NewsRoom>.

Siegel, Larry J., and Chris McCormick. *Criminology in Canada.* Scarborough, ON: ITP Nelson, 1999.

Toughill, Kelly. Adapted from "Mercy Mixed with Justice." *Toronto Star* 3 Feb. 2001: K3.

CONCEPTS, THEORIES, AND THEORISTS

LEARNING EXPECTATIONS

After reading this chapter, you will be able to:

- interpret legal concepts such as democracy, justice, equity, equality, and sovereignty
- analyze the views of historical and contemporary philosophers of law
- evaluate the strengths and weaknesses of different theories of law
- explain the concept of justice as defined by philosophers and legal scholars

FIGURE 3.1 Socrates, as well as other early philosophers took up the question of the "nature" of law. They believed that the boundaries set out in the natural world should serve as a guide for human laws. Natural law supporters believe that people are basically "good" by nature. Socrates, shown here in prison, was sentenced to death for imparting his views to the youth of Athens, Greece. Do you believe people are generally good-natured? If so, why then is it necessary to have laws?

You can tell whether a man is clever by his answers. You can tell whether a man is wise by his questions.

—Naguib Mahfouz, Egyptian novelist, 1911

■ I N T R O D U C T I O N ■

In a sense, we are all philosophers. Throughout history, human beings have asked questions about life's small and large mysteries, such as, What is a truth? and Why do we exist? Our legal system lends itself particularly well to questions and analysis. *Is law necessary?* and *What does "liberty" mean?* are but a few of the questions that early and contemporary philosophers have tried to answer.

We may find philosophers' ideas and explanations somewhat challenging to understand, but that is one of their goals—to stimulate others to think about issues in depth. Historical legal philosophy can shed light on many of the law-based concerns of contemporary society. In your study of the legal concepts, philosophies, and philosophers in this chapter, your task is to try to gain a better understanding of the law by asking relevant questions and digging deeper to find the best answers.

Legal Concepts

Throughout history there have been many responses to the question, *What is law?* For example, some have said it is the will of God, while others have suggested it is an expression of class struggle. Our understanding of the concept of law depends on our perspective and circumstances. There are those who would argue that law is what those in power say it is, as well as those who suggest that law is force or the threat of force.

Assuming that human society is one beset by continual conflict, we must develop a system for conflict resolution in order to survive. One of the key purposes of law, therefore, is to act as such a system, balancing the interests of individuals against those of the community. We also recognize that societies have certain values in common. Therefore, another key purpose of the law is to uphold these shared values while resolving conflicts.

Law uses many abstract concepts to form rules and systems. Relating these concepts to one another is known as **judicial reasoning**. For example, in civil law a person may be held liable based on a negligent act, and in criminal law on whether the act was committed intentionally. Concepts such as "motive" and "intention" are used to determine the existence and extent of liability or criminal responsibility. What should the basis of criminal responsibility be, and when should someone be excused from punishment? Why should it be possible to use an excuse in the first place? Perhaps the actions and consequences should be the criteria for criminal responsibility. Why aren't they? Why should insanity or drunkenness be permitted as a legal defence? Legal

Law is the highest reason implanted in nature which commands what ought to be done and forbids the opposite.

—Cicero
(106–43 BCE)

scholars continually engage in judicial reasoning by refining these types of questions in an attempt to properly evaluate our law and legal institutions.

The essence of law is understanding the relationship between certain similar, yet different, legal concepts: democracy, sovereignty, and jurisdiction; power and authority; legitimacy and ownership; rights and duties; equality and equity; morality and humanity; and the key concepts of law and justice. There are no clear-cut definitions of these legal concepts, but an understanding of their role in our legal system is necessary in order to evaluate the law effectively.

Democracy

Democracy can be defined as a form of government in which the power resides in, and is exercised by, the people through a system of representation. However, the concept of democracy requires a broader examination. Some nations tend to believe that they are democratic because the masses can vote for representatives who will make laws on their behalf. It may be argued, however, that once elected, representatives can impose laws that the majority would not necessarily support. For example, the majority likely would not have voted in support of taxes, such as the goods and services tax (GST) and provincial sales tax (PST), if a referendum had been held on the matter.

Socialists and capitalists disagree on which of their rival systems is more democratic. Socialists might argue that "one person, one vote" is meaningless if the wealthy can unfairly influence the system. Capitalists might counter that socialism inevitably limits political and individual freedoms.

Democracy is also criticized because the freedom given to the majority may be used to harm a minority, as was the case with slavery in the United States. The fight for self-government by Aboriginal peoples in Canada also reflects the problems of being a minority within a majority in a democracy.

Democracy is the worst form of government in the world—except for all the other forms.
—British Prime Minister Winston Churchill (1874–1965)

Sovereignty and Jurisdiction

Sovereignty

Sovereignty and jurisdiction are closely related but are not the same. The concept of **sovereignty** is comparatively recent. It is the principle that nation-states (societies with defined boundaries and laws) are free to impose whatever laws they choose within their own territories. This concept dates back to the 1648 *Treaty of Westphalia* between Germany and the monarchs of Spain, France, Sweden, and the Netherlands. The treaty established, for the first time, that sovereign powers possessed the freedom to act as they wished within their own defined borders without interference from the neighbouring countries.

Sovereignty remained intact until the end of World War II, when it was challenged. It was felt that the world had stood by while Germany

FIGURE 3.2 This space in a Baghdad courtroom will house suspects when the war-crimes tribunal begins hearing cases in 2005. Should war criminals face justice in courts in their own country, or should the international community be responsible for bringing war criminals to justice in United Nations tribunals?

killed millions of its own citizens and that this was unacceptable. In 1945, the **United Nations** was set up as an international organization to promote peace, in part, by limiting the sovereignty of those nation-states that agreed to membership. Nation-states that committed acts of **genocide**, that is, the systematic killing of an entire group of human beings based on their ethnicity or religion, or **war crimes** (crimes violating the international laws of war) could be subject to intervention by the member states of the United Nations. The idea that international law could act as a guarantor of individuals' rights against the abuses of sovereign states has, to some extent, limited the concept of sovereignty.

Jurisdiction

Jurisdiction has a number of legal meanings, but in a general sense, it refers to the parameters within which power or authority may be exercised. Sovereignty refers to national boundaries, but jurisdiction is more limited. For example, the *British North America Act* sets out the powers and authority of different levels of government in Canada. The federal government has jurisdiction over criminal law; the provincial governments of Canada may make recommendations, but they cannot make unilateral changes to the *Criminal Code of Canada*. In addition to jurisdiction applying to levels of authority, it can also refer to geographical limits on authority. For example, a school board has authority to make decisions for all the schools within its jurisdiction, an area that has physical boundaries.

Power and Authority

Power and authority are also concepts that are similar but not the same. **Power** is the ability to act or refrain from acting. This ability is often derived from legal authority. In Canada, the **authority**, or the legal right, to make laws is granted to government by the *British North America Act*. Government also has the power to enforce the laws it makes because it has various methods and means of enforcement available,

including police officers and punishments such as fines or imprisonment. However, power can be acquired without legal authority. For example, a police officer may have the authority and the power to arrest a criminal, but if the criminal takes the officer's weapon, the criminal has the power to act, even though he or she has no legal authority to do so.

Legitimacy and Ownership

The concept of **legitimacy** has various meanings in law. It refers to the lawful right to inherit either property or title. It can also mean that which is lawful or recognized by law. For example, only a legitimate heir to the throne can become king or queen. The head of state of Canada, for example, can only be the legitimate heir to the throne of England. Determining who is a legitimate heir is a matter of relationship to and position within the royal family.

Ownership is another interesting concept. It can mean being the legitimate owner; that is, one who has legal title to a property or possession. Since the concept of ownership depends greatly on context, some people might disagree with this definition. For example, it is customary in certain Canadian families for parents to will their property to their children and to assume that land will stay in the same family for generations. This idea of ownership may differ considerably from that held by Communists, who reject the concept of private ownership in favour of state ownership and allocation of resources. There are still others, such as some Aboriginal peoples, who believe humans merely inhabit the earth but cannot own it and therefore would not be able to delegate ownership after death.

Some people are highly critical of the fact that many nation-states have acquired land and property through conquest and war. For example, Aboriginal communities in Canada have long argued that Europeans took advantage of Aboriginal views on the concept of ownership that differed from theirs to acquire large tracts of land.

FIGURE 3.3   A painting by Canadian A. Bruce Stapleton shows Treaty No. 7 negotiations between British immigrants and Aboriginal people in the southern part of present-day Alberta. This was the last of the numbered treaties negotiated and signed during the 1870s. Aboriginal people and Europeans had and still have differing ideas on the concept of land ownership.

The debate over the meaning of ownership continues. We still argue over who, if anyone, can claim ownership of outer space, the fish in the sea, the bottom of the ocean, and even the air above our heads. At one time in various countries, slavery was legal and "owning" people was acceptable. Just as ownership of people is now illegal, in the future, the ownership of land may also become illegal.

Rights and Duties

The concept of a **right** can be interpreted in many ways. In the abstract, it can refer to that which is correct or just, or it can mean a legal entitlement to a particular property or possession. The term "right" is often misused. For example, you may claim it is your right to watch television or drive a car. Many people claim they have a right to free speech or to join a union. However, a right is more often connected with duty. A legal right implies that the state is obligated or has a duty to provide or enable that privilege or service. For example, you do not have a right to watch television because the state does not obligate anyone to provide you with a television to watch. You may join a union, but there is no law that says you have a right to belong to a union. The state is obligated to ensure that you are able to exercise your right to free speech, and if another party denies you that right, the state will intervene on your behalf.

A legal right, therefore, is meaningless unless there is an equal duty to provide the right. For example, under certain circumstances, an accused has the right to a jury trial. This right would be meaningless if the state could not impose a duty on citizens to sit on a jury. A right, therefore, generally must come with a corresponding obligation or duty if it is to have validity in law.

SHIFTING PERSPECTIVES: Should Animals Have Rights?

Some people would argue that, in Canada, we treat our pets better than we treat some people. On the other hand, ever since humans and animals have co-existed, humans have eaten animals, bought and sold them, bred and experimented with them, hunted them for sport, and made their body parts into trinkets and trophies. Animal-rights activists in Canada are now arguing that animals deserve more protection in law. Some have gone so far as to suggest that certain animals should have equal status to humans to enjoy life and liberty. A group of animal-rights lawyers and advocates have argued that our closest biological connection, the chimpanzee, should be given three fundamental rights: the right to life, the right not to be tortured, and the right not to be imprisoned. Animal-rights activists point to the fact that scientific discoveries have led us to an increased awareness that many animals have a much higher level of thinking skills and social development than was previously believed.

Canada's federal laws on animal cruelty have not changed since 1892, and in response to changing attitudes and more concern for the well-being of animals, the Canadian government tabled Bill C-10B in October 2002, with the intention of strengthening the present animal-cruelty legislation. Acceptance of the legislation would mean that those convicted of causing "unnecessary pain and suffering or injury to an animal," could face maximum jail sentences of up to 5 years and a $10 000 fine. The present maximum penalty for animal cruelty is a $2000 fine and 6 months in jail. In part, the bill reads as follows:

182.1 In this Part, "animal" means a vertebrate, other than a human being, and any other animal that has the capacity to feel pain.

182.2 (1) Every one commits an offence who, wilfully and recklessly,

(a) causes or, being the owner, permits to be caused, unnecessary pain, suffering or indignity to an animal;

(b) kills an animal or, being the owner, permits an animal to be killed brutally or viciously, regardless of whether the animal dies immediately;

(c) kills an animal without lawful excuse;

(d) without lawful excuse, poisons an animal, places poison in such a position that it may be easily consumed by an animal or, being the owner, permits anyone to do any of those things.

The House of Commons passed the bill, but the Senate refused to pass it unless the government adopted the Senate's proposed changes. The original bill defined an animal as "a vertebrate, other than a human being, and any other animal that has the capacity to feel pain." The Senate committee proposed amending the definition of "animal" to read "a vertebrate, other than a human being." The term "vertebrate" refers to species with a backbone, such as fish, birds, mammals, and amphibians. Using that word would exclude creatures such as octopuses, squids, lobsters, and crabs. The Senate argued that "the definition in Bill C-10B feeds into concerns that the bill adheres to animal rights philosophy and that an ideological shift is taking place in favour of the emancipation of animals" (Lunman 2003).

The Senate is also considering exemptions for hunters, trappers, scientific researchers acting under "generally accepted standards," those who practise animal husbandry or slaughter, and natives who practise "traditional hunting, trapping or fishing."

Advocates for various animal-based businesses have appeared before the committee to ask that their industries be exempt from the bill. They want assurances that people who use humane methods to kill animals will not be subject to attempts by animal-rights groups to prosecute them privately. Experts on pain also appeared before the Senate committee and testified that a lobster being boiled does not feel pain.

Animal-rights advocates accuse the Senate committee of giving in to the animal-industry lobby and losing sight of the very serious problem of animal cruelty in Canada. David Loan, campaign manager for the International Fund for Animal Welfare said, "I'm hoping the Senate will take a step back and remember what this law is for. They're setting it back prior to 1892" (Lunman 2003).

FIGURE 3.4   Valerie Roberton (centre) from the animals' rights group Voice for Animals holds an inflatable dolphin during a protest aimed at the owners of West Edmonton Mall in 2003. The group is unhappy with the mall's treatment of Howard the dolphin following the death of another dolphin recently. Do you believe rights laws are needed to protect animals in Canada?

SOURCES: Adapted from Tizon, Alex. "Apes in the Courtroom: A Group of Lawyers Is Fighting for Recognition of Apes as Legal Persons." *National Post* 1 Apr. 2000;

Adapted from Lunman, Kim. "Definition of 'Animal' May Hold Up Cruelty Law." *The Globe and Mail* 22 Apr. 2003.

Your Perspective

1. The Senate committee suggested that an "ideological shift is taking place in favour of the emancipation of animals." What evidence could you offer to show that the senators are correct?
2. Scientists are now discovering that fish feel pain, elephants show compassion, and dolphins display intelligence. Will we look back 100 years from now and see our cruelty and use of animals as barbaric, just as we now view the enslavement of people? Discuss.
3. Read the above excerpts from Bill C-10B. Would you pass the bill into law? Why or why not?
4. Draw up your own Bill of Rights for Animals.
5. Some philosophers argue that people who do not know they have a right or are incapable of understanding what a right is cannot exercise their rights. Do you agree with this argument? Does this mean that animals can never have rights? Explain.

Equality and Equity

The terms "equality" and "equity" are often used interchangeably, yet, in certain instances, they could have the opposite meaning. **Equality** means treating everyone in the same manner, while **equity** means treating people according to the principles of fairness. Sometimes treating people equally results in fairness, but other times it would appear that it does not. For example, it might not be fair to treat a child the same as an adult in all circumstances. However, we would consider it unfair if a woman were paid a different salary than a man for doing the same job. Equity generally means treating like cases alike and different cases differently in the spirit of fairness, justice, and doing what is right. Equality means treating everyone the same even if equal treatment may yield unfair results. Equality can mean a strict application of the rules of law, while equity permits a judge to depart from a strict application of the law in the interest of fairness.

Morality and Humanity

The concepts of morality and humanity are closely connected. **Humanity** generally refers to kindness toward humankind. International law defines **crimes against humanity** as crimes that are so terrible that they warrant condemnation by all humans. Genocide and war crimes are examples.

Morality refers to that which might render an action right or wrong. Determining whether an action is right or wrong may be personal; that is, an individual has his or her own sense of right or wrong. Alternatively, the standard of moral conduct could be determined by religious, cultural, or other societal beliefs. While our legal system recognizes the right of individuals to their own moral sense, our laws are more concerned with applying the values of the community. For example, one of the tests used to determine whether or not something is obscene is the **community standards test**. If the courts determine that the material would offend the community, it may be considered obscene even if certain members of that community would not be offended.

At the same time, the law often acts as the arbiter, or judge, of moral standards and imposes moral standards that may not be supported by the majority of people. Although many Canadians support the death penalty, our law does not apply this most severe punishment, believing it to be cruel and against the moral values of the legal system. As Canadian society widens to include a diversity of communities, our laws will continue to be questioned, discussed, and amended.

Landmark CASE

Towne Cinema Theatres Ltd. v. The Queen, [1985] 1 S.C.R. 494

Read the following case, which attempted to clarify what the courts meant by the application of the "community standard of tolerance" in a situation involving obscenity. The concurring judges in this case argued that the test for obscenity was not what Canadian citizens would think was right for themselves to see, but what they would tolerate other Canadians seeing. Do you agree with the need to apply this test? Assume that you disagree with the decision in this case, and write a possible dissent.

Facts: The appellant, the owner of an Edmonton theatre, was charged with presenting an obscene motion picture contrary to s. 163 of the *Criminal Code*. At trial, the defence was able to show that the film had been approved and classified by the Alberta Censor Board as a restricted adult movie, and that it had been previously shown in Alberta to a large audience with no complaints being made to the board. The evidence further showed that the film had been similarly approved and classified by the other provincial censor boards across the country. The trial judge said he found the film immoral, indecent, and obscene and convicted the appellant. The Court of Appeal upheld that decision. This appeal is to determine whether the trial judge applied the proper test in finding the appellant guilty of presenting an obscene entertainment.

Issue: Assuming that "undue exploitation of sex" is to be assessed on the basis of community standards, do these standards refer to what one would find acceptable for oneself to see or read, or to what one would tolerate others seeing or reading?

Criminal Code: 163 (2) Every one commits an offence who knowingly, without lawful justification or excuse,
(a) sells, exposes to public view or has in his possession for such a purpose any obscene written matter, picture, model, phonograph record or other thing whatever;
(3) No person shall be convicted of an offence under this section if the public good was served by the acts that are alleged to constitute the offence and if the acts alleged did not extend beyond what served the public good.
(8) For the purposes of this Act, any publication a dominant characteristic of which is the undue exploitation of sex, or of sex and any one or more of the following subjects, namely, crime, horror, cruelty and violence, shall be deemed to be obscene.

Held: The appeal should be allowed and a new trial ordered.

Ratio Decidendi: (Dickson C.J. and Lamer and Le Dain JJ.) "A film is obscene under s. 163 (8) of the *Criminal Code* if it contains as a dominant characteristic the 'undue exploitation of sex.' To determine 'undueness,' one of the tests to be applied is whether the accepted standards of tolerance in the contemporary Canadian community, taken as a whole, have been exceeded. In applying the community standards of tolerance, what matters is not what Canadians think is right for themselves to see. What matters is what Canadians would not abide other Canadians seeing because it would be beyond the contemporary Canadian standard of tolerance to allow them to see it. Relevant to that determination is, among other factors, the audience to which the film is targeted, since the community may tolerate different things for different groups of people depending on the circumstances.

"The trier of fact must formulate an opinion of what the contemporary Canadian community will tolerate in order to determine 'undueness' by the community standards test....The trier of fact's personal view regarding the film is irrelevant.

"In the case at bar, the trial judge applied his own subjective standards of taste and not the community's standard of tolerance. He did not direct his mind to the question whether most people would tolerate others seeing the film in question, and he failed to consider the fact that the film was restricted to adults only and that only those who chose to see it would be exposed to it. He should not have rejected it without explanation."

CONFIRM YOUR UNDERSTANDING

1. Democracy has been referred to as the "tyranny of the majority." What do you think this means? Do you agree? Explain your answer.

2. Explain the difference between jurisdiction and sovereignty in your own words.

3. Explain how international law limits the concept of sovereignty.

4. Since the *Declaration of Human Rights* in 1948, many nations, from South Africa to Serbia, have violated the rights of their own people.

   a) What criteria would you suggest that international bodies, such as the United Nations, use to determine whether or not to interfere with the actions of a sovereign state?

   b) Other than going to war, what suggestions would you make to stop a nation-state from violating human rights within its own borders?

5. a) Create a Venn diagram showing the relationship between power and authority.

   b) Is it possible to have power but not authority? Give an example.

6. Provide a definition of the concept of legitimacy. Illustrate your definition with a recent example.

7. An agreement called the *Outer Space Treaty* was signed by 120 countries in 1967. This treaty barred any nation or government from claiming title to the solar system. However, the treaty failed to mention anything about individual ownership, and in 1980 an entrepreneur named Dennis Hope filed a declaration of ownership with the United Nations and United States government claiming title to the moon, all the planets, and their moons. He sold parcels of the moon to 2.2 million people in 180 countries. Former US presidents Jimmy Carter and Ronald Reagan and the original cast members of the TV show "Star Trek" all purchased a piece of the lunar landscape from Mr. Hope.

   a) How would you define "ownership"?

   b) Do the people referred to above really own the moon? Make an argument that they do. Make an equally convincing argument that they do not.

   c) There is no right to property in the Canadian Constitution. Does that mean the government could expropriate your property (i.e., buy your land even if you are unwilling to sell)? Discuss.

8. Is it possible to have a right without a corresponding obligation or duty? Explain.

9. According to the *Charter of Rights and Freedoms*, all Canadians have the "right to life." Does this mean the state must provide food to someone who is starving to death or shelter to someone who is dying from cold? Discuss.

10. Explain the difference between equality and equity. Provide an example to support your answer.

Law and Justice

We know that law is not the same thing as justice. In fact, we often speak of these two concepts as though they are opposed to each other. The idea of law, however, has always been associated with the idea of justice. Most legal scholars agree that justice represents the ultimate goal to which the law should strive. The Statue of Justice (as seen on p. 290) symbolizes the view that law must be integrated with justice, and that law without justice is a mockery. Yet the perception that these two concepts are at odds with each other remains.

Law	Justice
Law provides order in society.	Justice provides fairness and equity.
The rule of law is of supreme value.	Civil disobedience is valid if the laws are unjust and contrary to what is fair.
The law incorporates a way of resolving disputes.	A judge can depart from the law in an unusual case by setting a precedent.
The role of law is to defend persons, property, and rights.	To be just, law must be consistent with moral law and law inspired by God(s).

FIGURE 3.5 This chart compares the characteristics of law and justice. In your own words, give an explanation of each row.

Characteristics of Justice

Law, as you have learned, is a set of rules, impartially applied, for regulating human behaviour and settling disputes. Law and justice can be contrasted more easily using a chart (see Figure 3.5).

Justice is a more elusive concept than law. British philosopher Thomas Hobbes said that the only standard of **justice** is the law itself, so whatever rule the law lays down must be just. On the other hand, Greek philosopher Plato thought that justice was the most important concept of the moral world. More cynical people have suggested that justice is the personal point of view an individual holds on a particular issue. Philosophers have struggled for years with the idea of justice, and law-makers have attempted to use their ideas to reach an ideal balance between justice and the law. Over the years, certain characteristics have come to be accepted in determining what justice means.

Most people would argue that the idea of justice should be linked with equality of treatment. This means that all people, regardless of ethnicity, religion, or social standing, should be treated without discrimination. However, the principle of equality comes with qualifications. For example, we would usually consider it unjust to give the same punishment to a child as we would give to an adult. Therefore, the basic principle of justice is to treat like cases alike and different cases differently. Justice, therefore,

should facilitate a certain amount of respect for all people by maintaining a balance of equality and equity.

Conceptions of justice have varied through the centuries and from society to society. Since ancient Greeks believed that there was a natural inequality among people, they did not think justice was meant to attain or promote equality. Today, Canadians believe it would be unjust to treat members of society differently based on, for example, their gender. Our society would consider it extremely unjust to make a university education available to boys but not to girls, yet other current societies consider such a limitation perfectly just, as did our own society over 100 years ago.

Justice is often more concerned with how law is applied than with the substantive law itself. The vast majority of people may view a particular law negatively, yet if it is justly applied, it may become less objectionable. For example, most people do not like paying taxes, but as long as all of us are equally subject to the tax laws, most of us would not consider those laws unjust.

Although justice involves the distribution of benefits and burdens within a group, justice is not necessarily the same as fairness. For example, it would be *fair* to set the same standards of testing for all individuals who wish to become firefighters. However, when one particular group, such as women, tend not to have the same physical strength as most men, it might be considered *just* to judge the scores of female applicants on the physical test differently from the scores of male applicants. This may not seem fair to a man who scores well on the physical test but is denied admittance so that a woman can be admitted.

We consider it unjust if a law discriminates on the basis of irrelevant characteristics. For example, it may be considered just if a person is denied the opportunity to become a police officer because he or she lacks the necessary mental skills. However, if a person were denied the opportunity to apply because he or she failed to meet a certain height requirement that had no bearing on the ability of officers to do their job, and this height requirement meant certain people could never apply to the police force, then we would consider such a requirement unjust.

Justice should also apply to both **substantive** and **procedural law**. For example, the substantive law ensures that the standard that determines whether a driver should be subject to a breath test is the same for all drivers. Procedural law stipulates that the police officer administering the test will proceed in the same way no matter who the driver is.

The administration of justice, according to many legal scholars, deals with what is called **distributive justice**—the idea that there should be a fair distribution of honours and rewards by the state to the people according to merit, or worth. This concept applies to the idea of reward and punishment: we assume that the fundamental role of law and justice should be to reward good and punish evil. This concept of justice was articulated by the Greek philosopher Aristotle and by the Roman emperor Justinian, who said that justice consists of giving each person his or her due. The difficulties arise in determining one's "due" and assessing merit.

There is a constant tension in law between stability and certainty and equity and fairness, and finding the perfect balance has proved difficult. This has not deterred many of the legal scholars you will study in this chapter from continuing to seek the elusive goal of ideal justice.

FIGURE 3.6 Canadian female ice hockey player Hayley Wickenheiser is pictured during a game in Finland in January 2003. Wickenheiser was the first woman to play ice hockey in a men's league, when she signed with the Salamat (Lightnings) of Kirkkonummi. Many companies and universities have been expected to provide accommodations to permit women to join the workforce or academia. Should sports teams be expected to make similar adjustments to ensure women can play on men's sports teams?

Philosophies of Law

There are many philosophies about the nature of law, and although each stands on its own, law may encompass all of them to a greater or lesser extent. There continues to be a great deal of debate about these various theories. Is law merely the expression of the will of the leader? Are there boundaries set by nature and reason that should serve as a guide? Does law derive from the word of God? Historical theories of law include divine, natural, and positive law.

Divine Law

The earliest forms of law were likely based on religious doctrines. Divine law rests on the belief of divine intervention, meaning that all law comes from God(s). Those who support **divine law** principles say that law is the product of God's will, which people incorporated into their own legal codes. Since supporters of divine law believe that law is derived from God(s), they say that it cannot be changed or overruled, and that human laws that violate the laws of God(s) are invalid.

Natural Law

In the fifth century BCE, Socrates, as well as Plato and Aristotle who came after him, took up the question of the nature of law. These philosophers recognized that there was a distinction between ideas and rules existing in nature and those created by humans. Socrates, Plato, and Aristotle believed that there were boundaries set out by nature, such as birth, death, and the tides of the ocean, which should serve as a guide to human-made laws.

Natural law supporters assume that it is human nature to be good, that all people strive to be good, and that goodness is essential to our well-being. Natural law is assumed to be universal, in that it applies to all humankind. It also imposes a moral responsibility on a society to give each person his or her due, regardless of the laws in place. Philosophers of natural law always try to seek out the meaning of truth, which they believe can be discovered by constantly questioning the meaning and purpose of law.

Positive Law

Later, in the sixteenth century, philosophers such as Thomas Hobbes and Jeremy Bentham rejected this idea of natural law. They argued that law was based on the principles of positive law. **Positive law** supporters argued that law and justice were not the same thing and that law was nothing more than the opinion of whoever held power at that moment. As a result, positive law supporters agreed that positive law (also called social law) could be based on the principles of natural law but did not have to be. Some positive law supporters argued that law is coercive, or forceful, in order to preserve order. Hobbes, for example, argued that obedience to the existing law was essential, even if it meant that justice was not done.

CONFIRM YOUR UNDERSTANDING

1. Law is sometimes referred to as "reason" and justice is sometimes referred to as "fairness." What other concepts do you think relate to law and justice? Explain.

2. How would you argue that law is different from justice?

3. Explain three characteristics of justice. Provide an example of each characteristic.

4. How does justice apply to substantive and procedural law?

5. Read the facts of the following edited case.
   a) What would you decide? Write a brief _ratio decidendi_.
   b) Indicate how you would decide this case if you were to apply the principles of justice, and how your answer would differ if you were to apply only the letter of the law.

Riggs v. Palmer 115 N.Y. Court of Appeals 506 (1889)
Facts: Elmer Palmer murdered his grandfather Francis B. Palmer in order to benefit from his grandfather's will. Francis B. Palmer, Elmer's grandfather, in a will dated August 13, 1880, left most of his estate to his grandson, Elmer. Elmer decided to kill his grandfather to inherit the estate earlier and to prevent his grandfather's new wife from any possible share in Elmer's inheritance. Elmer was convicted of murdering his grandfather, but he still insisted on receiving the inheritance that his grandfather had legally willed to him.
Issue: Must the wishes of a testator (the person who wrote the will) be upheld even if the beneficiary killed the testator to benefit

early from the will? (Dyzenhaus and Ripstein 1996)

6. Complete the following statements:
   a) Divine law is correct because…
   b) Natural law is correct because…
   c) Positive law is correct because…

7. During World War II, a number of people collaborated with the Nazis and turned in ordinary citizens for speaking out against Hitler. This was in accordance with a law at the time that stated it was illegal to make negative statements about Hitler or the Third Reich (the Nazi regime). Most of the people

who were denounced under the law were either executed or sent to concentration camps. After the war, there was a desire to punish the informants for their actions. A number of these informants were put on trial.

   a) Assume the informants in these cases were found guilty. Do you think the judges who tried these cases considered natural or positive law in making their decisions? Explain.

   b) What problems do you foresee with the judges' decisions in such cases? Explain.

Philosophers of Law

What is law? If good is to be rewarded and evil punished, how do we define good and evil? Should we obey the law, no matter what its content? What if the law itself is evil? Who should we entrust with making the law? There are no perfect answers to these questions; the importance lies in the asking. The hope is that by posing questions and building up a jigsaw puzzle of answers, we will finally be able to see the whole picture of the meaning of law.

The philosophers you will learn about are but a few of the most influential legal thinkers of their day. They represent ancient, historical, and contemporary philosophies and all have influenced jurisprudence and contemporary legal thought in North America.

Plato (428–348 BCE)

We know of the work of Plato through his famous books, such as *Dialogues* and *The Republic*, and through the writings of his pupil Aristotle. In *Dialogues*, Plato tried to explain justice through a series of question-and-answer conversations with Socrates. The Greek society that Plato observed did not appear to meet his standards of justice: "I declare that justice is

nothing else than that which is advantageous to the stronger. It follows that the just man disregards them [laws]. But the subject who obeys hurts himself and promotes the good of others. It pays therefore to act unjustly" (Griffith 1997).

Plato believed that the just person was a reflection of the just society. An ideal or just society, according to Plato, would be one in which everyone performed to the best of his or her abilities. Since Plato believed that people were unequal, such a society would not rest on equal treatment of all members. The ideal ruler of this society would be a "philosopher king," who would be wise enough to administer justice. This philosopher king would be selected not by birth but based on his or her achievements, education, and ability to rule.

Initially, Plato thought that justice should be administered without law because he felt that the law was too abstract and general and failed to observe the differences among people. He eventually realized that it would be difficult to find a philosopher king, and without one, who could rule with justice without being corrupted? There was, therefore, a need for law.

FIGURE 3.7   Socrates was put on trial and subsequently sentenced to death by drinking poison (held in the bowl) for corrupting the youth of Athens, Greece. He would not go along with a planned prison break due to his beliefs on law and justice (see Asking Key Questions, below). If a wrongfully convicted Canadian had a chance to escape from prison, should he or she do so? Explain.

ASKING KEY QUESTIONS

Socrates and Crito Discuss a Prison Break

The great philosopher Socrates, born in Athens in 420 BCE, actually left no legal writings of his own. We know his views through Plato's *Dialogues*. Socrates' method of intellectual inquiry was to raise and discuss searching questions about customs, morals, and religious and political behaviours with the young men from the leading families in Athens.

His actions soon came to the attention of the authorities, and Socrates was asked to stop challenging the status quo. Socrates refused and was put on trial for allegedly corrupting the youth of Athens. At his trial, Socrates was unrepentant. Instead of apologizing, which would likely have

saved his life, Socrates argued that Athens should award him the honours normally bestowed on Olympic athletes. Annoyed by his arrogance, the court sentenced him to death by poisoning. While Socrates was in prison awaiting the time he had to drink the poison, his friend and student Crito came to visit. Crito told Socrates that a jailbreak was all arranged. In an extended dialogue with Crito, Socrates explained why he could not escape and had to abide by the laws of Athens. The following is an excerpt of that dialogue.

Socrates: We should not then think so much of what the majority will say about us, but what he will say who understands justice and injustice, the one, that is, and the truth itself. So that, in the first place, you were wrong to believe that we should care for the opinion of the many about what is just, beautiful, good, and their opposites. But, someone might say that the majority is able to put us to death.

Crito: That too is obvious, Socrates, and someone might well say so.

Socrates: And, my admirable friend, that argument that we have gone through remains, I think as before. Examine the following statement, in turn, as to whether it stays the same or not, that the most important thing is not life, but the good life.

Crito: It stays the same.

Socrates: And the good life, the beautiful life, and the just life are the same, does that still hold or not?

Crito: It does hold.

Socrates: As we have agreed so far, we must examine next whether it is right for me to try to get out of here when the Athenians have not acquitted me. If it is seen to be right, we will try to do so; if it is not, we will abandon the idea…. For us, however, since our argument leads to this, the only valid consideration is whether we should be acting rightly in giving money and gratitude to those who will lead me out of here, and ourselves helping with the escape, or whether in truth we shall do wrong in doing all this. If it appears that we shall be acting unjustly, then we have no need at all to take into account whether we shall have to die if we stay here and keep quiet, or suffer in another way, rather than do wrong….

Crito: I think you put that beautifully, Socrates, but see what we should do.

Socrates: Then I state the next point, or rather I ask you: When one has come to an agreement that is just with someone, should one fulfill it or cheat on it?

Crito: One should fulfill it.

Socrates: See what follows from this: If we leave here without the city's permission, are we injuring people whom we should least injure? And are we sticking to a just agreement or not?

Crito: I cannot answer your question, Socrates. I do not know…

Socrates: …Shall we say, "The city wronged me, and its decision was not right?" Shall we say that or what?

Crito: Yes, by Zeus, Socrates, that is our answer.

Socrates: Then what if the law said: …Is your wisdom such as not to realize that your country is to be honoured more than your mother, your father and all your ancestors…. You must either persuade it or obey its orders, and endure in silence whatever it instructs you to endure, whether blows or bonds and if it leads you into war to be wounded or killed, you must obey…. One must obey the commands of one's city and country, or persuade it as to the nature of justice.

Source: Grube, C.M.A., trans. *Plato: Five Dialogues*. Indianapolis: Hackett Publishing Company. 1981. pp. 50–53.

Form Your Questions

Perhaps Socrates could have been swayed from his decision to accept his fate if Crito had asked more thoughtful, challenging questions. Assume the role of Crito, and think of three questions that might have persuaded Socrates that it is sometimes justified to break an unjust law.

Aristotle (384–322 BCE)

Aristotle was one of the early Greek philosophers. He was only 17 when he left home to study at the Academy at Athens. There he became one of Plato's favourite students. Aristotle had a different approach to the questions of jurisprudence than Plato. He believed that justice should aspire to equality. He stated, "The 'just' therefore means that which is lawful and that which is equal or fair" (Morris 1981). He believed that the hardships of humankind could be cured by equity, by which he meant the fair sharing of resources among members of a community.

However, he could not envision, nor would he have supported, an egalitarian society in which everyone would share equally in the resources of the world. Justice, according to Aristotle, was to be exercised in the distribution of wealth and honour, and could be allotted in equal or unequal shares depending on the worthiness of the recipient. He argued that if persons are unequal they may be "allotted unequal shares" (Morris 1981).

Allotment, according to Aristotle, should not be dependent on the luck of being born into a wealthy or powerful family. Aristotle was opposed to an **oligarchy**, which, in his time, was a form of government in which only those born into the upper class could rule. Rather Aristotle was in favour of a **meritocracy**, that is, a society in which individuals are rewarded based on their own merit and performance of their civic duties. Aristotle also believed that, in regard to law, justice should be done with equity. For example, he would have permitted a judge to depart from the law in a difficult case, such as in the trial of Socrates.

Cicero (106–43 BCE)

Cicero was a young Roman lawyer, who wrote his thoughts on law and justice during the time of Julius Caesar's reign. Cicero was opposed to what he saw as Caesar's dictatorship. Although he was a friend of Brutus's, and Brutus eventually killed Caesar, Cicero was not part of that conspiracy.

FIGURE 3.8 Aristotle was a student and friend of Plato, but they disagreed on the meaning of justice. With which of these philosophers' ideas are you more inclined to agree? Why?

Nevertheless, he was ultimately declared a traitor to Rome and was later executed.

Cicero took the ideas of natural law and justice, which were established by the early Greek philosophers, and introduced them to the early Christian and European scholars. Cicero, therefore, established the principle that justice, right, equality, and fairness should underlie all law.

Cicero did not agree completely with Aristotle's view that a person could live a proper life only if he or she obeyed the state, which, Aristotle believed, knew what was best for its citizens. "Law," wrote Cicero in his treatise *De Republica*, "is a natural force; it is the mind and reason of the intelligent man, the standard by which justice and injustice are measured" (Morris 1981). But law is not the product of only the *human* mind, according to Cicero. He wrote that law and justice exist "both in man and God, the first common possession of man and God is reason" (Morris 1981).

Cicero agreed with Aristotle that the state should represent the collective will of its citizens, who are united by common agreement about laws and rights. They are also united by the desire to participate in governance and benefit from being members of a nation-state. However, the state could not enact "evil" laws—that is, laws not in the common interest, such as robbery or adultery—even if these acts were approved by the collective will of the people because the laws of nature would not support such activities. It would be permissible, according to Cicero, for citizens to withdraw their support from a government that enacted evil laws.

Justinian (483–565 CE)

Justinian was another Roman philosopher whose writings influenced legal thinking. Because of his role as emperor, he was able to put in place a codified version of Roman law, which came to be known as "Justinian's code." Justinian believed that law had two parts: the universal laws of nature, which were observed by all people, and civil laws, which may be specific to a particular society or community.

Natural law, according to Justinian, ensured that all people were born free. Therefore, laws that permitted slavery violated these universal laws of nature and should be struck down. Justinian applied these principles to reform unjust Roman laws. For example, a husband was no longer permitted to sell his wife into slavery to pay a debt, nor could a father, in his role as head of the family, kill his son, sell his children, or force his daughter to marry.

Saint Augustine (354–430 CE)

Saint Augustine was a Christian bishop in the city of Hippo, in Algeria, for 34 years. He believed in divine law and that God would punish evil and reward good. He thought that "ideal justice" could be achieved only when the "City of God" came on earth, meaning when God came back to earth and Christian justice reigned supreme. He

FIGURE 3.9 This painting shows the building of the "City of God" from a 1486 French copy of Saint Augustine's famous book of the same name. He believed it should be the responsibility of the Church to keep an eye on the actions of the state. In contemporary Canadian society, whom does this responsibility fall to?

thought that the Church had a moral duty and authority to act as a check on the abuses of the state. He argued that it was the responsibility of the Church to exercise a moral veto over any actions that violated God's law. He claimed, "The only perfect law is Eternal Law, God's law. Justice being taken away, then, what are the kingdoms but great robberies?" (*City of God*, Book IV 2003).

Thomas Aquinas (1225–1274)

Aquinas came from a very wealthy family who sent him to the University of Naples to study the liberal arts. His parents were astounded when, for a short time, instead of studying he became a begging Dominican friar. Aquinas went on to study theology at the University of Paris, becoming an expert in philosophy and, in particular, the works of Aristotle.

To Aristotle's argument, "Whatsoever pleaseth the sovereign has force of law," Aquinas replied, "On the contrary, it belongs to the law to command and to forbid" (Morris 1981). He argued, "Law is chiefly ordained to the common good," and that the intention of the law-maker should be to "lead men to virtue." He did not assume that law makes people good but rather "that a man obeys a law is due to his being good." A tyrannical law would not be a law, but rather "a perversion of law." The first rule of law, according to Aquinas, is that "good is to be done and pursued, and evil is to be avoided. All other precepts of the natural law are based on this" (Morris 1981).

Thomas Hobbes (1588–1679)

As a student at Oxford University in England, Thomas Hobbes was as interested in mathematics as he was in philosophy. In 1651, Hobbes wrote *Leviathan*, his best-known work, which was inspired by the political events of his time. Hobbes was both an **atheist**, meaning he did not believe in God, and a Republican. Although he supported Oliver Cromwell, a Republican, over King Charles II, the king still brought him to court and gave him the opportunity to discuss his theories. Hobbes wrote about the life of a human in *Leviathan* as "solitary, poor, nasty, brutish, and short" (Morris 1981), and many people of his era would likely have agreed with him. As well as the poor conditions prevalent at that time, England was involved in a civil war between Oliver Cromwell's Republicans and the monarchy.

Security and the preservation of peace, according to Hobbes, were fundamental to political and social justice. He believed that human-made law was much more important than natural law. Justice, he thought, depended largely on the existence of a superior power. In other words, a sovereign or ruler must have the authority to take whatever steps are necessary to protect life, property, and contract.

Hobbes stated, "If we could suppose a great multitude of men to consent in the observation of justice…without a common power to keep them all in awe, we might as well suppose all mankind to do the same; then there neither would be nor need to be any civil government or commonwealth at all" (Morris 1981). In this quotation, Hobbes pointed out an obvious impossibility to illustrate the fact that people need government to legislate, or enact, laws in order to regulate their relationships with one another.

Citizens, according to Hobbes, make an agreement, a social contract in which they surrender the right to govern themselves to the ruling power (a monarch or parliament, for example). Having transferred their right to govern to the ruler, the people can no longer claim a right to control that ruler. Justice, therefore, depends largely on people's obedience to civil law. Consequently, Hobbes declared, "No action can be unjust. But when a covenant [contract or promise] is made, then to break it is unjust: And the definition of Injustice is no other than the not performance of a covenant" (Morris 1981).

John Locke (1632–1704)

John Locke was another English philosopher who studied at Oxford University. His political book *Two Treatises of Civil Government* influenced the political landscape of England at the time. There is no doubt that Locke's ideas on political philosophy expanded the knowledge base in this field and changed people's way of thinking.

He did not agree that collective rights were more important than individual rights. According to Locke, the positive law of the state was embedded in a constitution, but that constitution had to be based on natural law, which emphasized individual rights. He believed that all people had the right to self-preservation but that the law should restrain people from "doing hurt to one another."

While he acknowledged the supremacy of a legislative power, Locke believed it should be subject to reasonable natural law and the fundamental rights of individuals to life, liberty, and property. Locke, therefore, believed there was a need to set limits on the power of the state. He wrote, "The legislative...cannot assume to itself a power to rule by...arbitrary decrees." For Locke, the fundamental right to own property did not mean that governments should be expected to redistribute resources, such as land and money. He believed that individuals were free to apply their minds and bodies to gain wealth or property. It was only natural therefore, according to him, that some people would accumulate more property than others.

Locke believed that the sole purpose of government was to protect individuals against the arbitrary acts of others who would interfere with their freedom. This constitutional, liberal, democratic theory of Locke's led to the French and American revolutions and is the foundation of Canadian constitutional law.

Jean-Jacques Rousseau (1712–1778)

Jean-Jacques Rousseau, a French philosopher, was born in Geneva. Until he was 18, his life was poor and miserable. Then he went to Venice where he met important literary scholars, such as Denis Diderot and Immanuel Kant. Rousseau wrote a number of important social and political works, but his most important ones were *The Social Contract* and *Discourse on the Origin of Inequality*. The first is a radical criticism of society, and the second contains his description of a just and good society. In *The Social Contract*, Rousseau opens with these famous lines: "Man is born free; and everywhere he is in chains.... How did this change come about?" Rousseau argued that civilization had a corrupting influence on humans. He suggested that the social structure that encouraged self-interest instead of goodwill toward others had corrupted human nature and ruined our way of life and our search for happiness.

At the same time, Rousseau recognized the necessity of the state in governing. He advocated the idea of a contract between citizens and the state. The state, he believed, should govern according to what he referred to as the "general will" of the people. It would be a mutually beneficial relationship in which the state could be removed if the people willed it. The difficulty lay in determining exactly what Rousseau meant by the "general will" of the people—a definition many philosophers have questioned over the years. Despite this uncertainty, Rousseau's writings continue to influence social and political thought.

Jeremy Bentham (1748–1832)

Jeremy Bentham, an English philosopher, was the first person to support **utilitarianism**—a theory that laws should be based on what is practical and realistic rather than on an idealistic moral view. His views were shaped by the Industrial Revolution and the kind of society he saw around him. He dismissed all natural law. He said the only way to assess a law was to measure its utility or expedience, that is, the extent to which it benefits the community and the individual members of the community.

Bentham's primary concern as a philosopher was legal and social reform. The law in the

FIGURE 3.10 Jeremy Bentham's views on law were formed mainly in reaction to the Industrial Revolution as illustrated in this 1835 drawing of women and child labourers in a cotton factory.

eighteenth century was a mix of precedents and unjust laws. For example, many crimes of a minor nature carried the death penalty, and there was no access to any kind of legal support or advice. Bentham attempted to sort out the law using a rational system of principles. The key principle, according to Bentham, was that of utility. Law, he explained, was simply a means of social control and had nothing to do with morality. The law was simply the best way of ensuring the good of all, or, as he put it, "the greatest good for the greatest number."

John Austin (1790–1859)

John Austin, an English philosopher, was influenced by the views of Jeremy Bentham. He believed that the main purpose of government and of law was to enable "the greatest possible advancement of human happiness" (Morris 1981). Justice meant lawfulness, yet law and justice were considered separate and distinct according to Austin. He believed that no positive law could be unjust, because the positive law itself was the measure of what was just or unjust.

Austin believed that acts of law, such as criminal codes, could also be measured or judged against the rules of morality or by divine law, but he argued that these are subjective measures. The function of law—what it is designed or intended to do—was just as important as the quality of the law. He believed that the acts of individuals were to be tried against an objective standard of law and that ethics or morality should play no part in determining whether a law was good or bad. Austin claimed that the extent to which one violated the legal norms determined whether that person was just or unjust.

John Stuart Mill (1806–1873)

Mill's concept of justice was also designed around the idea of utilitarianism. John Stuart Mill's father had been a disciple of Bentham's, and Mill acknowledged his father and Bentham as early influences. Laws, according to Mill, should serve a utilitarian (or useful) function in society. He stated, "Actions are right in proportion as they tend to promote happiness; wrong as they tend to produce the reverse of happiness" (Mill 1986).

Mill's notion of happiness was not strictly centred on emotion but more on the pleasures of the intellect, art, music, literature, and helping others. Mill advocated a doctrine of happiness that was altruistic, that is, being more concerned for the well-being of others than oneself. He believed in social good and argued that ideal happiness was the "happiness for all concerned" (Mill 1986).

FIGURE 3.11 Three ladies present a petition to John Stuart Mill in Westminster Hall in 1865. The women were seeking a change in laws that would allow females to vote, attend university, and enter previously male-only professions. Knowing Mill's views on law and justice, do you think he would have signed the petition?

VIEWPOINTS: Do we do good because we are good?

Fyodor Dostoevsky's (1821-1881) book *Crime and Punishment* is one of the most powerful novels ever written. Although the novel dealt with many issues, the fundamental question Dostoevsky asked was, Why be good? What is the motivation or point of pursuing a life of good when there are so many other options that would be more pleasurable or would allow advantage over others?

Some philosophers have argued fear of punishment, either by God(s) or by the justice system, makes us obey the law. Others argue it is the desire for reward either in an afterlife or on Earth as the approval of society that encourages people to be good. The philosopher Immanuel Kant (1724-1804) said we do good because of "the moral law within," but more recent scientific discoveries argue that we do good because we are good.

Craig Packer, a professor of ecology and evolution at the University of Minnesota said, "There is a grandness in the human species that is so striking and so profoundly different from what we see in other animals." Yet other animals do demonstrate altruistic behaviour. Richard Wrangham, a primatologist at Harvard cites the example of red colobus monkeys who, when the group is attacked, sacrifice themselves to save the weaker members. Biologists and social scientists are now doing studies to determine what causes humans to sacrifice themselves for strangers. Some argue that there is a basic mechanism in humans to cooperate and to reward behaviours that strengthen the group or community. This same mechanism allows for selflessness to thrive and multiply. Altruism and heroism define our humanity and some studies suggest these traits may be less of a choice in humans than a biological imperative that ultimately works to ensure the survival of our species.

SOURCE: Natalie Angier. "Heroism Innate in Humans". *Toronto Star* 23 Sept. 2001.

Up for Debate

1. Choose a philosopher that would support and one that would oppose the position that humans are ultimately good. Compare and contrast the two views.
2. With a partner assume the role of the philosophers you choose for Question 1 and have a dialogue in which you question and respond to one another on the statement: "Humans do good because they are naturally good."

CONFIRM YOUR UNDERSTANDING

1. What do you think Plato meant when he said, "It pays therefore to act unjustly"?

2. Explain the difference among Plato's, Aristotle's, and Cicero's views of what is just.

3. The Canadian government has initiated many social programs, such as welfare, universal health care, and education, to ensure a fair allocation of resources. These programs ensure that families with limited means have equal access to certain services. Would Plato have supported these measures? Explain.

4. What criteria would Justinian, Saint Augustine, and Aquinas have used to determine whether a law was just or unjust? Explain.

5. What do you think Saint Augustine meant when he said, "Justice being taken away, then, what are kingdoms but great robberies"?

6. The first precept of law, according to Aquinas, was that "good is to be done and pursued, and evil is to be avoided." What arguments could you make against such a view?

7. Assume we elected a government based on its promise to lower taxes. Once elected, the government raised taxes by 10 percent. What recourse would the public have in such circumstances according to the following philosophers? Choose a suitable quotation from each philosopher to illustrate his point of view.
   a) Rousseau   b) Hobbes   c) Locke

8. Bentham, Austin, and Mill are all considered positivists. What does this mean?

9. What is meant by the term "utilitarian"?

10. John Stuart Mill said, "Actions are right in proportion as they tend to promote happiness; wrong as they tend to produce the reverse of happiness." What did Mill mean by "happiness"?

11. According to Bentham, law should ensure "the greatest good for the greatest number." What problems do you foresee with this argument?

Contemporary Legal Theories

Modern legal theorists have accepted many of the principles and ideas provided by the historical philosophers. However, they have also challenged many of the historical views of jurisprudence and added their own contributions to the body of legal thought. Although there are many schools of legal thought, some of the more prominent ones are outlined on the following pages.

Legal Formalism

Legal formalism treats law as though it were a science or math. Formalists believe that law consists of a body of rules and nothing more; they believe that judges should merely apply the law and have no authority to act outside it. Unlike some natural-law proponents, legal formalists argue that judges cannot depart from the law or use their discretion in an unusual case; they must apply the rules made by the state and its agencies.

Law, according to formalists, is enacted by a legislature and derived from the state. The role of the judge is to be remote and disinterested and to apply the law. It is not the judge's role to make social policy. New cases should be decided according to a scientific application of legal precedent. This conservative view of the law was widely supported in Britain and Canada until recently. The introduction of the *Canadian Charter of Rights and Freedoms* in 1982 challenged the principles of legal formalism. The *Charter* opened a debate between those who support the view that judges should merely apply the law and those who argue that the role of judges is to make law.

Legal Realism

Legal realism rejects the principles of legal formalism. Supporters of this theory argue that the law, itself, is often uncertain, vague, and based on the judge's own view. Some argue that legal decisions are often the result of the judge's mood or personal prejudices. Contrary to the formalist position that judges should merely apply the law, realists argue that judges, in fact, are the real authors of law. They say it is the court, not Parliament, which in reality makes the law. They also argue that the "scientific application of precedent" is an illusion and that judges shape precedents to support their own conclusions.

Critical Legal Studies

The theory of **critical legal studies** (**CLS**) shares some of the views of legal realism, but goes further in its criticism of accepted legal theories. Supporters of CLS argue that law is not neutral or value-free; rather it is about value choices. The law, according to CLS theory, exists to support the interests of the people in power and can be a powerful instrument for injustice and oppression. According to CLS, judicial decisions are the result of ideological and historical struggles, such as the fight for civil rights or Aboriginal land claims.

Supporters argue that the law should be used as a tool to achieve social justice. CLS supporters point out that the state provides for the health and welfare of its citizens through law, and therefore judges can and should exercise discretion in ensuring that the law also achieves justice.

Feminist Jurisprudence

Feminist jurisprudence is a philosophy of law based on the argument that the legal system upholds political, economic, and social inequality for women. Supporters argue that the logic and language of the law create and reinforce male values. Even laws supposedly put in place to protect women and children, instead support the view that women are the property of men.

FIGURE 3.12   Feminist legal scholar and anti-pornography activist Catharine MacKinnon shown here outside an American porn theatre in 1993. MacKinnon, along with Andrea Dworkin, Lenore Walker, and Susan Estrich are leading current supporters of feminist jurisprudence philosophy.

For example, supporters of this philosophy argue that laws such as those that dealt with rape were put in place to protect the value of a woman as a marriageable commodity rather than to protect a woman from a violent act.

Supporters of feminist jurisprudence argue that the prevailing theories of law reinforce and preserve male authority at the expense of women. The criticisms voiced by supporters have led to changes in laws affecting employment, divorce, domestic violence, and sexual harassment in North America.

Law Based on Economics

Instead of examining issues of law and justice, some legal theorists argue that the discipline of economics offers the best explanation for how the law functions or should function. Embracing many ideas and views, this theory of law includes the study of laws dealing with property, torts, and contracts. Those who believe law is based on economics argue that the purpose of all law is resource allocation. In a world where there are scarce resources, they believe that the function of law is to determine how resources should be divided.

Some economic theorists suggest that law should be used as a social tool to ensure the fair allocation of resources. Others argue that the laws should be evaluated purely from a func-

tional perspective. For example, a law that imposed a fine on individuals who failed to wear bicycle helmets would be considered successful only if it saved more money through fewer people's use of health services due to injuries than it cost to enforce the law. Supporters of law based on economics argue that judges should consider economics in all their decisions rather than such subjective issues as morality and justice.

CONFIRM YOUR UNDERSTANDING

1. Choose three of the following legal theories, and explain their meaning in your own words.
   a) legal formalism
   b) legal realism
   c) critical legal studies
   d) feminist jurisprudence
   e) law based on economics
2. How has the _Canadian Charter of Rights and Freedoms_ challenged the principles of legal formalism?
3. In keeping with the critical legal studies theory, you could argue that the right for

women to vote was the result of ideological struggle. Suggest one other example that demonstrates that law was changed not by judges but by historical and ideological struggles.
4. Which historical philosophers would have been most likely to support the view of those who argue that law should be based on economic principles? Explain.
5. Provide two examples in law that would justify the arguments of those who support feminist jurisprudence.

Contemporary Theorists

You will find that many of these modern philosophers share either a natural or positivist perspective on law and justice. However, unlike the more historical philosophers, they are not radically different in their thinking from one another. These contemporary philosophers recognize that there are valid aspects to most theories and that many different perspectives can enhance our knowledge about law.

H.L.A. Hart (1907–1992)

Hart was an English legal writer who believed that the purpose of law was to coerce, or force, people to do certain things and not do others. In any legal system, he believed, there must be rules

of general application, such as following the speed limit, backed by threats given by people who are generally obeyed, such as police officers or judges.

Hart broke down rules or laws into primary and secondary categories. Primary rules define what individuals must or must not do. Secondary rules set out how primary rules are defined and how they are to be applied, removed, changed, or enforced. Hart also recognized that it would be difficult to apply this approach to the broad range of human conduct, so he proposed an "open texture of law," arguing that judges should strike a balance between competing interests and could be flexible in certain circumstances.

John Rawls (1921–)

John Rawls based his concept of law on the idea that "justice is fairness." In his book *A Theory of Justice*, Rawls argues that the only way the legal system could achieve fairness and ensure that decisions are rational and unbiased is if no one in the society knew his or her own status or the extent of his or her own wealth. If this were possible, the justice system could operate behind what Rawls calls "a veil of ignorance." Rawls believes that legal systems should strive toward this ideal. In Ontario, for example, people who are accused of crimes and cannot afford a lawyer are provided with a legal-aid certificate, which they can present to any lawyer who will accept them as a client. In court, the jury is not aware that the accused is being defended by a free legal-aid lawyer. Therefore, it is assumed that the jury could not be influenced by the social status of the accused.

Richard A. Posner (1939–)

Posner, an American philosopher, is known as a modern utilitarian. He argues that law must reflect certain economic realities. He believes that law should be assessed on the basis of its effectiveness in altering negative behaviours. For example, smoking bylaws should be assessed purely on their effectiveness in reducing smoking and the expenses associated with smoking-related illnesses versus the cost to the government of collecting cigarette taxes.

Noam Chomsky (1948–)

One of the most famous and controversial present-day legal philosophers, Noam Chomsky is an American linguist and political activist who has written extensively about law and politics. Chomsky believes that law primarily serves the purposes of those in power. He believes there is co-operation between the elite class of society and the law-makers to make laws that maintain the status quo and the wealth and power of the elite. Chomsky believes that the media play a part in this by withholding serious information from the public, thereby keeping the masses happy but ill-informed. In this way, according to Chomsky, the elite class makes all the true decisions in its own favour.

FIGURE 3.13 Noam Chomsky photographed at his office at MIT, 2002. Do you agree with Chomsky's views on role of the media in law in contemporary North American society? Explain.

1. What did H.L.A. Hart mean when he said that the purpose of law is to be coercive? What other historical philosophers would you most associate with the ideas of H.L.A. Hart?

2. Assume our government enacted a law making it an offence to chew gum. What arguments would Posner have against such a law?

3. What criticisms would you make of Rawls's argument that law should operate behind a "veil of ignorance"?

4. Noam Chomsky argues, "As long as authority, power and decision-making are narrowly concentrated, you don't have a democratic society" (Chomsky 2002). Would you agree or disagree with this statement? Explain.

5. Which of the contemporary philosophers whom you have studied would you most likely support? Explain.

In Closing

The concepts discussed in this chapter—jurisdiction and sovereignty, rights and duties, legitimacy and ownership, power and authority, equality and equity—have general meanings. The concept of a right, for example, is dependent on point of view and social context. In addition, many of these concepts are related to one another, whether they have similar meanings, such as "right" and "duty," or opposite meanings, such as "equality" and "equity."

Legal analysis, as you have discovered, requires that we go beyond the general and, with some degree of precision, find the distinctive features of these concepts that make their meanings clearer. Legal analysis requires us to explain how jurisdiction differs from sovereignty or how we might apply equity to achieve equality. Legal scholars and law-makers are constantly refining the meaning of these concepts so that they better inform our thinking on law and justice.

The philosophers and philosophies described in this chapter often express conflicting views on law and justice. Saint Augustine and Aquinas viewed law as a reflection of the word of God. For these philosophers, law was unchanging and there was an obligation on the part of each citizen to disobey a state-imposed law that violated the law of God. Other philosophers, such as Cicero, saw law as a reflection of human nature, that is, a "natural force" found in the mind and reason of the intelligent person.

These historical Greek and Roman philosophers spoke to the society in which they lived, and their philosophies reflected their observations. Theorists, such as Hobbes, Bentham, and Austin, whose views were shaped by the inequities of seventeenth-century England or the poverty caused by the Industrial Revolution, held different views on law and justice. Legal theorists, such as Locke and Rousseau, had their own unique views on law and justice. Their views on the role of government in law can be detected today in our own rights-based justice system and in our *Canadian Charter of Rights and Freedoms*.

Contemporary theories of law, such as legal formalism and feminist jurisprudence, have added to the debate on law and justice and what justice means in today's society. Modern philosophers, such as Hart, Rawls, Posner, and Chomsky, have added their voices to our present body of legal knowledge.

The philosophers and philosophies you have read about in this chapter have all attempted to show the relevance of law to human problems. The problem of balancing the competing interests of law and justice is complex and will likely always be with us in one form or another. Over the course of time, new theories have added to our understanding, but the process is unending. Legal theory must be continually rethought by every age as new scientific knowledge sheds light on our views about justice and law.

CHAPTER ACTIVITIES

Extend Your Legal Knowledge

1. In the 1950s the federal government enacted legislation that forcibly removed some Inuit groups from their land and relocated them to Ellesmere and Cornwallis Islands in the Far North.

a) What argument would Cicero have offered against such legislation?

b) According to Austin, why would such legislation be acceptable?

c) Would this plan be contrary to Mill's theory of utilitarianism? Explain.

d) Hobbes and Aquinas would have had opposing views on this issue. What would they have said about this legislation?

2. Create an organizational chart showing the legal concepts studied (pp. 75–82), their definitions, and a contemporary example that best illustrates each concept.

3. What is meant by the term "crime against humanity"?

4. During World War II, the Canadian government enacted legislation that put many Japanese Canadians in prisoner-of-war camps and confiscated their property, fearing they might be spies or might collaborate with the enemy. What would Aristotle, Plato, or Cicero have thought about such legislation? Explain.

5. Aristotle supported a legal or governmental system based on a meritocracy rather than an oligarchy.

a) What do these terms mean today?

b) Is Canada's governmental system based on a meritocracy or an oligarchy? Explain.

6. Carefully read each of the following statements. Choose the legal concept that you believe best applies to each. Briefly explain your reasoning.

a) The law is the law; it should be fixed and clear, otherwise it means nothing.

b) Singers who, in their lyrics, advocate hatred of women should not be permitted to perform in Canada or have their CDs sold here.

c) The rulers of Afghanistan argue that the United States has no business coming to their land to capture an alleged terrorist who has possibly committed a crime in the United States but has done nothing illegal in Afghanistan.

d) A massive relief operation will be put in place, supported by almost every nation, to help refugees displaced by war.

e) If the principal suspects that a student has drugs or weapons on his or her person, the principal can search the student and the student's locker.

f) A person who is arrested is entitled to be informed of the reasons for his or her arrest.

g) The winnings from a lottery ticket are the property of the person who purchased the ticket.

h) The provincial government cannot claim it will bring in laws that will result in a reduction in the crime rate, since it is the federal government's responsibility to deal with criminal law.

7. Identify which of these philosophers made the statements that follow:

Hobbes, Aristotle, Plato, Austin, Cicero, Aquinas, Bentham, or Saint Augustine.

a) "No positive law is legally unjust."

b) "The first precept of law is that good is to be done and pursued, and evil is to be avoided."

c) "Justice being taken away, then, what are kingdoms but great robberies?"

d) "No action can be unjust. But when a covenant is made, then to break it is unjust."

e) "I declare that justice is nothing else than that which is advantageous to the stronger. It follows that the just man disregards them [laws]."

f) "The purpose of law is to ensure the greatest good for the greatest number."

g) "Law is a natural force; it is in the mind and reason of the intelligent man, the standard by which justice and injustice are measured."

h) "If persons are not equal, they will not have equal share."

8. If you were to summarize the key legal theory of John Locke in one sentence, you could say that for Locke the purpose of law was to protect citizens' rights and to ensure equality. Review the theories of the following contemporary theorists, and summarize their key ideas in one sentence.
   a) Posner
   b) Rawls
   c) Chomsky

9. In your own words, explain the key differences between legal formalism and legal realism.

Think About the Law

10. The philosopher Cicero argued that if a government put evil statutes in place, the people could disobey the law. Indicate, in your own words, how Hobbes would have replied to such an argument.

11. What do you think Rousseau meant by the "general will"? How does the idea of the general will differ from majority rule?

12. What evidence do you see of Locke's views in Canada's political system?

13. Identify which of the following statements would relate to the concept of sovereignty and which to the concept of jurisdiction. Give reasons for your answers.
   a) Paul Bernardo would have been arrested for the murders of Leslie Mahaffy and Kristen French much earlier if there had been more co-operation between the police forces in Toronto and the Niagara Region.
   b) NATO (North American Treaty Organization) launched a bombing campaign against the former Yugoslavia with the expressed aim of preventing genocide in Kosovo.
   c) St. Pierre and Miquelon are located off the coast of Canada, but they belong to France.
   d) Parents of students who live across the street from a brand new school are incensed that the school board created boundaries for the new school that excluded their side of the street.
   e) When speaking to the General Assembly of the United Nations, Secretary-General Kofi Annan said that the world could not accept that national borders protect tyrants who inflict horrors on their own people.

14. During the 1900s, Canada sent shipping expeditions to the Arctic islands in order to ensure its sovereignty over all the territory between the northern coast of mainland Canada and the North Pole. Why do you think Canada would want sovereignty over such a vast, almost uninhabitable landscape?

15. Following the defeat of Nazi Germany in World War II, the Allies put some of the Nazi officers on trial at Nuremberg, Germany. Lord Elwyn Jones, former Lord Chancellor of Britain, was a prosecutor at these trials. He said, "Before Nuremberg, the doctrine and approach of international law was that the way a government treated its own people was entirely a matter for the sovereign decisions of that sovereign state. After the war and the creation of an international code of human rights (1948), the position of the individual human being was transformed as a matter of law from being a mere object of compassion to being a subject of rights" (Watson and Barber 1988). Do you think an international body such as the United Nations should have the power to intervene in a matter involving a democratically elected government of a sovereign state? Explain.

16. Read the following letter to the editor, and answer these questions.
   a) Is Ms. Peddle a natural or positive law supporter? Explain.
   b) Which philosophers would be most likely to support Ms. Peddle's view?
   c) Which philosophers would be most likely to oppose Ms. Peddle's view?

Challenging the Rule of Law

Western civilization has progressed primarily as a result of the rule of law. Within this framework, laws can be changed in accordance with the will of the people through our democratic and legal process. Our entire legal and political system has been based on the rule of law, and I find it difficult to believe people support and encourage groups taking the law into their own hands as we are witnessing every day in the media.

Whether it is anti-poverty protesters invading city hall, globalization protesters climbing fences at the Québec summit, animal-rights activists releasing research animals or spraying people wearing fur coats, or any other groups who continue to break the law in the name of a higher good, the principles remain the same. It is perfectly legitimate in a democratic country to exercise the right to freedom of expression and to demonstrate in order to change the legal and political system, but it is unacceptable for these groups to challenge our existing law by setting up barricades and taking over empty houses. No government can, or should, surrender to this type of intimidation.

I do not care whether these groups have legitimate grievances; there are ways of airing their views in a legal manner. The government cannot set a precedent and permit these protesters to go free. They must be subject to the same rule of law as everyone else.

—D. Peddle

17. In your opinion, is there ever an obligation on the part of citizens to disobey an unjust law? Provide examples to support your position, and name at least two philosophers who would support your point of view.

18. Canada's justice system is not perfect. Many people have been wrongfully convicted over the years, including Donald Marshall, David Milgaard, Guy Paul Morin, and Thomas Sophonow. Considering the characteristics of justice you have read about, make an argument that despite their wrongful convictions, these individuals received their due.

19. In Pope John Paul II's thirteenth encyclical letter, *Fides et Ratio* (Faith and Reason), he said that "Humanity has to accept certain truths rather than embrace ethical relativism where quick success is rewarded and the search for ultimate truth is shunned as archaic" (*Toronto Star* "Pope Urges…" 1990).
   a) Of the philosophers you have studied so far, which would agree with Pope John Paul II? Explain.
   b) What do you think the pope meant by "ethical relativism"? Do you think there is such as thing as an ultimate (or, universal) truth? Discuss.
   c) One might argue that religious leaders should lead humanity to virtue, but Aquinas argued that the purpose of law should also be to "lead men to virtue." Do you agree with Aquinas that our law-makers should lead us to virtue? Explain.

Communicate About the Law

20. Assume you had to define the concept of morality to someone who had no understanding of the term. Write out your definition of the concept, and compare it with the definitions of your classmates.

21. The *Youth Criminal Justice Act* treats young people aged 12 to 18 differently than those over 18 in most cases.
   a) Is our legal system treating young people with equity or equality? Explain.
   b) Do you think young offenders should be treated differently than adult offenders who commit the same crime?

22. Read the following situations involving justice. Keeping in mind the characteristics of justice, write a brief account of each case indicating whether or not you believe justice was served. Discuss your view with a partner or with the rest of the class.
   a) Jan, aged 19, drove home after a party despite the fact that she was quite drunk. She refused to let a friend drive her. On her way home, she drove into another car, killing

a mother and her two young children. Jan survived. The judge suspended her licence for five years and sentenced her to imprisonment for two years less a day. Matthew, also 19, was sentenced by the same judge for sexually assaulting a female. Matthew received a six-year prison term. Consider Jan's and Matthew's punishment.

b) A well-known tobacco company has been ordered to pay fines in the billions of dollars to compensate individuals who became ill as a result of many years of smoking. The lawyers in the class-action suit claimed the tobacco company knew its product was deadly and yet continued, through advertising, etc., to influence people to buy their product.

c) Ms. Simeon was admitted to law school despite the fact that her grades were not as high as those of some of the males who applied. The law school had adopted a quota policy that set aside a certain number of spots for female candidates in order to maintain a 4 to 1 ratio of males to females.

d) Andrew Lee, 15, and Daniel Roy, 19, were both convicted of second-degree murder in the beating death of a 14-year-old schoolmate. Lee, as a young offender, received a penalty of three years in a detention centre. Roy was sentenced to life imprisonment with no chance of parole for 10 years.

e) Jake Bruhn was serving a life sentence for the murder of two young children. Bruhn at 68 years old needed a heart transplant in order to survive. A heart transplant costs $1 million. Critics argued that Bruhn should be denied a transplant because there was a waiting list of people who had not committed crimes who should be given priority. Bruhn's lawyer successfully argued that Bruhn was entitled to equal treatment—the same as everyone else. Bruhn received his transplant.

23. Read the two views of sovereignty below. Choose one of the views presented, and then research, prepare, and present a debate in class.

The sovereignty of states remains a fundamental tenet and key measure of peace and security, but it is neither absolute nor is it a shield behind which the most egregious violations of human rights and fundamental freedoms can be protected.

—Lloyd Axworthy, former Canadian foreign affairs minister speaking at the United Nations

When the sovereignty of a country is put in jeopardy, its human rights can hardly be protected.

—Tang Jiaxuan, former Chinese foreign minister speaking at the United Nations

Apply the Law

24. In the Robert Latimer case, detailed on pages 351–352, Robert Latimer killed his daughter because he believed she was so severely disabled that she would never have a pain-free life. Believing she would never be cured, Latimer thought her death was the best way to end her suffering. Our _Criminal Code_ makes it clear that such a crime is first-degree murder, for which the penalty is life imprisonment with no possibility of parole for 25 years. Assume that there were five judges deciding this case: Cicero, Hobbes, Austin, Aquinas, and you. Write a judgment that would indicate the philosophy of law held by each of these judges, including your own judgment.

25. In 1993, Private Kyle Brown, along with another soldier, Corporal Clayton Matchee, were stationed in Somalia with the now-disbanded Canadian Airborne Regiment. Private Brown was convicted of manslaughter and torture in the death of a Somali teenager, Abukar Shidane Arone. Arone was discovered hiding in the Canadian camp, likely searching for food. Brown, Matchee, and other members of the regiment allegedly caught Arone, tortured him, and took "trophy" photographs of themselves and the boy. When the photographs of the torture were discovered and released to the public, Kyle Brown and Clayton Matchee became the first Canadians to be charged with war crimes. Should soldiers who are trained to kill in times of war be subject to the same rules of law as civilians? Explain.

a) The International Court of Justice at The Hague has tried a number of war criminals, including the former president of Yugoslavia, Slobodan Milosovic. Critics argue that this is unjust because both sides in a war commit atrocities, but only those who lose the war are subject to trial. Do you agree? How should law and justice be applied in times of war? Should both sides be subject to penalties for war crimes?

b) Assume you were responsible for making up rules of war to be followed by Canadian soldiers. What kind of rules would you put in place?

c) Research the cases of Kyle Brown and William Calley, the American soldier also convicted of war crimes in My Lai, Vietnam, during the Vietnam War. Compare the trials and sentencing of the two men. Present a report to the class on your findings.

BIBLIOGRAPHY

Canadian Legal Information Institute. Accessed 3 Nov. 2003. <www.canlii.org>.

Chomsky, Noam and Edward Herman. *Manufacturing Consent: The Political Economy of the Mass Media.* New York: Pantheon Books, 2002.

Dyzenhaus, David, and Arthur Ripstein (eds.). *Law and Morality: Readings in Legal Philosophy.* Toronto: University of Toronto Press, 1996.

Fuller, Lon L. *The Morality of Law.* New Haven, CT: Yale University Press, 1969.

Golding, Martin P. *Philosophy of Law.* Englewood Cliffs, NJ: Prentice-Hall: 1975.

Griffith, Tom (ed.). *Plato—Symposium and the Death of Socrates.* Hertfordshire, UK: Woodsworth Editions Limited, 1997.

Lloyd, Dennis. *The Idea of Law.* London: Penguin Books, 1987.

Mill, John Stuart. *On Liberty.* Ed. Currin V. Shields. Indianapolis, IN: Bobbs-Merrill Company Inc., 1986.

Morris, C. (ed.). *The Great Legal Philosophers: Selected Readings in Jurisprudence.* Philadelphia, PA: University of Pennsylvania Press, 1981.

"Pope Urges Humanity to Search for Truth!" *Toronto Star* 10 Oct. 1990: A22.

Powell, Betsy. "Moonstruck Woman Vanishes." *Toronto Star* 15 Nov. 2003: A12.

Rousseau, Jean-Jacques. *Discourse on the Origin of Inequality.* Ed. J. Miller. Indianapolis, IN: Hackett Publishing Company, 1992.

———. *The Social Contract.* Ed. Lester Crocker. New York: Washington Square Press, 1974.

Waddams, S.M. *The Study of Law.* Scarborough, ON: Thomson Canada Limited, 1997.

Watson, Patrick, and B. Barber. *The Struggle for Democracy.* Toronto: Lester & Orpen Dennys Ltd., 1988.

LAW, SOCIETY, AND LEGAL REFORM

LEARNING EXPECTATIONS

After reading this chapter, you will be able to:

- explain the interrelation of law, religion, and morality
- understand how law expresses social values
- analyze possible conflicts between law and societal values
- evaluate the influence of individual citizens on law reform
- assess the role of collective action on law reform

FIGURE 4.1 Demonstrators in Ottawa protest the Canadian *Firearms Act*. This federal gun control legislation was passed in 1995. It required all gun owners to obtain a gun licence by January 1, 2001, and to register ownership of their guns by January 1, 2003. Anti-gun-control lobbyists challenged the *Firearms Act*, saying that the law intruded too much into the lives of law-abiding gun owners and would not reduce criminal violence. Why do you think law reform is sometimes contrary to the wishes of certain segments of society?

> *The Law, like the traveler, must be ready for the morrow; it must have a principle of growth.*
>
> —American Justice Benjamin N. Cardozo (1870–1938)

▪ I N T R O D U C T I O N ▪

As you read in Chapter 2, at one time, anyone in Canada who tried to commit suicide could have been charged with a crime. This was so because throughout history, both religion and morality have helped to shape the law. The Judeo-Christian tradition has maintained that suicide is an offence against God's creation. As the religious taboo against suicide became part of the prevailing moral code, people who tried to commit suicide, as well as the family members of those who succeeded, often found themselves stigmatized. The formal expression of this religious and moral taboo was reflected in the *Criminal Code* until 1972. Today, most people believe that those who are desperate enough to kill themselves should be viewed with compassion rather than condemnation. While some faith groups still treat suicide as a serious offence with spiritual consequences, the moral consensus is that suicide should not be criminalized. Correspondingly, Canadian laws no longer view attempted suicide as a crime.

From this brief example, it is possible to see how religious, social, and moral values have extensive influence on the legal system. Other factors also play a role in the evolution of the legal system. Technological and social advances, the actions of individuals and groups, and the forces of globalization all play a part in shaping the law and the legal process. Often the changes meet the developing needs of society; sometimes, however, they bring different segments of society into conflict with each other. This chapter will help you decide to what extent these influences have provoked or exacerbated conflict, and whether or not the resulting legal reform has promoted more or less harmony between the law and society.

Connections and Conflict

Religion and the Law

In contemporary Canada, most people think of the law as **secular**, that is, having a non-religious basis. As you have just read, however, certain laws have been influenced by **religion** (a formal system of belief and worship) and **morality** (a standard of right and wrong). At one time, attitudes about the law differed substantially from the contemporary view. The legal system was assumed to have an authority based on divine origin. Indeed, for thousands of years, monarchs and emperors around the world believed that they had been divinely chosen by God to lead their people. This view was upheld by the fourth-century Christian writer Saint Augustine, who wrote that even if kings were bad leaders, they had come to power for some good reason known by God. This notion was formalized by the seventeenth century as the theory of the **divine right of kings**. The sovereign or king imposed laws upon his subjects because he had the divine, or God-given, right to do so. These laws were assumed to be rooted in religion and could appeal to divine sanction for their validity. As a result, both laws and law-makers enjoyed a certain commanding authority.

The Hebrew prophets strengthened the connection between the law and religion. To the Hebrews, God's will dictated the moral pattern for all humankind. Obedience to that will was ensured by the divine punishment of offenders. As you read in Chapter 2, many contemporary laws can be traced directly to Hebraic laws found in the Bible, in the book of Exodus. For example, Canada's *Criminal Code* reflects many of the same prohibitions found in the Ten Commandments, such as "You shall not murder" and "You shall not steal."

The extent to which religious prohibitions should continue to inform law is still being debated. For example, the preamble to the Canadian Constitution states that Canada was founded on principles that recognize the rule of law and the Supremacy of God. Increasingly, however, the inclusion of the word "God" has been scrutinized. The Canadian Supreme Court has been asked to determine, among other issues, whether the recitation of the Lord's Prayer in public school or the custom of swearing on the Bible in court violates the right to exercise religious freedom.

Many prohibitions identified in the Ten Commandments are also no longer part of the *Criminal Code*. For example, the Commandment "Honour your father and mother" may be morally acceptable to Canadian society, but

children who do not honour their parents are not considered criminals. Similarly, the Commandment "You shall not commit adultery" makes it clear that the God of Moses condemns marital infidelity, but the *Criminal Code* no longer cites adultery as a criminal offence.

However, the law still does recognize the prohibitions of the Ten Commandments in some fashion. Although it is not considered criminal for children to fail to honour their parents, the *Family Law Act* recognizes that adult children have a responsibility to take care of their parents if their parents are in need. Criminal law also recognizes the special relationship between parents and children when it allows parents to use corporal punishment as a form of discipline. Similarly, while adultery is no longer an offence in the *Criminal Code*, it is still considered a ground for divorce under the *Divorce Act*. Even the Judeo-Christian view of marriage as **monogamous** (being married to only one person at a time) is reflected in the *Criminal Code* offences of **bigamy** (being married to two persons at one time) and **polygamy** (being married to more than two persons at one time).

Canada is not the only country struggling with questions regarding religion and the law. In the United States, the establishment clause of the First Amendment reads, "Government shall make no law respecting an establishment of religion." This would seem to prevent religion from interfering with law-making altogether, and yet conflicts persist. In August 2003, the Supreme Court of the United States rejected arguments from a chief justice of Alabama that he should be able to place a two-and-a-half-tonne granite monument engraved with the Ten Commandments in the Alabama State Judicial Building. Chief Justice Roy Moore argued that the monument was an acknowledgment of the Judeo-Christian God as the moral foundation of American law. The Supreme Court of the United States determined that this might be so. Nevertheless, it ruled that the monument still interfered with the First Amendment clause that separates Church and state.

On December 18, 2003, French president Jacques Chirac announced that his government would ban the use of religious symbols in public schools, including the wearing of the hijab for Muslim girls and women, the yarmulke for Jewish boys and men, and any large crucifix jewellery worn by Christians. The announcement was criticized by some religious leaders, who said that the presence of such symbols merely indicated that France was a diverse society. However, Chirac said he believed that "clothing and signs which conspicuously show membership of a religion must be forbidden in schools." He noted that the teaching of religion is banned in France's public school system and that the system "must remain secular."

Many nations around the world can trace their legal roots back to ancient philosophies and religions. Around the sixth century, while Europe was learning from the philosophers of Athens and the Hebrew prophets, the people and laws of Asia were being influenced by many great faiths such as Hinduism, Buddhism, and Confucianism. For example, Buddhism, which was founded 2500 years ago in India, focused on "The Eightfold Path of Liberation"—a code for living. The fourth tenet of this code, called "right action," sets out five basic precepts for moral conduct: "avoid destroying life, stealing, sexual misconduct, lying and intoxicants" (Fisher 1994).

The writings of K'ung Fu-tzu (known to Westerners as Confucius) also offered ways to help people create a lawful and just society. Confucianism became highly influential in China and spread to many parts of the world. The Confucian virtues include innate goodness, love, benevolence, perfect virtue, and humanity. Confucius argued that people must have faith in their rulers, and to earn this faith rulers should not lead by force but by personal virtue. Peace, according to Confucius, begins with cultivating a moral sense within the individual and the family, which would in turn impact society and the government.

It is important to point out that although morality is often connected with various religious

FIGURE 4.2 Young Muslim girls demonstrate in favour of the Islamic hijab during a march in Strasbourg, France, December 20, 2003. A few days earlier, France's president, Jacques Chirac, had called for a law banning Islamic headscarves and other religious symbols in public schools, despite protests from Muslims in France and across the world. The banner reads: "One veil = 1 voice."

codes from around the globe, many atheists, or people who do not believe in God, also have strong moral codes and values.

Morality and the Law

The Greek philosopher Socrates was sentenced to die because he had allegedly corrupted the youth of Athens by teaching them philosophy. Socrates was prepared to accept this punishment because he felt obliged to obey the state even if its laws were immoral and unjust. Socrates believed that the state itself embodied superior morality, and there was no room for individual judgment of its laws. Most people would agree that a citizen, for the most part, should obey the law. What happens, though, when extreme situations result from objectionable laws, such as the anti-Semitic legislation passed by the Nazis in Germany during the 1930s? Should citizens in South Africa have obeyed that country's laws on apartheid between 1948 and 1994? Were American citizens obliged to inform authorities of the whereabouts of enslaved people fleeing to freedom, as the law demanded until the 1880s? It becomes much more difficult to argue for obedience to a law that seems morally wrong.

The debate on the relationship between law and morality is ongoing. Philosophers and legal scholars tend to fall into two broad camps. On the one hand, **positive law** supporters, such as Thomas Hobbes, John Stuart Mill, Jeremy Bentham, and H.L.A. Hart, say that laws can be established without reference to morality. Opposed to the positivists are the **natural law** defenders, such as Thomas Aquinas and the English legal scholar Patrick Devlin, who argue that fundamental moral principles must be at the heart of any legal system.

The Positivists

The view of the positivists can be summed up by these words, spoken by John Stuart Mill: "The only purpose for which power can be rightfully exercised over any member of a civilized community, against his will, is to prevent harm to others. His own good, either physical or moral, is not a warrant." Many contemporary legal scholars, such as H.L.A. Hart, support the idea that the role of government should be limited to preventing harm to others. Positivists argue that the connection between law and morality is arbitrary. For example, they point out that the crime of murder is viewed as morally wrong *and* criminally wrong. The *Criminal Code* says that murder occurs only if the victim dies within one year and one day of the incident that caused the injury. Morally, it matters little whether the victim dies on Day 366 or Day 367, yet the legal system draws this distinction—not on moral grounds, but because it must draw a line somewhere. Similarly, most people would morally condemn someone who could have saved a drowning child but chose instead to ignore him or her. However, the law imposes no legal obligation to help. Positivists also argue that the criminal law is unfair in its application. For example, the law

does not object if someone gambles away his or her family's savings on the stock market or in a government-run lottery, but it does object to private or "off-track" betting.

Enforcing morality on a reluctant population has also proven to be difficult. It often results in police engaging in undercover work, for example, acting as "johns" or prostitutes, drug dealers or buyers, to catch criminals. Such actions, especially when there is little discernable evidence that they reduce the crime rate, bring the administration of justice into disrepute, according to positivists. They maintain that criminal law is an ineffective and expensive way to impose moral values—that by using criminal law to impose morality, the state criminalizes people who would not otherwise be classified as criminals, such as individuals who have been charged with possession of very small amounts of narcotics. Finally, positivists argue that it is too difficult to determine *whose* morality should be used to determine which behaviours are criminal. In a diverse society such as Canada, with its Aboriginal and immigrant traditions, the positivists might argue that different groups of people would have different sensibilities about a wide range of moral issues.

The Naturalists

The naturalist view is well summed up in the words of English judge Patrick Devlin in his 1965 report, *Morals and the Criminal Law*. He argues that a society is defined by its communal moral and value system. Devlin and the natural law supporters point out that morality and the law are inextricably joined, and that the law's function has never been limited to preventing "harm to others." Devlin notes that if that were so, the law would not concern itself with offences involving victims who consented. For example, consent of the victim is no defence for murder. Someone who ends a person's life solely upon the request or consent of that person may not pose a threat to others but, as Devlin argues, he or she does threaten "one of the great moral principles upon which society is based, that is, the sanctity of human life." Naturalists also say that the law must be concerned about private matters because private matters do affect society. For example, society is not likely to be overly concerned about one gambler but if half the population were gambling, such a situation would have an enormous impact on society.

Natural law supporters agree that views on morality can evolve, but they maintain that the evolution of morality should not prevent lawmakers from considering moral issues in making law. Natural law supporters note that laws often change because small groups of determined individuals have acted to change public views by creating a shift in public feeling. For example, laws dealing with the protection of children, cruelty to animals, abortion, homosexuality, and same-sex marriage have changed in Canada because of changing views about morality as well

as for legal reasons. In response to the positivist argument that it is too difficult to find common ground when it comes to morality, natural law proponents agree that it is difficult but not impossible. They argue that society has a right to determine what it deems morally unacceptable and to use the law to formally express its view.

Both positivists and natural law proponents agree that a variety of strategies besides criminal law should be used to curb unwanted behaviour. For example, Canada's response to smoking has incorporated a number of strategies, including public education, regulation, and fines. Both sides also agree that the *Criminal Code* should be used in a very limited way to impose moral values and that governments, in co-operation with citizens, must search for alternative interventions when society wishes to discourage certain actions.

CONNECTIONS: Law and Literature

In his novella *Billy Budd, Sailor*, American author Herman Melville (1819–91) tells the story of a young sailor who strikes a superior officer after being severely provoked. By chance, the officer dies from the injury, although the blow would not generally be considered fatal. The central theme of the novella is the relationship between morality and justice. The captain of the ship, Captain Vere, witnesses the death and decides that Budd must be executed even though he considers Billy to be morally innocent. Despite the fact that he regards the law as morally unjust in this instance, Vere feels compelled to enforce it. The following excerpt from the novella contains Captain Vere's arguments for Budd's execution:

> But your scruples: do they move as in a dusk? Challenge them. Make them advance and declare themselves. Come now: do they import something like this? If, mindless of palliating circumstances, we are bound to regard the death of the master-at-arms as the prisoner's deed, then does that deed constitute a capital crime whereof the penalty is a mortal one? But in natural justice is nothing but the prisoner's overt act to be considered? How can we adjudge to summary and shameful death a fellow creature innocent before God, and whom we feel to be so? Does that state it aright? You sign your sad assent. Well, I too feel that, the full force of that. It is Nature. But do these buttons that we wear attest that our allegiance is to Nature? No, to the King. When war is declared are we the commissioned fighters previously consulted? We fight at command. If our judgements approve the war, that is but coincidence. So now....Our avowed responsibility is in this: That however pitilessly that law may operate, we nevertheless adhere to it and administer it.

But the exceptional in the matter moves the hearts within you. Even so too is mine moved. But let not warm hearts betray heads that should be cool....

But something in your aspect seems to urge that it is not solely the heart that moves in you, but also the conscience, the private conscience. But tell me whether or not, occupying the position we do, private conscience should not yield to that imperial one formulated in the code under which alone we officially proceed? (Melville 1861)

Questions
1. Summarize in your own words Captain Vere's argument for executing Budd.
2. Would Captain Vere belong to the positivist or naturalist school of thought with regard to the law? Explain.
3. Assume that you are acting on behalf of Billy Budd. Create an argument that would counteract the argument of Captain Vere.

Key Influences on Law Reform

Law is made in the powerful chambers of elected officials and the courts. These may seem far removed from ordinary people and everyday life, yet courts and law-makers must reflect society's changing attitudes and values. In the following pages, you will examine some of the strongest forces and relationships that have shaped legal reforms.

Society and the Law

In the 1950s, birth control, abortion, and homosexual acts were outlawed in the *Criminal Code*. The notion of legal rights for gay men and lesbians—let alone full marital status for same-sex couples—would have struck most Canadians as outrageous. Since the conservatism of the 1950s, however, social values have become less restrictive.

One force driving social and legal change has been the movement for women's rights. Canadian women did not have the right to vote until the federal election of 1917. Even then, only the wives, mothers, and daughters of Canadian servicemen fighting overseas in

And to those who would ask why the word [persons] should include females, the obvious answer is, why should it not?
—Lord Sankey, Lord Chancellor of the Privy Council, October 18, 1929

World War I could vote. It took another 12 years for Canadian women to win their battle to be recognized as legal "persons," which gave them the right to hold public office. As a result of these events, women began to exert more influence in shaping society's views about their roles. They pushed for new laws that paved the way for new opportunities and new social attitudes, which in turn resulted in more legal reform.

When Canada's political leaders were drafting the *Canadian Charter of Rights and Freedoms* in the early 1980s, it soon became obvious that women were absent. Women's rights were not on the negotiating tables. In 1982, in response to pressure from women's groups and nationwide protests, the government changed equality provisions of the proposed constitution. Section 28 of the *Charter* now guarantees equality to both sexes:

28. Notwithstanding anything in this *Charter*, the rights and freedoms referred to in it are guaranteed equally to male and female persons.

Family law also reflects the social changes that have occurred in recent decades, especially in the division of property. In 1973, a legal decision involving women's property rights provoked a public outcry. The Supreme Court of Canada ruled that Irene Murdoch was not entitled to any share of the family property after her husband sold their farm and their marriage broke down. Murdoch had helped to build and run the farm for more than 25 years, yet the all-male court ruled she was not entitled to any part of it, not even her own clothing. People across Canada disagreed with the decision and lobbied the government to have the law changed. Since the 1980s, family law on property division has generally come to divide assets equally in the case of separation or divorce.

Changing social attitudes have also affected Canada's abortion laws. In 1969, the *Criminal Code* was amended to allow for legal abortion, but only if the pregnancy threatened the health of the mother and the procedure was approved by a hospital therapeutic abortion committee. Henry Morgentaler, a physician, believed that women should have the right to make the decision themselves and have access to abortion on demand. That same year, he opened an abortion clinic in Montréal, openly defying the law. Years of police searches, criminal charges, and court battles followed, along with heated debates and protests across Canada. Eventually, three different juries acquitted Morgentaler. It became obvious that the *Criminal Code* abortion law, whatever its intrinsic value, was widely opposed and largely unenforceable.

The enactment of the *Charter* in 1982 shifted the legal ground as the Morgentaler case worked its way through the courts. When the case came before the Supreme Court in 1988, the court found that the *Criminal Code* violated the constitutional rights of Canadian women:

Forcing a woman, by threat of criminal sanction, to carry a fetus to term unless she meets certain criteria unrelated to her own priorities and aspirations, is a profound interference with a woman's body and thus a violation of her security of the person.

Citing the *Charter*, the Supreme Court **struck down** the *Criminal Code*'s abortion law, which means it can no longer be enforced. Since then, Canadian politicians have been unable to reach consensus on a new law.

FIGURE 4.3   Pierre Trudeau was Canada's "swinging" new Prime Minister as he danced with his future wife, Margaret Sinclair, in 1969. In 1967, as justice minister, Trudeau introduced *Criminal Code* reforms that would, among other things, decriminalize homosexual acts between consenting adults. At the time, he told reporters, "There's no place for the state in the bedrooms of the nation." What is done in private between two consenting adults, he said, "does not concern the *Criminal Code*." Controversy greeted both his comments and the reforms. What does the fact that Trudeau was later elected prime minister say about social values at the time?

Accommodating Diversity

In the last few decades, immigration has made Canada a truly pluralistic society. Laws must reflect the country's diverse multicultural realities

FIGURE 4.4 In 2002, the Québec Supreme Court ruled that 12-year-old Gurbaj Singh could wear his kirpan to school in Montréal, as long as it was encased within a wooden sheath. When he returned to class in a Montréal public school, Singh was escorted by police and was insulted by local residents who disagreed with the court. Months later, Singh's parents enrolled him in a private school. What does this case say to you about social attitudes within the courts and Canadian society?

and changing collective values. Newcomers to Canada bring their own cultures, customs, faiths, and values. As they become part of Canadian society, they help to redefine mores, creating change in public policies. Ultimately, Canada's law-makers must respect the country's legal traditions while also recognizing the needs and rights of new Canadians.

Complex cases have tested the legal system and the *Charter* about what is, or should be, reasonable accommodation of diversity. Courts and human rights tribunals have had to determine, for example, whether Christian public holidays unfairly discriminate against non-Christians. Should non-Christians be entitled to time off for their religious holidays? Courts have also been asked to resolve cases involving restrictions on the wearing of traditional clothing—for

example, turbans for RCMP officers, and the hijab for Islamic young women in school. Courts have had to decide whether Sikh Canadians have the right to wear the traditional kirpan, a symbolic sword, or whether the sword must be removed in public schools, airports, and courts to ensure public safety. Canada's legal system must apply the law equally to citizens of all cultures and faiths while recognizing the needs of cultural minorities. The challenge is to resolve complex issues of faith and custom without compromising the common good.

Technology and the Law

Each breakthrough in technology brings with it changes and the need for new law. When the airplane took its first tentative flight just over 100 years ago, no one could have predicted the thousands of national and international laws that would result. The same is true of the automobile. Today, laws regulating motor vehicles are part of the *Criminal Code*, highway traffic acts, tort law, contract law, consumer safety laws, and so on.

In this new millennium, computers have fuelled a technological revolution that is racing ahead of society and its legal institutions. Scientific research and genetic engineering have improved health care and increased agricultural production, and they may soon create a kind of artificial intelligence that we cannot yet imagine. Biotechnology has led to cures for some diseases and to hopes for more miracle drugs and treatments. Animals can be cloned, and human fetuses can be modified both inside and outside the womb. Through reproductive technology, babies can be engineered.

These advances raise difficult ethical questions and pose unknown risks. What limits should laws impose? Should it be legal to clone human beings? Stem cell research promises enormous progress in treating disease, and fetuses are the primary source of stem cells. Is it socially acceptable to "grow" fetuses only to harvest their stem cells? If this is to be legal, what conditions must apply? In 1993, after years of study, the Royal

Commission on New Reproductive Technologies issued a 1300-page report dealing with questions such as these. More than ten years later, its 293 recommendations are still mired in controversy. By 2004, Parliament was split on the answers to these questions and had yet to vote on Bill C-13, a draft bill that would have put some of the recommendations into law.

Because biotechnology can modify life itself, governments and courts must decide if and when life forms can be claimed as exclusive intellectual property. In 2002, for example, the Supreme Court of Canada rejected an application from Harvard University for a **patent** (a grant or right to exclude others from making, using, or selling one's invention) on the OncoMouse®, a mouse that had been genetically modified to be cancer-prone for cancer research. Other countries had recognized the university's right to claim the mouse as its intellectual property. Governments and courts will also have to decide who is responsible if genetically modified organisms prove to be dangerous to the environment and to the public good. The rights of private business must be carefully balanced against the concern for public good.

Landmark CASE

R. v. S.A.B., 2003 SCC 60

Technology is providing some new and sophisticated investigative tools to law enforcement officials. One of those tools is DNA matching. (DNA, or deoxyribonucleic acid, is located in every cell and is unique to an individual.) Civil libertarians argue that insisting that suspects give a sample of their DNA for matching purposes violates a person's right not to self-incriminate. Read the opinions of Justices Arbour and Berger in this case. Write an argument indicating which opinion you would support and why.

Facts: The complainant, a 14-year old girl, discovered that she was pregnant and told her mother that the accused had sexually assaulted her. The complainant had an abortion and the police seized fetal tissue for DNA testing. The police obtained a warrant and seized a blood sample from the accused. Analysis showed that five of the seven DNA samples taken from the blood sample established the probability that the accused was *not* the father to be 1 in 10 million. The accused argued that the DNA warrant provision violated s. 7 of the *Charter* (the right to be free of unreasonable search and seizure), as well as s. 8 (against self-incrimination). The accused was convicted and he appealed to the Supreme Court of Canada.

Issue: Do ss. 487.04 to 487.09 (special procedures and powers re: sufficiency of warrant) of the *Criminal Code* violate *Charter* ss. 7 and 8?

Held: The appeal should be dismissed.

Ratio Decidendi: (Arbour J.) The court accepted that the *Charter* right against self-incrimination limits the extent to which an accused person can be used as a source of information about his own criminal conduct. However, the court held that balancing the interests of the accused with the need for the government to promote law enforcement finds that the DNA warrant procedure is fair and does not violate the accused person's expectation of privacy.

Justice Arbour said: "The state's interest in the scheme is significant. DNA evidence has enormous power as an investigative tool and may exonerate an accused.

Effective law enforcement benefits society and law enforcement is interested in arriving at the truth in order to bring offenders to justice and avoid wrongful convictions. Under a DNA warrant, the degree of offence to the physical integrity of the person is relatively modest. DNA searches are specific to an accused and may exonerate him early in the investigative process."

Dissent: (Berger J.) "The standard of reasonable probability was insufficient for this kind of search. The case law has repeatedly recognized the intrusive nature of searches involving interference with a person's bodily integrity. A DNA warrant should only be issued if a judge is concerned on a balance of probabilities by clear, cogent and compelling evidence that the information in support of a DNA sample is justified. Failure to apply such a high standard results in a violation of the principle against self-incrimination and the deprivation of liberty and security of the person. DNA because of its conscriptive nature should have been excluded pursuant to s. 24 (2) of the *Charter of Rights and Freedoms*."

Brave New Crimes

Some believe computers have fuelled technological discovery and given Canadians greater personal freedom and power. However, while computer banking, debit cards, and automated teller machines are convenient, they also leave a trail of transactions that computer hackers can trace to steal banking and other personal data. Using the Internet, hackers can also break into other computers and databases. In 2000, for example, a Montreal teenager known as "Mafiaboy" hacked into some of the Internet's largest Web sites, including Amazon, Yahoo, and CNN, and brought their traffic to a halt. His actions prevented the sites from doing business, creating an estimated loss of more than a billion dollars in revenues. The maximum penalty for his crime would have been two years in prison and a $1000 fine. Mafiaboy was sentenced to eight months in a youth detention facility.

When legislators created laws against theft and break and enter, they could never have foreseen the activities of hackers. Downloading music, another new kind of theft, is so widespread as to seem unstoppable. Moreover, the Internet, or cyberspace, is choked with gambling and pornography sites, some of them

FIGURE 4.5 The computer hacker known as "Mafiaboy" walks with his lawyer during his trial. He was accused of disrupting traffic for hours at a time on several major Web sites. The 16-year-old pleaded guilty to most of the charges of mischief filed against him. Do you think the eight-month sentence that Mafiaboy received was too lenient, considering the implications of his crime?

linked to organized crime. Cyberspace represents a whole new area for law, a kind of faceless new world that is virtually borderless. It has created controversies that will challenge lawmakers to enact laws that balance privacy rights with enforcement.

CONFIRM YOUR UNDERSTANDING

1. It has been argued that as society's attitudes become more open-minded, laws become more tolerant. Cite two changes in the law that appear to reflect this change.

2. In some cases, it can be argued that social attitudes and laws have become less tolerant of certain behaviours or activities, such as smoking. Cite two other behaviours of which society and the law seem to have become less tolerant.

3. Why was it significant that three juries acquitted Dr. Henry Morgentaler although he clearly broke the existing law?

4. a) The quotes that follow reflect social attitudes of their time. Compare them with s. 28 of the *Charter*.

"The male is by nature superior, and the female inferior; and the one rules and the other is ruled; this principle, of necessity, extends to all mankind."

—Aristotle, fourth century BCE

"By marriage, the husband and wife are one person in law; that is the very being or legal existence of the woman is suspended during marriage….But though our law in general considers man and wife as one person, yet there are some instances in which she is separately considered as inferior to him….and therefore all deeds done by her….are void."

—Sir William Blackstone, *Commentaries on the Laws of England* (1769)

"Notwithstanding anything in this *Charter*, the rights and freedoms referred to in it are guaranteed equally to male and female persons."

—The *Canadian Charter of Rights and Freedoms*, s. 28.

b) Do you think that s. 28 of the *Charter* adequately reflects Canadian society's attitude toward women today? Explain.

5. The following news article appeared in the *National Post* on December 30, 2003.

Careful, Your Car Could Be Spying On You
By Chris Wattie and John Schwartz

New cars now come equipped with OnStar security systems that offer services such as built-in global positioning, and help in finding your car in the parking lot. But the same technology and others like it can also be used for other purposes. On-board computers record information on drivers, and their vehicles, all without the knowledge of most motorists. Authorities are now using this information to catch hit-and-run drivers. Black box sensors that are now in millions of new cars can record data such as speed, seatbelt use and driver actions before a collision. This information is being used by insurance companies in traffic accidents. Privacy advocates say the car should be the last refuge for privacy but believe the car is now turning into "Big Brother."

a) Should data recorded by automobile security and tracking devices be used as evidence in court against drivers? Explain.

b) What positive uses can these new technologies have in terms of the law?

c) Some toll roads use recording devices to bill clients, but data from these devices can be introduced in court as evidence to determine whereabouts, the validity of alibis, and so on. What other uses of these technologies might violate individual rights?

d) What challenges do law-makers face in responding to new technologies such as these?

e) Provide three examples of how technology has changed our laws.

The Courts and the Law

In 1982, when the *Canadian Charter of Rights and Freedoms* became law, Canada's courts received a greater role in law reform. Prior to this time, the courts could declare a law invalid only if it went beyond the scope of a legislature's authority. After 1982, a court could strike down any law that infringed on the rights listed in the *Charter*. One of the first cases to come before the courts involved an individual's legal rights (ss. 7–14).

For years, a great many Canadians wrongly assumed that the law guaranteed they would be informed of their right to a lawyer if ever arrested. That practice was a regular occurrence in popular US movies and television shows, in which police read the accused their rights (the "Miranda warning") before arresting them. "Miranda" applied only in the United States, not Canada. The situation would change, however, after the passage of the *Charter* led to the precedent-setting case *R. v. Therens*, [1985] 1 S.C.R. 613.

In 1982, one week after the *Charter* took effect, 24-year-old Paul Mathew Therens of Moose Jaw, Saskatchewan, was drinking at a birthday party. After he learned that two friends had been killed while canoeing, he consumed more drinks. While driving home, he smashed his car into a tree. Police at the scene demanded that Therens come to the station and provide a breath sample for analysis. They didn't tell him of his right to seek a lawyer, and Therens did not ask for one. He went to the station and gave the sample, which revealed excessive blood-alcohol levels. Therens was charged with and later convicted of impaired driving. Therens's lawyer launched a *Charter* challenge. He argued that Therens had been detained in the police station and denied his right to a lawyer, which is guaranteed in s. 10 of the *Charter*. The Supreme Court agreed. In 1985, it overturned the conviction, ruling that the test results were wrongly obtained; to admit them would bring the administration of justice into disrepute. The ruling was controversial, but it sent out a message: The Supreme Court would exclude evidence if *Charter* rights were not respected in obtaining it.

In another landmark case, *R. v. Butler*, [1992] 1 S.C.R. 452 (see p. 206), the Supreme Court upheld the law criminalizing "obscene" pornography, despite the *Charter*'s guarantee of freedom of expression. The court cited the limiting clause in s. 1 of the *Charter* and described its decision as a "reasonable limit" of free expression on the grounds that degrading or dehumanizing sexually violent materials were obscene because they cause harm. They potentially victimize women and children and negatively influence social attitudes and behaviour, the court reasoned. Critics called the *Code*'s obscenity provisions outdated and illogical.

In other landmark cases, the court has upheld the equality rights of women, and extended *Charter* protections to gay men and lesbians and to those who are not Canadian citizens. Court rulings involving sexual orientation are often flashpoints. For example, in 1990, Delwin Vriend was fired from his job at a Christian college in Alberta because of his homosexuality. Alberta's human rights legislation did not include sexual orientation as a prohibited ground of discrimination. To fight his termination, Vriend had to take his case to the Supreme Court. Eventually, in 1998, the court heard the case and read sexual orientation into the *Alberta Individual Rights Protection Act*. The Alberta government threatened to invoke the notwithstanding clause (s. 33) of the *Constitution Act, 1982* to sidestep the ruling, but did not do so.

In addition to the responsibility of ensuring that laws do not infringe on Canadians' rights, the *Charter* also gave courts the role of prescribing remedies when rights are violated. Many such rulings have been far-reaching. In *R. v. Askov* (see p. 11), the Supreme Court ruled that the accused's right to a fair trial had been violated by unreasonable delays. As a result, tens of thousands of other cases were tossed out of court because the Crown had taken too long to bring them to trial.

FIGURE 4.6   Delwin Vriend, a gay man from Alberta, arrives at a news conference in Edmonton. The Supreme Court of Canada ruled against the Alberta government in Vriend's favour, and declared that the province must recognize sexual orientation as a prohibited ground of discrimination under the *Charter of Rights and Freedoms*.

Canada's constitutional jurisprudence is still in its youth and often shocks many Canadians. Some critics argue that the courts are being overly aggressive in protecting the equality rights of Canadians and the rights of the accused. They say the courts are taking the law beyond the intent of law-makers and the wishes of the majority of Canadians. Others argue that the courts must force Parliament to think more carefully about civil liberties and human and minority rights in drafting legislation. There is no argument that, since taking effect, the *Charter* has profoundly changed the relationship between courts and the law. Because of Supreme Court rulings, police must not only advise an accused

of the right to counsel, they must do so before taking any evidence, or before telling someone to stand for a line-up. The Supreme Court has also ruled that taking an involuntary blood sample is an unreasonable seizure, and that police taping of private communications, without judicial authorization, violates the *Charter*.

The Supreme Court has been condemned as being both too liberal and too conservative in interpreting rights law, but its power is not without limits. For example, the notwithstanding clause, mentioned above, applies to only a few sections of the *Charter* and lets provincial and territorial governments pass laws that may be contrary to the *Charter*. As well, s. 1 of the *Charter* states that rights and freedoms are "subject only to such reasonable limits prescribed by law as can be demonstrably justified in a free and democratic society." This limits the power of Canadian courts, which must strive to balance individual/group rights and the common good. In light of heightened concerns about public security, and with new laws such as the *Anti-Terrorism Act* and the *Firearms Act,* finding that balance will be a demanding challenge.

Government and the Law

The legislature and the courts are the chief sources of law in Canada. However, the elected legislature has the constitutional authority to make law, and is the chief instrument of law reform. As you will read in Chapter 5, a bill becomes law when it has been enacted by the legislature and has received royal assent. All federal and provincial statutes are published in annual volumes and some are available on computer databases.

It would be virtually impossible for someone to become familiar with all the laws of Canada. The *Criminal Code* alone has more than 700 sections, and there are more than 20 000 federal offences, 20 000 provincial offences, and thousands of municipal bylaws! Needless to say, critics often charge that Canada has too many laws, and governments are constantly being urged to streamline legislation. Yet this is no easy task. Law-makers must respond to the changing needs of the population, as well as to new technologies and international developments—and this often means a new law.

The Law Commission of Canada

To help determine when and how to reform the law, the Canadian government established the Law Reform Commission. In March 1976, the commission published *Our Criminal Law*, a report that described the scope of criminal law and suggested a number of ways to reform it. Government cutbacks led to the demise of the Law Reform Commission, but it was re-established in 1996 as the Law Commission of Canada. The commission is once again pursuing its mandate to review Canadian laws and determine whether they meet Canada's needs. It is charged with the responsibility to

- initiate and supervise independent research;
- examine proposed legislation dispassionately;
- point out possible problems that might arise with a new law or laws;
- engage Canadians in the process of reforming laws so that they are relevant, just, and equally accessible to all.

In 2003, the commission published a discussion paper entitled "What is a Crime?" Its purpose is to engage Canadians in questioning the contradictions and ambiguities that currently exist in Canadian law.

Criminal Law Reform

The *Criminal Code* is approximately 1500 pages long. It lists thousands of criminal offences, which are constantly under review. Recently, however, the Canadian government announced that there would be a full-scale overhaul of the *Code* because government lawyers were finding that many of its provisions were outdated. The

SHIFTING PERSPECTIVES: The Gambling Revolution

Gambling has long been considered a social nuisance that contributes to immorality, organized crime, and poverty. Criminal jurisprudence reflected this attitude, and Canadian law once prohibited all games of chance and outlawed establishments that engaged in gambling. Before World War I (1914–1919), most Canadian communities frowned upon gambling as a social and moral evil. When "gambling dens" appeared, law enforcement officials, including the Northwest Mounted Police, were often called in to disrupt the proceedings and haul the offenders off to jail.

Even today, you might be committing a criminal offence if you bet on a game of poker in your own house. *Technically*, if you placed a bet on behalf of another person and received payment for so doing, you would have committed an indictable offence. Such laws, still on the books, reflect the serious view of gambling once held by the government.

Because gambling was so heavily restricted, the public response to it evolved in much the same way as it did with other so-called "sin" offences. By the 1950s, fewer people were persuaded by moral arguments against gambling. As gamblers turned to illegal gambling venues, organized crime moved in to provide a variety of gambling services. Critics argued that making gambling an offence encouraged more illegal trade and set the stage for corruption. They claimed that the public would be better served by regulated gambling, which would be safer.

According to University of Toronto law professor Alan Young, the government's attitude toward gambling changed not as a result of changes in public opinion, but because of a simple business proposition. In 1985, the federal government needed money for the 1986

Winter Olympics. The provinces agreed to give them $100 million in exchange for the "exclusive jurisdiction to conduct and manage permitted lotteries" (Young 2003). Since that time, the Canadian government has enjoyed billions of dollars in revenue from the proceeds of gambling.

Today, there are myriad gambling opportunities—from legal casinos to government-run lotteries. The government even advertises legal gambling on television. In fact, buying lottery tickets, betting at the racetrack, and spending money at the casino are encouraged as healthy recreation. However, Professor Young continues to criticize the government's involvement in gambling. He argues that reforming Canada's gambling laws had nothing to do with sound public policy but occurred to accommodate business interests. He also criticizes the fact that the government continues to punish people who gamble outside the "sanctioned venues" while remaining morally oblivious to the consequences of promoting legal gambling. He notes that the government should be offering programs to assist people for whom gambling has become a serious social and financial problem. He also argues that underground gambling should be treated no differently than fishing without a licence.

FIGURE 4.7   A ferry boat en route to Nova Scotia provides slot machines for its passengers. Critics of Canada's gambling laws have argued that gambling opportunities have become too numerous, and that many individuals and families are suffering as a result. On-line gambling in particular has received heavy criticism, as it can be carried on in the privacy of one's home. Do you think certain kinds of gambling should be banned? Why or why not?

SOURCE: Young, Alan. "Gambling with People's Lives." *Toronto Star* 31 Aug. 2003.

Your Perspective

1. How have attitudes toward gambling changed over the years? Why do you think gambling was considered both a social evil and a crime in the past?
2. Is gambling a behaviour that is harmful only to the individual who may lose money? Make an argument that gambling should retain its criminal status because it also harms society.
3. One of the fastest-growing gambling outlets is the Internet. Many on-line gambling services are provided by organizations outside of Canadian jurisdiction. What problems do you foresee for the Canadian government in making new laws around the issue of Internet gambling?
4. Government-run lotteries and regulated casinos amass large revenues for the government. Critics argue that these forms of gambling are highly addictive and can cause serious personal problems. Recently, several individuals have filed lawsuits claiming their lives have been ruined by government-sanctioned gambling. Does the government have any responsibility to these individuals? Explain.
5. Gambling offences are found in Part VII, Disorderly Houses, Gaming and Betting, *Criminal Code of Canada*. Read the gambling offences contained in the *Code* and speculate whether any of these offences should be included in a reformed *Criminal Code*.

intent of this massive reform is to send fewer people to jail and to soften, eliminate, or streamline provisions that have existed for decades. One of the complaints is that current criminal law has become too confusing and that too many new offences have been created as a result of the government's desire to be harder on crime. Another complaint is that too many Canadian laws are no longer in step with society, such as the laws on prostitution, euthanasia, gambling, and possession of marijuana.

The task of reforming Canada's *Criminal Code* is not an easy one, since many people have strong views on criminal behaviour and appropriate sanctions. Marc David, a spokesman for the Canadian Bar Association says, "The *Criminal Code*, if you think about what it represents in society, is a code of morality, it is our reference point." David notes that the *Code* has become increasingly tough over the past two decades: "It's very much more repressive, and it's not blowing in the direction of liberty and liberal values" (Tibbets 2002).

Others have observed that, while the *Criminal Code* should be reformed, there should also be more uniformity in sentencing—even going so far as to suggest that judges follow a standard formula for determining sentences. Moreover, many members of the public believe the criminal justice system is not working because the courts are too lenient on criminals. For example, some critics point out that the offence of murder is too often plea-bargained to the lesser offence of manslaughter. While the maximum penalty for manslaughter is imprisonment for life, such a severe penalty is rarely imposed.

Attempting to balance these competing views is a formidable task that citizens and law-makers will likely be engaged in for years to come. While citizens need to make informed decisions on matters of law reform, Canada's law-makers need to develop a criminal system that is clearer, more streamlined, and more easily understood by the general public.

Landmark CASE

Rodriguez v. Attorney General of British Columbia (1993), 85 CCC (3d) 15 (S.C.C.)

Many people feel that Canada's laws regarding assisted suicide are outdated, although the courts disagree. In the case below, four Supreme Court of Canada judges concurred with the Supreme Court of British Columbia's decision to dismiss the appeal of Sue Rodriguez, but three judges dissented. Assume the role of a dissenting judge. What arguments would you make to counter the position of the concurring judges in this case?

Facts: Sue Rodriguez is a 42-year old woman living in British Columbia. She is married and the mother of a young son. Rodriguez suffers from amyotrophic lateral sclerosis (ALS) and is expected to live between 2 and 14 months.

She is fully aware that very soon she will lose her capacity to breathe and eat without medical intervention and will become confined to bed. Rodriguez wishes to live only so long as she can enjoy life and to control when and how she will die. By the time she is no longer able to enjoy life, however, she will be unable to end her life without assistance. Rodriguez seeks a legal order that will allow a qualified medical practitioner to set up a device that will allow her, at the time she chooses, to end her own life.

Ms. Rodriguez appealed to the Supreme Court of British Columbia for an order that s. 241(b) of the *Criminal Code* be declared invalid pursuant to s. 24 (1) of the *Charter*, on the grounds that it violates her rights under ss. 7, 12 and 15 (1) of the *Charter*.

Issue: Does s. 241(b) of the *Criminal Code* infringe or deny the rights and freedoms guaranteed by ss. 7, 12, and 15 (1) of the *Charter*? If it does, can this be justified under s. 1 of the *Charter* and therefore be consistent with the *Constitution Act, 1982*?

Criminal Code: 241. Everyone who (a) counsels a person to commit suicide, or (b) aids or abets a person to commit suicide, whether suicide ensues or not, is guilty of an indictable offence and liable to imprisonment for a term not exceeding fourteen years.

Held: Appeal is dismissed.

Ratio Decidendi: (La Forest, Sopinka, Gonthier, Iacobucci, and Major JJ.) "The most substantial issue in this appeal is whether s. 241(b) infringes s. 7 in that it inhibits the appellant in controlling the timing and manner of her death. While we have the utmost sympathy for the appellant and her family it must be concluded that while s. 241(b) impinges on the security interest of the appellant, the resulting deprivation is not contrary to the principles of fundamental justice. The appellant seeks a remedy which would assure her some control over the time and manner of her death. She supports her claim on the ground that her liberty and security of the person are infringed. But a consideration of these interests cannot be divorced from the sanctity of life, which is one of the three *Charter* values protected by s. 7.

"The argument focuses on the generally held and deeply rooted belief in our society

that human life is sacred or inviolable. The appellant suggests that for the terminally ill the choice is over time and manner of death rather than death itself, since the latter is inevitable. But surely it is rather a matter of choosing death instead of allowing natural forces to take their course.

"S. 242(b) does deprive the appellant of autonomy over her person and may cause stress in a manner which impinges on her security of the person. It is necessary therefore to determine whether there has been any deprivation thereof that is not in accordance with the principles of fundamental justice. The principles of fundamental justice leave a great deal of scope for personal judgment and the court must be careful that they do not become principles which are fundamental justice in the eye of the beholder only. In this case in general s. 241(b) is valid and desirable legislation which fulfills government objectives of preserving life and protecting the vulnerable.

"Regardless of one's personal views, there is a consensus that human life must be respected and we must be careful not to undermine the institution that protects it. It cannot therefore be said that the prohibition on assisted suicide is arbitrary or unfair or that it is not reflective of fundamental values in our society. Therefore, no principles of fundamental justice are violated and the appeal is dismissed."

Laws in Response to Crisis

It may be argued that ensuring the peace and security of Canadians is not the sole function of government. However, most would agree that it is a fundamental responsibility. Times of crisis, especially those of public emergencies and threats, have often prompted the government to

create new legislation in order to fulfill this responsibility. Such security measures have not come without a cost—or controversy. For example, the Canadian government has been forced to suspend civil liberties to protect collective security many times in Canada's history. In 1914, World War I had begun and Canada was at war with the Austro-Hungarian Empire. Canada passed the _War Measures Act_, giving the federal government sweeping emergency powers during this time of war, invasion, and rebellion. The act severely limited individual rights and freedoms and resulted in the internment of thousands of Canadians who had recently emigrated from the Austro-Hungarian Empire. They were considered **enemy aliens** (citizens of a country at war with the country in which they are currently residing or traveling). Those who were not imprisoned were forced to report to local authorities on a regular basis.

A few weeks following the Japanese attack on Pearl Harbour in December 1941, the Canadian government invoked the _War Measures Act_ once again. This time, Japanese Canadians were classified as enemy aliens. The government ordered all Canadians of Japanese descent to be moved to detention camps in the interior of British Columbia, Alberta, and Manitoba. The government confiscated homes, cars, boats, and other belongings, which were never returned. Joy

Kogawa, who was a child at the time, has described some of these experiences in her autobiographical novel, _Obasan_. Narrated by a 35-year-old Japanese Canadian who lived through the events and is determined to ignore her past, the novel focuses on the importance of memory as a means of exposing historical injustice.

The _War Measures Act_ was used again in Québec during the FLQ crisis of 1971. The FLQ—_Front de Libération du Québec_—was a radical group that had committed violence and vowed to overthrow the Québec government. As well as making membership in the FLQ a criminal offence, the act allowed police to arrest, question, and detain suspects without charge for up to 90 days. More than 400 people were placed in jail during the crisis, on the grounds that they threatened the security of Canada. Twenty people were later charged with various offences.

In 2001, Canada passed the _Anti-Terrorism Act_ in response to security fears following the attacks on the World Trade Center in New York City on September 11, 2001. The stated purpose of this

None of this bears remembering. "You have to remember," Aunt Emily said. "You are your history. Don't deny the past. Remember everything."
—Joy Kogawa, _Obasan_

FIGURE 4.8 Several children watch armed soldiers in Québec City during the FLQ crisis. In invoking the _War Measures Act_ during the FLQ crisis of 1971, Prime Minister Trudeau said that the government was not acting out of fear, but to prevent "fear from spreading." Days before, the FLQ had kidnapped a British trade commissioner to Canada as well as Québec's labour minister (who would later be killed). What alternatives do you think the government had under these circumstances?

act is to "take steps to combat terrorism and terrorist activities at home and abroad." The act amends and strengthens the power of the government in a number of other pieces of legislation, including the *Criminal Code*, the *Official Secrets Act*, the *Canada Evidence Act*, and the *Proceeds of Crime Act*. The *Criminal Code* has also been amended to include new offences that make it a crime to knowingly collect or provide funds, directly or indirectly, that could be used to carry out terrorist activities. The *Anti-Terrorism Act* also makes it easier for police to use electronic surveillance against terrorist organizations and creates the power of "preventative arrest," which enables

police to arrest and impose conditions of release on those suspected of terrorist activity. These sweeping powers have been criticized by various individuals and civil rights organizations, who argue that these powers are much too broad and violate individual rights guaranteed under the *Canadian Charter of Rights and Freedoms*.

It is very likely that the *Anti-Terrorism Act* will be the subject of a *Charter* challenge in the near future. At that time, the Supreme Court of Canada will be given the difficult task of determining to what extent it is permissible to violate individual freedoms in exchange for collective security.

CONFIRM YOUR UNDERSTANDING

1. How did the Therens case change arrest procedures in Canada?

2. In Canadian courts some judges are throwing out cases because the accused has been held too long in custody while awaiting a **bail hearing** (held to determine if the accused should be released until trial). What case would the judges likely cite as precedent for their decisions? Explain why.

3. Explain how the courts and government act as a check and balance to our rights in Canada.

4. Why do you think governments supported the addition of the notwithstanding clause to our Constitution?

5. What are the main arguments both for and against the Supreme Court's role in interpreting the law since the introduction of the *Canadian Charter of Rights and Freedoms*?

6. Identify three key changes to our law that have been made as a result of Supreme Court rulings since 1982.

7. In the 1998 *Vriend v. Alberta* case, critics argued that the Supreme Court "read in" amendments to Alberta's *Human Rights Code* to make sexual orientation a prohibited ground of discrimination despite the objections of the Alberta government. What do you think they meant by "read in"?

8. What is the purpose of the Law Commission of Canada? Do you think it serves a useful purpose? Explain.

9. Do you agree with Marc David's statement that the *Criminal Code* has become increasingly tough over the past two decades? Explain.

10. Under what circumstances has the government of Canada been able to suspend civil liberties?

Individual Action and the Law

On Thursday, December 1, 1955, a young woman named Rosa Parks returned home after a hard day's work at a downtown department store in Montgomery, Alabama. Glad to spot a seat on the bus, she sat down under a sign that said, "Whites only." At the time in Alabama, African-Americans were allowed to sit in these seats only

until a white passenger boarded the bus, at which point they were expected to give up the seat and go to the back of the bus. When some white passengers got on a few stops later, the bus driver told Rosa and other African-Americans sitting up front to move. All except Rosa moved. Rosa did not have any great dream of changing the law that day; she was tired and simply didn't want to move. She was arrested and fined for breaking one of Montgomery's segregation laws. Rosa's action sparked Dr. Martin Luther King, a minister in Alabama, and other African-American leaders to organize a boycott of Alabama's buses. This action ignited a **civil rights movement** (a body of people who organize to protest what they perceive as a violation of rights) that influenced American law and societies all over the world.

Although Rosa Parks's action had an extraordinary impact on the US civil rights movement, individual action rarely results in this kind of legal reform. Still, some determined individuals have managed to leave a lasting impact on Canadian law. As you read earlier, before 1929, women in Canada did not have the status of "persons" under the law. It took the efforts of five individuals—Emily Murphy, Nellie McClung, Louise McKinney, Irene Parlby, and Henrietta Muir Edwards—to challenge the 1928 Supreme Court ruling that limited the meaning of "person" to males only. The women sought justice before the Judicial Committee of the Privy Council of Great Britain. On October 18, 1929, the Lord Chancellor affirmed that "the word person includes members of the male and female sex and that therefore the question propounded by the Governor General must be answered in the affirmative and that women are eligible to be summoned and become members of the Senate of Canada."

Women's equality before the law was challenged again in 1981 when the *Canadian Charter of Rights and Freedoms* seemed to exclude women. Marilou McPhedran, a Toronto lawyer, and several other women fought this oversight and drafted the sexual-equality statement found in our 1982 *Charter of Rights and Freedoms*.

Mary Two-Axe Earley (1911–1996), born in Kahnawake, Québec, was another woman who took action to redress an injustice—this time, against Aboriginal women. In 1932, she married a non-Aboriginal man and immediately lost her Indian status. (At the time, the *Indian Act* stated that women who married non-Aboriginal men lost their status; however, Aboriginal men did not

lose their status if they married non-Aboriginal women.) The battle over the loss of status for Aboriginal women went to the Supreme Court in 1971. At this time, the court ruled that another woman who had experienced the same loss of status (Jeannette Corbière Lavell, discussed in Chapter 6) was not discriminated against because the *Indian Act* treated all Aboriginal women the same way. Mary Two-Axe Earley was so upset by this ruling, and by the treatment of other women who had married non-Aboriginal men, that she formed an organization called Equal Rights for Indian Women. As a result of her lobbying efforts, in 1985, Parliament passed Bill C-31, which removed the section of the *Indian Act* that took away a woman's status if she married a non-Aboriginal man. Two weeks later, Mary became the first woman to have her Indian status officially restored.

Individuals who influence law reform can sometimes be a "flashpoint" for issues that divide or engage Canadians. For example, Canadian abortion law would not have changed with-

FIGURE 4.9 Mary Two-Axe Early fought for the right of Aboriginal women to retain their Indian status if they married non-Aboriginal men.

out the persistence of Henry Morgentaler. Morgentaler, who challenged the inclusion of abortion in the *Criminal Code* by performing abortions at his own clinic, was willing to go to prison for his beliefs. His actions brought the debate on abortion into the public eye and before the courts. Since the Supreme Court struck down the law in 1988 as violating women's *Charter* rights, the issue of legal abortion has remained controversial, and attempts have been made to introduce a new abortion law. However, in Canada today, abortion remains a medical and not a legal matter.

Another individual who was brave enough to stand his ground despite much pressure is Elijah Harper, an Aboriginal member of the Manitoba legislature, who challenged the **ratification** (confirmation) of the Meech Lake Accord. By June 23, 1990, eight out of ten provinces had agreed to ratify the accord, a constitutional agreement that recognized Québec as a distinct society. When the Manitoba Legislature voted to ratify the accord, Harper voted no, saying he did not believe the accord sufficiently addressed Aboriginal concerns, especially land claims. His single "no" vote meant the death of the accord. It also meant that the province of Québec remained outside the Canadian Constitution, and left other constitutional issues unresolved.

Collective Action and the Law

Although individuals can be the impetus for law reform, the support of groups and organizations is often necessary. Such "collective action" can be a small group of like-minded individuals working together to change a law, or it can be a sophisticated **lobby group** with ample funding and resources to lobby all members of Parliament, seek and use media attention, and engage the public consciousness in creative ways. Some lobbyists act on behalf of other groups or corporations. Some act on behalf of non-profit organizations. Lobbyists always try to influence legislators to pass laws that are favourable to their interests. They work in such diverse fields as business, human rights, environment, labour, peace, and public policy.

It was collective action sparked by outrage that led to a change in Canada's gun laws. On December 6, 1989, Marc Lepine killed 14 women at École Polytechnique de Montréal after acquiring a semi-automatic military weapon. Horrified individuals across Canada saw the tragedy as one more example of the problems with the nation's gun laws. Organizations such as the Coalition for Gun Control, the Canadian Association of Police Chiefs, Citizens Against Violence Everywhere Advocating its Termination (CAVEAT), and many others lobbied the government to change the law. In 1995, Canada passed the *Firearms Act*. It required all gun owners to obtain a gun licence by January 1, 2001, and to register ownership of their guns by January 1, 2003. Anti-gun-control lobbyists immediately challenged the *Firearms Act*, but on June 15, 2000, in response to a challenge by the government of Alberta, the Supreme Court of Canada ruled that the new law was legal.

Other lobby groups, such as Mothers Against Drunk Driving (MADD), have been equally successful. MADD not only succeeded in changing the laws governing drunk driving, it also changed public attitudes toward drinking and driving. Various other lobby groups have been successful in reforming laws—and attitudes—about such diverse issues as seatbelts, child custody, and the environment.

Not everyone supports the notion that collective action should result in a change of law; some argue that activism can encourage civil disobedience and even lead to anarchy. However, one of the hallmarks of a healthy democracy is that citizens are free to express public judgment and actively debate the kinds of laws by which they live.

Globalization and the Law

Globalization and free trade are forces that are interconnected. Together, they have a huge impact on the social, cultural, and economic reality of all communities. In Canada, as in many countries, the rule of law supports the structure of democracy and reflects the citizens' belief in their country as a sovereign nation. However, as

According to the federal government, 75 percent of all gun owners met the deadline, registering 5.8 million of the estimated 8 million unrestricted firearms in Canada. But that didn't stop gun owners and politicians from expressing opposition.

—CBC News Backgrounder, January 2003

FIGURE 4.10   The US *Patriot Act* was signed into law in October 2001. It gave the American government new power to use wiretaps, electronic and computer eavesdropping and searches, and the authority to access a wide range of financial and personal information. Canada's *Anti-Terrorism Act* follows the *Patriot Act* in many of its provisions. Do you think it is necessary for governments to have such sweeping powers in order to protect national security?

Canada becomes a larger player in the global economy, it may be subject to international rules, norms, and standards that clash with its own. Multinational and transnational corporations, as well as new economic blocs such as NAFTA and the European Union, are changing the world by creating highly mobile and flexible workforces; challenging standards in environmental protection and attitudes about human rights; and redefining the whole notion of national loyalty and government power. In the future, the idea of national citizenship may disappear, to be replaced with a concept of global citizenship that recognizes the benefits of international co-operation.

As Canada stands at the threshold of the twenty-first century, it may find that its greatest challenges in law reform come not from within, but from the global community. The development of international norms, standards, and laws in business will have an impact on Canada's own laws. For example, in 2002, Canada formally adopted the **Kyoto Protocol**, an international agreement to reduce global warming. The *Kyoto Protocol* commits many industrialized nations to reducing their greenhouse gas emissions between 2008 and 2012 to a level that is 5.2 percent below 1990 levels. Greenhouse gases pollute the environment and result from burning fossil fuels, such as coal, petrol, and diesel. As a result of the protocol, many nations, including Canada, are now in the process of passing new regulations regarding emissions from power plants and vehicles.

The *Kyoto Protocol* is just one example of how international pressure is influencing legislative development of Canada. Another area of concern is national security in the wake of the Setpember 11, 2001, attacks in the United States. Canada's new *Anti-Terrorism Act* is closely patterned on the US *Patriot Act* and the anti-terrorism laws of Great Britain. As a result of this legislation, these nations can collaborate more easily to share intelligence about terrorist organizations, track their funding, and dismantle terrorist cells. On the other hand, citizens of all three nations have criticized these laws as a blow to personal liberty. Balancing the need for national security against the individual's right to liberty is likely to engage citizens and legislators for years to come.

CONFIRM YOUR UNDERSTANDING

1. Choose three of the individuals discussed in this chapter whose actions precipitated changes to our law. Assess their impact on changing the law.
2. What is the role of lobby groups on changing law?
3. Some argue that powerful lobby groups have too much influence on governments and force changes that are at odds with the wishes of the silent majority. With reference to the lobby groups discussed in your text do you agree with this assessment? Explain.
4. What impact will the forces of globalization and international law have on law-making in Canada?

In Closing

The extent to which religion and morality should inform law is not an idle debate. Those who subscribe to the view upheld by Mill—that the law should intervene in matters of private moral conduct as little as necessary—will not make the same laws as those who argue that the law must express the moral standards of the community.

The law is a reflection of religious and moral traditions, and each generation must determine what values it wishes to promote and preserve. Reforming the law to meet the needs of each new generation is a formidable task. The legislature, which is the chief instrument of law reform, must ensure that the law does not trail too far behind—or jump ahead of—prevailing social attitudes. Law-makers must consider the impact of technology and make laws that protect privacy but do not stifle innovation in science or technology. They must attempt to balance minority and majority rights, as well as individual liberties

versus collective security. They must respond both to critics who claim there are too many laws and to those who claim there are too few. Finally, governments and law-makers must consider the role of international law and the demands of the global economy.

Making new law or changing old law can create enormous tension and conflict in society, but laws must constantly be re-analyzed to remain in touch with contemporary society. At the same time, law-makers must not be concerned only with the future—they must also consider the important values and traditions represented by the past. The scope and purpose of law is reflected in religious values, beliefs, morals, and fundamental assumptions about what should be prohibited or upheld as acceptable. The important task of changing law cannot be left solely in the hands of law-makers because future generations will judge our society by the laws we have allowed to be enacted on our behalf.

CHAPTER ACTIVITIES

Extend Your Legal Knowledge

1. Positivists concede that legal systems are often based on moral values, but they argue that those moral values merely reflect the views of those with the power to make the law. Assume the role of a natural law proponent and make an argument against the positivist position.

2. Create a timeline showing significant changes in the law regarding women, starting with the 1929 decision by the Judicial Committee of the Privy Council that declared women to be persons under the law.

3. What was the significance of the Therens case (p. 118) in changing the role of the Supreme Court of Canada? Research and report on one other case that illustrates the influence of the Supreme Court in changing or amending our law.

4. The film industry has been lobbying the government to make new law regarding the illegal

videotaping of movies. In the United States, such laws have already been passed. For example, the state of Ohio has passed a law that allows police to arrest people for videotaping movies in theatres. Do you think it is necessary to employ criminal law to curb the practice of illegal videotaping? Explain. What other strategies would you employ? What problems would you foresee in applying this type of law?

5. The *War Measures Act* has been replaced with the *Emergency Measures Act*, which gives government wide powers in public emergencies. For example, the government can order people to leave their homes in the case of flooding or forest fires. What safeguards does Canada have in place to ensure our government does not abuse this power?

6. International treaty agreements such as NAFTA (the North American Free Trade Agreement

between Canada, the United States, and Mexico) have been criticized because they interfere with national sovereignty in terms of the environment, worker rights, and economic security. Do you agree that international agreements such as NAFTA interfere with national sovereignty? Explain.

7. The United States has refused to sign the *Kyoto Protocol*. Research the reasons behind this decision and state whether you agree or disagree with them.

Think About the Law

8. On January 2, 2004, the federal government's new *Personal Information Protection and Electronic Documents Act* came into effect. The law says that companies must create new systems to ensure that customer information is secure, accurate, gathered with appropriate consent, and not to be used beyond a stated purpose. Critics argue the act will place too much of a burden on business and will be too costly to implement. They also argue that Canada is putting such a law in place to meet standards imposed by the European Union. Do you think a law is needed to protect the abuse of personal information, or are there other methods that may be more appropriate to deal with this matter? Explain.

9. Should Canadians be concerned about the influence of international developments on Canadian law? Discuss.

10. Speculate on the possibility of a concept of worldwide citizenship and common standards of criminal, environmental, labour, and contract law.

11. Discuss the following statement with reference to the *Anti-Terrorism Act*:

"Any new law is some restriction on liberty, but not all restrictions are threats to it."

Communicate About the Law

12. Prepare and present a debate on either of the following statements:

"The use of the criminal law to enforce morals has tended to be inefficient, to produce handicaps for enforcement against genuinely threatening conduct."

or

"Society cannot ignore the morality of the individual any more than it can its loyalty; it flourishes on both and without either it dies."

13. Many individuals have fought to change the law in such diverse areas as family law and gun control. Research and evaluate the influence of an individual who has helped to change the law.

14. Immigration patterns have always influenced law. Speculate on how present immigration to Canada will change our laws in the future.

15. There are dangers inherent in all new technologies. For example, the Internet has fostered new problems such as easy access to child pornography and the pirating of music. Evaluate the pros and cons of using the criminal justice system to regulate these new technologies.

Apply the Law

16. The *Firearms Act* has resulted in intense lobbying by those in favour of gun control and those against. Assume the role of a member of the Coalition for Gun Control. Prepare an argument that could be used to convince the government that the *Firearms Act* should be amended to make all guns, with the exception of those used for hunting animals, illegal. Assume the role of a gun collector and make an argument that the *Firearms Act* should be repealed and the registration of firearms ended.

17. The Law Commission of Canada released a discussion paper in 2003 entitled "What is a Crime?" The purpose of the paper is to engage Canadians in thinking about alternative strategies to curb unwanted behaviour in society other than through the criminal justice system. Read the following excerpt:

A liberal democracy is as concerned with the means of intervening in unwanted behaviour as it is with the ends. In considering how we can promote a good and safe society, we must reflect on the strategies we use to confront unwanted behaviour. Any society must have the tools to realize the vision that it has of itself: a just, safe, prosperous and egalitarian society.

Our comparative use of criminal law, regulation, surveillance, community control, therapy, public education and reward programs says a lot about our society, about its structure of governance and about its values....We invite Canadians to reflect on their role in a democracy that is searching for intervention strategies that are efficient, equal and just.

a) Keeping in mind the goals mentioned above, examine the following behaviours that are prohibited in our *Criminal Code*. Suggest other strategies that might be more appropriate in limiting such behaviour.

b) Do any of these behaviours warrant inclusion in our criminal law? Explain.

c) Make your own list of behaviours now prohibited in the *Criminal Code* that might benefit from alternative intervention strategies.

- Nudity in a public place: s. 174 (1)
- Spreading false news: s. 181
- Keeping a gaming or betting house: s. 201 (1)
- Failure to stop at scene of accident: s. 252 (1)
- Bigamy and polygamy: s. 290 (1) and s. 293 (1)
- Counselling or aiding a suicide: s. 241(a)(b)
- Possession of marijuana (substance): s. 4, *Controlled Drugs and Substances Act*

18. It is difficult to create laws regulating the use of new medical technologies. One of the most controversial technologies concerns stem cell research. Should researchers be allowed to use human embryos discarded from the *in vitro* fertilization process for stem cell research? Should there be laws preventing scientists from creating embryos for stem cell research to treat illnesses such as Parkinson's disease? The government has been asked to enact new laws controlling this type of research but has not yet passed any legislation. Assume you have the task of drafting new legislation on these issues. What laws would you propose?

BIBLIOGRAPHY

Canadian Legal Information Institute. Accessed Jan. 2004. <www.canlii.org>

Coomber, Jan, and Rosemary Evans. *Women Changing Canada*. Toronto: Oxford University Press, 1997.

Dyzenhaus, David, and Arthur Ripstein (eds.). *Law and Morality: Readings in Legal Philosophy*. Toronto: University of Toronto Press, 2001.

Fisher, Mary Pat. *Living Religions*. Englewood Cliffs, New Jersey: Prentice-Hall. 1994.

The Law Commission of Canada. "What is a Crime?" Discussion Paper. 2003.

Melville, Herman. *Billy Budd and Other Tales*. New York: Signet Classics, 1961.

Taylor, A.E. (ed.). *The Laws: The Collected Dialogues of Plato*. Princeton, NJ: Princeton University Press, 1961.

Tibbetts, Janice. "Cauchon Set to Liberalize Criminal Laws." *National Post* 24 Sept. 2002.

Young, Alan. "Gambling with People's Lives." *Toronto Star* 31 Aug. 2003.

Watson, Patrick, and Benjamin Barber. *The Struggle for Democracy*. Toronto: Lester and Orpen Dennys Limited, 1988.

UNIT ONE CULMINATING ACTIVITY

At the Philosophers' Table

Introduction

For centuries philosophers have grappled with the complexities of understanding law and justice. Now that you have completed Unit 1, your challenge is to analyze and effectively summarize the philosophy of justice for a particular philosopher and to interpret the merits of actual or proposed laws based on that person's theories.

In addition to addressing the Overall Learning Expectations outlined at the beginning of this unit, this culminating activity requires you to use a number of legal inquiry skills. You may want to consult Chapter 1 "The Legal Handbook" (on the pages indicated by the icons) to review each of these skills.

Your Task

1. Select a legal philosopher studied in class or one found through independent research of your own.

2. Using library resources and/or the Internet, research your chosen philosopher and his or her views regarding law and justice. (You may want to consult "Conducting Law Research on the Internet" in the Legal Handbook.)

3. Write a clear and concise one-page summary highlighting five main points to explain your chosen philosopher's ideas on law and justice. Support your points by including examples to illustrate each.

4. For each of the actual or proposed laws listed below, summarize what you think your chosen philosopher's view would have been. Prepare written arguments for or against each actual or proposed law based on this view. (You may want to consult "Tips for Writing an Argumentative Essay" in the Legal Handbook.)

   - A law that allows the use of random spot checks to catch possibly impaired drivers.

   - A law that permits euthanasia.

   - A proposal by the government to legalize theft.

   - A proposed new law that would permit the government to take DNA samples from all newborns in order to maintain a databank that could be used to match DNA from a crime scene.

   - A proposed new law that permits members of certain ethnic groups to be arrested and interrogated without legal representation for a period of time in order to combat terrorism.

   - A proposed law that would limit lawyer–client privilege and force defence lawyers to disclose to the Crown if their client confessed to a serious crime.

   - A proposed new law that would decriminalize crimes such as possession of drugs, prostitution, and all gambling.

5. Host a class "panel discussion" in which each proposed law becomes a topic for debate. You will state and debate the merits and/or flaws of the law according to the opinions of your chosen philosopher. Try to be convincing and logical in the presentation of your arguments, while staying as true as possible to what you believe the philosopher's views would be.

Present your information in a clear and engaging manner. Ensure that your information is accurate, relevant, and properly connected to the ideas of the philosopher you are representing. (You may want to consult "Delivering an Oral Presentation" and "Honing your Debating Skills" in the Legal Handbook.)

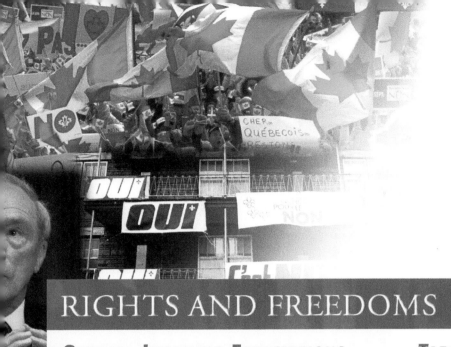

UNIT 2

RIGHTS AND FREEDOMS

OVERALL LEARNING EXPECTATIONS

By the end of this unit, you will be able to:

- demonstrate an understanding of the historical development of human rights legislation in Canada
- explain the development of constitutional law in Canada
- demonstrate an understanding of the rights and responsibilities of individuals under the *Canadian Charter of Rights and Freedoms*
- explain the role of the legislature and the judiciary in defining, interpreting, and enforcing *Charter* rights in Canada
- analyze the conflicts between rights and freedoms and between minority and majority rights in a democratic society and describe the methods available to resolve these conflicts

TABLE OF CONTENTS

Chapter 5

CONSTITUTIONAL LAW

LEARNING EXPECTATIONS

After reading this chapter, you will be able to:

- explain what a constitution is and why it is necessary
- distinguish among the law-making jurisdictions of the federal, provincial, and municipal governments
- understand the role of the courts in law-making in Canada
- identify key events in the history of Canada's Constitution

FIGURE 5.1 The construction of Canada's first Parliament Building in Ottawa in 1865 symbolized the unifying of Canada under Confederation. But it is our Constitution, with its entrenched *Charter of Rights and Freedoms*, that defines Canada as a nation, and demonstrates our commitment to the principles of democracy. How does Canada's Constitution act as a framework or guideline for our nation?

It was a feature of the 1960s to search for Canada's identity by finding differences from the United States. In fact, countries are not constituted by myths; countries exist as units of government over a geographical base. What makes Canada is its constitution. This is the bedrock on which myths may or may not be erected.

—William Johnson, *Montreal Gazette*, January 20, 1996

■ I N T R O D U C T I O N ■

Conflict and compromise: these are the cornerstones of Canada's constitutional history. It is not surprising, then, that our Constitution is wielded almost daily as both a weapon and a shield. Scan the pages of any national newspaper and you will no doubt find the term *unconstitutional* at the heart of many stories dealing with parliamentary debates or judicial proceedings.

So why is it that the very thing that is supposed to ensure the smooth, peaceful operation of our country is the source of so much strife? Is it because of what it says or doesn't say? Whom it empowers or doesn't empower? What it guarantees or doesn't guarantee? The simple answer to all of these questions is "yes."

The Canadian Constitution is not a static document, but rather an evolving entity. Its capacity for interpretation and change is what keeps it relevant and powerful.

In this chapter, you will explore the historical evolution of Canada's Constitution and how it informs law-making powers and jurisdictions. You will also examine the basic foundations and key institutions that create and maintain the constitutional framework in Canada.

Sources of the Canadian Constitution and Constitutional Law

A **constitution** is a legal framework or guideline that establishes how power and authority within a country is exercised. It also assigns the limits of that power. Consider your school's student council. Without rules governing the roles of elected individuals, your student council would be an ineffective body, unable to make decisions or achieve goals. For nations that have weak democratic traditions and institutions, the consequences can be much more severe. Without strong guidelines embodied in a constitution to assign the powers of the state, the threat of civil war may emerge, with rival interest groups fighting to gain power and control of the country.

Constitutional law comprises the principles of the constitution, the powers that are assigned by it and how they are implemented through a country's legal and political institutions, and the roles of the people who operate within those institutions.

Many nations around the world are held to account by a constitution. Most constitutions consist of a written document that lays down the fundamental principles and rules for how a country governs itself. For example, the United States upholds the Constitution of 1787 and its amendments. Most constitutions have a provision for making amendments so that the basic framework of power can be adjusted to address changing needs in a country. A case in point is the text of the Italian Constitution of 1948, which has been amended 13 times. France is on its fifth constitution and has made a number of amendments to the current one.

There are several countries that do not have written constitutions, however. Britain and Israel are two examples. In both cases, traditions and customs help guide the operation of the country and the division of power. Despite the absence of a formal constitution—a central law that delegates the use of authority—these countries run smoothly as democratic nations. Conversely, there are countries that have formal constitutions, but they are unconnected to the needs, wishes, and values of the general public. Thus, these constitutions are easily manipulated and of no force or effect. For example, the military in Turkey amended its constitution in 1982 with an article indicating that the people accepted military rule. In Chile, the constitution has been written to ensure the military and other political groups hold the balance of power at the expense of a democratically elected legislature.

Since the constitution of a democratic country is often regarded as the supreme law of the land, it must be a reflection of the collective views and values cherished by the people of that land. In Canada, the views and values that we uphold as a nation and wish to protect span the political, legal, social, and economic spectrum. However, not all of the principles that characterize Canada's Constitution are written down and not all of the

written principles can be found in one particular document. In fact, the Canadian Constitution is a combination of many unwritten rules and written documents, added over time, much like links in a chain.

You may recall from a course in civics or history that Canada was originally established in 1867 as an act of British Parliament. Our Constitution is, therefore, based on the British model. The complex web of principles governing the federation of Canada is not codified in one single written document, but rather in

- constitutional documents, which establish the structure of government, the division of powers, and the rights of individuals;
- **conventions**, or unwritten rules followed primarily for reasons of tradition rather than law, which provide the details of how our government operates; and
- common law (or case law), which addresses constitutional disputes and establishes precedents upheld by our legal system.

Constitutional Documents

Constitutional documents are the most concrete source of Canada's Constitution. Although some of these documents have greater importance or relevancy than others, they each have their place in shaping and informing Canada's legal system.

The British North America Act

When the Fathers of Confederation made the decision in 1867 to create a new national entity called Canada, the various parts of Canada at that time (consisting of what are now Ontario, Québec, New Brunswick, and Nova Scotia) were colonial dependents of Great Britain. The act passed by British Parliament, which created the federation of Canada, was called the *British North America Act* (*BNA Act*) and it served as the main document in Canada's Constitution. The *BNA Act*, which became known as the *Constitution Act, 1867*, established that Canada would be modelled on the same principles as that of Great Britain, implying that it would operate as a parliamentary-style democracy. The document

FIGURE 5.2   Leaders of the various colonies in British North America convened in 1864 to construct an arrangement that would see the creation of the federal government and the country known as Canada. Why do you think creating a larger political union would have been a goal of the leaders of the colonies at this time?

also outlined the division of powers between the federal and provincial governments. But the *BNA Act* was equally noteworthy for what it did not say. For example, the roles of the prime minister and the Cabinet were not made explicit because, following the British model, most of these issues were to be addressed by conventions. The document also did not have a formula or mechanism for amending Canada's Constitution. This meant that whenever Canadians wanted or needed to make a change to their constitution, the federal government had to ask British Parliament to pass a bill implementing that change.

British Parliament passed a number of bills after 1867, amending the *BNA Act*. Changes were required for a variety of reasons, such as when new provinces entered Confederation or new powers were assigned federal or provincial jurisdiction. All of the individual bills passed by Britain since 1867 are considered constitutional documents in their own right and are linked to the original 1867 document.

As our nation grew and matured, we became dissatisfied with having to involve a foreign parliament in any changes, additions, or deletions

we wanted to make to our Constitution. A series of discussions and conferences about an acceptable amending formula took place between the federal and provincial governments over the course of about 50 years. (On constitutional matters, the federal government speaks on behalf of the territories. Since the territories are not yet organized into provinces, they do not have constitutional standing or powers granted to them by the Constitution.) Most of these discussions ended in a failure to reach a compromise. Among the obstacles was a feeling on the part of the province of Québec as well as Aboriginal peoples that their concerns were not being adequately addressed in each draft document.

Initially, when no agreement on a suitable amending formula could be reached, the federal government attempted to **patriate** (bring under the authority of the country to which the laws apply) the Constitution on its own, without provincial consent. The provinces took the federal government to court. The Supreme Court of Canada ruled that, although it would not be illegal for the federal government to patriate the Constitution on its own, to do so without substantial provincial support would flout an unwritten convention. However, in 1981, a new amending formula was agreed upon by the federal government and 9 out of the 10 provinces. Québec walked out of the negotiations, citing the compromise deal as insufficient in addressing its concerns and meeting its demands. Canada's Constitution was patriated and renamed the *Constitution Act, 1982*. However, this event did not mark an end to Canada's constitutional evolution. In fact, it was just the beginning.

The Constitution Act, 1982

Three forces were at work during the patriation debates of the late 1970s and early 1980s. The first was the need to create an amending formula so that Canada would no longer require Britain's involvement to change its Constitution.

The second involved growing concerns over Québec nationalism and that province's desire to separate. Québec politicians often cited the federal structure as an impediment to Québecers completely controlling their own destiny. Separatists concluded that leaving Canada was the only way to solve these issues. Federalist

I wish simply that the bringing home of our Constitution marks the end of a long winter, the breaking up of the ice jams and the beginning of a new spring. What we are celebrating today is not so much the completion of our task, but the renewal of our hope—not so much an ending, but a fresh beginning.

—Pierre Elliott Trudeau,
at Canada's
patriation ceremony,
April 17, 1982

politicians in Québec argued that renewing the federation and remaining in Canada was the best way to protect Québec culture and interests. The need to address Canada's Constitution became even more urgent when, in 1976, Québec elected its first separatist party, led by René Lévesque. Premier Lévesque promised to hold a **referendum**, which is the process of referring a political question to the electorate for a direct vote, on Québec separation from Canada. Prime Minister Pierre Trudeau, who was a staunch federalist and the driving force behind patriation, promised Québecers that if they defeated the separation referendum in 1980, he would work to renew the federation to better meet Québec's concerns. The referendum resulted in a "no" vote, and a new round of constitutional discussions took place.

The third and final force was Trudeau's commitment to the protection of human rights. Much like Prime Minister John Diefenbaker, Trudeau believed that the rights of all Canadians needed to be better protected by law. In his opinion, the best way to achieve that goal was to **entrench** these rights, or safeguard them in perpetuity from political or legal interference, within Canada's Constitution.

The final package—the *Canada Act, 1982*—was proclaimed the *Constitution Act, 1982* and was officially signed in Ottawa by Queen Elizabeth II on April 17, 1982. The *Constitution Act, 1982* comprises seven parts

I   *Canadian Charter of Rights and Freedoms*
II Rights of the Aboriginal Peoples of Canada
III Equalization and Regional Disparities
IV Constitutional Conferences
V   Procedure for Amending Constitution of Canada
VI Amendment to the *Constitution Act, 1867*
VII General

Four of the seven parts of the *Constitution Act, 1982*, have played a significant role in the evolution of Canada's legal system, primarily because they deal directly with the rights of citizens. Arguably, the component that has had the

FIGURE 5.3 The signing of the *Constitution Act, 1982* by Queen Elizabeth II marks the official end of British control over Canada's Constitution. Why is it important that Canada have complete control over its Constitution?

greatest impact on Canadian law since patriation is Part I: *Canadian Charter of Rights and Freedoms*. The *Charter* codified and guaranteed rights for all Canadians that could not be infringed on by government. Furthermore, any law passed by any government could be challenged if it infringed on any *Charter* right. (The *Charter* will be covered in greater detail in Chapters 6 and 7.) Part III outlines the concept of equalization, the principle of which is intended to strengthen federation. This component of the act commits the federal parliament to providing equalization payments to provincial and territorial governments, if necessary, to ensure there are sufficient revenues in all regions to provide reasonably comparable levels of public services at reasonably comparable levels of taxation. Part V, the new amending formula, outlines the procedure for changing aspects of Canada's Constitution. Part VI amends the *Constitution Act, 1867*, strengthening certain provincial rights in the areas of non-renewable natural resources such as oil, natural gas, and metals.

Other Constitutional Acts

There are several other documents passed before and after the *BNA Act* that, although they are less well known, in some cases still have legal force, and in all cases are important to the constitutional development and evolution of Canada.

The *Royal Proclamation, 1763* made the common law of England applicable to all British-controlled territory in North America. The act also established that the government or the Crown owned all non-privately held land, and it set out certain rights of Aboriginal peoples. Specifically, it outlined that the relationship between the Crown and Aboriginal peoples would be nation to nation and that although the Crown would control the land, it granted to Aboriginal peoples title to use and occupy the land. The *Royal Proclamation* prevented anyone from negotiating land deals with Aboriginal peoples without authority from the British Crown. To this day, the *Royal Proclamation* is used to uphold the rights of Aboriginal peoples in

Canada, as in the case of *R. v. Sparrow*, [1990] 1 S.C.R. 1075. Ronald Sparrow, a member of the Musqueam group, was charged under the *Fisheries Act* with violating federal fishing regulations while fishing off-reserve in the lower Fraser River in British Columbia. On appeal, the Supreme Court ruled that Aboriginal rights and title to fish for food continue to exist in non-treaty areas. This ruling found basis in the *Royal Proclamation* and in the principle that all lands traditionally used by Aboriginal peoples can continue to be so used for the purposes of hunting and fishing. Although the government had the right to limit and regulate fishing by Aboriginal peoples, common law and the *Royal Proclamation* guaranteed that the right could not be **extinguished**, or cancelled.

The *Québec Act of 1774* outlines the right of Québec to have and administer the French legal system's practice of **civil law**, which comprises codified laws rather than case law as the basis of regulating matters of a private nature among citizens, rather than the English common law. This right still exists today in Québec. The impact this legal distinction has on Canada is that three of the nine Supreme Court Justices are appointed from Québec because of their expertise and experience with the *Civil Code of Québec*.

The *Constitution Act, 1791* divided the British North American colony into Upper Canada (Ontario) and Lower Canada (Québec), thus enshrining the separate character of Québec. The act was created in response to a demand from settlers fleeing the American Revolutionary War for representative government in their new land based on British traditions and customs. The first legislature of Upper Canada convened at Newark (Niagara-on-the-Lake) in September of 1792. Although representatives were elected to the Legislative Assembly by a small number of land-owning men, the executive (comprising the Lieutenant-Governor and his appointed cabinet ministers, none of whom were elected) were not responsible to the Legislative Assembly nor to the people who elected those representatives, and were not required to follow their advice.

Figure 5.4 Lieutenant-Governor Sir John Graves Simcoe addresses the first legislature of Upper Canada in 1792. Why do you think the leadership of the legislature at this time was not accountable to the elected members of the assembly or the voting public?

The *Act of Union, 1840* joined the colonies of Upper and Lower Canada into one province. A true form of responsible government was now established, whereby the executive (again, the Lieutenant-Governor and his appointed cabinet ministers) became accountable to an elected legislature. Cabinet ministers were appointed from among those elected to the Legislative Assembly, and the Lieutenant-Governor was now required to implement the will of the assembly and the laws it passed. This change laid the foundation for the current political model in Canada, which follows a British parliamentary-style democracy. The only change left to make was to add representation by population to the election process so that each seat represented the same number of citizens.

The *Statute of Westminster, 1931* officially ended Canada's colonial status. Canada was no longer required to follow and apply regular laws passed by the British Parliament. The Canadian Parliament also gained the authority to change previously passed acts of British Parliament that applied to Canada, excluding constitutional documents that outlined the basic features of the federation. The statute transferred legal authority to former colonial dependents of Britain, such as Australia and New Zealand, conferring on them the power to change their own constitutions. However, because the federal government and the provinces in Canada could not agree to an amending formula once the country was in control of its Constitution, the British Parliament continued to have the authority to change the *Constitution Act, 1867*.

In 1949, the Canadian Parliament was granted a very narrowly defined power to change the *BNA Act* without having to seek the approval of the British Parliament.

Conventions

Conventions, which are essentially unwritten rules, are another major source of Canada's Constitution. Although the courts cannot legally enforce them, conventions are adhered to by government leaders out of fear of a political backlash by the voting public. If, for example, the government ignored the long-standing convention of appointing members to the Senate or Supreme Court in a manner that fairly represents Canada's regions, it would likely be punished with negative attention in the media and with a lack of support in the next election from voters in excluded regions.

Think of the Constitution as the engine of a car: the constitutional documents are the component parts, and conventions are the fluids that keep the parts running smoothly. Unlike the Constitution of the United States, which outlines in detail how the government works and who the political figures are, the *Constitution Act, 1867* and all the other constitutional documents provide a general structure of how our government is set up. All the details of how our government operates are the function of conventions.

When the *Constitution Act, 1867* was created, there was no attempt to write in or explain conventions. It was assumed that Canada would follow the practices and conventions of Britain. Since the Fathers of Confederation at Canada's birth were part of, and therefore familiar with, British parliamentary systems, no explanation was necessary.

The fact that Canada functions as a democracy is a product of convention rather than law. The Canadian Constitution does not stipulate, either in the *Constitution Act, 1867* or in any other document, that Canada must function as a democracy. There are many countries around the world that claim to be democracies and have the concept written into their constitutions, but they are less democratic than Canada, which adheres to a democratic process solely out of British tradition.

Similarly, there is no formal written principle of responsible government whereby, if the party in power cannot keep the confidence or carry the vote of the House of Commons on major government bills, an election must be called. One compelling example of conventions at work took place in 1979 when the Progressive Conservative government under Prime Minister Joe Clark failed to pass its budget in the House of Commons. Clark immediately rose from his seat and informed the Speaker of the House that he was going to ask the Governor General (the Queen's representative in Canada) to dissolve Parliament and call an election. Although there was nothing in writing mandating Clark to dissolve the government and call an election, a conventional rule of parliamentary democracy obligated him to do so.

Conventions also exist outside of our parliamentary democracy. To a certain extent, the relationship between the federal and provincial governments relies on conventional practice. For example, if the federal government attempts to exercise power within its jurisdiction that will affect a particular province, by convention the federal government will usually attempt to exercise its authority in conjunction with provincial co-operation. This is why, when the federal government wanted to make changes to Canada's Constitution prior to 1982, it consulted with the provincial governments before requesting a change from the British Parliament.

Conventions are regularly at work behind the scenes in the operation of our government. For example, by convention the Senate cannot veto bills passed by the House of Commons because the Senate is not an elected body. Theoretically, however, the Senate has the authority to block any legislation. Another convention prevents the Opposition from unduly delaying or blocking the passage of legislation of a minority government. Further, there is an expectation by convention that the leader of any political party will seek a seat in the House of Commons as soon as is practical.

Common Law

The four pillars of constitutional law in Canada are constitutional documents, conventions, **statutes** (laws passed by federal or provincial governments), and common law. As you learned in Chapter 2, **common law** can also be described as judge-made law or case law. Common law is an extremely important component in Canadian jurisprudence, as it is in most Commonwealth countries.

Generally speaking, most constitutional documents and statutes are written in very general and sometimes vague language. When a dispute arises or a clarification is necessary, the courts

FIGURE 5.5 In 1979, Prime Minister Joe Clark was compelled by convention to dissolve Parliament and call an election after losing a vote on a budget bill. What is the purpose of such a convention?

create principles that become part of the large body of common law. Over time, the courts clarify the language of the Constitution and set out clear interpretations of what the language of the Constitution means. The courts keep adding to earlier decisions or make slight changes and modifications to them. Since common law is not explicitly written in one document, it is flexible. The principles can be altered over time if the views and opinions of society change. This makes common law a powerful tool in modernizing and adapting the Constitution to reflect more recent views within Canada.

Before the advent of the *Canadian Charter of Rights and Freedoms* in 1982, there was essentially no written constitutional document outlining and guaranteeing the rights of individual Canadians. Whether it was freedom of speech or freedom of association, or even some fundamental legal protection—the right to a fair trial, the right not to be subjected to cruel and unusual punishment—no written codification of these rights existed in our Constitution. However, these rights were still protected by the large body of common law that dated back hundreds of years.

For example, in the Supreme Court of Canada case *Reference re Alberta Statutes*, [1938] S.C.R. 100, the Alberta government attempted to restrict the press from reporting on the government's economic policies. The court eventually ruled that while provinces have the ability to regulate businesses operating within the province, the province could not infringe on the basic right of free press. To allow such actions by the government could undermine the concept of democratic government itself.

Although there is some case law that attempted to protect the fundamental rights of citizens from government infringement, this was not always so; hence, the movement throughout the twentieth century toward guaranteeing rights, both domestically and internationally. Written documents entrenching the rights of individuals became a major feature of constitutions in Canada and throughout the world. You will learn more about these written documents in Chapter 6.

CONFIRM YOUR UNDERSTANDING

1. What is a constitution? Develop a concept web to answer this question. Explain why it is important for a democratic nation to have a constitution.

2. Identify three components of Canada's Constitution. Briefly explain each one.

3. Explain the purpose and importance of the *BNA Act*. How did the lack of an amending formula pose a problem for the development of Canada's Constitution?

4. What three forces influenced the patriation debates?

5. Explain the significance of the *Royal Proclamation, 1763*.

6. Explain why conventions are integral to the functioning of Canada's Constitution.

7. Identify three advantages and three disadvantages of having a constitution that comprises some unwritten conventions and common law.

8. According to some political scientists, the best check against a government that ignores conventional practice is an election. Explain the principles that would lead to this conclusion.

9. The common law is said to be a flexible feature of Canada's Constitution. Why is this so? Would it be better to move principles established in common law into a constitutional document? Explain.

Components of the Canadian Constitution

After the *Act of Union, 1840* merged Upper and Lower Canada into one province, it became apparent that competing political interests—in this case, French-speaking Lower Canada and English-speaking Upper Canada—could make it impossible to reach a compromise on a variety of issues. In order to minimize regional rivalries and differences within the larger political unit, the Fathers of Confederation decided to set up the new nation as a federal state that would operate as a parliamentary democracy.

Jurisdictional Powers

Sir John A. Macdonald, Canada's first prime minister, was a leading politician in Upper Canada and a strong advocate of the union of the British colonies in British North America. He regarded confederation as a way to thwart American expansionism and strengthen the economic and military unity of the colonies against any possible American threat. At the same time, Macdonald wanted to avoid the mistakes that, in his view, caused the devastating American Civil War. He believed that the decentralized American federation, in which the major powers and those powers not specified in the US Constitution belonged to the states rather than to the federal government, was a flaw that led to the war. To avoid this perceived weakness, the Canadian Confederation would assign jurisdiction of the most important powers to the federal government and designate powers of a local nature to the provinces. Macdonald's vision of Canada consisted of a strong central government and substantially weaker provinces. The division of power was to follow that of other governments in the late 1800s.

In 1867, the areas of health, education, and social services—three areas that today grip the voting public on an almost daily basis, employ thousands, and require billions of dollars to administer—were not considered of sufficient importance to warrant federal jurisdiction. The job of overseeing and setting policy in these areas

was given to the provinces. With time, especially as the welfare state grew after the Great Depression, the powers assigned to the provinces became increasingly important to the daily lives of Canadians, effectively shifting the balance of power from a centralized government to the regions. Macdonald's vision for Canada was turned on its head.

Federal and Provincial Powers

A federal arrangement is one in which the powers of the state are distributed among different levels of government. This division of power is usually based on geographic areas. In Canada, power is distributed between the federal parliament and the provincial legislatures. Other countries that have federal systems of government include Australia, India, and the United States. A federal arrangement is common in geographically large nations that have diverse peoples or interests because it has the ability to unite different regions for the purpose of achieving common goals and

A bone of contention.

FIGURE 5.6 The provinces have always exercised vigilance over the authority and power granted to them by the *Constitution Act, 1867*. Whenever the federal government has attempted to implement public policy or social programs that infringed on provincial powers, the provinces have collectively ensured that their powers were not diminished. Do you think that a strict division of powers is in the best interest of Canadians?

objectives. The opposite of a federal state is a **unitary state**, meaning there is only one national parliament and it has the authority to make law. Examples of unitary states include New Zealand, France, and Ireland. Britain has historically been a unitary state with the parliament in London making law for all of the United Kingdom. Since the 1990s, however, the British Parliament has created through statute regional assemblies for Scotland, Wales, and Northern Ireland with powers to address regional issues.

It is important to remember that our federal parliament does not have supremacy over provincial legislatures, and provincial legislatures do not gain their authority from the federal parliament. A federation means that each level of government is given specific authority to make laws in certain areas without interference from another level of government. Legally, therefore, each level of government is supreme in the area of law over

which it has jurisdiction. The division of powers is exclusive of the other level of government. In practice, however, there is a great deal of federal–provincial co-operation when governments exercise authority in their jurisdictions. For example, the federal government will seek input and co-operation from the provinces over issues related to immigration and settlement.

The authority to make laws in Canada comes from the *Constitution Act, 1867*. This act outlines the division of powers between the federal and provincial governments. Specifically, s. 91 outlines the powers of the federal parliament and s. 92 outlines the powers of the provincial legislatures. Section 93 assigns jurisdiction and exclusive power to make laws related to education to the provinces. It also protects the religious Catholic minority in Ontario and the Protestant minority in Québec by enabling them to have their own separate school systems.

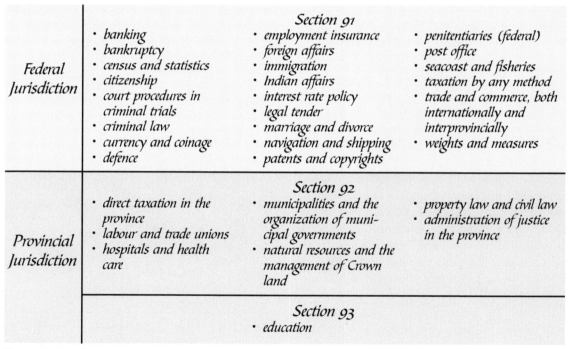

	Section 91		
Federal Jurisdiction	• banking • bankruptcy • census and statistics • citizenship • court procedures in criminal trials • criminal law • currency and coinage • defence	• employment insurance • foreign affairs • immigration • Indian affairs • interest rate policy • legal tender • marriage and divorce • navigation and shipping • patents and copyrights	• penitentiaries (federal) • post office • seacoast and fisheries • taxation by any method • trade and commerce, both internationally and interprovincially • weights and measures
	Section 92		
Provincial Jurisdiction	• direct taxation in the province • labour and trade unions • hospitals and health care	• municipalities and the organization of municipal governments • natural resources and the management of Crown land	• property law and civil law • administration of justice in the province
	Section 93 • education		

FIGURE 5.7   The intention in 1867 was to establish a strong central government that would have very little, if anything, to do with the economic and social lives of the people. But as the twentieth century unfolded, the demands on government at all levels to become more involved in issues directly affecting individual citizens increased. As this table shows, the provinces have jurisdiction over some of the most important elements of day-to-day life. How might you adjust the division of powers created in 1867 to reflect the realities of the twenty-first century?

The drafters of the Constitution attempted to keep issues of national importance at the federal level and issues of a local or private matter at the provincial level. Any other issue that was not delegated to the provinces and not specifically listed anywhere would fall under federal jurisdiction. This is called **residual power**.

Intra Vires *and* Ultra Vires

The *Constitution Act, 1867* set out the jurisdiction and division of powers for the two levels of government in the Canadian federation. But what happens if there is a disagreement over an area of law that is claimed by both levels of government as their jurisdiction, and they both attempt to legislate in that area? When the *Constitution Act, 1867* is silent on an area that is claimed by both the federal and the provincial governments, it becomes a matter for the courts to decide whether a legislature is acting outside the scope of its jurisdiction. If an action by a legislature, either federal or provincial, is within its jurisdiction, that legislature has acted **intra vires** its authority. If the action by a government is outside of its legal authority or jurisdiction, then it has acted **ultra vires** its authority.

At the time of Confederation, it was not possible to completely foresee all of the powers that would need to be delegated to either the provincial or federal level of government. For example, air travel did not exist, and once this technology was invented and the need to regulate the industry became apparent, it fell to the federal government because of its residual power. Whenever there is a dispute over which level of government has jurisdiction over a particular area, the issue is referred to the courts for clarification. More often, however, it is one government or private individual who initiates a hearing to settle jurisdiction. In cases where the authority of a level of government to act is in question, it is the courts that must ultimately decide whether or not the action is legal. The courts will measure the action of that government against the assigned jurisdictions listed in ss. 91 to 93 of the *Constitution Act, 1867*. If it is not listed, then it is considered a residual power that belongs to the federal government. The court will also use what is called the **pith and substance** doctrine (the overriding purpose or intent of the law) to determine whether or not the action is legal in areas where both levels of government have legitimate claims of authority in a jurisdictional dispute. (The pith and substance doctrine is covered in greater detail on p. 146.)

In the case *Re Protection of Children Involved in Prostitution Act,* [2000] ABPC 113, two 17-year-old females—the applicants—were apprehended by Calgary Police Service officers on September 13, 1999, in accordance with the *Protection of Children Involved in Prostitution Act.* The applicants were taken by police to a "protective safe house" where they were confined for two days. On September 15, 1999, they were brought before the Provincial Court of Alberta as required by the act, for the director to show cause for their confinement. The constitutionality of the law itself was challenged, one component being the authority of the provincial legislature to pass what seemed to be a detention similar to that found in criminal law.

The court had to determine whether the *Protection of Children Involved in Prostitution Act* was *ultra vires* the legislature of Alberta because the pith and substance of the legislation fell under criminal law, and therefore, within the exclusive legislative authority of the federal parliament. The court eventually ruled that the act fell within the authority of the Alberta Legislature and was, therefore, *intra vires*. The basis of the ruling follows:

> It is not axiomatic that the legislation is penal or criminal law because it authorizes the apprehension and detention of children engaged in prostitution. If the only reason for trying to eradicate this activity were moral, it would follow that legislation directed at this purpose would be criminal law....
>
> There are, however, valid reasons for trying to eliminate prostitution in which children are involved which are not based in morality.

Prostitution is a dangerous enterprise; female participants, whether children or adult, are subject to serious harm and even death at the hands of both pimps and johns. Alcoholism and drug addiction are widespread within the trade. The risk of sexually transmitted disease is so high as to be a significant public health risk....

Confinement of children to protect them from sexual abuse while working as under-age prostitutes falls within the same category as confinement to prevent harm from potentially abusive parents....Attempts to control and or eliminate child prostitution can be compared with tobacco control legislation....

...[T]he pith and substance of the _Protection of Children Involved in Prostitution Act_ is the protection of children from the sexual abuse and other risks inherent in the sex trade [particularly in relation to health, safety, and child welfare matters that are under provincial jurisdiction]. It does not invade the domain of the criminal law. It is within the legislative competence of the Legislature of Alberta....

In many cases, provincial and federal governments work out power-sharing arrangements in some areas of uncertainty rather than having jurisdictions clarified by the courts.

Pith and Substance

Most issues of disagreement regarding legislative authority are not clear cases of whether a power is listed in s. 91 or s. 92. More commonly, a law passed by government can very easily be classified under both ss. 91 _and_ 92. So, how do the courts determine which level of government has authority if the issue in question falls under both sections? This is where the pith and substance doctrine comes in.

As stated earlier, the pith and substance of law is concerned with the overriding purpose or intent of the law. As Justice Lamer stated in _R. v. Swain_, [1991] 1 S.C.R. 933, "In order to determine the pith and substance of any particular legislative provision, it is necessary to examine that provision in its overall legislative context...[and]...'to identify the **dominant** or **most important** characteristic of the challenged law' (Hogg, _Constitutional Law of Canada_ [2nd ed.], p. 313, [emphasis added])."

The court is interested in finding out what the purpose of the law is rather than the effect of ruling whether or not the law is _intra vires_ or _ultra vires_. In areas where both levels of government can exercise a legitimate claim of jurisdiction, the courts must determine what the main purpose of the bill or government action is. For example, if the action is related to criminal law, it falls under federal jurisdiction, but if it is concerned with the regulation of business, then it falls under the authority of provincial legislation. Once the main purpose of the bill is determined, the courts must then confirm what level of government has the authority to legislate in that area based on the powers listed under ss. 91 to 93 of the _Constitution Act, 1867_.

The case _Reference re Firearms Act (Can.)_, [2000] 1 S.C.R. 783 illustrates the pith and substance doctrine at work. In this case, the federal government enacted the _Firearms Act_ in 1995, which changed the classification of some firearms and required all owners to obtain licences and register their firearms. The _Constitution Act, 1867_ gives the power of criminal law to the federal government, but clearly gives regulatory power of property and licensing to the provinces. The Alberta government challenged the federal legislation in the Alberta Court of Appeal because it believed the federal law was merely regulating lawful property, which could not be considered criminal law.

The case was appealed to the Supreme Court of Canada. The court ruled that in pith and substance the _Firearms Act_ was concerned with public safety, which has traditionally been viewed as a criminal law matter. Even though the law did affect provincial rights to regulate and license property, because the purpose of the _Firearms Act_ was to address the misuse of firearms and their potential risk to public safety, the law was upheld.

Municipal Powers

Local governments do not have any constitutional status. Section 92 gives provincial governments the sole authority to arrange and oversee municipal institutions within their borders. Therefore, municipalities and cities are created by the provinces and can be altered or even abolished at their will.

A major conflict occurred in Ontario when the provincial government introduced the *City of Toronto Act, 1997*—legislation that would amalgamate six local municipalities and their councils into one mega-city. This one large municipality would comprise East York, Etobicoke, North York, Scarborough, Toronto, and York, and would be known as the City of Toronto. Many local citizens mobilized to oppose this legislative initiative, not only by voting against the proposed mega-city in a referendum, but also by launching legal challenges that questioned the province's jurisdictional authority to impose amalgamation on the six municipalities. The Ontario Court dismissed the challenge, as did the Ontario Court of Appeal. The Court of Appeal agreed with the lower court's ruling that municipal governance is conferred on the municipalities by the provincial government.

The increasing urbanization of Canadian society has led some to call for a review of the status of cities. Cities have become increasingly important as centres of economic and job growth, especially as Canada moves from a resource- to a knowledge-based economy. Furthermore, municipal governments provide a range of essential services to people and communities, but they do not have the same taxing authority as provincial governments to meet the growing needs and demands. For example, health and emergency services (police, fire, and ambulance) are administered by municipal governments, as are social assistance and subsidized housing. The demands placed on municipal resources far exceed the cities'

FIGURE 5.8 Municipalities are an essential and important part of daily life in Canada, although they do not have any constitutional authority of their own. What functions does your municipality perform?

ability to fund them, thus leading to the deterioration or outright loss of services. Cities have argued for additional authority to levy taxes in order to fund the services expected of them. Some provincial governments have responded by offering additional access to provincial gas taxes. Some mayors of larger municipalities have even argued for constitutional status so that their cities are no longer under the authority or control of provincial governments. This would leave them free to address the pressing needs of their citizens and to implement the tax framework necessary to fund the increased demand for services.

CONNECTIONS: Law and Non-Profit Corporations

The Constitutions of Non-Profit Organizations

By definition, a constitution is the body of fundamental principles according to which a state or organization is governed. Based on this definition, almost any organization can have a constitution to govern its affairs in an orderly manner.

Non-profit or charitable organizations are corporations like any other business, but they are not allowed to make a profit. Non-profit organizations are generally founded to perform a public good or good works in the community for an identified need that is not otherwise being met.

All provincially registered charities and non-profit organizations are required to follow the *Corporations Act* that stipulates the need to set bylaws or establish a constitution to govern the organization. A constitution in this case functions similarly to Canada's Constitution. It builds and defines the relationships among the members within the organization and between the organization and the general public. These links are important because they become the basis for legal accountability in cases where wrongdoing or mismanagement occurs. For example, to incorporate a charity in Ontario, a minimum of three people must be listed on the board of directors when registering with the government under the authority of the *Corporations Act*. Those listed directors then become legally liable for acts undertaken in the name and authority of the non-profit organization. Once the organization is incorporated, a founding meeting must occur at which the general membership must elect a board of directors beyond the original three.

The constitution of a non-profit corporation holds the directors accountable for all aspects of the organization's operation. "In properly fulfilling their duties as directors, they must:
- ensure the objects [purposes] of the corporation are properly carried out
- ensure the corporation does not undertake activities outside its corporate objects
- provide adequate authority for the activities that the corporation does undertake
- set long-range objectives and strategic plans for the corporation
- ensure the corporation's financial stability and overall performance
- hire and supervise management and staff to do the day-to-day work of the corporation" (Connor 2002)

A non-profit organization must have an objective when registering. For example, a community youth organization might draft its objectives as:
- promoting the best interests of teenagers in the specified community;
- promoting interest in athletics, sports, and recreation, and establishing and maintaining facilities and equipment for same; and
- pursuing other complementary purposes not inconsistent with these objectives (Ministry of the Attorney General, Ontario "Part 3…").

The actions of a non-profit organization must be consistent with its founding principles, and the directors must ensure that any actions the charity takes are consistent with those principles.

Unfortunately, there are those in our society who use the guise of a charity to prey on the goodwill of the general public for their own personal benefit, rather than to help people in need. For example, the stated purpose of the National Society for Abused Women and Children, an incorporated charity, was to provide family support services, counselling, and public education concerning abused women and children, and to assist shelters and related organizations (Goodman 2002). After a newspaper article revealed that thousands of dollars had been donated to the organization but no funds had been spent on the objectives of the charity, provincial officials became suspicious. When the public began to complain about the organization, the Office of the Public Guardian and Trustee (OPGT), the provincial body in Ontario responsible for protecting the public interest in accordance with the *Charities Accounting Act*, obtained all documents related to the financial operations of the charity.

The National Society for Abused Women and Children had entered into three fundraising contracts to raise money for the organization. Investigators discovered that one of the fundraising companies involved was owned by two of the National Society's directors. The accounts showed that the National Society had raised about

FIGURE 5.9   In accordance with the Corporation Act, all registered non-profit organizations, such as the Youth Assisting Youth program, must be governed by a set of bylaws or a constitution.

$905 000, but had spent only $1365 on charitable objectives. The fundraising companies had charged the National Society between 75 and 80 percent of the gross income for fundraising expenses. The courts were not willing to approve the accounts of the National Society and ruled that the directors had profited from a conflict of interest. The directors were required to repay all monies received from the National Society for expenses, excluding expenses that could be supported with proper documentation. In addition, the two directors who owned the one fundraising company were ordered to return all profits received by their company (Goodman 2002).

This decision helped to clarify the responsibilities of charities. Contracts and third-party fundraisers are not accountable to the public, but they are accountable to the charity's board of directors. The board of directors is accountable to the public, and it is their duty to ensure that the monies collected in the name of the charity are disbursed appropriately and in accordance with the objectives of the organization's constitution and bylaws.

Charities and non-profit organizations have an essential role to play in a modern, civil society, as they contribute in areas where government assistance is lacking or non-existent. They are extensions of—and exist because of—the goodwill and support of the general public, offered through the donation of time or money. To maintain the public's trust, and thus the effectiveness of non-profit organizations, a strong legal framework is needed to govern their operations.

SOURCES: Connor, Jacqueline. *Part I: Directors' Legal Duties and Liabilities*. Not-for-Profit Board Management Series. 24 Sept. 2002. Accessed 20 Dec. 2003 <www.carters.ca/pub/seminar/charity/2002/jmc0924.pdf>;

Goodman, Kenneth R. *2002 Church and The Law Seminar: The Public Guardian & Trustee & the Courts on the Limits of Fundraising in Ontario*. 5 Nov. 2002. Accessed 20 Dec. 2003 <www.carters.ca/pub/seminar/chrchlaw/2002/goodman.pdf>;

Ministry of the Attorney General, Ontario. *Not for Profit Incorporator's Handbook—Part 5: Corporate Maintenance*. Accessed 20 Dec. 2003 <www.attorneygeneral.jus.gov.on.ca/english/family/pgt/nfpinc/corpmaintain.asp>;

———. —— *Part 3: Incorporation*. Accessed 20 Dec. 2003 <www.attorneygeneral.jus.gov.on.ca/english/family/pgt/nfpinc/incorp.asp>.

Questions

1. Explain the purpose of a constitution for a non-profit organization.
2. How is accountability maintained in fundraising charities? How can consumers protect themselves from charitable scams?
3. Assume you are to set up a non-profit corporation. How would you ensure that a strong legal framework is established to govern the operations of the organization? Summarize the mandate for your directors.

CONFIRM YOUR UNDERSTANDING

1. Identify two advantages and two disadvantages of a federal style of government.

2. Explain the concept of residual power and why it was allocated to the federal government. Do you think residual power would be better allocated to the provincial level of government? Explain why or why not.

3. Distinguish between *intra vires* and *ultra vires*. Explain how these concepts are used to resolve issues regarding the division of powers.

4. Explain how the pith and substance doctrine was used in the *Reference re Firearms Act (Can.)*, [2000] 1 S.C.R. 783 in making a final judgment regarding the legality of the federal action.

5. Refer to the case *Re Protection of Children Involved in Prostitution Act* on pages 145–146.

    a) Explain why the Alberta provincial government took action in this case.

    b) Explain why the court ultimately decided that the Alberta statute to protect children involved in prostitution did not infringe on the federal power to make criminal law.

    c) Identify some of the issues the judge raised relating to public health and the dangers experienced by child prostitutes. In what ways might these issues be addressed outside of the act in question?

Parliamentary Democracy

As stated earlier, Canada is governed as a parliamentary democracy. This means that the fundamental principles of our Constitution are upheld by federal and provincial governments that are responsible and accountable to the public. There are many democracies in the world, but each one functions in slightly different ways, and the institutions that represent the people differ from country to country.

Canada follows the parliamentary model inherited from Britain, commonly called the Westminster Parliament. Other countries that operate on this British model include Australia,

Jamaica and, until 1999, Hong Kong, when control was transferred back to China. The main features of our parliamentary democracy include a general election held at least once every five years. The party that earns the most seats in the election forms the government, and the leader of that party becomes Prime Minister. Those elected from opposing parties sit in the House of Commons or provincial legislature and form the Opposition. Their role is to hold the government to account for its handling of issues. The Prime Minister appoints his or her **Cabinet** (individuals who oversee the various departments of government) from those party members elected to Parliament. The government presents **bills** (draft legislation) to Parliament (the House of Commons) for consideration, most of which are passed and become law.

The head of state in Canada is the British monarch, who is represented by the Governor General; however, since most power rests with the Prime Minister and Cabinet, the role of the British monarch and the Governor General is primarily ceremonial. Much of how Westminster-style parliamentary democracies function is based on conventions, as described earlier. Countries that follow this democratic model usually do not have extensive, detailed constitutions describing how the mechanisms of the political institutions work.

The Three Branches of Government

Also in keeping with the British model are Canada's three branches of government: the executive, the legislative, and the judicial. Almost every modern form of government in the world breaks the functions of the state into these three distinct parts, although the power and relationship among the branches can differ significantly from nation to nation. In Canada, the executive is responsible to an elected legislative assembly that makes the law, and an independent judiciary adjudicates disputes without interference from the other two branches.

The Legislative Branch

The main purpose of the legislative branch of government is simply to make law. All statute laws have their origin in either the federal or provincial parliaments. The legislative branch is the only body that can approve or reject what laws Canada will have. (See also Law-making in Canada, beginning on p. 163.)

The legislative branch of the federal government comprises all members who are elected to the House of Commons, as well as those who are appointed to the Senate. The federally elected members are called members of

FIGURE 5.10 Rosemary Brown, seen here in 1990, became the first Black woman member of any Canadian parliamentary body when she was elected to the British Columbia provincial legislature in 1972. She had a distinguished career as a social worker, academic, politician, and feminist, who was dedicated to achieving justice and equality for women and minorities. How many women currently serve as members of your provincial or territorial legislature?

Parliament (MPs). Together, the House of Commons and the Senate make up the federal parliament. Provincial and territorial governments consist of members who are elected to the Legislative Assembly (there is no senate at the provincial level). Québec's is called the National Assembly and Newfoundland and Labrador's is called the House of Assembly. Members elected provincially or territorially are called either members of provincial parliament (MPPs) or members of the Legislative Assembly (MLAs). In Québec, they are called members of the National Assembly (MNAs) and in Newfoundland and Labrador, members of the House of Assembly (MHAs).

The Senate is also part of the legislative branch of the federal government. But unlike members of the House of Commons, members of the Senate are appointed rather than elected. The Senate also differs from the House in that it is not a body based on representation by population. Seats in the Senate are assigned on a regional basis. So although Ontario and Québec together hold more than half the seats in the House of Commons, they hold fewer than half of the seats in the Senate. The Senate thus provides a regional counterbalance to the dominance of the more populous provinces in the House.

Traditionally, the Senate's role was intended as a check on laws passed by the House to ensure specific interests, particularly regional interests, were not overlooked in draft legislation. For bills to become law, the Senate must approve the draft legislation submitted to it by the House of Commons. Without Senate approval, a bill passed by the House cannot become law.

The legitimacy of the Senate became an issue in the second half of the twentieth century, however. An unelected body vetoing the will of an elected House is in conflict with conventions and the principles of democracy. Also, because members of the Senate are appointed by the prime minister, there is the risk that regional interests may be superseded by allegiance to the political party in power at the time of the appointment. For these reasons, the Senate almost never vetoes legislation passed by the House, begging the question: Why have a Senate at all? Calls to reform or even abolish the Senate have been put forth in recent years, especially from provinces in western Canada that feel that the federal government focuses on issues affecting central Canada (Ontario and Québec) while ignoring the needs of the other provinces. Much of this sentiment stems from the federal government's policies in the early 1980s regarding Alberta's resources—in particular, oil—that benefited Ontario and Québec at the expense of Albertans. Western Canada believes that an effective Senate, constructed to represent the provinces equally, would counterbalance central Canadian power in the House of Commons.

The Executive Branch

The day-to-day management and operation of the government is the responsibility of the executive branch. This branch is also responsible for recommending bills to the legislative branch for consideration, and for implementing the laws that are passed. The executive branch is the primary generator of draft laws and bills, but without the assent of Parliament, the executive has no legal authority to act. Members of the executive branch at the federal level include the prime minister and his or her cabinet ministers. The Governor General is the symbolic head of the executive. Together, they form the executive cabinet or council. At the provincial level, it is the premier and his or her cabinet who form the executive branch, and it is the Lieutenant-Governor who serves as the symbolic head of this branch.

The executive relies on a politically neutral civil service that has expertise in various departments of government. The **civil service** comprises people hired to perform the various day-to-day functions of government, and includes nurses, inspectors, customs officers, and other frontline workers who provide government services to the public. The civil service also includes people who help administer the functions of government, such as office workers and managers of various government ministries. This group is often referred to as the government bureaucracy.

The senior members of the civil service, usually the deputy minister and a number of assistant deputy ministers, present cabinet ministers with public-policy options and recommendations. These ideas do not always originate within the civil service, but quite often are initiated by the party in power or the general public. Nevertheless, the senior members of the bureaucracy are always the managers of the ideas and their flow through the government process. Cabinet ministers rely heavily on these unelected senior bureaucrats because they are the most familiar with the way government institutions operate. Because this top echelon of senior bureaucrats controls the flow of information to Cabinet and Cabinet relies on it when making decisions, it is very powerful and influential. The Secretary of Cabinet is the chief civil servant who ensures that the decisions of Cabinet and the House are implemented by the bureaucracy.

The United States has a slightly different structure that more strictly separates the various branches of government. In the Presidential–Republican system, the legislative and executive branches are divided by separate elections. The president (the head of the executive) has no control over Congress (the legislative branch) because members of each branch are elected separately. The president must therefore compromise in order to implement his governing agenda. State governments in the United States follow the same model as the federal government, similar to how provincial governments in Canada follow the same model as our federal government (with the exception that there are no senates at the provincial level).

In Canada, the prime minister is much more in control of the legislative agenda and hence, exerts a greater influence on public policy debate. This relative power of the executive branch of our government both federally and provincially is a unique feature of our style of parliamentary democracy inherited from Britain. In fact, it is a feature of all British-style parliaments. Members of the executive branch not only run the government, but they also belong to the legislative branch, sitting as members of Parliament (MPs) in the House of Commons, or members of provincial parliament (MPPs) representing the riding that elected them. This overlap of the legislative and executive branches enables the ruling party, led by the prime minister or the premier, to control the agenda of the government. By controlling his or her party members in the legislature, the prime minister or premier can ensure that vital bills get passed. This is particularly important for the smooth operation of the country because, as you may recall from earlier in this chapter, if the ruling party cannot carry a

vote in the House, by convention, an election must be called.

The Judicial Branch

Th role of the judiciary is to act as an independent third party to settle disputes or to clarify the law. Since this branch performs an extremely important function, there is a strictly understood principle of non-interference from the other two branches. This principle is, in many ways, related to the rule of law, which was introduced in Chapter 3. In the simplest of terms, the **rule of law** means (1) that the government must follow the law that it makes; (2) that no one is exempt from the law and that it applies equally to all; and (3) that no action can be taken unless authorized by law. The importance of the rule of law is that it is a safeguard against the exercise of arbitrary government action. In order for the government to carry out any activity, it must have the authority to do so, either granted in statute law passed by Parliament or provided for within the common law. If the actions of government have not been authorized by law, then those actions are considered to be a breach of this principle and hence illegal. An integral part of this principle is the right to challenge the actions of government in court if one feels that the principle of the rule of law has been infringed upon, as in the case of *Roncarelli v. Duplessis*, which you will read about in Chapter 6 (p. 172).

If government officials were able to interfere or pressure court officials, then the public would have no assurance that the laws were being applied fairly and evenly. Without independence, the impartiality of the court could be called into question. In certain countries where this division may not be clear, it is possible that court officials might even be ruling out of fear and intimidation. In Canada, once judges are appointed, they cannot be removed by government, which strengthens the independence of the judiciary since it does not have to worry about changing political dynamics of the government of the day.

Canada's court system is a reflection of the division of powers. The *Constitution Act, 1867* gives the provinces and territories the authority to organize the main elements of the legal system, including the police and the court system. The RCMP, however, is a federal police force, and is therefore governed by federal legislation. Although the court system is organized and funded by the provinces and territories, the federal government does make appointments to these courts.

The judicial system in the provinces and territories deals with most issues, and consists of three tiers:

- Courts of first appearance, such as the Ontario Court of Justice
- Superior trial courts, such as the Superior Court of Justice
- Courts of Appeal, such as the Ontario Court of Appeal

In addition, Canada has federal courts, which are specialized courts dealing with specific issues of law, and the Supreme Court of Canada, which is the final Court of Appeal for issues stemming from both the provincial courts and the federal courts.

Courts of first appearance, which are the provincial and territorial courts, decide very little civil law. They hear most criminal cases with the exception of a few serious offences, such as murder, treason, and piracy, which are heard in the Superior Courts of Justice. These provincial and territorial courts also hold preliminary inquiries when necessary. A preliminary inquiry is a hearing by a judge alone to determine whether there is enough evidence to recommend a full trial. If so, the accused can elect a method of trial in either the provincial or superior court. There are no jury trials at this level. Youth criminal court is also administered by this tier of the court system, meaning there are no juries present in youth criminal trials. Justices of these courts are appointed by the corresponding provincial or territorial government.

Superior trial courts hear virtually all civil law cases and the most serious of criminal offences. These courts are also Courts of Appeal for **summary conviction offences** (criminal offences that are minor in nature and have consequences much less severe than indictable offences) from the provincial or territorial courts. Justices are appointed by the federal government.

Courts of Appeal are the highest courts in the provinces and territories and have jurisdiction to hear cases from all lower courts. The chief justice of the province is a member of this court, which sits in panels of three when it hears cases. Appellate courts do not retry a case; rather, they review legal issues that are the basis of appeals. Courts of Appeal can dismiss a lower ruling, uphold a lower ruling, change a ruling, or order a new trial. Justices are appointed by the federal government.

Federal courts are special courts created by statute to hear cases within specific areas of law, often because of the unique expertise required by the justices hearing the cases. Once created, these courts will travel to hear cases throughout Canada; the parties involved are not required to travel to Ottawa to have their cases heard. The Tax Court of Canada, for example, hears all issues related to the *Income Tax Act* and any disputes with the Canada Revenue Agency. The Federal Court of Canada has exclusive jurisdiction over issues related to patents, copyright and trademarks, shipping and navigation, and some lawsuits against the federal government itself. The Federal Court of Appeal is the Court of Appeal for all cases arising in the federal courts. Another special federal court—the courts martial—was created by the *National Defence Act* and has the exclusive authority to hear all cases related to members of the armed forces who have committed offences while in uniform or while discharging their duties on behalf of the Canadian Armed Forces.

The **Supreme Court of Canada** (**SCC**) is the final Court of Appeal for all cases from the provincial and territorial courts and the federal courts. But this was not always so. Prior to 1949, the final Court of Appeal for cases originating in Canada and in other countries in the British Empire was the Judicial Committee of the Privy Council (JCPC). This committee is a component of the British political and legal system. But once the Supreme Court of Canada became the last Court of Appeal for both criminal and civil cases, it was no longer necessary for Canadians to appeal cases to the JCPC. Nevertheless, there are many colonial territories of Britain that continue to retain the JCPC as their last Court of Appeal, including Bermuda, the Cayman Islands, Gibraltar, and Montserrat.

The impact that the JCPC had on Canada's constitutional history is noteworthy. As explained earlier, case law, or rulings by the judiciary, helps form the basis of the common law and provides the guiding principles for future similar cases. The JCPC heard a number of cases in the early history of Canada's *Constitution Act, 1867*. Sir John A. Macdonald, George-Étienne Cartier, and other key framers of the 1867 document believed that they had established a constitutional framework that produced a strong central government within the federation, one that retained the most important powers. But as cases involving jurisdictional powers made their way to the JCPC, the resultant rulings tended to increase the authority and autonomy of the provinces, producing a less centralized federal system than the framers of the Constitution had intended and desired.

Among the advantages of having the JCPC as Canada's last Court of Appeal was its remoteness from the nation's political pressures. Consisting of British judges, the council could dispense rulings without interference from short-term political interests. For example, it was the JCPC that ruled in 1929 that women were "persons" under the law and legally entitled to serve in the Senate, overturning Canadian courts that had ruled otherwise. (See Chapter 8, p. 228, for more information on this landmark decision.) Over time, however, it became clear that Canada wanted to control its constitutional development. Adhering to the decisions of judges who were unconnected to, and perhaps unaware of, the legal and political realities of the issues about which they were ruling did not complement Canada's constitutional aspirations.

FIGURE 5.11 The Judicial Committee of the Privy Council's ruling in the 1929 "Persons Case" paved the way for women to serve in the Senate. In February 1930, Cairine Wilson became Canada's first woman senator, appointed by Prime Minister Mackenzie King. How many female senators does Canada have today?

Today, the Supreme Court of Canada consists of nine justices, among them the chief justice of Canada. It is the responsibility of the prime minister of Canada to appoint these justices, who take their place at the court until a maximum age of 75. By convention, three of the nine justices are appointed from Québec because of their knowledge of that province's *Civil Code* in areas of civil law. The remaining six justices are chosen to ensure regional representation across Canada.

The Supreme Court of Canada hears appeals from the provincial or territorial Courts of Appeal, and the Federal Court of Appeal. In most instances, permission to have a case heard by the SCC must first be obtained from a panel of three judges of the court. This process is called "leave to appeal." Cases for which permission is not required (classified as "appeals as of right") are criminal cases. The third way cases make their way to the SCC is by the referral power of the federal government. In these cases, the SCC is required to give an opinion on questions referred to it by the government (see the Landmark Case on pp. 161–163).

Legislative Supremacy

A key feature of Canada's democratic system is the principle of **legislative supremacy**. This simply means that the ultimate authority to make and unmake law in Canada resides with the federal or provincial parliament under whose jurisdiction the law falls. It is not the role of the judiciary to question the substance or morality of any law passed by a democratically elected government, but rather, to ensure that the law itself is being applied equally and fairly. This principle is tied to the idea that only democratically elected parliaments can shape public policy. If citizens feel that a particular statute is substantively wrong, then it is their right and their responsibility to lobby Parliament to amend that law.

However, the principle of legislative supremacy substantially changed with the patriation of the Constitution and the creation of the *Canadian Charter of Rights and Freedoms*. Prior to 1982, most constitutional issues were related to the division of powers. After 1982, the *Charter* became the focal point of most constitutional issues and debate.

The Canadian Charter of Rights and Freedoms

The *Charter* empowered the courts because all law passed by Parliament or provincial and territorial legislatures now has to subscribe to the principles listed in the *Charter*. Before the *Charter*, the courts would only rule laws invalid if they were outside a legislature's jurisdictional power; that is, *ultra vires* that government's authority. After 1982, the courts gained the power to declare laws invalid and illegal if they infringed on a *Charter* right. Citizens who feel that their rights are being infringed upon can bypass the traditional political avenues of change and apply directly to the courts to rule on the validity and constitutionality of any law passed by Parliament.

ASKING KEY QUESTIONS

The Constitutionality of Canada's Marijuana Law

The perspective we have on law often depends on the questions we ask related to the principles and facts that are before the court. In December 2003, the Supreme Court of Canada was required to rule on the constitutionality of Canada's drug laws, specifically, the laws that criminalize the possession of marijuana under the *Narcotic Control Act*.

This first *Charter* test of marijuana laws at the Supreme Court level involved three men who had failed to persuade the lower courts of the unconstitutionality of the marijuana law. In a collective attack, the appellants—David Malmo-

Levine, Victor Caine, and Christopher Clay—asked the court to declare the law unconstitutional. They argued that marijuana is virtually harmless and that criminal sanctions of the substance violate their *Charter* right to "life, liberty and security of the person." A *Globe and Mail* article dated December 23, 2003, cited statistics estimating that 100 000 Canadians use the substance on a daily basis and claiming that over 600 000 Canadians have a criminal record for marijuana possession.

Lawyers for the appellants used a two-pronged approach in the appeal. The first called on the government "to show serious harm to the health of marijuana users in order to justify a law that deprives offenders of their liberty. They stressed that marijuana is a unique case, since a host of doctors and government-appointed inquiries have concluded that the drug is relatively safe" (Makin 2003). The second argued that health is a provincial responsibility; the federal government has no jurisdiction to initiate sanctions in this area.

In the end, all the legal arguments put forth by the appellants failed. The Supreme Court upheld the constitutionality of the legislation criminalizing marijuana possession. The court came to its conclusion by asking a set of specific and relevant questions to answer the legal assertions of the appellants. The role of the court was to test the legality and constitutionality of the marijuana prohibition and ultimately, the *Narcotic Control Act*, not the merits or wisdom of the government drug strategy or the policy itself.

Philippe Luca, with the Vancouver Island Compassion Society, said the court had an opportunity to issue a ruling "based on science and reason."

"I'm disappointed that instead we're going to be spending another $340 million or so this year on maintaining cannabis prohibition and criminalizing another 50 000 Canadians for behaviour that's neither harmful to themselves nor society" (Hunter 2003).

Supporters of the federal law were pleased with the outcome. Tony Cannavino, president of the Canadian Professional Police Association, said that the "rulings send at least a clear message about the legitimacy of our current laws

pertaining to marijuana. Over the past years the ongoing debate about the decriminalization of marijuana and more recently around Bill C-38 (the Marijuana Bill), have unfortunately fed the perception of a higher tolerance towards marijuana possession and trafficking."

Cannavino went on to say that "the CPPA's position pertaining to the liberalization of marijuana has always been very clear: Before bringing any significant legislative change, Canada first needs a fully funded National Drug Strategy that invests in research, enforcement, and innovative prevention and treatment. Police officers need the right tools and training to combat impaired driving by drugs. We also need to send a clear message to our youth: Marijuana is a harmful drug and the only right choice for them is to stay 'drug-free'. "

SOURCES: "The Canadian Professional Police Association Pleased by Today's Supreme Court Marijuana Rulings." Canadian Professional Police Association 23 Dec. 2003. Accessed 30 Dec. 2003 <www.cppa-acpp.ca/index-english.htm>;

Hunter, Stuart. "Parliament Has the Right to Ban Pot, Court Decides." *The Province* 24 Dec. 2003. Accessed 30 Dec. 2003 <www.canada.com/search/story.aspx?id=9a45b233-ef48-4ceb-9781-bae4d953b85d>;

Makin, Kirk. "Pot Ban Is Constitutional, Supreme Court Rules." *The Globe and Mail* 23 Dec. 2003. Accessed 30 Dec. 2003 <www.globeandmail.com/servlet/story/RTGAM.20031223.wpott1223_5/BNStory/National/?query=marijuana>;

———. "Pot Laws Don't Breach Charter: Supreme Court." *The Globe and Mail* 23 Dec. 2003. Accessed 30 Dec. 2003 <www.globeandmail.com/servlet/story/RTGAM.20031223. wpott1223_4/BNStory/National/?query=marijuana>.

Form Your Questions

The issue above raises many questions. For example, should there be an overall drug strategy before the government entertains any idea of marijuana decriminalization? What other questions might you ask regarding marijuana laws? Think of three questions. Share your questions with the rest of the class, and discuss possible answers or solutions.

The *Charter* incorporates most of the principles found in common law, but because it is a constitutional document, it serves as the supreme guide to determining the constitutionality of all laws passed in Canada by all levels of government. However, there is one component of the *Charter* that provides for the traditional concept of legislative supremacy. Section 33, otherwise known as the notwithstanding clause, enables Parliament and the provincial legislatures to retain a degree of control in enacting laws.

In addition to protecting the individual rights of Canadians, the *Charter* also protects specific collective group rights. In the *Constitution Act, 1867*, specific provisions were made for the protection of the English-speaking minority in Québec and the French-speaking minority in Ontario. Both of these groups are entitled to education rights based on religious affiliation in both provinces. There are also provisions guaranteeing the official status of the English and French languages within the federal parliament

FIGURE 5.12   Canada's *Charter of Rights and Freedoms* entrenched the rights of citizens. What are the benefits of entrenching citizens' rights in a constitutional document?

and the courts. (For more information on *Charter* rights, see Chapter 7.)

Amending the Constitution

Prior to 1982, most significant changes to the *Constitution Act, 1867* were made as acts of the British Parliament. With patriation, however, Canada had a specific, agreed-upon formula for amending the formal written components of our Constitution. This formula can be found in the *Constitution Act, 1982*. The formula itself is rather complex and differs depending on what is being amended and what jurisdiction is affected by the change.

The unwritten parts of the Constitution continue to be changed or amended as they always have been through decisions of the courts that add to or alter the common law. In the case of conventions, changing expectations and priorities have led to the need to alter conventional practices.

Amending Formula

The general amending formula applies to the division of power between the federal and provincial governments. Any changes require the approval of the House of Commons and the Senate (the federal government) and two-thirds of the provincial Legislative Assemblies representing 50 percent of the population. This translates into seven provinces representing a total of at least 50 percent of the population in provinces. The territories are not part of the amending formula because, as stated earlier, on constitutional matters the federal government speaks on their behalf.

If an amendment affects only the federal parliament, then only the federal parliament would need to approve the change. This amending formula would apply in instances where, for example, the mandatory retirement age for senators was to change, or the number of seats in the House of Commons assigned to each province needed to change as a result of census data.

If an amendment has an impact on only one province, then the federal parliament and that province would need to agree to the change. For example, in 1998 Newfoundland changed the structure of its education system to move away from funding based on religious denomination to one that is secular and publicly funded. This constitutional change required the consent of only the Newfoundland House of Assembly and the federal parliament.

If an amendment affects the office of the Queen, the Governor General, or the Lieutenant-Governor, the composition of the Supreme Court, or the use of official languages, then the federal parliament and all provinces must agree to the amendment. If, for example, the number of Supreme Court justices were to be increased, then this formula would be used.

CONFIRM YOUR UNDERSTANDING

1. Distinguish among the roles of the three branches of government and explain the significance of each.

2. Explain why it is important for the judicial branch to be independent of the other branches of government.

3. Describe the principle of legislative supremacy. What impact did the patriation of the Constitution have on this principle?

4. The position of the prime minister has sometimes been referred to as a "benign dictatorship." Explain what is meant by this term.

5. Explain in your own words how Canada's Constitution is amended.

6. How does the amending formula give greater power to the more populated provinces of Ontario and Québec? Should all provinces have equal power in amending Canada's Constitution? Explain why or why not.

Constitutional Renewal

Québec did not sign the 1982 constitutional document and hence a rift occurred in the basic framework of Canada's constitutional structure. A major province within the federation was subject to constitutional rules to which it did not consent. Most politicians and political observers believed that, over the long term, it was necessary to have Québec agree to the *Constitution Act, 1982*. In 1984, Brian Mulroney, then leader of the federal Progressive Conservative Party, promised that if elected prime minister he would attempt to get Québec to join Canada's constitutional family.

Québec was concerned with the potential negative effect that the *Charter* could have on protecting French language and culture in the province. Another concern was the need to be able to veto any constitutional changes. Québec demanded the following before it would agree

to sign on to the 1982 document:
* recognition as a distinct society
* a greater role in immigration to the province
* a role in appointments to the Supreme Court
* limitations on the ability of the federal government to spend money in areas of provincial jurisdiction
* **veto power** over, or power to reject, all constitutional changes

Prime Minister Mulroney and the provincial premiers held negotiations to address Québec's five concerns, which were eventually incorporated into the 1987 Meech Lake Accord. The "distinct society" status that Québec wanted written into the Constitution was granted. In addition, the accord not only granted Québec the other listed demands, it also gave those powers to the other provinces. Supreme Court justices would be appointed from a list provided by the provinces, and Québec would be constitutionally guaranteed three members on the Supreme Court. All of the provinces would be allowed to opt out of new federal social programs. Every province would be given a constitutional veto, and the provinces would have a greater role to play in immigration policy.

At first, Canadians welcomed the agreement, but as more people questioned the specifics of the accord, support for it declined. The main concerns raised included the fact that the agreement only addressed Québec's concerns in a renewed federalism. Aboriginal peoples were concerned about their outright exclusion from the Meech Lake Accord, and women's groups, who were seeking greater equality provisions in the Constitution, were also dissatisfied. Others argued that the accord would dramatically weaken the power of the federal government, which could lead to disunity if the national government became ineffective in addressing the needs of Canadians. Some argued that "distinct society" would be interpreted in the courts as granting additional powers to Québec that would not be available to the other provinces.

In order to become law, the Meech Lake Accord had to be **ratified**, or officially approved and passed in a formal legal process, by the federal parliament and all the provinces. A change in government in Manitoba and Newfoundland, two provinces that were sympathetic to the concerns raised, caused the agreement to fail. In Manitoba, legislative policy called for unanimous approval in order for the accord to be brought forward for final debate. Since the majority of the legislature was in favour of the Meech Lake Accord, most people assumed that the agreement would be tabled. However, an elected member named Elijah Harper cast a deciding "no" vote that ultimately prevented the Manitoba Legislature from ratifying the agreement. Elijah Harper, a Cree from northern Manitoba, did not agree with the negotiation process that had excluded the issues Aboriginal peoples had with the

Never in Canadian history has a single word carried so much political weight.

—Pauline Comeau, *The Canadian Forum,* commenting on MPP Elijah Harper's repeated "no" vote that led to the failure of the Meech Lake Accord

FIGURE 5.13   Elijah Harper, as a member of the Manitoba Legislature, played a key role in the defeat of the Meech Lake Accord because it failed to address ongoing issues of concern to Canada's Aboriginal community. How did Elijah Harper prevent the Manitoba Legislature from ratifying the agreement?

federal government with regard to addressing land claims and self-government.

With the failure of the Meech Lake Accord, Québec nationalism began to increase, causing some federalist politicians to become separatists. Another attempt at constitutional renewal began with more discussions that were broader in scope to address the concerns raised by those opposed to the Meech Lake Accord. By August of 1992, a new agreement was reached by the provinces and included the main elements of Meech Lake, but went even further in addressing the needs and concerns of Aboriginal peoples and others. This new agreement was called the Charlottetown Accord and, in addition to the provisions of the Meech Lake agreement, called for:

- self-government for Aboriginal peoples
- Senate reform
- strengthened equality for male and female persons in the Constitution

- a recognition of group rights in addition to individual rights
- a minimum representation of 25 percent in the House of Commons for Québec

The final agreement was put to a national **referendum**, which is a process by which the general population or electorate can voice their opinion on a public-policy question. This was regarded as a unique way of broadening the participation of Canadians. As Canadians became more knowledgeable about the specifics of the agreement leading up to the referendum, an increasing number of them became wary of some of the provisions in the accord. The accord had addressed so many issues that there were many people who would agree, in principle, to maybe

all but one provision, and that one provision would become the stumbling block that would lead them to vote "no." Compounding the reluctance of Canadians to vote in favour of the accord was the fact that many of the provisions were vaguely worded. This was done intentionally by the government to allow for further negotiations once the accord was approved in the referendum, but it only served to heighten suspicions about the extent of the consequences if the agreement were to be ratified.

Fifty-four percent of Canadians voted "no" to the Charlottetown Accord in the 1992 referendum. Attempts at renewing the federation through direct amendment of the Constitution have since been put aside.

Landmark CASE

Reference re Secession of Québec, [1998] 2 S.C.R. 217

A **reference** is a procedure by which the government of Canada or a province refers legal or factual questions it considers important to the Supreme Court of Canada for the court to hear and to consider. The court answers the questions and gives reasons for its opinion.

Read the following Supreme Court of Canada ruling and write a concurring decision.

Issue: In September of 1994, the Parti Québecois led by Jacques Parizeau won the Québec election and promised to hold a referendum on Québec separation. The referendum would not be on outright separation but on a mandate to negotiate a new economic and political partnership with Canada. The polls indicated strong support for this initiative. The result of the referendum in October 1995 was a slim defeat of the initiative by 50.6% to 49.4%. The close-

ness of the referendum caused the federal government to become more prepared in case another referendum were to take place in the future and succeed. Many legal questions were outstanding if such a scenario were to take place. In order to address these legal questions, and rather than leave the issue unresolved and risk future political instability and legal uncertainty, the federal government made a reference to the Supreme Court on a series of three questions related to Québec separation:

1. Under the Constitution of Canada, can the National Assembly, legislature or government of Québec effect the secession of Québec from Canada unilaterally?

2. Does international law give the National Assembly, legislature or government of Québec the right to effect the secession of Québec from Canada unilaterally? In this regard, is there a right to self-determination under international law that would give the National Assembly, legislature or government of

Québec the right to effect the secession of Québec from Canada unilaterally?

3. In the event of a conflict between domestic and international law on the right of the National Assembly, legislature or government of Québec to effect the secession of Québec from Canada unilaterally, which would take precedence in Canada?

Held:

Question 1

"The Constitution is more than a written text. It embraces the entire global system of rules and principles which govern the exercise of constitutional authority.... It is necessary to make a more profound investigation of the underlying principles animating the whole of the Constitution, including the principles of federalism, democracy, constitutionalism and the rule of law, and respect for minorities. Those principles must inform our overall appreciation of the constitutional rights and obligations that would come into play in the event that a clear majority of Québecers votes on a clear question in favour of secession.

"... Arguments in support of the existence of such a right were primarily based on the principle of democracy. Democracy, however, means more than simple majority rule.... Since Confederation, the people of the provinces and territories have created close ties of interdependence (economic, social, political and cultural) based on shared values that include federalism, democracy, constitutionalism and the rule of law, and respect for minorities. A democratic decision of Québecers in favour of secession would put those relationships at risk. The Constitution vouchsafes [ensures] order and stability, and accordingly secession of a province 'under the Constitution' could not be achieved unilaterally, that is, without principled negotiation with other participants in Confederation

within the existing constitutional framework....

"Québec could not, despite a clear referendum result, purport [attempt] to invoke a right of self-determination to dictate the terms of a proposed secession to the other parties to the federation. The democratic vote, by however strong a majority, would have no legal effect on its own and could not push aside the principles of federalism and the rule of law, the rights of individuals and minorities, or the operation of democracy in the other provinces or in Canada as a whole. Democratic rights under the Constitution cannot be divorced from constitutional obligations. Nor, however, can the reverse proposition be accepted: the continued existence and operation of the Canadian constitutional order could not be indifferent to a clear expression of a clear majority of Québecers that they no longer wish to remain in Canada. The other provinces and the federal government would have no basis to deny the right of the government of Québec to pursue secession should a clear majority of the people of Québec choose that goal, so long as in doing so, Québec respects the rights of others....

"The negotiation process would require the reconciliation of various rights and obligations by negotiation between two legitimate majorities, namely, the majority of the population of Québec, and that of Canada as a whole. A political majority at either level that does not act in accordance with the underlying constitutional principles puts at risk the legitimacy of its exercise of its rights, and the ultimate acceptance of the result by the international community...."

Question 2

"The Court was also required to consider whether a right to unilateral secession exists under international law.... Québec does not meet the threshold of a colonial people or an oppressed people, nor can it be suggested that Québecers have been denied meaningful access to government to pursue their political, economic, cultural and social development. In the circumstances, the 'National Assembly, the legislature or the government of Québec' do not enjoy a right at international law to effect the secession of Québec from Canada unilaterally.

"Although there is no right, under the Constitution or at international law, to unilateral secession, the possibility of an unconstitutional declaration of secession leading to a *de facto* secession [a separate nation of Québec, whether recognized legally domestically] is not ruled out. The ultimate success of such a secession would be dependent on recognition by the international community, which is likely to consider the legality and legitimacy of secession having regard to, amongst other facts, the conduct of Québec and Canada, in determining whether to grant or withhold recognition.…"

Question 3
"In view of the answers to Questions 1 and 2, there is no conflict between domestic and international law to be addressed in the context of this Reference."

SOURCES: *Canadian Legal Information Institute.*
Accessed Dec. 2003
<www.canlii.org/ca/cas/scc/1998/1998scc63.html>;

Department of Justice, Canada. Accessed Dec. 2003
<www.canada.justice.gc.ca/en/ps/const/bck2.html>.

CONFIRM YOUR UNDERSTANDING

1. Compare the terms of the Meech Lake and Charlottetown Accords.

2. Explain the role Elijah Harper played in the failure of the Meech Lake Accord.

3. In what ways did the Charlottetown Accord attempt to address the needs of Québec?

4. Explain the purpose of a constitutional referendum.

Law-making in Canada

As a democracy, the government of Canada operates under the authority and legitimacy given it by the people through open and free elections. Part of the job of government is to change, create, or remove outdated laws to address the needs and issues facing the nation and its citizens. Making laws is one of the most fundamental jobs of government. A course in civics has taught you that there is a specific process for how laws are created in Canada. What follows will not only serve as a review of that process, but will also provide insight into how ideas make it to the legislature to become laws.

How a Bill Becomes Law

You are probably well aware of the general steps that a proposed bill takes in order to become a law. Most history and civics courses explain these steps. However, there are significant decisions made before a bill makes it to Parliament. These decisions are made during the pre-legislative stages of a bill or draft law (see Figure 5.14 on the following page).

Pre-Legislative Stages

Before a bill is introduced into the House of Commons, the general purpose and character of

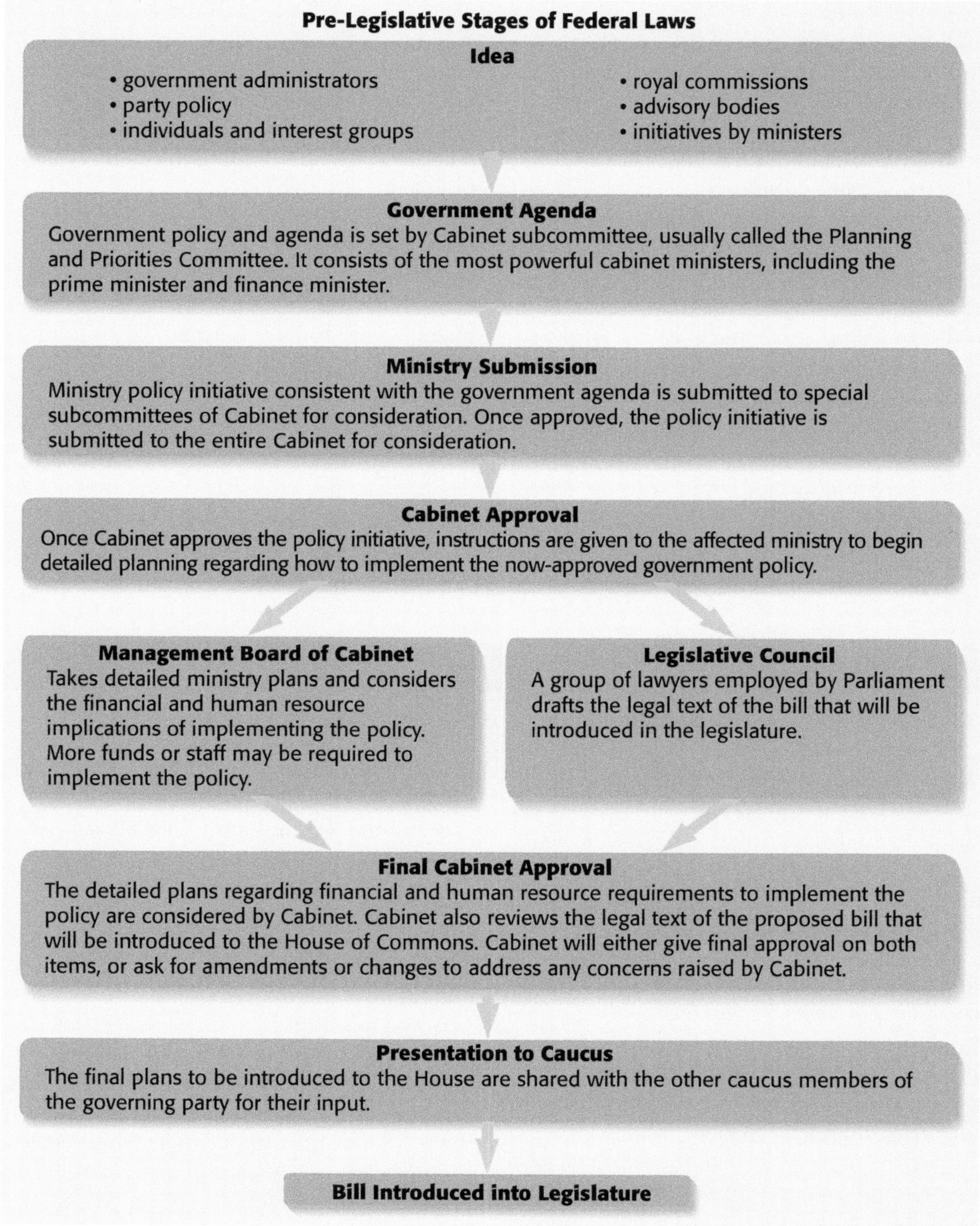

Pre-Legislative Stages of Federal Laws

Idea
- government administrators
- party policy
- individuals and interest groups
- royal commissions
- advisory bodies
- initiatives by ministers

Government Agenda
Government policy and agenda is set by Cabinet subcommittee, usually called the Planning and Priorities Committee. It consists of the most powerful cabinet ministers, including the prime minister and finance minister.

Ministry Submission
Ministry policy initiative consistent with the government agenda is submitted to special subcommittees of Cabinet for consideration. Once approved, the policy initiative is submitted to the entire Cabinet for consideration.

Cabinet Approval
Once Cabinet approves the policy initiative, instructions are given to the affected ministry to begin detailed planning regarding how to implement the now-approved government policy.

Management Board of Cabinet
Takes detailed ministry plans and considers the financial and human resource implications of implementing the policy. More funds or staff may be required to implement the policy.

Legislative Council
A group of lawyers employed by Parliament drafts the legal text of the bill that will be introduced in the legislature.

Final Cabinet Approval
The detailed plans regarding financial and human resource requirements to implement the policy are considered by Cabinet. Cabinet also reviews the legal text of the proposed bill that will be introduced to the House of Commons. Cabinet will either give final approval on both items, or ask for amendments or changes to address any concerns raised by Cabinet.

Presentation to Caucus
The final plans to be introduced to the House are shared with the other caucus members of the governing party for their input.

Bill Introduced into Legislature

FIGURE 5.14 The process that a bill goes through before it is introduced for debate in the House of Commons is a long and arduous one, generally hidden from the public eye. Why do you think public input is reserved for until much later in the process of a bill becoming law?

the bill has already been decided outside of public view. Ideas for government consideration can come from a host of sources. Common sources include government administrators, party policy, election promises, interest groups, and advisory bodies of government.

These ideas are usually reviewed by the inner Cabinet. This is a subcommittee of Cabinet and usually consists of ministers from the most important and powerful ministries. The prime minister and finance minister are usually on this subcommittee. Once this inner Cabinet has agreed in principle to an idea, the affected ministry puts together a presentation outlining all the possible options in implementing the idea, which it will submit to the entire Cabinet. This ministry submission is usually very detailed and is prepared by the bureaucrats in the civil service.

The detailed ministry submission is presented to all of Cabinet to be debated. It is during this process that the general policy and character of the idea are moulded to fit a variety of factors, one of which is the political bias of the party in power. It is common for Cabinet to recommend to the ministry changes in the direction of the policy. It is usually at this stage that government policy is leaked to the public. This is usually done deliberately so that the government can gauge the electorate's relative acceptance of, or hostility toward, the particular policy and idea. If the public reception is negative, the government can deny that the idea is government policy because it has not yet been approved by Cabinet. If the reception is positive, then the government is likely to move forward, comfortable that there will be little controversy. Once the idea is approved by Cabinet, it is sent to government lawyers who draft the legal text of the bill to be presented to Parliament. At the same time, another powerful ministry called the Management Board (also known as Treasury Board) considers the financial and human resources necessary to implement the policy.

The final package is then presented again to Cabinet, including a report from the Management Board and a draft of the legal text of the bill. Once Cabinet gives final approval, the bill is shared with the rest of the government caucus and then presented to the legislature for debate at first reading.

Legislative Stages

The draft legislation goes through a series of readings in the House of Commons.

First Reading
- Bill is introduced to Parliament and given first reading
- Ministers may discuss the purpose of the bill
- Background information is supplied to opposition parties.
- Bill is printed and distributed

Second Reading
- Principle of the bill is debated
- Bill may be referred to a committee for further examination. The committee is open to the general public and anyone is entitled to make a presentation before the committee. On important bills, the committee will travel to hear views from around the country or province.
- The committee may amend the draft legislation before sending it back to the House

Third Reading
- Debate is restricted to the content of the bill
- No amendments can be made at this point

Once a bill has passed the House of Commons, it is submitted to the Senate for consideration. To gain approval in the Senate, the bill goes through the same process of three readings as it does in the House. Once the bill is approved, it is submitted to the Governor General for proclamation to become law. Since provincial governments do not have a senate, once approval of the Legislative Assembly occurs, the bill is sent to the Lieutenant-Governor of the province for royal proclamation to become law.

CONFIRM YOUR UNDERSTANDING

1. Summarize the pre-legislative stages in how a bill becomes a law.

2. What concerns might be raised regarding the rather secretive way in which ideas are debated and moulded in the pre-legislative stages? How could these concerns be addressed?

3. Why are the ideas that are debated by Cabinet and the upper bureaucracy often leaked to the public?

4. Summarize the steps in the legislative process.

In Closing

Canada's Constitution is not a static document. It has evolved and changed with each new social, economic, political, and legal challenge, and it will continue to do so as long as Canada remains a democratic nation, responsive and accountable to the needs and wants of the electorate. Furthermore, the structure of our parliamentary democracy, with its rich heritage of common law and conventions, will also continue to grow and adapt to the ever-changing relationship between citizen and state.

This chapter has traced the history of Canada's constitutional development, exploring not only the importance of the division of powers between the federal and provincial governments, but also introducing the role of the judiciary in interpreting and making law. It has also touched on the importance of the *Canadian Charter of Rights and Freedoms* and the central role it plays in all challenges to legislation passed by all levels of government. Establishing the *Charter* as a constitutional document has given individual Canadians, through the medium of the courts, a voice in the laws that affect their day-to-day lives.

Chapters 6 through 8 examine the *Charter* in greater detail, providing further insight into how Canadian attitudes and laws are influenced and shaped by this very powerful document. The specific rights guaranteed by the *Charter* and the approach to reconciling competing rights in a free and democratic society are also highlighted. But as you delve further into your study of the *Charter*, it is important to remember the foundation on which it was established: the foundation of conflict and compromise at the heart of Canada's constitutional evolution.

CHAPTER ACTIVITIES

Extend Your Legal Knowledge

1. Outline Canada's constitutional evolution from the *Royal Proclamation, 1763* to the *Constitution Act, 1982*. Briefly explain the significance of each document.

2. Distinguish between a written and an unwritten constitution. Provide examples of countries that have each form of constitution.

3. Describe the role of the judiciary with respect to law-making in Canada.

4. Explain the significance of the Québec secession reference.

Think About the Law

5. Why does the constitution of a democratic country act as the supreme law of the land and as a framework for the structure of power?

6. Canada's Constitution is considered to be flexible, fluid, and organic because of its unwritten components. How important are these features for the evolution of Canada's Constitution? Explain.

7. Does the *Charter of Rights and Freedoms* make Canada's Constitution more flexible or inflexible? Explain.

8. Should the legislative branch of government be more distinct and separate from the executive branch of government (i.e., similar in style to that of the United States)? Support your opinion.

9. What issues would be raised if the Senate decided to block a bill passed by the House of Commons? What convention if any would be broken by this action? Explain why this action by the Senate would or would not be reasonable in your opinion.

10. Compare the structure of the government in Canada with another country of your choice. Describe how that country's government is different from ours and give your opinions on the positive and negative aspects of that

arrangement. What elements of that country's system of government would you like to see incorporated into our system of government, if any?

11. Examine the constitution of your school's student council. Describe the rules that govern the roles and responsibilities of those elected. If applicable, explain the procedure for amending your student government constitution.

Communicate About the Law

12. Select an important constitutional document other than the *Constitution Act, 1867* or *1982*. Research and write a one-page summary of the significance of that document to Canada's Constitution.

13. The principle of legislative supremacy has been an important feature of Canadian and British constitutional practice. Should legislative supremacy retain its significance or should it be curbed by other checks within the Constitution?

14. Research either the Meech Lake Accord or the Charlottetown Accord. Consider the various terms highlighted in the accord you have chosen. Select one of these terms and examine it in greater detail. Comment on the extent to which you believe changes should be made to the Constitution in this area.

15. Conduct research that compares Canada's amending formula with the amending formula from another nation's constitution. Would you recommend the other nation's amending formula for Canada's Constitution? Support your opinion. (Refer to the Legal Handbook for information regarding conducting research on the Internet.)

16. Select either the first or second legal question referred to in the Landmark Case on page 161. Prepare a commentary that either supports or refutes the rationale given by the Supreme Court.

LEGAL *p. 23* HANDBOOK

Apply the Law

17. In the case of *Ward v. Canada (Attorney General)*, [2002] 1 S.C.R. 569, Ford Ward held a commercial sealing licence issued under the federal *Fisheries Act*. This licence permitted him to harvest hooded and harp seals. On a seal hunt in 1996, Ward harvested approximately 50 seals, including a number of bluebacks, or young seals, which were not authorized by his licence. He was charged with selling blueback pelts contrary to s. 27 of the federal *Marine Mammal Regulations*, which prohibits the sale, trade, or barter of young seals. Ward argued that s. 27 was *ultra vires* Parliament's constitutional authority and was a power that belonged to the provincial government since it dealt with regulating commerce and business within a province.

a) Refer to the division of powers listed in Figure 5.7 on page 144. Prepare arguments using the division of powers and the pith and substance principles to defend or support the action of the federal government in the *Ward v. Canada* case.

b) Should the federal power to regulate fisheries in this case supersede a province's ability to license and regulate trade and business? Explain.

18. In the case of *R. v. Hydro-Québec*, [1997] 3 S.C.R. 213, Hydro-Québec allegedly dumped polychlorinated biphenyls (PCBs) into a river in early 1990, and was charged with two infractions under regulations of the federal *Canadian Environmental Protection Act*. Hydro-Québec brought a motion seeking to have relevant regulations and certain sections of the act declared *ultra vires* the Parliament of Canada on the grounds that they do not fall within the authority of the federal government set out in s. 91 of the *Constitution Act, 1867*. The Attorney General of Québec intervened in support of Hydro-Québec's position. The motion was granted in the Court of Québec, and an appeal to the Superior Court was dismissed. A further appeal to the Court of Appeal was also dismissed.

The federal government argued that the regulations and the act itself formed a part of the criminal law because of the nature and danger of the substances in question. It argued that it needed to regulate these chemicals under its criminal law authority because of the danger to the environment and to human health posed by these toxins.

The Québec government argued that the authority to control and regulate industry belongs to the provinces as indicated under s. 92 of the *Constitution Act, 1867*.

a) Explain whether the action of the federal government in this case was *intra vires* or *ultra vires* Parliament.

b) Explain how the pith and substance doctrine could be applied in this case.

c) How would you decide this case? Provide a rationale for your decision.

BIBLIOGRAPHY

Banks, Margaret A. *Understanding Canada's Constitution.* London, ON: The University of Western Ontario , 1991.

Bryant, Michael, and Lorne Sossin. *Public Law.* Toronto: The Carswell Company, 2002.

Canadian Legal Information Institute Accessed 15 Dec. 2003 <www.canlii.org >.

"The Canadian Professional Police Association Pleased by Today's Supreme Court Marijuana Rulings." Canadian Professional Police Association. News Release. 23 Dec. 2003. Accessed 30 Dec. 2003 <www.cppa-acpp.ca/index-english.htm>.

Connor, Jacqueline. *Part I: Directors' Legal Duties and Liabilities.* Not-for-Profit Board Management Series. Orangeville, ON: Carter & Associates, 24 Sept. 2002. Accessed 20 Dec. 2003 <www.carters.ca/pub/seminar/charity/2002/jmc0924.pdf>.

Dawson, R. MacGregor, and W.F. Dawson. *Democratic Government in Canada.* Toronto: University of Toronto Press, 1971.

Department of Justice Canada. "Quebec Secession Reference." 24 Apr. 2003. Accessed Aug. 2003 <www.canada.justice.gc.ca/en/ps/const/bck2.html>.

Finkelstein, Neil. *Laskin's Canadian Constitutional Law.* 5th ed. Vol. 1. Toronto: The Carswell Company, 1986.

Funston, Bernard W., and Eugene Meehan. *Canada's Constitutional Law in a Nutshell.* Toronto: The Carswell Company, 1994.

Goodman, Kenneth R. *2002 Church and The Law Seminar: The Public Guardian & Trustee & the Courts on the Limits of Fundraising in Ontario.* Orangeville, ON: Carter & Associates, 5 Nov. 2002. Accessed 20 Dec. 2003 <www.carters.ca/pub/seminar/chrchlaw/2002/goodman.pdf>.

Heard, Andrew. *Canadian Constitutional Conventions: The Marriage of Law and Politics.* Toronto: Oxford University Press, 1991.

Hogg, Peter W. *Constitutional Law of Canada.* 4th ed. Toronto: The Carswell Company, 1997.

Hunter, Stuart. "Parliament Has the Right to Ban Pot, Court Decides." *The Province* 24 Dec. 2003. Accessed 30 Dec. 2003 <www.canada.com/search/story.aspx?id=9a45b233-ef48-4ceb-9781-bae4d953b85d>.

Macklem, Patrick. *Canadian Constitutional Law.* 2nd ed. Toronto: Emond Montgomery Publications Limited, 1997.

Makin, Kirk. "Pot Ban is Constitutional, Supreme Court Rules." *The Globe and Mail* 23 Dec. 2003. Accessed 30 Dec. 2003 <www.globeandmail.com/servlet/story/RTGAM.20031223.wpott1223_5/BNStory/National/?query=marijuana>.

———. "Pot Laws Don't Breach Charter: Supreme Court." *The Globe and Mail* 23 Dec. 2003. Accessed 30 Dec. 2003 <www.globeandmail.com/servlet/story/RTGAM.20031223.wpott1223_4/BNStory/National/?query=marijuana>.

Ministry of the Attorney General, Ontario. *Not for Profit Incorporator's Handbook—Part 5: Corporate Maintenance.* 20 Dec. 2002. Accessed 20 Dec. 2003 <www.attorneygeneral.jus.gov.on.ca/english/family/pgt/nfpinc/corpmaintain.asp>.

———. ——— *Part 3: Incorporation.* 14 Jan. 2003. Accessed 20 Dec. 2003 <www.attorneygeneral.jus.gov.on.ca/english/family/pgt/nfpinc/incorp.asp>.

Monahan, Patrick. *Constitutional Law.* Essentials of Canadian Law Series. Toronto: Irwin Law Inc., 2002.

Ontario Legislative Library. "How a Government Bill Becomes Law (Pre-Legislative Stages)." Toronto: Office of the Legislative Assembly of Ontario, 2 May 2002. Accessed 26 Oct. 2003 <www.ontla.on.ca/library/billsresources/preleg.pdf>.

Sharpe, Robert, Katherine Swinton, and Kent Roach. *The Charter of Rights and Freedoms.* Essentials of Canadian Law Series. Toronto: Irwin Law Inc., 2002.

Chapter 6

HUMAN RIGHTS IN CANADA

LEARNING EXPECTATIONS

After reading this chapter, you will be able to:

- identify how Canadian human rights legislation has evolved from English common law to the *Canadian Bill of Rights* and then to the *Canadian Charter of Rights and Freedoms*

- understand the meaning of entrenching rights in a written constitution

- evaluate the protection provided by federal and provincial human rights legislation

FIGURE 6.1 Canada's diversity is a source of national pride. In order to promote tolerance and respect, laws have been passed that demonstrate our commitment to human rights protection. What laws exist in Canada today to prevent discrimination?

> *No one can be above the law. And no one can be forgotten by the law or denied its protection. Human rights not only protect individuals from abuse, they empower them to contribute fully and creatively to building a stronger society.*
>
> —Prime Minister Jean Chrétien, 2001

∎ I N T R O D U C T I O N ∎

Although we all live under the umbrella of Canadian society, our unique differences are protected by rights legislation. In this chapter, you will explore the evolution of Canadian human rights legislation and discover how law and justice have developed in Canadian society so that human rights are safeguarded. Education and understanding are the keys to promoting tolerance and respect. Yet it is through action that citizens demonstrate a commitment to upholding human rights laws. By analyzing the protections provided under the *Canadian Human Rights Act* and provincial human rights legislation, in particular, the Ontario *Human Rights Code*, you will assess the extent to which our laws currently promote tolerance and address discrimination issues.

The Evolution of Canadian Human Rights Law

Human rights protection in Canada has been a developmental process. Canadians did not always have rights and **civil liberties** (actions exercised without government interference) guaranteed and protected as part of our Constitution. In fact, barely two decades have passed since our rights were **entrenched**, that is, firmly established, in a constitutional framework as part of the *Canadian Charter of Rights and Freedoms*. Does that mean that Canadians were left to the mercy of our government with no protections prior to 1982? On the contrary, Canada has had legislated rights protection for actions falling under federal jurisdiction since 1960, with the *Canadian Bill of Rights*. This document had its limitations, but it at least demonstrated a solid commitment to rights protection. Prior to this, civil liberties were protected, but

not necessarily guaranteed, by our rich inheritance of English common law.

Common Law Rights

As discussed in Chapter 2, Canada's system of law developed from two distinct legal traditions: the common law from England, and civil law from France. Although our legal heritage is founded on these laws, it was the English system of common law that was predominant in the colonies of British North America. In England, civil liberties were protected by the rules of common law, and there were no constitutional or legislative guarantees. The common law, itself, did not expressly provide for a guarantee of civil liberties. Constitutional law expert Peter Hogg, in *Constitutional Law in Canada*, states that "the common law's position is that a person is free to

FIGURE 6.2 Premier Maurice Duplessis of Québec was sued by a Montréal restauranteur in the 1950s. How did Duplessis act beyond his scope of power in the *Roncarelli v. Duplessis* case?

do anything that is not positively prohibited, and various doctrines help to narrow the scope of what is positively prohibited" (Hogg 1985). He further adds that "civil liberties do not derive from positive law [law enacted by a government authority] or governmental action, but from an absence of positive law or governmental action."

Therefore, an individual has the freedom of speech as long as exercising that freedom does not conflict with laws that regulate speech, such as laws on **defamation** (making false or malicious statements that injure a person's reputation), contempt of court, obscenity, fraud, or hate propaganda, to name a few. Canadians did not gain a constitutional guarantee of civil liberties from England, but we did inherit the principles of common law and allowed our courts to interpret how they were to apply.

A well-known case that illustrates common law principles and the protection of civil liberties, in addition to the rule of law (see Chapter 5, p. 153), is that of *Roncarelli v. Duplessis*, [1959] S.C.R. 121. The two common law principles

evident in this case are (1) **validity**, meaning that government action must be justified by law, and (2) **redress** for injuries, meaning that those who are injured by government action can seek remedies. Frank Roncarelli was a Jehovah's Witness who owned a café in Montréal. Contrary to the wishes of Premier Maurice Duplessis of Québec, Roncarelli regularly posted bail for other Jehovah's Witnesses arrested for breaching municipal laws prohibiting them from distributing their literature. Duplessis then ordered the cancellation of Roncarelli's liquor licence. The Supreme Court of Canada awarded damages to Roncarelli after it was determined that the premier was not acting within the scope of his legal authority when he made the decision to cancel Roncarelli's liquor licence. The common law principles were interpreted and applied by the courts to remedy a situation in which a violation of civil liberties was evident. This application of common law principles continued in the absence of formal written rights protection legislation. However, a shift in favour of formal protections was soon to occur.

The *Canadian Bill of Rights*

The horror and shame of racially discriminatory actions reached a peak during World War II, not only in Europe, but also in Canada. Canada accepted very few Jewish refugees fleeing Nazi persecution. Aboriginal peoples and Black Canadians volunteering for active service were barred from joining the air force or the navy. They were permitted to join only the infantry. After the bombing of Pearl Harbor in 1941, the Canadian government, under the authority of the *War Measures Act*, seized the property and possessions of Japanese Canadians and separated families, sending family members to various internment camps in remote parts of Alberta and British Columbia.

The systematic brutality associated with World War II demonstrated a complete disregard for human worth and dignity. In 1948, the United Nations attempted to reaffirm faith in fundamental human rights by drafting a docu-

FIGURE 6.3   Imagine that your property and possessions were seized and that you were placed in an internment camp because of your ethnicity like this Japanese family was during World War II. What form of redress from the Canadian government do you feel would be just?

ment called the *Universal Declaration of Human Rights*. Canada, as a signatory to this document, embraced its underlying principles—the inherent dignity and worth of a human being and the importance of establishing laws protecting human rights. This UN Declaration influenced the development of many modern-day human rights documents and spurred on legislation for rights protection in Canada.

In 1960, a strong movement led by Prime Minister John G. Diefenbaker reached its goal of establishing written protection of rights and freedoms with the passing of the *Canadian Bill of Rights*. In order not to negate any of the common law rulings or suggest that Canadians didn't have rights prior to the enactment of this legislation, the document was carefully worded to indicate that human rights and fundamental freedoms had been part of our legal heritage and would continue to exist. Section 1 of the *Canadian Bill of Rights* lists some major tenets, as follows:

1. It is hereby recognized and declared that in Canada there have existed and shall continue to exist without discrimination by reason of race, national origin, colour, religion or sex, the following human rights and fundamental freedoms, namely,

(a) the right of the individual to life, liberty, security of the person and enjoyment of property, and the right not to be deprived thereof except by due process of law;

(b) the right of the individual to equality before the law and the protection of the law;

(c) freedom of religion;

(d) freedom of speech;

(e) freedom of assembly and association; and

(f) freedom of the press.

It would now be left to the courts to interpret the meaning of the various protections provided under the *Bill of Rights* legislation. The case of *Attorney General of Canada v. Lavell*, [1974] S.C.R. 1349 clearly indicates the limited scope

Born in Canada, brought up on big-band jazz, Fred Astaire and the novels of Rider Haggard, I had perceived myself to be as Canadian as the beaver. I hated rice. I had committed no crime. I was never charged, tried or convicted of anything. Yet I was fingerprinted and interned.

—Ken Adachi,
Toronto Star,
September 24, 1988

FIGURE 6.4 Jeanette Lavell (left) and her daughter stand outside the Supreme Court of Canada in March 2004. Why did Lavell challenge the validity of the *Indian Act* 30 years earlier?

of the *Bill of Rights* legislation when it came to rights protection and the interpretation of equality rights. Jeannette Corbière Lavell challenged the validity of s. 12.1(b) of the *Indian Act*, which provided that a status Indian woman who married a non-status man would lose her Indian status. The situation was different for a status Indian man. He did not lose his status by marrying a non-status woman. When Lavell married a non-Indian, her name was struck from the Indian Register. Her appeal was rejected at the Ontario Court of Appeal. On appeal to the Federal Court, the court declared that the *Indian Act* was discriminatory on the basis of gender, as an Indian man did not lose his status if he married a non-Indian woman. This section of the *Indian Act* was declared inconsistent with the *Canadian Bill of Rights*. However, the case was appealed to the Supreme Court of Canada. The Supreme Court held that there was no violation of the equality provision under the *Bill of Rights*. The meaning given to

the term "equality" was to be consistent with the time period of the enactment of the bill; it was defined in terms of the equal administration of the law. Therefore, "equality" as it applied to the Lavell case meant that all Indian women were to be treated the same and all Indian men were to be treated the same. The *Canadian Bill of Rights* was not used to override the *Indian Act*, and Lavell lost her case.

This narrow interpretation of the term "equality" under the *Bill of Rights* would be criticized and would reinforce the need for clarity in interpreting equality rights in Canada. In addition to its narrow interpretation of rights, the *Canadian Bill of Rights* also had several other limitations. First, it was an ordinary federal statute that could be amended or revoked. Further, it did not apply to the provincial or territorial governments. The *Bill of Rights* also did not confer any ability to create new rights nor was it part of any constitutional document. Shifting tides of public opinion were soon to support the efforts of Prime Minister Pierre Elliott Trudeau. Not only was there growing public support for **patriating** our Constitution (bring under the authority of the country to which the laws apply), but there was also a desire to provide a rights protection document that was fully entrenched in our constitutional framework, thus protecting rights regardless of the level of government action. The signing in 1982 of the *Canadian Charter of Rights and Freedoms* as part of our Constitution heralded a new era in Canadian constitutional law.

The *Canadian Charter of Rights and Freedoms*

As you learned in Chapter 5, the *Canada Act* was proclaimed on April 17, 1982, thereby enacting the *Constitution Act, 1982* and the new *Canadian Charter of Rights and Freedoms*. No longer would rights be interpreted solely within the narrow confines of the *Canadian Bill of Rights* and federal jurisdiction. Rights protection would now apply to citizens in their interaction with provincial and territorial governments as well. Further, rights

FIGURE 6.5 "We must now establish the basic principles, the basic values and beliefs which hold us together as Canadians so that beyond our regional loyalties there is a way of life and a system of values which make us proud of the country that has given us freedom and such immeasurable joy."
—Pierre Elliott Trudeau, 1981

and freedoms would now be entrenched in the Constitution, meaning that they could not be repealed or changed without using the constitutional amendment provision in s. 38 of the Constitution. This amending process requires the agreement of the federal parliament and the legislatures of two-thirds of the provinces having at least 50 percent of the population, rendering constitutional amendment a formidable task.

The guarantees in the *Charter* specifically entrench the four fundamental freedoms of religion, expression, peaceful assembly, and association; they also guarantee democratic, mobility, legal, equality, language, and Aboriginal and treaty rights. Canadian citizens now had a voice that could be used in challenging government action where it appeared to violate rights and freedoms. The judiciary would be given the controversial new task of interpreting rights and considering the scope of rights protection in Canada. The courts would make determinations regarding, for example, the meaning of freedom of expression or unreasonable search and seizure under the *Charter*. (A more extensive analysis of *Charter* provisions, case law, and the controversial relationship between the legislature and the judiciary is the focus of Chapter 7.)

What happens to a law that violates the *Charter*? The *Charter* has the authority of constitutional supremacy, so any law that is inconsistent with the provisions of the *Charter* can be declared of no force or effect. If legislation or the action of a government agency were considered to violate a *Charter* right, it could be challenged in a court of law. For example, if a provision in a provincial family law act prevented same-sex couples from receiving spousal support, the law could be challenged on the basis of a denial of equality rights to same-sex couples. The remedy may require the province to amend the law to include spousal support for same-sex couples. This means that the ability for judges to interpret the scope of the *Charter* is balanced within the context of the current social and political climate. Through the process of judicial review, there is the opportunity for the protection of rights and freedoms to evolve.

The case of *M. v. H.*, [1999] 2 S.C.R. 3 illustrates how courts are involved in interpreting legislation. The parties to the action, M. and H., had lived together in a same-sex relationship for 10 years. When the relationship ended, M. sought spousal support under Ontario's *Family Law Act*. The definition of "spouse" in the act did not provide for same-sex couples. When challenged in court, the Ontario Court of Justice ruled that the words "man and woman" in the definition of spouse should be replaced by the words "two persons" and declared the *Family Law Act* invalid. The Court of Appeal agreed with the trial decision. The Attorney General for Ontario appealed the decision to the Supreme

Court of Canada, where, in a 9 to 0 judgment, the court declared the *Family Law Act* to be of no force or effect. Subsequent to this ruling, the federal government passed the *Modernization of Benefits and Obligations Act*. This act required that the words "opposite sex" be replaced by "survivor" in federal legislation. The Ontario government also responded by amending 67 statutes in order to prevent discrimination against same-sex couples.

What does having the *Charter* within our Constitution mean for us today? As you learned in Chapter 5, a constitution may suggest a rigid framework for the jurisdictional separation of powers. However, the *Charter* allows our Constitution some flexibility and provides for the development of a broader understanding of rights protection for the benefit of individual Canadians.

CONFIRM YOUR UNDERSTANDING

1. How would freedom of speech be restricted by common law?
2. Discuss how the common law concept of validity was used in the *Roncarelli v. Duplessis* case.
3. Explain the circumstances that led to the development of the *Canadian Bill of Rights* and discuss its limitations.
4. How was "equality" interpreted in the *Attorney General of Canada v. Lavell* case?
5. Explain the significance of entrenching rights in a constitution.
6. How did the *Bill of Rights* differ from the *Charter* with respect to legislative authority?
7. Explain what is meant by "constitutional supremacy." Provide an example.

Human Rights in Canada

More often than not, disadvantage arises from the way in which society treats particular individuals, rather than from any characteristic inherent in those individuals.

—Justice La Forest in *Egan v. Canada*, [1995] 2 S.C.R. 513

You have just learned that the *Charter* applies to governments and their agencies in the exercise of their actions but that human rights legislation in Canada applies to individuals. Human rights safeguard equality rights in certain areas (such as access to goods, services, or facilities; accommodation; and employment) and opportunities are provided for redress in instances in which discrimination has occurred.

Human rights are protected in Canada by both the federal and the provincial and territorial governments. The federal government has enacted the *Canadian Human Rights Act* to provide protection against discrimination for those areas falling within the scope of federal authority, such as regulating airlines and their employees. Similarly, all provinces and territories have enacted their own human rights legislation to deal with discrimination within the confines of their jurisdiction and authority. Both levels of

government offer protections that are intended to deal with discrimination effectively.

The *Canadian Human Rights Act*

The *Canadian Human Rights Act* (CHRA) was passed in 1977 to provide protection from discrimination and harassment. The CHRA applies to federal government departments, such as the postal service, and to businesses that fall under federal jurisdiction, such as airlines and chartered banks. The prohibited grounds for discrimination under the CHRA are similar to those provided for under provincial and territorial human rights legislation, but there are some slight distinctions among the grounds that are specifically protected. Under s. 3, the CHRA prohibits discrimination on the grounds of race, national or ethnic origin, colour, religion, age, sex, sexual orientation, marital status, family status, disability, and conviction for which a pardon has been granted.

In this section, selected grounds for discrimination are examined in order to broaden your understanding of the scope of discrimination, to highlight some of the issues dealt with by the Canadian Human Rights Commission, and to familiarize you with terms that are significant in discrimination case law.

Under the CHRA, disability does not exclusively refer to a physical incapacity. Section 25 of the act specifically defines "disability" as including "any previous or existing mental or physical disability and includes disfigurement and previous or existing dependence on alcohol or a drug." The Canadian Civil Liberties Association was involved in a nine-year court battle with the Toronto Dominion Bank over its mandatory pre-employment urinary drug-testing program. In 1998, the Federal Court of Canada (which has jurisdiction to hear appeals from federally appointed tribunals and boards and to try civil cases involving federal employees) ruled that the policy was discriminatory and referred the case back to the human rights tribunal for a decision regarding the remedy. The Toronto Dominion Bank subsequently withdrew the policy.

Both the CHRA and provincial and territorial human rights legislation allow for the development of affirmative-action programs designed to address inequities experienced by Aboriginal peoples, women, people with disabilities, and visible minorities. They also prevent retaliation against an individual who files a complaint of discrimination.

Section 15 of the CHRA provides for the justification of a bona fide occupational requirement and requires that accommodations be considered. Simply speaking, a **bona fide occupational requirement** is one that is deemed to be reasonably necessary for the safe and efficient performance of a job. **Accommodation** requires that an employer eliminate or adapt an existing requirement in order for a person to carry out the essential aspects of the activity or job.

A landmark ruling of the Canadian Human Rights Commission, the federal body responsible for enforcing the *Canadian Human Rights Act*, considered a claim of religious discrimination. In *Bhinder and the Canadian Human Rights Commission v. Canadian National Railway Company*, [1985] 2 S.C.R. (4th) 561, the complainant, Karnail Singh Bhinder, a Sikh, challenged the mandatory hard-hat rule used by the Canadian National Railway (CNR). His religion required him to wear a turban, and he argued that the CNR's hard-hat rule infringed on his religious freedom. The court held that the hard-hat rule was a bona fide occupational requirement necessary for safety on the job and that it was not necessary to accommodate Mr. Bhinder.

Arguments of bona fide occupational requirements are not always successful. Sometimes accommodations are made in order to protect religious freedom. In 1988, Baltej Singh Dhillon was told that he could join the RCMP only if he did not wear the turban required by his Sikh religion. Dhillon challenged this requirement, and the RCMP removed the ban in 1990. Despite this decision, a group of retired RCMP officers challenged the right of Sikhs to wear turbans, but the Supreme Court of Canada rejected their application in 1996.

FIGURE 6.6 Baltej Singh Dhillon challenged a ban that prevented Sikhs from wearing turbans in the RCMP. The RCMP removed the ban in 1990. How do Canadian laws prevent religious discrimination?

Section 11 of the CHRA specifies equal pay for male and female employees in the same establishment who perform work of equal value. Complaints can be filed with the Canadian Human Rights Commission if an individual feels he or she has been the victim of a pay inequity covered by the act. Generally speaking, in pay equity claims, jobs within the same industry are compared on the basis of four criteria: skill, effort, responsibility, and working conditions. The value of one job is then compared with the value and wages of another job. Should it be found that a female's job is of similar value to the job of a male but the pay is lower, the employer is ordered to remedy the imbalance.

Many cases have been fought in the courts to remedy wage gaps. According to the Canadian Human Rights Commission, in 1990, federal public servants received a back-pay settlement of $317 million with an additional $76 million in salary adjustments. In 1995, a group of 1700 nurses received a $12.7 million settlement. In 2002, it was reported that clerical and sales staff at Bell Canada settled for $178 million. While pay equity advances have been made, the Canadian Human Rights Commission has been concerned with the complaint mechanism used

to achieve pay equity, and with the long and expensive legal challenges that have resulted. The telephone operators at Bell Canada have been involved in a legal battle for over a decade in their efforts to achieve pay equity. The legislation that is used to implement pay equity may require review in order to improve the mechanisms used to settle pay equity complaints.

Technological change sometimes affects legislation as well. In 1988, the CHRA was amended to make communication of hate messages by telephone or telecommunication facilities a discriminatory practice. Occasionally a situation will arise that leads to further amendments. In the wake of the September 11, 2001, terrorist attacks, the *Canadian Human Rights Act* was updated to include communication of hate messages by computer, groups of computers, and the Internet. Discriminatory practices have been perpetuated by the Internet. While human rights complaints and court actions might be difficult to pursue in this area, primarily because it is difficult to trace the perpetrators, the fact remains that circumstances necessitated the broadening of the act to clarify actions that would be considered discriminatory.

CONFIRM YOUR UNDERSTANDING

1. Outline the scope of the *Canadian Human Rights Act*.

2. Discuss whether drug and alcohol testing should be allowed in the workplace. Justify your opinion.

3. Explain how pay equity is achieved.

4. How was the CHRA amended to deal with discriminatory practices perpetuated on the Internet?

Provincial Human Rights Legislation

The Ontario *Human Rights Code*, originally drafted in 1962, was strongly influenced by the *Universal Declaration of Human Rights*. This influence is evident in the Preamble of the Ontario *Human Rights Code* (see Figure 6.7).

The Ontario *Human Rights Code* (the *Code*) specifically protects everyone from discrimination and harassment in Ontario. All legislation in Ontario must be consistent with the provisions of the *Code*. Legislation that is not consistent may be challenged or declared invalid. Individuals can file complaints with the Ontario Human Rights

> *Preamble*
>
> *Whereas recognition of the inherent dignity and the equal and inalienable rights of all members of the human family is the foundation of freedom, justice and peace in the world and is in accord with the Universal Declaration of Human Rights as proclaimed by the United Nations;*
>
> *And Whereas it is public policy in Ontario to recognize the dignity and worth of every person and to provide for equal rights and opportunities without discrimination that is contrary to law, and having as its aim the creation of a climate of understanding and mutual respect for the dignity and worth of each person so that each person feels a part of the community and able to contribute fully to the development and well-being of the community and the Province;*
>
> *And Whereas these principles have been confirmed in Ontario by a number of enactments of the Legislature and it is desirable to revise and extend the protection of human rights in Ontario;*
>
> *Therefore, Her Majesty, by and with the advice and consent of the Legislative Assembly of the Province of Ontario, enacts as follows....*

FIGURE 6.7   This preamble to the Ontario *Human Rights Code* indicates that the recognition of rights is public policy and must be accomplished without discrimination. Summarize the main principles included in the preamble.

Commission (the provincial body responsible for enforcing the Ontario *Human Rights Code*) if they feel that they have been discriminated against or harassed. Indeed, if the situation is warranted, the commission may initiate a complaint itself (e.g., an investigation into the issue of racial profiling).

Scope and Grounds of Discrimination

When individuals complain of unfair or unequal treatment, it is important to recognize that these inequities must occur within an area that is covered by the scope of the Ontario *Human Rights Code*. Equal rights apply specifically to five areas under the *Code* as follows:

* access to services, goods, and facilities
* accommodation
* the right to contract
* employment
* occupational associations

You therefore have the right to be free from discrimination and harassment in many of the areas in which you conduct your daily life. Whether you attend school, shop at the mall,

access hospital services, or work at a part-time job, you are protected under the scope of the Ontario *Human Rights Code*.

Many of the distinct grounds for discrimination are highlighted in s. 1 of the *Code*, which states that "Every person has a right to equal treatment with respect to services, goods and facilities, without discrimination because of race, ancestry, place of origin, colour, ethnic origin, citizenship, creed, sex, sexual orientation, age, marital status, same-sex partnership status, family status or disability." The prohibited grounds specified in s. 1 apply to services, goods, and facilities. Under the *Code*, the grounds vary slightly depending on the particular area of focus. For example, under employment, the prohibited grounds are expanded to include record of offences, meaning conviction for an offence for which a pardon has been granted and not revoked, or an offence involving conviction for an infraction of a provincial enactment, such as the *Highway Traffic Act*. Under accommodation, the grounds are broadened to include receipt of public assistance. Because fair treatment of individuals is essential, the *Code* broadly encompasses many grounds in order to secure mutual respect for the dignity and worth of the parties involved.

All provincial and territorial human rights legislation identifies specific grounds of discrimination, but the grounds may differ somewhat in each jurisdiction. For example, under the Nova Scotia *Human Rights Act*, an individual or class of individuals cannot be discriminated against "on account of age; race; colour; religion; creed; sex; sexual orientation; physical disability or mental disability; an irrational fear of contracting an illness or disease; ethnic, national or aboriginal origin; family status; marital status; source of income; political belief, affiliation or activity." Prohibited grounds under s. 6 of the Yukon *Human Rights Act* include discrimination toward an individual or group on the basis of ancestry, including colour and race; national origin or ethnic or linguistic background or origin; religion, creed, religious belief, religious association, or religious activity; age; sex, including pregnancy, and pregnancy-related conditions; sexual orientation; physical or mental disability; criminal charges or criminal record; political belief, political association, or political activity; marital or family status; and actual or presumed association with other individuals or groups whose identity or membership is determined by any of the grounds listed.

To evaluate the protections provided by human rights legislation in Ontario, you must become familiar with the terminology of human rights cases. Some terms are specifically defined under the *Code*, such as "age," "disability," and "harassment." Other terms, such as "accommodation" and "bona fide occupational requirement," have been interpreted through case law. The sections that follow will familiarize you with human rights terminology and will show you how the law is applied in discrimination cases. Four particular grounds of discrimination will be highlighted for the purpose of this analysis: sex discrimination, discrimination on

the basis of disability, age discrimination, and racial discrimination. Enforcement of rights under the Ontario *Human Rights Code* will also be addressed.

Discrimination on the Basis of Sex

When human rights legislation is applied to the workplace, discrimination based on sex can take one of two forms: direct discrimination or adverse-effect discrimination. **Direct discrimination** involves a practice or behaviour that is overt and clearly discriminatory. **Adverse-effect discrimination** involves a requirement or standard that may appear neutral but is, in fact, discriminatory in effect toward an individual or group protected under the Ontario *Human Rights Code*. For example, an employer who advertises for an electrician but refuses to consider a female applicant solely because she is a woman could be subject to a complaint of direct discrimination on the basis of sex. If that same employer hires women but then insists that they meet a standard test requiring all electricians to carry 70 kg of cabling while working, thus barring many women from holding this job, female applicants could lodge a complaint of adverse-effect discrimination.

Direct discrimination cases are often easier to prove because the action or behaviour is overt. Indirect or unintentional cases, such as those involving adverse-effect discrimination, are often more difficult to prove. The law generally requires the complainant to establish a ***prima facie* case** of discrimination, meaning one in which there is sufficient evidence to justify a finding of discrimination for the complainant in the absence of evidence from the respondent. Then, the burden shifts to the employer to establish that the standard or qualification is necessary as a bona fide occupational requirement.

The Landmark Case beginning on the opposite page clearly addresses the issue of sex discrimination and outlines a three-step test to determine if a standard is a bona fide occupational requirement in cases where discrimination is at issue.

Landmark CASE

British Columbia (Public Service Employee Relations Commission) v. BCGSEU, [1999] 3 S.C.R. 3

Read the case analysis that follows. Show you understand the nature of the ruling by applying the **precedent** to a case scenario that you create involving a similar situation (e.g., a case requiring aptitude or fitness testing, or height/weight requirements). Clearly outline your rationale for each of the three steps in identifying whether a standard is a bona fide occupational requirement. Identify the accommodations that should be made, if any.

Facts: In 1992, Tawney Meiorin was hired by the Province of British Columbia to fight forest fires. She worked satisfactorily in her job for two years, but when the government adopted a series of tests that set minimum fitness standards for firefighters, Meiorin failed to meet the aerobic standard test. The test required firefighters to run 2.4 km in 11 minutes. Meiorin made four attempts but missed the minimum standard by 49.4 seconds and was dismissed for failing to meet the required fitness standard.

After Meiorin filed a grievance, an arbitrator found that Meiorin had established a *prima facie* case of adverse-effect discrimination as the aerobic standard had a disproportionate negative effect on women as a group. The arbitrator accepted evidence of physiological differences between men and women, particularly that most women have lower aerobic capacity than men and that even extra training would not enable Meiorin to meet the aerobic standard. No credible evidence was given by the government to indicate that the particular aerobic standard was required in

order for a firefighter to carry out his or her job safely and efficiently. The government was unable to establish that the test was a bona fide occupational requirement. Nor was it able to show that it had accommodated Meiorin to the point of **undue hardship**, meaning that the cost of making the accommodation would have a negative effect on, or alter the very the nature of the business—in this case, fire-fighting. The arbitrator made an order to reinstate Meiorin and directed that she receive compensation for lost wages and benefits.

The case was appealed to the Court of Appeal for British Columbia where the arbitrator's decision was overturned. The Court of Appeal did not distinguish between direct or adverse-effect discrimination. It held that as long as a standard was necessary for safe and efficient performance and the same standard applied to all individualized testing, then there was no discrimination. The case was appealed to the Supreme Court of Canada.

FIGURE 6.8 Tawney Meiorin won her case at the Supreme Court of Canada and was reinstated in her job as a firefighter. How was Ms. Meiorin discriminated against?

Issue: Was the standard test discriminatory? If so, was it justifiable as a bona fide occupational requirement?

Held: Appeal allowed.

Ratio Decidendi: (McLachlin J.) In her ruling, Justice McLachlin at paragraph 54 proposed a three-step test for determining whether a *prima facie* discriminatory standard is a bona fide occupational requirement:

"An employer may justify the impugned standard [the standard being challenged or questioned] by establishing on the **balance of probabilities** [the standard of proof required for the believability of an argument]:

(1) that the employer adopted the standard for a purpose rationally connected to the performance of the job;

(2) that the employer adopted the particular standard in an honest and good faith belief that it was necessary to the fulfillment of that legitimate work-related purpose; and

(3) that the standard is reasonably necessary to the accomplishment of that legitimate work-related purpose."

The court added that "[t]o show that the standard is reasonably necessary, it must be demonstrated that it is impossible to accommodate individual employees sharing the characteristics of the claimant without imposing undue hardship upon the employer."

The first two steps of the test were met. The general purpose in imposing the aerobic standard was clearly connected to the performance of the job. The BC government also met the good faith test for adopting the standard since they had researchers from the University of Victoria study the issue in order to ensure the test would not be discriminatory toward women. However, the government was unable to satisfy the third step of the test. It failed to show that for a firefighter to perform his or her job safely and efficiently, the minimum aerobic standard qualification was necessary. The government was also unable to produce evidence of accommodation to the point of undue hardship. The Supreme Court of Canada ordered the province to reinstate Meiorin and to revise its fitness tests.

The goal of human rights legislation as it applies to the workplace is to protect both employers and employees. Although employees may want to carry out their jobs successfully on the basis of their merits and capabilities, employers must balance this interest with their own responsibility to set standards for safe and efficient job performance. But how far should an employer be expected to go in making accommodations? In the Meiorin case, Justice McLachlin discussed the nature of accommodation at paragraph 64:

Courts and tribunals should be sensitive to the various ways in which individual capabilities can be accommodated. Apart from individual testing to determine whether the person has the aptitude or qualification that is necessary to perform the work, the possibility that there may be different ways to perform the job while still accomplishing the employers' legitimate work-related purpose should be considered in appropriate cases. The skills, capabilities and potential contributions of the individual claimant and others like him or her must be respected as much as possible. Employers, courts and tribunals should be innovative yet practical when considering how this may best be done in particular circumstances.

Not only must accommodations be made in order to prevent discrimination under human rights legislation, but they must also be made to the point of undue hardship. The concept of undue hardship and how it is determined under human rights law is explained within the context of discrimination based on disability.

Discrimination on the Basis of Disability

Section 10 of the Ontario *Human Rights Code* defines "disability" as including a physical disability, a condition of mental impairment or a developmental disability, a learning disability, a mental disorder, or an injury or disability claiming support under the *Workplace Safety and Insurance Act, 1997.* All provincial and territorial human rights documents, such as *The Saskatchewan Human Rights Code*, the Yukon *Human Rights Act*, the New Brunswick *Human Rights Act*, and the Nova Scotia *Human Rights Act*

also include mental and physical disability as protected categories.

In 2002, 66 percent of the complaints filed with the Ontario Human Rights Commission cited discrimination based on disability as the grounds for submission. Such a high level of complaints may mean that Ontario is not doing enough to address the needs of people with disabilities. It could also mean that the number of people with disabilities has risen in Ontario and that there is an increased need to accommodate their needs. During the 2002–2003 fiscal year, the Ontario Human Rights Commission was involved in public consultations on disability in order to consider areas where people with disabilities face discrimination, such as the accessibility of restaurants and of public transit.

The term "equality" does not imply treating everyone in the same manner. In fact, to do so to someone with a disability would, in effect, perpetuate inequality. Rather, it is ensuring

The essence of equality is to be treated according to one's own merit, capabilities and circumstances. True equality requires that differences be accommodated....

—Justice McLachlin in Meiorin case ruling

When you give to United Way, you're helping people with disabilities overcome barriers by providing things like home support, rehabilitation services and skills development. With 200 United Way-funded agencies helping so many in our community, making a difference is easier than you think. Call 416-777-2001 or visit www.unitedwaytoronto.com

WITHOUT YOU, THERE WOULD BE NO WAY

United Way of Greater Toronto

FIGURE 6.9 Accessibility to buildings continues to be a concern for people with disabilities. The United Way champions such causes with ads such as this. What has been done to address the issue of accessibility in your community? What has yet to be done?

equality of access that is crucial to preventing discrimination on the basis of disability. Wheelchair ramps, closed captioning, braille in elevators, sign-language interpretation, and books on tape demonstrate that some progress has been made. Yet there are still many services and premises that remain inaccessible to people with disabilities.

Consider the massive power failure that affected much of the eastern seaboard and all of Ontario in August of 2003. Most elevators shut down in a power outage due to the interruption of electricity. However, some buildings, equipped with emergency generators, continue to supply power to one elevator during a power outage. To uphold equality of access for people with disabilities, all buildings should be required to have this feature. But under the Ontario *Human Rights Code*, the duty to accommodate exists only to the point of undue hardship. So, would the cost of installing and maintaining an emergency generator on one elevator be regarded as undue hardship on the part of building owners?

There are three considerations in making an assessment of undue hardship: (1) cost, (2) outside sources of funding, and (3) health and safety requirements. In considering undue hardship, the Ontario Human Rights Commission, in their "Policy and Guidelines on Disability and the Duty to Accommodate," states that the cost must be quantifiable and so substantial that it would affect the survival of the business or change its essential nature. As well, outside sources of funding, such as government grants and loans, may be available to offset the costs. Finally, the nature of the health or safety risk must be determined through objective evidence and a consideration made under Ontario's health and safety laws as to whether any requirements can be changed or modified.

The case of *Turnbull, et al. v. Famous Players* (2001), 40 C.H.R.R. D/333 (Ont. Bd. Inq.) demonstrates how a victory from the Ontario Human Rights Commission can be short-lived. In 2001, journalist Barbara Turnbull, along with four other complainants, launched a human rights

complaint against Famous Players Inc., alleging discrimination on the basis of disability. Not only did the board learn that several Famous Players theatres in downtown Toronto were inaccessible to patrons in wheelchairs, but testimony in the case revealed further discriminatory practices on the part of theatre workers. Turnbull, who became a quadriplegic in 1983 after being shot during a robbery at the convenience store where she worked, stated that she went to one theatre to watch a specific movie. The theatre was advertised as accessible, but it, in fact, was not. Turnbull was instructed by theatre employees to see a different movie. Another

FIGURE 6.10 The Uptown Theatre in Toronto was one of three Famous Players theatres involved in a 2001 human rights complaint over wheelchair accessibility. What factors are considered when determining whether an employer has suffered undue hardship?

complainant testified that after being admitted to an inaccessible theatre, he was told by the manager to leave before the movie started. Yet another complainant had asked in advance for theatre staff to assist her in navigating some stairs at the end of the movie, but no one showed up to help her after the movie was over.

The Board of Inquiry ruled that Famous Players had to make the theatres fully wheelchair-accessible and awarded damages to each of the complainants for infringement of their rights and mental anguish. Subsequent to the ruling, Famous Players reviewed the financial reality and implications of the board's decision and announced that the company was closing down the three theatres. The Uptown Theatre, one of the prime locations for the Toronto International Film Festival, closed its doors in September 2003 after being sold by Famous Players to a developer for $10 million.

The number of human rights complaints filed on the grounds of disability is increasing. As our society ages, this trend will likely continue unless further measures are taken to eliminate the barriers in achieving equality for people with disabilities.

CONFIRM YOUR UNDERSTANDING

1. Distinguish between direct discrimination and adverse-effect discrimination by providing an example of each.

2. Briefly summarize how a case of discrimination would be proven in court.

3. Explain in your own words the three steps used in the Meiorin case to determine whether a standard is a bona fide occupational requirement.

4. Describe the competing interests between employer and employee where accommodation is concerned.

5. Describe the means by which undue hardship could be established by an employer. Provide examples.

6. Give examples of the types of questions that should be asked of an employer to determine if proper accommodation for employees with disabilities is being made.

CONNECTIONS: Law and Genetics

Privacy vs. Access to Information

Designer babies, human clones, genetically modified foods: these are not simply concepts mined from the imaginations of science-fiction authors or Hollywood scriptwriters. These developments indicate the direction in which science and technology are leading us as a society. We are now faced with the legal and ethical implications of this new reality.

Diagnostic and genetic testing, which profiles donor DNA, uncovers information about a person that may be of interest to more than just the patient and his or her health practitioner. If genetic testing revealed your predisposition to diabetes, Parkinson's disease, or cancer, should a prospective employer or insurance company be allowed access to that information? Armed with that information, an employer may deny you access to the company's health benefits plan or refuse to hire you altogether. Similarly, an insurance company, with access to

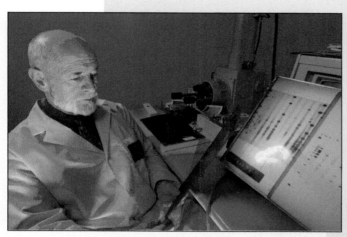

FIGURE 6.11 A scientist analyzes donor DNA. Who should have access to this genetic information?

your private health information, could deny your application for disability and life insurance coverage. Should these businesses have a right to protect themselves from economic liability should you become chronically ill or, worse, die? Or should your right to privacy take precedence?

In a 2001 survey conducted in Canada, 90 percent of respondents felt that strict rules should govern access to genetic information.

Genome Canada is sponsoring research projects to delve into these complex issues relating to genomics (the study of the genes and their function in living organisms). The GE³LS symposium held in Montréal in February 2003 discussed the ethical, environmental, economic, legal, and social issues relating to genomics. Over 200 researchers and policy-makers from the social sciences, humanities, genomics, and law fields discussed such issues as genes and patents, access to genetic information, stem cell research and cloning, and the labelling of genetically modified foods.

While advances in science and technology provide hope for many individuals, the ethical and legal implications of such progress must be considered on balance.

SOURCES: *Genome Canada*. Brunk, Conrad, and Timothy Caulfield. "Summary of Canada's First GE³LS Symposium." 8 Feb. 2003. Genome Canada Articles and Transcripts. Accessed 21 Aug. 2003 <www.genomecanada.ca>;

"Gene Patents, Genetic Diseases, GMO Labelling…First GE³LS Winter Symposium." News Release. 5 Feb. 2003. Accessed 21 Aug. 2003 <www.genomecanada.ca>.

Questions

1. Explain the pros and cons of insurance companies having access to genetic information.
2. What kinds of rules should be put into place regarding access to genetic information?
3. Should companies be allowed to patent genetic coding (e.g., the SARS coronavirus and its genetic material)? Justify your opinion.

Discrimination on the Basis of Age

According to s. 10 (1) of the Ontario *Human Rights Code*, " 'age' means an age that is eighteen years or more, except in subsection 5 (1) where 'age' means an age that is eighteen years or more and less than sixty-five years." Under the *Code*, you cannot be discriminated against on the basis of age in areas such as health care, transportation, education, housing, contracts, and associations or affiliations. In fact, only in the area of employment—the area covered by subsection 5 (1) of the *Code*—are some

discriminatory practices toward individuals over the age of 65 permissible. For example, employees over age 65 cannot launch a complaint with the Human Rights Commission if they are excluded from company health and insurance benefits, are treated differently in terms of remuneration and vacation time, or are forced to retire.

However, statistics show that our society is aging, resulting in an increased need to respond to the conditions of this ever-expanding demographic group. In its efforts to be proactive and to

Nobody has a shelf life.

The only thing that's out of date is the idea that older people don't deserve the same respect and opportunities as everyone else. Let's stop age discrimination. It's old news.

If you think you have encountered age discrimination, call 1-800-387-9080. TTY 1-800-308-5561 or visit www.ohrc.on.ca or www.fifty-plus.net

FIGURE 6.12 This 2003 Ontario Human Rights Commission campaign targeted age discrimination. Are employers guilty of reinforcing stereotypical attitudes about the ability of older workers? Does mandatory retirement negatively assume that older workers cannot contribute? Explain.

isolate what may be an emerging area for human rights concerns, the Ontario Human Rights Commission developed its "Policy on Discrimination Against Older Persons Because of Age" in 2001, which addressed attitudes toward aging and how age discrimination is approached. The commission launched a public awareness campaign, targeting four distinct areas in which older people face barriers: employment, health care, housing, and transportation. The commission cited mandatory retirement as a key area of concern for older Ontarians.

Since the *Code* sets a minimum age of 18, you might think you could argue age discrimination if you are prohibited from buying alcohol or cigarettes at age 18. However, the *Human Rights Code* yields to two pieces of legislation: the *Liquor Licence Act*, which regulates a minimum drinking age of 19, and the *Tobacco Control Act*, which regulates the sale and supply of tobacco to those under the age of 19.

Students often complain that their auto insurance rates are too high and that they are being discriminated against. If your auto insurance rates are higher than those of your 28-year-old cousin, could you launch an age discrimination complaint? Section 22 of the *Human Rights Code* allows for such distinctions to be made by insurers for insurance purposes. Statistical data regarding accident claims is used by insurance companies to assess risks, and this data is then used to justify the setting of rates.

The *Code* also provides an exception under s. 4 that allows individuals who are 16 and 17 and have withdrawn from the control of their parents/legal guardians to have equal treatment with respect to accommodation and contracting for accommodation. They cannot be discriminated against because they are under 18, but they also cannot use the fact of their youth to shield them from their contractual obligations. For example, a 16-year-old might rent accommodation and then try to get out of the lease. In this case, a contract may be held enforceable against the youth as if he or she were 18.

Discrimination on the Basis of Race

The Canadian Census of 2001 indicated that between 1991 and 2001, there were 1.8 million new immigrants to Canada. More than half of these immigrants settled in Ontario. The demographic makeup of our cities is changing. In fact, according to the 2001 Census, 36.8 percent of the 4.6 million people in the Greater Toronto Area were visible minorities. As Ontario is becoming a more racially diverse province, it is ever more pressing for tolerance and respect to be valued in our society. The Honourable R. Roy McMurtry, chief justice of Ontario, voiced these sentiments at the Iroquois Ridge High School Law Symposium in late 2002:

Canadians should take much pride in the fact that so many people of diverse racial, ethnic, cultural, and religious backgrounds have chosen and will choose Canada as their home. This choice often demanded great courage in facing the challenges of a different culture, language, and a sometimes hostile climate. I think, therefore, that more Canadians should reflect more frequently on the respect that is due to those who made that choice and who, in so doing, have helped make ours a truly remarkable country, despite our ongoing challenges.

However, it is most regrettable that this sense of respect is not shared by all our citizens. Recent reports of the Canadian Human Rights Commission have warned of an increase in racism in Canada. It is therefore required that we all continue to commit to strengthening the relatively fragile fabric of our pluralistic society. This is particularly important in times of economic uncertainty when traditionally there are malevolent forces looking for scapegoats and which historically often focus on the newer, more vulnerable members of minorities whose cultures do not appear to fit the mainstream stereotype.

The concern of the individual citizen is vital because we must recognize that all the laws in the world and all the human rights codes count for little if we are not prepared to make a personal commitment to tolerance, to understanding, and above all, to fighting intolerance and bigotry at every opportunity.

The Ontario *Human Rights Code* prohibits discrimination on the basis of race, colour, and ethnic origin in areas such as accommodation, professional associations, and employment. Similar provisions are found in other provincial human rights legislation, such as in the Alberta *Human Rights, Citizenship and Multiculturalism Act*. However, in the area of accommodation, the Ontario *Human Rights Code* specifically protects individuals from harassment. Under s. 2 (2) of the *Code*, "Every person who occupies

accommodation has a right to freedom from harassment by the landlord or agent of the landlord or by an occupant of the same building because of race, ancestry, place of origin, colour, ethnic origin, citizenship, creed, age, marital status, same-sex partnership status, family status, disability or the receipt of public assistance." With respect to professional association, the *Code* allows for exceptions for restricted membership in religious, philanthropic, social, educational, or fraternal organizations if the focus of the group is to serve the interests of that identifiable group. Also, recreational clubs may restrict access or give preferences with respect to membership because of age, sex, marital status, same-sex partnership status, or family status.

While much publicity is often given to sexual harassment, racial harassment is also of concern. The *Code* defines "harassment" in s. 10 as "engaging in a course of vexatious comment or conduct that is known or ought reasonably to be known to be unwelcome." Other provincial governments, such as Manitoba in its *Human Rights Act*, also use this general description of harassment.

As population demographics change, so, too, must efforts to prevent harassment in all areas. Discriminatory behaviour, which may take the form of racial slurs, jokes, ridicule, or insults, is degrading and is considered a form of harassment. When such activities take place in the work environment, they can be especially threatening. In addition to overt behaviour, images or pictures placed in the work environment can be another form of harassment. All of these actions may be considered to have "poisoned" the work environment, thereby creating an atmosphere that is discriminatory.

Another controversial issue is racial profiling. In 2003, the Ontario Human Rights Commission launched a public inquiry and investigation into the effects of racial profiling. The commission has the power to investigate and launch new actions under s. 29 of the Ontario *Human Rights Code*, which states:

It is the function of the Commission…

(f) to inquire into incidents of and conditions leading or tending to lead to tension or conflict based upon identification by a prohibited ground of discrimination and take appropriate action to eliminate the source of tension or conflict;

(g) to initiate investigations into problems based upon identification by a prohibited ground of discrimination that may arise in a community, and encourage and co-ordinate plans, programs and activities to reduce or prevent such problems….

The commission defines racial profiling as "any action undertaken for reasons of safety, security or public protection, that relies on stereotypes about race, colour, ethnicity, ancestry, religion, or place of origin, or a combination of these, rather than on reasonable suspicion, to single out an individual for greater scrutiny or different treatment." It further states that racial profiling "assumes that the personal characteristics of an individual are indicative of his or her actions or of a tendency to be engaged in illegal activity." For example, if a police officer pulled over a Black driver because the tail lights of his or her vehicle were not working but then demanded to search the vehicle for drugs for no particular reason, the conduct of that police officer could be questioned and the issue of racial profiling might be raised.

The issue of racial profiling was raised as a defence in the case of *R. v. Brown*, (2003-04-16) ONCA Docket C37818, in which a Toronto Raptors basketball player, Decovan ("Dee") Brown, was stopped by police and subsequently arrested and charged with impaired driving contrary to s. 253(b) of the *Criminal Code*. The defence counsel raised the issue of racial profiling and argued that stopping Brown was an arbitrary detention. The trial judge did not entertain the defence of racial profiling and convicted Brown. As part of his sentencing, the trial judge suggested that Brown should apologize to the officer. On appeal, Justice Morden concluded that there was a reasonable apprehension of bias. He wrote at paragraph 104: "The suggestion of an apology, an act that is not part of the proper judicial function, was consistent with the judge's expression of distaste and reinforces the appearance of the primacy of his concerns for the effect of the application on the officer. It can only be seen as being demeaning to the respondent who had given evidence that, if accepted, supported a finding of racial profiling."

While the case hung mainly on the issue of judicial bias, the fact remains that the issue of racial profiling was acknowledged in a higher-level Court of Appeal in Ontario. It will be left to future cases to determine whether a defence of racial profiling can be argued successfully in the courts.

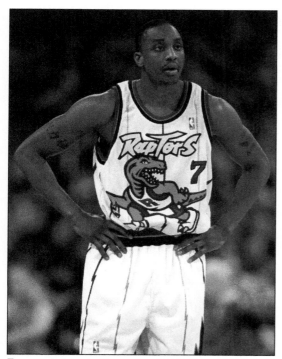

FIGURE 6.13 In November 1999, Toronto Raptors basketball player Dee Brown was arrested for impaired driving. The defence alleged that he was arbitrarily stopped because of racial profiling. How is racial profiling discriminatory?

ASKING KEY QUESTIONS

Racial Profiling

In February 2003, the Ontario Human Rights Commission launched a province-wide inquiry into the effects of racial profiling. The particular emphasis of the investigation was to study the effects of racial profiling on individuals, families, and communities. Individuals were asked to submit first-hand accounts of their experiences. In a news release from the Canadian Race Relations Foundation (CRRF), Lincoln Alexander, chair of the CRRF, applauded the move of the Ontario Human Rights Commission "as it affects victims in a human rights context." He further commented, "I strongly encourage all people who have been affected by racial profiling to have their say at this inquiry. It is another step towards assessing its impact and effectively addressing the issue."

Mr. Alexander had been present at a meeting of politicians and community leaders in November 2002, during which issues of race and racial profiling were discussed. A consensus was reached at the November meeting for a

"review of zero tolerance for racism, racial discrimination and 'racially biased policing,' with an emphasis on racial profiling and the importance of understanding it." Three months later, the issues were discussed again at a closed-door meeting in which Alexander indicated that he was encouraged by the progress being made in addressing race relations and policing. "On the question of racial profiling, while we need to be concerned with the morale of police officers, most of whom do their jobs ethically, honorably and professionally, we have to remain concerned with the community's reality, especially youth."

Dr. Karen Mock, Executive Director of the CRRF, voiced her concerns. "We should not lose sight of the real-life incidents of racial profiling experienced by a disproportionate number of members of the community." She further added, "The first step towards a solution is to validate these experiences and not to deny the existence of racial profiling and systemic racism."

Source: Canadian Race Relations Foundation News Releases. February 2003.

Form Your Questions

Now that you have read the CRRF's viewpoint on racial profiling, particularly as it relates to law enforcement, develop three possible questions that you would ask the speakers to further clarify the issue. Share your questions with the rest of the class and discuss possible answers or solutions.

Enforcement Under Human Rights Legislation

There are several options available for enforcement under provincial and territorial human rights legislation. According to the Ontario *Human Rights Code*, an individual must file a complaint within six months of the last incident involving the alleged discrimination. The same limitation period of six months is mandated

under the Yukon *Human Rights Act*. The limitation period for filing a complaint may vary from jurisdiction to jurisdiction. For example, in Alberta, the complaint must be filed within 12 months of the alleged violation under that province's *Human Rights, Citizenship and Multiculturalism Act*. Similarly, under the New Brunswick *Human Rights Act*, the complaint must be filed within one year of the incident. The

Saskatchewan *Human Rights Code* allows complainants to file within two years of the alleged discrimination.

In Ontario, the Ontario Human Rights Commission has full discretion to deal with a complaint under s. 34 of the *Code*. It may choose not to do so if the complaint is considered to be frivolous or vexatious, or not within the jurisdiction of the commission. Also, other avenues may be available in advance of commission involvement, such as grievance procedures in labour law. **Mediation** services were introduced to the Ontario Human Rights Commission in 1997. The mediation process is generally used as the first mechanism for resolving a complaint. According to figures from the Ontario Human Rights Commission, between 65 and 70 percent of complaints, on average, are settled successfully when mediation is attempted as a mechanism for dispute resolution. If mediation is not successful, an investigation may take place.

In Alberta, the Human Rights and Citizenship Commission also uses a conciliation process as a mechanism for dispute resolution. **Conciliation** is a voluntary method of settling disputes where a neutral third party, usually a representative of the human rights commission, helps the parties to identify and discuss the issues, and then to resolve the conflict. A settlement may take place during the conciliation stage. Conciliation can also occur in Ontario.

Cases in Ontario not resolved by mediation or conciliation may then be referred to the commission to determine if there is sufficient evidence of discrimination. Should sufficient evidence be found, the commission has the power to refer the complaint to a Board of Inquiry for a hearing. (In Alberta, the case would be referred to a body called a Human Rights Panel, while the Yukon would use a Human Rights Board of Adjudication.) The board must determine whether there was a violation of a right under the Ontario *Human Rights Code* and then decide on the appropriate remedy.

In many circumstances, the remedy will be an order requiring that the alleged discriminator comply with the *Code* and refrain from the discriminatory practice. The remedy could be very specific, such as requiring an employer to reinstate an employee. Other possible remedies include ordering an organization to develop harassment or discrimination policies, or requiring an employer to provide human rights training for employees. Compensation could also be ordered. Under the Ontario *Human Rights Code*, the maximum monetary award is $10 000 for mental anguish. In other jurisdictions, remedies may vary. For example, the Nova Scotia Human Rights Commission indicates that settlements in human rights discrimination cases may include any or all of the following remedies: "an apology; a positive reference letter; an agreement to change discriminatory policies and practices; compensation for lost wages; compensation for out-of-pocket expenses, such as medical bills; and compensation for humiliation and loss of dignity."

Ultimately, if a complainant is not satisfied with the decision, there is a right to appeal from the Board of Inquiry to a Divisional Court and then to the Supreme Court of Ontario. Other provincial and territorial jurisdictions also provide the option of appealing to the courts.

CONFIRM YOUR UNDERSTANDING

1. Identify four areas in which barriers to equality may be evident for older people. Provide examples of age discrimination that could occur in each area.

2. If the mandatory retirement age of 65 were to be extended or made more flexible, explain the positive or negative effects that this change would have on younger workers entering the workforce.

CONFIRM YOUR UNDERSTANDING (continued)

3. Explain the exceptions under the Ontario *Human Rights Code* to the minimum age requirement of 18 for age discrimination.

4. What should employers do to prevent racial harassment in the workplace?

5. Explain your understanding of the term "racial profiling" and how it amounts to discrimination on the basis of race.

6. What implications do you think the *R. v. Brown* case might have for law enforcement? Explain.

7. Mediation is often the first conflict resolution method used in human rights complaints. Why do you think this is the case?

8. a) Explain the types of remedies available under provincial and territorial human rights legislation.

    b) Do you think there should be a maximum award for mental anguish? Discuss.

In Closing

As we become more respectful of individual differences and can recognize actions and behaviours that are discriminatory, the scope and grounds for human rights protection may be broadened. For example, if the economic gap continues to widen between those that have income and resources in our society and those that live below the poverty line, legislators may be compelled to include poverty as grounds for discrimination under human rights codes. As courts and human rights tribunals strive for clarity in determining what constitutes discrimination, we at least have the comfort of knowing that great effort is being made to safeguard human rights in Canada.

Equality is valued in our struggle to achieve a fair and just society. It is even more important as Canada's population demographics continue to change. The new cultural reality shows that as immigration trends continue, we are increasingly becoming a racially diverse society, but with this comes the potential for an increase in complaints of discrimination based on race. Human rights commissions might face increased demands to investigate incidents of discrimination and must

therefore be given the resources and tools to effectively deal with complaints. In addition, as demographics indicate, the Canadian population is aging. It is therefore possible that human rights commissions will face an increased number of complaints of discrimination on the basis of age.

Not only will our human rights codes be called upon to reflect our social realities, but, as you will see in subsequent chapters, our laws will also be challenged to broaden the concept of equality rights under the *Canadian Charter of Rights and Freedoms*. We have the legal framework of both provincial and territorial human rights legislation and the *Charter* to safeguard rights in Canada. A continual commitment on the part of individuals to value diversity is crucial.

Public education is essential to highlight what constitutes discrimination and to teach individuals about tolerance and respect for individual differences. We know that discrimination is not tolerated under our human rights laws in Canada. However, we must remember that it is ultimately through our actions that we demonstrate our commitment to upholding human rights legislation.

CHAPTER ACTIVITIES

Extend Your Legal Knowledge

1. Explain the difference among rights protection afforded under common law, the *Bill of Rights*, and the *Charter of Rights and Freedoms*.

2. Would a municipal bylaw that prohibits certain groups from handing out their literature door to door be acceptable today? Explain.

3. Distinguish between the jurisdictions of the *Canadian Human Rights Act* and provincial human rights legislation.

4. Explain the "equal pay for equal work" provisions under the *Canadian Human Rights Act.*

5. Explain how a bona fide occupational requirement might be used to justify what would otherwise be considered discrimination.

Think About the Law

6. Analyze the statistical data in the charts that follow, and then answer the questions on page 194.

New Complaints Filed by Social Area and Grounds Cited
Total Number of Complaints Filed = 1776

	Accommodation	Contracts	Employment	Services	Vocational Associations	Total Grounds	Percent of Ground Cited	Percent of Total Complaints Filed
Age	6		105	13	1	**125**	3.74	7.04
Ancestry	5		98	23		**126**	3.77	7.09
Association	6		6	6	2	**20**	0.60	1.13
Breach of Settlement			6			**6**	0.18	0.34
Citizenship			26			**26**	0.78	1.46
Creed	4	1	49	25	2	**81**	2.42	4.56
Disability	29	1	745	390	7	**1172**	35.05	65.99
Ethnic Origin	7	1	177	32		**217**	6.49	12.22
Family Status	32		61	8	1	**102**	3.05	5.74
Marital Status	30		26	4		**60**	1.79	3.38
Place of Origin	5	1	153	29		**188**	5.62	10.59
Public Assistance	38			2		**40**	1.20	2.25
Race & Colour	10		337	53		**400**	11.96	22.52
Record of Offences			2			**2**	0.06	0.11
Reprisal	2	1	161	6		**170**	5.08	9.57
Sex & Pregnancy	32		383	19	1	**435**	13.01	24.49
Sexual Harassment	1		132	6	1	**140**	4.19	7.88
Sexual Orientation			28	6		**34**	1.02	1.91
Sum of Categories	**207**	**5**	**2495**	**622**	**15**	**3344**	**100%**	**188.29**
Total for All Complaints per Social Area	82	2	1226	456	10	**1776**		
Percentage of All Complaints	4.62	0.11	69.03	25.68	0.56	**100.0**		

Note: Because complaints can involve multiple grounds, the sum by grounds exceeds the total for all complaints filed, and the corresponding percentages of total complaints exceed 100%.

SOURCE: Ontario Human Rights Commission. *Annual Report 2002–2003,* Table 1, p. 57.

Complaints Closed by Disposition and Grounds
Total Number of Complaints Closed = 1,954

	Dismissed	Failed to Provide Evidence	Not Dealt With (s. 34)	Referred to Human Rights Tribunal	Resolved	Settled	Withdrawn	Total	Percentage
Age	16		19	3	24	66	16	**144**	3.86
Ancestry	37	1	20	6	12	51	9	**136**	3.65
Association	6	1	4		10	11	2	**34**	0.91
Breach of Settlement	1		2		1		1	**5**	0.13
Citizenship	2					1	2	**5**	0.13
Creed	15	2	8	2	12	40	12	**91**	2.44
Disability	125	27	113	17	185	550	89	**1106**	29.68
Ethnic Origin	60	6	39	8	30	100	23	**266**	7.14
Family Status	8	3	10	4	10	33	15	**83**	2.23
Marital Status	3	2	8	1	11	18	10	**53**	1.42
Place of Origin	47	3	23	4	21	63	21	**182**	4.88
Public Assistance	4		2	3	3	6	2	**20**	0.54
Race & Colour	119	13	82	22	71	244	42	**593**	15.92
Record of Offences			3		1	2		**6**	0.16
Reprisal	18	2	18	12	40	102	18	**210**	5.64
Sex & Pregnancy	59	8	36	38	102	277	43	**563**	15.11
Sexual Harassment	14	2	8	11	25	92	11	**163**	4.37
Sexual Orientation	18	1	6	3	9	22	7	**66**	1.77
Sum of Categories	**552**	**71**	**401**	**134**	**567**	**1678**	**323**	**3726**	**100.0**
Total for All Complaints	271	40	185	58	324	909	167	**1954**	
Percentage of All Complaints	13.87	2.05	9.47	2.97	16.58	46.52	8.55	**100.0**	

Note: Because complaints can involve multiple grounds, the sum by grounds exceeds the total for all complaints filed.

SOURCE: Ontario Human Rights Commission. *Annual Report 2002–2003*, Table 3, p. 58.

a) What questions would you ask about the statistics shown before you draw any conclusions about their reliability?

b) What conclusions can you draw from the data available in the chart?

c) Explain how this information would be useful to the Ontario Human Rights Commission.

d) Explain how this information would be useful to advocacy groups protecting rights (e.g., the Canadian Race Relations Foundation or an advocacy group for people with disabilities).

7. Should human rights legislation be amended to include poverty as a prohibited ground of discrimination? Justify your opinion.

8. Does equality mean treating individuals in exactly the same way? Explain using examples from the text and other sources to support your opinion.

9. a) Prepare an argument in support of the claim that we are using human rights codes to justify making too many accommodations and that the test of undue hardship is too extreme. Are we overly accommodating (e.g., legislating scribes for all testing, interpreters for people with hearing impairments, and structural changes to the physical layout of buildings)?

   b) Prepare a counter-argument that indicates we have not gone far enough in making accommodations.

Communicate About the Law

10. Why is it important to have laws that prevent discrimination? Write a one-page justification for having human rights legislation in Canada.

11. In a news release issued by the Ontario Human Rights Commission in May 2003, Keith Norton, Chief Commissioner of the Ontario Human Rights Commission, praised a government bill regarding retirement age: "Older workers have the right to be treated as individuals, assessed on the basis of actual skills and abilities and given the same opportunities and benefits as everyone else." Research and prepare a debate on the following statement: "The Ontario *Human Rights Code* should be amended to remove the upper age limit of 65." Be certain to prepare arguments both for and against this proposed legislative change to the Ontario *Human Rights Code*.

12. Jane Jacobs, in *The Nature of Economies*, suggests that societies who practise discrimination actually stifle creativity and ultimately affect the entire economic well-being of the country.

Now, suppose portions of a population are prevented from exercising economic creativity and initiative because of discrimination attached to gender, race, caste, religion, social class, ideology, or whatever. This means that the kinds of work those people do are automatically sterilized, so to speak—they can't be generalities from which new differentiations emerge. If categories of people doing specific kinds of work can't use those kinds of work as bases for development, it's unlikely anyone else in that economy will....People don't need to be geniuses or even extraordinarily talented to develop their work. The requirements are initiative and resourcefulness—qualities abundant in the human race when they aren't discouraged or suppressed. (2001)

Comment on the extent to which you agree or disagree with Jacobs's viewpoint. Provide evidence to support your opinion (e.g., research countries that oppress individuals, such as women and people with disabilities, and comment on the state of the economy in these countries).

13. Write a dissenting opinion for the case of *Attorney General of Canada v. Lavell* (see pp. 173–174). Elaborate on the meaning of "equality rights" from the perspective of your current understanding. (Refer to s. 15 of the *Canadian Charter of Rights and Freedoms* on p. 515 of the Appendix for a broader definition of equality. You might also review "Creating case briefs" on p. 13 of the Legal Handbook, focusing in particular on a dissent in a case decision.)

LEGAL HANDBOOK p. 13

Apply the Law

14. Public education is key to promoting tolerance and respect. In order to promote and defend human rights in Ontario, select a particular area of discrimination and launch a public awareness campaign. Prepare a pamphlet summarizing the law on discrimination, key areas of concern, and ways that individuals can be non-discriminatory in their actions. Consult the Ontario *Human Rights Code*. Refer to the statistical chart on page 193, and use annual reports or fact sheets available from the Ontario Human Rights Commission for your research.

15. In the Canadian Human Rights Tribunal decision of *Ede v. (Canada) Canadian Armed Forces*, [1990] 11 C.H.R.R. D/439, James Ede filed a complaint against the Armed Forces alleging discrimination on the grounds of disability. He met all the qualifications for hiring except that he was shorter than the minimum height standard required for the Armed Forces. James Ede was 143 cm tall while the army had a minimum height requirement of 152 cm. The army successfully argued that the minimum size requirement was a bona fide occupational qualification.

Contrast this ruling with the Meiorin case on pages 181–182. Review the three-step test for a bona fide occupational requirement and the issue of accommodation in the Meiorin case. Prepare an argument for or against allowing the army's minimum height requirement as a bona fide occupational requirement.

16. Often human rights interests are balanced with economic realities. Do you agree with the Board of Inquiry's decision in the *Turnbull et al. v. Famous Players Inc.* case (see pp. 184–185)? Explain.

17. Harassment in the workplace is a serious human rights violation. What happens if your employment situation involves a poisoned work environment?

Michael McKinnon, a person of Aboriginal ancestry, was employed as a correctional officer with the Metro East Detention Centre in Toronto. He filed two separate complaints of discrimination: the first in 1988 and the second in 1990. The Board of Inquiry in *McKinnon v. Ontario* (Ministry of Correctional Services) (No. 3) (1998), 32 C.H.R.R. D/1 agreed that McKinnon had suffered from racial discrimination, harassment, and reprisals, and that his workplace was a poisoned environment. The board ordered the Ministry of Correctional Services to establish a human rights program. Even though the program was delivered to the employees in 1999, the discrimination continued. When McKinnon complained again, the board reviewed the evidence and determined that the ministry had failed to clean up the "racially poisoned workplace." In addition to appointing external investigators to monitor discrimination and complaints, the board ordered the Ministry of Correctional Services to have mandatory training for its senior management.

Assume that you have been hired to design the race and harassment training program for the senior administration. You understand that there are great difficulties in promoting racial tolerance in a workplace that has been deemed a poisoned environment. What types of education and programs would you include as part of the training (e.g., the design and implementation of a policy on harassment)?

BIBLIOGRAPHY

Age Discrimination: Your Rights & Responsibilities. Toronto: Ontario Human Rights Commission, 2003.

Alberta Human Rights and Citizenship Commission. Accessed Nov. 2003 <www.albertahumanrights.ab.ca>.

Brunk, Conrad, and Timothy Caulfield. "Summary of Canada's First GE³LS Symposium." 8 February 2003. Genome Canada Articles and Transcripts. Accessed 21 August 2003 <www.genomecanada.ca>.

Canadian Civil Liberties Association. Accessed Nov. 2003 <www.ccla.org>.

The *Canadian Human Rights Act* [R.S. 1985 c. H-6]. *Canadian Legal Information Institute.* Accessed Nov. 2003 <www.canlii.org/ca/sta/h-6>.

Canadian Human Rights Commission. Accessed Nov. 2003 <www.chrc-ccdp.ca>.

———."Time for Action—Special Report to Parliament on Pay Equity." Executive Summary. Accessed 26 Aug. 2003 <www.chrc-ccdp.ca/pe-ps/SRPE_S_RSPS.asp?l=e>.

Canadian Human Rights Tribunal. Accessed Nov. 2003 <www.chrt-tcdp.gc.ca>.

Canadian Legal Information Institute. Accessed Nov. 2003 <www.canlii.org>.

Canadian Race Relations Foundation. Accessed Aug. 2003 <www.crr.ca>

———. "The Canadian Race Relations Foundation Commends the OHRC on Initiative to Hear Racial Profiling Incidents." News Release. 17 Feb. 2003. Accessed Aug. 2003 <www.crr.ca/EN/MediaCentre/NewsReleases/eMedCen_NewsRel20030217.htm>

———. "CRRF Concerned with Continued Denial of Racial Profiling." News Release. 21 Feb. 2003. Accessed 26 Aug. 2003 <www.crr.ca>

———. "Honourable Lincoln Alexander Encouraged By Summit Outcome—Much Progress Achieved in Addressing Race Relations and Policing." News Release. 25 Feb. 2003. Accessed 26 Aug. 2003 <www.crr.ca/EN/MediaCentre/NewsReleases/eMedCen_NewsRel20030225.htm>

———. "Summit on Policing, Race Relations and Racial Profiling: Opening Remarks by Lincoln Alexander." 25 Feb. 2003 <www.crr.ca>

The Commission: What You Need to Know. Toronto: Ontario Human Rights Commission, 2000.

"Gene Patents, Genetic Diseases, GMO Labelling… First GE³LS Winter Symposium." *Genome Canada.* News Release. 5 Feb. 2003. Accessed 21 Aug. 2003 <www.genomecanada.ca>.

Hogg, Peter W. *Constitutional Law of Canada.* Toronto: The Carswell Company Limited, 1985.

Jacobs, Jane. *Nature of Economies.* Toronto: Vintage Canada, 2001.

Magnet, Joseph Eliot. *Constitutional Law of Canada: Cases, Notes, and Materials.* Toronto: The Carswell Company Limited, 1983.

Manitoba Human Rights Commission. Accessed Nov. 2003 <www.gov.mb.ca/hrc/>.

McMurtry, R. Roy. Iroquois Ridge High School Law Symposium. *Ontario Justice Education Network.* Accessed Nov. 2003 <www.ontariocourts.on.ca/ojen/index.htm>.

New Brunswick Human Rights Commission. Accessed Nov. 2003 <www.gnb.ca/hrc-cdp/e/>.

Nova Scotia Human Rights Act. Accessed Nov. 2003 <www.gov.ns.ca/legi/legc/statutes/humanrt.htm>.

Nova Scotia Human Rights Commission. Accessed Nov. 2003 <www.gov.ns.ca/humanrights/>.

Ontario Courts. Accessed 26 Aug. 2003 <www.ontariocourts.on.ca>.

Ontario Human Rights Code [R.S.O. 1990, c. H.19]. Accessed Nov. 2003 <http://192.75.156.68/DBLaws/Statutes/English/90h19_e.htm>.

Ontario Human Rights Commission. Accessed Nov. 2003 <www.ohrc.on.ca>.

———."Policy and Guidelines on Disability and the Duty to Accommodate. Fact Sheet #4: How far does the duty to accommodate go?" Accessed 20 Aug. 2003 <www.ohrc.on.ca/english/publications/disability-policy-policy-fact4.shtml>.

Ontario Human Rights Commission Annual Report 2002–2003. Toronto: Ontario Human Rights Commission, 2003.

Racial Harassment: Your Rights and Responsibilities. Toronto: Ontario Human Rights Commission, 2001.

Saskatchewan Human Rights Commission. Accessed Nov. 2003 <www.gov.sk.ca/shrc/>.

Yukon Human Rights Commission. Accessed Nov. 2003 <www.yhrc.yk.ca/>.

THE CANADIAN *CHARTER*, THE LEGISLATURE, AND THE JUDICIARY

LEARNING EXPECTATIONS

After reading this chapter, you will be able to:

- identify how *Charter* rights are accompanied by corresponding responsibilities or obligations

- explain how citizens can exercise their rights under the *Charter* and how *Charter* rights are enforced

- understand how rights may be limited or overruled by certain sections of the *Charter*

- define legal rights, fundamental freedoms, and democratic, language, equality, and mobility rights under the *Charter*

- evaluate the role of the courts and tribunals in interpreting *Charter* rights

FIGURE 7.1 The *Canadian Charter of Rights and Freedoms* forms an essential part of Canada's Constitution. What rights and freedoms are protected? What is the role of the courts in interpreting *Charter* rights, and how does this role compare with that of the legislature?

The Charter is a uniquely Canadian document and a product of our distinctive history. It is also the product, not just of politicians, but of ordinary Canadians who worked tirelessly to ensure that it would reflect their vision of Canada—a Canada that recognizes respectful tolerance of one another, the interests of individuals as well as groups, and the balance between individual rights and the well-being of the country as a whole.

—The Right Honourable Chief Justice of Canada Beverley McLachlin

■ I N T R O D U C T I O N ■

What if a law were passed allowing the government to censor all music sold in stores across Canada and a CD by a popular performer were pulled from the shelves? Not only might the buying public strongly protest, but the performer might also be outraged and launch a legal challenge, claiming a violation of freedom of expression. This chapter will focus on the use of the *Canadian Charter of Rights and Freedoms* as a mechanism for rights protection in Canada, specifically as it applies to the relationship between individuals and the government. It will also examine the guarantees of rights and freedoms available under the *Charter* and explore how *Charter* rights are enforced.

In analyzing cases in which an alleged violation of *Charter* rights has been at issue, you will discover how courts have been challenged to interpret the meaning of the various *Charter* provisions. You will find out that some decisions have been the subject of great public attention because rights were interpreted broadly, while other decisions have been scrutinized because rights have been limited. When the courts use their power of unbiased judicial review to strike down laws that violate the *Charter*, the courts, in effect, have law-making ability. Some would argue, however, that this power should rest solely in the hands of our democratically elected representatives in the legislature.

Applying the *Charter*

When enacted in 1982, the *Canadian Charter of Rights and Freedoms* entrenched in the Constitution the rights and freedoms of all Canadians. For over 20 years, the *Charter* has influenced law in Canada and allowed our Constitution to grow like a living tree. It is through the interpretations placed on these constitutionally protected rights that we have provided an opportunity for our Constitution to evolve.

The *Charter* guarantees four fundamental freedoms: freedom of religion, freedom of expression, freedom of peaceful assembly, and freedom of association. It also expressly protects democratic rights, mobility rights, legal rights, equality rights, language rights, and Aboriginal

Section 1:	Guarantee of Rights and Freedoms
Section 2:	Fundamental Freedoms
Sections 3–5:	Democratic Rights
Section 6:	Mobility Rights
Sections 7–14:	Legal Rights
Section 15:	Equality Rights
Sections 16–22:	Official Languages of Canada
Section 23:	Minority Language Education Rights
Section 24:	Enforcement
Sections 25–31:	General (including Aboriginal Rights and Multicultural Heritage)
Sections 32–33:	Application of *Charter*

FIGURE 7.2   These are the main sections in the *Canadian Charter of Rights and Freedoms*. A complete copy of the *Charter* is provided on page 514 of the Appendix.

and multicultural heritage rights. (See Chapter 8 for more detail on Aboriginal and multicultural heritage rights.)

Under the *Charter*, some rights apply to everyone, such as those stated under Fundamental Freedoms. Others, however, apply only to citizens of Canada, such as democratic and mobility rights. But through an analysis of s. 1 of the *Charter*—the reasonable limits clause—you will discover that there are limitations on your fundamental guarantees of rights and freedoms. Further, by studying s. 33 of the *Charter*—the notwithstanding clause—you will see that, in some cases, governments may pass laws that override certain rights and freedoms in the *Charter*.

Limitations of Fundamental Freedoms and Rights

Can you imagine what our society would be like if you were allowed to say anything that you wanted? In Canada, you are prevented from

freely expressing yourself in some circumstances because your actions would not be tolerated or justified in our free and democratic society. For example, you are not allowed to **defame** someone (that is, make a false or malicious statement that injures a person's reputation), spread hate messages across the Internet, or make or distribute depictions of children in pornographic settings. If you were free to express your views and opinions on anything at all and in any manner in which you saw fit, it could infringe on the rights of others. With the guarantee of rights comes a corresponding obligation that you will not use these rights to harm others in any way. The irony of guaranteeing rights and freedoms in our society is that we sometimes have to restrict these same rights and freedoms.

Section 1 of the *Charter* specifically mandates that individual rights can be subject to limitations. In addition, s. 33 of the *Charter* gives government the power to pass laws that might be considered totally inconsistent with the rights in the *Charter* and, in effect, override them.

Section 1

Section 1 of the *Charter* is referred to as the reasonable limits clause and reads as follows: "The *Canadian Charter of Rights and Freedoms* guarantees the rights and freedoms set out in it subject only to such reasonable limits prescribed by law as can be demonstrably justified in a free and democratic society."

When the *Charter* was first enacted, the terms "reasonable" and "demonstrably justified" were not defined in the legislation. Rather, it was left up to the courts to interpret their meanings. Not surprisingly, there has been substantial litigation in this area of the law.

In the case of *R. v. Oakes*, [1986] 1 S.C.R. 103, the judges of the Supreme Court of Canada laid down a test for whether an action, which would otherwise be considered a violation of rights, could be justified under s. 1, in effect limiting individual rights. David Oakes was charged with possession of a narcotic for the purpose of trafficking. Once the Crown proved that the accused was in possession of the narcotic, the responsibility shifted to Oakes to prove that he did not have the narcotic for the purpose of trafficking. Oakes argued that this shift of responsibility, or **reverse onus provision**, violated his right to be presumed innocent until proven guilty. The Supreme Court of Canada held that s. 8 of the *Narcotic Control Act* (now called the *Controlled Drugs and Substances Act*) was unconstitutional and violated the rights of the accused.

The first criterion of the two-part test laid down by the Supreme Court in the Oakes case (which is often referred to as the Oakes test) is whether a limit on rights and freedoms can be justified. The courts must decide if the provision of the law in question is "sufficiently important to warrant overriding a constitutionally protected right or freedom." In determining whether the objective is of sufficient importance, the court will ask if it relates to "societal concerns which are pressing and substantial in a free and democratic society." Once the objective of the legislation meets the criterion of sufficient importance (i.e., it is pressing and substantial), the court must then determine if the limitations on an individual's rights satisfy a **proportionality test**, which is a weighing of the interests of society against those of individuals and groups in determining whether to limit rights. The proportionality test is the second criterion laid down by the Supreme Court in the Oakes case and consists of three parts, as follows:

1. Is there a rational connection between the limitation of rights and the objective of the legislation?
2. Does the limitation impair rights or freedoms as little as possible?
3. Are the effects of the limitation proportional to the objective?

In the Oakes case, the Supreme Court characterized Parliament's concern with reducing trafficking as substantial and pressing, and cited societal concern with drug trafficking as a sufficient justification for overriding constitutionally protected rights. However, the court held that the reverse onus provision of the law did not meet the rational connection component of the proportionality test. It held that there was no "rational connection between the basic fact of possession and the presumed fact of possession for the purpose of trafficking." The court held that "it would be irrational to infer that a person had an intent to traffic on the basis of his or her possession of a very small quantity of narcotics."

In any *Charter* case, the burden is on the individual to first establish that a *Charter* right or freedom has been violated. The burden then shifts to the government to show that the limit is justified. The Oakes test continues to be the means by which the validity of limiting a person's rights or freedoms is determined, as you will see in the Landmark Case decision on page 207. The **rational connection** component of the proportionality test suggests that the connection must not be unfair or arbitrary. The **minimal impairment** component provides that laws and government action will interfere with rights and freedoms as little as possible. The final proportionality component requires the court to find a balance between the objective of the legislation and limiting rights.

The Honourable R. Roy McMurtry, chief justice of Ontario, referred to this proportionality test in comments regarding the potential for challenges to Canada's anti-terrorism legislation passed after the September 11, 2001, attacks on the World Trade Center:

In particular, the objective of the legislation must be of sufficient importance to warrant overriding a constitutionally protected right or freedom. The objective must be "pressing and substantial." The task of the legislature and perhaps the courts will be to balance the strength of the concern around terrorism against the reasonableness and rationality of the means selected to combat it. This test of proportionality and balance includes a consideration of whether there is a rational connection between the threat and the response, whether the response impairs constitutional freedoms as little as possible, and whether there is a balance between the deleterious effects of the measures and their salutary effects. (McMurtry 2001)

Section 33

In order to have all provinces sign the Constitution in 1982, a compromise section was added to the *Charter* to enable the federal and provincial governments to override some of the rights and freedoms in the *Charter*. Section 33 (1), often referred to as an override clause or a notwithstanding clause, enables governments to limit the application of the *Charter*. It reads as follows: "Parliament or the legislature of a province may expressly declare in an Act of Parliament or of the legislature, as the case may be, that the Act or a provision thereof shall operate notwithstanding a provision included in section 2 or sections 7 to 15 of this *Charter*."

Invoking the notwithstanding clause allows the federal and provincial governments to pass legislation that is inconsistent with the rights and freedoms set out in s. 2 (Fundamental Freedoms) and ss. 7 to 15 (Legal and Equality Rights) of the *Charter*. As a safeguard, however, the legislation must be reviewed every five years. The drafters of the notwithstanding clause could not have predicted, however, that Québec would pass all of its legislation notwithstanding the *Charter*. Although Québec did not sign the *Constitution Act, 1982*, the Constitution still came into force and Québec was, therefore, bound by its terms. Therefore, the *Charter*, as part of the Constitution, still applied.

A significant case illustrating the application of the notwithstanding clause is *Ford v. Québec (Attorney General)*, [1988] 2 S.C.R. 712 where s. 33 of the *Charter* was used in Québec to validate a French-language-only sign law. Essentially, Québec's Bill 101 had required that all public signs were to be only in the French language. This law was challenged in the Supreme Court and held to be unconstitutional. Valerie Ford was one of five business owners who challenged the validity of Québec's *Charter of the French Language* requiring public signs and posters and commercial advertising to be only in the French language. The Québec government subsequently responded by passing Bill C-178, which allowed the French-language sign laws to exist and not to contravene the *Canadian Charter of Rights and Freedoms*.

The Saskatchewan government also used s. 33 in an effort to ensure the validity of back-to-work legislation in 1986. The government was concerned about the potential for a long, protracted strike involving dairy workers, and so it passed legislation ordering the workers to return to their jobs. The government of Alberta threatened to use the nothwithstanding clause when the Alberta Marriage Act was amended in 2000 to provide a definition of marriage as a contract between a man and a woman, thereby preventing legally recognizing same-sex marriages.

FIGURE 7.3   In Québec, signage for commercial establishments must be in the French language. How was the notwithstanding clause used in Québec to legislate French-language-only signs?

CONFIRM YOUR UNDERSTANDING

1. In your own words, summarize the meaning of s. 1 of the *Charter*.

2. How do the courts determine if the objective of legislation is of sufficient importance to warrant overriding a constitutionally protected right or freedom?

3. Explain the difference between the rational connection component and the minimal impairment component of the proportionality test.

4. Explain what is meant by the notwithstanding clause in the *Charter*.

5. In 2003, there were substantial debates across Canada with respect to the issue of same-sex marriages. Some provinces insisted that if the federal government passed a law allowing the definition of marriage to include same-sex partners, then they would use the notwithstanding clause to limit its application. If a province were to pass such a law, how often would it have to be reviewed? What is the purpose of such a review?

Charter Violations

Individuals may initiate a *Charter* challenge if laws or government action are considered to violate their rights. Not only can the *Charter* be used to declare a law unconstitutional, but it can also be used to provide a remedy should rights and freedoms be violated.

Challenges Under the Charter

If a law violates a *Charter* right and cannot be justified under the reasonable limits clause, the court may declare the law unconstitutional. Section 52 (1) of the Constitution is called the supremacy clause, and it reads as follows: "The Constitution of Canada is the supreme law of Canada, and any law that is inconsistent with the provisions of the Constitution is, to the extent of the inconsistency, of no force or effect."

When a court declares a law unconstitutional, it has several options. It can strike down an entire law or cut the particular provision that is at issue. Further, the court can use a process of **reading down** the legislation. If the law in question has been interpreted too broadly, the court will narrow the interpretation given to the section. For example, in the case of *R. v. Butler*, [1992] 1 S.C.R. 452, which is outlined on pages 206–207, the courts read down the obscenity legislation in order to specifically restrict the type of actions that were considered to be obscene.

The court can also use a process of **reading in** a term so that the legislation will stand and the court will not have to strike it down. In the case of *Vriend v. Alberta*, [1998] 1 S.C.R. 493 (see Chapter 4, p. 118), Delwin Vriend had been fired from a Christian college in Alberta because he was a homosexual. He attempted to file a human rights complaint in Alberta but was prevented from doing so because the province's human rights legislation did not contain the term "sexual orientation." In ruling that the Alberta legislation violated equality rights under the *Charter*, but not wanting to declare Alberta's entire *Individual's Rights Protection Act* unconstitutional, the Supreme Court chose to read in the term "sexual orientation" as a prohibited ground of discrimination.

Sometimes the court will make a declaration that a law is unconstitutional but give the appropriate government body a certain time period in which to change the law. This declaration procedure was used in the case of *M. v. H.*, [1999] 2 S.C.R. 3 (see Chapter 6, pp. 175–176). In this case, the Supreme Court of Canada declared s. 29 of Ontario's *Family Law Act* to be of no force or effect. The effect of the declaration was temporarily suspended for six months to provide time for the Ontario government to amend the legislation. The case set a precedent, and subsequently many federal and provincial pieces of legislation were amended so as not to discriminate against same-sex couples.

While many *Charter* cases involve the validity of a law, other cases question the actions of the government in applying a law. In *Eldridge v. British Columbia (Attorney General)*, [1997] 3 S.C.R. 624, the BC government had denied sign-language interpreters for deaf individuals as a benefit under the provincial health-care plan. The court granted a declaration that the action was unconstitutional and allowed the government time to remedy the situation. (For more on this case, see p. 213.)

Remedies Under the *Charter*

The *Charter* provides for a remedy in some criminal cases in which a violation of legal rights has occurred. It may be that a complainant was arrested and not told of the reason for the arrest. It may be that evidence was obtained illegally or that a proper legal search was not conducted. Should a court determine that an individual's rights have been violated, he or she can apply to the court for a remedy under s. 24 of the *Charter*, which states:

> 24 (1) Anyone whose rights or freedoms, as guaranteed by this *Charter*, have been infringed or denied, may apply to a court of competent jurisdiction to obtain such remedy as the court considers appropriate and just in the circumstances.
>
> 24 (2) Where, in proceedings under subsection (1), a court concludes that evidence was obtained in a manner that infringed or denied any rights or freedoms guaranteed by this *Charter*, the evidence shall be excluded if it is established that, having regard to all the circumstances, the admission of it in the proceedings would bring the administration of justice into disrepute.

If a complaint made in accordance with s. 24 (1) of the *Charter* is successful, the court has the option of issuing an injunction or awarding damages as a possible remedy. An **injunction** is a court order requiring a specified party to take or not take a particular action. The Supreme Court has been reluctant to issue injunctions in situations that would require the activity to be

FIGURE 7.4   Police investigations may involve a search and subsequent seizure of evidence. If this search were deemed to be illegal, how might the court deal with the drug evidence?

specifically monitored by the courts. **Damages** are court-ordered monetary awards given as compensation for loss or injury. Damage awards under *Charter* litigation are not common.

Remedies under s. 24 (2) may take the form of a **stay of proceedings**, meaning that the court can stop the proceedings against the accused if continuing the action would be considered prejudicial to the accused. Anyone whose rights have been infringed or denied may apply to the court to have evidence excluded. The court must then decide whether allowing the evidence into a proceeding would bring the "administration of justice into disrepute." For example, if evidence was obtained in an investigation and it was later determined that there had been an unreasonable search and seizure under the *Charter*, an application could be made to have the evidence excluded. In deciding whether to allow or exclude evidence, the judge will carefully consider all the circumstances and try to determine whether allowing the evidence in such a case would make the trial unfair.

CONFIRM YOUR UNDERSTANDING

1. Summarize the remedies available to the court should the validity of a law be successfully challenged.

2. Why do courts use the process of "reading in" or "reading down" legislation?

3. Under what circumstances can s. 24 (1) of the *Charter* be used?

4. In your own words, explain the meaning of "bring the administration of justice into disrepute."

Fundamental Freedoms

How our laws reflect societal values is demonstrated in key decisions made under s. 2 of the *Charter*. The courts, in interpreting these *Charter* provisions, may, for example, decide to uphold freedom of religion even if so doing affects the religious freedom of others. They may curtail an individual's freedom of expression if his or her actions are deemed harmful to society as a whole. They may accept freedom of peaceful assembly as a defence for protests initiated by bike gangs or radical activists. One challenge the courts face in cases involving s. 2 of the *Charter* is balancing the freedoms of all parties involved.

Freedom of Religion

Challenges under s. 2(a) of the *Charter* usually involve one of two situations: either an individual feels his or her right to religious customs or practices is being infringed upon, or there is evidence to suggest that one religious viewpoint is overriding others. The leading case on freedom of religion occurred in 1985 in the case of *R. v. Big M Drug Mart Ltd.*, [1985] 1 S.C.R. 295. Big M Drug Mart was charged with unlawfully carrying on the sale of goods on a Sunday, contrary to the *Lord's Day Act*. Big M was acquitted at trial, and the law was held to be unconstitutional. An appeal by the Attorney General to the Alberta Court of Appeal was dismissed. On a subsequent appeal to the Supreme Court of Canada, the court held that the requirements of the *Lord's Day Act* infringed on the freedom of religion provision in the *Charter*. In determining whether the legislative objective of the *Lord's Day Act* was

1. Has a right or freedom been infringed?

2. Does s. 1 of the *Charter* justify the infringement as a reasonable limit?

3. Is there a remedy available under s. 24?

FIGURE 7.5   An analysis of a *Charter* case should include these questions.

valid, the court held that the act discriminated against non-Christian Canadians. Compelling all individuals to observe Sunday as a day of rest was considered discriminatory. In recent case law, the courts have held that employers must accommodate the interests of employees with respect to the observance of their religious days.

Freedom of Expression

Section 2(b) of the *Charter* guarantees freedom of thought, belief, opinion, and expression, including freedom of the press and other media of communication. However, the right to express yourself through speech, media, literary forms of expression, and so on, may at times violate the law. The freedom of expression provisions have been challenged under the hate law sections of the *Criminal Code*.

FIGURE 7.6 Activist Judy Rebick addresses a crowd of students outside Concordia University in November 2002. Under what circumstances might a person's freedom of expression be limited?

In the case of *R. v. Keegstra,* [1990] 3 S.C.R. 697, Alberta high-school teacher James Keegstra was charged with wilfully promoting hatred against an identifiable group. The *Criminal Code* defines an identifiable group as "any section of the public distinguished by colour, race, religion, or ethnic origin." In teaching that the Holocaust never happened, Keegstra expected students to reflect his views in class work and examinations. Although convicted at trial, Keegstra was successful in his appeal. The court held that the *Criminal Code's* hate law provisions were a violation of freedom of expression. The Crown appealed the case to the Supreme Court of

Canada, where, in a landmark judgment, the appeal was allowed. While the court agreed that the section of the *Code* violated Keegstra's freedom of expression under s. 2(b) of the *Charter*, the majority of the court, in a narrow 4 to 3 decision, held that the limit on freedom of speech was justifiable.

In 2003, a private member's bill was introduced by MP Svend Robinson to amend hate laws to include sexual orientation. The bill to amend the hate propaganda section of the *Criminal Code* passed in September 2003 by a vote of 143 to 110. Under the *Criminal Code*, an identifiable group was previously distinguished on the basis of only colour, race, religion, or ethnic origin. An identifiable group now includes any section of the public distinguished by sexual orientation, and anyone who incites or wilfully promotes hatred against this identifiable group can be charged under the *Criminal Code*.

Obscenity laws under the *Criminal Code* have also restricted the freedom of expression provision. The leading case on obscenity laws is *R. v. Butler,* [1992] 1 S.C.R. 452 (see below), in which the Supreme Court of Canada developed a three-part test for obscenity.

Freedom of expression laws may be expanded in the years to come, or they may be limited as new cases are brought before the courts. The task of the courts will be to balance the rights guaranteed under s. 2(b) of the *Charter* with society's views of what is acceptable and tolerable.

Landmark CASE

R. v. Butler, [1992] 1 S.C.R. 452

Read the following case analysis. The facts, issue, and *ratio decidendi* have been provided for you.

Assume that you agree with the *R. v. Butler* decision, and write a concurring judgment.

Facts: The appellant, Donald Butler, ran a boutique in Winnipeg, Manitoba, which sold and rented hard-core video material and magazines, and sexual paraphernalia. He was charged under s. 159 (now s. 163) of the

Criminal Code with selling obscene material contrary to the *Code*, possessing obscene material for the purposes of distribution contrary to the *Code*, and exposing obscene material to the public contrary to the *Code*. The *Criminal Code* had defined "obscene" as "any publication a dominant characteristic of which is the undue exploitation of sex, or of sex and any one or more of the following subjects, namely, crime, horror, cruelty and violence." At trial, Butler was convicted on eight counts and acquitted on the other 242 charges. The trial judge held that much of the material in question was covered by the freedom of expression provision of the *Charter*. On appeal by the Crown, Butler was convicted on all counts. In rejecting the freedom of expression argument, the Court of Appeal held that the material "involved the undue exploitation of sex and the degradation of human sexuality." The accused appealed to the Supreme Court of Canada.

Issue: Does the definition of "obscenity" in the *Criminal Code* infringe on s. 2(b) of the *Charter*? If so, is it justified under s. 1 of the *Charter*?

Held: The appeal was allowed and a new trial directed.

Ratio Decidendi: (Lamer C.J. and La Forest, Sopinka, Cory, McLachlin, Stevenson, and Iacobucci JJ.) While the court held that the obscenity provision infringed on s. 2(b) of the *Charter*, it was a reasonable limit demonstrably justified in a free and democratic society. The court upheld the constitutional validity of the obscenity provisions but read down the legislation to specifically restrict the definition of obscenity to three categories.

Material may be considered obscene if it contains (1) explicit sex with violence, (2) explicit sex without violence but that is degrading or dehumanizing, or (3) explicit sex that does not contain violence, is not degrading or dehumanizing, but employs children in producing it.

The Supreme Court further outlined a "community standard of tolerance" test. This test is intended to indicate what the community will not tolerate other Canadians being exposed to. The material in question may be saved by a defence of artistic merit, that is, a justification that the material in question has an artistic purpose. In making the decision, the court held that the overriding objective of the legislation was to avoid harm to society and held that it was pressing and substantial to justify the restriction of freedom of expression.

In considering the proportionality test, the court held that there was a rational connection for making such actions criminal as it demonstrated societal concern with the victimization of, and violence against, women. It also considered the negative effects such material could have on changing people's attitudes and beliefs. The court further held that the obscenity provision in the *Criminal Code* minimally impaired freedom of expression because it classified as obscene only sexually explicit material involving violence and materials that were degrading and dehumanizing. Any material that had as its central purpose an artistic or literary theme would not be caught by the obscenity provision. Finally, the court weighed the context of the situation and whether the exploitation was undue. In weighing the harm to society and the threat to fundamental values, the court held that the infringement of s. 2(b) was justified.

Freedom of Association and Peaceful Assembly

The Supreme Court of Canada has been called upon to interpret the meaning of "freedom of association" under s. 2(c) of the *Charter* in the field of labour law. The court has upheld the rights of individuals to join together in groups, but it has not allowed the section to be used as a guarantee of the right to strike or the right to conduct **collective bargaining** (a term used in labour law to describe the formal process of negotiating conditions of employment between an employer and a union) as part of labour relations. The court also guarantees the freedom of peaceful assembly. The critical word in this provision is "peaceful." While Canadians have enjoyed the right to demonstrate their discontent with many government actions, their freedom to join together in mass protest demonstrations is limited by their ability to keep the gathering peaceful and lawful.

Some people like to express their dissatisfaction with issues by being involved in protests. For example, environmental protesters may condemn the logging of old-growth forests, social justice activists may rally against world trade talks, and local anti-poverty groups may actively criticize government inaction regarding low-cost housing. The nature of the assembly, however, is limited by the ability of the organizers to keep the demonstration peaceful and lawful. Should the gathering be in violation of an injunction (perhaps the group was ordered by the court to refrain from protesting in a particular area or to avoid certain actions), charges of contempt of court could be laid. The *Criminal Code* also includes further restrictions on assemblies. Under s. 63 of the *Code*, three or more persons who gather with the intent to carry out a common purpose and cause others to fear that the peace will be tumultuously disturbed (in a manner that gives rise to an atmosphere of violence), could be charged with unlawful assembly.

A more serious riot charge could be laid if the unlawful assembly has actually begun to disturb the peace tumultuously.

FIGURE 7.7   A protest of a World Trade Organization meeting in Montréal on July 28, 2003, was marred by violence and vandalism. More than 200 protesters were charged with participating in an illegal demonstration. When can an individual be charged with unlawful assembly?

Democratic Rights and Mobility Rights

Under s. 3 of the *Charter*, "Every citizen of Canada has the right to vote in an election of members of the House of Commons or of a legislative assembly and to be qualified for membership therein."

Canadian citizens aged 18 and over are eligible to vote in Canada. However, when citizens choose not to exercise their right to vote, they deny themselves a voice in the resulting government. According to a report commissioned by Elections Canada, only 22.4 percent of voters between the ages of 18 and 20 cast their ballot in the 2000 federal election, compared with over 80 percent of voters above the age of 58. On the other hand, citizens who have been denied the right to vote, such as federal inmates, have waged legal challenges arguing a violation of democratic rights. In fact, there was a constitutional challenge regarding the denial of voting rights to federal inmates. In 2002, the Supreme Court of Canada released its 5 to 4 decision allowing federal inmates—that is, those serving sentences of two years or more—the right to vote in federal elections. While the majority of the court held that s. 51(e) of the *Canada Elections Act* violated s. 3 of the *Charter* and could not be justified under s. 1, the dissenting judges felt that s. 1 of the *Charter* could be used to justify limiting a prisoner's right to vote. (For more on this legal challenge, refer to the Sauvé case in question 17 on p. 223.)

The *Charter* also provides for mobility rights under s. 6: "Every citizen of Canada has the right to enter, remain in and leave Canada." Further, every Canadian citizen and those having permanent resident status in Canada have the right to move to and take up residence in any province or territory and can pursue a livelihood there as well. The argument of a violation of mobility rights is often raised in cases involving **extradition**, that is, the legal surrender by one jurisdiction of a person to another jurisdiction to face criminal prosecution. In the case of *United States v. Burns*, [2001] 1 S.C.R. 283, 2001 S.C.C. 7, two Canadian citizens—Glen Sebastian Burns and Atif Ahmad Rafay—were wanted for murder in the United States. They were arrested in Canada, and the American authorities wanted them extradited to the United States. Generally, in extradition cases, Canada will seek assurances that the death penalty will not be used on anyone seeking refuge in Canada, whether or not the person is a citizen. In this case, Canada's minister of justice did not seek these assurances,

FIGURE 7.8   Statistics show that voter apathy among Canadian youth is at an all-time high. To address this concern, Kids Voting Canada organized mock student voting in over 1000 schools in fall 2003. What else could be done to improve voter turnout for citizens aged 18 to 24?

so the appellants argued that their mobility rights would be violated should they be extradited from Canada. Although s. 6 was argued, the Supreme Court accepted a s. 7 argument (under the legal rights provisions, which is the focus of the next section) in ruling against the extradition of Burns and Rafay. The court stated that a violation of s. 7—the right "to life, liberty and security of the person"—was a more appropriate argument in this case than was an argument based on an infringement of mobility rights. (For more information on this case, see p. 446 in Chapter 14.)

CONFIRM YOUR UNDERSTANDING

1. How was freedom of religion violated in the Big M Drug Mart case?
2. What limits exist on freedom of expression? Explain by providing examples.
3. Using the definition for "obscenity" in the Butler case, describe the restrictions that could be placed on literary or artistic works.

How could an artist or writer justify his or her freedom of expression rights?
4. What laws under the *Charter* and the *Criminal Code* can be used to limit the actions of protesters who assemble in public?
5. Explain mobility rights under the *Charter*, and provide an example.

Legal Rights

Under ss. 7 to 14 of the *Charter*, you are guaranteed legal rights at all stages of the criminal justice process. But as you learned earlier in this chapter, you also have a right to a legal remedy under s. 24 of the *Charter* if one of your legal rights is violated.

Life, Liberty, and Security of the Person

Under s. 7 of the *Charter*, you are entitled "to life, liberty and security of the person and the right not to be deprived thereof except in accordance with the principles of fundamental justice." This means that your rights under s. 7 are guaranteed, but they may also be restricted in certain circumstances. Consider seatbelt legislation. As a driver, you may choose not to buckle up, but if a police officer catches you or your passengers without a seatbelt, you will be fined.

The meaning of "security of the person" is less clear and, in fact, the courts have wrestled with the interpretation of this phrase. For example, technological advances have led to unrestricted access to information, raising issues of personal privacy. The challenge facing the courts is to balance the rights of the individual with the rights of the majority when it comes to such issues as public health and safety. It could be argued that red-light cameras at major road intersections are demonstrably justified in a free and democratic society, or that they are an invasion of privacy. In the same vein, international identity cards are being implemented as an anti-terrorism measure, but what abuses to "security of the person" could result?

You may recall from Chapter 4 that the right to security of the person was used to challenge s. 251 of the *Criminal Code* in *R. v. Morgentaler*, [1988] 1 S.C.R. 30. Although the Supreme Court of Canada struck down the abortion law in this case, there was tremendous controversy subsequent to the decision because the courts had ruled on a matter of significant public policy. In response, the federal government, under the leadership of Prime Minister Kim Campbell, attempted to pass legislation that would provide for some restrictions concerning abortions, but the legislation was defeated in the Senate in 1991. Since the 1988 decision, there has been no criminal law in Canada prohibiting or restricting abortions.

If s. 7 upholds your right to life, liberty, and security of the person, does this imply that you have the right to die whenever and however you wish, and for whatever reason? In *Rodriguez v. British Columbia (Attorney General)*, [1993] 3 S.C.R. 519, the appellant argued that the *Criminal Code* section on aiding and assisting suicide was a violation of s. 7 because it prevented a terminally ill patient from seeking assistance to commit suicide. The Supreme Court of Canada ruled that the section was constitutional as the *Code* protects those who are vulnerable in society. (For more on the Rodriguez case, see p. 122 in Chapter 4.)

As explained on page 209, the courts in the Burns case accepted the s. 7 argument regarding the right to life, liberty, and security of the person. In refusing to grant the extradition of Burns and Rafay to the United States to face murder charges and possibly the death penalty, the courts demonstrated Canada's commitment to the principles of s. 7.

Unreasonable Search and Seizure

Section 8 of the *Charter* states, "Everyone has the right to be secure against unreasonable search or seizure." In cases involving s. 8, it is up to the courts to determine the meaning of "unreasonable" and what constitutes a legitimate search and seizure. Drug-related cases often require an interpretation of this section of the *Charter*. For example, if drug evidence is obtained in a manner that violates the principles of a legitimate search, an application can be made under s. 24 to have it excluded as evidence. Consider this scenario: A driver is pulled over for a routine traffic violation, such as failing to use a turn signal. The police officer subsequently asks the driver to step out of the vehicle. If the officer proceeds to turn the vehicle inside out looking

Save the community and you will save the individual. Teach the man his responsibilities, and his rights will take care of themselves.

—W.W. Campbell, poet, from Preface of *Poems of Loyalty by British and Canadian Authors* (1913)

for drugs without having reasonable and probable grounds for doing so, the driver may raise the argument of unreasonable search and seizure. Even if the police officer does find drugs in the vehicle, an application can be made under s. 24 of the *Charter* to have the evidence thrown out. The court will consider the circumstances and decide whether admitting the evidence would make the trial unfair. (For more information on the scope and limits of search and seizure powers, see Chapter 10.)

Arbitrary Detention

Section 9 of the *Charter* protects citizens from being arbitrarily detained or imprisoned. Generally speaking, in law the word "**arbitrary**" means having no justifiable reason for an action. Very early on in *Charter* litigation, the word "detained" also had to be interpreted.

At one time, random police spot checks were considered a violation of rights. In the case of *R. v. Hufsky*, [1988] 1 S.C.R. 621, Werner Hufsky was stopped during a random police spot check; he was not driving in any unusual manner. Hufsky was asked to provide his licence and proof of insurance. The police officer then detected the smell of alcohol on Hufsky's breath and noticed that his speech was somewhat slurred. He requested that Hufsky complete a roadside Breathalyzer test, and then made a formal demand for Hufsky to comply. When Hufsky refused, he was charged under the *Criminal Code* with refusing to provide a breath sample. Hufsky argued in court that the random stopping of motor vehicles violated his s. 9 rights. While the court agreed that Hufsky was detained in accordance with the meaning of s. 9 as the police officer was exercising control over Hufsky's movements, it held that this was a reasonable limit under s. 1 of the *Charter* for the purpose of highway safety.

Police officers cannot use the pretext of a spot-check program to engage in a fishing expedition to search your vehicle for evidence of other criminal activity unless they have reasonable and probable grounds for doing so. Should you be detained or arrested, you have the right to be informed of the reason and the right to retain and instruct legal counsel. Therefore, police officers must be aware of what constitutes a detention under the law and remember to inform an individual of his or her rights.

Being Arrested and Charged

You are probably familiar with TV police dramas in which a suspect is arrested for a specified crime and read his or her rights while being folded into a waiting police car. The next scene usually involves the dingy interrogation room where the accused calmly refuses to answer questions and demands the right to legal counsel. And then there's the brief court appearance, where the accused hears the charges against him or her and enters a plea of guilty or not guilty. This scenario illustrates ss. 10 and 11 of the *Charter*, which provide for the rights of an accused at both the arrest and charging stages of the legal process.

Once arrested or detained, everyone has the right to be informed of the reason for the arrest or detention, the right to retain and instruct legal counsel, and the right to have the lawful validity of the detention determined by way of *habeas corpus*, which is a court order that involves bringing a person to court to determine if he or

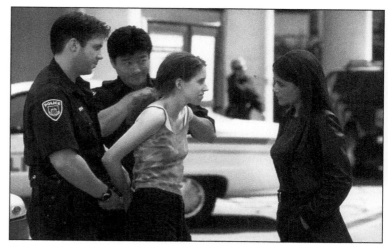

Figure 7.9   This scene from an episode of *Da Vinci's Inquest* shows the arrest stage of the legal process. What rights do you have on arrest under s. 10 of the *Charter*?

she is being detained legally. In addition, an accused has rights on being charged with an offence, including the right to be informed of the specific offence, to be tried within a reasonable time, and to be presumed innocent until proven guilty. (These legal rights will be discussed in detail in Chapter 10.)

Additional Legal Rights

The *Charter* provides for additional legal rights, as follows:
- Section 12: the right not to be subjected to cruel and unusual treatment or punishment
- Section 13: the right of a witness who testifies not to have any **incriminating** evidence (evidence that establishes or infers guilt) used to incriminate that witness in subsequent proceedings, unless it is used to show that the witness committed **perjury** (lied under oath) or gave contradictory evidence
- Section 14: the right to the assistance of an interpreter for those who do not understand or speak the language, or who are deaf

Canadians have very specific views as to what constitutes proper punishment. As our views have changed over time, so too have our laws. Corporal punishment, which was once part of the *Criminal Code* and allowed offenders to be subjected to such treatments as whipping and paddling, was abolished in 1972. Capital punishment was also once accepted as a valid form of punishment, but it was abolished in 1976. The Supreme Court of Canada, most recently in the case of *United States v. Burns*, has strongly condemned the death penalty.

The legal rights provisions under the *Charter* ensure that the trial process is conducted fairly and that sentencing procedures (discussed in detail in Chapter 11) reflect our social conscience and attitudes toward punishment.

Equality Rights

As you learned in Chapter 6, equality does not mean that everyone should be treated the same, but rather that everyone should be given equal access to the same opportunities. In order to uphold this definition of equality, sometimes accommodations must be made to the point of undue hardship. The *Charter* entrenches our right to equality in s. 15 (1):

> Every individual is equal before and under the law and has the right to the equal protection and equal benefit of the law without discrimination and, in particular, without discrimination based on race, national or ethnic origin, colour, religion, sex, age or mental or physical disability.

The first test of s. 15 was heard in the Supreme Court of Canada in the case of *Andrews v. Law Society of British Columbia*, [1989] 1 S.C.R. 143. Mark Andrews was a British subject and a permanent resident of Canada. He met all the requirements for the practice of law in British Columbia except for the Canadian citizenship requirement. At trial, Andrews argued that this citizenship requirement denied him equality rights under s. 15 (1) of the *Charter*. At trial, the action was dismissed, but a subsequent appeal was allowed. The Court of Appeal for British Columbia held that the citizenship requirement for practising law violated the *Charter*. The Law Society of British Columbia was then granted leave to appeal the case to the Supreme Court of Canada, where the majority of the court once again held that the citizenship requirement violated s. 15 (1) of the *Charter*. In his ruling, Justice McIntyre described discrimination as follows:

> …a distinction which, whether intentional or not but based on grounds relating to personal characteristics of the individual or group, has an effect which imposes disadvantages not imposed upon others or which withholds or limits access to advantages available to other members of society. Distinctions based on personal characteristics attributed to an individual solely on the basis of association with a group will rarely escape the charge of discrimination, while those based on an individual's merits and capacities will rarely be so classed.

Canada tries to protect minority rights and safeguard human rights not only through human rights legislation, but also through the discrimination provisions of the *Charter*. While equality rights were guaranteed under the *Bill of Rights* legislation, definitions of equality based on narrow interpretations of the term meant that the law did not always adequately respond to the changing needs of our society. The court hearing the Lavell case demonstrated the narrow interpretation of equality rights (see Chapter 6, pp. 173–174). In effect, individuals within certain groups or classes were treated alike, while other individuals outside that particular group or class were not. Rarely were laws struck down under the *Bill of Rights* legislation.

Other cases also drew criticism under the *Bill of Rights* legislation. In *Bliss v. Attorney General of Canada*, [1979] 1 S.C.R. 183, the court held that a woman would be denied unemployment insurance benefits if her employment were interrupted by pregnancy. The court held that pregnancy did not amount to discrimination on the grounds of sex. Interpretations of equality were to change once the equality rights provisions in the *Charter* were guaranteed.

The lobby for the equality rights provisions of the *Charter* was strong. When discussions were complete, the *Charter* had guaranteed equality rights by providing equality before the law, equality under the law, equal benefit, and equal protection of the law. In effect, the four components of s. 15 were attempts to ensure the true attainment of equality rights in Canada. The equality rights provisions did not come into effect until three years after the *Charter* was enacted in order to give legislatures time to bring their statutes in line with s. 15. The courts have been interpreting the meaning of the term "equality" ever since.

Canada's perspective on the nature and scope of equality rights is an evolving process. How far do you think Canadians are willing to take equality rights legislation to prevent discrimination? The definition of "equality" could be expanded to include discrimination on the basis of weight or size, potentially forcing airlines to make accommodations for overweight individuals. Airlines would have to prove undue hardship in order to avoid making such accommodations. There have been rulings against accommodations of a bona fide occupational requirement when these might pose a threat to safety or security, as you learned in Chapter 6 in the case of *Bhinder and the Canadian Human Rights Commission v. Canadian National Railway Company*.

The equality provisions under the *Charter* allow for affirmative-action programs, which are designed to remedy inequities experienced by women, minorities, Aboriginal peoples, and people with disabilities. (For more on the issue of affirmative action, see Chapter 8.)

Sometimes, the actions of government violate equality rights. If an institution is acting on behalf of the government, then the *Charter* applies. In the case of *Eldridge v. British Columbia (Attorney General)*, [1997] 3 S.C.R. 624, the court considered an equality rights challenge. As you read earlier in this chapter, hospitals in British Columbia failed to provide sign-language interpreters as a benefit under the BC health-care plan. The court held that this action violated equality rights. As a remedy, the court made a

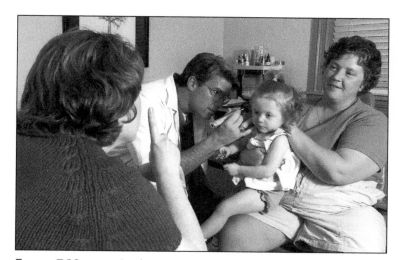

FIGURE 7.10   On what basis would the failure to provide sign-language interpreters in the health-care system be considered a violation of *Charter* rights?

declaration that the failure to provide the services was unconstitutional and gave the government six months to remedy the situation by providing sign-language interpreters when delivering medical services to individuals who are deaf. The impact this decision will have on providing equal access to health care will likely be long-term. It is possible that access to health care will become the next major hurdle in the interpretation of equality rights, compelling government bodies to accommodate the needs of more individuals in order to achieve equality.

The courts do not always interpret equality rights broadly. In *Law v. Canada (Minister of Employment and Immigration)*, [1999] 1 S.C.R. 497, the Supreme Court of Canada used a new test referred to as the human dignity test in holding that it was not a denial of equality rights to refuse a claim by a 30-year-old widow to the Canada Pension Plan for survivor benefits. The Canada Pension Plan allows for survivor benefits to become payable to a surviving spouse after he or she reaches age 65. If the surviving spouse is between the ages of 45 and 64 with dependent children or is (or becomes) disabled, he or she is entitled to the full pension. For widows and widowers who are between the ages of 35 and 45, are not disabled, and have no dependent children, the pension benefit is gradually reduced by an additional $1/120^{th}$ for each month that a claimant is below the age of 45 at the time of his or her spouse's death. However, a surviving spouse who is under age 35 at the time of the contributor's death, has no dependent children, and is not disabled is denied a survivor's pension until he or she reaches age 65, unless the surviving spouse becomes disabled. Nancy Law had no dependent children nor was she disabled at the time of her spouse's death. She argued age discrimination under s. 15 of the *Charter*, but the court held that the law governing the reduction of survivor pension benefits to widows and widowers who met specific criteria would not result in unfair treatment.

Our understanding of equality rights will continue to evolve. Rosalie Silberman Abella, Justice of the Court of Appeal for Ontario, commented on some future areas where there will be demands under the *Charter*:

> By adding the *Charter* in the last 20 years to the public's arsenal of rights protectors, we have not only thereby added more rights, but have also added expectations that more needs will be treated as rights and not merely as aspirations. Globalization, technology, diversity, and deficits, the foundational quartet conducting public policy before terrorism got to the podium, are not about to leave the stage anytime soon. And it will not be long before they spawn a deluge of repercussive rights demands, primarily about access—to health, to education, to physical and economic security, to privacy, and, of course, to justice itself. (Abella 2002)

As society embraces tolerance, respects individuality, and places a high value on protection of equality rights, our courts will be called on to ensure that a legal view of equality mirrors the societal view.

Language Rights

The *Charter* guarantees French and English as the official languages of Canada in ss. 16 to 22. These rights include having parliamentary debates in English or French, recording all statutes and records of Parliament in both languages, and allowing court proceedings in either language. The *Charter* also specifically protects minority language education rights under s. 23, as you will learn in the case of *Doucet-Boudreau v. Nova Scotia (Minister of Education)*, 2003 S.C.C. 62 on page 218 of this chapter.

CONFIRM YOUR UNDERSTANDING

1. Assume the Canadian government authorized the police to install and monitor video surveillance cameras on street corners, in schools, at special events, and in public parks, as is the case in some cities in the United States and Europe. What objective do you think would be served by such legislation? How would this infringe on your rights?

2. Does your right to liberty mean that you cannot be given a jail sentence? Explain.

3. a) Are you detained within the meaning of the *Charter* when you are stopped for a random police spot check? Explain.
   b) Should road safety override individual rights? Support your opinion.

4. Assume that drug evidence was obtained during an illegal search and seizure. Would the evidence automatically be excluded? Explain.

5. Explain how your rights could be violated under s. 10 of the *Charter*.

6. Identify the changes made to the definition of "equality" from the *Bill of Rights* to the *Charter of Rights and Freedoms*.

7. Summarize the equality rights challenge in the case of *Andrews v. Law Society of British Columbia*.

8. Under what circumstances could you foresee a *Charter* challenge on the basis of a denial of equality rights in the area of health care?

9. Think about future *Charter* challenges that could arise with respect to equality rights, and outline the issues involved.

The Legislature and the Judiciary

You may recall from Chapter 5 that the legislature and the judiciary were established as separate and distinct bodies. The legislature was empowered to make and change the laws, while the courts were given the mandate to resolve issues regarding division of powers. All of that changed in 1982 when the courts were given the power to rule as to whether or not legislation was unconstitutional and, therefore, of no force or effect. The courts, in essence, developed a new law-making power in interpreting the scope of government laws.

Role of the Courts and Tribunals

Traditionally, law-making power has been the domain of the legislative arm of government. We elect politicians to represent our interests. They measure political and social support, and then decide whether or not to enact changes to the law. However, when the *Charter* was passed, it

FIGURE 7.11   The Supreme Court of Canada in Ottawa is Canada's final Court of Appeal. What role does the judiciary play in our democratic society?

was understood that the judiciary would assume tremendous power in interpreting the provisions.

On the one hand, this system of judicial interpretation provides an excellent safeguard for civil rights, especially if governments can be compelled to change, amend, repeal, or modify existing laws. However, the role of the courts and **tribunals** (any governmental body or official group of people sitting in a less formal setting than a court and engaged in resolving a dispute involving such issues as human rights complaints and landlord–tenant matters) is often examined when groups of citizens strongly disagree with their decisions. During such times, the extent of the courts' power is challenged and each case becomes the subject of debate.

ASKING KEY QUESTIONS

Is Judicial Activism Alive in Canada?

The *Canadian Charter of Rights and Freedoms* has allowed our Constitution to evolve, but the price has been criticism and controversy. Our system of parliamentary democracy in Canada provides a formal law-making procedure in which the legislatures have the key role. However, our Supreme Court may interpret the laws in cases challenged under the *Charter*. Additionally, there are circumstances in which the Supreme Court is asked to provide an interpretation even before a law is enacted. Sometimes, the Supreme Court will hear a reference case and make a ruling on a potential law (see the Landmark Case in Chapter 5, p. 161).

The Supreme Court of Canada has ruled on issues such as abortion, obscenity, and drunkenness as a defence in sexual assault cases. The Courts of Appeal have made decisions relating to same-sex marriage and allowed artistic merit to be a defence in suspected cases of pornography. Some decisions have met with public support, while others have faced public outcry.

"Judicial activism" is a term that describes how courts broadly interpret laws under the *Charter* in their case rulings. When judges rule on cases and these decisions become public, they are often examined in light of whether policy decisions are being made. Courts are accused of wielding their decision-making power as a weapon of judicial activism. Supporters of legislative supremacy argue that legislation should be able to stand since it is enacted by a duly elected legislature. Supporters of the judiciary argue that the court, in reflecting on all considerations, should be able to interpret a law as unconstitutional if it is deemed to violate the *Charter*.

Justice Abella, in commenting on the controversial nature of the judiciary, defended the power of the courts:

> [W]hen the *Charter* was in its teens, parts of the nation started to rebel. Almost imperceptibly at first, when the *Charter* became an adolescent, public pride in its grasp seemed to turn into strident fear over its reach. That is when we got the panic attacks about the fate of democracy. What had always been seen as a complementary relationship between the legislature and the judiciary, was recast as a competitive one.
>
> And to what end? To stop the flow of rights streaming from the courts. But the criticisms would prove to be a finger in the dike. They could stop neither the

flow nor the people along the shore cheering the progressive currents.

The Honourable R. Roy McMurtry, Chief Justice of Ontario, in speaking about the role of the courts in cases involving constitutional challenges to the anti-terrorism legislation, stated:

> In the past decade, some Canadian commentators have argued that the *Charter* has given the courts too much power to enforce the rights of minorities and criminals. They state that courts have generally become too activist and give too liberal a meaning to the expression of the rights and freedoms in the *Charter*.

In justifying the interpretive role that the court plays, he added:

> Some of the criticism simply ignores what is necessarily involved in the process of judicial interpretation. It often assumes that in every case that comes before the court, there is a simple right answer in the Constitution awaiting discovery by judges. There is no validity to this assumption as the key words and expressions in the *Charter of Rights* are very general, such as "freedoms of thought, belief, opinion and expression," the "right to liberty and security of the person," the "principles of fundamental justice," "unreasonable search and seizure," etc., etc. These terms are inherently indeterminate in that they are often susceptible to more than one reasonable meaning.

Justice McMurtry summed up the role of the courts and legislature as follows: "If there is a dispute as to the constitutionality of any legislation, the conflict should not be viewed as between the court and Parliament, but between Parliament and the Constitution."

Justice Abella, in elaborating on her positive view of the role of the courts and the *Charter*, stated:

> And twenty years from now, those demands [for rights] in turn will lead, as now, to people who criticize the courts for doing too much and the legislature for doing too little to stop them. But as we grow more comfortable, as we should, with the inevitability of the criticisms, the more both the courts and the legislature will comfortably do what they have to do without looking over their shoulders, confident in the knowledge that the rights business is booming and that there is more than enough to go around.

SOURCES: Abella, Rosie Silberman. "The Future After Twenty Years Under the *Charter*." Canadian Rights and Freedoms: 20 Years Under the *Charter*. The Association for Canadian Studies, Closing Session, Ottawa: 20 Apr. 2002. Accessed 11 Aug. 2003 <www.ontariocourts.on.ca/court_of_appeal/speeches/future.htm>;

McMurtry, R. Roy. "The Role of the Courts in Turbulent Times." The Canadian Club. Ontario Justice Education Network. 3 Dec. 2001. Accessed 26 June 2003 <www.ontariocourts.on.ca/ojen/speeches/role.htm>.

Form Your Questions

Do our courts have too much power? Assume you have the opportunity to interview the speakers in this feature. What questions might you ask to further clarify the issue? Think of at least three possible questions. Share your questions with the rest of the class, and discuss possible answers or solutions.

The case of *Doucet-Boudreau v. Nova Scotia (Minister of Education)*, 2003 S.C.C. 62 raised the issue of judicial activism. Francophone parents challenged the Nova Scotia government, arguing that the government was violating their minority language rights by failing to provide French-language facilities and programs at the secondary school level. The trial judge agreed and ordered the province to take steps to provide the necessary facilities and programs. In granting a remedy, the trial judge maintained jurisdiction in the case by requesting that the government report on its progress and by requiring the parties to return to the court to report on the status of the work. The Attorney General challenged the jurisdiction of the trial judge to hear status reports and launched an appeal. The majority of the Nova Scotia Court of Appeal allowed the appeal and held that the trial judge did not have jurisdiction to see that the remedy was enforced. However, the Supreme Court of Canada, in a 5 to 4 decision, held that the trial judge used an appropriate remedy in requiring the Nova Scotia government to report back to the court.

This case was used as a focal point for debating the issue of judicial activism in a newspaper editorial entitled "The Expanding Court." The editorial included a quotation from the minority judges of the Supreme Court: "Courts should not unduly encroach on areas which should remain the responsibility of public administration and should avoid turning themselves into managers of the public service" (*The Globe and Mail* 2003). The majority of judges, however, felt that the trial judge had exercised proper judicial discretion. According to the editorial, "The majority said the trial judge was on solid ground: that he was just borrowing remedies from other areas of law, that his pragmatism achieved the desired end, that the right he upheld was particularly valuable and that enforcing minority language rights in particular may require 'novel remedies.'" In commenting on the term "novel remedies," the issue of judicial activism was

> *They that can give up essential liberty to obtain a little temporary safety deserve neither liberty nor safety.*
> —Benjamin Franklin (1706–1790), US politician and scientist

summed up as follows: "The words amount to a colourful bow on a defence for an unsettling expansion of judicial power."

As well as being criticized for their role in controversial case decisions, the courts are also considered to be major players in matters of national security as they interpret anti-terrorism legislation in light of *Charter* provisions.

In speaking about anti-terrorism legislation and the role of the courts and Parliament, Deputy Minister of Justice Morris Rosenberg acknowledged that the courts will play a key role in the discussion of the impact of security on **civil liberties** (actions exercised without government interference) and recognized that there could be challenges in court to the *Anti-Terrorism Act*:

> Those who see this issue primarily in terms of the impact of a security focus on civil liberties, will see the courts as the key forum for discussion. But others in our society are concerned that an over-reliance on the courts weakens the primary role of Cabinet and Parliament to take policy leadership. For Canada to find policy balance in the area of national security, there needs to be what Peter Hogg, Dean of the Osgoode Hall Law School, has characterized as an active dialogue between the courts and Parliament. This dialogue is a metaphor for the relationship between these two institutions. It is a relationship that works best when it is characterized on both sides by respect for, and consideration of, the perspective the other side brings.
>
> The challenge for us is not only to encourage the discussion, but to ensure that it is a balanced and informed one. The combination of the media, an independent bar, an active academic community, and a vigorous civil society will ensure that government action will be closely scrutinized and properly criticized. But how will citizens, Parliament or the courts judge whether proposed government actions are appropriate? …
>
> We all need a greater understanding of the national security context, and of the threats

we are facing. An informed citizenry, Parliament and judiciary increase the likelihood that our responses will be appropriate and measured…. (Rosenberg 2002)

The courts may be open to claims of judicial activism when they interpret rights and freedoms under the *Charter*. However, new situations will require both institutions—the legislature and the judiciary—to balance their roles in order to reflect a commitment to participate in this "active dialogue."

VIEWPOINTS: Security versus Civil Liberties

In August 2003, federal officers working under the Public Security and Anti-Terrorism (PSAT) unit arrested 19 people in the Toronto area as part of an anti-terrorism investigation called Project Thread. Some were held without charges as officials checked out their links to terrorist groups. After being held for six weeks, many of the men were released as Citizenship and Immigration Canada no longer believed that they were a security risk or posed a threat to Canada.

In the aftermath of September 11, 2001, all freedom-loving, democratic countries were compelled to address one overriding issue: Should the protection of society as a whole supersede individual rights?

In response to the events of 9/11, Canada passed Bill C-36, the *Anti-Terrorism Act*, in the late fall of 2001. In order to combat terrorism and promote national security, this new act allowed for amendments to be made to the *Criminal Code*, including making it an offence to participate in any activity of a terrorist group, use property for terrorist purposes, finance a terrorist activity, or facilitate a terrorist activity. The *Criminal Code* was also amended to allow investigative hearings that would require individuals with relevant information

FIGURE 7.12 How has 9/11 affected privacy rights in Canada?

related to an investigation of a terrorist activity to appear before a judge and disclose that information, in effect compelling a person to provide testimony. The *Code* was further amended to allow peace officers to detain individuals in order to prevent terrorist activities from being carried out. The haste with which this anti-terrorism legislation was passed allowed very little time to debate the issues, chiefly, the curtailing of individual rights in Canada.

Perceived threats to security are also covered by Canada's immigration legislation. Under Bill C-11, the *Immigration and Refugee Protection Act*, the federal government can detain, without charges, **foreign nationals** (people in Canada who are not citizens or permanent residents) or those with permanent resident status if they are considered a threat to national security. Some people rank security as a priority and believe strongly that protecting society as a whole is worth sacrificing the rights of a few. Civil libertarians, however, view the new legislative powers of preventive detention and compulsory testimony as a threat to civil liberties.

Edward L. Greenspan, one of Canada's top criminal defence lawyers, warned that due process (i.e., procedural fairness) may be suspect in cases in which the minister of immigration and the Solicitor General, under the authority of the *Immigration and Refugee Protection Act*, sign a "security certificate" against foreign visitors or individuals who have permanent resident status. Such certificates, when issued, would have the effect of declaring a person inadmissible to Canada on the basis of being considered a danger to the security of Canada. In the act, security concerns also include "engaging in terrorism, or acts of violence that would or might endanger the lives or safety of persons in Canada." Greenspan's concerns relate to the fact that a foreign visitor can be immediately arrested and held without bail for an indefinite period of time. As well, an individual with permanent resident status can also be detained, but a federal court judge must begin a review procedure within 48 hours of that detention. If this detention is considered to be valid, the permanent resident can be held for up to six months without review. While the act does provide for a federal court judge to review both cases of detention by the seventh day of custody, the accused or the lawyer is not involved in the process of reviewing the evidence of the government. Eventually, a summary of the evidence is provided to the accused, but if a judge rules that providing certain information would pose a threat to national security, then the information can be withheld. When the accused is finally given the opportunity to be heard, the judge's main job is to assess the "reasonability" of issuing the security certificate, not to determine whether the accused is actually a security threat. A further criticism of the security certificate process is that the accused is not given a right to appeal and may even be deported from Canada. If the lawyer is not privy to the evidence against his or her client, a solid legal defence cannot be provided. Greenspan warned of having blind trust in government action:

> It's astounding that we are living under a government that, in defence of freedom and liberty, can keep someone not charged with any crime in solitary confinement for years based on secret information. It's terrible to contemplate that people can lose their livelihood based on information they cannot question. It's unthinkable that such people have absolutely no right of appeal or review, a glaring violation of a basic tenet of the rule of law: the right to appeal the decisions of a lower court.
>
> We are living in a time when the defeat of terrorism is on everyone's mind. But that doesn't mean we are supposed to simply trust the government to act wisely on correct information. The rule of law is the bedrock of our nation, not blind faith in the unchecked judgment of government officials. Any country that lives by a rule of "trust us, there is no need for due process," is totalitarian....
>
> The challenge is to figure out a way to deal with the threat of terrorism without losing the freedoms that make Canada the great nation it is. Everyone

must be able to respond to their accusers, whether in the realm of a criminal trial or a security hearing. We must demand that persons threatened with loss of liberty, livelihood and possibly life, be provided with someone in this process who can protect them from false and unsupported allegations.

Greenspan emphasized the importance of legal representation and warned of serious consequences if mistakes were made in security cases based on false information. He warned that sacrificing fundamental freedoms could come at a high cost:

> In the global struggle against terrorism, Canadians are in possession of the ultimate weapon. It's the weapon of an unassailable idea—individual rights, liberty and the dignity of the individual. It would be a tragic paradox if we should surrender any part of this heritage, for we should then have done to ourselves from within what we fear most from without. We must remain forever vigilant about any encroachment on personal freedom and individual liberty, of citizens and non-citizens alike….If we really believe in democracy, we must have faith enough to fight for its preservation with the tools of freedom.

SOURCE: Greenspan, Edward. "In Defence of Freedom." *Maclean's*. 28 July 2003.

Up for Debate

After studying the viewpoint of Edward Greenspan, carefully conduct your own research on the issues. Then prepare a debate based on the following resolution: "Be it resolved that national security at the cost of civil liberties is demonstrably justified in a post-9/11 world."

CONFIRM YOUR UNDERSTANDING

1. Briefly compare and contrast the role of the legislature with that of the judiciary.

2. Explain the concept of judicial activism.

3. Explain the concept of "active dialogue" as used by Peter Hogg.

In Closing

In this chapter, you have not only learned about the guarantees of rights and freedoms under the *Charter*, but you also now understand the challenge of balancing these rights and freedoms within the context of each situation. Rights are not absolute, and sometimes restrictions are placed on their use and application.

The *Charter* has indeed allowed our Constitution to grow and will continue to do so as our judiciary is given the task of balancing these rights and freedoms within the restrictions of the reasonable limits section of the *Charter*. Concepts such as liberty, security, and equality will continue to evolve as we are challenged to interpret our rights and freedoms within the context of a free and democratic society.

CHAPTER ACTIVITIES

Extend Your Legal Knowledge

1. Explain how rights in the *Charter* are balanced by corresponding responsibilities or obligations.
2. Outline the steps in the proportionality test used to determine the validity of limiting individual rights under the *Charter*.
3. Describe three situations in which rights have been justifiably limited under the *Charter*, and then comment on the extent to which you support the limits.
4. Explain how the *Charter* can be used to provide remedies when rights violations have occurred.
5. Explain why the Supreme Court has been criticized for judicial activism.

Think About the Law

6. "The freedom of no one is safe unless the freedom of everyone is safe" (Canadian Civil Liberties Association). Explain, in your own words, what is meant by this statement. Do you agree? Give reasons for your opinion.
7. How would you define the term "reasonable" as used in s. 1 of the *Charter*? Use *Charter* cases cited in this chapter to support your explanation.
8. Research the internment of Japanese Canadians during World War II. Had the *Charter of Rights and Freedoms* been in force then, what sections could you argue were violated?
9. How could you use the proportionality test to justify limiting your rights during a random police spot-check program? Explain your reasoning for each step of the test.
10. In his speech "The Role of the Courts in Turbulent Times," the Honourable Justice R. Roy McMurtry observed that Canada's anti-terrorism legislation "may well be tested in our courtrooms and as a result the role of judges could be subjected to closer scrutiny than at any time before in our nation's history. While the accountability of any important institution is essential in a democratic society, it is appropriate that it occur with an understanding of the basic principles of judicial interpretation of our Constitution." As part of Canada's anti-terrorism legislation, individuals can be detained without charges if they are considered to pose a threat to national security.
    a) What potential *Charter* violations could be argued?
    b) Using the three-part proportionality test (see p. 201), justify or refute the validity of a detention under Canada's anti-terrorist legislation.

Communicate About the Law

11. Read the following opinion piece on the role of our Supreme Court.

    The federal government's reference to the Supreme Court of Canada of a draft bill on same-sex marriages underscores the need to change Canadian democracy.

    Parliament, in the Age of the *Charter of Rights and Freedoms*, is increasingly an institution of secondary importance, while the Supreme Court and the provincial superior courts have become those of primary importance.

    Canada should therefore stop living the fiction that the courts check Parliament and recognize in democratic practice that the courts rule in wide areas of public policy.

    Parliament (and legislatures) now waste a lot of time grappling with issues that the courts eventually decide. The whole political process could be streamlined if we recognized the importance of the courts, turned over directly to them important areas of public policy, then allowed Parliament to fine-tune what the courts have decided.

    Submitting proposed draft legislation to the Supreme Court first is one method. Referring general issues of public policy, with the reference appropriately framed as in the

Québec secession reference case, is another method.

Any innovative way would be an improvement on the current situation in which Canadian citizens labour under the illusion that their elected officials are making decisions, when in fact the courts are.... (Simpson 2003)

Write a counter-argument that justifies the validity of our elected legislatures. Support your opinion.

12. Research a newspaper article that deals with a *Charter* issue. Prepare a legal analysis of the issue using the Legal Quest Research Model in the Legal Handbook.

13. Write an argument that defends the protection of civil liberties at all costs.

14. Some argue that the courts should have the ultimate power to interpret the *Charter* in matters relating to fundamental rights and freedoms. Others argue that the use of the override clause protects society from improper interpretations by the court. Assuming that the Supreme Court erred in interpreting rights in a case, the only option for addressing the error would be to wait for a subsequent case decision in which the court could reverse an earlier ruling or make a constitutional amendment. The power of the federal and provincial governments to pass laws that will operate notwithstanding the *Charter* allows legislatures to exercise their legitimate role in the area of rights protection.

a) Do you support the use of s. 33 (the notwithstanding clause)? Support your opinion.

b) Should s. 33 have a five-year limitation period? Support your opinion.

Apply the Law

15. Use the Internet to research a Supreme Court of Canada decision on a *Charter* issue. Prepare a case analysis using the Case Study Method in the Legal Handbook. Where possible, highlight

the extent to which the reasonable limits clause (s. 1) was applied to the decision.

16. In the case of *Ramsden v. Peterborough (City)*, [1993] 2 S.C.R. 1084, Kenneth Ramsden was charged with violating a municipal bylaw that absolutely prohibited putting posters on public property. The city argued that the bylaw was designed to prevent such consequences as litter, aesthetic blights, and traffic hazards. The court held that the effect of the bylaw was to restrict expression and was therefore unconstitutional.

a) What section of the *Charter* could be argued as being violated in this case?

b) How could you use the steps of the proportionality test under the *Charter* to justify an infringement of your rights under s. 1?

17. Richard Sauvé was an inmate of a federal prison, serving a sentence of more than two years. In the case of *Sauvé v. Canada (Chief Electoral Officer)*, [2002] 3 S.C.R. 519, 2002 SCC 68, Sauvé argued that because s. 51(e) of the *Canada Elections Act* denied federal inmates serving sentences of more than two years the right to vote in elections, his rights and the rights of all prisoners were violated. According to the *Charter*, all citizens have a constitutional right to vote. The Canadian government argued that denying inmates in federal penitentiaries the right to vote was a reasonable limit according to s. 1 of the *Charter*. Nine judges of the Supreme Court of Canada heard the case. Five judges concurred with Sauvé and argued that s. 51(e) of the *Canada Elections Act* did violate the constitutional right to vote and could not be justified by s. 1 of the *Charter*. Four judges disagreed with the majority and held that it was a reasonable limit.

A brief synopsis of the judges' decisions is presented on the following page. It is not uncommon for judges to disagree with one another. Assume the role of a tenth judge. How would you have argued this case?

McLachlin, Iacobucci, Binnie, Arbour, and LeBel JJ. (concurring)

To justify a *Charter* infringement under s. 1, the infringement must achieve a constitutionally valid purpose and must be reasonably and demonstrably justified. Denying the right to vote as a matter of social and political philosophy is rejected. The right to vote, which is fundamental to democracy and the rule of law, cannot be ignored. Framers of the *Charter* gave a special importance to the right by exempting it from s. 33 (the notwithstanding clause). The position of the government is that denying prisoners the right to vote enhances civic responsibility and respect for the rule of law. Withdrawing the right to vote recognizes that voting is a privilege accorded to those who have not committed crimes. This position must be rejected. There is no rational connection between the right to vote and its objectives. Prisoners are already being punished by virtue of being imprisoned. Not being able to vote is an additional punishment. Denying the vote is more likely to undermine than uphold civic responsibility.

L'Heureux-Dubé, Gonthier, Major, and Bastarache JJ. (dissenting)

Philosophical, political, and social considerations are not able to be proved scientifically. Limiting the right to vote is based on an argument of principle or value statements. Section 1 of the *Charter* suggests that if social, political, or philosophical advancement by Parliament reasonably justifies a limit of a right in the context of a free and democratic society, then it should be upheld as constitutional. Section 51(e) of the *Canada Elections Act* denying the right to vote to federal inmates indicates that Parliament has drawn a line. Society rejects serious crime, and **disenfranchisement** (taking away one's right to vote) is a civil disability derived from the criminal conviction. In the opinion of the dissenting judges, s. 51(e) meets the proportionality test that the legislation is rationally connected to the objective. Reason, logic, and common sense support a connection between disenfranchising those imprisoned for serious crimes and the objective of promoting civic responsibility and the rule of law. Those who commit serious crimes will lose one aspect of political equality of citizenship. It is a temporary disadvantage and the impairment is minimal. It is a valid object for Parliament to apply **sanctions** (disciplinary actions or restrictions, limitations, suspensions, or terminations of normal privileges) for a serious crime. Disenfranchisement is one sanction and is a reasonable limit in a democratic society.

BIBLIOGRAPHY

Abella, Rosalie Silberman. "The Future After Twenty Years Under the Charter." Canadian Rights and Freedoms: 20 Years Under the Charter. The Association for Canadian Studies, Closing Session, Ottawa. 20 Apr. 2002. Accessed 11 Aug. 2003 <www.ontariocourts.on.ca/court_of_appeal/speeches/future.htm>.

Borovoy, A. Alan. "The Fundamentals of Our Fundamental Freedoms: A Primer on Civil Liberties and Democracy." Toronto: Canadian Civil Liberties Education Trust.

Canadian Civil Liberties Association. Accessed Sept.–Dec. 2003 <www.ccla.org>.

Canadian Legal Information Institute. Accessed Sept.–Dec. 2003 <www.canlii.org>.

Department of Justice Canada. Accessed Sept.–Dec. 2003 <www.canada.justice.gc.ca/en/index.html>.

Elections Canada On-line. "Youth Electoral Participation —Survey and Analysis of Canadian Trends." Accessed 1 Dec. 2003 <www.elections.ca/content.asp?section=med&document=survey&dir=eveyou/forum&lang=e&textonly=false>.

"The Expanding Court." Editorial. *The Globe and Mail* 8 Nov. 2003: A26.

Greenspan, Edward. "In Defence of Freedom." *Maclean's.* 28 July 2003: 30–31.

Hogg, Peter W. *Constitutional Law of Canada.* 2nd ed. Toronto: The Carswell Company Limited, 1985.

Guide to Ontario Courts. Accessed Sept.–Dec. 2003 <www.ontariocourts.on.ca>.

Macklem, Patrick. *Canadian Constitutional Law.* 2nd ed. Toronto: Emond Montgomery Publications Limited, 1997.

McMurtry, R. Roy. "The Role of the Courts in Turbulent Times." The Canadian Club. Ontario Justice Education Network. 3 Dec. 2001. Accessed 26 June 2003 <www.ontariocourts.on.ca/ojen/speeches/role.htm>.

Rosenberg, Morris. "An Effective Canadian Legal Framework to Meet Emerging Threats to National Security." The Canadian Association for Intelligence and Security Studies. 26 Sept. 2002. Accessed 13 Sept. 2003 <http://canada.justice.gc.ca/en/news/sp/2002/doc_30694.html>.

Sharpe, Robert J., Katherine E. Swinton, and Kent Roach. *The Charter of Rights and Freedoms.* 2nd ed. Toronto: Irwin Law Inc., 2002.

Simpson, Jeffrey. "Why Don't We Just Turn Policy Over to Courts?" *The Globe and Mail* 22 July 2003: A15.

Supreme Court of Canada. Accessed Sept.–Dec. 2003 <www.lexum.umontreal.ca/csc-scc/en/>.

Chapter 8

CONFLICTS AND RESOLUTIONS IN A DEMOCRATIC SOCIETY

LEARNING EXPECTATIONS

After reading this chapter, you will be able to:

- identify the historical and contemporary barriers to the equal enjoyment of human rights in Canada, and analyze the effects of these barriers

- analyze historical and contemporary conflicts between minority and majority rights

- demonstrate an understanding of the difficulty of balancing rights in a democracy

- assess the political and legal avenues for resolving conflicts (e.g., referendums, the courts, tribunals)

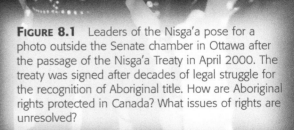

FIGURE 8.1 Leaders of the Nisga'a pose for a photo outside the Senate chamber in Ottawa after the passage of the Nisga'a Treaty in April 2000. The treaty was signed after decades of legal struggle for the recognition of Aboriginal title. How are Aboriginal rights protected in Canada? What issues of rights are unresolved?

> *If all people are equal, it follows that all people are equally entitled to freedom, fair treatment, and respect. The rights are easily stated. The more difficult problem is to move them off the sterile page and into the reality of people's lives.*
>
> —The Right Honourable Chief Justice of Canada Beverley McLachlin

■ I N T R O D U C T I O N ■

Canada is regarded around the world as a country that recognizes and upholds the importance of human rights. The protections provided for in provincial and territorial human rights legislation, as well as the guarantees entrenched in the *Charter,* are evidence of this. A historical perspective on Canada's human rights record reveals a very different picture, however. Indeed, even today, there are barriers to the equal enjoyment of human rights among Canadians. For women, Aboriginal peoples, immigrants, and others, the struggle to achieve equality in Canadian society is ongoing. So, too, is the struggle to balance minority and majority rights in Canada. The Canadian government has allowed individual citizens and groups to voice their concerns about inequities and, in some instances, has taken action to protect minority rights. For example, some Aboriginal hunting and fishing rights have been guaranteed, pay equity legislation has been implemented, and affirmative-action programs have been developed. But despite Canada's efforts to address inequities, there are still those in our society who claim that their rights have not been given sufficient recognition. And there are others who claim that minority rights protection has been extended too far.

Since the task of balancing rights in a democratic society is clearly a difficult one, it is not surprising that the political and legal methods for resolving conflicts are rarely simple or straightforward. Consider the political process of referendums used in the Québec sovereignty debate or the legal process of settling Aboriginal land claims. Each issue brings with it a new set of challenges that stem from different perspectives. Through the conflict resolution process, it becomes apparent that the rights and interests of the majority may conflict with the rights and interests of the minority, and vice versa. The question then remains: How do we recognize the rights and interests of everyone in Canadian society and still achieve justice?

Barriers to the Equal Enjoyment of Human Rights

Some of the laws that Canada has enacted or applied in the past would be considered discriminatory by today's standards. An examination of historical records reveals the multitude of inequities experienced by women, Aboriginal peoples, immigrants, people with disabilities, and others. Current laws, however, demonstrate Canada's commitment to removing barriers to equality.

Women

Historically, women were considered property. They had neither voting nor political rights. Until the early part of the twentieth century, women in Canada were excluded from holding political office, sitting in the Senate, and becoming judges. They were not considered "persons" under Canadian law until 1929. The historic case of *Edwards v. Attorney General for Canada*, [1930] A.C. 124 (often referred to as the "Persons Case") is proof that even our Supreme Court was not prepared to define women as "qualified persons" so that they could be appointed to a position in the Senate. Emily Murphy, Canada's first female judge, wanted to secure a position in the Senate, but the interpretation given to a section of our Constitution blocked her initial efforts. Essentially, the *BNA Act* allowed only qualified persons to be appointed to the Senate.

Murphy engaged four other women— Henrietta Muir Edwards, Louise McKinney, Irene Parlby, and Nellie McClung—to launch a reference to the Supreme Court. At the time this case was heard, there existed a provision that five people who had an interest in the same matter could initiate a **reference** (that is, submit a question to the Supreme Court of Canada concerning a constitutional issue) by petitioning the Governor-General-in-Council (the federal Cabinet). The Governor-General-in-Council would then refer the question to the Supreme Court. (Today, a reference is a procedure by which the government of Canada refers an important legal or factual question to the Supreme Court of Canada for the court to hear and to consider. The Supreme Court can also hear references that provincial governments have made to their Courts of Appeal.) The issue to be determined in this case was whether the word "persons" under s. 24 of the *BNA Act* included female persons. In 1928, the Supreme Court rendered a verdict against the five women, a ruling that appears outrageous by today's standards. The Famous Five, as they became known, subsequently launched an appeal to the Judicial Committee of the Privy Council of Britain. In 1929, the Privy Council declared: women were indeed persons.

Voting rights for women were also attained only through the struggles and efforts of advocates such as Nellie McClung and Emily Murphy. The

FIGURE 8.2   Former PM Jean Chrétien and Adrienne Clarkson looked on as this statue of Emily Murphy was unveiled in Ottawa in 2000. It is part of a monument honouring the Famous Five who fought for over 10 years to have women legally declared "persons." How did Emily Murphy contribute to the development of women's rights in Canada?

first province to legislate a woman's right to vote was Manitoba, in 1916, and other provinces soon followed suit.

As more women entered the workforce during and after World War II, further barriers to equality arose. Inequities became apparent in situations in which women were performing comparable work to that of men but were being paid significantly less. As noted in Chapter 6, the *Canadian Human Rights Act* protected employees working under federal jurisdiction (e.g., employees in banks, airlines, and postal services) from discrimination. Section 11 (1) of the *Canadian Human Rights Act* states that "it is a discriminatory practice for an employer to establish or maintain differences in wages between male and female employees employed in the same establishment who are performing work of equal value." In order to remedy pay inequities, governments enacted legislation to protect women from this form of discrimination. For example, Ontario and New Brunswick enacted their specific pay equity legislation in the 1980s.

In order to achieve **pay equity**, or equal pay for work of equal value, the value of a predominantly female job must be compared to the value of a predominantly male job in the same establishment. For example, if a company employs a female receptionist and a male warehouse worker, a job evaluation must be conducted to determine the value of the work being performed. An evaluation allows for a comparison of the different jobs on the basis of skill, effort, responsibility, and working conditions. Points are assigned to each of the four categories, and a value for each job is determined based on the total score. After the job evaluations are complete, the job values and wages are compared. If the point values for the jobs are equal, then the wages are compared. If the woman's wage is below that of the man's in a comparable job, then, in accordance with pay equity legislation, the employer is obligated to remedy the wage discrepancy.

Generally, the salary is raised immediately upon evaluation, submission, and approval of the documents by the government. In some instances, however, there are issues of back pay, which can take years to resolve. Pay equity is designed to remedy wage inequities for underpaid female job classes. If the job evaluation comparison indicates that the value of the work is comparable but that it is the male who is underpaid, then the wages are not adjusted.

Many gains have been made in the area of pay equity for women. Since the *Canadian Human Rights Act* was enacted in 1977, the Canadian Human Rights Commission has dealt with over 400 complaints initiated by individuals or small groups of employees. One of the criticisms of pay equity legislation, however, has been that many of the claims have required extensive litigation in the courts, which is not only costly but also time-consuming. For example, a legal battle for pay equity that was launched in 1983 by the predominantly female clerical staff of the federal public service, who made less than the predominantly male administrative group, is still ongoing.

Another criticism of pay equity legislation, this one coming from advocates of the policy, is that it is somewhat limited in its ability to remedy inequities for women in the workforce. A report submitted in March 2003 by the Canadian Human Rights Commission to the Pay Equity Task Force acknowledged the need for a broader approach to securing equality rights for female workers:

> Equitable wages are a fundamental aspect of equality, but they are not sufficient to redress the inequality suffered by women and other disadvantaged groups in employment. A coordinated and concerted strategy is needed to transform the systems and practices that continue to exist. Only part of this transformation can be achieved through employment equity and anti-discrimination initiatives. A specialized, human rights-based and proactive approach to pay equity is also needed. Where pay equity is achieved, it can add to a synergy that sparks changes not only in pay, but in the systemic attitudes and practices towards women and others. This flow-

through effect results from the interconnectedness of human rights. An institutional framework that deals with wage discrimination in isolation from human rights machinery is ill-equipped to foster this kind of transformation. (Canadian Human Rights Commission, "Submission...")

Pay equity legislation aims to remedy pay disparities in the workforce, but sometimes there is an actual imbalance in the number of women represented in certain areas of the job market. The federal *Employment Equity Act*, which came into force in 1996, provides for the development of employment equity or **affirmative-action** programs in workplaces that fall under federal jurisdiction. These affirmative-action programs specifically target women, Aboriginal peoples, people with disabilities, and visible minorities in order to address discriminatory hiring practices. However, these programs are surrounded by controversy, as you will learn later in this chapter.

Equality rights for women have been aided by the extension of maternity leaves and the addition of paternal leaves. These changes have alleviated some of the stress on mothers from having to choose between going back to work and staying home during the first few months following the birth or adoption of a child. However, the issue of daycare for children is of primary concern to many working mothers. The unavailability of suitable daycare arrangements can be a critical barrier to women entering or returning to the workforce when their children are still young. The inability or reluctance on the part of federal and provincial governments to provide universal free daycare might also be viewed as a barrier to equality. Employers who are faced with staffing shortages may have to consider offering the incentive of paid or subsidized daycare in order to entice people to work for their organizations. Any program that serves to eliminate employment barriers aids in the promotion of equality rights in the workplace.

Although efforts to broaden equality rights for women have been successful in many areas, pursuing changes and remedies through the court system can be time-consuming and extremely costly. The challenge facing the courts, on the other hand, is determining how far constitutional guarantees of equality rights should be extended.

Organizations such as the Women's Legal Education and Action Fund (LEAF)—a group formed to advance equality rights for women and girls through a focus on law reform, public education, and court advocacy—are finding it increasingly difficult to fund their intervention work at the Supreme Court level. LEAF has intervened in over 140 cases since it was formed in 1985, and judgments have considered such issues as violence against women, sexual harassment, and spousal support. LEAF's advocacy work in cases where there was a perceived denial of equality rights was highlighted in the widely publicized case of *Doe v. Metropolitan Toronto (Municipality) Commissioners of Police*, [1998] 39 O.R. (3d) 487, (Ont. Ct. Gen. Div.).

Jane Doe launched a civil suit against the Toronto police after she was the victim of a serial rapist who had been targeting an area in downtown Toronto where she lived in the summer of 1986. She successfully sued for damages on the grounds that the police, in failing to warn women in the area of the presence of the "balcony rapist" were, in effect, using them as bait to catch the predator. Doe cited an infringement of her equality rights under s. 15 (1) of the *Charter*, which states, "Every individual is equal before and under the law and has the right to the equal protection and equal benefit of the law without discrimination and, in particular, without discrimination based on race, national or ethnic origin, colour, religion, sex, age or mental or physical disability." Doe also claimed that the police had breached her legal right under s. 7 "to life, liberty and security of the person." In her decision, Justice Jean MacFarland had this to say:

> In my view, the conduct of this investigation and the failure to warn in particular, was moti-

vated and informed by the adherence to rape myths as well as sexist stereotypical reasoning about rape, about women and about women who are raped. The plaintiff therefore has been discriminated against by reason of her gender and as the result the plaintiff's right to equal protection and equal benefit of the law were compromised.

Immigrants

Canada has an enviable reputation on the world stage as being a peace-loving, open-minded, tolerant nation. A rich tapestry of peoples has contributed greatly to both our economic and cultural development. However, Canada has not always been so welcoming, and, in fact, many of our laws have perpetuated discrimination against, and inequality for, those people trying to escape similar treatment elsewhere.

Chinese immigrants were subject to inequity very early in Canadian history. The Canadian Pacific Railway, which opened up Canada to settlement, trade, and commerce, was built in large part by Chinese immigrant labourers who were paid significantly less than workers of European descent. After the last spike of the transcontinental railway was driven into the ground in 1885, the Canadian government began imposing a **head tax**—a fee to be paid by an immigrant on admission to Canada—of $50 on Chinese immigrants. This fee continued to increase, reaching $100 in 1900 and $500 in 1903, the equivalent of about two years' wages for a Chinese labourer living in Canada. The head tax was eventually abolished in 1923, but, in that same year, the government passed the *Chinese Exclusion Act*, which had the effect of excluding people of Chinese descent from entering Canada. After World War II, many Chinese Canadian war veterans fought to have this discriminatory act repealed. Although the act was revoked in 1947, it remains a solid reminder of Canada's disgraceful treatment of Chinese immigrants.

In addition to entrance conditions, Chinese immigrants were restricted in their ability to practise certain professions, such as law, and in their hiring practices if they were business owners. In *Quong-Wing v. The King* (1914), 49 S.C.R. 440, a Saskatchewan law prohibited the employment of white females in businesses "owned, kept or managed by any Japanese, Chinaman or other Oriental person." Quong-Wing challenged the law preventing him from employing two white female waitresses in his restaurant, arguing that the law was **ultra vires**, or outside the authority of, provincial jurisdiction. He argued that the subject matter of the law related to "naturalization and aliens," a matter under federal jurisdiction. The Supreme Court held that the subject matter of the law was **intra vires**, or within the authority of, provincial jurisdiction as a matter of property and civil rights. The **pith and substance** (overriding purpose or intent) of the law was held to be for the protection of white women and girls. The court made a constitutional ruling, holding that the Saskatchewan government had the exclusive authority to pass the law.

In the late nineteenth century, British Columbia did not allow Chinese and Japanese Canadians or Aboriginal peoples to vote in provincial elections. In British Columbia in 1895, the *Provincial Elections Act* stated, "No Chinaman, Japanese or Indian shall have his name placed on the Register of Voters for any Electoral District, or be entitled to vote at any election."

The start of World War II led to further discrimination against people of Japanese descent. Regarded as "enemy aliens," their homes and businesses were confiscated and auctioned off at a fraction of their worth. Then, under the authority of the *War Measures Act*, Japanese Canadians were moved to internment camps and work camps. In September 1988, the Canadian government acknowledged its ill treatment of Japanese Canadians, issuing a public apology for their internment and seizure of property, and providing a compensation package worth $400 million in total.

The text of the *Japanese Canadian Redress Agreement* serves as a painful reminder to future generations of this dark period in Canada's history:

> Despite perceived military necessities at the time, the forced removal and internment of Japanese Canadians during World War II, and their deportation and expulsion following the war, was unjust. In retrospect, government policies of disenfranchisement, detention, confiscation and sale of private and community property, expulsion, deportation and restriction of movement, which continued after the war, were influenced by discriminatory attitudes. Japanese Canadians who were interned had their property liquidated and the proceeds of sale were used to pay for their own internment.
>
> The acknowledgement of these injustices serves notice to all Canadians that the excesses of the past are condemned and that the principles of justice and equality in Canada are reaffirmed…(Canadian Race Relations Foundation, "Terms of Agreement…")

The monetary compensation provided for in the agreement included $21 000 for individual survivor redress, $12 million for the Japanese Canadian community for the promotion of human rights education, and $12 million for the creation of a Canadian Race Relations Foundation. Roger Obata, a Japanese Canadian and human rights activist, was instrumental in negotiating the redress agreement with the federal government and was a signatory to the agreement. He was awarded the Order of Canada in 1990, which read, "He has enriched Canada and all of her ethnocultural communities with his contribution to a new ledger in race relations, a ledger in which any future incoming peoples to this country can write their history without fear and without prejudice" (Keung 2002).

Not all ethnic groups that have experienced systemic discrimination in Canada have received compensation packages. Since 1984, the Chinese Canadian National Council has been urging the federal government to compensate surviving Chinese immigrants who were forced to pay the head tax. They also requested an apology be issued to Chinese Canadians for their ill treatment, but the apology has yet to be given. Then in 2000, a class-action lawsuit was launched by some individuals who had paid the head tax, as well as by spouses and descendants of those who had paid the head tax.

In the case of *Mack v. Canada (Attorney General)*, (2002-09-13) ONCA Docket C36799, the plaintiffs sought reimbursement for the head taxes paid, plus interest and damages for pain and suffering. The claim amounted to $23 million of head-tax revenues collected during that time. The plaintiffs argued that the head-tax laws violated equality rights under the *Charter* and that the government of Canada was "unjustly enriched" at the expense of Chinese immigrants by the revenues gained from this tax. The Ontario Court of Appeal held that the facts giving rise to the *Japanese Canadian Redress Agreement* were completely different from those giving rise to this compensation claim. It also held that the *Charter* could not be applied retroactively to this situation. As the head-tax law was valid when it was enacted, the plaintiffs were unable to succeed in their argument of unjust enrichment. The Ontario Court of Appeal agreed with the decision of the Ontario Superior Court of Justice that the statement of claim "disclosed no reasonable cause of action." The case was appealed to the Supreme Court of Canada, but leave to appeal was denied in April 2003.

There have been efforts on the part of other communities in Canada to claim redress for discriminatory treatment. For example, the Italian Canadian community has sought an apology and compensation from the federal government for interning people of Italian descent during World War II. Similarly, the Ukrainian Canadian community has lobbied for compensation for the internment of members of their community during World War I. Undeniably, the laws that allowed for internment had a discriminatory effect.

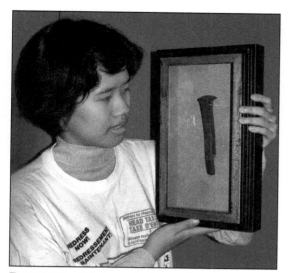

FIGURE 8.3 This framed railway spike was part of a 2003 cross-Canada campaign to raise awareness about the injustices suffered by Chinese immigrants in the early part of the twentieth century. What differences exist between the facts giving rise to the Chinese Canadian claim for compensation and the facts giving rise to the *Japanese Canadian Redress Agreement?*

As you learned in Chapter 6, the aftermath of World War II exposed human rights violations and discrimination worldwide. The creation of the United Nations and its *Universal Declaration of Human Rights* were to influence the development of Canadian rights legislation. Shortly after World War II, in 1947, Chinese Canadians were given the right to vote in federal and provincial elections. The right to vote in federal elections was extended to Japanese Canadians in 1949. The federal government passed its own rights legislation, the *Canadian Bill of Rights*, in 1960. The provinces, beginning with Ontario in 1962, began to enact human rights legislation that would protect individuals against discriminatory treatment. Today, all provinces have human rights laws that address issues of discrimination. In addition, the *Canadian Charter of Rights and Freedoms* entrenches equality rights in the Constitution.

Despite human rights legislation, immigrants continue to face barriers to equality. According to the 2001 Census, almost half of Toronto's population—43.7 percent—was born outside of Canada. In fact, Toronto has the highest immigrant population of any city in North America. Statistics also reveal that the unemployment rate in Toronto for recent immigrants aged 25 to 44 is 10.7 percent, compared to an unemployment rate for the non-immigrant population of 3.7 percent. Immigrants are often unable to find work that measures up to their background or training. The inability of skilled and educated workers to find meaningful employment is a barrier that perpetuates inequality.

Despite the laws designed to prevent discrimination, the fact remains that discrimination still exists in Canada. Between April and August 2002, 42 500 people from across Canada took part in an Ethnic Diversity Survey. The survey results revealed that "[o]ne-in-five (20%) people aged 15 and over who were part of a visible minority, or an estimated 587 000 people, said they felt that they had experienced discrimination or unfair treatment sometimes or often in the five years prior to the survey because of their ethnicity, culture, race, skin colour, language, accent or religion" (Statistics Canada).

In September 2003, Doudou Diène, the United Nations Special Rapporteur on Racism, Racial Discrimination, Xenophobia, and Related Intolerance, toured Ottawa, Montréal, Halifax, Regina, and Toronto over a two-week period and received over 200 submissions from Canadian citizens regarding racism. Topics of the submissions concerned "conditions of Aboriginals on reserves and in urban communities, anti-Black racism, the impact of the demolition of Africville [a community outside of Halifax originally established in 1840 by Black Americans, which became the target of extreme prejudice and discrimination], the post–September 11th climate on Muslims, the phenomenon of racial profiling and its impact on racialized groups, anti-Semitism, hate and the Chinese head tax, among other manifestations of racism and racial discrimination" (Canadian Race Relations Foundation, "Racism Still Exists..."). In announcing his preliminary findings, Diène commented that racism still exists in Canada.

Aboriginal Peoples

Many misconceptions about Aboriginal peoples have made them a target of discriminatory practices for well over a century. Among the primary misconceptions is the belief that they are all members of one group of people. The Assembly of First Nations defines Aboriginal peoples as encompassing First Nations, Inuit, and Métis, each having their own separate and distinct history, culture, and political structure. First Nations peoples are legally registered under the terms of the *Indian Act* as "status Indians." There are over 600 First Nations representing numerous cultural groups (nations) and languages, such as Cree, Dene, and Blackfoot. Their rights, although constitutionally protected, are still subject to regulations. "Non-status Indians" are Aboriginal peoples (excluding Inuit and Métis) who are, for various reasons, not registered under the terms of the *Indian Act*. You may recall from Chapter 6 that Jeannette Corbière Lavell lost her Indian status by marrying a non-Indian. Unfortunately, many First Nations peoples, particularly women, became non-status Indians as a result of discriminatory practices.

The 2001 Census defines a "treaty Indian" as an individual who is registered under the *Indian Act* and can show descent from a band that signed a treaty with the federal government. Continuing use of the outdated term "Indian" to describe an indigenous person, whether status Indian, non-status Indian, or treaty Indian, is an issue of ongoing controversy. Not only has the term "Indian" been used indiscriminately, but the term "Eskimo" has also been used incorrectly to describe the Inuit of Canada. Inuit are those Aboriginal peoples who live north of the treeline in Nunavut, the Northwest Territories, and Northern Québec and Labrador. In the Inuit language of Inuktitut, the term "Inuit" means "people." The singular form of Inuit is "Inuk."

The Métis of Canada are also considered Aboriginal people. The term "Métis" is used to identify those of mixed Aboriginal/European heritage and to refer to the Métis Nation of the central and northwestern parts of Canada, a group that numbered approximately 300 000 people in 2003.

Canada's record with respect to the treatment of Aboriginal peoples has been closely examined in recent years. Oral and written documentation verify that Aboriginal peoples have been the target of prejudice and discriminatory practices throughout Canada's history. After Confederation, the federal government implemented a policy of assimilation that was designed to absorb Aboriginal peoples into Canadian society. Not only were many of them moved from their land to reserves (lands set aside and designated by the federal government for occupation by Aboriginal peoples), but children were also separated from their families and forced to attend residential schools. The goal of these institutions was to ensure the assimilation of Aboriginal children into Canadian society. However, the numerous cases of physical, sexual, and emotional abuse that the victims, now adults, have launched in the past decade or so serve as evidence of just how mishandled and ill-conceived this goal of assimilation was.

The 1996 Royal Commission on Aboriginal Peoples raised the profile of the issue of residential-school abuse and spoke of a time period of negotiation and renewal. A compensation package for victims of residential-school abuse was negotiated in 2000, and a system of mediation was recommended for the settlement of claims. In June 2001, the Canadian government announced the creation of Indian Residential Schools Resolution Canada, a federal department with the mandate to resolve claims connected with physical and sexual abuse in the residential-school system.

Although this acknowledgment of past abuses is an important step in the process of healing relationships between the government and Aboriginal peoples, the loss of Aboriginal languages that resulted from the federal education policy remains an issue of some significance. We now know that Aboriginal children who attended residential schools or were victims

of forced adoptions were frequently punished for using their own language. We also know that the loss of the languages of Aboriginal peoples has compounded their difficulty in maintaining their cultures, especially since much of their histories and cultures have been passed down through generations by an oral tradition. This loss of language and culture has been referred to as "cultural genocide."

In order to prevent further erosion of Aboriginal languages, individual bands now offer classes to educate people in their own language. Some communities are also preserving their language through language laws. In January 2002, one Mohawk community in Québec— Kahnawà:ke (Kahnawake), near Montréal— passed its own language law requiring all government institutions within the Mohawk territory to have a language policy for their employees and to provide assurances that these employees could perform their work in the Mohawk language. The language law also upholds the right to have court proceedings within the Mohawk jurisdiction conducted in Mohawk, and it stipulates that those who apply

FIGURE 8.4 Mohawk language classes for adults aim to preserve Mohawk identity and culture. According to Mark Abley, who was consulted for an October 2003 *Toronto Star* article titled "Languages on Life Support," there are 53 Aboriginal languages spoken in Canada, but only Cree, Ojibway, and Inuktitut are in no danger of disappearing. However, 10 other Aboriginal languages are being used on a limited basis, and 40 are on the brink of elimination. What impact might losing Aboriginal languages have on Aboriginal peoples and Canada as a whole?

for public-sector jobs must either speak the language or promise to learn it (Abley 2003).

For its 2001 Aboriginal Peoples Survey, Statistics Canada interviewed 117 000 First Nations, Inuit, and Métis peoples about issues of health, housing, language, and education for those living off-reserve. Among the concerns cited by some participants were crowded living conditions, unsafe drinking water, substandard health care, and a decline in completion rates for secondary and post-secondary education. Phil Fontaine, the national chief of the Assembly of First Nations, had this to say about the survey results:

> We need greater First Nations control of First Nations education to ensure the curriculum and classroom are relevant to our youth so that they stay in school. Our post-secondary students say they need more resources and

FIGURE 8.5 Phil Fontaine was head of the Assembly of First Nations in 1997 and became leader again in 2003. His goal as leader is to strengthen relations with the federal government in order to secure better conditions for his people. What current barriers to equality are faced by Aboriginal peoples?

better access to child care so they can stay in school. And we must do more to support our languages because the survey shows they are in danger of disappearing. These are all priorities that require urgent attention. (Assembly of First Nations, "AFN National Chief States…")

Social issues continue to be of primary concern for Aboriginal leaders such as Fontaine. The 2001 Census results indicated that the Aboriginal population of Canada comprised approximately 3.3 percent of Canada's total population, or slightly less than 1 million people. As of 2003, approximately 700 000 Aboriginal peoples were living off-reserve, and, according to Fontaine, "Poverty is the overriding concern. It's a plague and it's an enormous cost on all" (Girard 2003). He also cited the need for adequate housing and attributed Canada's drop from third to eighth spot on the 2003 United Nations' Human Development Index to this fact.

Although employment equity programs have been put into place to remedy the imbalance of representation of Aboriginal peoples in the Canadian workplace, unemployment continues to be a major concern.

Given current circumstances, efforts to eliminate barriers to equality for Aboriginal peoples in Canada—especially as they relate to such social issues as employment, education, housing, and health care—will likely continue well into the twenty-first century. Issues of Aboriginal self-government, land claims, and harvesting rights will also play a dominant role. In recent years, the courts have considered Aboriginal claims to recover the land that was taken from them and have also ruled on First Nations' rights to hunting, fishing, and harvesting timber. Yet many of the resolutions to past injustices have been achieved with great difficulty by Aboriginal peoples through litigation, as you will learn later in this chapter. (The issue of balancing minority and majority rights and the process of resolving the resulting conflicts are examined in detail beginning on p. 241 of this chapter.)

Subsequent to the Royal Commission on Aboriginal Peoples in 1996, the federal government created a long-term action plan for its dealings with Aboriginal peoples. The document *Gathering Strength: Canada's Aboriginal Action Plan* included a "Statement of Reconciliation" by the Government of Canada acknowledging the injustices faced by Aboriginal peoples:

> Sadly, our history with respect to the treatment of Aboriginal people is not something in which we can take pride. Attitudes of racial and cultural superiority led to a suppression of Aboriginal culture and values. As a country, we are burdened by past actions that resulted in weakening the identity of Aboriginal peoples, suppressing their languages and cultures, and outlawing spiritual practices. We must recognize the impact of these actions on the once self-sustaining nations that were disaggregated, disrupted, limited or even destroyed by the dispossession of traditional territory, by the relocation of Aboriginal people, and by some provisions of the *Indian Act*. We must acknowledge that the result of these actions was the erosion of the political, economic and social systems of Aboriginal people and nations.
>
> Against the backdrop of these historical legacies, it is a remarkable tribute to the strength and endurance of Aboriginal people that they have maintained their historic diversity and identity. The Government of Canada today formally expresses to all Aboriginal people in Canada our profound regret for past actions of the federal government which have contributed to these difficult pages in the history of our relationship together. (Indian Residential Schools Resolution Canada 2003)

The injustices and inequities suffered by Canada's Aboriginal peoples serve as a constant reminder that policies designed to suit one purpose may have far-reaching and negative consequences. The suppression of cultures and the erosion of languages stemming from the government's assimilation policy have affected the heritage of Aboriginal peoples. To ensure history does not repeat itself, it is important to foster tolerance and acceptance of differences and to combat present barriers to equality.

Other Groups

The equal enjoyment of human rights is an issue for other segments of Canada's population besides women, immigrants, and Aboriginal peoples. Barriers to equality also exist for people with disabilities, people living with poverty, and same-sex couples. Although Canada has made progress in recent years in attempting to remove some of these barriers, some segments of our population still suffer from a lack of equality.

Some of the struggles for recognition of rights and interests have taken place in the courts, for example, the recognition of benefits for same-sex couples or the responsibility of employers to accommodate people who have disabilities to the point of undue hardship. The list of gains, however, is far outweighed by the goals still to be achieved. For people with disabilities, many buildings remain inaccessible, employment opportunities are limited, and cutbacks to government services directly affect their quality of life. Human rights legislation does allow individuals to lodge complaints and provides redress should a case of discrimination on the basis of disability be proven. However, a more proactive approach is needed to address potential discrimination issues before they occur. This would include more emphasis being placed on the rights of people with disabilities, including improved access to housing, transportation, and employment. More court cases are likely to occur as people with disabilities continue their fight for equality.

Some disadvantaged segments of our population have depended on advocacy groups and the media to showcase their struggle. For example, people who are homeless and people living with poverty would have difficulty raising the necessary funds to cover the legal costs to mount a rights challenge. Therefore, anti-poverty demonstrations have been used to focus public attention on the need for better access to health care, shelters for people who are homeless, and low-income housing. Although access to low-income housing is a concern for many Canadians, government cuts to affordable housing and other social programs can have severe consequences for individuals who are homeless or living with poverty.

Some laws can adversely affect people who are homeless or living with poverty. In 1999, the Ontario government passed the *Safe Streets Act*, which made it illegal to solicit in an aggressive manner. While the law was designed to control safety on the streets, it also affected the livelihood of many young people who were homeless or living with poverty. In Toronto, specifically, these youths had been offering to clean windshields of vehicles that were stopped in traffic.

The *Safe Streets Act* was passed to prevent these so-called "squeegee kids" from doing so.

Any gains to be made in achieving equality for people living with poverty must be weighed against the costs associated with providing affordable housing and expanding the social safety net. Ignoring the issue only further perpetuates the barriers to equality for this group.

With respect to the rights achieved by gay men and lesbian women in Canada, there has been progress. Gay men and lesbian women have long experienced unfair treatment and discriminatory practices; however, recent court litigation involving same-sex issues has broadened the scope of equality rights. (See Shifting Perspectives on p. 239 for an examination of the evolution of equality rights for gay men and lesbian women in Canadian society.)

In the 1999 case of *M. v. H.* (see Chapter 6, p. 175), there was an application under Ontario's *Family Law Act* to have benefits apply to same-sex couples. The Supreme Court held that to deny benefits to same-sex couples was a violation of equality rights under the *Charter*. The decision had a major effect on legislation at both the federal and provincial levels of government. In order to ensure that common-law relationships between opposite- and same-sex couples had equal treatment under the law, the federal government passed the *Modernization of Benefits and Obligations Act*. In effect, this statute required the amendment of 68 federal statutes involving more than 20 federal departments to include same-sex couples, thereby broadening the scope of rights protection. Changes were made to such statutes as the *Income Tax Act* and the *Canada Pension Act* so that benefits would apply to same-sex common-law partners. The case of *M. v. H.* did not change the definition of marriage, but the issue of same-sex marriage was soon to come to the forefront of social and political discussions. As the debate over the issue of same-sex marriage has shown, Canada's definitions of equality will continually be put to the test, and the concept of equality will be forced to evolve.

FIGURE 8.6   The aim of the Ontario *Safe Streets Act, 1999* was to prohibit soliciting in an aggressive manner. The law effectively made it illegal for squeegee cleaners to carry on their activities on the streets of Toronto. What barriers to equality do people who are homeless face?

SHIFTING PERSPECTIVES: Same-Sex Issues

Historically in Canada, homosexuality was considered criminal behaviour and was sanctioned under the *Criminal Code*. In 1967, however, Pierre Trudeau's declaration as justice minister that "the state has no place in the bedrooms of the nation" heralded a shift in opinion regarding the criminalizing of behaviours. In 1968, the *Criminal Code* was amended.

While the Ontario *Human Rights Code* originally included discrimination only on the basis of sex, it was later amended to include sexual orientation as a prohibited ground. In 1996, the federal *Canadian Human Rights Act* was also amended to include sexual orientation. Even as late as 1998, sexual orientation was read into Alberta's *Individual's Rights Protection Act*. While s. 15 of the *Charter* refers to discrimination only on the basis of sex under the equality provisions, sexual orientation has been interpreted as being an analogous ground, that is, one sufficiently related to afford protection.

While human rights laws have provided increased protection from discrimination for gay men and lesbian women, there were lobbies for the law to provide even more. Since 1981, MP Svend Robinson has lobbied the government for changes to Canada's hate propaganda laws to include sexual orientation as an area for which protection must be afforded under criminal law. In 2003, a bill was passed in Parliament to amend the hate provisions under the *Criminal Code* to protect gay men and lesbian women from being the target of hatred.

People continued to challenge government laws and actions as it became apparent that many pieces of legislation denied equality to same-sex couples, particularly with respect to benefits and pensions. Such laws were challenged in the courts on the basis of a violation of equality rights under the *Charter*, and support was granted in favour of same-sex couples. After the landmark decision of *M. v. H.*, governments were given time to amend statutes so that they did not violate equality rights. Changes in public opinion and increased tolerance also became evident in the debate over same-sex marriage.

In 2002, many courts heard cases arguing that marriage laws were discriminatory because they did not apply to same-sex couples. Marriage acts were challenged as discriminatory in several jurisdictions with the resulting court verdicts that governments should amend their legislation. In May 2003, the British Columbia government ruled that marriage laws were discriminatory. Similarly, in June 2003, the Ontario Court of Appeal struck down marriage laws as being unconstitutional. The argument in both cases focused on the definition of marriage, which, prior to these decisions, had been defined in common law as "the union of one man and one woman, to the exclusion of all others." Both courts considered the definition to be a violation of equality rights on the grounds of sexual orientation. In comments made during the Ontario Court of Appeal case of *Halpern v. Canada (Attorney General)* (2003-06-10) ONCA Docket C39172; C39174, Chief Justice Roy McMurtry indicated that the issue "is ultimately about the recognition and protection of human dignity and equality in the context of the social structures available to conjugal couples in Canada."

Instead of appealing the decisions of the British Columbia and Ontario governments, the federal government announced in June 2003 that it would formulate draft legislation that would allow for same-sex marriages. Prior to having a debate on the issues, the legislation was referred to the Supreme Court of Canada to determine the constitutionality of the draft bill. A July 2003 press release from the Department of Justice summarized the three reference questions as follows:

1. Is the draft bill within the exclusive legislative authority of the Parliament of Canada?
2. Is the section of the draft bill that extends capacity to marry to persons of the same sex consistent with the *Canadian Charter of Rights and Freedoms*?
3. Does the freedom of religion guaranteed by the *Charter* protect religious officials from being compelled to perform a marriage between two persons of the same sex that is contrary to their religious beliefs? (Department of Justice, "Minister of Justice…")

The essence of the bill was first to recognize same-sex marriage and then to allow religious groups the right to refuse to perform ceremonies contrary to their beliefs.

The issue of changing the definition of marriage was hotly debated in 2003 as those for and against changing the definition of marriage argued their particular view. In September 2003, the former Canadian Alliance Party presented a motion to the House of Commons asking it to uphold the traditional definition of marriage as "the union of one man and one woman, to the exclusion of all others." The motion to uphold the traditional definition of marriage was struck down by a narrow margin of 137 to 132. Other groups expressed their disapproval. In July 2003, the Vatican issued an edict for world opposition to same-sex marriages. The Supreme Court decision regarding the constitutionality of the draft legislation was set for a spring 2004 release.

In commenting about the debate over same-sex marriages, federal Minister of Justice Martin Cauchon stated, "I believe that Canada has become a beacon to the world in our acceptance of minorities, and our respect for human rights and dignity. The Government of Canada is showing leadership on the issue of same-sex marriage by seeking a balanced solution that will work for all Canadians" (Department of Justice, "Notes…").

SOURCES: Department of Justice Canada. "Minister of Justice Announces Reference to the Supreme Court of Canada." Ottawa: 17 July 2003. Accessed 31 Aug. 2003 <http://canada.justice.gc.ca/en/news/nr/2003/doc_30944.html>;

———. "Notes for an Address by The Honourable Martin Cauchon, PC, MP, Minister of Justice and Attorney General of Canada." Canadian Bar Association, Montréal: 18 Aug. 2003. Accessed 31 Aug. 2003 <http://canada.justice.gc.ca/en/news/sp/2003/doc_30966.html>.

Your Perspective

1. Summarize the development of equality rights for gay men and lesbian women.
2. Explain the significance of a reference regarding the definition of same-sex marriage.
3. Explain the impact of changing societal values on laws.

CONFIRM YOUR UNDERSTANDING

1. Identify historical examples of inequality for Aboriginal peoples.
2. Summarize the current issues facing Aboriginal peoples in Canada.
3. Reread the "Statement of Reconciliation" on page 237. How do you think such an apology was viewed by Aboriginal peoples?
4. Describe the barriers to equality faced by people with disabilities.
5. Should "squeegee kids" be allowed to earn a livelihood on the streets of Toronto? Explain.
6. Explain the significance of the *M. v. H.* decision.

Balancing Minority and Majority Rights

Minority rights are recognized in Canada and protected in the Canadian Constitution. Laws have been passed and agreements have been negotiated that demonstrate a commitment to this constitutional recognition. In examining contemporary issues relating to Aboriginal peoples, such as land claims, self-government, and harvesting rights; affirmative-action programs; and Québec sovereignty, you will discover some of the challenges in balancing minority and majority rights in Canada.

Aboriginal Rights

Prior to the patriation of the Constitution in 1982, there were three primary documents governing Aboriginal rights: the *Royal Proclamation, 1763*; federal government authority under s. 91 of the *Constitution Act, 1867* to pass laws relating to "Indians"; and the common law relating to **Aboriginal title** (a specific Aboriginal right relating to land claims). The *Royal Proclamation, 1763* guaranteed protection for Aboriginal lands, but it did not create Aboriginal title to those lands; rather, it was the Crown that regulated the transfer of land involving Aboriginal peoples. Under the proclamation, Aboriginal peoples could sell or sign over their lands to the Crown, but their land could not be taken away by force or fraud. Subsequent treaties between Aboriginal peoples and the Crown were negotiated whereby Aboriginal land was traded to the Crown in return for protection and treaty benefits, such as the right to hunt, fish, and be educated.

The federal government also had constitutional authority to enact laws relating to Aboriginal peoples, and in 1876, the first *Indian Act* was created. Essentially, the *Indian Act* set out the role of the federal government in its dealings with Aboriginal peoples and created a distinct category of status Indians for whom benefits would be provided.

The last source of law stems from the common law of Aboriginal title, which refers to the nego-tiation of specific treaties between the Crown and Aboriginal peoples. There were many Aboriginal treaties across Canada. However, prior to 1982, Aboriginal rights could be **extinguished**, or cancelled, by their surrender to the Crown, by constitutional enactment, or by federal legislation that specifically stated as its purpose the extinguishing of Aboriginal rights. As a result, a great deal of time is often spent by the courts in determining whether, in fact, Aboriginal rights were surrendered to the Crown or there was a clear purpose in federal legislation to extinguish specific Aboriginal rights.

Aboriginal Land Claims

During the period when the Canadian government tried to assimilate Aboriginal peoples through such measures as the reserve system and residential schools, no effort was made to recognize the distinct nature of Aboriginal societies. In fact, in 1969, the federal government launched a White Paper, or policy document, which aimed to end the special status of Aboriginal peoples and called for the repeal of the *Indian Act* in an effort to end any legal distinction between Aboriginal peoples and other Canadians. The White Paper, however, met with strong opposition from Aboriginal peoples and, as a result, did not become law.

The decision in the 1973 case of *Calder v. Attorney General of British Columbia*, [1973] S.C.R. 313 led to a turning point in the recognition of Aboriginal land claims. While the case involved a claim by the Nisga'a in British Columbia for Aboriginal title to their land, no ruling was made to allocate lands at that time. The Calder case was significant because it recognized a common-law right of Aboriginal title that existed independent of the *Royal Proclamation, 1763*. Subsequent to the Calder decision, the federal government set up a policy that allowed for the negotiation of land-claim settlements. This meant that Aboriginal title could be shown when there was proof of occupation of the land by Aboriginal peoples before the **assumption of sovereignty** (the time period in which European control was said to have taken place). The Calder case influenced the Canadian and British Columbia governments in their decisions to begin negotiation for a land-claim settlement with the Nisga'a. It wasn't until 2000 that a Nisga'a treaty was negotiated and the _Nisga'a Final Agreement Act_ was passed. Not only did the agreement allow for the transfer of approximately 2000 km² of land to the Nisga'a Nation, but it also provided for a system of Aboriginal self-government. In short, the Nisga'a gained legal title to the land, assumed control over the structure of their government, and acquired the right to make certain laws. They would also receive government funding for programs relating to health care, education, and housing.

Not until 1982 were Aboriginal rights entrenched in the Constitution, under s. 35 of the _Constitution Act_, shown in Figure 8.7, below:

> ### Part II
> ### Rights of the Aboriginal
> ### Peoples of Canada
>
> (1) _The existing aboriginal and treaty rights of the aboriginal peoples of Canada are hereby recognized and affirmed._
>
> (2) _In this Act, "aboriginal peoples of Canada" includes the Indian, Inuit and Métis peoples of Canada._
>
> (3) _For greater certainty, in subsection (1) "treaty rights" includes rights that now exist by way of land claims agreements or may be so acquired._
>
> (4) _Notwithstanding any other provision of this Act, the aboriginal and treaty rights referred to in subsection (1) are guaranteed equally to male and female persons._

FIGURE 8.7 Section 35 of the _Constitution Act_ recognizes existing Aboriginal and treaty rights. However, these existing rights were not defined in the Constitution; rather, they were to be interpreted by the courts. How has the _Constitution Act_ safeguarded Aboriginal rights?

Further, the _Charter_ recognizes and supports Aboriginal rights in s. 25:

> The guarantee in this _Charter_ of certain rights and freedoms shall not be construed so as to abrogate or derogate from any aboriginal, treaty or other rights or freedoms that pertain to the aboriginal peoples of Canada, including
>
> a) any rights or freedoms that have been recognized by the Royal Proclamation of October 7, 1763; and
>
> b) any rights or freedoms that now exist by way of land claims agreements or may be so acquired.

The Constitution protections set the stage for a series of cases to be heard in the courts on the nature and scope of Aboriginal rights and particularly the settlement of land-claim issues. In the case of _Guerin v. The Queen_, [1984] 2 S.C.R. 335, an official of the Indian Affairs Department of the federal government had been involved in negotiating a lease of Musqueam land to a golf club. The terms of the deal turned out to be less favourable than had originally been approved by the Musqueam group at the surrender meeting. The court held that Aboriginal title gave rise to a **fiduciary duty**, that is, a duty developed by nature of a trust relationship, on the part of the Crown in its dealings with Aboriginal peoples. This fiduciary duty required that the Crown not take advantage of its position when dealing with Aboriginal peoples. Other significant Supreme Court decisions soon followed that aided the advancement of Aboriginal rights and treaty rights claims. In _R. v. Sparrow_, [1990] 1 S.C.R. 1075, Ronald Sparrow, a member of the Musqueam band, was charged under s. 61 (1) of the _Fisheries Act_ with using a drift net longer than that permitted by the band's food-fishing licence. While Sparrow admitted that this was true, he argued that he had an Aboriginal right to hunt and fish for food and that the net length restriction was invalid. The Supreme Court of Canada held that s. 35 (1) should be given a "generous and liberal interpretation in favour of Aboriginal peoples." In effect, if there is doubt as to what falls within the scope of s. 35 (1), it is resolved in favour of Aboriginal peoples. The Supreme Court overturned Sparrow's conviction and ordered a new trial.

A leading case on Aboriginal title is *Delgamuukw v. British Columbia*, [1997] 3 S.C.R. 1010. In this case, the Gitxsan and Wet'suwet'en peoples of British Columbia made a claim for Aboriginal title over their lands, the various parcels of which amounted to 57 000 km². While the court did not make a ruling on title of the lands and sent the issue back to trial, an important test for establishing Aboriginal title was set out at paragraph 143: "In order to make out a claim for Aboriginal title, the aboriginal group asserting the title must satisfy the following criteria: (i) the land must have been occupied prior to sovereignty, (ii) if present occupation is relied on as proof of occupation pre-sovereignty, there must be a continuity between present and pre-sovereignty occupation, and (iii) at sovereignty that occupation must have been exclusive."

The other significance of the Delgamuukw decision was that Chief Justice Lamer highlighted that the laws of evidence must take into consideration the oral traditions of Aboriginal peoples. At paragraph 84, he stated, "In practical terms, this requires the courts to come to terms with the oral histories of aboriginal societies, which, for many aboriginal nations, are the only record of their past." Clearly, there are difficulties in trying to make a historical claim without written documentation. Requiring a presentation of written evidence would have prevented Aboriginal communities from being able to assert their rights, so it was important for the court to recognize the importance of oral traditions and to make accommodations for them.

FIGURE 8.8 The Gitxsan dancers perform in front of the Supreme Court of Canada in 1997 while the land claims case of *Delgamuukw v. British Columbia* is being presented to the court. The Supreme Court established a test for determining Aboriginal title and also emphasized that oral histories of Aboriginal peoples be given the same weight as written evidence. How does the acknowledgment of oral traditions help to safeguard Aboriginal rights?

As Aboriginal communities continue their struggle to achieve land-claim settlements and to secure self-government, many of the principles stemming from case decisions, interpretations of s. 35, and the acknowledgment of oral histories will be applied in order to address and safeguard minority rights.

Aboriginal Harvesting Rights

In addition to land-claim and self-government issues, Aboriginal peoples are also working to gain recognition of harvesting rights. These rights include activities related to their occupations of the land, such as hunting and fishing. In the leading case of _R. v. Van der Peet_, [1996] 2 S.C.R. 507, Dorothy Van der Peet was charged with selling salmon contrary to the British Columbia (General) Fishery regulations. Her husband had caught the fish legally in accordance with his status-Indian fishing licence; however, the regulations prohibited the sale of fish caught in accordance with this licence. Van der Peet argued that her Aboriginal right to fish also included a right to sell the fish and that the government laws violated her constitutional rights under s. 35 (1). Chief Justice Lamer discussed the constitutional significance of s. 35 (1):

> In my view, the doctrine of aboriginal rights exists, and is recognized and affirmed by s. 35 (1), because of one simple fact: when Europeans arrived in North America, aboriginal peoples _were already here_, living in communities on the land, and participating in distinctive cultures, as they had done for centuries. It is this fact, and this fact above all others, which separates aboriginal peoples from all other minority groups in Canadian society and which mandates their special legal, and now constitutional, status.
>
> More specifically, what s. 35 (1) does is provide the constitutional framework through which the fact that aboriginals lived on the land in distinctive societies, with their own practices, traditions and cultures, is acknowledged and reconciled with the sovereignty of the Crown. The substantive rights which fall

within the provision must be defined in light of this purpose; the aboriginal rights recognized and affirmed by s. 35 (1) must be directed towards the reconciliation of the pre-existence of aboriginal societies with the sovereignty of the Crown.

In order to consider the nature of the Aboriginal right, Chief Justice Lamer indicated that you had to look at the activities of the Aboriginal societies prior to the arrival of Europeans. The test used by Chief Justice Lamer indicated that "an activity must be an element of a practice, custom or tradition integral to the distinctive culture of the aboriginal group claiming the right." He also considered whether the right had been extinguished by any other federal legislation. In this case, the court held that fisheries legislation had not specifically extinguished Aboriginal rights. Therefore, the selling of the fish was considered to be an activity associated with the Aboriginal right to fish.

Another landmark Supreme Court of Canada decision occurred in 1999 in the case of _R. v. Marshall_, [1999] 3 S.C.R. 456. Donald Marshall Jr., a Mi'kmaw fisherman, had been charged with catching and selling fish out of season. Marshall argued that a 1760 treaty gave Mi'kmaq and Maliseet people the right to hunt and fish. The Supreme Court agreed. This decision was to affect fishing rights for all Aboriginal communities by requiring government fisheries enforcement officers to recognize Aboriginal fishing rights.

Many of the major Supreme Court of Canada decisions have addressed the constitutional protections for First Nations, but how have the Métis been protected? Many people associate the Métis with a struggle for rights headed by leader Louis Riel. Riel helped to develop the _Manitoba Act_, which led to the inclusion of Manitoba in Canada in 1870. He was also instrumental in the fight for Métis land claims. In an 1885 uprising against the government over land issues, Riel was captured, forced to stand trial for treason, and subsequently executed. In recent years, the federal government has acknowledged its wrongdoing with regard to Riel. As part of the

"Statement of Reconciliation" (also referred to on p. 237), the federal government issued an official apology:

> No attempt at reconciliation with Aboriginal people can be complete without reference to the sad events culminating in the death of Métis leader Louis Riel. These events cannot be undone; however, we can and will continue to look for ways of affirming the contributions of Métis people in Canada and of reflecting Louis Riel's proper place in Canada's history. (Indian Residential Schools Resolution Canada 2003)

While status Indians have had their Aboriginal rights to hunt and fish protected, the rights of the Métis have, in the past, not been similarly protected. The Constitution recognizes the Métis as one of the Aboriginal peoples of Canada; however, there is an inherent difficulty in applying the pre-sovereignty occupation test to the Métis. Such a test would be impossible to pass because the very nature of the Métis identity required contact with Europeans. (Refer to the Landmark Case that follows to see how this pre-sovereignty occupation test was modified in the Powley decision.)

In 2003, the Supreme Court of Canada released a landmark judgment for the Métis. The judgment affirmed their recognition as Aboriginal people by the Constitution and ruled that the Aboriginal right to hunt for food was also extended to members of a Métis community. Jean Teillet, Louis Riel's great-grandniece and a lawyer representing the Powleys, had this to say after successfully winning her 10-year legal battle: "I feel I have brought some justice back. It's a happy day for the Métis people of Canada and it's a happy day for me personally" (Lunman 2003).

Landmark CASE

R. v. Powley, 2003 S.C.C. 43

Read the following case analysis. The facts, issue, and *ratio decidendi* have been provided for you. Assume that you agree with the decision. Consider the implications of the Powley decision, and apply the precedent to a new situation.

Facts: In October 1993, two Métis hunters, Steve and Roddy Powley, were charged with unlawfully hunting a moose without a licence and knowingly possessing game contrary to ss. 46 and 47 (1) of the Ontario *Game and Fish Act*. The Powleys argued that they had a constitutional right to hunt for food in the Sault Ste. Marie area and that the government could not infringe on this right unless there was proper justification for doing so. At trial, they were acquitted on the grounds that the court recog-

FIGURE 8.9 Métis lawyers representing their nation in the *R. v. Powley* case are shown in the foyer of the Supreme Court of Canada. From left to right, they are Clem Chartier, Jean Teillet (great-grandniece of Louis Riel), and Jason Madden. What Aboriginal right was recognized in the Powley decision?

nized an Aboriginal right to hunt for food that was constitutionally protected under s. 35 of the _Constitution Act, 1982._ On appeal to the Superior Court of Justice and the Court of Appeal, the acquittals were upheld. The case was appealed to the Supreme Court of Canada.

Issue: Do the provisions of the _Game and Fish Act_, which prohibit moose hunting without a licence, violate the Aboriginal right to hunt for food under section 35 (1) of the _Constitution Act, 1982_?

Held: Appeal dismissed.

Ratio Decidendi: (McLachlin C.J. and Gonthier, Iacobucci, Major, Bastarache, Binnie, Arbour, LeBel, and Deschamps JJ.) In a 9 to 0 decision, the court held that the Métis had a historic right to hunt for food in the Sault Ste. Marie area and that this right was protected under s. 35 (1). The appellant had

argued that the law was justified for reasons of conservation (i.e., wildlife stocks would be threatened), but the court rejected that argument. The court described the Métis community as "a group of Métis with a distinctive collective identity, living together in the same geographic area and sharing a common way of life."

In applying the Van der Peet pre-sovereignty occupation test (see p. 244) but modifying the pre-contact requirement to reflect the distinct history of the Métis (the culture of the Métis developed _after_ contact with Europeans), the court held that the Powleys had established an Aboriginal right that had not been extinguished. The court set out a three-part standard for determining Métis identity that required proof or evidence of (1) self-identification as a member of a Métis community; (2) an ancestral connection to a historic Métis community; and (3) acceptance by a modern Métis community.

CONFIRM YOUR UNDERSTANDING

1. Compare the types of Aboriginal rights in Canada before and after the patriation of the Constitution.
2. Explain what the court meant when it concluded that the Crown held a fiduciary relationship with the Aboriginal peoples of Canada.
3. Why would traditional requirements for written evidence be prejudicial to Aboriginal peoples in Canada when they are trying to assert their rights to title in land claims?
4. Explain the significance of the Powley decision for the Métis community.

Affirmative-Action Programs

Employment equity legislation aims to remedy employment inequities by requiring all employers to develop plans to address hiring practices that may be perceived as discriminatory. These plans—widely known as **affirmative-action programs** (programs designed to remedy disadvantages faced by designated groups)— encourage employers to make hiring decisions that increase the proportional representation of diverse peoples in the workplace.

Employers who fall under the jurisdiction of the federal _Employment Equity Act,_ such as the public service of Canada and federally regulated organizations and businesses, must survey their workforce to determine if employees are among any of the designated groups (identified as women, Aboriginal peoples, people with disabilities, and members of visible minorities). Self-identification in one or more of the designated groups by an employee is voluntary. Once the surveys are completed, employers must then analyze their workforce to determine if under-representation exists. Should this be the case, employers are required to develop an employment equity plan designed to remove barriers to equality and establish short- and long-term goals for hiring, training, and promotion related to the under-represented group or groups.

The purpose of the federal *Employment Equity Act* is to achieve equality in the workplace by correcting the conditions of disadvantage experienced in employment by women, Aboriginal peoples, people with disabilities, and members of visible minorities. The act requires that employers consider accommodation of differences; however, it does not compel them to hire unqualified job candidates.

Support for affirmative-action programs is provided in s. 15 of the *Charter*:

(1) Every individual is equal before the law and under the law and has the right to the equal protection and equal benefit of the law without discrimination and, in particular, without discrimination based on race, national or ethnic origin, colour, religion, sex, age or mental or physical disability.

(2) Subsection (1) does not preclude any law, program or activity that has as its object the amelioration [improvement] of conditions of disadvantaged individuals or groups including those that are disadvantaged because of race, national or ethnic origin, colour, religion, sex, age or mental or physical disability.

Further support for employment equity is contained in s. 16 of the *Canadian Human Rights Act*:

(1) It is not a discriminatory practice for a person to adopt or carry out a special

FIGURE 8.10   Employment equity programs attempt to remedy the disadvantages experienced by women, Aboriginal peoples, members of visible minorities, and people with disabilities. How can employers address the inequities faced by these designated groups?

program, plan or arrangement designed to prevent disadvantages that are likely to be suffered by, or to eliminate or reduce disadvantages that are suffered by, any group of individuals when those disadvantages would be based on or related to the prohibited grounds of discrimination, by improving opportunities respecting goods, services, facilities, accommodation or employment in relation to that group.

Employment equity policies and practices of employment (hiring, training, and promotion) have been criticized as a form of reverse discrimination in that they perpetuate discrimination against all those who are not part of the designated groups. (See Connections on p. 248 for more discussion about reverse discrimination.) While some people see affirmative-action programs as an outright denial of equal opportunity for all to contribute to the workforce, others see these programs as a praiseworthy attempt to remedy past and present inequities for the four designated groups.

CONNECTIONS: Law and Affirmative Action

How might affirmative-action programs affect you in the job market? Consider this scenario. An organization or business has an affirmative-action policy and places a want ad for prospective job candidates. Specifically, the application process for the job may give candidates the opportunity to self-identify as a member of one of the four designated groups. The employer might take membership in one of these groups into account when making a hiring decision. It may be that two candidates are vying for the same job, but the employer has an under-representation of visible minorities in his or her workplace. An affirmative-action policy might require a hiring decision to be made in favour of the candidate who is a member of a visible minority, in order to increase the proportional representation of visible minorities in the organization.

While the programs have helped members of these groups make employment gains, some people have argued that the use of such representational hiring is a form of reverse discrimination. An unsuccessful job candidate could argue that he or she was suitably qualified for a particular job but was unable to secure the position because it was awarded to someone else to fulfill a mandated affirmative-action hiring policy. In May 2002, a Declaration of Policy from the former Canadian Alliance indicated the party's disapproval of affirmative-action programs. In discussing economic and fiscal schemes, the Canadian Alliance declared:

> We will encourage the entrepreneurial sector by eliminating unnecessary regulations and minimizing government interference in the labour market, including the elimination of discriminatory hiring and promotion policies for federally regulated employees. Every job shall go to the most qualified applicant without the use of affirmative action or any other type of discriminatory quota system.

Others, after reflecting on the difficult struggle of the identified groups to reach proportional representation in employment and recognizing their historical disadvantages, argue that affirmative-action programs are the only way to ensure there are opportunities to achieve equality. The federal public service investigated the participation of visible minorities in its workplace in 2000 and discovered that this designated group was seriously under-represented. In the study "Embracing Change in the Federal Public Service—Task Force on the Participation of Visible Minorities in the Federal Public Service," an action plan recommended the implementation of a benchmark or target for recruiting and advancing the participation of visible minorities. The benchmark or target was set at 1 in 5 or 20 percent participation of visible minorities in all sectors of the federal public service.

The concept of equality is used in a contradictory fashion when dealing with affirmative action. The outcome of trying to remedy inequities for disadvantaged individuals or groups through affirmative-action programs may create tension and resentment with other groups who are adversely affected by these policies and programs. However, it is likely that many employers will continue to use affirmative-action programs until there are no more barriers to equality in the workplace.

Sources: *Canadian Alliance Party.* "Declaration of Policy." May 2002. Accessed 28 Oct. 2003
<www.canadianalliance.ca/english/policy/index.asp>;

Treasury Board of Canada Secretariat. "Embracing Change in the Federal Public Service—Task Force on
the Participation of Visible Minorities in the Federal Public Service." Accessed 23 Oct. 2003
<http://www.tbs-sct.gc.ca/pubs_pol/hrpubs/tb_852/ecfps2_e.asp>.

Questions

1. Explain the purpose of affirmative-action programs.
2. Explain the steps involved in implementing an employment equity program under the *Employment Equity Act*.

Québec Sovereignty

It is difficult to comprehend the Québec sovereignty movement without having a clear understanding of the historical and social context in which it developed. History has chronicled significant conflict between England and France, which was transplanted to the New World. After the fall of the French fortress of Louisbourg on Cape Breton Island in 1758, Québec became the main focus of the British military offensive. In 1759, British forces took control of Québec City and the surrounding area in the famous battle on the Plains of Abraham. By 1763, the British had achieved victory over the French.

Under British rule during the late eighteenth and early nineteenth centuries, the French in Québec were allowed a degree of freedom to speak their own language and to practise the Catholic religion. In 1867, French Canada played a key role in Confederation, but despite participating in the process of establishing the nation of Canada, French Québecers (Québécois) felt that their language, culture, and religion set them apart from other Canadians.

Twentieth-century industrialization transformed Canadian society, and as Québec shifted from an agrarian to an industrial society, there was an influx of industry and investment from English-speaking Canada and from the United States. French Québecers were not major partners in this process of rapid industrialization. Therefore, further tensions developed between French- and English-speaking citizens of Québec. English was the official working language in industry. Top positions in business were awarded to English-speaking Québecers. Even public signs were in English. These factors and the continued threats to the survival of the French language in Québec continued to foster resentment among French Québecers.

Not only was the conflict regarding Québec sovereignty influenced by the desire to protect both French culture and French language in Québec, but it was also driven by a desire for more provincial autonomy. Québec was uncomfortable with, and felt threatened by, the power of a centralized federal government. When the federal government passed conscription legislation in 1918 during WWI, French opposition led to anti-conscription riots in Québec. Québec continued its opposition to conscription during World War II, which further fuelled the fire of Québec nationalism. After 1945, more power was centralized in the hands of the federal government, much to the dismay of Québecers who adhered to the desire for provincial autonomy.

The 1960s were characterized by increased urbanization and technological growth. Population demographics were changing in Québec through increased immigration and declining birth rates, thus posing further threats to the survival of the French culture and language. The tensions that had been developing in Québec among the French-speaking population and the desire for more provincial autonomy led to what became known as the "Quiet Revolution." Under the leadership of Premier Jean Lesage and his Liberal government, many social reforms were implemented, including the establishment of a provincial Ministry of Education, controlling both Catholic and Protestant systems of education. Nationalist sentiment grew throughout the 1960s as the Québec government took control of all privately owned hydroelectric companies and formed Hydro-Québec. The expression "_maîtres chez nous_" (masters in our own house) was continually used by Québec politicians to focus attention on political decision making in Québec. This continuous upsurge in Québec nationalism eventually led to the formation of the Parti Québécois in 1968.

The Parti Québécois became a formidable political entity within Québec and a force to be reckoned with in subsequent constitutional dialogues with both the federal and provincial governments. Under the leadership of René Lévesque, the Parti Québécois focused on an independent Québec based on a policy of **sovereignty association**, which allows independence but maintains economic and political ties with Canada.

The federal government was conscious of growing Québec nationalism. In recognizing the concerns about protecting the French language, the Royal Commission on Bilingualism and Biculturalism was established. This commission recommended that Canada become a bilingual country, and in 1969, the federal government under Prime Minister Trudeau responded by enacting the _Official Languages Act_, giving both the French and English languages equal status in Canada at the federal level. Both French and English would now become the official languages of Parliament, the federal courts, and federal government services, although this official-language status was not entrenched in the Constitution at this time. Despite some measures taken at the federal level to appease francophone interests, tensions continued to mount in Québec, and the early 1970s became

Vive le Québec libre !
(Long live free Québec!)
–Charles de Gaulle, president of France, on a visit to Montréal in 1967 (This public declaration fanned the flames of Québec nationalism.)

a time of unsurpassed political turmoil. Strong resentment and tension among the French resulting from generations of perceived domination by the English escalated into violence.

In 1970, the _Front de Libération du Québec_ (FLQ), an extremist group that advocated separatist goals, was the focus of national attention during what became known as the "October Crisis." The FLQ kidnapped British Trade Commissioner James Cross and Québec Labour Minister Pierre Laporte. Trudeau took a strong

FIGURE 8.11 Armed soldiers march past Montréal city hall on October 16, 1970. The October Crisis, as it came to be known, prompted the federal government to invoke the _War Measures Act_. Why was this act passed? What effect did it have on civil liberties?

stance against the actions of the FLQ by invoking the *War Measures Act*, thus allowing for enforced curfews, police raids, arrests, and detentions. Although the *War Measures Act* severely curtailed civil liberties, the federal government felt it was a necessary step in order to ensure some degree of safety and security during an extremely volatile situation. Unfortunately, the government's response did not prevent the FLQ from murdering Laporte. The FLQ was denounced for its violent actions, but the October Crisis still succeeded in focusing national and world attention on the conflict in Québec.

As the 1970s unfolded, the Parti Québécois tried to distance itself from the October Crisis and renewed its focus on the protection of the French culture and language. Québec was not completely satisfied with the extent of language protection granted under the *Official Languages Act*, so in 1974, the provincial government passed Bill 22, legislating French as the official language of government in Québec. Bill 22 also restricted access to English-language schooling in the province by requiring families who wanted their children to attend English schools to pass an English-language proficiency test. During this time period, the Parti Québécois gained ever-increasing popularity in Québec.

In 1976, the Parti Québécois, under the leadership of René Lévesque, won the Québec provincial election. Soon after, the Parti Québécois government passed Bill 101, requiring that French become the primary language of business and industry and that public signs be written in only the French language. The Parti Québécois pursued a separatist agenda—that is, the goal of an independent Québec—and in 1980 planned a referendum based on the concept of sovereignty association. In Canada, one of the constitutionally significant methods for resolving conflict is the referendum process. In a democratic referendum, the electorate votes in support of or against a particular issue. The referendum question in 1980 required voters to consider a proposal of Québec sovereignty and was worded as follows:

The Government of Québec has made public its proposal to negotiate a new agreement with the rest of Canada, based on the equality of nations; this agreement would enable Québec to acquire the exclusive power to make its laws, levy its taxes and establish relations abroad—in other words, sovereignty—and at the same time to maintain with Canada an economic association including a common currency; no change in political status resulting from these negotiations will be effected without approval by the people through another referendum; on these terms, do you give the Government of Québec the mandate to negotiate the proposed agreement between Québec and Canada? (Government of Canada, Privy Council Office "Questions and Results...")

The referendum on Québec sovereignty was defeated, with 40.4 percent of Québecers voting "yes" to the proposal of negotiating a new agreement with Canada and 59.6 percent voting "no."

Tensions continued to exist between the federal government and Québec. When Trudeau pushed for the patriation of the Constitution, Québec was the only dissenting province. Despite entrenching minority language rights, guaranteeing French and English as official languages, and adding the notwithstanding clause to the *Charter of Rights and Freedoms*, the Constitution was patriated without Québec's consent or signature. Even after the patriation of the Constitution, there was a continued push for the recognition of Québec as a distinct society. However, the constitutional dialogues with the federal and provincial governments, such as the 1987 Meech Lake Accord and the 1992 Charlottetown Accord (discussed in Chapter 5 on pp. 159–161) did not bring Québec any closer to achieving distinct recognition status.

In 1994, the Parti Québécois continued to gain momentum and again captured the leadership of the Québec government. Premier Jacques Parizeau put forward a draft bill on sovereignty and scheduled a sovereignty referendum for October 30, 1995. The question put to voters was somewhat different this time around: "Do you agree that Québec should become sovereign after having made a formal offer to Canada for a new economic and political partnership within the scope of the bill respecting the future of Québec and of the agreement signed on June 12, 1995?" (Government of Canada, Privy Council Office, "Questions and Results...").

The result of the 1995 referendum was very close, with 49.4 percent voting "yes" and 50.6 percent voting "no" to establishing a different relationship with Canada. Having won by only a slight majority in the referendum vote, the federal government was concerned about Québec's continual assertions of independence. In 1998, the federal government launched a reference to the Supreme Court of Canada to consider the constitutional validity of the secession arguments. (The Québec Secession Reference case is highlighted in Chapter 5, beginning on p. 161.) The decision of the Supreme Court in the Québec Secession Reference indicated that neither Québec nor the other provinces have the legal right to unilaterally secede from Canada. (See Asking Key Questions on p. 253 for a further discussion of the Québec Secession Reference.) The federal government also responded to the Supreme Court of Canada decision by passing the *Clarity Act* in 2000. This act was an attempt by the federal government to ensure that, prior to engaging in negotiations for secession, there was a formal determination that (1) any referendum question submitted to voters about proposed secession was clear, and (2) a clear majority of a province's population expressed a clear desire to secede from Canada. The following is an excerpt from the *Clarity Act*:

1. (1) The House of Commons shall, within thirty days after the government of a province tables in its legislative assembly or otherwise officially releases the question that it intends to submit to its voters in a referendum relating to the proposed secession of the province from Canada, consider the question and, by resolution, set out its determination on whether the question is clear.

2. (4) The Government of Canada shall not enter into negotiations on the terms on which a province might cease to be part of Canada unless the House of Commons determines, pursuant to this section, that there has been a clear expression of a will by a clear majority of the population of that province that the province cease to be part of Canada.

If Québec holds another referendum in the future regarding secession, no agreement will be negotiated without first establishing that the criteria for clarity have been met.

The sovereignty debate is likely to continue for some time. If the French–English conflict gains momentum and there is a resurgence of intense Québec nationalism in support of separation, then the Supreme Court of Canada has set the stage for resolution by outlining the legality of the process and the procedures that must be followed.

FIGURE 8.12 Just days before the October 30, 1995, referendum on Québec sovereignty, thousands of people from all across Canada rallied in support of national unity. How might a Québecer have reacted to this outpouring of concern?

ASKING KEY QUESTIONS

Québec Secession Reference

In an excerpt from "Reflections on the Opinion of the Supreme Court of Canada in the Québec Secession Reference," Mary Dawson, Q.C., lead legal advisor for the federal government on the issue of Québec's secession concludes:

> The Supreme Court of Canada has given answers to some fundamental questions. We now have it confirmed from the highest legal authority in the land that the unilateral secession of a province from Canada would be a secession that takes place outside the law. This would apply to Québec or to any other province. We are told, as well, that under international law there is no basis upon which to found a right for the governing institutions of Québec to take Québec out of Canada. We have seen that Québecers are full participants in the democratic governance of Canada.
>
> The Court has gone beyond the questions asked to provide additional advice. It has found a duty to negotiate the secession of a province if it is the clear will of the population of that province that it secede from Canada. The Court has found that this duty to negotiate is a reciprocal one that binds all parties to Confederation, including the government proposing to secede. It has been inclusive in describing the rights and interests that would have [to] be addressed and reconciled in these negotiations. The Court has said that there is no guarantee that negotiations would succeed. It has said further, however, that the legitimacy of the position of any of the participants

> in the negotiations would be seriously compromised if that participant did not conduct its negotiations in a principled way.
>
> The Court has made it clear that a constitutional amendment would be required to effect the secession of a province within the law. The negotiations just referred to would be a necessary condition of such an amendment.
>
> The Court has identified four constitutional principles—federalism, democracy, constitutionalism and the rule of law, and respect for minority rights—that would bear on the secession of a province from Canada. These principles form the rationale for the conclusions of the Court. They must also, the Court tells us, inform the way negotiations relating to the secession of a province must be carried out. Finally, the Court has given us guidance on what issues are appropriate for the courts and what issues must stay with political actors.
>
> In short, the Court has provided us with a legal framework within which the secession of Québec, or of any other province, would have to take place in the unhappy event that its population expressed a clear desire to leave....
>
> This does not mean that we should be lulled into tranquillity. As we have seen before in this country, the public mood can change quickly. Most Canadians fervently hope and expect that Canada will remain united. They see Québec and Québecers as an integral part of their identity as

Canadians. However, should the future hold something different for us, it is important that, whatever happens, we act within the orderly framework that only the rule of law can provide. For this reason, the guidance that the Court has given us is very important indeed.

There has not been a referendum in Québec since 1995. However, polling firms will periodically survey public opinion in Québec about the issue of sovereignty. Generally, the surveys are conducted during periods in which dissatisfaction with the provincial government in power is evident. In January 2004, Léger Marketing surveyed 1000 Québecers on the issue of sovereignty. The results showed that 47 percent of those surveyed were in support of sovereignty as long as there was a political and economic partnership with Canada. However, the support for sovereignty dropped to 28 percent when those surveyed were asked whether they would favour sovereignty without an economic and political partnership.

Jean-Marc Léger, president of the polling firm, commented, "What this shows is that when Quebeckers are confronted with two radical options, sovereignty or status-quo federalism, we find that the majority find themselves somewhere in between. They don't want outright sovereignty and they are not happy that things remain the same" (Séguin 2004).

SOURCES: Dawson, Mary. "Reflections on the Opinion of the Supreme Court of Canada in the Quebec Secession Reference." *National Journal of Constitutional Law*. November 1999. Accessed 26 Jan. 2004 <http://canada.justice.gc.ca/en/ps/const/journal-pt6.html>;

Séguin, Rhéal. "Voter Dismay Fuels Sovereignty Support." *The Globe and Mail* 23 Jan. 2004. Accessed 26 Jan. 2004 <www.globeandmail.com/servlet/ArticleNews/TPStory/LAC/20040123/QUEBEC23/National/Idx>.

Form Your Questions

The information above raises many questions. For example, what legal framework must be followed before secession of a province could occur? What other questions might you ask regarding the issue of Québec sovereignty? Think of three questions. Share your questions with the rest of the class, and discuss possible answers or solutions.

CONFIRM YOUR UNDERSTANDING

1. How do affirmative-action programs achieve equality?

2. Identify the inequities perceived by the French population of Québec that led to the goal of sovereignty.

3. a) How did the Québec government work to protect French-language rights?

b) How does the Constitution protect the French language?

4. Explain how referendums were used in the Québec sovereignty debates.

5. Why did the federal government seek a ruling from the Supreme Court on the legality of Québec independence?

Conflict Resolution

In Canada, there are various legal and political avenues available to resolve conflicts. The referendum process provides one method to resolve political conflicts. Other options for legal resolution of conflict include courtroom litigation, tribunal hearings, and the dispute resolution process of mediation.

The **referendum process** is one of the strongest political avenues for conflict resolution. As demonstrated in the Québec sovereignty debates, the referendum is a critical reminder of the democracy in which we live because it allows individual citizens to vote on matters of importance. The referendum process has been used both federally and provincially as a means of giving the public a direct voice in legislative decision making. For example, in 1898, a national vote on the prohibition of alcohol sales was conducted, and in 1942, there was a vote on conscription. The national referendum that took place in October 1992 resulted in the defeat of the Charlottetown Accord (see Chapter 5, p. 161). A series of significant provincial referendums took place in Newfoundland prior to 1949, which asked the voting public to decide whether Newfoundland should join Confederation. The referendum as a means of conflict resolution is not necessarily an indicator of public opinion on a given issue, however. This is especially the case when the wording of the issue to be decided on is ambiguous. In addition, a referendum may prove to be a risky method for resolving an issue, particularly in situations where there are uncertainties as to voter support for the government's position on the issue. But if the issues are clearly stated, the referendum process reveals where the majority of a given population stands on a particular issue.

FIGURE 8.13 During the 1980 referendum on Québec sovereignty, strong support existed for both sides of the issue. However, the referendum was defeated by a vote of 40.4 percent for the "yes" side and 59.6 percent for the "no" side. How does a referendum contribute to the process of conflict resolution?

Courts and tribunals have long been used as a legal mechanism for conflict resolution. The **adversarial trial system** involves two opposing sides arguing the merits of a case. Generally speaking, after all the arguments are presented, there is an individual (or group) who succeeds in proving his or her case and another party who is not so fortunate. The system works in the sense that individuals have an opportunity to litigate if they feel that their rights have been violated. Cases of alleged discrimination may appear before a human rights tribunal and be resolved. The tribunal can order a remedy and the complainant can seek to have the remedy enforced. Similarly, with the enactment of the _Charter_, individuals now have the right to have their day in court if government laws or actions violate their rights and freedoms. The fact that there is an avenue for addressing rights infringement is deserving of praise. However, high litigation costs and substantial delays in resolving complaints may serve as deterrents to individuals seeking redress through the courts.

In an attempt to address concerns of cost, lengthy delays, and the argumentative and, at times, antagonistic process that can be part of court litigation, alternative methods of conflict resolution have been developed. One method of alternative dispute resolution (ADR) focuses on **mediation**, a process by which the parties attempt to negotiate a resolution to their dispute. Essentially, mediation involves the participation of an appointed neutral third party who assists the parties in resolving their dispute. In many provincial human rights offices, complaints are investigated and resolved by the mediation process rather than by means of a court proceeding. If the parties agree to a settlement, the mediation has been successful and there will be no need for further action. The advantage of mediation is that both parties have the opportunity to discuss the issues in a non-threatening, informal environment. This method is lower in cost and substantially quicker than taking a case to court. For example, the federal government's Office of Indian Residential Schools Resolution Canada is currently using the mediation process in its efforts to settle thousands of sexual and physical abuse claims from former students of residential schools. It is hoped that this process will aid in reconciliation and healing for the victims of abuse.

While mediation has its merits, it is not always the best method for dispute resolution. Sometimes, the issues are too complex and the interests of the parties are too divergent for mediation to work. In such cases, the parties may choose the formal court process.

Whether a dispute is resolved through the mediation process, the court system, or the political referendum process, the fact remains that, as Canadians, we are fortunate to have both political and legal avenues available for resolving conflicts.

CONFIRM YOUR UNDERSTANDING

1. a) Explain the significance of a referendum in resolving conflict.

b) Identify the advantages and disadvantages of holding a referendum.

2. Compare court litigation with the process of mediation. Outline the advantages and disadvantages of each.

3. Why would the mediation process be quicker than court proceedings?

4. Why do you think mediation is being used as a means of settling residential-school abuse claims?

In Closing

While it is apparent that Canada has not always recognized or acknowledged inequities in the treatment of its citizens, progress is being made to remove barriers to equality. But the challenge of upholding the rights and interests of individuals and groups within society while balancing those with the rights of the majority of Canadian citizens is a difficult one that often leads to conflict.

Clarifying the concept of equality is, like the law itself, an evolving process. Current public opinion, beliefs, and values can alter the borderline between minority and majority rights, but shifting perspectives of equality can also broaden our understanding of justice. If Canada wishes to present itself as a nation that values individual rights, it must also reflect openness, respect, tolerance, and empathy. Some segments of the population will continue to seek recognition of their rights within Canadian society, and governments and courts will aim to establish a balance between minority and majority rights. Whether political or legal avenues are chosen as methods of conflict resolution, the challenge of balancing rights in our democracy will continue.

CHAPTER ACTIVITIES

Extend Your Legal Knowledge

1. Create an organizational chart that outlines the historical barriers to achieving equality rights for women, immigrants, Aboriginal peoples, and people with disabilities.

2. Highlight contemporary barriers to equality faced by designated segments of Canada's population. Provide examples to illustrate current barriers faced by each segment.

3. Differentiate between pay equity and employment equity (affirmative-action programs), and then outline the advantages and disadvantages of each program.

4. Outline advantages and disadvantages of using the various political and legal methods of conflict resolution.

Think About the Law

5. Select one of the designated groups identified in this chapter for which contemporary barriers to equality exist. Research the barriers that this group currently faces, and assess the extent to which laws should change to ensure better access to equality rights. Refer to the Legal Handbook for guidelines on Conducting Research on the Internet.

LEGAL
p. 23
HANDBOOK

6. Read the following excerpt from *Peace, Power, Righteousness* by leading Mohawk scholar and activist Taiaiake Alfred.

The present crisis reflects our frustration over cultural loss, anger at the mainstream's lack of respect for our rights, and disappointment in those of our own people who have turned their backs on tradition. And I believe it is heightened because the choices we make today will determine whether or not we survive as indigenous peoples beyond the next generation. No one can deny that our cultures have been eroded and our languages lost, that most of our communities subsist in a state of abject economic dependency, that our governments are weak, and that white encroachment on our lands continues. We can, of course, choose to ignore these realities and simply accede to the dissolution of our cultures and nations. Or we can commit ourselves to a different path, one that honours the memory of those who have sacrificed, fought, and died to preserve the integrity of our nations. This path, the opposite of the one we are on now, leads to a renewed political and social life based on our traditional values. (Alfred 1999)

Conduct extended research on the present-day reality for Aboriginal peoples. Select one of the following areas for further examination, and write a report outlining its significance for Aboriginal peoples in Canada. Then, identify how the government is addressing this area.

- contemporary realities for reserves (health, education, clean water)
- Aboriginal land-claim cases
- Aboriginal language issues
- Aboriginal self-government
- sentencing circles and other forms of restorative justice

7. The loss of a language can accelerate the loss of a culture. Read the following excerpt from "Spoken Here" by Mark Abley. Then, assuming the role of a leader of the Mohawk territory, prepare a speech justifying the development of a language law that promotes your native language as the primary language of communication. Refer to the Legal Handbook for guidelines on Delivering an Oral Presentation.

> And so, in January 2002, Kahnawà:ke became the first Mohawk territory to put its own language law into effect. *Kaianerehnserón:ni ne Onkwawenna'ón:we Aóntston ne Kahnawà:ke* [the Kahnawà:ke language law] arose from a declaration made by the community's elders in the winter of 1998. "Fearful of the loss of our beautiful Kanien'kéha language," the elders urged the Mohawk Council of Kahnawà:ke to take action. What emerged was a law that sets out "to revive and restore the Kanien'kéha language as the primary language of communication, education, ceremony, government and business within the Mohawk Territory of Kahnawà:ke." (Abley 2003)

Communicate About the Law

8. Read the following excerpt from "The *Canadian Charter of Rights and Freedoms* at Twenty: The Ongoing Search for Balance Between Individual and Collective Rights" delivered in April 2002 by the Honourable Stéphane Dion, President of the Privy Council and Minister of Intergovernmental Affairs, to the Director's Forum, Woodrow Wilson International Center for Scholars, in Washington, DC. Then, summarize the excerpt in your own words, and explain the need for the constitutional protection of minority rights.

> Individuals in society maintain or develop affinities from the fact that they share tastes, beliefs, interests or that they have common traits. Some of these affinities are based on ethnicity, race, language, culture or religion, and find expression in collective identities. Others are based mainly on sharing the same territory over generations and are rooted in local or regional identities. Sometimes, all these sources of identity converge, mutually reinforce each other, and take the form of specific national identities within the society as a whole.
>
> In this way, a society includes minorities of different kinds, and these minorities are inclined to believe that constitutions and charters exist not only to protect individuals against the unfettered power of the state, but also to protect minorities against the domination or negligence of the majority.

9. Prepare an argument for or against conservation rights as a justification for limiting Aboriginal hunting and fishing rights. Support your opinion.

10. Review the section of this chapter that focuses on pay equity, paying particular attention to the quoted passage that appears at the bottom of page 229. Write an argument justifying the merits of pay equity or a counter-argument justifying your disapproval of the current pay-equity system.

11. The "Statement of Reconciliation" developed by the federal government in 1997 to acknowledge the injustices faced by Aboriginal peoples also expressed a formal apology to victims of residential-school abuse:

> One aspect of our relationship with Aboriginal people over this period that requires particular attention is the Residential School system. This system separated many children from their families and communities and prevented them from speaking their own languages and from learning about their heritage and cultures. In the worst cases, it left legacies of personal pain and distress that continue to reverberate in Aboriginal communities to this day. Tragically, some children were the victims of physical and sexual abuse.
>
> The Government of Canada acknowledges the role it played in the development and administration of these schools. Particularly to those individuals who experienced the tragedy of sexual and physical abuse at residential schools, and who have carried this burden believing that in some way they must be responsible, we wish to emphasize that what you experienced was not your fault and should never have happened. To those of you who suffered this tragedy at residential schools, we are deeply sorry. (Indian Residential Schools Resolution Canada 2003)

Conduct research and prepare a report on the issue of residential-school abuse. Highlight the nature and scope of the abuse and the current status regarding the resolution of claims.

Apply the Law

12. Harvesting rights not only cover the rights of Aboriginal peoples to hunt and fish, but they have also been extended to include timber rights. In 2003, the New Brunswick Court of Appeal, in *R. v. Bernard*, 2003 N.B.C.A. 55, considered an application by a Mi'kmaw logger who claimed he had a treaty right to harvest and sell timber on Crown land. Joshua Bernard had been convicted under New Brunswick's *Crown Lands and Forests Act* of the illegal possession of timber. Justice Daigle considered four steps in analyzing Aboriginal rights under s. 35 (1) of the *Constitution Act*: (1) Does an Aboriginal right to title exist? (2) Has this right or title been extinguished? (3) If not extinguished, has the Aboriginal right to title been infringed? and (4) Is the infringement justified? The Bernard case rested on the interpretation of treaty rights. The court held that Mr. Bernard did indeed have a treaty right to harvest and sell timber and that the infringement by the law could not be justified.

What implications do you think this decision will have across Canada? Explain.

13. Immigration is changing the composition of Canada's population and compelling us to focus on the increased diversity of our nation.

a) Visit the Statistics Canada Web site at <www.statscan.ca>, and examine Canada's most recent immigration statistics. Search the general index under the keyword "population," and narrow your focus to the data relating to immigrant population. What questions would you ask about these statistics before you could draw any conclusions about their reliability?

b) What conclusions can you draw from the Statistics Canada figures?

c) Choose one aspect of the statistical information provided on the Web site, and speculate as to how it could be used to justify the enactment of particular laws or programs in Canada.

BIBLIOGRAPHY

Abley, Mark. "Spoken Here." *Canadian Geographic.* Sept.–Oct. 2003: 78–86.

Alfred, Taiaiake. *Peace, Power, Righteousness.* Toronto: Oxford University Press, 1999.

Assembly of First Nations. "AFN National Chief States That Aboriginal Peoples Survey Provides Further Evidence of Need to Address Key First Nations Issues." 24 Sept. 2003. Accessed 28 Oct. 2003 <www.afn.ca/Media/2003/sept/september_24_03 .htm>.

———. "Fact Sheet: Top Misconceptions About Aboriginal Peoples." Ottawa, May 2002.

Canadian Alliance Party. "Declaration of Policy." May 2002. Accessed 24 Oct. 2003 <www.canadian alliance.ca/english/policy/index.asp>.

Canadian Human Rights Commission. "Submission of the Canadian Human Rights Commission to the Pay Equity Task Force." March 2003: 4. Accessed 28 Oct. 2003 <www.chrc-ccdp.ca/pe-ps/ PayEquity Submission.asp?l=e>.

Canadian Legal Information Institute. Accessed Aug.–Oct. 2003 <www.canlii.org>.

Canadian Race Relations Foundation. "Fact Sheet: Leading Aboriginal Rights Cases." Accessed Oct. 2003 <www.crr.ca/EN/ MediaCentre/FactSheets/FactAboutCases.pdf>.

———. "Fact Sheet: Leading Aboriginal Treaty Rights Cases." Accessed Oct. 2003 <www.crr.ca/EN/ MediaCentre/FactSheets/FactAboutTreaty.pdf>.

———. "From Racism to Redress: The Japanese Canadian Experience." Accessed 25 Jan. 2004 <www.crr.ca/en/MediaCentre/FactSheets/ eMedCen_FacShtFromRacismToRedress.htm>.

———. "'Racism Still Exists in Canada,' Says UN Special Rapporteur." 26 Sept. 2003. Accessed 4 Oct. 2003 <www.crr.ca/EN/MediaCentre/News Releases/eMedCen_NewsRel20030926b.htm>.

———. "Terms of Agreement Between the Government of Canada and the National Association of Japanese Canadians." Accessed 25 Jan. 2004 <www.crr.ca/en/FAQs/Redress Agreement/eFaq_RedressAgreement.htm>.

Cardin, Jean-Francois. *A History of the Canadian Constitution: From 1984 to the Present.* Montréal: Global Vision Publishing Company, 1996.

Cockburn, Neco. "Equality-Rights Cases Strain Group's Funds." *Toronto Star* 18 Oct. 2003: B2.

Dawson, Mary. "Reflections on the Opinion of the Supreme Court of Canada in the Quebec Secession Reference." *National Journal of Constitutional Law.* November 1999. Accessed 26 Jan. 2004 <canada.justice.gc.ca/en/ps/const/ journal-pt6.html>.

Department of Justice Canada. Accessed Aug. 2003 <www.canada.justice.gc.ca>.

———. "Minister of Justice Announces Reference to the Supreme Court of Canada." Ottawa: 17 July 2003. Accessed 31 Aug. 2003 <http://canada. justice.gc.ca/en/news/nr/2003/doc_30944.html>.

———. "Notes for an Address by The Honourable Martin Cauchon, PC, MP, Minister of Justice and Attorney General of Canada." Canadian Bar Association, Montréal: 18 Aug. 2003. Accessed 31 Aug. 2003 <http://canada.justice.gc.ca/en/ news/sp/2003/doc_30966.html>.

———. "Reference to the Supreme Court of Canada." July 2003. Accessed Aug. 2003 <http://canada. justice.gc.ca/en/news/nr/2003/doc_30946.html>.

Girard, Daniel. "Fontaine Steers to the Mainstream." *Toronto Star* 19 July 2003: E3.

Government of Canada, Privy Council Office. "The *Canadian Charter of Rights and Freedoms* at Twenty: The Ongoing Search for Balance Between Individual and Collective Rights." By Stéphane Dion. Washington, DC: Director's Forum, Woodrow Wilson International Center for Scholars. 2 Apr. 2002. Accessed 11 Oct. 2003 <www.pco-bcp.gc.ca/aia/default.asp? Language=E&page=pressroom&sub=speeches& doc=20020402_e.htm>.

———. "Questions and Results 1980 and 1995 Referenda." Updated 15 Feb. 2001. Accessed 2 Feb. 2004 <www.pco-bcp.gc.ca/aia/default.asp? Language=E&Page=consfile&Sub= ReferendaQuestionsandRes>.

Hogg, Peter W. *Constitutional Law of Canada.* 2nd ed. Toronto: The Carswell Company Limited, 1985.

Indian and Northern Affairs Canada. "Fact Sheet: The Nisga'a Treaty." Updated 30 Dec. 2002. Accessed 27 Oct. 2003 <www.ainc-inac.gc.ca/pr/info/ nit_e.html>.

———. *Gathering Strength: Canada's Aboriginal Action Plan.* Ottawa: Minister of Public Works and Government Services Canada, 1997. Updated

19 Dec. 2002. Accessed 28 Oct. 2003 <www.ainc-inac.gc.ca/gs/chg_e.html>.

————. "Information: Definitions." March 2000. Accessed 28 Oct. 2003 <www.ainc-inac.gc.ca/pr/info/info 101_e.pdf>.

Indian Residential Schools Resolution Canada. "Statement of Reconciliation." Updated 4 Apr. 2003. Accessed 28 Oct. 2003 <www.irsr.gc.ca/english/reconciliation.html>.

Keung, Nicholas. "Activist Sought Rights for Japanese Canadians." *Toronto Star* 4 June 2002: B6.

Linteau, Paul-Andre. *Le Québec Depuis 1930.* Montréal: Les Éditions du Boréal Express, 1986.

Lunman, Kim. "Lawyer Wins Key Court Case for the Métis and Her Family." *The Globe and Mail* 20 Sept. 2003: A4. Accessed 26 Sept. 2003 <www.globeandmail.com/servlet/ArticleNews/TPPrint/LAC/20030920/UJEANN/National/>.

Métis Nation. "The Powley Appeal: A Case Summary." Accessed 28 Oct. 2003 <www.metisnation.ca/POWLEY/home.html>.

Séguin, Rhéal. "Voter Dismay Fuels Sovereignty Support." *The Globe and Mail* 23 Jan. 2004.
Accessed 26 Jan. 2004 <www.globeandmail.com/servlet/ArticleNews/TPStory/LAC/20040123/QUEBEC23/National/Idx>.

Statistics Canada. Accessed Jan. 2004 <www.statscan.ca>.

————. "Ethnic Diversity Survey." *The Daily* 29 Sept. 2003. Accessed 25 Jan. 2004 <www.statscan.ca/Daily/English/030929/d030929a.htm>.

Stoffman, Judy. "Languages on Life Support." *Toronto Star* 4 Oct. 2003: J15.

Teillet, Jean. "Metis Law Summary—2003." *The Métis Nation of Ontario.* Accessed Oct. 2003 <www.metisnation.org/news/POWLEYsupremecourt/index.html>.

Treasury Board of Canada Secretariat. "Embracing Change in the Federal Public Service—Task Force on the Participation of Visible Minorities in the Federal Public Service." 17 Apr. 2000. Accessed 23 Oct. 2003 <www.tbs-sct.gc.ca/pubs_pol/hrpubs/tb_852/ecfps2_e.asp>.

Wilkes, Jim. "Railway Spike Used in Redress Effort." *Toronto Star* 4 Oct. 2003: H2.

UNIT TWO CULMINATING ACTIVITY

Charter Case Analysis

Introduction

The *Charter* has had a significant impact on law-making in Canada. Now that you have completed Unit 2, your challenge is to select a precedent-setting *Charter* case that has made a difference in Canadian law. Highlight key aspects of the case decision and indicate how the decision has affected the law and Canadian citizens.

In addition to addressing the Overall Learning Expectations outlined at the beginning of this unit, this culminating activity requires you to use a number of legal inquiry skills. You may want to consult Chapter 1 "The Legal Handbook" (on the pages indicated by the icons) to review each of these skills.

Your Task

1. Select one of the Supreme Court of Canada *Charter* cases identified below for your analysis. Or, you may choose one of the cases discussed in class or found through extended research using an Internet case-reporting site. Alternatively, your teacher may select the case to be analyzed.

   ***R. v. Big M Drug Mart Ltd.,* [1985] 1 S.C.R. 295**
   Struck down the federal *Lord's Day Act* as an unjustifiable violation of freedom of religion.

   ***R. v. Oakes,* [1986] 1 S.C.R. 103**
   Established how the courts could determine if a *Charter* violation can be justified "in a free and democratic society."

   ***R. v. Smith (Edward Dewey),* [1987] 1 S.C.R. 1045**
   Ruled that a mandatory minimum sentence of seven years for importing narcotics constituted cruel and unusual punishment.

   ***Andrews v. Law Society of British Columbia,* [1989] 1 S.C.R. 143**
   Applied equality rights to citizens and non-citizens.

   ***R. v. Askov,* [1990] 2 S.C.R. 1199**
   Ruled that an accused is entitled to a trial within a reasonable time.

   ***R. v. Stinchcombe,* [1991] 3 S.C.R. 326**
   Ruled that prosecutors must disclose all relevant evidence to the defence before a trial.

   ***Vriend v. Alberta,* [1998] 1 S.C.R. 493**
   Ruled that the Alberta *Human Rights Code* must "read in" sexual orientation as a prohibited ground of discrimination.

   ***M. v. H.,* [1999] 2 S.C.R. 3**
   Ruled that sections of Ontario's *Family Law Act* that restricted the definition of "spouse" to heterosexual couples violated the *Charter*'s equality provisions.

   ***Corbiere v. Canada,* [1999] 2 S.C.R. 203**
   Ruled that voting in Aboriginal band elections cannot be limited only to band members living on reserves.

   ***United States v. Burns,* [2001] 1 S.C.R. 283, 2001 SCC 7**
   Ruled that sending two Canadians to face the death penalty in the United States violates fundamental justice.

2. Prepare a case analysis by ensuring each of the following components is included:
   - Proper case citation
   - Summary of facts
   - Issue to be decided
   - Decision of the Supreme Court of Canada
   - Reason for the decision

   (You may want to review all topics in "Understanding Case Law" in the Legal Handbook.)

3. State your opinion of the judgment and justify your views. (You may want to review the "Analyzing a Court Decision" skill in the Legal Handbook.)

4. In a two-page written essay, explain the impact of the judicial decision of your case on Canadian law and the rights of citizens. (You may want to review "Tips for Writing an Argumentative Esssay" in the Legal Handbook.)

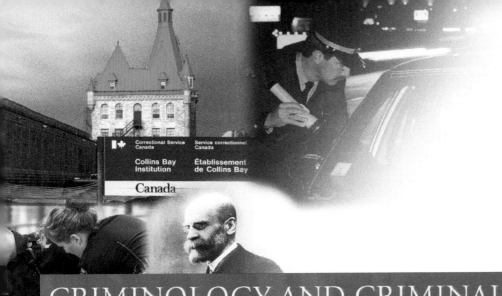

UNIT 3

CRIMINOLOGY AND CRIMINAL PROCEDURES

OVERALL LEARNING EXPECTATIONS

By the end of this unit, you will be able to:

- analyze theories about criminal conduct and the nature of criminal behaviour and explain what constitutes a crime in Canadian law
- analyze the Canadian criminal trial process
- demonstrate an understanding of the competing concepts of justice as they apply to the criminal justice system

TABLE OF CONTENTS

Chapter

9

LEARNING EXPECTATIONS

After reading this chapter, you will be able to:

- understand and evaluate the key theories experts use to explain criminal deviance
- explain the relationship between law and morality
- understand the purpose of criminal law
- identify what is a crime in Canada and the concepts of *actus reus, mens rea,* and absolute liability
- explain key offences found in the Canadian *Criminal Code*
- explain how the concept of justice relates to criminal law

FIGURE 9.1 Matti Baranovski was a 15-year-old high school student beaten to death by a group of young men in 1999 in the Toronto park shown here. Two members of the group were charged with second-degree murder. Why do certain members of society commit crimes such as murder, while others obey the laws of our *Criminal Code?*

> *Evil is unspectacular and always human*
> *And shares our bed and eats at our table.*
>
> —W.H. Auden, (1907–1973)
> British Poet, quoted from "Detective Story"

◼ I N T R O D U C T I O N ◼

We are both fascinated and repelled by criminal behaviour. The media feed our fascination with seemingly endless coverage of crime and profiles on criminals, who sometimes become household names. It is perhaps not surprising that some of us worry more about becoming a victim of crime than any other possible misfortune. Why do people commit criminal acts? Why do we consider certain behaviours criminal and others merely "bad"? How can our society reduce criminal activity? The attempt to answer these complex questions is the basis of **criminology**. Criminologists analyze the nature, causes, and means of dealing with crime, and, as you will learn, they do not always agree. This chapter will explore some of the historical and contemporary theories relating to our criminal justice system.

Historical Perspectives on Criminology

Classical Criminology

Cultures around the globe have unique perspectives on criminal law and justice. You have already explored, for example, Iroquoian and Babylonian origins of law in Chapter 2. The theories on criminology presented in this chapter come from Europe, where Canadian criminal law also has its roots.

Classical theories of criminology came about in response to the chaotic systems of justice in Europe during the eighteenth and early nineteenth centuries. The two most famous proponents of the classical school of thought were Italian theorist Cesare Beccaria (1738–1794) and English philosopher Jeremy Bentham (1748–1832). Beccaria and Bentham were interested in how law-making and the legal process affected the incidence of crime in society.

In his book *On Crimes and Punishments*, Beccaria argued that human beings were driven primarily by self-interest, but that they would be rational in their actions. Weighing the possible consequences of their actions, individuals would conclude that it was ultimately in their best interests to limit some of their freedoms. For example, people would forfeit the freedom to drive through a red light in exchange for their personal peace and security. Beccaria suggested that the role of government should be to act on behalf and in the best interest of all citizens; therefore, each citizen should be prepared to forgo a certain amount of personal freedom in exchange for the protection of the state. He believed the very existence of the law should act as a sufficient deterrent to those likely to break it, and the punishment enacted should be proportionately greater than the pleasure derived from a criminal gain.

Jeremy Bentham's view was based on the philosophy of **utilitarianism**, which is the belief that law should ensure the greatest good for the greatest number of people. Law, according to Bentham, should be based on a social contract between the government and the people, with each side accepting certain consequences if the contract were broken. Bentham argued that it was the role of government to make clear what sorts of behaviours would be considered criminal and to establish limits on the degree to which government could use its power to punish citizens.

Bentham and Beccaria both believed that government could control crime by enacting laws that were seen by people as being in the best interests of society. The government would also have to ensure the enforcement of these laws through the use of swift and certain punishment.

Positivism

During the late nineteenth century, a new movement began that would challenge the classical position. The **positivist** school of thought focused on biological and psychological factors—rather than the legal system—to explain criminal behaviour. Adherents to this movement attempted to support their theories by applying scientific methods to their study of human behaviour. The importance of the positivists' theories lies not in how right they were, but in how incredibly wrong some of them were.

One of the better-known positivists was Italian physician and psychiatrist Cesare Lombroso (1835–1909). Lombroso studied the cadavers of executed criminals in an effort to determine scientifically whether criminals were physically any different from non-criminals. Lombroso argued that serious offenders had inherited criminal traits. He believed that there was such a person as a "born criminal" and that specific physical features reflected a criminal mind. The features that criminals Lombroso studied had in common included, for example, enormous jaws and strong canine teeth.

During the 1960s, criminologists of the positivist school argued that the explanation for criminal behaviour might lie in chromosomal abnormalities. The XYY theory argued that

It is obviously impossible for criminality to be inherited as such, for crime is defined by acts of legislature and these vary independently of the biological inheritance of the violators of the law.

—Sutherland and Cressey, 1924

violent male criminals have an abnormal XYY chromosome (XY is the normal pattern in males). However, researchers soon discovered this was not true: many male criminals did not have the abnormality, and some men who did have the abnormality had never committed any crimes.

The notion that criminals were *born* rather than *made* continued over the past century but fell out of favour in part due to the moral implications. If criminals were born, it would simply be a fact of life for which no one—not parents, society, or even the criminals themselves—could be blamed. At the same time as some of the positivist theories were being discredited, new theories emphasizing "nurture" over "nature" as the cause of crime began to be explored.

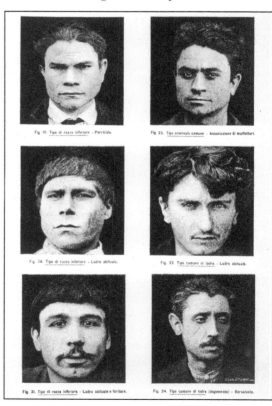

FIGURE 9.2 Lombroso wrongly believed that a person could be trained to recognize criminals based on their common facial features. He developed charts in which various faces were classified into categories of criminals. The faces in this group, for example, were murderers. What criticisms can you make of this classification system?

Sociological Perspectives

Other criminologists began to focus their research not on the individual or the legal system, but on external physical and environmental factors as major contributors to criminal behaviour.

Theory of Anomie

One of the first exponents of the **anomie theory** was French sociologist Emile Durkheim (1858–1917), who argued that as society moved from a rural to an urban setting, the traditional values and bonds that regulated an individual's behaviour within the group were weakened. From this shift flowed what Durkheim called "anomie," a concept describing the individual's isolation in an urban setting. No longer restrained by the norms of society and given the anonymity that comes with living in a big city, certain individuals, according to Durkheim, turned to crime.

In another theory, Durkheim argued that since crime has always existed and is found in all communities, both wealthy and economically challenged, it might serve a useful function. If there were no crime, it would mean that everyone in society was the same and agreed on what was right and wrong. A society in which no one challenged the prevailing opinion would be too conforming. Durkheim pointed to the Greek philosopher Socrates, who, as you read in Chapter 3, was considered a criminal and sentenced to death for challenging the social order. Individuals, such as Socrates, who challenge the prevailing view often force society to change for the better.

Ecological School

During the 1930s, scholars at the University of Chicago took Durkheim's ideas further, arguing that criminal behaviour was indeed fostered and encouraged in certain environments. The **ecological school** studied a number of poor or transient neighbourhoods and concluded that communities that suffered from high rates of poverty and social disintegration were more likely to condone

FIGURE 9.3 Emile Durkheim believed that urban living afforded people a level of anonymity that allowed them to commit crimes. When you think of present-day cities, do you think his theory holds more or less merit than it did when Durkheim developed it back at the turn of the twentieth century?

criminal activity than were more affluent neighbourhoods. This idea was soon countered by theories pointing to capitalism as the true cause of crime.

Social conflict theories of the mid-nineteenth century arose from the theories of Karl Marx and Frederick Engels who argued that in a capitalist society, which encouraged competition for resources and wealth, crime was inevitable. Also, in a capitalist society, those in political power controlled the definition of crime and, therefore, were more likely to punish criminals who were economically disadvantaged than criminals belonging to the corporate elite. According to Marxist theorists, our justice system protects those with power and property against those who have little of either.

Consensus Theory

Other criminologists disagree with the social conflict theories, arguing that crime is not a politically defined concept; rather, crimes are behaviours that most people would consider wrong. **Consensus theorists** assume there is a universal definition of right and wrong and that criminal laws reflect this consensus. They argue that criminal laws prohibit behaviours that society has agreed are harmful, and that these collective prohibitions are applied to all classes of people. Criminal codes, for example, outline crimes against property but also include laws banning insider trading, fraud, and other types of white-collar crimes. Criminals, according to supporters of the consensus theory, choose not to accept the view of the majority.

CONFIRM YOUR UNDERSTANDING

1. What evidence do you see for Beccaria's or Bentham's views in the following quotation from the American Declaration of Independence of 1776?

> We hold these truths to be self-evident, that all men are created equal, that they are endowed by their Creator with certain inalienable Rights, that among these are Life, Liberty, and the pursuit of Happiness….That to secure these rights, Governments are instituted among Men, deriving their just powers from the consent of the governed….That whenever any Form of Government becomes destructive of these ends, it is the Right of the People to alter or to abolish it, and to institute new Government, laying its foundation on such principles, and organizing its powers in such form, as to them shall seem most likely to effect their Safety and Happiness….

2. Examine the _Canadian Charter of Rights and Freedoms_ (pp. 514–517). Identify evidence of classical theory in our _Charter_ and explain your choices.

3. The classical theory suggests that criminal behaviour is the result of rational choice and that people will be deterred by punishment. What arguments would you use to counter this position?

4. Create a comparison chart highlighting the key arguments of classical and positivist criminology.

5. Explain Durkheim's theory of anomie. Provide three counter-arguments to this theory.

6. a) Explain the key differences between the following criminal theories: ecological school, social conflict theory, and consensus theory.

b) Write a short argument outlining which of the above theories you would be most likely to support.

Contemporary Theories of Criminal Deviance

Newer theories of criminal deviance employ more sophisticated methods of data collection and interpretation but still echo many of the theories of the past. Classical theory has evolved into **rational choice** and **deterrence theories**. They suggest that many criminals carefully calculate the costs and benefits of engaging in criminal activity. Persons who are likely to commit crime value the excitement and thrill of breaking the law and are willing to take greater chances than other people. However, if the risks outweigh the benefits and punishment is almost certain, only the most irrational person would continue to break the law.

Sociological Theories

Some criminologists argue that people commit crimes when they believe they cannot achieve their desires and goals through legitimate means. This is known as the **strain theory** and has its roots in the ideas of Emile Durkheim. Modern supporters of this theory suggest that in current societies that stress the goals of acquiring wealth, success, and power, the means to achieve these goals, such as education or economic resources, are denied to those who are economically disadvantaged or have little opportunity for formal education.

Social psychologists place more emphasis on the **socialization theory**; they suggest that the key influences leading to criminal behaviour are found in upbringing, peer groups, and role models. **Social conflict theorists** continue to be influenced by Marxist economic views that the root cause of crime is in the unfair economic structures of capitalism.

Contemporary Biological Theories

Positivist theories have also been revisited as a result of the enormous research now being done in biology and genetics. The modern version, sometimes referred to as **biological trait theory**, argues that certain human traits, such as intelligence, personality, and chemical and genetic makeup, may predispose certain individuals to engage in criminal behaviour. Biochemical research suggests that poor diet; the influence of hormones, especially male hormones (androgens); or exposure to alcohol or drugs while in the womb could cause a person to become a criminal. Defence lawyers have used this view to excuse their clients' criminal conduct. For example, in 1979 lawyers for Daniel White, the confessed killer of the mayor of San Francisco, argued White's actions were caused by an addiction to sugar-laden junk food. This so-called "Twinkie defence" was successful in reducing White's sentence.

Neurophysiological theorists focus on the study of brain activity and argue that certain neurological dysfunctions are connected with criminal activity. Others have pointed out the connections between crime and genetics. Some studies done on identical and fraternal twins suggest the tendency to engage in criminal behaviour may have a genetic component. Other studies argue that the evidence is inconclusive, pointing out that the results of the twin studies are weak since not enough attention was paid to other possible influences, such as upbringing and environment.

The controversy over what makes some individuals turn to crime continues. Most criminologists today recognize that the answer is extremely complex and that it is unlikely that a single trait or inherited characteristic can explain crime. However, many are convinced that biological and mental traits interact with environmental factors to influence human behaviour, including criminality.

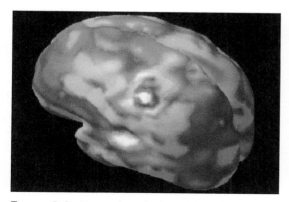 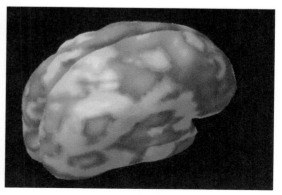

FIGURE 9.4 Research on brain activity is done at the University of Montréal using 3-D scans. These images are examples of the types of 3-D scans researchers use to study neurological dysfunctions. (The photo on the right is a normal brain showing glucose consumption with sensory activity, while the photo on the left shows glucose consumption without sensory activity.) Explain why you feel it is, or is not, a good idea for researchers to work on discovering connections between neurological dysfunction and criminal activity.

1. How does classical theory relate to the contemporary theories of rational choice and deterrence?

2. How would the strain theory of crime explain white-collar crimes such as insider trading and fraud?

3. Prepare a Venn diagram showing the difference/connection between the sociological and biological contemporary theories of crime.

The Purpose of Criminal Law

First and foremost, the job of any government is to provide its citizens with a reasonable degree of security. The main purpose of criminal law, therefore, is to control and prevent conduct that society believes may be harmful or potentially harmful. But should criminal law control conduct that may be offensive or merely a nuisance? Is it the job of government to protect you from harming yourself? What conduct should be considered so repugnant that it warrants depriving individuals of their liberty? In Canada, crimes and punishments are defined in our *Criminal Code*. Unlike the United States, where each state may have its own unique criminal code, in Canada responsibility for criminal law falls under the jurisdiction of the federal government. The definition and range of punishments for a crime in Kamloops, British Columbia, are exactly the same as they are in Cobourg, Ontario.

When citizens give to their government the power to make and enforce criminal law, they agree to restrict their own personal liberties in exchange for peace and security. In assuming this considerable power, including the employment of agents, such as police, to help uphold laws, governments are obliged to establish limits on the degree to which they can use this power to punish citizens. Finding a balance between personal liberty and the protection of society is an ever-present challenge in criminal law.

Functions of Our *Criminal Code*

Our *Criminal Code* has several different functions. The most important ones are as follows:
- preventing harm to people and property
- preventing action that challenges government authority and institutions
- discouraging personal revenge
- preventing harm to oneself
- expressing and enforcing morality

Some of these functions are widely accepted without debate. For example, most people agree that the law should prohibit behaviours harmful to others, such as physically injuring another person, taking another person's possession, or damaging another person's property. Similarly, it is acceptable that criminal law should prevent actions that challenge legitimate government, such as treason or inciting riots. The punishments for such offences should be sufficient to deter potential violators. Other functions of our criminal law, such as deterring personal revenge, legal paternalism, and the enforcement of morality, are more controversial.

Deterring Personal Revenge

Although revenge may not be an acceptable motive for criminal behaviour, we nevertheless have more sympathy for the parent who avenges the killer of his or her child than for the person who kills a stranger in cold blood. At the same time, we recognize that private retribution could lead to anarchy, and so we give government the responsibility for punishing people who harm others. To deter **vigilantism**, or acts of personal revenge, government must be able to demonstrate that it is capable of apprehending and punishing criminals.

Legal Paternalism

One of the more controversial criticisms of criminal law is the concept of **legal paternalism**. This refers to the idea of government as a kind of father figure and involves crimes that prohibit people from harming themselves. Examples of these types of crimes include possession of drugs, possession of obscene material, and enlisting someone's help to commit suicide. Do these types of crimes warrant inclusion in the *Criminal Code*, or should criminal codes reflect only the most serious crimes or those crimes that directly harm others? At one time, for example, our *Criminal Code* included the crime of attempted suicide. Most people today would see people who were feeling so depressed that they wanted to kill themselves as individuals who needed help, not as criminals.

Nevertheless, we understand that many people may believe that committing suicide does diminish respect for life, and we can understand how attempted suicide may have been considered a crime at one time. However, the reason for its inclusion in our *Criminal Code* may have been less moral than we might assume. Some argue that the historical reason for including attempted suicide as a crime had more to do with the interest of the state than the protection of the public or the individual. Prohibition of suicide stemmed from the idea that an individual was a subject of the king, and to deprive the king of a subject was to deprive the king of an asset and, therefore, was a crime against the king. Families in which a member committed suicide were often obliged to turn over their assets to the king in compensation.

FIGURE 9.5 In 2002, the Netherlands became the first country in the world to legalize assisted suicide, or mercy killings. However, this move did not come without controversy, as the above protest photo shows. Do you think Canada should follow the Dutch lead?

Laws that prohibit possession of certain drugs are also controversial. The argument that laws prohibiting drug use prevent social harm is countered by the argument that many other actions, such as cigarette smoking, also cause social harm but are not considered criminal.

The Expression and Enforcement of Morality

Our *Criminal Code* also functions as a reflection of our moral values. Crimes such as murder or robbery are prohibited in most societies, but other offences shift with changing attitudes and values. This has become one of the most controversial aspects of criminal law. How does criminal law determine and reflect the moral values of the majority, while at the same time protect the differing opinions of the minorities? Should the enormous power of the state to punish and take away liberty be used to enforce laws against behaviours many people may consider more nuisances than harmful? Should criminal laws impose or merely reflect morality? What should be the connection between law and morality?

Morality is the custom of one's country and the current feeling of one's peers. Cannibalism is moral in a cannibal country.

—Samuel Butler (1612–1680), English writer and poet

SHIFTING PERSPECTIVES: Who Should Butt Out?

Smoking is a custom loathsome to the eye, hateful to the nose, harmful to the brain, dangerous to the lungs, and in the black, stinking fume thereof, nearest resembles the horrible stygian smoke of the pit that is bottomless.

—King James I, seventeenth-century England

Reach for a Lucky, not a sweet.

—Lucky Strike cigarette advertisement, 1950

You are all so much above this. You are intelligent. You are energetic…. Any dream you have is possible. But if you walk the path I walked, this is the path you will walk. And I don't want any of you to ever walk this walk.

—Barb Tarbox, 41, ex-model, talking to Edmonton students before she died of smoking-related cancer, 2003

As the above quotations illustrate, few topics have been the subject of such changing perspectives over time as our views on smoking. Our laws have reflected our changing attitudes. By 2004, almost every province in Canada had enacted laws placing bans on smoking in all public places, including restaurants and bars. Tobacco advertising has been severely restricted. Tobacco companies have been successfully sued by smokers suffering from smoking-related diseases, and governments are now in the process of suing tobacco manufacturers in an attempt to recoup smoking-related health-care costs.

Tobacco was first introduced in North America in the seventeenth century, and although it was controversial even then, it still clearly increased in popularity over the years. By the 1950s, tobacco companies were seriously recommending smoking as a cure for migraines, stress, toothaches, and even cancer! It was not until 1964, when the Surgeon General of the US Public Health Service released a report called "Smoking and Health," that the connection between cancer and smoking was clearly spelled out to the general public.

A more significant shift came in the 1980s, during one of the many lawsuits against the Philip Morris Company, with the discovery of confidential documents suggesting that tobacco companies were targeting adolescents. There was also evidence to suggest these companies were aware of the cancer-causing properties of their product.

By 1999, even large companies such as Philip Morris were forced to admit that their product could cause lung cancer, emphysema, and heart disease, and that cigarettes were, indeed, addictive. Despite the controversy, the tobacco industry made over $160 billion worldwide during that same year, showing that tobacco companies were still very much in business.

Recognizing their obligations regarding smoking and the concern about second-hand smoke, both provincial and municipal governments in Canada have enacted laws and

FIGURE 9.6   Photo of an early 1950s ad proclaiming the virtues of Lucky Strike cigarettes

bylaws restricting smoking. Most provinces and municipalities have already banned smoking in public buildings and are beginning to severely restrict smoking in private businesses. By 2003, all restaurants were 100 percent smoke-free in Toronto (although there was the option of a designated smoking room), and initiatives were underway to ban smoking from all bars and bingo halls as well.

The legislation and the lawsuits have had an effect—smoking in Canada has been reduced—but the issue remains controversial. The tobacco companies continue to fight back, and in 1995 the Supreme Court of Canada struck down a ban on tobacco ads under the *Tobacco Product Control Act*, which stated, "No person shall advertise any tobacco product offered for sale in Canada." The court argued that this ban violated the *Charter* right to freedom of speech. The law was changed to permit tobacco advertising in publications that have adult readership, but the ban remained in effect in public places. Imperial Tobacco is now challenging the legality of the legislation in the Québec Court of Appeal.

In addition, organizations such as PUBCO (the Pub and Bar Coalition of Ontario) have been complaining about the loss of business due to the smoking ban and have pointed out that since April 2003, when Ottawa's anti-smoking bylaw went into effect, numerous bars and pubs have been forced to close.

Some lawyers and individuals are now arguing that governments have gone too far and that the laws banning smoking are violating the rights of smokers. They argue that alcohol is equally harmful to individuals and society, yet it is not subject to the same restrictions. They also argue that the government seems to be trying to make smoking illegal without actually declaring it illegal.

SOURCE: Khoo, Lisa. "Banning the Butt: Global Anti-smoking Effort." *CBC News Online.* Accessed Jan. 2004 <www.cbc.ca/news/indepth/background/smokingbans.html>.

Your Perspective

1. In keeping with society's changing perspective on cigarettes over the past century, the Canadian government has enacted many pieces of legislation dealing with smoking and the tobacco industry.
   a) Create a timeline on which you record the enactment of six new laws put forth by the government in an attempt to curb tobacco consumption.
   b) Continue your timeline with three additions of your own that indicate what you think the government will or should do next.
2. "Anti-smoking legislation is 'legal paternalism' and does not conform to the principles of positive law." Write a few paragraphs explaining this statement and whether or not you agree with it.
3. Those opposed to smoking laws argue that government is slowly moving to make tobacco an illegal drug subject to the same penalties as certain other drugs under the *Controlled Drugs and Substances Act* or the *Food and Drug Act* found in the *Criminal Code*.
   a) Using your classroom copy of the *Criminal Code*, examine what kinds of drugs are controlled or limited under these two acts.
   b) Assume the role of the legislature intending to add tobacco to one of these acts. Which act would tobacco best fall under in your opinion?
   c) Prepare an argument that the possession, sale, and distribution of tobacco products should be part of criminal law.

Law and Morality

Few people would debate the argument that people who kill or physically injure other people should be punished. We can sympathize with the victims, and we want to make sure such behaviours are prevented. However, if there is no victim, should there be no crime? Prostitutes willingly engage in sexual acts, and one might argue that the law should be involved only if one party fails to uphold the contract by refusing to pay or provide services, or by forcing the other party into non-consensual activity. Individuals who have in their possession obscene or pornographic material generally knew what they were purchasing, so they are not victims. Similarly, those who knowingly purchase illegal drugs do not meet the criteria of victim any more than the purchasers of alcohol or tobacco. Many of these offences are referred to as "victimless crimes." However, others would argue that the victim is, in fact, society. Critics of the "victimless crime" argument would suggest that the actions of individuals always impact on society. They point to the fact that those who use or abuse drugs may be a financial burden on the heath-care system. Opponents of prostitution or pornography argue that it "dehumanizes" women and others, turning them into products and commodities. They also point to the fact that young runaways and drug addicts are often exploited and coerced into prostitution.

The fact that offences regarding prostitution or drug use are found in our *Criminal Code* sends a message that such acts are not to be tolerated because they will ultimately erode the moral fabric of our society. In his essay "Morals and the Criminal Law," English judge and legal philosopher Patrick Devlin wrote, "What makes a society of any sort is a community of ideas…about the way its members should behave and govern their lives; these ideas are its morality" (Dyzenhaus 2001). His view argues that one of the purposes of criminal law is to express public morality. The problem created by this argument is that it is an almost impossible task to define morality. At various times in the past, Canada has permitted slavery, placed Aboriginal children in residential

schools far from their families, and denied women the right to vote.

Defining morality becomes even more challenging in a multicultural society such as our own. In a democracy, should the majority dictate how all should live? Adding even more confusion to the argument is the fact that some things many people would consider immoral are not crimes—gluttony, adultery, and child poverty, for example. It is not a crime to ignore the cries of a drowning child, though many of us would consider such behaviour highly immoral. At the same time, we consider criminal the actions of people whose intentions may have been moral. Robert Latimer, who is discussed in Chapter 11, killed his daughter to end her suffering, but he was convicted of murder.

The most compelling argument that so-called victimless crimes cause social harm is also debatable. We know that drug use causes harm to the user, but we are also aware of the enormous social cost to families and our health-care system. We acknowledge the harm prostitution may do to local neighbourhoods where prostitutes ply their trade. However, the same arguments could be made regarding activities that are not illegal, such as alcohol or tobacco use.

Criminal law has always reflected the moral values of society, and when the laws are out of step with public opinion, the results are apparent. An example is the Morgentaler case, which took place in 1988. The *Criminal Code* prohibited abortion except as approved by a therapeutic abortion committee. Dr. Henry Morgentaler openly defied the law by performing abortions that were not approved. He was prosecuted and acquitted by a jury. On appeal, the Québec Court of Appeal substituted a conviction, which was upheld by the Supreme Court of Canada. A new trial was ordered, and Dr. Morgentaler was again acquitted by a jury. He was also charged in Ontario and again acquitted. On appeal, the Supreme Court of Canada held that the relevant provision of the *Criminal Code* was invalid because it conflicted with the *Canadian Charter of Rights and Freedoms* (*R. v. Morgentaler*, [1988] 1 S.C.R. 30).

1. What are the key functions of criminal law? Can you think of any others?

2. What is "legal paternalism"? Why is it controversial?

3. Is it ever necessary to take the law into your own hands? Explain.

4. What evidence is there that our criminal law reflects our moral values? Search the newspapers to find two legal cases that support your view.

5. English philosopher John Stuart Mill (1807–1873) said, "Law should not intervene in matters of private moral conduct more than necessary to preserve public order and to protect citizens against what is injurious." Compare this view with that of Patrick Devlin on page 274. With which legal philosopher do you most agree? Why?

What Is a Crime?

A simple legal definition of crime is anything that is defined as criminal within the Canadian *Criminal Code* and related federal statutes such as the *Food and Drugs Act, Youth Criminal Justice Act,* and *Controlled Drugs and Substances Act.* Even without consulting the *Code,* most people intuitively know what the serious crimes are. Offences such as murder, assault, and theft violate standards in a community to such an extent that we are prepared to impose serious sanctions on those who engage in such acts. The Law Reform Commission of Canada's 1976 report on criminal law stated, "Criminal law must be an instrument of last resort. It must be used as little as possible." Yet, as we have discussed, our *Criminal Code* imposes sanctions on conduct that many would argue is more annoying than criminal. For example, our *Criminal Code* includes such offences as pretending to practise witchcraft and disturbing an oyster bed. Thus defining what constitutes criminal conduct is one of the more difficult tasks of criminal law.

In addition, there are other offences that fall under provincial jurisdiction, such as failing to wear a seatbelt, speeding, or drinking under age. These offences are enforced by the courts and may result in substantial penalties, but they are not crimes. They are sometimes referred to as **quasi-criminal offences**, and although they may

be considered serious offences, they do not warrant a criminal record.

In order to be convicted of a crime in Canada, two elements must be proven: that the crime occurred—the *guilty act*—and that the defendant not only engaged in the criminal act, but intended to do so—the *guilty mind.* The Latin terms for these two elements are ***actus reus*** (guilty act) and ***mens rea*** (guilty mind).

Actus Reus

The *actus reus* of a criminal offence is found in its *Criminal Code* definition. For example, s. 265 of the *Criminal Code* defines assault:

(1) A person commits an assault when

(a) without the consent of another person, he applies force intentionally to that other person, directly or indirectly.

To prove *actus reus,* the Crown would have to demonstrate that (a) there was no consent, and (b) force was applied.

Sometimes the *actus reus* of the offence is not in doing something, but in failing to do something that is one's duty to do. For example, you have a legal duty to assist a police officer when required to do so. Section 129 of the *Criminal Code* states:

Every one who

(b) omits, without reasonable excuse, to

assist a public officer or peace officer in the execution of his duty...., after having reasonable notice that he is required to do so

(d) is guilty of an indictable offence....

The *actus reus* of a criminal act must be voluntary. For example, if someone shoots another while having a seizure or heart attack or while sleepwalking, he or she may not be criminally liable. The central issue of whether or not an action was voluntary depends on whether the accused had control over his or her actions. In 1992, the Supreme Court of Canada upheld the acquittal of Kenneth Parks, who drove to the home of his parents-in-law some 20 km away, stabbed his mother-in-law to death, and seriously injured his father-in-law. His defence successfully argued that Mr. Parks was sleepwalking at the time and thus acted involuntarily.

FIGURE 9.7   Kenneth Parks, charged with the murder and attempted murder of his in-laws, claimed to have been sleepwalking throughout the incident. His lawyer Marlys Edwardh (on the left) used the defence of automatism. "Automatism" means an action performed involuntarily. How would such an action relate to the *actus reus* component of criminal liability?

ASKING KEY QUESTIONS

Free Will, Determinism, and Criminal Law

Introduction

In the American movie *Minority Report*, the main character is able to predict crimes and prevent them from happening by accessing the visions of three telepathic muses who are able to see future potential crimes. The premise is somewhat far-fetched, but the movie asks interesting legal questions about the concepts of *mens rea* and *actus reus*. In the hypothetical world of *Minority Report*, a person could be arrested for planning to commit a crime, even though he or she had not actually carried it out. Under our current *Criminal Code*, this same person could not be convicted due to the necessity of proving *actus reus*.

The Scientific View

Advances in science may present us with an equally controversial view of the nature of crim-

inal behaviour. In his article "A Vision of the Future," Steven I. Friedland posits that breakthroughs in genetics will alter our whole system of criminal law. He points to the fact that defence lawyers are already citing genetic explanations, such as alcoholism and certain anti-social disorders, to excuse the conduct of their clients. He writes that the real question "is not whether genetic evidence will ever be admitted into court, but when and under what kinds of circumstances." Friedland argues that as the Human Genome Project advances, the focus of criminal law may change from the concept of free will, which assumes rational choice, to a return to the ideas of positivism or biological trait theory.

Friedland suggests that this will have enormous implications for criminal law, which currently determines guilt by examining "blameworthiness." As he points out, if defendants claim their genes caused them to commit the crime, they cannot be blamed for actions over which they had no control. His arguments suggest that our justice system, which is based on rehabilitation, may be rendered useless since these individuals cannot be rehabilitated by any of our traditional methods. If we accept Friedland's view from a legal philosophy perspective, then a "geneticized" criminal law system would challenge our concept of morality. If there is no free will, can there be a moral choice?

Friedland says that if the discoveries of the Human Genome Project reveal that genetics play a large role in determining criminal behaviour, our legal system may begin to emphasize a biological basis of conduct rather than our current psychological or sociological basis. His argument raises the possibility of defence lawyers and Crown attorneys arguing over not who actually committed the crime, but just how much influence an individual's genetic makeup had on the crime committed.

Friedland suggests that an even more controversial consequence of citing genetic evidence as a defence for criminal conduct may be the development of DNA Identification Cards. These cards, he says, may be developed along with Genetic Propensity Cards, which could be used to determine sentencing, among other things. "The length of the defendant's sentence might be affected by his or her dangerous quotient" (Friedland 1997).

Is there actual scientific support for this new determinism, or will we look back 100 years from today with the same sense of disbelief as we now look at the theories of Cesare Lombroso?

Research does indicate a correlation between biological conditions and criminal behaviour. Dutch researchers have been studying several generations of a Dutch family in which primarily the male members seemed to display significant levels of anti-social and criminal behaviour. The researchers found that these males were deficient in a particular enzyme in the brain associated with levels of the neurotransmitter serotonin. They concluded that there was a link between this genetic abnormality and the family's anti-social behaviour (Gallagher 2001). Other researchers have come to the conclusion that the small groups of individuals who commit the majority of crimes have a genetic marker causing them to act in a violent manner (Gallagher 2001).

Our present criminal justice system is based on the concept of *mens rea*, or guilty mind. If the Human Genome Project ultimately proves that criminal behaviour has a significant genetic component, its implications for the criminal justice system will be significant. However, Friedland suggests that criminal law should explore the ramifications of a genetically reordered system but must not use genetics and science as "a substitute for the necessary and imprecise social aspect of the criminal law" (Friedland 1997).

SOURCES: Friedland, Steven I. "A Vision of the Future." Excerpted from "The Criminal Law Implications of the Human Genome Project: Reimagining a Genetically Oriented Criminal Justice System." *Kentucky Law Journal* 86 (1997): 303–366.

Gallagher, Winifred. "How We Become What We Are." *The Atlantic Monthly*. Sept. 1994.

Form Your Questions

The information above raises many questions. For example, should individuals with a genetic propensity to violence be treated, possibly against their will, *before* they demonstrate violent behaviour?

What other questions might you ask regarding the impact of genetics on our criminal justice system? Think of three key questions. Share your questions with the rest of the class, and discuss possible answers or solutions.

Mens Rea

Some would argue that since it is impossible to prove the mental state of a person, as the margin quotation suggests, individuals who engage in criminal conduct should be judged on the consequences of their actions rather than on their intent. However, this is not the case in Canada. To meet the legal definition of a crime in this country, the guilty act must be done with criminal intent or *mens rea*. "Intent," in the legal sense, can mean to carry out an act with intent, with knowledge, or by being reckless or wilfully blind to the consequences of the act.

In criminal law, "intent" is defined in the precise detail of each offence. For example, "robbery" is defined as "theft committed with violence." The decision to act or threaten violence is the intent of the crime.

General Intent Versus Specific Intent

Some crimes require what is called general intent, and others require specific intent. The type of intent varies depending on how the crime is defined in the *Criminal Code*. For most crimes, it must be shown that the accused *meant* to commit the crime. This is the **general intent**. For example, if Brian swings his golf club and hits John, he is guilty of assault if he meant to hit John, but if it was an accident, there is no assault.

Specific intent involves intent in addition to the *general intent* to commit the crime. For example, burglary is the breaking and entering of a dwelling-house with "intent to commit an indictable offence." The "break and enter" aspect requires a general intent, but the "intent to commit an indictable offence" is a specific intent.

Intent and Motive

The concept of *mens rea* and **intent** is not to be confused with **motive**. *Intent* refers to the state of mind with which an act is done or not done, but *motive* is what prompts or causes a person to act or not act. For example, in the Robert Latimer case mentioned on page 351, Robert Latimer's motive may have been honourable—he wanted to end his

daughter's suffering—but his intention was still to commit murder, the fact that led to his conviction. In some cases, as you will learn in Chapter 11, motive may be considered in determining if an accused has a legal defence, or it may be taken into consideration in the sentencing of the guilty party.

Mens rea also applies if the accused intended to commit a crime against one person but injured another instead. This is referred to as the **doctrine of transferred intent**, that is, the original criminal intent is transferred to the unintended victim.

Knowledge

In order to have the requisite *mens rea* to commit a crime, the courts assume a person must have some knowledge of the *actus reus* of the crime. This is sometimes indicated by the words "knowing" or "knowingly" in the definition of the crime. For example, s. 251 of the *Criminal Code* says:

(1) Every one who knowingly
(b) sends an aircraft on a flight or operates an aircraft that is not fit and safe for flight
…is guilty of an indictable offence….

Recklessness and Wilful Blindness

Recklessness and **wilful blindness** are also types of *mens rea*. A person is said to be reckless when he or she is extremely careless or heedless of apparent danger. Some *Criminal Code* offences clearly require recklessness by including the words "reckless" or "recklessness" in the definition of the crime. For example, s. 219 on criminal negligence states:

(1) Every one is criminally negligent who
(a) in doing anything, or
(b) in omitting to do anything that it is his duty to do, shows wanton *or* reckless disregard for the lives and safety of other persons.

For a person to be convicted of reckless conduct, it must be shown that the accused was aware of the danger involved even if he or she did not intend the consequence. For example, if someone were to shoot a pellet gun into a crowd of children, injuring one seriously, that person may not have intended harm but should have foreseen the possibility and was taking a risk.

Wilful blindness is related to recklessness but is a somewhat more complex concept. A person could be said to be wilfully blind when he or she suspects a harmful or criminal outcome but prefers not to ask the questions that would confirm these suspicions. For example, in *R. v. Blondin*, [1970] 2 C.C.C. (2d) 118 (B.C.C.A.), the accused was charged with importing narcotics. The drugs were found in scuba-diving equipment that the accused was trying to bring into Canada. The accused admitted he knew there was something illegal in the tank but did not attempt to find out what it was. The courts found him guilty of the offence even though the *actus reus* of the offence requires knowledge that the substance being imported was a narcotic. The court found that the accused was wilfully blind to what was in the tank, and therefore the knowledge requirement was satisfied.

Mens Rea and the Subjective/ Objective Distinction

As a result of many *Charter* challenges, there is still ambiguity and confusion about the definition of *mens rea*. A central issue is whether the intent meets the **subjective** or **objective standard**. The Supreme Court judgments you read in *R. v. Vaillancourt* (p. 15) and *R. v. Martineau* (p. 39) make it clear that there should be a clear distinction between the *subjective* standard—did the accused know the consequences of his or her actions?—and the *objective* standard—measured against a reasonable person, should the accused *ought* to have been able to foresee the consequences of his or her actions? It is more challenging for the Crown to prove the subjective standard since it is difficult to know what is in a person's mind at any given time. For most criminal cases, the circumstances make it clear that the conduct was deliberate. However, in borderline cases, such as *R. v. Tutton and Tutton*, it is more difficult to determine whether or not the conduct was deliberate.

Mr. and Mrs. Tutton were charged with crim-

inal negligence causing death (*R. v. Tutton and Tutton*, [1989] 1 S.C.R. 1392, 48 C.C.C. (3d) 129). Their young son was a diabetic in need of insulin, but the Tuttons believed he would be cured by faith and stopped giving him his medication. The child died and the parents were charged with criminal negligence. Lawyers for the parents argued that the parents were acting in the best interests of their child and were therefore not negligent. The Crown argued that any reasonable parent would have been able to foresee that without his required medication, the child would die, and since the parents failed to provide medical treatment for their child, they were guilty of negligence. The case was appealed to the Supreme Court of Canada, and the fact that the judges were split three to three on their decision indicates the complexity of the concept of *mens rea*. The following excerpts are taken from the decisions given by the concurring and dissenting judges:

The Objective Argument (McIntyre, Lamer, L'Heureux-Dubé JJ.)
The words of s. 202 of the *Criminal Code* make it clear that one is criminally negligent who, in doing anything or in omitting to do anything that is in his duty to do, *shows* wanton or reckless disregard for the lives and safety of other persons. The objective test must therefore be employed where criminal negligence is considered for it is the conduct of the accused, as opposed to his intention or mental state which is examined in this inquiry…. The attribution of criminal liability without proof of such a blameworthy state raises serious concerns. Nonetheless, negligence has been accepted as a factor that may lead to criminal liability and strong arguments can be raised in its favour. It must be observed at once that what is made criminal is negligence. Negligence connotes the opposite of thought-directed action. This leads to the conclusion that what is sought to be restrained by punishment, under s. 202 of the *Criminal Code*, is not the state of mind, but the consequences of mindless action.

The Subjective Argument (Dickson C.J. and Wilson, Le Dain JJ.)

I wish to deal with the implication of my colleagues' approach in this case. By concluding that s. 202 of the *Criminal Code* prohibits conduct and the consequences of mindless action absent any blameworthy state of mind, they have in effect held that the crime of criminal negligence is an absolute liability offence…. The presumption when we are dealing with a serious criminal offence should be in favour of a requirement of some degree of mental blameworthiness. The phrase "wanton and reckless disregard for the lives and safety of other persons" signifies more than gross negligence in the

Landmark CASE

R. v. Hamilton, 2002 ABQB 15

Read the following case analysis. The facts, issue, and *ratio* have been provided for you. Assume, however, that you disagree with the decision. Write a possible dissent for this controversial case.

Facts: Mr. Hamilton was charged under s. 464 of the *Criminal Code* with counselling four indictable offences that were, in fact, not committed. Mr. Hamilton had purchased a Web site called "Top Secret Files." This site included titles such as *How to Break into a House* and *An Anarchist's Guide to Airports*. The key issue dealt with credit card fraud. Part of the Web site offered a program that generated credit card numbers. Mr. Hamilton sent ads to a large number of computer users offering to sell these files. The ads included the following statements:

> Produce credit card numbers! All valid and fully functional. Imagine the things you could do with this program….This software is for educational purposes only and is to be treated as such. If you use the software, you take full responsibility for your actions. Looking forward to seeing you well on your way to a wealthy lifestyle.

Although some people had purchased the program, there was no evidence of any actual fraud using the instructions in the program. Credit card company officials pointed out that the numbers alone would not be sufficient to be able to use the cards. However, "Top Secret Files" did contain information explaining how to commit offences.

Criminal Code: At trial, the Crown and defence agreed that statements such as "looking forward to seeing you well on your way to a wealthy lifestyle" constituted the *actus reus* of the offence. They disagreed on the *mens rea* of the offence.

22. (1) Where a person counsels another person to be a party to an offence and that other person is afterwards a party to that offence, the person who counselled is a party to that offence, notwithstanding that the offence was committed in a way different from that which was counselled.

(2) Every one who counsels another person to be a party to an offence is a party to every offence that the other commits in consequence of the counselling that the person who counselled knew or ought to have known was likely to be committed in consequence of the counselling.

(3) For the purposes of this Act, "counsel" includes procure, solicit or incite.

464. Except where otherwise expressly provided by law, the following provisions apply in respect of persons who counsel other persons to commit offences, namely,

(a) every one who counsels another person to commit an indictable offence is, if the offence is not committed, guilty of an indictable offence and liable to the same punishment to which a person who attempts to commit that offence is liable....

Issue: Must the subjective standard be applied to "intent to counsel"?

Held: The accused should be acquitted.

Ratio Decidendi: (Smith J.) "I find that Mr. Hamilton ought to have known he was counselling fraud. The teaser and his subjective knowledge that the use of the false credit card numbers is illegal make this conclusion irresistible. However, I have a doubt that Hamilton had subjective intent to counsel fraud. His motivation was monetary, and he sought to pique the curiosity of readers who might acquire the information in the same way that he was initially attracted to the information. Further, he struck me as utterly unsophisticated and naive to the point that he cannot be said to have been wilfully blind or reckless. I also find that Mr. Hamilton did not intend the fraud be carried out nor was he wilfully blind or reckless as to the risk of deprivation which would result. In my view, the evidence points to a conclusion that Mr. Hamilton was inviting others to do as he had done—to satisfy their curiosity by seeing how easy it is to generate numbers and to expect that they cannot use them without the expiry date. In other words, he did not specifically intend that the fraud would be carried out. Nor, in all of the circumstances, ought he to have known that the fraud would be carried out. It follows that there could not be a conclusion that he was wilfully blind or reckless as to the consequences of the fraud. In my view, on all of the evidence, it cannot be found that he counselled fraud."

objective sense. It requires some degree of awareness to the threat to the lives and safety of others or alternatively a wilful blindness to that threat which is culpable in light of the gravity of the risk that is prohibited. In the absence of clear statutory language and purpose to the contrary, this court should, in my view, be most reluctant to interpret a serious criminal offence as an absolute liability offence.

Strict and Absolute Liability

For the most part, the two elements—*mens rea* and *actus reus*—must be present to secure a conviction in criminal law. However, some crimes defined by statutes do not require *mens rea*. For these offences, the Crown need prove only the *actus reus* of the offence. In the case of **strict liability** offences, the accused will be convicted unless they can demonstrate that they acted with **due diligence**, that is, they acted as any reasonable person would under the circumstances. Strict liability offences generally deal with health and safety issues or offences dealing with the general welfare of the public.

Absolute liability offences allow for no defence, fault is not an issue, and the accused will be convicted based on the *actus reus* of the offence as defined in the statute. In *R. v. Pontes*, [1995] 100 C.C.C. (3d) 353 (S.C.C.), the accused was convicted of driving while prohibited, that is, he had already had his licence to drive removed due to a previous conviction. The *British Columbia Motor Vehicles Act* provided that a person convicted of such an offence could be sentenced automatically without notice and fined up to $2000. Pontes appealed his conviction, arguing that the law violated s. 7 of the *Charter*, denying him liberty without following the

principles of fundamental justice. The Supreme Court denied the appeal and upheld the absolute liability offence on the grounds that the accused was not in danger of imprisonment and thus his liberty was not at risk.

CONFIRM YOUR UNDERSTANDING

1. Explain the two main elements required for the legal definition of a crime.
2. What is the difference between specific and general intent? Provide an example of transferred intent.
3. Explain what is meant by recklessness and wilful blindness in reference to *mens rea*.
4. Some defence lawyers argue that absolute and strict liability offences should be removed from the *Criminal Code* as they violate the right to be presumed innocent under the *Charter of Rights and Freedoms*. Write a brief counter-argument defending the inclusion of strict and absolute liability offences in the *Criminal Code*.

5. a) After carefully reading the Objective Argument (p. 279), sum up the argument in your own words.
   b) What problems do you foresee with the decision? Write a brief counter-argument.
   c) Read the Subjective Argument (pp. 280–281) carefully, and then sum up the key points in your own words.
6. The *R. v. Tutton and Tutton* case on page 279 pointed to the difficulty of using an equal number of judges to decide a case. In important precedent cases, do you think the decisions should be unanimous? Explain your position.

The *Criminal Code*

As you have read in previous chapters, many societies wrote down their penal law in the form of a code. Canada's *Criminal Code* is rooted in the common law of England. (To learn about Aboriginal and other cultures' approaches to law, please see Chapter 2 pp. 57–62.) By the eighteenth century, England still did not have a codified criminal law. As a result, criminal law had, according to former Canadian Federal Court Judge Allen Linden, evolved into a "bottomless pit of complex case law, petty anachronistic offences and harsh punishments" (Linden 1990). Jeremy Bentham was one of the first legal philosophers to argue the merits of a written code "to set forth the whole of the penal law with such simplicity and clarity that the average citizen would be able to understand it and the average judge would be

unable not to" (Bentham 1789). Some would argue that the present Canadian *Criminal Code* is still a far cry from Bentham's ideal.

In the Canadian Constitution, the federal government was given the authority to codify the criminal law. In 1892, Canada achieved its first criminal code thanks to Sir John A. Macdonald, our first prime minister. He believed strongly in the need for a unified system of criminal law for the whole country. This first criminal code wasn't exactly a model of clarity, and we would be shocked today at some of its provisions. Punishments were severe: "Where whipping may be awarded for any offence...the number of strokes shall be specified at sentencing... the instrument shall be a cat-o'-nine-tails" (www.Duhaime.org).

Our Current *Criminal Code*

Our present *Criminal Code* is the result of numerous amendments to accommodate the needs of changing times. Just 40 years ago, birth control was illegal in Canada, and abortion was a crime until 1988 (before this time, women could receive a legal abortion only after being granted approval by a special hospital committee). Attempting to commit suicide was, at one time, a criminal act, yet incest was not.

Today our *Criminal Code* contains some 28 parts and includes a range of offences from s. 49 "intending to alarm Her Majesty" to s. 71 (c) "accepts a challenge to fight a duel" to very serious offences such as murder. It is a complex and challenging read even for lawyers and judges. Section 2 of the *Code* provides definitions for many of the terms used in the *Code*, but, as you can see, defining a simple term such as "dwelling-house" is more complex than you might think:

2. ..."dwelling-house" means the whole or any part of a building or structure that is kept or occupied as a permanent or temporary residence, and includes

(a) a building within the curtilage of a dwelling-house that is connected to it by a doorway or by a covered and enclosed passage-way, and

(b) a unit that is designed to be mobile and to be used as a permanent or temporary residence and that is being used as such a residence.

Indictable, Summary Conviction, and Hybrid Offences

Crimes were formerly described as treasons, felonies, and misdemeanours, terms you may find familiar from American TV or movies since they are still in common use in the United States today. In Canada, crimes are referred to as indictable, summary conviction, or hybrid. **Indictable offences** are more serious offences such as aggravated assault; **summary conviction offences** are less serious offences such as water skiing at night, common assault, or theft under a certain amount. **Hybrid offences** include a wide range of offences that may be designated indictable or summary conviction offences at the option of the Crown. Depending on whether an accused is charged with a summary conviction or indictable offence, he or

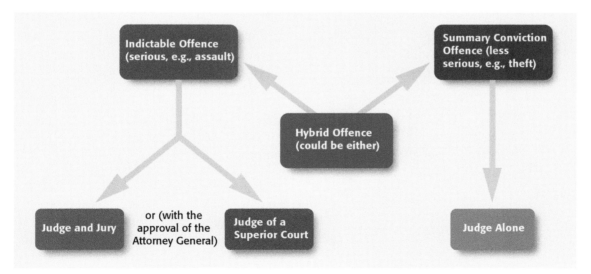

FIGURE 9.8 In the case of a summary conviction offence, the accused has no option but to be tried by a judge alone. If the charge is a serious indictable offence such as murder, the accused must be tried by a judge and jury, though in some cases, with the approval of the Attorney General, the accused may elect to be tried without a jury by a judge of a superior court of criminal jurisdiction. For other less serious indictable offences, the accused has the options of being tried by a judge alone or by a judge and jury.

she has a number of trial options, as Figure 9.8 shows.

Judicial Interpretation of the Code

The annotated version of the *Criminal Code* includes not only the definition of crimes and punishments, but also cases of relevant decisions. Cases are included because, as you read in Chapter 4, statute law, such as the *Criminal Code*, is often open to judicial interpretation. For example, in the offence of assault:

> 265. (1) A person commits an assault when
> (a) without the consent of another person, he applies force intentionally to that other person, directly or indirectly.

Does this mean a hockey player who seriously injures another player during the game can use the defence of consent? Perhaps. The *Criminal Code* includes a variety of cases involving fights during legitimate sporting events. Although there may be implied consent in contact sports such as hockey, the *Code* concludes: "Contact which

FIGURE 9.9 Marty McSorley was convicted in 2001 of an assault on a fellow player, Donald Brashear, during a hockey game. What factors do you think a judge or jury would have considered in determining guilt in this case?

evinces a deliberate purpose to inflict injury will generally be held to be outside of the immunity provided by implied consent in sporting events" (*R. v. Cey*, [1989] 48 C.C.C. (3d) 480).

As you read in earlier chapters, the judge's interpretation of such cases becomes part of the precedent and will be examined in future cases concerning assaults during sporting events. For example, the Boston Bruins' Marty McSorley was convicted of assault in the slashing of rival Vancouver Canuck Donald Brashear during a National Hockey League game. Although McSorley's lawyer tried to argue that violence was part of the game of hockey and "the laws of the land don't typically apply," the Crown successfully argued that "the act depicted is such an excessive act of violence and so gross in its delivery that it must engage criminal law" (Girard 2000).

Examples of Serious Offences

To include all the crimes defined in our *Criminal Code* is beyond the scope of this text, but to give you an idea of how our laws have changed to reflect public and legislative concerns, we will examine in detail two offences: stalking and the use of firearms.

Although the presence of dangerous stalkers has always existed, it was in the early 1990s in North America that movie and TV stars started complaining in the media about being stalked by overzealous or sometimes deranged fans. Soon more individuals began to complain about work colleagues, ex-boyfriends, or mere acquaintances who made them fearful due to persistent stalking. Until recently, such behaviour was considered a nuisance rather than a crime, and until there was actual evidence of harm or threat of harm, the criminal justice system refused to get involved. Slowly, the police and the courts recognized that this behaviour was more serious than first thought. This change of attitude, helped along by lobbying from various groups, including victims, led to the amendment of the *Criminal Code* to include **stalking** or **criminal harassment**.

264. (1) No person shall, without lawful authority and knowing that another person is harassed or recklessly as to whether the other person is harassed, engage in conduct referred to in subsection (2) that causes that other person reasonably, in all the circumstances, to fear for their safety or the safety of anyone known to them.

(2) The conduct mentioned in subsection (1) consists of

(a) repeatedly following from place to place the other person or anyone known to them;

(b) repeatedly communicating with, either directly or indirectly, the other person or anyone known to them;

(c) besetting or watching the dwelling-house, or place where the other person, or anyone known to them, resides, works, carries on business or happens to be; or

(d) engaging in threatening conduct directed at the other person or any member of their family.

(3) Every person who contravenes this section is guilty of

(a) an indictable offence and is liable to imprisonment for a term not exceeding five years; or

(b) an offence punishable on summary conviction.

Public concern about the use of firearms has created offences in the *Criminal Code* that impose severe penalties on those who use guns as weapons. For the purpose of this offence, a firearm may include an air gun or pistol.

244.1. Every person who, with intent

(a) to wound, maim or disfigure any person,

(b) to endanger the life of any person, or

(c) to prevent the detention of any person,

discharges an air or compressed gas gun or pistol at any person, whether or not that person is the person mentioned in paragraph (a), (b), or (c), is guilty of an indictable offence and liable to imprisonment for a term not exceeding fourteen years.

CONNECTIONS: Law and the Media

Media Wave or Crime Wave?

If a person were to focus on the news programs, headlines, and TV shows about crime and our criminal justice system in Canada, he or she might get the impression that this is a very dangerous country in which to live. In actuality, instances of serious crimes such as murder are relatively rare, yet the dramatic and extensive play they receive in the media ensure that they stay in our consciousness long after the fact.

Polls done by the British Crime Survey in June 2003 showed that although the risk of being a victim of crime was at a 20-year low, 70 percent of Britons believed that crime had risen in the two years prior, while only 4 percent believed it had declined (Hurst 2003). Similar misperceptions are held in Canada. Figures released recently by Statistics Canada show that between 1992 and 2002, youth offences fell by 33 percent. But in a national survey done for the federal Solicitor General's office in 2000, 74 percent of respondents said they thought crime by young offenders had increased during the previous five years (Hurst 2003).

Some experts argue that these false impressions are due to fear-mongering by the media. Canadian criminologist Julian Roberts said that the media present a "constant stream of little crime stories about real people, real victims, usually involving serious personal injury. They

FIGURE 9.10 This is a scene from the American crime show *Law & Order*. What level of impact, if any, do you feel fictional television dramas have on the viewers' perception of the amount of crime happening in their community?

have a cumulative effect on how people perceive the amount of crime around them" (Hurst 2003). Statistics suggest that TV programs portraying crime in Canada often present a distorted image of reality. For instance, the plots of many police dramas seem to suggest that most crimes are ultimately solved and the perpetrators are brought to justice. In reality, 80 percent of murders are solved, but less than 20 percent of burglaries are solved. For another example, in 1999 Statistics Canada reported that guns were used in only 3.3 percent of all violent crimes, yet the National Media Archive suggests that a much higher percentage of the violent incidents shown on TV programs involved the use of guns.

Nevertheless, one could argue that the purpose of violent crime shows is to entertain, not to educate. But what about information concerning crime and the justice system provided in the news media?

The public depends on the media for information about crime and the justice system, yet there is evidence that suggests TV news sensationalizes reports on crime, skews reality, and fuels fear. The National Media Archive monitored CBC and CTV newscasts from 1989 to 1995 and found that stories about murders increased, while the murder rate during the same period decreased. The 1996 report of the National Media Archive noted that although for the first time in four years the coverage of murder had gone down, in the authors' opinion TV news continued to distort the public's perception of murder. For example, the authors of the report pointed out that the news continued to focus on murders perpetrated by strangers. In 2000, 44 percent of homicides reported on CBC and 48 percent of those reported on CTV were committed by a stranger. However, for the same year, Statistics Canada reported that only 12 percent of Canadian murders were committed by a stranger to the victim.

The role of the media in reporting crime is important since public perception leads to public outcry, which in turn can influence our laws. Public perceptions of youth violence, for example, have contributed to the enactment of a new *Youth Criminal Justice Act* in Canada. The *Young Offenders Act* permitted media coverage of trials (though they could not publish names), and much of that coverage focused on the sensational crimes. Meanwhile, the fact that statistical evidence showed the decline of youth crime was not always apparent in media reports. In 1997, an Angus-Reid poll showed that 72 percent of the public had no confidence in the *Young Offenders Act*. The *Youth Criminal Justice Act*, which came into effect in 2003, places more focus on protecting society and introduced new measures such as empowering judges in youth court to impose adult sentences for serious violent offences.

Certainly the public has a responsibility to be sufficiently informed so that we can distinguish between entertainment and information. However, since journalists and their employers are the main source of crime news for the general public, should they accept responsibility for ensuring we receive a realistic picture of the criminal landscape of our country?

SOURCES: Hurst, Lynda. "Why Fear Remains High as Crime Rates Fall." *Toronto Star* 26 July 2003.
The National Media Archive. *On Balance* Volume 9, Number 8 (1996);
Volume 10, Number 8 (1997).
Statistics Canada. *Canadian Crime Statistics*, 1999.

Questions

1. To determine whether a crime should be reported in the evening news, the news editor may evaluate the crime in terms of its national importance. Assuming the role of a news editor, develop a list of three other criteria you would consider to determine whether a crime should be included in the evening's newscast.

2. According to some reports, there is a considerable amount of violent content in the media, yet the crime rate is down. Does this mean that, contrary to public opinion, the more we read about and see crimes, the less likely we are to commit crimes? Discuss.

3. Choose two TV news stations (both either local or national), and make notes on the evening news of each station for one week. Compare and contrast the number of crime stories reported. Provide a statistical analysis of the number of crime stories and the difference (if any) between the two news reports.

Reforming Our *Criminal Code*

Our *Criminal Code* is an evolving document challenged by changes in social mores. When the *Charter of Rights and Freedoms* was introduced in 1982, it created new opportunities for challenge. Each piece of the *Criminal Code* was now subject to a test of its constitutionality. As we have seen, the law, in part, reflects public opinion: what was a crime 40 years ago may not be considered so today. The crime of possessing marijuana, for example, may be decriminalized, and gambling, once an illegal offence, has been almost totally legalized and is even practised by government in the form of lotteries.

With respect to some other laws, however, penalties have been toughened, especially for violent crimes such as sexual assault or spousal assault. In other instances, laws are being relaxed or changed. For example, the laws on assisted suicide or euthanasia are being removed from some jurisdictions. In the United States, Oregon has a *Death with Dignity Act*, which allows physician-assisted suicide. The Netherlands also permits physician-assisted suicide, and in Switzerland an organization called Dignitas offers physician-assisted suicide for foreign tourists who wish to end their life. In Chapter 4, you learned that Canadian Sue Rodriguez was denied the right to assisted suicide, and our laws prohibiting aiding and abetting a suicide remain in place. However, Canada's stance may be changing. The most recent case was challenged in 1998 when Dr. Nancy Morrison, a respirologist at Victoria General Hospital in Halifax, Nova Scotia, was charged with ending the life of a terminally ill cancer patient after he had been taken off life support. Morrison was acquitted, an outcome that may reflect changing public opinion on this issue.

The criminal law is undergoing constant reform and must continue to address social and technological change. The thousands of criminal offences in the *Criminal Code* are constantly under review, and the Department of Justice is in the process of a full-scale review and overhaul of the *Code*. The review will examine numerous potential changes, including loosening mandatory minimum sentences and altering potentially outdated laws that no longer reflect our society's values. Regardless of the proposed amendments, the most compelling challenge for law-makers will continue to be the attempt to balance the competing concepts of law and justice.

VIEWPOINTS: In Defence of Self-defence

(editorial in *National Post*, 2003)

On the night of Aug. 22, 1999, Tony Martin was home alone on his remote farm in Norfolk, England, when two burglars invaded his house. Being more than 30 minutes by car from the nearest police station and fearing for his life, Mr. Martin grabbed his shotgun and fired, injuring one intruder and killing the other. To us, this seems like a clear case of self-defence. But a British court judged it to be murder.

Mr. Martin received a life sentence. At trial, the presiding judge claimed British law does not countenance the use of lethal force to defend one's person or property, and therefore instructed the jurors to find Mr. Martin guilty. An appeal court later reduced Mr. Martin's sentence to five years for manslaughter.

The latest news is that British government lawyers are arguing Mr. Martin should not be granted mandatory release this summer, though he has served two-thirds of his sentence, because he refuses to guarantee he will not do the same thing again if presented with similar circumstances. Crown lawyers told a London court Monday that burglars are "members of the public" who "need protection" from homeowners like Tony Martin, even "whilst committing their offences."

It gets worse. The burglar who survived Mr. Martin's shotgun blast has been given $12,000 in legal aid to sue for personal injury. As well, this "victim" has been granted the right to appear at Mr. Martin's parole hearing to offer his views on whether or not the jailed farmer is fit to be released—even though he himself has 34 criminal convictions and is currently in prison for 18 months for trafficking in heroin....

Tragically, Canadian law may be headed in the same dangerous direction. In early March, two thieves drove a stolen SUV through the front window of an Edmonton stereo store. As they were attempting to release a high-end, big-screen television from its wall mounts, the shop owner arrived brandishing a firearm. Shand King is alleged then to have fired, wounding one of the perpetrators. Edmonton police have cut a deal with one of the burglars—a lighter sentence in return for testimony against Mr. King for offences against federal gun control laws.

Moreover, since June, 1998, the Department of Justice has been working off and on to weaken the *Criminal Code* sections that permit actions conducted in defence of oneself or one's property. The Law Commission of Canada and Canadian Heritage's human rights program, several law journal authors and participants at academic seminars have all speculated that society has progressed beyond the need for armed self-defence.

This is nonsense, of course. Violent crime is still a problem in most parts of this country. (In the last two weeks, for instance, a trio of violent crooks has invaded eight

Toronto homes.) And so it is absurd to suggest that our society has graduated into some sort of post-criminal utopia. Self-defence—even armed and lethal self-defence, provided circumstances justify it—has for centuries been a right of law-abiding citizens in common law countries, including Canada. We are aware of no reason why this right should be extinguished.

SOURCE: Editorial. *National Post* 8 May 2003.

Up for Debate

1. After examining the relevant section in the *Criminal Code* below, why do you think Shand King was convicted? Do you think that Mr. Martin would have been convicted if he had been tried in Canada? Explain.

    > Defence of dwelling   40. Every one who is in peaceable possession of a dwelling-house or real property, ... is justified in using force to prevent any person from trespassing on the dwelling-house or real property, or to remove a trespasser therefrom, if he uses no more force than is necessary.

2. Should the right to defend oneself be extinguished or has the need for armed self-defence become all the more crucial in today's society? Choose either side and write an argumentative essay defending your position. (You may want to refer to the Legal Handbook to review "Tips for Writing an Argumentative Essay.")

LEGAL HANDBOOK p. 29

CONFIRM YOUR UNDERSTANDING

1. Could a person be convicted of stalking (criminal harassment) if there was only one incident?

2. There have been a number of incidents of harassment over the Internet. Examine the law on criminal harassment (p. 285), and then decide if sending repeated messages via e-mail would be considered harassment. What factors would you consider to determine if such an act was criminal?

3. What is the *mens rea* of the offence of "discharging a firearm"?

4. Why do you think it was necessary to have a separate offence for injuring someone using a firearm?

5. Reread the definition of "dwelling-house" in the *Criminal Code* on page 283. Police officers generally require a search warrant to enter a dwelling-house. According to this definition, would the following be considered dwelling-houses under the law and therefore require police officers to obtain a search warrant in order to enter? Explain your answers.

 (a) a hotel room rented for the evening
 (b) a houseboat
 (c) a passenger's room on a cruise ship
 (d) a trailer in a trailer park
 (e) a van lived in by a homeless person

6. As you read, there have been many changes to our *Criminal Code* since 1982. Look forward 10 years into the future. Speculate on three possible new crimes that may be added to the *Code*.

7. In response to such cases as that of Dr. Nancy Morrison (p. 287), recommendations have been made to amend the *Criminal Code* to include a defence of "compassionate homicide." Would you be in favour of such an amendment? Explain your position.

Concepts of Justice

> *Sarah Jayne Kendall stormed from a Toronto courthouse, yelling "injustice," moments after a teenager accused of shooting her 5-year-old son in the eye with a pellet gun was freed on bail.*
>
> —*Toronto Star*, Aug. 9, 2003

You have read about the characteristics of justice in Chapter 3. However, nowhere is the concept of justice more scrutinized than in its application to criminal law. The strong feelings that people have about justice and the indignation that they feel toward injustice are perhaps more compelling in the area of criminal law than in any other branch of law. The Statue of Justice is a symbol of the purpose of justice, which is to restore a balance that has been shifted or broken. The scales suggest that all interests will be equally weighed,

FIGURE 9.11 Lady Justice, as shown in this poster, is often used as a symbol of justice. Justice is often referred to as a two-edged sword. What do you think this means? Do you agree?

and the fact that the statue is blindfolded implies that all legal judgments will be made without discrimination. Our hope is that justice will repair the wrong that has been done, console those who have been injured, and try to arrange an outcome that will restore peace and avoid repetition of the wrongdoing. However, many people, including victims such as Sarah Jayne Kendall and her son, often feel that justice in our criminal courts does not restore, repair, or do much to avoid repetition.

Victims' rights groups suggest that, in our system, the scales of justice are tilted in favour of the accused. Others argue that, in our justice system, all interests are not equally weighed and justice often sides with the rich and powerful. Advocates for social justice point out that the higher incidence of convictions for certain visible minorities suggests that justice is not necessarily blind, while the wrongfully convicted remind us that justice is often blind to the truth.

The Law and Justice

What is the relationship of justice to criminal law? Some legal philosophers argue that there is no relationship; law and justice are separate. Others claim there must be a close connection between law and justice. Sir William Blackstone, in his famous study of English common law, wrote, "Law is a vehicle for justice." The word "justice" comes from the Latin word *justus*, meaning upright or lawful, but the English concept of criminal justice likely arose from the blood feud. Human passion for vengeance is described everywhere in the plays of Shakespeare, religious documents, and the pages of your local newspaper.

Justice for some, even today, means **retributive justice**—an eye for an eye, meaning that the punishment should fit the crime.

The Greeks were one culture to give birth to a more rights-based model of justice in which equity and fairness were the main goals. **Restorative justice**, as in the Canadian system, is a modern reflection of this idea. Rather than punish an offender, supporters of restorative justice advocate that the offender must "restore" justice by recognizing, accepting, and taking real responsibility for his or her actions. The philosopher John Rawls outlined his views on justice in his book *A Theory of Justice* (1971) by presenting a hypothetical argument of a just society as one that "rational but mutually disinterested people would unanimously choose to belong to if such a choice were available."

The view of some Aboriginal peoples in Canada asserts that justice is a healing concept unlike the ideas of justice described in the retributive and restorative models. Some believe the difference between this perspective and the current Canadian justice system with respect to fundamental issues, such as the substantive content of justice and the process of achieving justice, results in negative impacts on Aboriginal peoples. In the document *Bridging the Cultural Divide*, the Royal Commission on Aboriginal Peoples included the following conclusion: "The Canadian criminal justice system has failed the Aboriginal Peoples of Canada—First Nations, Inuit and Métis people, on-reserve and off-reserve, urban and rural—in all territorial and governmental jurisdictions."

The Canadian criminal justice system, though imperfect, does strive to provide fair procedures and to be both rational and consistent. The voices of victims of crime are being heard and supported with initiatives such as financial assistance and counselling for the victims and their families. Family members of murder victims are now permitted to attend parole hearings of those convicted of the murder, and victims are given the opportunity to make victim impact statements prior to

FIGURE 9.12 Donald Marshall Jr. was wrongfully convicted of the murder of Sandy Seale in Nova Scotia in 1971. Marshall is a member of the Mi'kmaq and was only 17 years old at the time of his arrest. He was acquitted by the Nova Scotia Court of Appeal and released in 1983. What effect do you think wrongful convictions such as this have on the public's belief that justice is being done in this country?

sentencing. The *Canadian Charter of Rights and Freedoms* helps ensure that criminal laws and those who enforce the laws act within the principles of fundamental justice and do not deprive accused individuals of their rights. Better crime investigation tools, such as DNA analysis and improved training of investigative officers, are being used to reduce the incidence of wrongfully accused persons.

There will always be tension between substantive criminal law, represented by stability, certainty, and predictability, and justice, represented by equity and fairness. Difficult cases, those that reach the level of the Supreme Court of Canada, and those that we learn about in the media, bring these tensions into focus and compel courts to make a choice. Should convicted pedophiles who have completed their sentence be forced to register with the police upon release, or does this violate their rights to liberty and security of the person under the *Charter*? Should someone who kills three people while driving home drunk from a New Year's Eve party receive the same sentence as a mass murderer? Should a person suspected of terrorist activities be detained without bail? Regardless of the decision made in these controversial situations, some will argue that the outcome represents a miscarriage of justice.

The concept of justice continues to be debated by legal scholars, but, especially in the area of criminal law, we must be aware that justice is not an abstract ideal. Rather it is a concrete reality for all those who find themselves confronting our criminal justice system.

CONFIRM YOUR UNDERSTANDING

1. What is the difference between retributive and restorative justice? What advantages and disadvantages do you see for each type?
2. The *Canadian Charter of Rights and Freedoms* says that the rights of an accused cannot be removed except in accordance with the principles of fundamental justice.

How would you describe the principles of fundamental justice?
3. The Greek philosopher Aristotle said that justice was receiving one's due. How would you argue that wrongfully accused Canadians such as Donald Marshall Jr., David Milgaard, and Guy Paul Morin received their due?

In Closing

In Canadian society, it seems to be a trend that people assume each upcoming generation is more crime-ridden than the generations that came before. Statistics tell us, however, that crime is not rampant and serious crimes, such as murders, remain rare. Still, we seek to understand why some people continue to commit criminal acts and what we can do within the justice system to try to limit such behaviour.

Criminologists aim to make our system safer for citizens and fair to those accused of crimes, and there are many challenges ahead for them in our criminal justice system. For example, in the

last few years new scientific discoveries on brain theory have raised questions about genetic and biological factors that could be linked to criminal behaviour. Also, ongoing reform of our *Criminal Code* has required criminologists and society at large to re-evaluate what constitutes a crime and warrants inclusion in the *Code*, and what is merely annoying or offensive. It is the job of the criminologist to apply the principles of scientific analysis and rigorous investigation to assist those involved in the law to find the best answers to these complex questions.

CHAPTER ACTIVITIES

Extend Your Legal Knowledge

1. What research methods would criminologists use to collect information on crime?
2. Create an organizational chart illustrating the connections between historical and contemporary theories of criminal behaviour.
3. Give an example of a biochemical condition that is thought to influence a specific criminal behaviour. Elaborate on how the condition is thought to be related to the crime.
4. Explain what is meant by a "quasi-criminal offence." Provide two examples of a quasi-criminal offence.

5. Explain the distinction between intent and motive. Provide an example that would illustrate your explanation.

Think About the Law

6. What type of social policies would you put in place to combat crime? Use your text and other research to support your opinion.

7. You have read about the many theories that explain why people commit crimes. Most people do not commit crimes. Why do you think people obey the law?

8. Marxist and social conflict theorists argue that the capitalist system is the root cause of crime. What criticisms could you make of this argument? How would you argue in support?

9. Discuss the rationale for studying twins to understand the effects of genetics on criminal behaviour.

10. Evaluate the roles of family, peers, and the education system as they relate to criminal behaviour.

11. Unlike the United States, Canada does not have a statute of limitations, or a time limit, on prosecutions of serious crimes. British and Canadian law have no time limit as to when the state can prosecute an individual for serious crimes due to the belief that criminal offences are so serious that they must always be open for prosecution. As a result, convictions in Canada have taken place even though the crimes may have occurred many years before. Larry Fisher, the actual killer in the David Milgaard case, was convicted some 27 years after Gail Miller, the victim, was murdered. Some defence lawyers are arguing that the *Criminal Code* should be amended to include limitation periods on all crimes. They argue that an accused cannot receive a fair trial many years after the crime took place because memories fade, witnesses die, and evidence may be lost or contaminated.
a) What do you think? Should there be an amendment to the *Criminal Code* that would impose a time limit on the prosecution of serious crimes?
b) What crimes would you suggest be covered by the amendment? Who should decide when it is too late to pursue justice? What problems do you foresee with such an amendment?

Communicate About the Law

12. Criminologists have proposed many theories about why people commit crimes. The labelling theory, for example, suggests that people behave as criminals because they are labelled by society as criminals due to their age, race, gender, faith, etc. Research and prepare a debate on the following statement: "The deviant is one to whom that label has successfully been applied."

13. English writer G.K. Chesterton (1874–1936) said, "Art, like morality, is the drawing of a line." Is morality, like art, the drawing of a line? Is the purpose of our criminal law to draw the line for us, or should the law serve simply to protect peace and security? Prepare a research paper discussing the relationship between criminal law and morality. Support your research with information from the text and other sources.

14. The sociologist Emile Durkheim, whom you read about on page 267, defined crime as a normal and necessary social event and an "integral part of all healthy societies." What evidence could you offer to support Durkheim's position?

15. In 2003, Toronto Police Chief Julian Fantino proposed that the government enact a law requiring hospitals to report all gunshot wounds to police. Rights advocates said such a law should be rejected because it violates an individual's right to privacy and security of the person. Make an argument for and against such a proposition.

16. Our criminal law is often reformed not by lawmakers but by changing social attitudes. Think about our present laws, and explain which

Criminal Code offences you think are subject to changing social attitudes.

Apply the Law

17. Read the following case concerning the elements of *mens rea* and *actus reus*. Apply your knowledge of *mens rea* and *actus reus* to answer the following questions:

a) Explain the *mens rea* and *actus reus* of this offence.

b) Assume the role of the Crown in this case. What would you argue to uphold Fagan's conviction?

Fagan v. Commissioner of Metropolitan Police, [1969] 1 Q.B. 439 (C.A.)

Facts: The appellant, Vincent Martel Fagan, was convicted of assaulting a police constable in the execution of his duty. The accused was reversing his car when Constable Morris, who knew Fagan as a petty criminal, stopped him and directed him to drive the car forward and park.

Fagan did not park as close to the curb as Morris had requested, so Morris instructed him to park closer and directed him to a specific spot. Fagan drove forward and accidentally drove the wheel onto the constable's foot. The constable asked Fagan to move the car as it was on his foot. Fagan yelled an obscenity and said, "You can wait." The engine of the car stopped running because either Fagan turned it off or the engine went off by itself. The constable, in considerable pain, again asked Fagan to remove the car from his foot. Fagan restarted the car and drove the car off the constable's foot.

Lawyers representing Fagan appealed the case, arguing that at the time the vehicle rested on the constable's foot, there was no *mens rea* of assault. At the point at which Fagan unnecessarily allowed the car to rest on the constable's foot, there was no *actus reus*. The two elements must come together to constitute a crime. In this instance, they did not, so Mr. Fagan should be acquitted.

265. (1) A person commits an assault when
(a) without the consent of another person, he applies force intentionally to that other person, directly or indirectly;
(b) he attempts or threatens, by an act or a gesture, to apply force to another person, if he has, or causes that other person to believe upon reasonable grounds that he has, present ability to effect his purpose....

18. A survey taken in 2000 asked respondents if they thought crime involving youthful offenders had increased, decreased, or remained the same during the past five years. Seventy-four percent said it had increased. In fact, most recent figures released by Statistics Canada show that, between 1992 and 2002, youth offences actually fell by 33 percent.

Canadian analysts say there are serious consequences of such misperception. Quality of life is affected. People stay home at night. People distrust strangers. They become fearful and intolerant of young people. (Hurst 2003)

a) Why do you think there is such a misperception about the incidence of youth crime? Has it been your perception that the crime rate for young people is higher than it was when your parents or grandparents were young?

b) Conduct your own survey on perceptions of public safety. What percentage of people at your school are afraid to walk at night in their neighbourhood? Break down your survey by age and gender. Are there any differences?

19. Statistics Canada reported that violent crime in Toronto in 2001 had dropped by 6.8 percent, a figure that was disputed by Toronto police who said the decline for the City of Toronto itself was only 4.8 percent. Statistics Canada figures included Metropolitan Toronto and surrounding areas, while the Toronto police figures centred on the city itself. Thus the context of all statistical data should be analyzed in detail and understood in their entirety before they are used.

a) Examine the most recent crime figures released by Statistics Canada at the following Web site: <www.statcan.ca>. What questions would you ask about these statistics before you could draw any conclusions about their reliability?

b) What conclusion regarding the increase or decrease in crime could you draw from the Statistics Canada figures?

c) Choose one aspect of the statistical information provided on the site (e.g., difference in adult vs. youth crime, increase or decrease in property or violent crimes, incidence of female crime), and present a report on your findings. Include graphs and charts to illustrate your report.

BIBLIOGRAPHY

Barnhorst, Sherrie, L.L.B., and Richard Barnhorst, L.L.B. *Criminal Law and the Canadian Criminal Code.* 3rd ed. Toronto: McGraw-Hill Ryerson Limited, 1996.

Beccaria, Cesare. *On Crimes and Punishments.* Indianapolis, IN: Bobbs-Merrill Co., 1963.

Bentham, Jeremy. *Introduction to the Principles of Morals and Legislation.* Ed. Laurence J. LaFleur. New York: Prometheus Books, 1970.

Canadian Legal Information Institute. Accessed 5 Sept. 2003 <www.canlii.org>.

Devlin, Patrick. "Morals and the Criminal Law." *Law and Morality: Readings in Legal Philosophy.* Eds. David Dyzenhaus and Arthur Ripstein. Toronto: University of Toronto Press, 2001.

Duhaime and Company. Accessed Nov. 2003 <www.duhaime.org>.

Dyzenhaus, David, and Arthur Ripstein (eds.). *Law and Morality: Readings in Legal Philosophy.* Toronto: University of Toronto Press, 2001.

Friedland, Steven I. "A Vision of the Future." Excerpted from "The Criminal Law Implications of the Human Genome Project: Reimagining a Genetically Oriented Criminal Justice System." *Kentucky Law Journal* 86 (1997): 303-366.

Gallagher, Winifred. "How We Become What We Are." *The Atlantic Monthly.* Sept. 1994.

Girard, Daniel. "McSorley's Slash Called Criminal Act." *Toronto Star* 30 Sept. 2000.

Hurst, Lynda. "Why Fear Remains High as Crime Rates Fall." *Toronto Star* 26 July 2003.

"In Defence of Self-defence." Editorial. *National Post* 8 May 2003.

Khoo, Lisa. "Banning the Butt: Global Anti-smoking Efforts." *CBC News Online.* Accessed Jan. 2004 <www.cbc.ca/news/indepth/background/smokingbans.html>.

Lloyd, Dennis. *The Idea of Law.* London: Penguin Books, 1987.

Rawls, John. "Civil Disobedience." *Law and Morality: Readings in Legal Philosophy.* Eds. David Dyzenhaus and Arthur Ripstein. Toronto: University of Toronto Press, 2001.

Royal Commission on Aboriginal Peoples. *Bridging the Cultural Divide: A Report on Aboriginal People and Criminal Justice in Canada.* Canada Communication Group, 1996.

Siegel, Larry J., and Chris McCormick. *Criminology in Canada.* Scarborough, ON: ITP Nelson, 1999.

Statistics Canada. *Canadian Crime Statistics.* 1999.

Tebbit, Mark. *Philosophy of Law: An Introduction.* London: Routledge, 2000.

The National Media Archive. *On Balance* Vol. 9, Number 8 (1996).

The National Media Archive. *On Balance* Vol. 10, Number 8 (1997).

PRE-TRIAL AND TRIAL PROCEDURES

LEARNING EXPECTATIONS

After reading this chapter, you will be able to:

- explain the processes of police investigation, arrest, search, and interrogation of suspects
- explain pre-trial procedures, including plea bargaining and release procedures
- explain the purpose of key features of the criminal trial process
- analyze situations in Canadian law in which the principles of justice conflict
- analyze cases in which the principles of justice have been violated

FIGURE 10.1 Police officers are shown in a scuffle with a man resisting arrest. After the arrest, charges were laid for uttering threats and resisting arrest. Ultimately, the accused will have to answer to these charges in a criminal court. How does the criminal justice system protect the rights of the accused during pre-trial procedures and during the criminal trial process?

No form of human judgment is perfect. Criminal proceedings run the risk of making two kinds of errors: they can exonerate the guilty or convict the innocent. While both are judicial miscarriages, the legal system, in keeping with the presumption of innocence principle, has sought to avoid false convictions even if this has meant that some criminals go free.

—Thomas Gabor and Julian Roberts, professors of criminology, University of Ottawa

■ I N T R O D U C T I O N ■

All too often, the nightly news leads with a story about a crime that grips the attention of the viewing public. Maybe the police have made a record drug bust, seizing millions of dollars' worth of cocaine. Or a custody dispute has resulted in the parental abduction of a child. Maybe a disgruntled employee turns to arson to avenge perceived mistreatment by a former employer. Or a quiet suburb has been the target of a sexual predator. When arrests are made in connection with each of these crimes, the public breathes a collective sigh of relief. Rarely do we, as a society, question the process by which these individuals have come to be arrested, charged, and given their day in court. It is only when we learn that procedures have been ignored or carried out incorrectly that we re-examine the safeguards designed to protect all of us from becoming victims of injustice. Canada's justice system is structured in a way that prevents random arrests and indefinite prison sentences. It protects the rights of the accused at all stages of the process and strives for procedural fairness. The system, however, is not immune to criticism, particularly when rights have been denied or when procedural unfairness has occurred. A democratic society has a vested interest in ensuring that procedural safeguards are followed prior to and during a trial so that an accused is given his or her day in court and the correct verdict is rendered.

By examining the criminal justice system, you will discover how the rights of an accused are protected during pre-trial procedures and the criminal trial process. Pre-trial procedures consist of police investigations, searches, arrests, interrogations, plea bargains, and release procedures. The criminal trial process involves key legal principles in criminal law, such as the burden of proof, the presumption of innocence, rights after being charged, the roles of participants in the trial process, and the admissibility of evidence.

What happens when the principles of justice are violated? Ultimately, when the proper rules and procedures are not followed, claims of miscarriage of justice may result. Society and particularly the victim of a crime are outraged when the guilty person walks free. Procedural errors may have even more devastating consequences for an individual who is wrongly convicted. Improper procedures may also result in cases being thrown out of court. This chapter explores the mechanisms used in the criminal justice system so that the accused, the victim, and society may pursue their rights to fundamental justice with procedural fairness.

Pre-trial Procedures

To ensure procedural fairness and to maintain the integrity of the criminal justice system in Canada, all citizens are afforded certain rights, which law enforcement officers must constantly keep in mind when carrying out their duties. Evidence that is gathered during a lawful search may lead police to arrest and interrogate a citizen about possible involvement in a criminal activity. At all times, however, an accused must be treated in accordance with **due process** of the law, that is, judicial procedures conducted properly. The legal rights section of the *Charter* provides for procedural safeguards in the criminal justice system, specifically with respect to the legality of searches and to detention, arrest, interrogation, and other pre-trial procedures.

Criminal Investigation and Search and Seizure

Images of police officers and special investigators combing a specific area and carrying away bags that are presumably filled with evidence are often the first indicator that a crime has occurred. Law enforcement officers engage in investigating and searching crime scenes in the hope of finding evidence to use in prosecuting a case.

After a crime has been committed, the crime scene is **secured**, meaning that it is sealed off so that no one, except those required to complete the investigation, can enter. Evidence found at the crime scene may help investigators to determine what happened, may lead to the identification of the perpetrator of the crime, or may lead officers to consider other locations for further investigation. Police may search for such items

as hair and fibre samples, blood, and chemical residue, or for signs of forced entry or a physical struggle. They may discover a weapon at the scene of the crime or uncover fingerprint or footprint evidence. All the painstaking work of gathering evidence must be completed carefully to ensure the samples are preserved for analysis

FIGURE 10.2   RCMP officers carry away bags of evidence from a crime scene. The officers are conducting a search for evidence as part of the criminal investigation process. How might this evidence be used?

and the evidence is considered credible in court. Evidence collected at the scene of the crime is often referred to as "forensic evidence." Forensic analysis involves the scientific study of the crime scene. While the procedure of dusting for finger-print evidence has been traditionally used in criminal investigations, recent advances in DNA technology have enhanced investigators' ability to pinpoint potential suspects with close to 100 percent accuracy. Blood, semen, saliva, hair, and even bone and teeth samples can be collected for DNA analysis. (Refer to Admissibility of Evidence on p. 315 for further details on forensic evidence.)

Criminal investigations include not only the collection and preservation of physical evidence but also the questioning of witnesses. Officers interview witnesses about their knowledge of the crime or the parties involved and record these statements as part of the investigation process. Photographs must be taken of the crime scene to serve as a permanent record and to help investigators piece together all available information about the crime. Once the evidence is collected, it must be analyzed and interpreted for use as evidence in court. For example, should bullet fragments be found at the crime scene, a ballistics expert might be enlisted to determine the type of firearm that was used, the trajectory (pathway) of the bullets, the distance from which the shots were fired, and other technical details. Should the case involve a violent homicide, a blood-spatter expert might be consulted to comment on the most likely sequence of events based on his or her technical interpretation of the physical evidence.

Securing the crime scene and collecting evidence for the purpose of a criminal investigation must be done carefully and with regard to the law governing search and seizure. Section 8 of the *Charter* states that "Everyone has the right to be secure against unreasonable search or seizure." Although the *Charter* does not use the word "privacy" in any of its sections, we, as Canadians, value and uphold the concept of privacy, at times going to extreme lengths and expense to prevent others from invading our personal space and property. However, there is a balance that must be struck between protecting an individual's right to a reasonable expectation of privacy and keeping our society safe from criminal activity. The large number of criminal cases challenging the legality of a search or seizure indicates the range of interpretations that can be given to this section of the *Charter*. It is the role of the courts to determine if there has been an unreasonable search and seizure. They must also rule on any application made to have evidence excluded should it be established that to admit the evidence would bring the administration of justice into disrepute. These applications are submitted under s. 24 (2) of the *Charter*:

> Where, in proceedings under subsection (1) [the subsection of the *Charter* dealing with the enforcement of guaranteed rights and freedoms], a court concludes that evidence was obtained in a manner that infringed or denied any rights or freedoms guaranteed by this *Charter*, the evidence shall be excluded if it is established that, having regard to all the circumstances, the admission of it in the proceedings would bring the administration of justice into disrepute.

In the case of *R. v. Collins,* [1987] 1 S.C.R. 265, Ruby Collins was charged with possession of heroin for the purpose of trafficking. She and her husband had been under surveillance by two police officers. When Collins's husband left a pub with a friend, he was arrested, searched, and found to be in possession of heroin. The officers returned to the pub and saw Ruby sitting with another woman at a table. The officers approached the table. Fearing that Collins might try to swallow any drugs she was in possession of, one officer used a choke-hold procedure on her, which is a drug seizure technique designed to prevent the swallowing of any suspected drugs. Collins did not have any drugs in her mouth; the heroin was in her hand, contained in a green balloon. The trial focused on the issue of the validity of the search and seizure and the admissibility of the drug evidence. The officers did not have reasonable and probable grounds for believing that she was in possession of the drugs. The Supreme Court set out a test for a reasonable search: "A search will be reasonable if it is authorized by law, if the law itself is reasonable and if the manner in which the search was carried out is reasonable."

The court held that the search and seizure in this case was unreasonable. They struggled with whether the evidence should be excluded under the authority of s. 24 (2) of the *Charter*. Ultimately, the majority of the court decided that it would bring the administration of justice into disrepute if the drug evidence were allowed. In deciding whether to exclude the evidence, the court considered many factors, including the seriousness of the offence (i.e., the seriousness of the charge of "possession of heroin for the purpose of trafficking") and the unfairness to the trial. In other words, would admitting the drug evidence adversely affect Collins's chances of receiving a fair trial and would it cast a negative light on the justice system?

In another case involving a search, the accused, Theodore Mellenthin, was pulled over by the RCMP and detained under an "Alberta Check Stop" (*R. v. Mellenthin*, [1992] 3 S.C.R. 615). The primary purpose of the program was to check for driver sobriety; valid licence, insurance, and registration; and the mechanical fitness of the vehicle. The accused complied with the request to produce his licence, registration, and insurance papers. The officer shone his flashlight into the interior of the vehicle and noticed an open gym bag on the front seat. The gym bag contained a brown bag with another plastic bag inside. When asked about the contents of the bag, the accused replied that there was food inside the bag and showed the officer a brown paper bag with a plastic sandwich bag inside. The officer saw a reflection of what he thought was glass inside the bag. Becoming suspicious that there might be narcotics inside the bag, the officer asked Mellenthin what was inside. Mellenthin subsequently produced a plastic bag that contained empty glass vials, which the officer recognized as those often used to store cannabis resin.

The officer asked Mellenthin to get out of the car. He then searched the brown bag and found that it did indeed contain cannabis resin. The accused was arrested for possession of a narcotic. A further search of the vehicle turned up vials of hash oil and cannabis resin cigarettes.

The Alberta Court of Queen's Bench held at trial that the search was unreasonable and excluded the evidence under s. 24 (2) of the *Charter*. The Alberta Court of Appeal agreed that the search was improper but allowed that admitting the drug evidence would not bring the administration of justice into disrepute. A new trial was ordered, which the accused appealed to the Supreme Court of Canada on the grounds that a new trial in which the drug evidence would be allowed would undoubtedly lead to a conviction. Mellenthin's lawyers wanted both the search and the admissibility of the evidence to be held invalid. The Supreme Court ruled that the questions pertaining to the gym bag were improper and that the search was unreasonable. The Supreme Court made it clear that a check-stop program cannot be used as a justification for searching all vehicles. The police must have reasonable and probable grounds for conducting a search, such as seeing drugs, alcohol, or weapons in plain view. The court added:

> It would surely affect the fairness of the trial should check stops be accepted as a basis for warrantless searches and the evidence derived from them was to be automatically admitted. To admit evidence obtained in an unreasonable and unjustified search carried out while a motorist was detained in a check stop would adversely and unfairly affect the trial process and most surely bring the administration of justice into disrepute.

Law enforcement officials are allowed to engage in search and seizure activities under the authority of the *Criminal Code* and other federal statutes, such as the *Controlled Drugs and Substances Act* and the *Income Tax Act*. In most cases, the police are required to appear before a judge to obtain a **search warrant**, which is a court document authorizing a law enforcement officer to enter a specified place in order to search for and seize specified evidence. (Under s. 489 of the *Criminal Code*, police may seize items that are not specifically mentioned in the warrant as long as they have reasonable and probable grounds to believe that the items were obtained by or used in the commission of an offence.) A search warrant is issued by a judge under the authority of s. 487 of the *Criminal Code*. The judge must be satisfied that there are reasonable and probable grounds for believing that the search is necessary under the conditions of s. 487 to search a building, place, or receptacle (container). Under s. 487, a search warrant will be issued if an offence is suspected to have been committed, if there are reasonable and probable grounds to believe that evidence about the offence or the whereabouts of the person believed to have committed the offence will be obtained, or if anything intended for the purpose of committing the offence could be found. A judge must be satisfied with the information presented by police before a search

FIGURE 10.3   A lawyer holds up a search warrant for the home of an *Ottawa Citizen* reporter in January 2004. The search was conducted in connection with an alleged information leak. What type of information is contained in a search warrant?

warrant is issued. In some cases in which time is of the essence and the search must be conducted immediately, the *Criminal Code* allows the police to obtain telewarrants. For example, a telewarrant may be necessary if the accused has committed an **indictable offence** (serious criminal offence) and is likely to destroy valuable evidence. Section 487.1 (1) allows police to request a warrant by phone or by other means of telecommunication, such as fax, if it would be impracticable in the interest of saving time to have to appear personally before the judge. The telewarrant must be followed up by a written police report requesting the warrant, stating when and where the warrant was executed, and listing what was seized.

In certain circumstances, a search can be executed without a warrant. The *Criminal Code* under s. 117.02 permits warrantless searches for offences involving weapons. The courts have also considered the common law right of search incidental to arrest where a warrant is not required. In the case of *Cloutier v. Langlois,* [1990] 1 S.C.R. 158, Montréal police constables Richard Langlois and Jean-Pierre Bédard stopped Pierre Cloutier for a traffic violation. On subsequent communication with police headquarters, it was apparent that there was a municipal court arrest warrant out for Cloutier for unpaid traffic fines. Cloutier was agitated and verbally abusive to police. He was subsequently arrested, frisked (which consisted of a pat-down search during which the accused's hands were placed on the police car and his legs were spread apart), and then taken to the police station. Cloutier argued that the police officers were not authorized to search him and that their actions were equivalent to assault. The summary convictions court judge and the superior court judge ruled against Cloutier. The Court of Appeal, however, found the officers guilty of common assault.

The officers appealed the decision to the Supreme Court of Canada. The issue to be determined was the legality of a search incidental to arrest. The court held that a frisk search incidental to arrest has limitations. Police officers have a discretionary right to search should they consider it necessary for applying the law; there must be a valid objective for the search, such as checking for objects that may pose a threat to safety or would allow the accused to escape; the purpose of the search cannot be to intimidate or pressure an accused into making an admission; and the search must not be conducted in an abusive manner. The Supreme Court held that the frisk search was justified, that the police had considered all the circumstances, including police safety, and that the search was not excessive.

A search without a warrant is also permissible under **exigent circumstances**. These include situations "where there is an imminent danger of loss, removal, destruction, or disappearance of the evidence if the search or seizure is delayed" (Barnhorst 1996). For example, if a plane needed to be searched before it was scheduled to depart for another location, this might amount to exigent circumstances since the time constraints would make it impracticable to obtain a search warrant. Under the *Criminal Code*, exigent circumstances are also understood to exist if police officers have reasonable grounds to suspect that they have to enter an individual's premises without a warrant in order to prevent imminent harm to, or the death of, someone.

Arrest and Detention

Both arrest and detention are covered by rights protections under ss. 9 and 10 of the *Charter*, which state:

9. Everyone has the right not to be arbitrarily detained or imprisoned.
10. Everyone has the right on arrest or detention
    (a) to be informed promptly of the reasons therefor;
    (b) to retain and instruct counsel without delay and to be informed of that right; and
    (c) to have the validity of the detention determined by way of *habeas corpus* and to be released if the detention is not lawful.

FIGURE 10.4 Police officers are permitted to conduct roadside spot checks to assess vehicle safety and driver sobriety. Why have the courts held that these roadside detentions are a reasonable limit on the rights of citizens?

There is, however, a distinct difference between arrest and detention. A formal arrest occurs when a law enforcement officer has reasonable and probable grounds to believe a person has committed or is about to commit an indictable offence. An officer may also arrest a person who is found committing an indictable offence or for whom there are reasonable grounds to believe that an arrest warrant is outstanding. A detention, on the other hand, may occur in the following ways: "by physical restraint; by psychological means (i.e., where a person is made to believe that he or she has no choice but to remain, even though no threat has been made); and by giving a demand or direction (i.e., where there will be legal consequences if the person refuses the demand or direction)" (Barnhorst 1996). Technically, when you are pulled over for a random police spot check during a vehicle safety blitz or a RIDE (Reduce Impaired Driving Everywhere) program, you are being detained. However, in the case of *R. v. Hufsky*, [1988] 1 S.C.R. 621, the Supreme Court of Canada held that roadside detentions conducted in the interests of public safety were a reasonable limit under s. 1 of the *Charter*. (For more on the Hufsky case, see p. 211 in Chapter 7.)

The right to retain and instruct counsel under s. 10(b) of the *Charter* includes the right to be advised of the availability of legal aid (see Figure 10.5, below). The right of **habeas corpus** (a court order that involves bringing a person to court to determine if he or she is being detained legally) under s. 10(c) is intended to prevent unlawful arrest and detention. Anyone who believes that his or her detention is unlawful or unreasonable can be brought before a judge to have the validity of the detention determined.

Under s. 10(b) of the *Charter*, it is not simply a question of informing an accused of his or her right to counsel. The accused must also be given an opportunity to exercise that right. A leading case on right to counsel was

---

Right to Counsel

I am arresting you for _____ [reasons for arrest are briefly described]. It is my duty to inform you that you have the right to retain and instruct counsel without delay. You have the right to telephone any lawyer you wish. You also have the right to free advice from a Legal Aid lawyer. If you are charged with an offence, you may apply to the Ontario Legal Aid Plan for assistance. 1-800-265-0451 is a toll-free number that will put you in contact with a Legal Aid duty counsel lawyer for free legal advice right now.

Do you understand? Do you wish to call a lawyer now?

Figure 10.5 At the time of the arrest, the police must advise the suspect of his or her right to legal counsel. This is referred to as the "police caution." In addition, the police provide a general caution as follows: "You (are charged, will be charged) with _____ [charge is described]. Do you wish to say anything in answer to the charge? You are not obliged to say anything unless you wish to do so, but whatever you say may be given in evidence." What could happen if the accused were not advised of his or her legal rights?

that of *R. v. Manninen*, [1987] 1 S.C.R. 1233. Ronald Manninen was charged with the armed robbery of a convenience store, as well as theft and possession of a stolen vehicle. A store employee stated that the robber had a gun and a knife and wore a hooded sweatshirt. An eyewitness saw a person fleeing the scene in a vehicle and recorded the licence plate number.

Police received information about the stolen vehicle and two days later, in an undercover investigation, went to a Toronto place of business and waited to see if anyone showed up in the stolen vehicle. Manninen drove up in a car that matched the description of the stolen vehicle used in the robbery. He got out of the car and went into the place of business, where one of the officers was waiting. The other officer investigated the car and noticed a gun protruding from under the driver's seat. Manninen was subsequently searched, arrested, and read the police caution. Manninen indicated a desire to remain silent and to see his lawyer. The police officers, however, continued to question Manninen with no lawyer present. It was during this questioning that Manninen made statements to the police that incriminated him.

The trial judge, in considering whether these statements could be admitted, found that Manninen's right to counsel had been infringed. However, the trial court allowed the statements, saying that this admission of evidence would not bring the administration of justice into disrepute. The Court of Appeal disagreed with the trial decision, allowed the appeal, and ordered a new trial. On subsequent appeal to the Supreme Court of Canada, the court ruled that Manninen was indeed denied his right to counsel. Since the use of the evidence involved a serious offence and would make the trial unfair, the court held that the evidence should be excluded and that a new trial should be ordered.

The implications of the violation of the right to counsel and of an improper arrest and search were considered in the case of *R. v. Feeney* (see the Landmark Case that follows).

Landmark CASE

R. v. Feeney, [1997] 2 S.C.R. 13

Read the following case analysis. The facts, issue, and *ratio decidendi* have been provided for you. Assume that you disagree with the court decision. Write a possible dissent for this controversial case.

Facts: During the 1991 investigation of the beating death of Frank Boyle, police received a tip that Michael Feeney had been seen walking by the victim's truck earlier that day. They subsequently went to Michael Feeney's trailer, knocked on the door, and, when no one answered, entered. They did not have an arrest warrant. The police roused Feeney from his bed so they could get a better look at him. They subsequently saw blood on his shirt and arrested him, advising him of his right to counsel. Although Feeney did not contact a lawyer at that time, the police continued to question him inside his trailer. His shirt was then seized for use as evidence, and he was brought to the RCMP detachment where he was unsuccessful in trying to contact a lawyer. After eight hours in an observation cell, detectives proceeded to question him further, even though Feeney had not yet contacted a lawyer. During the questioning, Feeney admitted to stealing Boyle's cigarettes, beer, and cash. A subsequent warrant enabled the police to

obtain the cash and cigarettes, as well as shoes, from the trailer. The Supreme Court of British Columbia convicted Feeney of second-degree murder. The Court of Appeal of British Columbia unanimously dismissed the appeal. Feeney then appealed to the Supreme Court of Canada.

Issue: Did the police violate ss. 8 and 10(b) of the *Charter*? If so, should the evidence be excluded under s. 24 (2) of the *Charter*?

Held: The Supreme Court set aside the conviction and ordered a new trial.

Ratio Decidendi: (La Forest, Sopinka, Cory, Iacobucci, and Major JJ.) The Supreme Court of Canada held that the police did not have grounds for a warrantless arrest. Since the arrest was unlawful, the subsequent search and seizure of the shirt was unlawful and violated s. 8 of the *Charter*. Furthermore, Feeney was detained the moment he was woken by the officers and asked to get out of bed. He should immediately have been read his rights and provided the opportunity to retain counsel. Feeney's statement about the cash, beer, and cigarettes was made after his s. 10(b) rights had been violated. To accept the statement as evidence would make the trial unfair. The court further held that to allow the use of the physical evidence, particularly the bloody shirt, would bring the administration of justice into disrepute.

CONFIRM YOUR UNDERSTANDING

1. Outline the requirements for a reasonable search and seizure.
2. Summarize the conditions under which a judge could issue a search warrant under s. 487 of the *Criminal Code*.
3. When can the police conduct a search without a warrant? Explain by providing examples.
4. Describe conditions that limit the common law right to search incidental to arrest.
5. Distinguish between arrest and detention.
6. Describe your *Charter* rights on arrest or detention. Provide examples of how these rights could be violated.

Interrogation of the Accused

Procedural fairness is a fundamental component of the interrogation process. When an individual is arrested, he or she cannot be forced into making a statement to authorities. Section 7 of the *Charter* ("the right to life, liberty and security of the person") has been used to assert the right of an accused to remain silent. Should an accused make a statement, this statement must be made voluntarily and with the understanding that it may be used as evidence. In the case of *R. v. Hebert,* [1990] 2 S.C.R. 151, the accused, Neil Hebert, was arrested and charged with robbery. After consulting a lawyer, Hebert indicated that he did not wish to make a statement to the police. However, when placed in a cell with an undercover police officer, Hebert was tricked into making statements that incriminated him in the robbery. At trial, the court ruled that Hebert's rights under ss. 7 and 10(b) had been violated. The statements Hebert had made in the cell were excluded as evidence, and he was acquitted. On appeal to the Court of Appeal for the Yukon Territory, the court held that Hebert's right to counsel as well as his right to remain silent had not been breached and that the actions of the undercover police officer did not violate the principles of justice.

The case was subsequently appealed to the Supreme Court of Canada where the court held that, in these circumstances, to admit the statements Hebert had made to the undercover officer as evidence would make the trial unfair. Justice McLachlin stated, "But where, as here, an accused is conscripted to give evidence against himself after clearly electing not to do so by use of an unfair trick practised by authorities, and where the resultant statement is the only evidence against him, one must surely conclude that reception of evidence would render the trial unfair."

False confessions can also pose problems because they can result in wrongful convictions. For this reason, police officers are well versed in the laws that govern the process of obtaining a confession and try to ensure their conduct does

Figure 10.6 This scene from the Canadian television drama *Da Vinci's Inquest* shows police interrogating a suspect. Police interrogations must be conducted properly in order to ensure procedural fairness and to safeguard the rights of an accused. What are your rights on being interrogated by the police?

not result in the inadmissibility of the confession under s. 24 (2) of the *Charter.* In cases in which an accused confesses, the courts are concerned not only with whether the confession was made voluntarily, but also with whether the police used threats or promises to induce the accused into making a statement. Procedural fairness prohibits the police from using harsh and threatening interrogation tactics, such as keeping an accused awake for 24 hours straight without food while pressuring him or her for a statement. An accused also cannot be interrogated in an oppressive atmosphere, such as a room without heat or adequate lighting. Similarly, police officers are prohibited from negotiating special deals with an accused, such as promising a reduced sentence, in order to extract a confession. A confession would also be regarded as questionable if the method used to gain the confession breached society's ethical standards, for example, a police officer posing as a minister in order to secure an admission of guilt from a suspect. Not only would such trickery to obtain a confession be clearly unfair to the accused, but it would also nullify the protections provided by privileged communication. Privileged communications are safeguarded from being introduced in court as evidence. Should an accused confide basic facts about a crime to a minister or to a lawyer, the information is considered privileged and does not have to be revealed.

CONNECTIONS: Law and Police Action

Law enforcement officers are mandated by government to protect society and to uphold and enforce laws. For example, if the police are involved in suppressing a riot, they may have to resort to severe measures in order to secure order. This could result in the legitimate use of tear gas and water cannons in order to disperse riotous crowds. Section 32 (1) of the *Criminal Code* allows the police to use such force as is necessary to suppress a riot:

> Every peace officer is justified in using or in ordering the use of as much force as the peace officer believes, in good faith and on reasonable grounds,
> (a) is necessary to suppress a riot; and
> (b) is not excessive, having regard to the danger to be apprehended from the continuance of the riot.

If a claim were made by those involved in a disturbance that the use of force by the police was excessive, then the police could argue that serious mischief, such as bodily harm and property damage, would have resulted if they had not acted. They might also argue that they perceived danger if the riot were allowed to continue. If police officers search and subsequently arrest those involved in a riot, they must act in accordance with the law; that is, the search and seizure must be reasonable, the police officers must notify those arrested of the reason for the arrest, and they must inform each accused of the right to contact legal counsel and then give the accused the opportunity to do so. All of these procedural safeguards are designed to protect the accused. Should these *Charter* rights be violated, an accused may apply for a court remedy under s. 24 of the *Charter*, which could result in having evidence excluded.

Law enforcement officers have the authority to make arrests; however, under the *Criminal Code*, those making an arrest can be held responsible for using excessive force. Section 26 of the *Criminal Code* states, "Everyone who is authorized by law to use force is criminally responsible for any excess thereof according to the nature and quality of the act that constitutes the excess." For example, should a suspect suffer severe abrasions to the head while being arrested, a complaint could be filed against the police officer for the excessive use of force, possibly leading to charges of criminal assault.

Police officers are investigated not only when there are allegations of the use of excessive force, but also when their actions result in the serious injury or death of a civilian. In Ontario, an independent civilian agency called the Special Investigations Unit (SIU) is responsible for investigating the circumstances surrounding these types of incidents. The SIU was created in 1990 and operates under the control of the Attorney General. The jurisdiction of the SIU covers 65 police service associations in Ontario, representing approximately 21 600 officers. The existence of an independent agency promotes the public's confidence in the law enforcement system since it eliminates the potential for accusations of police bias, which had previously occurred when the police force conducted its own internal investigations. In 2002, the SIU investigated 163 cases in Ontario, 5 of which resulted in criminal charges against the officers involved.

Although the role of the SIU is not to lay charges, if an investigation reveals that an officer or officers conducted themselves in a reckless or negligent manner, the Director of the SIU may recommend to the Attorney General that charges be laid. In October 2000, after an investigation by the SIU, four Toronto police officers were charged with manslaughter in connection with the death of Otto Vass. Vass, a 55-year-old man with a history of mental illness, had created a disturbance at a convenience store. When the police arrived, there was a struggle with Vass, which resulted in his death. A subsequent jury trial in 2003 acquitted the officers of any wrongdoing.

FIGURE 10.7   A Toronto police pursuit in October 2000 ended when the vehicle being pursued crashed head on into a police cruiser. One man was killed and seven others were injured, including two police officers. What types of actions are investigated by the Ontario Special Investigations Unit?

Complaints regarding police conduct that do not involve serious injury or death are first lodged with the police force itself. The Ontario Civilian Commission on Police Services (OCCPS), a civilian agency, might also be contacted to conduct an investigation and inquiry into police conduct. For example, a complaint could be made to the OCCPS to investigate the validity of a strip search subsequent to an arrest. Should an individual not be satisfied with the OCCPS review, he or she might consider launching a civil action for assault.

Not everyone is satisfied with the mechanisms designed to keep police actions in check. In speaking about the complaint process to the *Toronto Star*, Alan Young, a law professor and lawyer, commented that it "is as maze-like as possible to deter people from going forward with complaints, it's a process which tries to exclude more than embrace complainants." Nevertheless, there is at least a process or avenue to follow should you suspect that police conduct has affected you unfairly in the legal system.

SOURCES: Brennan, Richard. "Police Complaints System Will Face a Review." *Toronto Star* 3 Nov. 2003: A8; *Ontario Civilian Commission on Police Services (OCCPS)*. Accessed Nov. 2003 <www.occps.ca/>; *Special Investigations Unit (SIU)*. Accessed Nov. 2003 <www.siu.on.ca/home.asp>.

Questions

1. Explain the function of a law enforcement agency.
2. How does the *Charter* affect the role of a police officer in the execution of his or her duties?
3. Explain how police officers could be held accountable for the excessive use of force.
4. Distinguish between the jurisdiction of the SIU and that of the OCCPS.

Election of Trial Method and Judicial Release

After an accused is arrested and charged, he or she is not automatically released. Generally, the rule governing release procedures is that everyone should be released unless there are serious grounds for keeping the accused in custody. However, there are practical as well as legal reasons for releasing the majority of accused people. From a practical standpoint, there is just not enough room in our jails to keep everyone who has been charged with a minor or less serious offence in custody until his or her trial. Furthermore, under s. 11(d) of the *Charter*, an accused is presumed innocent until proven guilty. Therefore, a police officer who arrests someone for a **summary conviction offence** (a criminal offence that is minor in nature and carries consequences much less severe than an indictable offence) or a **hybrid offence** (an offence for which the Crown can elect to proceed by way of an indictable offence or a summary conviction offence) has the authority to release the accused under a **promise to appear**. This is an agreement the accused must sign, guaranteeing his or her appearance in court at a later date. The accused might also be allowed to enter into a **recognizance**, which is essentially a written promise to appear in court on a scheduled date or else pay a sum of money if he or she fails to show up. The recognizance can be issued with or without a **surety** (a person who agrees to pay an amount of money should the accused not show up in court). The police may also release the accused on an **undertaking**, which is an agreement with specific conditions attached, such as remaining within the jurisdiction or abstaining from drugs or alcohol.

When an accused enters a court of first appearance, the court clerk reads the charge and the accused must enter a plea of guilty or not guilty. Once the accused enters a plea, he or she may have the option of selecting a trial by judge alone or a trial by judge and jury, depending on the nature of the crime committed. For example,

if the crime is a summary conviction offence, the case will be heard in a summary conviction court by a judge alone. However, if the crime is an indictable offence that carries a penalty greater than five years (e.g., murder, aggravated sexual assault, kidnapping, robbery, impaired driving causing death, trafficking in cocaine), an accused has the option of electing a trial by judge and jury. After consulting with his or her lawyer, an accused may conclude that the odds of securing a "not guilty" verdict are better if the case is presented to a **jury of peers**. This is a group of 12 citizens who are selected to hear the evidence against the accused in a criminal trial. In other instances, an accused may choose to be tried by a judge alone, especially if there is a concern that jurors might be prejudiced in their views toward the accused due to the sensationalism of the case, or if the case involves factual details that are highly technical, such as insurance fraud. A defence lawyer might advise his or her client that inexperienced jurors might not be able to comprehend the nature of the details as well as a trial judge who has many years of experience hearing evidence.

If the police decide to hold the accused in custody until his or her trial, an application can be made for **bail**, which involves the posting of a sum of money in order to secure the release of the accused and to guarantee his or her appearance at trial. Section 11(e) of the *Charter* guarantees the right of the accused not to be denied reasonable bail without just cause. There are two grounds for prohibiting the release of an accused. The first is a belief on the part of law enforcement that the accused will not show up for trial. The second is a belief that the accused poses a danger to the public. It is the responsibility of the Crown to prove either one of these grounds. Judicial interim release is often referred to as a "show-cause hearing," because the burden is on the Crown to show why the accused should not be released on bail pending trial. Certain offences, such as drug trafficking or offences related to terrorist activities, carry a **reverse onus provision**, which is a shift in responsibility requiring the accused to justify or show cause why he or she should be released. In recent years, however, cases that involve crimes committed by offenders who have been released have led to closer scrutiny and criticism of the bail process.

In June 2000, Gillian Hadley was shot to death by her estranged husband, Ralph, who then took his own life. The couple had separated in 1999, but Ralph Hadley continued to harass Gillian Hadley. In early 2000, he was charged with assault and told not to contact his wife, but he continued to call her and threaten her. Ralph Hadley was charged with criminal harassment and ordered, as part of the bail conditions, not to contact his wife or go near Pickering, Ontario, where she lived. The conditions did not stop Ralph Hadley from entering her home and killing her. The Ontario chief coroner called for an inquest into the death of Gillian Hadley. The inquest jury studied how the events led to her death, and it made recommendations to prevent similar domestic violence situations from occurring in the future. The inquest jury recommended that, in cases involving an arrest for domestic violence, the granting of bail should be based on a reverse onus provision. In this way, more protection would be afforded to the victims of domestic violence.

No less troublesome than the possibility of suspected offenders committing crimes while out on bail is the overcrowding in detention centres of inmates who are awaiting trial. In recent years, the number of people held in pre-trial custody has doubled. According to Statistics Canada, pre-trial detention rose from 67 500 inmates in 1986 to 118 500 in 2001. Mr. Justice Marc Rosenberg of the Ontario Court of Appeal, in speaking to Queen's University Law School in October 2003, commented on the unfairness of detaining prisoners and keeping them in overcrowded conditions pending trial: "These threats to the rights of accused people to make full answer and defence and to be treated with humanity and fairness jeopardize the system of administration of criminal justice in this province" (Tyler 2003).

FIGURE 10.8 In December 2003, former NHL player Keith Magnuson was killed in a car driven by former Toronto Maple Leafs' captain Rob Ramage. Ramage was charged with impaired driving causing death and dangerous operation of a motor vehicle causing death. The maximum penalty for the first charge is life imprisonment; for the second charge, the maximum sentence is 14 years. In a show-cause hearing that took place at the hospital, Ramage was released from custody on $100 000 bail. What criteria do you think the courts use to determine the amount of money to be set for bail?

Although bail is designed to address the rights of the accused and society at large by establishing the criteria for release, the legal system is working on ways to address the rights of the accused while in custody. Since the conditions in some detention centres are deplorable, lawyers have asked judges in some cases to consider pre-trial incarceration in these facilities as time served when making their sentencing decisions.

Preliminary Inquiries and Plea Bargaining

If an accused is charged with an indictable offence, a preliminary inquiry may be held to determine if there is sufficient evidence for the case to be heard in a higher court, such as the Ontario Superior Court of Justice. The preliminary inquiry is held before a judge at the provincial court level, such as the Ontario Court of Justice, and gives the Crown an opportunity to assess the strength of its case. It also gives the defence an opportunity to discover the evidence that the Crown is planning to present at trial and to question Crown witnesses, which helps the defence to discover weaknesses in the Crown's case. If sufficient evidence is found during the preliminary inquiry, then the judge will determine a trial date. If the judge determines that there is insufficient evidence, the charges may be dropped. However, should evidence surface at a later date, the accused can be brought back to court to face charges. If an accused pleads guilty, a preliminary inquiry is not held.

Among the drawbacks of the preliminary inquiry is the negative effect it can have on victims and witnesses who are compelled to recount details of the crime even before the case goes to trial. An accused can also be negatively affected by the preliminary inquiry, especially if he or she has been falsely accused and must still be paraded in front of those attending court.

If a case proceeds to trial, there is an opportunity for Crown and defence lawyers to negotiate certain issues regarding the charge and the potential sentence prior to the trial date. The criminal justice system allows for a process of **plea bargaining** or **resolution discussion**, which can take several forms. It may involve the Crown agreeing to reduce the charge to a lesser charge, which would carry a lighter penalty. Or it may involve making recommendations for a reduced sentence in return for a guilty plea. Given the backlog of cases awaiting court dates and the cost both in time and money of a trial process, plea bargaining may seem to be a satisfactory remedy. However, many people, such as victims' rights advocates, view such bargains with contempt. In the case of Karla Holmolka, the public was outraged when, in 1993, she managed to successfully plea bargain for a reduced sentence in return for her testimony against her husband, Paul Bernardo, in the murders of Leslie Mahaffy and Kristen French. The criticism became even more pronounced once it was revealed that Homolka played a primary role in the crimes. On balance, the Crown and defence must weigh the circumstances to determine whether plea bargaining serves the best interests of the administration of justice.

CONFIRM YOUR UNDERSTANDING

1. Explain the right to remain silent. What *Charter* rights affirm this principle?
2. What factors would a defence lawyer consider in challenging the legality of a confession?
3. Should police officers be allowed to use trickery to obtain a confession? Support your opinion.
4. Why would an accused elect a trial by judge and jury rather than a trial by judge alone?
5. Distinguish between a promise to appear and a recognizance.
6. Should the onus be on the accused to prove why he or she should not remain in custody in all cases? Explain.
7. Explain the purpose of a preliminary inquiry.
8. Identify advantages and disadvantages of plea bargaining.
9. Should victims have input into whether plea bargaining is allowed? Explain.

Trial Procedures

In the pursuit of justice, our legal system strives to balance the rights of an accused with the interests of society in prosecuting criminal offenders. Today, legal principles are entrenched in the *Charter* to ensure procedural safeguards throughout the trial process. The adversarial system, on which our trial system is based, generates competition. Although there is the potential for abuse as both competitors—the Crown and the defence—seek justice, the burden of proof rests with the Crown prosecutor to prove his or her case beyond a reasonable doubt. The defence counsel, on the other hand, is charged with the responsibility of providing a proper legal defence for the accused. The Crown prosecutor, in seeking to prove the guilt of the accused, must face the defence counsel, who has worked to answer the charges and prepare the defence. Ultimately, the judge or judge and jury must weigh the facts and evidence to determine the guilt or innocence of the accused. In addition, the interests of society and the victim must be factored into any sentence in order to achieve justice.

Legal Principles

In Canada's criminal justice system, the **burden of proof** in a criminal trial rests with the Crown; that is, the Crown must prove the guilt of the accused beyond a reasonable doubt. Simply put, a **reasonable doubt** implies an honest or moral doubt as to whether the accused is guilty of the crime. If the Crown is unable to satisfy the court that this heavy burden has been met, then the accused must be **acquitted**, meaning declared to be not guilty. This principle is so important to the criminal justice process that a judge in a jury trial must instruct the jurors on the burden of proof prior to allowing them to deliberate on a verdict.

Tied closely to the burden of proof is a foundation principle of the criminal justice system—the presumption of innocence. The public sees a criminal arrested and taken to the police station to be charged. It is assumed then that justice will somehow be done: a trial will take place, the criminal will be sentenced, and the public will be protected. This is not always the case, however, in the face of the presumption of innocence principle. The arrested person is, at this point, innocent until he or she is either acquitted or convicted at trial. During the pre-trial process, an arrested person has the right to have a judge determine the validity of the arrest. Judicial release procedures also aim to protect the presumption of innocence by

allowing the release of the accused unless there is just cause for keeping him or her in custody pending trial.

In the case of *R. v. Oakes*, [1986] 1 S.C.R. 103 (see Chapter 7, p. 200–201), the principle of the presumption of innocence was violated. The charge of possession for the purpose of trafficking, which the police levied against David Oakes under the old *Narcotics Control Act*, involved a reverse onus provision. In effect, Oakes was required to prove that he did not have drugs for the purpose of trafficking, which was considered a violation of the presumption of innocence provision under the *Charter*. The reverse onus provision was therefore held to be unconstitutional. The presumption of innocence is a cornerstone of our judicial system, and every attempt is made to preserve the integrity of the system by its continued use.

Another important component of the criminal justice system is the principle of disclosure. **Disclosure** involves the Crown providing the defence with all relevant information to make a full answer and defence to a charge. Should disclosure of key information not be made to the defence, it could prejudice the case and, in the most serious of consequences, result in the wrongful conviction of the accused. In the case of *R. v. Stinchcombe*, [1991] 3 S.C.R. 326, the Crown failed to disclose statements made by a witness that were favourable to the defence and subsequently did not call that witness for the trial. The defence counsel requested disclosure of the statements, but the Crown refused. The Supreme Court of Canada directed a new trial and ordered that the statements be produced as evidence. In considering the timing of the disclosure, the court recommended that it should take place before the accused elects the method of trial (by judge alone or by judge and jury) and before a plea is entered. As Justice Sopinka stated, "The right to make a full answer and defence is one of the pillars of criminal justice on which we heavily depend to ensure that the innocent are not convicted."

The prospect of jailing an innocent person for someone else's crime has been considered more abhorrent to our sense of justice than a guilty person evading punishment.

—Thomas Gabor and Julian Roberts, professors of criminology, University of Ottawa

Rights on Being Charged

As stated earlier, the *Charter* guarantees certain rights to the accused when being charged with an offence. Under s. 11, an accused has the right to be informed of the offence without unreasonable delay, to be tried within a reasonable period of time, and to be presumed innocent until proven guilty. Without such rights, due process would not be provided for the accused, resulting in an improper and unfair trial.

Informing the accused of the specific offence at the time he or she is charged, in accordance with s. 11(a) of the *Charter*, gives the accused a clear understanding of the accusations, thus enabling him or her to mount an appropriate defence. An accused also has the right to be tried within a reasonable time under s. 11(b). The longer the accused goes without the opportunity to present a defence or answer the accusations, the longer his or her reputation is impugned by the charges laid. In addition, delays may cause evidence to be dated and even lead to inaccurate recollections in witness testimony.

An important, yet controversial, case clarifying the right to be tried within a reasonable time was addressed by the Supreme Court in *R. v. Askov*, [1990] 2 S.C.R. 1199 (see Chapter 1, p. 12). Askov had waited 24 months to go to trial on charges of conspiracy to commit extortion. The cause of the delay was attributed to a justice system that could not keep up with the number of trials being scheduled. The delay was not held to be the fault of any particular party. The court found the delay unreasonable and dropped the charges against Askov. As a result of this decision, more than 50 000 other charges were dropped because the delays extended beyond the 8- to 10-month time period the court had recommended as reasonable. This so outraged the general public that subsequent court rulings did not adhere to a strict application of the Askov case. Delays that exceed the 8- to 10-month recommendation do not always result in a **stay of proceedings**, which is a decision made by the court to stop the proceedings against the accused

if continuing the action would be considered prejudicial to the accused.

The courts will consider the cause of the delays, such as Crown and defence **motions for adjournment** (requests to put the hearing off to another time), before they rule that a constitutional right has been violated. Court delays are still a concern in the criminal justice system. In 2003, the Ontario *Provincial Auditor's Report* revealed that a significant backlog of criminal court cases continued to exist (see Figure 10.9, below). The risk associated with this backlog is that more criminals may go free if accused individuals successfully argue their *Charter* right to be tried within a reasonable time.

An accused is also protected from having to testify under s. 11(c) of the *Charter*, which states, "Any person charged with an offence has the right not to be compelled to be a witness in proceedings against that person in respect of the offence." In some cases, it may not be in the best

Backlog of Criminal Cases of the Ontario Court of Justice

Year	Total Cases	Cases Tried Within 8 Months	Cases Tried After 8 Months
1998	206 000	146 000	60 000
1999	207 000	148 000	59 000
2000	227 000	161 000	66 000
2001	262 000	174 000	88 000
2002	282 000	183 000	99 000

Source: Adapted from Ministry of the Attorney General, "3.01—Court Services." *2003 Annual Report of the Office of the Provincial Auditor of Ontario. Provincial Auditor's Report*, p. 33. Accessed 20 Feb. 2004 <www.auditor.on.ca/english/reports/en03/301en03.pdf>.

Figure 10.9 Over a five-year period, from March 1998 to February 2002, the number of criminal cases going to trial increased by about 37 percent. In that same period, however, the number of criminal cases exceeding the eight-month delay period increased by 65 percent. What factors do you think contribute to trial delays?

interests of the accused to testify, particularly if prior criminal behaviour might be questioned, or the defence attorney might decide that his or her client could not withstand the intense cross-examination by the Crown prosecutor. However, the fact that an accused does not have to take the stand to testify cannot be used against him or her as an admission of guilt.

The right to be presumed innocent until proven guilty is codified in s. 11(d) of the *Charter* and provides for a fair and public hearing by an independent and impartial tribunal. While open trials allow for greater public examination of the administration of justice, s. 486 of the *Criminal Code* assigns judges discretion to exclude the public for such reasons as protecting child witnesses or when matters of national security arising from terrorist activities are involved. Whenever the public is excluded from the administration of justice, however, confidence in the integrity of the system declines.

Participants in the Trial Process

Participants in the criminal trial process may have different impressions of the system depending on the nature of their involvement. To the accused, the trial may represent a system by which guilt or innocence is determined according to due process of the law. To the parties who work in the system, such as judges and lawyers, criminal trials may represent a complex network of rules and procedures designed to ensure not only that justice is served, but also that it is seen by the public as having been served. To the 12 people chosen to sit on the jury, the trial provides the opportunity to fulfill one of the duties of Canadian citizenship. Finally, to the victim, the trial process may represent a chance at closure, as justice is sought for the harm done. But the trial may also cause further emotional trauma for the victim since he or she is asked to testify and recount specific details of the crime under the examination of a questioning defence lawyer.

The judge, as a key participant in the criminal trial process, must remain **impartial**; that is, he or she must not be biased in the handling of the case. The role of a judge is to apply the law to the facts, and it is in this capacity that a judge is sometimes called the **trier of law**. In a trial without a jury, the judge is required to determine not only the credibility of the evidence, but the admissibility of it as well. At all times, the integrity of a judge is key to ensuring the public's confidence in the criminal justice system.

Similarly, the Crown must also exercise strict adherence to the rules and procedures governing the administration of justice.

> It cannot be over-emphasized that the purpose of a criminal prosecution is not to obtain a conviction, it is to lay before a jury what the Crown considers to be credible evidence relevant to what is alleged to be a crime. Counsel have a duty to see that all available legal proof of the facts is presented: it should be done firmly and pressed to its legitimate strength but it must also be done fairly. The role of prosecutor excludes any notion of winning or losing; his function is a matter of public duty than which in civil life there can be none charged with greater personal responsibility. It is to be efficiently performed with an ingrained sense of the dignity, the seriousness and the justness of judicial proceedings. (Justice Rand, *Boucher v. The Queen,* [1955], excerpted in *R. v. Stinchcombe*)

The role of the defence counsel is to prepare a proper legal defence for the accused. In addition to compiling statements from his or her client and from information disclosed by the Crown, the defence lawyer must also use his or her knowledge of case law to prepare a full answer and defence to the charge. As Edward Greenspan, a leading Canadian criminal defence lawyer, has commented:

> Under our adversary system—in a free society—the interests of the state are not absolute, or even paramount. The dignity of

A trial judge must display unremitting patience, consummate courtesy, diligence in research and preparation, complete integrity, great courage and a passionate sense of fairness.

–"The Inquiry Regarding Thomas Sophonow: The Role of the Trial Judge" the individual is respected to the point that even when the citizen is known by the state to have committed a heinous offence, the individual is nevertheless accorded such rights as counsel, trial by jury, due process, and the privilege against self-incrimination. I have always felt that a criminal lawyer can never excuse himself for accepting a defendant's confidence and then betraying it by a half-hearted defence. (Greenspan 1987)

If the accused elects a trial by judge and jury, then ordinary citizens must share the burden and responsibility of ensuring justice is served, not only to uphold the rights of the accused, but also to uphold the rights of the victim and society at large. Names of potential jurors are selected at random from the voters' list, and those selected are required to complete a questionnaire. A potential juror must meet several criteria in order to be further considered for jury duty. For example, he or she must be a Canadian citizen and must not have been convicted of an indictable offence. As well, a person may be exempted from serving as a juror if he or she is a police officer, lawyer, medical doctor, or veterinarian. Jurors must not be particularly skilled or knowledgeable in the area of the law. Twelve ordinary, reasonable people are selected from a **jury panel**, which is a large group of people who, after submitting a completed jury-duty questionnaire, are required to report to the courthouse on a particular day. A jury is selected by the Crown, the defence, and the accused. Prospective jurors can be **challenged**; that is, a claim is made by the Crown or the defence to remove a prospective juror from consideration. Challenges can take one of two forms: a **challenge for cause**, meaning a juror can be challenged for bias because he or she knows the accused, or a **peremptory challenge**, meaning a potential juror can be removed without any explanation. The Crown and defence have varying numbers of peremptory challenges available to them depending on the seriousness of the charge. For example, a

charge of first-degree murder, which carries an automatic sentence of life imprisonment if the accused is convicted, provides the Crown and defence with 20 peremptory challenges each, while a charge that carries a prison sentence of more than 5 years provides for 12 peremptory challenges. A charge for which the penalty is less than 5 years allows for 4 peremptory challenges. Challenges allow the Crown and defence to select the jurors for the case. In recent years, in an attempt to further screen jurors and prevent bias, judges have occasionally allowed potential jurors to be questioned by the defence counsel. However, the judge must examine the questions prior to allowing them to be asked during the jury selection process. Once selected, the jury is considered the trier of fact because the jurors assess the credibility and weight to be given to the facts presented. Before the jury **deliberates** (i.e., leaves the courtroom to determine a verdict after all the evidence has been presented), the judge must **charge the jury**, meaning he or she instructs the jury on the law and how it applies to the facts presented in the case. The judge's words must be chosen very carefully to ensure that no errors are made, since mistakes made in the charge to the jury could be used as grounds for an appeal.

Witnesses also play an important evidentiary role in the criminal trial process. Evidence must be introduced through the various Crown and defence witnesses, and the credibility of each witness is often key in assessing the extent to which information and evidence are reliable. Witnesses are used to substantiate claims being made in the trial. In order to protect witnesses in criminal prosecutions, s. 13 of the *Charter* protects witnesses who testify from having any incriminating evidence used against them in subsequent proceedings, subject to exceptions. If, for example, a witness lies on the stand, then the testimony could be used as evidence in a charge of **perjury**, that is, lying in court under oath or to show that the evidence given contradicted other evidence.

All witnesses do not have the same degree of credibility, as the inquiry into the wrongful conviction of Thomas Sophonow revealed. Sophonow was wrongfully convicted of murdering Barbara Stoppel in 1981 but was cleared on the basis of DNA evidence in 2000 (see p.p. 323–324). Justice Peter Cory, in a report on the investigation into Sophonow's wrongful conviction, was extremely critical of relying on the testimony of jailhouse informants:

> Jailhouse informants comprise the most deceitful and deceptive group of witnesses known to frequent the courts. The more notorious the case, the greater the number of prospective informants. They rush to testify like vultures to rotting flesh or sharks to blood. They are smooth and convincing liars. Whether they seek favours from the authorities, attention or notoriety they are in every instance completely unreliable. It will be seen how frequently they have been a major factor in the conviction of innocent people and how much they tend to corrupt the administration of justice. Usually, their presence as witnesses signals the end of any hope of providing a fair trial. ("The Inquiry Regarding Thomas Sophonow: Jailhouse Informants")

So much time and effort are spent on ensuring that the rights of the accused are not violated that victims may feel lost and forgotten in the process. Our adversarial court system may perpetuate their victimization by requiring them to testify in a criminal proceeding. This is especially difficult during a cross-examination in cases involving sexual assault. It is often extremely difficult for victims to relive a crime when they provide testimony. Efforts are being made, however, to address the needs of victims. The "Canadian Statement of Basic Principles of Justice for Victims of Crime, 2003" identifies principles for the fair treatment of victims (see Figure 10.11 on p. 316). In addition, there are many organizations in existence whose sole purpose is to help victims of crime. Such organizations include women's crisis centres, victim assistance programs, and groups such as Mothers Against Drunk Driving (MADD) that are focused on specific crimes. Victims are also being given the opportunity to provide input into the sentencing process by completing a **victim impact statement**, which is a statement outlining the harm done and the effects of the crime on the victim's life. Both the trial and sentencing process can exert an emotional toll on a victim. As victims seek their own claim for justice, they may or may not be satisfied with the verdict or the sentence provided in the criminal trial process.

Admissibility of Evidence

One of the most challenging aspects of a trial and a key responsibility of the trial judge is determining the admissibility of evidence. Evidence can be excluded not only when a violation of rights occurs, but also if proper procedures are not followed during the investigation stage. Police and forensic investigators must be diligent in ensuring that a crime scene is secured and that evidence is gathered, labelled, preserved, and packaged properly. Improper procedure may result in the inadmissibility of the proposed evidence in court.

FIGURE 10.10 Witnesses who testify in a criminal trial must withstand the scrutiny of intense cross-examination. Why is witness credibility important in the criminal trial process?

Canadian Statement of Basic Principles of Justice for Victims of Crime, 2003

The following principles are intended to promote fair treatment of victims and should be reflected in federal/provincial/territorial laws, policies, and procedures:

1. Victims of crime should be treated with courtesy, compassion, and respect.
2. The privacy of victims should be considered and respected to the greatest extent possible.
3. All reasonable measures should be taken to minimize inconvenience to victims.
4. The safety and security of victims should be considered at all stages of the criminal justice process and appropriate measures should be taken when necessary to protect victims from intimidation and retaliation.
5. Information should be provided to victims about the criminal justice system, the victim's role, and opportunities to participate in criminal justice processes.
6. Victims should be given information, in accordance with prevailing law, policies, and procedures, about the status of the investigation; the scheduling, progress and final outcome of the proceedings; and the status of the offender in the correctional system.
7. Information should be provided to victims about available victim assistance services, other programs and assistance available to them, and means of obtaining financial reparation.
8. The views, concerns and representations of victims are an important consideration in criminal justice processes and should be considered in accordance with prevailing law, policies and procedures.
9. The needs, concerns and diversity of victims should be considered in the development and delivery of programs and services, and in related education and training.
10. Information should be provided to victims about available options to raise their concerns when they believe that these principles have not been followed.

Source: Department of Justice Canada. "Canadian Statement of Basic Principles of Justice for Victims of Crime, 2003." Accessed 1 Dec. 2003 <www.canada.justice.gc.ca/en/ps/voc/publications/03/basic_prin.html>.

Figure 10.11 A new Canadian Statement of Basic Principles of Justice for Victims of Crime was endorsed by federal, provincial, and territorial ministers of justice in October 2003. Which of these principles would you consider to be the most important in promoting the fair treatment of victims in the pre-trial and trial processes?

There are many types of evidence that can be considered for use in the trial process: witness testimony, physical evidence, and circumstantial evidence. Witness testimony is often referred to as **direct evidence**. Either the Crown or the defence call witnesses to the stand in order to substantiate a fact in question. **Physical evidence** may include samples of bodily fluids, such as blood, semen, and saliva. It could also include hair and fibre samples, fingerprint evidence, and weapons found at the scene, such as guns or knives. **Circumstantial evidence** is indirect evidence that links the accused to the crime. For example, a wallet found at the crime scene belonging to the accused would be regarded as circumstantial evidence.

In recent years, DNA technology has had a significant impact on investigations and the analysis of evidence. DNA (deoxyribonucleic acid) is considered to be the hereditary building block of life. This genetic material is contained within the nucleus of a cell and organized into chromosomes. DNA analysis may be conducted on blood, semen, hair, saliva, and tissue samples. DNA is unique to all individuals except for identical twins. As part of a criminal investigation, investigators may collect biological samples from a suspect and prepare a DNA profile. A comparison might then be made between this DNA profile and the profile developed from the physical evidence that was collected at the crime scene. For example, a bloodstain found on a carpet at the crime scene could be collected and a DNA profile prepared. This DNA profile could then be compared with the DNA profile of a suspect. The purpose of DNA analysis is to exclude potential suspects from further consideration.

The ability of technicians who carry out DNA analysis to perfom their work effectively and produce reliable results is key to the use of forensic evidence in a trial. One of the main objectives of the Centre of Forensic Sciences in Ontario is to assist law enforcement agencies through "the production of evidence in a legally admissible form for law enforcement officers, crown attorneys, lawyers, coroners, pathologists and official investigative agencies by means of the scientific examination, analysis, evaluation and interpretation of physical objects and materials" (Centre of Forensic Sciences *Laboratory Guide...*1997).

The forensic expert conducts the tests on the evidence and compiles the results. This information is then introduced in court through the testimony of an expert witness, who is knowledgeable or skilled in a particular area. Either the Crown or the defence will call the expert witness to testify as to the validity of the evidence. For example, a fire marshal who has had experience investigating hundreds of suspicious fires may be called in as an expert witness in a suspected arson case. The witness must first be qualified as an expert, which means that both the Crown and defence counsel have an opportunity to either support or contest the qualification of a proposed expert witness prior to his or her testifying in court. Once the witness has been qualified as an expert, he or she is questioned about the evidence to be presented. The line of questioning may focus on the procedures used to collect the evidence, the tests that were conducted on the evidence, the potential for the evidence to have been tampered with prior to its introduction at

FIGURE 10.12   Once a crime has been discovered, police will secure the scene to ensure that nothing is removed or tampered with. To ensure that evidence does not become contaminated or destroyed, only authorized personnel, such as crime-scene experts and forensic investigators, are allowed to enter the contained area to collect evidence. What types of evidence may be found at a crime scene?

trial, margins for error in the results, and so on.

There are times when the defence or the Crown question whether certain evidence should be shown to the jury. If either side believes that the evidence should be inadmissible, the court uses a procedure called a *voir dire*, whereby the jury is removed from the courtroom while the lawyers argue over the admissibility of the evidence. For example, in a case involving a confession, the court would first have to consider whether the confession was given voluntarily before admitting it for a jury to consider. If the judge decided that the evidence was admissible, then the jury would be brought back into the courtroom and the trial would continue with the evidence in question.

Throughout the trial procedure, lawyers can object to questions being asked of witnesses by the opposing side by challenging the **relevance** of a question, that is, its legal connection or significance to the case. Similarly, **leading questions**—questions that suggest or imply the answer—may not be asked on direct examination of a witness. **Direct examination** refers to the questioning by a lawyer of his or her own witness. Leading questions are, however, permitted on cross-examination as long as the question relates to a fact that was established in the previous direct examination testimony.

Lawyers from both sides can also object to **hearsay evidence**, which is evidence given by a witness on the stand that relates to something another person heard or saw. All witnesses are prevented from testifying about anything that is not within their realm of knowledge or experience. To be deemed credible, this evidence would require a third party—that is, the person who actually heard or saw what happened—to testify as to its truth. By adhering to the rules of evidence, skilful lawyers can prevent certain evidence or testimony from being introduced into the trial process.

SHIFTING PERSPECTIVES: The Reliability of Evidence

In criminal law, if law enforcement officers catch a person who is in the act of committing a crime, or eyewitnesses identify a suspect, this can provide sufficient grounds for charging and prosecuting the person. Any eyewitness testimony could be used to support a conviction, but the reliability of eyewitness testimony must also be questioned in order to maintain a fair trial. It is possible that a witness may have poor vision or may have gotten only a partial view of the accused. The possibility also exists that the way in which police officers present lineups and photo packs showing potential suspects to witnesses may bias the witnesses toward identifying the accused as the prime suspect. When eyewitness testimony is introduced in court, lawyers are obligated to question the accuracy and reliability of the testimony.

In addition to eyewitness identification, fingerprint and hair comparison analyses are also used to identify and implicate an accused in a crime. However, the results of these analyses have not always been accurate or conclusive. Everyone's fingerprint patterns are unique. By analyzing certain characteristics in the fingerprint pattern, fingerprint analysis experts can testify as to the likelihood that the fingerprints of the suspect are those that have been lifted from the crime scene. The accuracy of fingerprint analysis can be diminished by such factors as the lifting of only a partial print from the crime scene. Similarly, experts can analyze hair samples found at the crime scene and identify specific characteristics. The hairs found at the crime scene can then be compared to hair samples from the suspect. Hair analysis experts, who are familiar with the requirements for recognizing the similarity of hair samples, can then testify as to the likelihood of the hairs belonging to a suspect if a suitable number of characteristics are present. The key thing to note about fingerprint and hair comparison analysis, however, is the word "likelihood." There are limitations to the accuracy of these techniques.

With the advent of DNA technology, some cases have been re-opened and evidence re-examined, particularly if further information comes to light that casts doubt on the innocence or guilt of an accused. One case involving hair comparison analysis for identification purposes was that of James Driskell, who was convicted in 1991 for the first-degree murder of Perry Dean Harder. A major source of evidence in the trial was three hair samples said to belong to the victim and taken from the backseat of Driskell's vehicle. In

2002, DNA tests performed on the three hairs determined that they did not come from the victim. The revelation that an informant was paid $20 000 for his services and that the Crown did not disclose the nature of its dealings with the informant to the defence also clouded the verdict and raised the spectre of wrongful conviction. The DNA forensic evidence and the non-disclosure of key information were enough to warrant a review of the case regarding a miscarriage of justice. Driskell was granted bail in November 2003 pending an inquiry into the allegations of a wrongful conviction.

More specialized science is being used today to collect and analyze DNA samples for use as evidence in court. According to the National DNA Data Bank,

FIGURE 10.13   Forensic DNA analysis has been used in criminal law to exclude and to link suspects to a crime. Should police be allowed to seize bodily samples from crime suspects in order to analyze their DNA?

> [t]he use of forensic DNA analysis in solving crime is proving to be as revolutionary as the introduction of fingerprint evidence in court more than a century ago. Remarkably, Canadian police have been using forensic DNA evidence for little more than a decade, yet it has emerged as one of the most powerful tools available to law enforcement agencies for the administration of justice. DNA analysis is the next generation of human identification in the science of police investigations and is considered a major enhancement for the safety of all Canadians.
>
> The value of DNA to police investigations is enormous. Biological samples collected from the crime scene can either link a suspect to the scene, or rule the suspect out as the donor of the DNA.

While advances in science and technology provide hope for both victims and those unjustly accused of crime, the ethical and legal implications of such progress must be considered on balance. In certain situations, under the authority of Bill C-104, the *DNA Warrant* legislation, investigators can obtain DNA samples from a suspect or an accused without his or her consent. While it may be argued that this seizure of DNA is a violation of privacy and amounts to an unreasonable search and seizure, the Supreme Court of Canada has upheld the constitutionality of DNA warrants, which allow police to force suspected criminals to provide samples of blood, hair, or saliva for use in DNA analysis. According to the Centre of Forensic Sciences, it remains to be seen what impact these new technologies will have on the criminal justice system and on society:

> The importance of forensic science in criminal and other investigations is almost impossible to assess with any accuracy. In some investigations and trials, its role

is relatively minor and often the outcome would be the same without any scientific evidence. There are, however, an increasing number of cases where forensic science can and does make a vital contribution. As the body of knowledge and techniques increases, scientific evidence becomes even more important in a greater proportion of cases. (*Laboratory Guide* 1997)

To ensure the reliability and admissibility of evidence, the forensic expert must be competent and qualified to conduct the tests and analyze the results. But society must also be prepared to accept the costs of time and money involved. With developments in technology comes the hope that fewer guilty individuals will go free and fewer innocent individuals will be wrongly convicted, thus providing peace of mind for victims of crime and alleviating the need to compensate victims of miscarriages of justice.

Sources: Centre of Forensic Sciences, Public Safety Division. *Laboratory Guide for the Investigator*. 5th ed. Toronto: Ministry of the Solicitor General and Correctional Services, 1997: 10; Chua, June. "Indepth: James Driskell." *CBC News Online*. Updated 26 Nov. 2003. Accessed 26 Nov. 2003 <www.cbc.ca/news/background/driskell/>; Jaimet, Kate. "Court Upholds Police Right to Seize DNA." *National Post* 1 Nov. 2003: A4; *National DNA Data Bank*. Accessed 13 Dec. 2003 <http://nddb-bndg.org/main_e.htm>; "Unreliable Evidence: Forensic Hair Analysis." *CBC News: Disclosure*. 26 Nov. 2003. Accessed 3 Dec. 2003 <www.cbc.ca/disclosure/archives/031126_evidence/hair.html>.

Your Perspective

1. Describe the potential challenges to eyewitness identification.
2. In what ways is new technology reducing the margin of error in the criminal justice system?
3. Should police officers be allowed to use a warrant to seize DNA samples from suspected criminals? Justify your opinion.

Confirm Your Understanding

1. Explain the significance of the burden of proof in a criminal trial.
2. In your own words, explain the significance of the presumption of innocence in Canada's criminal justice system.
3. Of what value is disclosure to the defence in a criminal trial?
4. What role does the judge play in the criminal justice system, and what constraints are placed on his or her duties?
5. Distinguish between the role of a Crown prosecutor and that of a defence lawyer.
6. How is the opportunity for bias reduced in the jury selection process?
7. Distinguish among the various types of evidence.
8. Describe how the testimony of an expert witness is used during a trial.
9. Explain the reasons for using the *voir dire* procedure in the criminal trial process.
10. Identify and explain the types of objections lawyers can make during the criminal trial process.

Miscarriage of Justice

To undertake an examination of the miscarriage of justice is to assume that there is some universal notion of justice. To some, justice may mean a verdict that renders to an accused what is due him or her. To others, justice may mean the protection of procedural rights. If the aim of a properly functioning criminal justice system is to achieve just results, then the degree of society's satisfaction with the system could be measured by the number of cases that have resulted in convictions or the number of cases in which all procedural rights have been protected. In an ideal system, it could be argued that justice is served when the guilty are convicted and the innocent go free. While the vast majority of cases in Canada's criminal justice system conclude with the proper verdict, there are still those that have eluded justice. A miscarriage of justice is considered to have occurred when innocent people are wrongly convicted or when guilty people have confessed to a crime and then walked away because of rights violations or procedural technicalities. In both situations, the credibility of the criminal justice system is weakened.

Canada's criminal justice system has not been immune to claims of injustice regarding wrongful convictions. In fact, the names Marshall, Morin, Milgaard, and Sophonow have become synonymous with the phrase "miscarriage of justice." All of these individuals were wrongly convicted for murder and subsequently released after having served many years in prison.

The case of Donald Marshall, Jr. (see Figure 9.12 in Chapter 9 on p. 291) was the first case in Canada to receive notable public attention regarding what can go wrong in the judicial system. Marshall, a Mi'kmaq from Nova Scotia, was wrongly convicted in the 1971 stabbing death of Sandy Seale. Marshall served 11 years of a life sentence in prison, yet always maintained his innocence. He was released when further investigation revealed that Roy Ebsary had actually committed the murder. An acquittal was entered in 1983, and in 1984,

Marshall was initially awarded a compensation package of $270 000, $100 000 of which was used to pay legal expenses.

A 1990 Royal Commission inquiry into Donald Marshall's conviction pointed out procedural problems. In addition to false testimonies and improper investigations, the case was also characterized by racism, which ultimately led to the wrongful conviction. In conjunction with the inquiry, Justice Gregory Evans reviewed Marshall's initial compensation package and subsequently ordered the lump sum payment of $200 000 in addition to a monthly annuity to be paid out over the course of Marshall's life.

Another miscarriage of justice involved Guy Paul Morin, who was charged with the murder of his 9-year-old neighbour, Christine Jessop. Morin was sentenced to life imprisonment in 1992, but in 1995, DNA evidence substantiated Morin's claims of innocence. A subsequent inquiry pointed to systemic problems in the criminal justice system,

FIGURE 10.14 A police officer carefully collects evidence from a crime scene. Why is the collection, preservation, labelling, packaging, and storing of evidence important in the criminal investigation process?

The Wrongful Conviction of Guy Paul Morin

Public hearings in the Guy Paul Morin inquiry began in February 1997 and lasted 146 days. During the trial, 120 witnesses were called and over 100 000 pages of documentation were considered, including trial transcripts and papers filed with the courts. "The Commission on Proceedings Involving Guy Paul Morin" investigated how an innocent person could be convicted and made recommendations to prevent further miscarriages of justice. An excerpt from the conclusion of the Honourable Fred Kaufman's report follows:

This Report ends where it started. An innocent person was convicted of a heinous crime he did not commit. Science helped convict him. Science exonerated him.

We will never know if Guy Paul Morin would ever have been exonerated had DNA results not been available. One can expect that there are other innocent persons, swept up in the criminal process, for whom DNA results are unavailable.

The case of Guy Paul Morin is not an aberration. By that, I do not mean that I can quantify the number of similar cases in Ontario or elsewhere, or that I can pass upon the frequency with which innocent persons are convicted in this province. We do not know. What I mean is that the causes of Mr. Morin's conviction are rooted in systemic problems, as well as the failings of individuals. It is no coincidence that the same systemic problems are those identified in wrongful convictions in other jurisdictions worldwide. It is

these systemic issues that must be addressed in the future. As to individual failings, it is to be hoped that they can be prevented by the revelation of what happened in Guy Paul Morin's case and by education as to the causes of wrongful convictions.

My conclusions should not be taken as a cynical or pessimistic view of the administration of criminal justice in Ontario. On the contrary, many aspects of Ontario's system of justice compare favourably to other jurisdictions. Most of its participants, police, forensic experts, Crown and defence counsel and the judiciary perform their roles with quiet distinction. These participants are justifiably proud of their roles in the administration of justice, and the roles performed by their colleagues. It is understandable, then, that a Report which focuses on systemic inadequacies may be viewed by some of them with dismay, if not frustration.

As several Crown counsel told me during the Inquiry, prosecuting someone who turns out to be innocent is a Crown attorney's "worst nightmare." I accept that. I also accept that no Crown counsel involved in this case, and no police officer involved in this case, ever intended to convict an innocent person. Although I have sometimes described the human failings that led to the conviction of Guy Paul Morin in very critical language, many of the failings which I have identified represent serious errors in judgment, often resulting from lack of objectivity, rather than outright malevolence.

> The challenge for all participants in the administration of justice in Ontario will be to draw upon this experience and learn from it.

SOURCE: Kaufman, Fred. "The Commission on Proceedings Involving Guy Paul Morin: Executive Summary and Recommendations." Ontario Ministry of the Attorney General, Queen's Printer for Ontario, 1998: 2, 43–44.

Form Your Questions

"The Commission on Proceedings Involving Guy Paul Morin" raises many questions. For example, what systemic problems exist in the criminal justice system that have led to wrongful convictions? Develop three possible questions that you would ask to further clarify the issue. Share your questions with the rest of the class, and discuss possible answers or solutions.

including flawed investigations, errors made by the Centre of Forensic Sciences, and false testimony provided by jailhouse informants. Morin was subsequently awarded a compensation package of $1.25 million.

Another prominent case involving wrongful conviction occurred in 1969 when David Milgaard was arrested and charged with the rape and stabbing death of Saskatchewan nursing assistant Gail Miller. Despite Milgaard's claim of innocence, he was convicted and sentenced to life imprisonment in 1970. Milgaard served almost 23 years in jail for the murder. During the time of his imprisonment, Milgaard appealed his conviction, and there was even a **reference** (a procedure by which the government of Canada refers an important legal or factual question to the Supreme Court of Canada for the court to hear and consider) regarding his trial and the alleged miscarriage of justice. Despite these processes, the courts maintained that there had been no miscarriage of justice and that a fair trial had taken place. However, in 1997, new evidence in the form of a DNA profile cast doubt on the reliability of Milgaard's conviction and implicated another with the murder. Larry Fisher, a known criminal who had committed similar crimes, matched a DNA profile from the blood found on the victim's underwear. Fisher

was found guilty of the offence in 2000 and sentenced to life imprisonment with parole eligibility after 10 years. On September 29, 2003, Fisher lost his bid to have the conviction overturned, and the next day the Saskatchewan government announced that a judicial inquiry would take place into Milgaard's wrongful conviction. The investigation would aim to determine how an innocent man went to jail for 23 years of his life. Milgaard had already been granted a compensation package of $10 million in 1999, the largest compensation package in Canadian history. In February 2004, Alberta Justice Edward MacCallum was appointed to head the public inquiry by the Saskatchewan government into the wrongful conviction of David Milgaard.

Thomas Sophonow was wrongfully convicted of the 1981 murder of Barbara Stoppel. He was tried three times and spent four years in prison before the Manitoba Court of Appeal overturned his conviction. In June 2000, DNA evidence cleared Sophonow of the murder. In the subsequent inquiry into the wrongful conviction, it was determined that the Crown had not disclosed significant and important information to the defence, including mistaken identifications made by the prime eyewitness. The failure to disclose key information seriously affected the fairness of the trial. The Commission of Inquiry stated, "Clearly, the failures resulted from the erroneous acts of Crown Counsel and the police, some of which were deliberate and some were inadvertent" ("The Inquiry Regarding Thomas Sophonow: Compensation—Failure to Disclose…").

Under the recommendations of the Commission of Inquiry, Sophonow received a compensation award of $2.6 million for the miscarriage of justice. The responsibility for paying the compensation was divided among the federal government, the Manitoba government, and the Winnipeg municipal government, in the amounts of 10 percent, 40 percent, and 50 percent, respectively. In considering the entitlement to such a compensation award, the inquiry judge, Justice Peter Cory, commented, "Thomas Sophonow has been deprived of his liberty; he has suffered irreparable damage to his reputation by being branded as a murderer; and he has suffered and will continue to suffer from the symptoms flowing from a post-traumatic stress disorder. In my opinion, there can be no doubt of his entitlement to compensation."

Determining compensation for those who have been wrongfully convicted is a difficult task and requires the careful consideration of many factors. In "The Inquiry Regarding Thomas Sophonow," Justice Cory borrowed from the factors identified in the 1990 Donald Marshall, Jr., Commission of Inquiry and considered such issues as losses of liberty, reputation, enjoyment of life, and civil rights. He also weighed the degree of humiliation and disgrace, and the pain and suffering, and even considered the danger of physical assaults while in prison to be a factor in determining compensation. In his recommendation regarding compensation for Sophonow, Justice Cory stated:

> To live in prison is to swim with sharks and to walk with tigers. Prisoners live in an atmosphere of high tension and resulting stress. There is the ever-present danger of physical attack. The constant threat of violence is palpable in a penitentiary setting. This is particularly true of a maximum-security facility but often equally true of overcrowded, understaffed remand centres. ("The Inquiry Regarding Thomas Sophonow: Compensation—Danger of Physical Assaults")

Wrongful convictions offend both our moral and legal sense of justice. The public outrage that arises when the innocent are convicted and the guilty go free cannot be overemphasized. Society will not abide any margin of error in this area, especially when even the slightest error can destroy so many lives. Criminal investigators and those involved in the legal profession must therefore be extremely careful to avoid some of the more common pitfalls that can lead to wrongful convictions. According to criminology professors Thomas Gabor and Julian Roberts, these include mistakes made in eyewitness identification, perjury, incompetence in the legal defence, false confessions, excessive eagerness on the part of police or prosecutors to convict, pressure by the community, the system of plea bargaining, and errors by medical or forensic experts. All of these factors must be examined in order to restore the

FIGURE 10.15 This 485-cell penitentiary in Kingston, Ontario, has been home to many convicted criminals. What if a wrongful conviction occurred and an innocent person were deprived of his or her liberty? What amount of money would you consider to be adequate compensation for years of freedom lost while in prison?

public's faith and confidence in the criminal justice system.

Other controversial miscarriage-of-justice cases can occur when a guilty person walks free based on procedural technicalities. Assume that an accused has been searched, arrested, and charged for a crime and then confesses to the crime, but due to a violation of rights, the evidence is excluded and the case is thrown out. *R. v. Hebert* and *R. v. Manninen*, which you read about earlier in this chapter (see pp. 305 and 303, respectively), are two such cases in which the evidence was excluded. In *R. v. Hebert,* the accused was acquitted. In *R. v. Manninen,* a new trial was ordered.

Although allowing a guilty person to go free due to a technicality is an intolerable prospect to most law-abiding citizens, consider the reverse. With no procedural safeguards to uphold the rights of citizens, each one of us would be subject to unreasonable searches, arbitrary detentions, and lack of access to legal counsel upon arrest. What is worse, we would be presumed guilty until proven innocent. The fact is that justice would also be denied in such circumstances.

The criminal justice system works to protect society and to ensure the proper administration of justice. In the majority of cases, the guilty are convicted and the innocent go free. But the enemy of the criminal justice system is complacency, which can lead to wrongful convictions. Professionals must perform their work with integrity and care so that errors do not result in a miscarriage of justice.

VIEWPOINTS: Roadside Drug Tests

The following excerpt from an October 2003 *Globe and Mail* article focuses on a government plan to allow roadside drug tests. Read the following excerpt and then consider the resolution for debate.

Ottawa is preparing to change the law as early as next year to allow police officers to test motorists suspected of driving under the influence of drugs.

"It's in the works," said Patrick Charette, a Justice Department spokesman. "Ideally, we'd like to be able to proceed with a bill in the New Year."

The federal government released a consultation paper…outlining amended legislation that would allow police to take saliva, blood, perspiration and urine samples to determine whether a driver has drugs, including marijuana, in his or her system.

In the document, the Justice Department outlined several options to allow police to administer the tests and gather evidence for possible criminal charges.

The proposed changes would create a legal drug limit, allow the collection of such samples and impose penalties for refusal to comply.

Under present laws, police officers can ask drivers only whether they have used drugs; they cannot administer a test.

Officers rely on symptoms of impairment such as driving behaviour and witness testimony to prosecute motorists.

"If officers do not have specific drug assessment training, this task can be nearly impossible," the document states.

Although it's illegal in Canada to drive while impaired by drugs or alcohol, no quick roadside test exists for drug use. Alcohol consumption can be measured by breath analysis.

The options outlined in the document would allow police officers to collect samples after concluding other sobriety tests, including eye examinations and physical examinations to search for injection sites.

"Based upon a reasonable suspicion of a drug in the body, a peace officer could be authorized to demand a saliva or sweat sample at road site," the document states....

SOURCE: Lunman, Kim. "Ottawa Plans to Let Police Conduct Roadside Drug Tests." *The Globe and Mail* 23 Oct. 2003: A6.

Up for Debate

Debate the following resolution: Be it resolved that roadside drug tests should be considered a violation of privacy and not be allowed.

CONFIRM YOUR UNDERSTANDING

1. Explain two types of situations that could lead to a miscarriage of justice in the criminal justice system.
2. a) What factors would lead to wrongful convictions and the miscarriage of justice?
   b) How could DNA technology assist in the reduction of wrongful conviction claims?
3. a) Identify some of the factors considered in determining the extent of a compensation package for those who are wrongly convicted.
   b) Assume you were awarding a compensation package in the David Milgaard case. Which factor(s) would you consider the most important? Justify your choice.

In Closing

Procedural safeguards are necessary in order to ensure the public's confidence in our justice system and to prevent grave injustices from occurring. Proper criminal investigation, search and seizure, arrest, detention, and interrogation procedures should help to ensure that evidence will withstand close examination by the court and not be declared inadmissible. The rights of the accused must be protected at all stages of the criminal trial process in order to maintain the integrity of our criminal justice system. Both society and technology are continually evolving.

As society evolves, with changing morals and values, some actions may be declared criminal while others might be decriminalized. Judges will be required to interpret new laws and apply them to the facts in a criminal trial. In addition, as technology changes, judges will be required to consider new scientific advancements as they rule on the admissibility of evidence. The challenge for legal professionals in the criminal justice system will be to keep up with the ever-increasing pace of change as they pursue the quest for justice.

CHAPTER ACTIVITIES

Extend Your Legal Knowledge

1. Explain what constitutes a reasonable search and seizure, and provide examples of unreasonable search and seizure.
2. Distinguish between arrest and detention, and explain the corresponding rights.
3. Explain what is meant by the "burden of proof" in a criminal trial.
4. Describe the presumption of innocence, and illustrate its importance to the criminal justice system.

Think About the Law

5. What restrictions are there on police powers of arrest?
6. Outline the risks involved in using jail informants to secure confessions.
7. Which do you consider a greater miscarriage of justice, when an innocent person is wrongly convicted or when a guilty person is freed on the basis of a technicality? Justify your choice.
8. As a judge, what factors would you consider in deciding on the admissibility of evidence?
9. In what ways do you think DNA technology could revolutionize issues involving evidence in the criminal justice system?
10. Police have used helicopters and infrared technology to detect unusual heat emissions from residential homes. This evidence is then used as the basis for establishing the reasonable and probable grounds necessary for a search warrant in order to determine if a resident is growing hydroponic drugs.
    a) How would you argue that the use of this technology is an unreasonable search and seizure?
    b) How would you argue that the search technique is justifiable?
11. Residential growing operations involving marijuana have been steadily increasing in recent years. In the case of *R. v. Plant*, [1993] 3 S.C.R. 281, when the police had received a tip about an in-home marijuana-growing operation, the residence of Robert Scott Plant came under suspicion. The police gained access to utility records and discovered that the home in question had four times the electrical consumption of similar houses in the area. The police used the electricity usage records to obtain a search warrant. Did the police use of the utility records amount to an unreasonable search and seizure? Explain the reasons for your decision.
12. Should police have expanded powers to search in the case of a missing child? Support your opinion.

Communicate About the Law

13. Select a case in which the principles of justice have been violated, and write a two-page report outlining the circumstances surrounding the wrongful conviction. Choose from the following miscarriage-of-justice cases: Donald Marshall, Jr., Guy Paul Morin, David Milgaard, Gregory Parsons, Thomas Sophonow, Steven Truscott, James Driskell, Romeo Phillion, or another individual who has been wrongfully convicted.
14. Prepare an argument against the death penalty using cases of wrongful conviction to support your reasoning.
15. What abuses might take place in our criminal justice system if an accused had no rights protections under the *Charter*? What fundamental concerns would you have about the proper administration of justice? Explain by providing examples.
16. Examine the principles that promote the fair treatment of victims within the criminal justice system (see Figure 10.11, p. 316). How might the criminal justice system better address the needs of victims?

Apply the Law

17. In the case of *R. v. M. (M.R.)*, [1998] 3 S.C.R. 393, a vice-principal of a Nova Scotia junior high

school was informed that one of his students was going to sell drugs at a dance. The vice-principal questioned the student and the student's friend about possession of drugs and announced he was going to search them. A plainclothes RCMP constable was also present but did not participate in the search. The vice-principal proceeded to conduct the search and found a bag of marijuana. The drug evidence was handed to the constable, and the accused was arrested and read his rights to counsel. The student's locker was then searched, but no drugs were found. The trial judge held that the search by the vice-principal was unreasonable and violated the rights of the accused. The Court of Appeal of Nova Scotia allowed the appeal and ordered a new trial. On appeal to the Supreme Court of Canada, the court held that the reasonable expectation of privacy is lower for a school due to the need to provide a safe environment for students and deemed the search legal.

a) Prepare an argument that would support a claim of unreasonable search and seizure and the exclusion of the evidence.

b) Prepare an argument that would justify the search as reasonable.

18. In the case of *R. v. Edwards*, [1996] 1 S.C.R. 128, the accused, Calhoun Edwards, was charged with possession of a narcotic for the purposes of trafficking. Police officers had convinced Edwards's girlfriend to allow them to search her apartment. She allowed the police into her apartment, and they found crack cocaine belonging to Edwards. The police arrested Edwards, impounded his vehicle, and took his cell phone. They intercepted phone calls involving requests for drugs. As Edwards's girlfriend had not been read her rights to counsel under s. 10(b) of the *Charter*, the court held that her rights had been violated. Edwards argued that his reasonable expectation of privacy was also violated.

a) Prepare an argument that would support a claim of unreasonable search and seizure and the exclusion of the evidence.

b) Prepare an argument that the search was reasonable and that the conviction should be upheld.

BIBLIOGRAPHY

Barnhorst, Sherrie. *Criminal Law and the Canadian Criminal Code.* 3rd ed. Toronto: McGraw-Hill Ryerson Limited, 1996.

Brennan, Richard. "Police Complaints System Will Face a Review." *Toronto Star* 3 Nov. 2003: A8.

Canadian Legal Information Institute. Accessed Oct.–Dec. 2003 <www.canlii.org>.

Centre of Forensic Sciences, Public Safety Division. *Laboratory Guide for the Investigator.* 5th ed. Toronto: Ministry of the Solicitor General and Correctional Services, 1997.

Chua, June. "Indepth: James Driskell." *CBC News Online.* 25 Nov. 2003. Accessed 26 Nov. 2003 <www.cbc.ca/news/background/driskell/>.

Department of Justice Canada. Accessed Nov.–Dec. 2003 <www.canada.justice.gc.ca/en/index.html>.

———. "Canadian Statement of Basic Principles of Justice for Victims of Crime, 2003." Accessed 1 Dec. 2003 <www.canada.justice.gc.ca/en/ps/voc/publications/03/basic_prin.html>.

Gabor, Thomas, and Julian Roberts. "How the Innocent End Up Behind Bars." *Toronto Star* 12 Jan. 1992.

Greenspan, Edward L. "The Role of the Defence Counsel in Canadian Society." The Empire Club Addresses. 19 Nov. 1987. Accessed 21 Feb. 2004 <www.empireclubfoundation.com/details.asp? SpeechID=641&FT=yes>.

Jaimet, Kate. "Court Upholds Police Right to Seize DNA." *National Post* 1 Nov. 2003: A4.

Kaufman, Fred. "The Commission on Proceedings Involving Guy Paul Morin: Executive Summary and Recommendations." Ontario Ministry of the Attorney General. Toronto: Queen's Printer for Ontario, 1998.

Lunman, Kim. "Ottawa Plans to Let Police Conduct Roadside Drug Tests." *The Globe and Mail* 23 Oct. 2003: A6.

Manitoba Justice. "The Inquiry Regarding Thomas Sophonow: Compensation—Danger of Physical Assaults." Accessed 26 Nov. 2003 <www.gov. mb.ca/justice/sophonow/compensation/dangerof. html>.

———. "The Inquiry Regarding Thomas Sophonow: Compensation—Entitlement to Compensation." Accessed 26 Nov. 2003 <www.gov.mb.ca/ justice/sophonow/compensation/entitlement.html>.

———. "The Inquiry Regarding Thomas Sophonow: Compensation—Failure to Disclose Matters Which Should Have Been Disclosed to Defence Counsel." Accessed 26 Nov. 2003 <www.gov.mb. ca/justice/sophonow/compensation/failure.html>.

———. "The Inquiry Regarding Thomas Sophonow: Jailhouse Informants, Their Unreliability and the Importance of Complete Crown Disclosure Pertaining to Them." Accessed 26 Nov. 2003 <www.gov.mb.ca/justice/sophonow/ jailhouse/index.html>.

———. "The Inquiry Regarding Thomas Sophonow: The Role of the Trial Judge." Accessed 26 Nov. 2003 <www.gov.mb.ca/justice/sophonow/judge/ index.html>.

McCarten, James. "Hadley Jury Urges Action on Domestic Violence." Canadian Press. *Toronto Star* 8 Feb. 2002. Accessed 13 Dec. 2003 <http:// fact.on.ca/news/news0202/ts020208.htm>.

Ministry of the Attorney General of Ontario: 3.01—Court Services. *2003 Annual Report of the Office of the Provincial Auditor of Ontario. Provincial Auditor's Report.* Accessed 20 Feb. 2004 <www.auditor. on.ca/english/reports/en03/301en03.pdf>.

National DNA Data Bank. Accessed 13 Dec. 2003 <http://nddb-bndg.org/main_e.htm>.

Ontario Civilian Commission on Police Services. Accessed 11 Dec. 2003 <www.occps.ca/englishwebsite/ aboutoccps/4membersofcommission.asp>.

Special Investigations Unit. Accessed 11 Dec. 2003 <www.siu.on.ca/sitemap.asp>.

Tyler, Tracey. "Judge Blasts Pre-Trial Custody System." *Toronto Star* 1 Nov. 2003: A12.

"Unreliable Evidence: Forensic Hair Analysis." *CBC News: Disclosure.* 26 Nov. 2003. Accessed 3 Dec. 2003 <http://www.cbc.ca/disclosure/archives/ 031126_evidence/hair.html>.

Chapter 11

DEFENCES AND SENTENCING

LEARNING EXPECTATIONS

After reading this chapter, you will be able to:

- outline legally acceptable defences to criminal conduct and evaluate some of the more controversial defences

- describe and evaluate the types and purposes of different sentences imposed in criminal law

- analyze situations in Canadian law in which principles of justice conflict (e.g., victims' rights versus the rights of the accused)

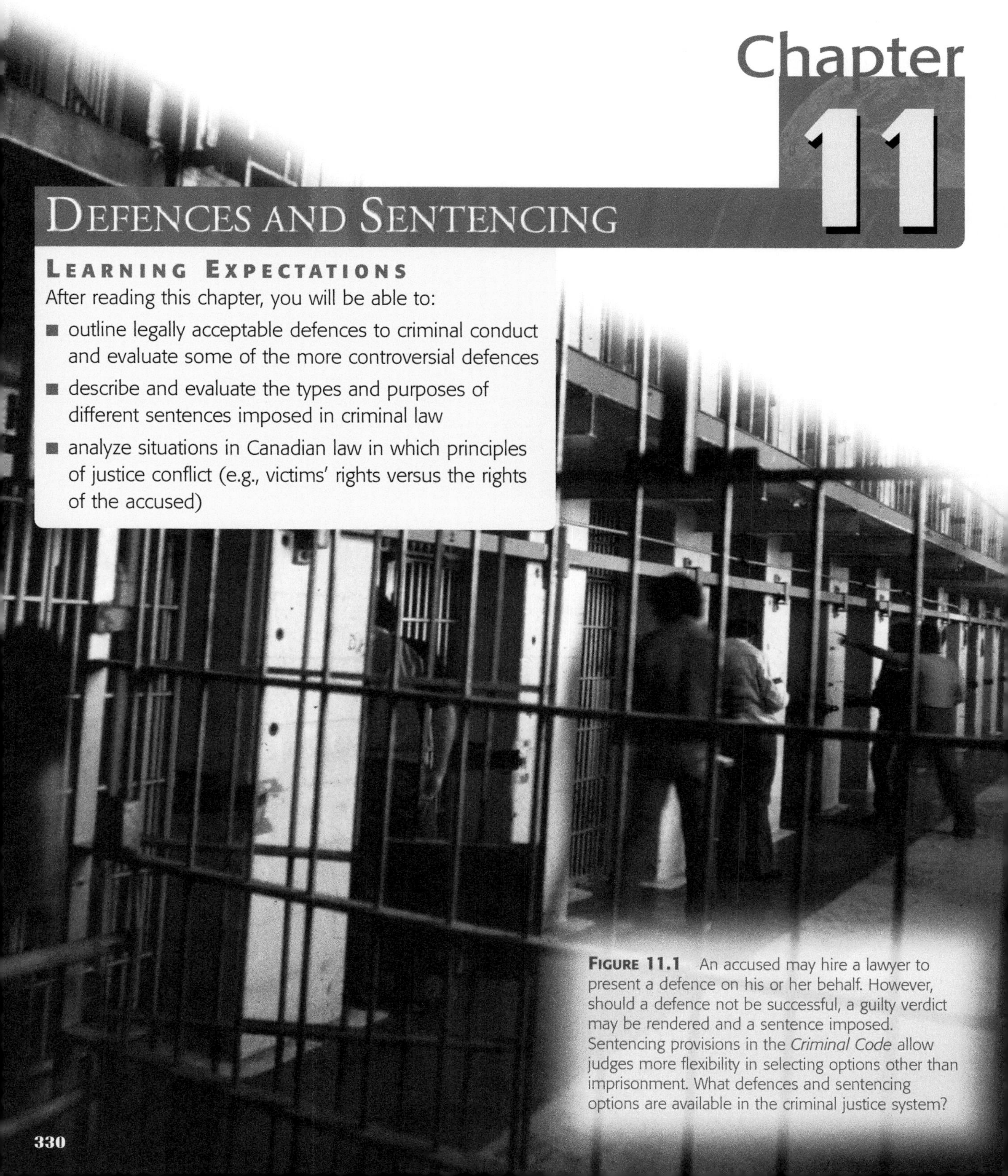

FIGURE 11.1 An accused may hire a lawyer to present a defence on his or her behalf. However, should a defence not be successful, a guilty verdict may be rendered and a sentence imposed. Sentencing provisions in the *Criminal Code* allow judges more flexibility in selecting options other than imprisonment. What defences and sentencing options are available in the criminal justice system?

> *Nothing is easier than to denounce the evil doer; nothing is more difficult than to understand him.*
>
> —Fyodor Dostoevsky, Russian Author (1821–1881)

■ INTRODUCTION ■

The Canadian legal system is based on the adversarial model of justice. Under this model, it is the responsibility of the Crown to prove the guilt of the accused. In theory, the accused does not have to offer any defence, but in practice, most people accused of crimes wish to absolve themselves of criminal responsibility. In Canada, there are a number of legitimate defences, but if they fail and a guilty verdict is rendered, the judge must then consider the sentence to impose on the offender. Sometimes the community reacts with acceptance to the sentence imposed, while other times the public may express shock or outrage at its perceived severity or leniency.

The process of determining a sentence can be challenging. In order to determine a just and appropriate sentence, a judge must not only consider the circumstances surrounding the crime, the character and background of the offender, and the harm done to the victim, but also sentencing objectives and principles.

This chapter will cover the common, legally accepted defences, as well as introduce you to some of the more controversial defences that pose a challenge for the Canadian legal system. It will also highlight the purpose and principles of sentencing. Further, it will detail various sentencing options available to a judge and also examine the role of the victim in the sentencing process.

Criminal Defences

The right to a criminal defence is one of our fundamental rights, known in Latin as *audi alterum partem*, meaning "to hear the other side," and can be traced back to British common law. Although the *Criminal Code* defines some defences available to the accused, it does not define them all. Many defences are found in case law and came into being as a result of judicial decisions, such as the **battered woman syndrome** defence used in the *R. v. Lavallee* case (p. 48). Between the *Code* and case law, the accused has a variety of lawful excuses or justifi-cations for escaping criminal responsibility even when there is overwhelming evidence against him or her. The statements "I didn't know it was a crime"; "I had no choice, it was me or him"; "I just couldn't take it anymore"; "I was drunk when it happened"; and, "I was sleeping when it happened," reflect the legally accepted defences of mistake of law, self-defence, provocation, intoxication, and sleepwalking. Other acceptable defences include mistake of fact, mental disorder, consent, duress, necessity, and entrapment.

Mistake of Fact

The defence of **mistake of fact** depends on the accused not having the *mens rea*, or guilty mind, necessary for the particular offence. For example, suppose a person was growing a plant in his or her garden that, unbeknownst to him or her, turned out to be marijuana. The Crown can charge the person with possession of marijuana; however, to convict, the Crown must prove that the accused knew the plant was marijuana. The accused can claim a defence of mistake of fact if he or she honestly believed that the plant was a harmless substance and not an illegal drug. The Crown cannot establish a fault element if the accused honestly, though not necessarily reasonably, was mistaken about whether the plant was marijuana.

The courts do not accept this defence under all circumstances, however. They have been less willing to apply this logic when an accused makes a mistake as to the nature of an illegal drug. For example, in the case of *R. v. Burgess*, [1970] 3 C.C.C. 268 (Ont. C.A.) the accused was convicted of possession of opium even though he thought the drug was hashish. Generally the accused can escape **culpability**, or criminal responsibility, if he or she can show: (a) the mistake was an honest one, and (b) no offence would have been committed had the circumstances been as the accused believed them to be. Thus, in *R. v. Burgess* the defence of mistake of fact failed because the accused was still knowingly in possession of a controlled or illegal substance, just not the one he thought he had.

Prior to the 1990s, mistake of fact was also used as a defence in sexual assault cases involving the issue of consent. In *R. v. Pappajohn*, [1980] 52 C.C.C. (2d) 481 (S.C.C.) a female real estate agent was sexually assaulted by a client. The accused claimed that since the woman had enjoyed an evening of drinking with him and had willingly returned to his home afterwards, he believed the sex was consensual. The Supreme Court held that the accused had a defence of an honest, but not necessarily reasonable, mistake that the complainant consented. This was a controversial decision, and in later cases the Supreme Court limited the defence by arguing that mistake of fact must be based on more than the mere assertion by the accused of a mistaken belief.

In 1992 the offence of sexual assault was amended to restrict the mistake of fact defence with regard to consent. Section 273.2 of the *Criminal Code* now states that the accused's belief that the complainant consented is not a defence if (a) it arose from the accused's (i) self-induced intoxication, or (ii) recklessness or wilful blindness, or (b) the accused did not take reasonable steps, in the circumstances known to the accused at the time, to ascertain that the complainant was consenting. If the Pappajohn case were being decided under these restrictions, it is unlikely that the accused would have been able to raise this defence at all.

Generally a mistake of fact assumes that the mistake must be honest and reasonable, but for some offences, such as absolute liability offences, even a reasonable mistake of fact could not be used as a defence. **Absolute liability** offences are those that require only an *actus reus* (illegal act) and not a *mens rea* (guilty mind), and include most regulatory offences. For example, you could not use a faulty speedometer to argue an honest, though mistaken, belief that you were driving within the speed limit.

Mistake of Law

Section 19 of the *Criminal Code* states: "Ignorance of the law by a person who commits an offence is not an excuse for committing an offence." Although people are expected to know the law, because of the enormous number of laws the court may actually permit the defence of **mistake of law** in certain circumstances. One such circumstance is if the accused relied upon incorrect legal advice from a government official. In *R. v. Baum and Baum* (1994), 32 C.R. (4th) 176 Ont. Ct. Gen. Div., a husband and wife were charged with operating a business out of their home contrary to the municipal bylaws. Mr. Baum had checked with the city planner to make sure it was legal to run the business out of his home, and the planner assured him that it was. In this case, the courts acquitted the Baums on the basis that the advice given by the city planner was reasonable and the law involved was complex.

Intoxication

It can be argued logically that a person who committed a crime while intoxicated from alcohol or drugs may not have been able to form criminal intent, or *mens rea*. Yet it is difficult to accept that an accused who commits a crime while intoxicated is morally innocent. This difficulty has been reflected not only in the attitude of the public toward the defence of **intoxication**, but also in the ambiguity of the courts.

The courts have attempted to limit the defence of intoxication by classifying crimes into those requiring general or specific intent. **General intent** requires that the accused intended to commit a criminal act but the prosecution need not prove that the accused intended all the harm that may have resulted from that act. For example, an accused may have intended to commit an assault but didn't intend to kill; nevertheless the victim died. **Specific intent** means having a deliberate aim to commit a particular offence, in addition to having the initial general intent to break the law. The type of intent required for a crime depends on how the crime is defined in the *Criminal Code*.

Since offences such as murder, theft, robbery, and aiding and abetting require a specific intent on the part of an accused, intoxication could be used as a defence. Other crimes such as common assault or manslaughter have been considered general intent offences and, therefore, intoxication could not be used as a defence. For example, if an accused is charged with murder and the evidence of intoxication raises reasonable doubt about whether the accused would have been able to form the intent to plan a murder, the accused may still be convicted of the general intent offence of manslaughter. However, such distinctions have proved confusing, and the courts seem to be moving toward a more logical, though

"My boy, ignorance of the law is no excuse for the losing barrister not to collect his fee."

FIGURE 11.2 What do you think would happen if the courts were much more lenient in allowing the defence of mistake of law?

perhaps more morally objectionable, argument that intoxication raises doubts as to the voluntary nature of any criminal conduct.

The very controversial case of *R. v. Daviault*, [1994] 3 S.C.R. 63, established that the defence of intoxication would apply only if the accused was *extremely* intoxicated. The Supreme Court ordered a new trial for Mr. Daviault, who was initially charged with sexually assaulting an elderly woman with a disability after consuming a large quantity of alcohol. In this case, the court required the accused to prove extreme intoxication as a defence to a general intent crime, based on a **balance of probabilities**—the likelihood that the defence is true. Justice Cory argued:

[T]hose who are a "little" drunk can readily form the requisite mental element to commit the offence. The alcohol-induced relaxation of both inhibitions and socially unacceptable behaviour has never been accepted as a factor or excuse in determining whether the accused possessed the requisite *mens rea*. Given the minimal nature of the mental element required for crimes of general intent, even those who are significantly drunk will usually be able to form the requisite *mens rea* and will be found to have acted voluntarily…

In his dissent, Justice Sopinka argued that those who voluntarily became intoxicated "deserved to be punished for their crimes" because their condition was voluntary and avoidable. Many people agreed with Sopinka, and in response to public outcry, the government amended the *Criminal Code*. Section 33.1 (1) and (2) of the *Criminal Code* now says that an accused cannot use intoxication as a defence for harming another person because:

> A person departs markedly from the standard of reasonable care generally recognized in Canadian society and is thereby criminally at fault where the person, while in a state of self-induced intoxication that renders the person unaware of, or incapable of consciously controlling, their behaviour, voluntarily or involuntarily interferes or threatens to interfere with the bodily integrity of another person.

The Daviault case and the government's response did not make the law regarding intoxication any less controversial or complex. The public, law-makers, and the courts still seem conflicted as to whether persons who commit serious crimes while intoxicated should be treated as not criminally responsible.

Mental Disorder

The defence of intoxication is particularly controversial because intoxication is self-induced, but persons suffering from a mental disorder are not responsible for causing their illness. Nevertheless, the defence of mental disorder is also complex and controversial.

Our laws dealing with mental disorder are derived from **M'Naghten's rules**. In 1843 Daniel

M'Naghten was found not guilty by reason of insanity for the murder of the secretary to then British Prime Minister, Robert Peel. M'Naghten suffered from delusions of persecution from the government. At that time, the House of Lords in Britain established the insanity defence, arguing that an accused could be found not guilty by reason of insanity if it was "clearly proved that, at the time of committing the act, the party accused was labouring under such a defect of reason, from disease of the mind, as not to know the nature and quality of the act he was doing" [M'Naghten's Case (1884), 8 E.R. 718 (House of Lords]. M'Naghten's rules were then incorporated, with some modifications, into our own *Criminal Code* as Section 16 (1), the insanity defence. This section was amended in 1992 and the insanity defence was renamed the **mental disorder defence** and the verdict "not guilty by reason of insanity" was changed to "not criminally responsible by reason of mental disorder."

There is a difference between the medical interpretation of a mental disorder and the legal interpretation. To be found not guilty by reason of a mental disorder, s. 16 of the *Criminal Code* states an accused must not only prove that he or she is suffering from a mental disorder, but also that the condition is of such severity that the person is "incapable of appreciating the nature and quality of the act." Canadian courts have stressed the significance of the word "appreciate" in this statement. It has been interpreted to mean that the accused not only had knowledge that the act was being committed, but also that he or she had the capacity to *measure and foresee* the consequences of the act. One test that can be applied is to ask if the accused would still commit the act if a police officer were standing by his or her side. For example, a psychopath may be mentally ill, but if he or she displays knowledge that an act is legally wrong, he or she would not be able to use the defence of mental disorder.

The second part of the mental disorder defence refers to the fact that the accused is "incapable of knowing that it is wrong." This statement is ambiguous because it does not make it clear whether an accused must not know that an act is *morally* wrong or *legally* wrong. In *R. v. Chaulk*, [1990] 3. S.C.R. 1303, the accused, two young boys, suffered from a psychosis that made them believe they had the power to rule the world and that killing was necessary. They believed they had the right to kill the victim because he was a "loser," although they knew that killing was wrong. The Supreme Court ruled that the accused could have an insanity defence if they were incapable of knowing that the act was *morally wrong* even if they were capable of knowing the act was *legally wrong.*

This decision raised the question of whether persons who had no moral conscience or whose value system differed from the norm could be found not criminally responsible for their acts. For example, could an offender who believed that the sexual assault of children was morally correct be found not guilty by reason of mental disorder? Judge Lamer, in the Chaulk decision, argued that this would not happen. He explained, "First, the incapacity to make moral judgments must be causally linked to a disease of the mind....Secondly, 'moral wrong' is not to be judged by the personal standards of the offender, but by his awareness that society regards the act as wrong…"

The mental disorder defence is not widely used in Canada for two main reasons. First, the law assumes that everyone is sane, thus the burden of proof lies with the defence to show, on a balance of probabilities, that their client is suffering from a disease of the mind that renders him or her incapable of "appreciating the nature and quality of the act." This argument can only

FIGURE 11.3 Diane Mitsuko Yano is led into court in Cranbrook, B.C., in November 1999. The Calgary mother was accused of drowning her two children, but was found not guilty by reason of a mental disorder in a one-day trial. What must the defence prove in order to secure a verdict of not guilty by reason of mental disorder?

be raised after the accused has been found guilty. Second, the insanity defence often becomes a battle between psychiatrists, with those for the defence arguing the accused is insane and the Crown's expert witnesses arguing the opposite. Psychiatrists attempt to provide an objective assessment using the *Diagnostic and Statistical Manual of Mental Disorders* (DSM-IV) to determine whether defendants are fit to stand trial, if they can understand criminal responsibility, and if they are a danger to themselves or others. However, the psychiatrists' testimonies are often conflicting and complex, and may be difficult for a jury to understand.

CONFIRM YOUR UNDERSTANDING

1. Explain the difference between mistake of fact and mistake of law. Provide an example to illustrate when an accused might be able to use each.

2. Identify three factors that prohibit using mistaken belief of consent as a defence to sexual assault.

3. Why can an accused not use mistake of fact for an absolute liability offence?

4. Explain the difference between specific and general intent offences.

Automatism

We have all experienced a mild form of automatism when we perform a routine task without thinking about our actions, such as brushing our teeth or tying a shoelace. In law, **automatism** refers to a state in which a person has no *conscious* control over his or her actions. Like the defences of intoxication and mental disorder, the defence of automatism applies to persons who commit criminal acts but who cannot be found criminally responsible because they were mentally impaired when the offence took place.

Automatism could be the result of a range of conditions, including hypnotism, sleepwalking, or having a brain tumor or epilepsy. *Non-insane automatism* means a mental disease did not cause the automatism; rather it was caused by some other temporary factor, such as a blow to the head, a severe psychological shock, or sleepwalking. In this case, the accused can be set free upon acquittal. *Insane automatism* falls under the defence of "mental disorder," and therefore even if the accused is acquitted, he or she may not be released into society.

In *R. v. Bleta*, [1965] 1 C.C.C.144 C.R. 193, the accused was charged with murder. During a fight, the accused either fell or was knocked down and struck his head on the sidewalk. The person he was fighting then walked away, but Bleta got up, followed him, and stabbed him with a knife. The accused argued that the blow to his head caused a state of automatism and he was therefore not criminally responsible for the attack. He was acquitted and the Crown appealed, but the Supreme Court of Canada upheld the acquittal and accepted the defence of automatism.

As you read in the *R. v. Parks* case in Chapter 9 (p. 276), the courts accepted the defence of automatism in this case of sleepwalking. In this controversial case, Mr. Parks was apparently sleepwalking when he drove 20 kilometres to his parents-in-law's home in the middle of the night, killed his mother-in-law, and seriously injured his father-in-law. His lawyers argued automatism, and brought in expert witnesses who testified that Mr. Parks did suffer from sleepwalking and that it was possible for him to commit such a crime while sleepwalking. Parks was acquitted and, although the Crown appealed arguing that the defence should have been mental disorder, the Supreme Court of Canada upheld the acquittal and the sleepwalking defence.

The Supreme Court arrived at the opposite decision in the equally controversial case of *R. v. Rabey*, [1980] 2 S.C.R. 513. The appellant, Rabey, was a 20-year-old university student who had feelings for a girl in his class. While snooping through her notebook, he found a letter she had written to a female friend in which she described the appellant as a "nothing." The appellant was deeply hurt. The next day he met the girl by chance as they walked across the university campus. During their conversation, the appellant asked the girl what she thought of him and she replied that he was a friend. The appellant suddenly struck the victim with a rock, which he had been carrying from geology class. He continued to strike her and began choking her before other students pulled him off. The defence introduced evidence to show that the appellant entered into a complete dissociative state during the conversation with the victim. This dissociative state was caused by the powerful emotional shock he had suffered when he read the letter. The appellant claimed the conversation the next day triggered the violent action.

Rabey was acquitted at trial and the Crown appealed to the Ontario Court of Appeal, which ordered a new trial saying that the defence should have been mental disorder, not automatism. However, before the new trial took place, a further appeal was made to the Supreme Court. The majority in the court decided that an accused would have a defence of non-insane automatism only if he or she went into an automatic state as a result of some extraordinary event, such as witnessing the death of a loved one. Rabey, who assaulted his fellow student simply because he discovered she had no romantic interest in him, could not have the defence of non-insane automatism. The judges argued that a person could not claim automatism because they were subject to "the ordinary stresses and disappointments of life, which are the common lot of mankind." However, the dissenting Supreme Court justice in this case, Judge Dickson, argued that the medical testimony showed that the accused did not suffer from any disease of the mind, and that his violence "was an isolated act" that he would be unlikely to repeat ever again.

The defence of automatism remains controversial. The general public may perceive it as a way for an accused to literally get away with murder. Meanwhile, the legal community must rely on the often-contradictory evidence of expert witnesses to determine whether the state of automatism actually existed at the time the accused committed the crime.

Self-Defence

The defences of intoxication, mental disorder, and automatism acknowledge that a crime has been committed but argue that, due to a lack of criminal intent, the accused should not be punished for the crime. The defence of **self-defence**, however, offers justification for the alleged criminal act. The accused is acknowledged as having the requisite *mens rea*, but it is believed that his or her actions were justified on the grounds that people have the right to defend themselves, defend their property, and defend others. This would seem to be a simple premise, yet the rules governing self-defence are very complex.

The law attempts to define the various circumstances in which an accused might act in self-defence. For example, the basic elements of all self-defence claims are twofold: (a) the accused believed he or she was about to be physically harmed, and (b) the accused used only the force required to avoid the threatened harm. If an accused uses more force than necessary, he or she may not have a defence. The *Criminal Code* sets out a person's criminal responsibility for excessive force in s. 26: "Everyone who is authorized by law to use force is criminally responsible for any excess thereof according to the nature and quality of the act that constitutes the excess." Depending on the circumstances, therefore, people who use excessive force to defend themselves may find themselves charged with assault or even murder.

The law also draws distinctions between those who use self-defence against an unprovoked assault and those who provoke the assault by, for example, taunting or assaulting the other person. The *Code* reads:

Section 34. (1) Everyone who is unlawfully assaulted without having provoked the assault is justified in repelling force by force if the force he uses is not intended to cause death or grievous bodily harm and is no more than necessary to enable him to defend himself.

Figure 11.4 In the Ontario town of Caledonia in February 2004, this variety store owner's German shepherd saved her and her husband from armed robbers when the couple released the dog from the back of the store. According to your understanding of the *Criminal Code*, under what circumstances, if any, could a store owner be in violation of the law for using a guard dog in self-defence?

The three tests of self-defence under s. 34 include (a) the existence of an unlawful assault, (b) a reasonable apprehension of a risk of death or serious bodily harm, and (c) a reasonable belief that it is not possible to save oneself from harm except by harming the other person. The defence relies on whether the person has a subjective belief as to all three tests and has a reasonable basis for that belief. In other words, the tests include both subjective and objective elements. However, in *R. v. Pétel*, [1994] 1 S.C.R. 3, the courts held that a person can qualify for the self-defence claim even if he or she was mistaken as to the existence of an unlawful assault. In this case, a woman who had been threatened by one of two men shot both of them after one of them had given her his gun. She claimed that she reasonably, though perhaps mistakenly, believed that they were both assaulting her.

Section 35 of the *Code* deals with situations of self-defence in which a person provokes an assault on another person:

Everyone who has without justification assaulted another but did not commence the assault with intent to cause death or grievous bodily harm, or has without justification provoked an assault upon himself by another, may justify the use of force subsequent to the assault if

(a) he uses the force:
   (i) under reasonable apprehension of death or grievous bodily harm from the violence of the person whom he has assaulted or provoked, and
   (ii) in the belief, on reasonable and probable grounds, that it is necessary in order to preserve himself from death or grievous bodily harm;

(b) he did not, at any time before the necessity of preserving himself from death or grievous bodily harm arose, endeavour to cause death or grievous bodily harm, and

(c) he declined further conflict and quitted or retreated from it as far as it was feasible to do so before the necessity of preserving himself from death or grievous harm arose.

The law also permits a person to use force to defend him or herself or a third party, again with the provision that he or she uses no more force than is necessary to prevent the assault or the repetition of it.

When it comes to the defence of one's property, the law permits a person to defend personal, moveable property only "if he does not strike or cause bodily harm to the trespasser," according to s. 38 (1). However, the law does permit the use of force to defend property such as a person's own home. Section 40 of the *Code* states that a person who is defending his or her dwelling-house is "...justified in using as much force *as necessary* to prevent any person from forcibly breaking into or forcibly entering the dwelling-house without lawful authority."

Landmark CASE

R. v. Cinous, [2002] 2 S.C.R. 3

The *R. v. Lavallee* case explained in Chapter 2 (p. 48) established a precedent in that it permitted the battered woman syndrome defence used by the Manitoba woman who shot her husband in self-defence. The court upheld the acquittal of Lavallee, despite the absence of an imminent threat from her husband, because she had a history of being abused by him. The precedent set in that case was relevant to Mr. Cinous's defence. Compare the two cases and indicate how the precedent could have applied and what implications this case may have on the future of the "imminent threat" or battered woman syndrome defences.

Facts: The accused was charged with first-degree murder. He and two other men were involved in a series of computer thefts. He became fearful of the others and told them he no longer wanted to participate in the thefts. Mr. Cinous claimed a string of suspicious events convinced him that his two partners were plotting to kill him. When they asked him to take part in just one more theft, he went along in order to determine the reality of the death threat. He testified that the other men acted strangely, wore surgical gloves of a type often used in bloody crimes, and that he believed them to be holding guns under their jackets. The accused drove his van to a gas station and purchased a bottle of washer fluid. He opened the back door of the van on the pretext of putting the bottle inside. This gave him the opportunity to shoot and kill Mr. Vancol, who was neither attacking him nor even looking at him. No explanation was ever given as to why he did not shoot both men.

The defence argued self-defence, claiming that the shooting was an instinctive reaction to a dangerous situation. It did not occur to the accused to flee or to turn to the police with his fears.

A jury rejected Mr. Cinous's claim of self-defence, but the Québec Court of Appeal ordered a new trial on the grounds that the judge improperly instructed the jury on the issue of self-defence. The Crown appealed, arguing that the jury should never have been permitted to consider self-defence because a "pre-emptive strike" can never meet the test of self-defence.

Held: The appeal should be allowed; the accused's conviction should be restored.

Issue: If an accused has only one defence, should the jury be permitted to hear that defence even if it has very little air of reality?

Ratio Decidendi: (McLachlin C.J. and L'Heureux-Dubé, Bastarache, and LeBel JJ.) "The trial judge must not keep from the jury any defence that lacks an 'air of reality' even if it is the only defence. The judge does not decide the merits of the defence; that is the task for the jurors. Self-defence was a weak defence in this case, but it had some reality to it. A jury acting reasonably could draw an inference from the circumstances described by the accused that he was going to be attacked. In this case, there was no evidence from which a jury could infer the reasonableness of a belief in the absence of alternatives. Where only one defence is raised and guilt is otherwise admitted, the 'air of reality' test should be limited to situations where there is a complete absence of evidence to support the defence."

Provocation

If successful, the defences of automatism or intoxication lead to a complete acquittal, but this is not so for the defence of provocation. **Provocation** is a partial defence that reduces the crime of murder to manslaughter providing the accused can show that he or she was provoked into killing the victim. Section 232 of the _Criminal Code_ states: "Culpable homicide that otherwise would be murder may be reduced to manslaughter if the person who committed it did so in _the heat of passion caused by sudden provocation_." The _Code_ then defines provocation in s. 232 (2) as a "wrongful act or insult that is of such a nature as to be sufficient to deprive an ordinary person of the power of self control."

The defence does have some restrictions. For example, it cannot be used if the victim who provoked the accused was exercising a legal right, such as a parking attendant giving the accused a parking ticket. Also, the act of alleged provocation must be a sudden act or insult and it must be sufficient enough to seriously upset a reasonable person.

The defence of provocation is very controversial. Although the accused is still convicted of an offence, the charge of manslaughter carries a maximum penalty of life, whereas murder carries life as the minimum penalty. As a result, many critics argue that the provocation defence allows deadly rage and violence to be treated less seriously than other deliberate killings.

FIGURE 11.5 Road rage is seen by some as a growing concern in large urban centres in North America. According to your understanding of the _Criminal Code_, are there situations that could occur while driving for which an accused could raise the defence of provocation? Explain.

CONFIRM YOUR UNDERSTANDING

1. Define the term "automatism." What are the key factors that distinguish "insane" from "non-insane" automatism?

2. Most people are skeptical of a sleepwalking defence. What questions would you raise to determine whether a defence of automatism during a sleepwalking episode was justified?

3. In the Rabey case, the majority denied Rabey the defence of non-insane automatism. Judge Dickson, however, disagreed and would have permitted the defence. What were the key arguments presented by the majority and by Judge Dickson?

4. Some defences are considered excuses for committing a crime, while others are considered justification for a criminal act. What is the difference between an excuse and a justification in relation to defences?

5. Explain the three tests of self-defence under s. 34 of the _Criminal Code_.

6. What does it mean that the tests for self-defence include subjective and objective elements?

7. Explain how murder may sometimes be reduced to manslaughter.

8. The defence of provocation is restricted. Explain the limitations of using this defence.

9. Why is the defence of provocation so controversial?

10. Some defence lawyers argue that the defence of provocation should be permitted for all crimes. Do you agree? Explain your views.

Entrapment

In general, the defence of **entrapment** is accepted only if the accused can show that he or she was "set-up," or trapped, by lawful authorities into doing something he or she would not otherwise have done. The precedent-setting case involving entrapment is *R. v. Mack*, [1988] 2 S.C.R. 903. Over a six-month period, an undercover police informer asked Mack numerous times to sell him drugs. The accused repeatedly refused and did so only when the informant threatened him. The court held that the police conduct was unacceptable and the charge was dropped.

As a result of the Mack case, the court established guidelines to determine if the defence of entrapment applies. For example, the courts now ask whether the authorities merely provided an opportunity to a person to commit an offence or whether they actually induced the commission of the offence. They also ask whether the police used certain inducements such as deceit, fraud, trickery, or reward; whether the police conduct involved an exploitation of human characteristics such as friendship; and whether the police exploited someone who was mentally impaired or had a drug addiction.

The defence of entrapment will only be accepted in the clearest of cases. For example, in the case of *R. v. Barnes*, [1991] 1 S.C.R. 449 the accused offered drugs to an undercover police officer. The accused was found guilty but tried to argue the defence of entrapment. The defence failed because the accused was caught in an area frequented by drug dealers that was already under investigation.

A finding of entrapment does not lead to an acquittal; rather it results in a permanent stay of proceedings. Entrapment can only be raised after the accused's guilt has been established, and the burden of proof of entrapment rests with the accused on a balance of probabilities. The judge, rather than the jury, then decides whether the defence of entrapment has been proven. If the judge determines the accused was entrapped, no finding of guilt or innocence is registered.

Necessity

Is it ever necessary to commit a crime? Generally the answer is no, and therefore the defence of **necessity** is rarely used. The courts have been reluctant to recognize necessity either as an excuse or as a justification, even when the crime was caused by dire circumstances or a life-threatening situation. In *R. v. Dudley and Stevens* (1884), 14 Q.B.D. 273 two men who killed a boy and resorted to cannibalism when lost at sea were convicted of murder. The court argued that the defence of necessity was dangerous and immoral and, although the accused had been subject to great suffering, they had no right to take the life of another. In *R. v. Berriman* (1987) 62 Nfld. & P.E.I.R. 239, Berriman claimed she had to exceed the speed limit because she believed an attacker was pursuing her, but the courts argued she had other options and her actions were not realistically unavoidable.

The Supreme Court of Canada finally recognized necessity as a common-law defence in the case of *R. v. Perka et al.* (1984), 14 C.C.C. (3d) 385 (S.C.C.). This case involved drug smugglers who were forced to come ashore in Canada because of rough and dangerous seas. The chief justice of the time, Brian Dickson, allowed the defence of necessity but stressed that necessity could only be used as an excuse in the face of immediate and urgent circumstances.

The defence of necessity was also successful for Dr. Henry Morgentaler when he challenged Canada's abortion law by arguing that, although the law forbade it, necessity compelled him to provide abortions for women.

Necessity as a defence is recognized in Canada only as an excuse and not as a justification for a criminal act. Justice Dickson further clarified that point in the Perka case, when he argued that necessity as an excuse "rests on a realistic assessment of human weakness, recognizing that a liberal and humane criminal law cannot hold people to the strict obedience of laws in emergency situations where normal human instincts, whether of self-preservation or of altruism, overwhelmingly impel disobedience."

FIGURE 11.6 Dr. Henry Morgentaler enters a press conference in Toronto in 1998 to mark the 10-year anniversary of the Supreme Court's decision to decriminalize abortion. What legal defence did Morgentaler use when he was charged with performing abortions prior to 1988?

Duress

The defence of **duress** makes the argument that an accused was forced to commit a criminal act under threat of personal injury or death. Section 17 of the _Criminal Code_ refers to duress as "compulsion by threats":

> A person who commits an offence under compulsion by threats of immediate death or bodily harm from a person who is present when the offence is committed is excused from committing the offence if the person believes the threats will be carried out.

However, the defence of duress is excluded if the crime was one that caused serious harm to another person, such as murder, abduction, or assault with a weapon. The courts have also been strict in their interpretation of whether the threats were immediate. For example, in the case of an inmate who was charged with damaging public property during a prison riot, his defence of duress was denied. The inmate argued that he had acted under duress because fellow prisoners threatened him with death or serious injury if he did not participate. The courts, however, concluded that the threats were not immediate because the prisoners issuing the threats were locked in their cells at the time.

But in the later case of _R. v. Ruzic_, (1998-08-28) ONCA Docket C20580, the courts recognized that a person who was morally innocent could be convicted under s. 17. The accused was charged with importing heroin after a person had threatened to kill her mother, who lived in a foreign country, if she did not import the drugs. The threat was not immediate and therefore, under s. 17, the accused could not use the defence of duress. However, the Supreme Court allowed that an accused could use the _common-law_ defence of duress. This defence does not require that the threats have to be made by a person who is present when the offence is committed, and they may apply to threats to third parties.

Other Controversial Defences

Defence lawyers are continually seeking novel excuses or justification for the criminal acts of their clients. Sometimes they are successful, as with the so-called "Twinkie defence," previously discussed in Chapter 9. In 1978, Dan White, a San Francisco city employee who was upset at the loss of his job, killed Mayor George Moscone and city employee Harvey Milk. His attorney raised the defence of "diminished responsibility" caused by White's addiction to junk food, in particular, Twinkies, claiming that too much sugar had caused White to suffer from depression. The defence was successful and White was convicted of the lesser charge of manslaughter.

In Canada, the appellant in the case of _R. v. Ly_ (1987), 33 C.C.C. (3d) 31 (B.C.C.A.) was born and raised in Vietnam. Defence lawyers argued that Ly's cultural background should have been considered when looking at the fact that he lost self-control when his wife refused to tell him where she had been for the evening. In this case the cultural defence was not successful. However, as Canada becomes more and more multicultural, some defence lawyers are arguing that an accused's cultural background should be considered.

Perhaps one of the most controversial defences to the charge of assault is that available under s. 43 of the *Criminal Code*. This section offers a defence to a parent (or one who acts on behalf of a parent, such as a guardian or teacher) who spanks his or her child. This is known as the **corporal punishment defence**, and it was upheld as constitutional by the Supreme Court of Canada in 2004, in the case *Canadian Foundation for Children, Youth and the Law v. Canada (Attorney General)*, 2004 S.C.C. 4. The defence justifies the hitting of a child for the purposes of correction, providing that the force used is reasonable under the circumstances. In its most recent finding the Supreme Court, while permitting the defence, established certain guidelines. Corporal punishment cannot

- be used against children under two,
- be used against children of any age who have a disability,
- cause harm or raise the prospect of harm to a child two or older,
- be degrading,
- be used on teenagers,
- involve the use of objects such as straps or belts,
- involve slaps or blows to the head.

Those who object to the defence argue that it is too broad and allows the corporal discipline of children when no other member of society would be subject to such a punishment.

FIGURE 11.7   In the years leading up to the Supreme Court ruling allowing the corporal punishment defence, there were vocal opponents on both sides of the issue. In this photo members of the Church of God wait outside the court in St. Thomas, Ont., in July 2001. The court ruled that seven children taken from their Aylmer, Ont. homes the week prior would remain in the custody of the Children's Aid Society. The children were removed amid allegations that the parents, also members of the Church of God, refused to promise not to spank them. Explain the meaning of the sign held by the young girl in this photo.

VIEWPOINTS: Defending Criminals

If I ever needed an education in defending an unpopular client, I received my degree with my defence of John Paul Roby.

Working with a wonderful team of lawyers, I have spent much of the past year defending the man described as the monster of Maple Leaf Gardens. I must say that, to the end, I always saw the human side of my client and preferred to leave matters of judgment of my client to a jury of his peers. A lawyer takes on a case, not a cause.

For a lawyer undertaking an unpopular case, there must be steely resolve not to be diverted from the task by the outpouring of anger and bitterness that constantly surround them. Whether it be the campaign of stares that greeted me regularly on my way to court or even the threats directed at me in the midst of my jury address, nothing moved me from my spot on the courtroom floor. The Roby trial brought to mind the description by Irving Stone in his biography of Clarence Darrow of a notorious case

Darrow participated in the early part of the twentieth century in Idaho: "The reception Darrow received in Boise would have poisoned a less hardy man, one less inured to the kind of universal condemnation, this all-pounding hatred; he would have shrivelled under it, become ill, been forced to flee. When he walked the streets, when he went into public buildings, when he entered restaurants, he found icy faces of loathing turned upon him or passionately burning eyes of aversion and contempt. 'He is defending the killer,' said Boise, 'so he must be in league with the killers.'"

It is precisely the unpopularity of the case, the tremendous stirring of public emotion and anger that sets the stage for a potential injustice. It is tempting to disregard principle for vengeance when the allegations are particularly stark and brutal. A democratic society cares about injustice in every case. In how many countries would Roby have received a fair trial?

Yet there will always be some, even political leaders, who will decry the "sympathy" defence counsel demonstrate toward their "criminal" clients and the great disservice they occasion on victims. It is only the verdict of the jury that dictates who the true victims and who the true criminals are.

As a society, we understandably condemn the imprisonment of the innocent. However, a system of justice devoid of rigid safeguards and checks and balances invites miscarriages of justice. The presumption of innocence becomes a hollow legal sham, unless we sustain the right of vigorous cross-examination to pierce the shield of deception worn by false complainants.

Most cases are decided on issues of credulity of witnesses, and miscarriages of justice will not always be rescued by magical potions of DNA. As I told the jury in Roby in my closing address, injustice is the drink that stirs the soul of the defence.

And yes, I do sleep well every night; yes, I can hold my head up high. I am very proud to call myself a criminal defence lawyer.

SOURCE: Skurka, Steven. "Defending a 'Monster.'" _Toronto Star_ 14 June 1999.

Up for Debate

1. Do you agree with the author that a defence lawyer "takes on a case, not a cause"?
2. What does the Clarence Darrow quote tell you about how the public views defence lawyers? Is the view justified or not? Explain.
3. Write an argumentative essay based on one of the following two quotes:
   "Injustice is the drink that stirs the soul of the defence."
   "The defence lawyer makes a living helping guilty people go free based on technicalities and ridiculous defences."

LEGAL
p. 29
HANDBOOK

CONFIRM YOUR UNDERSTANDING

1. What guidelines has the court established to determine whether the defence of entrapment applies?

2. Under what circumstances could a person caught selling drugs to an undercover police officer not use the defence of entrapment?

CONFIRM YOUR UNDERSTANDING (continued)

3. Under what circumstances can the defence of necessity be used?

4. Supreme Court of Canada Justice Dickson outlined in the Perka case described on p. 341 the following essential elements:

- Necessity is an excuse, not a justification for breaking the law.
- The accused must have been compelled to act by moral involuntariness.
- This involuntariness is measured on the basis of society's expectation of appropriate and normal resistance to pressure.
- The defence will fail if there were reasonable, legal alternatives available.

In the case of *R. v. Langlois* (1993), 80 C.C.C. (3d) 28 the accused was charged with trafficking in drugs when he smuggled drugs into a prison for an inmate after receiving anonymous phone calls from someone threatening to harm his family if he did not deliver the drugs. The accused argued the defence of duress. Do you think he would be successful in this defence? Use the bulleted guidelines to explain your answer.

5. The case of *R. v. Paul*, 2003 N.S.S.C. 211 took place just prior to the ruling in the "spanking" case. An argument between John Wesley Paul and his 17-year-old daughter escalated and the girl started swearing at her father. He warned her about speaking to her elders in such a disrespectful manner, and when she continued, he delivered a swift, single kick to her leg. The trial judge determined that there was sufficient evidence to support the finding that the father's action was one of "discipline and correction." The father was acquitted and the Crown appealed, arguing that standards had changed and the judge should have considered this in his decision. The appeal was dismissed and the acquittal upheld.

Review the guidelines outlined by the Supreme Court in the Canadian Foundation for Children case (p. 343). Assume this case was appealed to the Supreme Court. Do you think the acquittal would have been upheld? Explain.

Sentencing

> *The determination of a just and appropriate sentence is a delicate art which attempts to balance carefully the societal goals of sentencing against the moral blameworthiness of the offender and the circumstances of the offence, while at all times taking into account the needs and current conditions of and in the community. The discretion of a sentencing judge should thus not be interfered with lightly.*
>
> —Chief Justice Lamer, *R. v. M. (C.A.)*, [1996] 1 S.C.R. 500

Some may argue that the sole purpose of sentencing is to punish an accused for his or her criminal actions. Others may think that strong sentences will deliver a message to the accused not to become a repeat offender. Still others may see the need for counselling or treatment

_____ *Unit 3   Criminology and Criminal Procedures*

programs in order to rehabilitate the offender. Generally, a judge has great discretion in determining the appropriate sentence to fit a case, subject to offences for which there is a mandatory minimum sentence. The judge's discretion in the sentencing process is guided by principles and objectives of sentencing that are codified in the *Criminal Code* of Canada.

Purpose and Objectives of Sentencing

Sentencing in Canada has addressed various goals, such as protecting society, trying to prevent criminals from re-offending, and publicly condemning criminal acts. However, it is a widely accepted fact that the sentencing goal of "separating the offender from society" has resulted in a serious problem of over-incarceration in this country. Federal Supreme Court justices have commented on this problem:

> Canada is a world leader in many fields, particularly in the areas of progressive social policy and human rights. Unfortunately, our country is also distinguished as being a world leader in putting people in prison. Although the United States has by far the highest rate of incarceration among industrialized democracies, at over 600 inmates per 100,000 population, Canada's rate of approximately 130 inmates per 100,000 population places it second or third highest. (*R. v. Gladue*, [1999] 1 S.C.R. 688)

In response to this concern about over-incarceration and due to the wide variation of sentencing across the country, sentencing amendments were introduced in 1996. These amendments saw many of the purposes and principles of sentencing that had previously been considered in case law incorporated into the *Criminal Code*. Section 718.1 of the *Code* states:

> The fundamental purpose of sentencing is to contribute, along with crime prevention initiatives, to respect for the law and the maintenance of a just, peaceful and safe society by imposing just sanctions that have one or more of the following objectives:

(a) to denounce unlawful conduct;

(b) to deter the offender and other persons from committing offences;

(c) to separate offenders from society, where necessary;

(d) to assist in rehabilitating offenders;

(e) to provide reparations for harm done to victims or to the community; and

(f) to promote a sense of responsibility in offenders, and acknowledgment of the harm done to victims and to the community

In order to maintain law and order in society and to arrive at a just sentencing decision, a judge generally has discretion to consider the various objectives outlined in the *Criminal Code* above. However, there are also constraints placed on the decision-making process. Some offences require mandatory minimum sentences. For example, where a firearm is used in the commission of a robbery under s. 344(a) of the *Criminal Code*, the mandatory minimum sentence is four years. The offence of possession of weapons for the purpose of trafficking in weapons under s. 100 (2) of the *Criminal Code* also carries a mandatory, one-year minimum sentence. Some offences even have a mandatory minimum sentence before parole eligibility can be considered, such as the mandatory imprisonment of 10 years for second-degree murder. The *Code* also gives mandatory maximum sentences, such as life imprisonment for first-degree murder.

Judges must study the circumstances of each case carefully and consider all sentencing objectives and principles before choosing a sentencing option or combination of options. Judges are also required by law to state the reason(s) for imposing a particular sentence and must clearly state all the terms of the sentence.

Allan Manson, a law professor at Queen's University, comments on judges' discretion and the overall aim of the sentencing amendments in the *Criminal Code*:

> Discretion continues to be the hallmark of sentencing in Canada. The *Criminal Code* now contains statements of purpose, objectives,

and principles, which are more than a mere codification of accepted sentencing principles—they are intended to be a remedial response to the fact of over-incarceration. (Manson 2001)

The six sentencing objectives and principles are explained on the pages that follow.

Denunciation

The concept of **denunciation** allows the judge to take into account society's disdain for the crime committed as well as the offender's character and past actions when deciding on a sentence. The case of *R. v. M. (C.A.)*, [1996] 1 S.C.R. 500 illustrates the concept of denunciation. In November 1992, the accused pleaded guilty to numerous counts of sexual assault, incest, and assault with a weapon related to the sexual abuse of his children over a period of years. While none of the crimes in themselves carried a maximum penalty of life imprisonment, the magnitude of the crimes taken together compelled the Crown to request a cumulative sentence of more than 20 years. The trial judge agreed and sentenced M to a cumulative sentence of 25 years' imprisonment. On appeal to the British Columbia Court of Appeal, the sentence was reduced to imprisonment for a period of 18 years and 8 months. The Crown appealed to the Supreme Court of Canada. In reinstating the trial judge's sentencing decision, the Supreme Court commented on denunciation as a sentencing principle:

> The objective of denunciation mandates that a sentence should communicate society's condemnation of that particular offender's conduct. In short, a sentence with a denunciatory element represents a symbolic, collective statement that the offender's conduct should be punished for encroaching on our society's basic code of values as enshrined within our substantive criminal law.

In the *R. v. M.* case, the Supreme Court took into consideration the character of the accused and the background of the circumstances and concluded:

> The respondent committed a vile pattern of physical and sexual abuse against the very children he was entrusted to protect. The degree of violence exhibited in these crimes was disturbingly high, and the respondent's children will undoubtedly be scarred for life. The psychiatrist and psychologist who examined the respondent agree that he faces dim prospects of rehabilitation. Without doubt, the respondent deserves a severe sentence, which expresses the society's revulsion at his crimes.

The principle of denunciation weighs heavily in cases where the accused has deliberately planned the crime or where the actions of the offender are particularly offensive.

General and Specific Deterrence

The court's objective with **specific deterrence** is to impose a sentence that prevents an *individual* offender from re-offending. On the other hand, by using **general deterrence**, the courts are trying to discourage other members of *society* from committing the same crime by making an example of the offender. One or both of these forms of deterrence may be considered by a judge in sentencing an offender. In situations where incidences of certain types of crimes are escalating, a judge may be guided by general deterrence. For example, in drinking and driving cases, a judge may select a harsh sentence to serve as an example to others not to drink and drive. A judge could also be guided by specific deterrence, particularly if the offender is a repeat offender.

The case of *R. v. Stuckless*, (1998-08-10) ONCA Docket C28532, illustrates how both denunciation and general deterrence can be combined as a rationale for sentencing. Gordon Stuckless pleaded guilty in September 1997 to 24 counts of indecent assault and sexual assault against boys 10 to 15 years of age. The assaults took place over a period of almost 20 years. At trial, Stuckless was sentenced to two years less a day, and a period of three years probation. The Crown appealed the sentence. In denouncing the

FIGURE 11.8 Gordon Stuckless is taken into custody by police in February 1997. He was charged with numerous counts of indecent assault and sexual assault and subsequently convicted. What sentencing objectives were considered in the sentencing decision?

conduct of the accused and considering general deterrence, the court raised the sentence to six years. The court commented:

> These were not isolated acts worthy of compassionate review. They represented a deliberate, manipulative, destructive, and shameless pattern of sexual abuse. Pedophilia is an explanation, not a defence. Society is entitled to protection no less from pedophiles than from those who sexually abuse children without this tendency. General deterrence is a concept which seeks, in part, to protect the public by signalling, through imprisonment, a potential consequence to others of the condemned conduct.

Separation of Offender

Imprisonment serves the purpose of separating an offender from society, which meets a sentencing goal of protecting the public from the offender. No longer can offenders continue to pose a threat to personal safety or property if they are imprisoned. While we continue separating offenders from society by putting them in prison, the question to be considered is whether incar-

ceration is the best form of punishment for the various types of offences. The amendments to the *Criminal Code*'s sentencing provisions require judges to consider less restrictive measures than imprisonment if it is appropriate in the circumstances to do so.

Rehabilitation

What if the offender is suffering from a social problem such as an alcohol or drug addiction or has psychological and anger management problems? Should such factors be taken into account during sentencing? The goal of **rehabilitation** is to treat or improve the offender. It focuses on the needs of the offender in the particular circumstances of the case. Participation in a drug- or alcohol-abuse counselling program or anger management therapy may be helpful in treating the offender. An offender who is incarcerated may be ordered to participate in a treatment program in an attempt to reintegrate him or her back into society.

As with general deterrence, it can be difficult to determine whether the objective of rehabilitation has been successful. Given that sooner or later an offender will be released into the community, the objective of rehabilitation becomes all the more important for consideration. There are, however, still conflicting views about focusing sentencing on rehabilitation. Some people argue that judges should concentrate on the objectives of denunciation and deterrence in determining an appropriate **sanction** (a penalty or punishments imposed by the court on an offender). Others advocate a more holistic view of treating the offender, arguing that not only will the offender benefit from a focus on rehabilitation, but society will also be better served upon the offender's release into the community.

Reparations and Promoting Responsibility

The *Criminal Code* requires that judges also consider the objective of providing reparations for harm done to victims or to the community. Essentially, **reparations** are payment for injury or harm done. For example, if the offence involved a break-and-enter and subsequent theft of property, reparations could include paying the victim for the damage done to the property, as well as making payments for the items stolen.

The objective of promoting a sense of responsibility in offenders allows a judge to consider whether an offender has accepted that his or her actions were wrong and has acknowledged the harm done to the victim and community. Both of these sentencing objectives are designed to allow judges to expand their options for sentencing and to take into consideration restorative justice goals.

You will recall from Chapter 2 that **restorative justice** approaches to sentencing require that offenders accept responsibility for their actions and allow judges to consider creative sentencing based on the circumstances of the case. For example, the judge might consider community service, probation, or a conditional sentence (discussed on p. 356), which allows the offender to serve his or her sentence in the community. As government studies began to look at the over-incarceration of offenders in Canadian society, particularly with respect to Aboriginal offenders, new approaches such as these received more consideration. A judge may also consider new options for gathering community input on sentencing, such as the use of **sentencing circles**, a method that originally developed in an Aboriginal setting.

In sentencing circles, the offender is present in front of members of his or her community, including elders, peers, the victim, and their families. A judge, Crown and defence lawyers, and police officer also take part in the program. Sentencing circles allow all participants input in

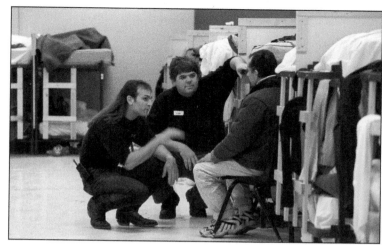

FIGURE 11.9 Two staff members of the O'Neill Program talk with a crack user at the Seaton House Hostel in Toronto. The program aims to lessen the harm crack addicts may do to themselves and eventually lead them into treatment. How might society as a whole benefit from drug or alcohol abuse programs aimed at offenders?

developing a sentence that not only fits the crime but also takes into account Aboriginal culture. The sentencing decision is reached by consensus. It may include such options as having the offender compensate the victim or perform community work. The judge may accept or reject the sentencing recommendation.

The restorative justice focus attempts a more holistic view of the harm caused by the offence and involves all those affected by it, including the offender, the victim, and members of the community. Rather than focus on traditional punishment, the restorative justice model seeks to restore the harmony and balance that existed among members of the community prior to the offence.

Confirm Your Understanding

1. Create a chart in which you summarize, in your own words, the objectives of sentencing.
2. Distinguish between denunciation and deterrence.
3. Differentiate between specific deterrence and general deterrence and provide an example of each.
4. Identify the advantages and disadvantages of rehabilitation as an objective of sentencing.
5. What sentencing objectives would you consider for a second-time offender charged with sexual assault? Justify your choice.

Other Sentencing Considerations

A trial judge has a complex task. After a guilty verdict is rendered, a trial judge must consider the objectives and principles outlined previously in order to select the appropriate sanction. Trial court judges have the advantage of having all testimony and evidence presented to them in court and are therefore given wide discretion in determining an appropriate sentence. However, the *Criminal Code* sets out additional principles that must be considered.

Cruel and Unusual Punishment

A constitutional law provision that must be considered when determining the extent and form of punishment is stated in s. 12 of the *Charter*: "Everyone has the right not to be subject to cruel and unusual punishment." In relation to this, a fundamental sentencing principle set out in s. 718.1 of the *Criminal Code* states: "A sentence must be proportionate to the gravity of the offence and the degree of responsibility of the offender." In considering **proportionality** the court must look at the harm done and how much blame to place on the offender for his or her actions. Therefore, if an offender feels his or her sentence is grossly disproportionate to the gravity of the crime, the offender can try to argue that the sentence amounts to cruel and unusual punishment under the *Charter*.

In the case of *R. v. Smith* (Edward Dewey), [1987] 1 S.C.R. 1045, Edward Smith pleaded guilty to importing 7.5 ounces of cocaine into Canada. He was charged under s. 5 (2) of the *Narcotic Control Act* (now the *Controlled Drugs and Substances Act*) with importing a narcotic. The act provided for a mandatory minimum sentence of seven years for importing or exporting a narcotic. Smith was sentenced to eight years at trial. He appealed the sentence to the Court of Appeal for British Columbia, which held the sentence to be appropriate. Smith then made a further appeal to the Supreme Court of Canada. While he admitted his guilt, he chal-lenged the mandatory minimum sentence of seven years as being a violation of s. 12 of the *Charter*. He argued that such a lengthy sentence amounted to cruel and unusual punishment.

Justice Lamer of the Supreme Court of Canada commented at paragraph 55:

> The test for review under s. 12 of the *Charter* is one of gross disproportionality, because it is aimed at punishments that are more than merely excessive. We should be careful not to stigmatize every disproportionate or excessive sentence as being a constitutional violation, and should leave to the usual sentencing appeal process the task of reviewing the fitness of a sentence. Section 12 will only be infringed where the sentence is so unfit having regard to the offence and the offender as to be grossly disproportionate.

The court raised a hypothetical situation whereby a first-time offender who had possession of a single joint of marijuana could be caught under this mandatory minimum penalty. It would be grossly disproportionate to sentence a small-time offender to such a penalty. The seven-year mandatory minimum sentence component was held to be unconstitutional and declared to be of no force and effect.

A constitutional argument based on cruel and unusual punishment was also raised in the case of *R. v. Morrisey*, [2000] 2 S.C.R. 90. Marty Morrisey had been drinking with his friend and his friend's father at an isolated cabin in the woods. Sometime during the evening they cut off a length of a rifle barrel. Morrisey left the cabin to drive his friend's father home. Upon returning to the cabin, he saw his friend lying on the top bunk. Holding the rifle and knowing it to be loaded, Morrisey jumped on the lower bunk to shake his friend. Morrisey lost his footing, the gun discharged and his friend was killed instantly. Morrisey pleaded guilty to the charges of criminal negligence causing death and unlaw-fully pointing a firearm. He was held in custody for five months pending the trial. The trial judge concluded that the four-year minimum sentence violated s. 12 of the *Charter* and sentenced

Morrisey to two years for criminal negligence and one year for unlawfully pointing the firearm. The trial judge took into consideration the time already spent in custody. The Crown appealed and the court imposed the mandatory four-year minimum sentence and would not allow consideration of any time spent in pre-trial custody.

The case was appealed to the Supreme Court of Canada. The court determined that the sentence was not disproportionate to the gravity of the crime as it resulted in serious consequences for the victim. Further, the actions of the accused were such that he had shown a reckless disregard for the lives and safety of others. The court held that the four-year mandatory minimum sentence for criminal negligence with a firearm did not violate s. 12 of the *Charter*.

ASKING KEY QUESTIONS

Mandatory Minimum Sentences

In 1993, Robert Latimer was charged with the first-degree murder of his 12-year-old, severely disabled daughter, Tracey. She died of carbon monoxide poisoning after being asphyxiated in Latimer's truck. Latimer had been concerned about Tracey's pain and wanted to end her misery. He was convicted at trial of second-degree murder. Despite the fact that second-degree murder carries a mandatory minimum sentence of 10 years, the trial court jury recommended a sentence of one year. The judge at trial granted Latimer a constitutional exemption and sentenced him to imprisonment for one year and one year probation.

The Crown appealed the sentencing decision. The Saskatchewan Court of Appeal reversed the decision and sentenced Latimer to life imprisonment without parole for 10 years. Latimer appealed his case to the Supreme Court of Canada arguing the defence of necessity and that the imposition of a mandatory minimum sentence of 10 years for second-degree murder amounted to cruel and unusual punishment under the *Charter*. The court rejected both arguments. In recognizing the principle of denunciation, the court held:

> Although in this case the sentencing principles of rehabilitation, specific deterrence, and protection are not triggered for consideration, the mandatory minimum sentence plays an important role in denouncing murder.

The Supreme Court further held that the mandatory minimum sentence was not grossly disproportionate to the offence of murder. In an excerpt from the case, the court commented on Latimer's actions:

> However, even if the gravity of second-degree murder is reduced in comparison to first-degree murder, it cannot be denied that second-degree murder is an offence accompanied by an extremely high degree of criminal culpability [responsibility]. In this case, therefore, the gravest possible consequences resulted from an act of the most serious and morally blameworthy intentionality.

The Latimer decision was met by mixed public reaction. Proponents for people with disabilities praised the decision, while others felt that the use of the mandatory minimum sentence was an undue hardship for Latimer.

Queen's University law professor Allan Manson, in his book *The Law of Sentencing*, wrote that the Latimer case exemplified the problem with mandatory minimum penalties. He stressed that the Canadian approach to sentencing is generally focused on the individual offender. That is, the judge considers such factors

as the offender's blameworthiness, the seriousness of the offence, the degree to which the
offender can be rehabilitated, and whether the
offender poses a great risk to the community.
Manson argues that, contrary to this, mandatory
minimum penalties provide an unrealistic "one
size fits all" approach to offenders. By forcing all
offenders with their differing individual circumstances into the same mould, "the mandated
sentence will produce unfair and individually
harsh responses" (Manson 2001).

Manson is critical of case law that allows the
successful argument for cruel and unusual

punishment if the sentence is grossly disproportionate. He argues that some sentences may
indeed be disproportionate and yet not "grossly"
disproportionate. He suggests that if society is
concerned with providing fair and just sentences,
then mandatory minimum sentences, which
promote long prison terms, shouldn't be used. He
argues that judges should be able to use their
own discretion to determine if the circumstances
warrant a harsh sentence.

SOURCE: Manson, Allan. _The Law of Sentencing._
Toronto: Irwin Law, 2001.

Form Your Questions

The information above raises many questions. For example, should Latimer have been
subject to a mandatory minimum sentence of 10 years before parole eligibility? What
other three questions might you ask regarding this issue of mandatory minimum
sentences? Share your questions with the rest of the class, and discuss possible answers
or solutions.

FIGURE 11.10   Robert Latimer was convicted of second-degree murder
in the death of his severely disabled daughter, Tracey, and sentenced to
10 years before the possibility of parole. Do you believe this was a just
sentence?

Aggravating and Mitigating Factors

Before imposing a sentence, a judge must also
take into consideration various **aggravating
factors** (those that would warrant a stronger
sentence) or **mitigating factors** (those that
would be considered in lessening the sentence)
related to the offence or the offender. A
sentencing hearing allows for the presentation of
this evidence. The _Criminal Code_ identifies some
of the factors that would be considered aggravating, but the list is not intended to be exhaus-
tive. Relevant aggravating factors under s. 718.2
(1) include:

- evidence that shows that the crime was motivated by prejudice or hate,
- evidence that the offender engaged in spousal
  or child abuse,
- evidence of abuse of trust in relation to the
  victim,
- evidence that the offence was committed for
  the benefit of a criminal organization, or

- evidence that the offence was an act of terrorism.

Should any of these circumstances exist, the judge may use his or her discretion to impose a stronger sentence.

The *Criminal Code* does not define mitigating factors. However, in case law the courts have considered many of the following factors in assessing mitigation of a sentence:

- whether the offender is a first-time offender,
- evidence of remorse by the accused,
- evidence that the offender is of good character,
- positive reputation of the offender in the community,
- evidence of a good record of employment, and
- whether the offender is engaged in a rehabilitation program.

Parity and Totality

Additional sentencing principles considered in the *Criminal Code* include parity and totality. The concept of **parity** ensures that judges do not give markedly different sentences to offenders in highly comparable cases. Parity is described in s. 718.2(b), which states, "A sentence should be similar to sentences imposed on similar offenders for similar offences committed in similar circumstances."

What if an offender is found guilty of more than one offence arising out of the same set of circumstances? The principle of **totality**, as codified in s. 718.2(c) of the *Criminal Code* requires that "where **consecutive** [one sentence term following the other] sentences are imposed, the combined sentence should not be unduly long or harsh." In sentencing an offender, both principles of parity and totality are considered in addition to all the objectives of sentencing.

Restraint

The principle of **restraint** encourages judges not to use incarceration if less restrictive sentencing options are available. In imposing a sentence, the court must consider the following principle under s. 718.2(d): "An offender should not be deprived of liberty, if less restrictive sanctions

FIGURE 11.11   Former Ontario Minister of Correctional Services Rob Sampson sits in a two-man cell during the official opening of the Maplehurst Correctional Complex in Milton in 2001. This "super jail" is the size of 110 football fields, with a capacity of 1,500 inmates. Ontario's Conservative government at that time suggested the complex would actually help cut the rate of crime. Was the government correct?

may be appropriate in the circumstances." Restraint is also considered in s. 718.2(e), which requires that imprisonment not be automatically considered as the best option, and allows the court to consider other available sentences, with particular attention to the circumstances of Aboriginal offenders. Additionally, the court may also consider sanctions other than imprisonment through the use of a restorative justice approach to sentencing.

When determining the interpretation to be given to s. 718.2(e) in the landmark case of *R. v. Gladue*, [1999] 1 S.C.R. 688, the Supreme Court of Canada recognized the problem of over-incarceration in Canada:

> Thus it may be seen that although imprisonment is intended to serve the traditional sentencing goals of separation, deterrence, denunciation, and rehabilitation, there is widespread consensus that imprisonment has not been successful in achieving some of its

goals. Over-incarceration is a long-standing problem that has been many times publicly acknowledged but never addressed in a systematic manner by Parliament. In recent years, compared to other countries, sentences of imprisonment in Canada have increased at an alarming rate. The 1996 sentencing reforms embodied in Part XXIII, and s. 718.2(e) in particular, must be understood as a reaction to the overuse of prison as a sanction, and must accordingly be given appropriate force as remedial action.

In regard to the particular problem of over-incarceration of Aboriginal peoples, the Supreme Court further stated:

In the mid-1980s, Aboriginal people were about 2 percent of the population of Canada, yet they made up 10 percent of the penitentiary population....By 1997, Aboriginal peoples constituted closer to 3 percent of the population of Canada and amounted to 12 percent of all federal inmates....This serious problem of Aboriginal overrepresentation in Canadian prisons is well documented. Like the general problem of over-incarceration itself, the excessive incarceration of Aboriginal peoples has received the attention of a large number of commissions and inquiries.

In the Gladue case, Jamie Tanis Gladue was charged in 1995 with the second-degree murder of her common-law husband. Gladue's husband had been having an affair with her older sister. When Gladue confronted her husband, he taunted and ridiculed her. Gladue subsequently stabbed her husband twice in the chest. At trial, Gladue pleaded guilty to manslaughter. During the sentencing hearing, the defence lawyer did not raise the issue of her Aboriginal background. At that time, Gladue was not living in a rural area or on a reserve and so the fact of her Aboriginal background was not considered. The court considered many mitigating factors in the sentencing process. Gladue was 20 years old with two children, had no criminal record, was attending alcohol-abuse counselling, and was

continuing her education. She was suffering from a hyperthyroid condition causing her to overreact emotionally to situations. The judge also considered the insulting behaviour and remarks made by her common-law husband as evidence of provocation. The fact that she entered a guilty plea and indicated remorse for her actions was also considered in mitigation. The aggravating factors were that she stabbed the victim twice, had intended to cause him harm, and was not in jeopardy herself. In considering the gravity of the offence and the concern for denunciation of the crime, the trial judge sentenced Gladue to three years in prison and added a 10-year weapons prohibition.

Gladue appealed to the Court of Appeal for British Columbia and the majority of the court dismissed her appeal. Gladue then appealed her case to the Supreme Court, the issue being the proper interpretation to be given to s. 718.2(e) of the *Criminal Code*.

The Supreme Court held that s. 718.2(e) should be applied broadly to include both Aboriginal and non-Aboriginal offenders. It further held that an Aboriginal offender did not have to live on a reserve to receive consideration of this section of the *Criminal Code*. Judges in sentencing must also keep in mind other sentencing principles such as denunciation, deterrence, and separation of the offender. When weighing the options under s. 718.2(e), the court held that the fundamental purpose of the section "is to treat Aboriginal offenders fairly by taking into account their differences."

The court also agreed that in sentencing Aboriginal offenders, the judge must take into consideration the following: "(a) the unique systemic or background factors that may have played a part in bringing the particular Aboriginal offender before the courts; and, (b) the types of sentencing procedures and sanctions that may be appropriate in the circumstances for the offender because of his or her particular Aboriginal heritage or connection."

The Supreme Court held that these relevant factors were not taken into consideration at trial or at the Court of Appeal. However, in considering the background and circumstances of the Aboriginal offender in this case, the judges at the Supreme Court held that the term of imprisonment in this case was not an unreasonable one. The appeal was therefore dismissed.

CONFIRM YOUR UNDERSTANDING

1. Differentiate between the principles of proportionality and parity in the sentencing process.
2. Distinguish between aggravating and mitigating factors in sentence determination. Provide examples of each.
3. How does the principle of restraint meet the goal of reduced incarceration? Outline the *Criminal Code* amendments specifically allowing for restraint.
4. Explain the criteria used in the *R. v. Gladue* case to interpret s. 718.2(e) of the *Criminal Code*.
5. How could s. 12 of the *Charter* be used as a basis for appealing a sentencing decision?

Sentencing Options

Once a judge has taken into consideration the various objectives and purposes of sentencing, he or she must select a form of sanction that will be appropriate to fit the circumstances of the case. While incarceration may come to mind as the most prominent form of sentencing, the *Criminal Code* also provides for a wide range of other sentencing options, including conditional and absolute discharge, fines, probation, restitution, and conditional sentencing.

Incarceration

Incarceration, or imprisonment, has been considered a fundamental sentencing option, particularly for serious offences. An offender can be placed in a federal penitentiary if his or her crime carries a penalty of more than two years, or in a provincial institution if the maximum penalty for the crime is less than two years. When an offence is less serious, and the term of imprisonment imposed by the judge is less than 90 days, an **intermittent** sentence can be used. This sentence enables an offender to continue in his or her employment and serve the sentence on weekends. Generally, there are conditions attached to such a sentence in order to monitor the offender's behaviour and actions carefully.

Offences described in the *Criminal Code* usually specify a maximum and in some cases minimum time for imprisonment. Exceptions can be made if the convicted person is declared a **dangerous offender**. This classification of criminals includes those who caused serious personal injury and who pose a continued threat to society, according to experts. Once designated a dangerous offender, the person is subject to an **indeterminate sentence**, or one for which no maximum is set. The status of the dangerous offender and his or her eligibility for **parole** (conditional release granted to an offender after he or she has served part or all of their sentence) is reviewed after seven years has expired from the time he or she was placed in custody. If parole is denied, the dangerous offender remains in prison, and the case is reviewed every two years thereafter until a decision is made to parole him or her.

Probation

A judge may decide to place an offender on probation. A probationary sentence allows the offender to live in the community as long as he or she meets specific conditions, such as keeping the peace, being of good behaviour, appearing before the court when required, and notifying the court of any change of name or address. The judge has discretion to attach other conditions, including reporting to a probation officer,

The myriad circumstances in which offences can be committed and the infinitely varied characters of the people who commit them require that sentencing be approached with an open mind.

—Allan Manson, *The Law of Sentencing*

remaining within the jurisdiction, abstaining from the consumption of alcohol or drugs, and performing up to 240 hours of community service within an 18-month period. Many of these conditions assist in the rehabilitation of offenders. A term of probation can be no more than three years. Should an offender fail or refuse to comply with the probation order, without providing a reasonable excuse, he or she can be subject to further criminal proceedings for breach of probation.

Absolute and Conditional Discharge

An offender may be granted a discharge—a sentencing option used by a judge whereby no conviction is recorded. A discharge is not granted if the offence requires a mandatory minimum sentence or if the offence is punishable by imprisonment for 14 years or life. The offender must have first pleaded guilty or have been found guilty of the criminal charge. The discharge is granted if it is in the best interests of the accused and is not contrary to public interest.

An individual who is given an **absolute discharge** as a sentence is deemed not to have been convicted. An absolute discharge results in no criminal record for the accused. An individual who is given a **conditional discharge** is subject to specific conditions under a probation order for a certain period of time. Should the offender breach the terms of the conditions, the conditional discharge may be revoked and the offender brought back to the court for a new sentence.

Restitution

In some cases, the court may order **restitution**, which essentially requires the offender to pay the victim for harm done. Restitution may require the offender to pay the replacement costs for property that was damaged or destroyed during the commission of the offence. In a case in which the victim suffered bodily harm as a result of the offence, the court may order the offender to pay the victim a sum of money to cover support or loss of income. Should the offence involve a situation in which the bodily harm or threat of harm

involved the offender's spouse, common-law partner, child, or other person living in the same home, the court may order the offender to cover reasonable expenses for moving the victim(s) out of the household. These expenses could include the cost of temporary housing, food, childcare, and transportation. Restitution is considered as a restorative justice option.

Fines

Fines require the offender to pay a sum of money to the court. A fine cannot be considered as the sole sentencing option for crimes requiring a mandatory minimum penalty, so if a fine is the sole sanction in a criminal case, it is likely that the offence was not very serious. However, the court has the authority to impose a prison term if an offender defaults on payment, that is, if an offender does not pay the fine within the time period set out in the court order.

In Canada, the maximum fine for a summary conviction offence is $2000, or a prison term, or both. A judge may also impose a fine for an indictable offence. Before imposing a fine, the judge must be satisfied that the offender is in a position to pay it. In some jurisdictions, offenders can participate in a program whereby they have up to two years to pay their financial obligations to the court, or they could have the fine deducted incrementally from their paycheque instead of paying cash.

Conditional Sentencing

When the 1996 sentencing amendments were made to the *Criminal Code*, conditional sentencing became a codified option. Under conditional sentencing, a term of imprisonment is imposed but the offender serves the sentence in the community. As long as the offender complies with the conditions attached to the conditional sentence order, he or she will not be incarcerated.

The *Criminal Code* criteria for conditional sentencing were highlighted in the landmark case of *R. v. Proulx*, [2000] 1 S.C.R. 61 (see p. 19). The offender, Jeromie Proulx, had consumed alcohol and then drove his unfit vehicle on slippery roads. While attempting to pass a vehicle, he drove his own vehicle erratically into the oncoming lane of traffic, side-swiping one car and then crashing into a second. A passenger was killed in his own car and another was seriously injured in the second car. Proulx almost died from his own injuries sustained as a result of the accident. He pleaded guilty to charges of dangerous driving causing death and dangerous driving causing bodily harm.

The trial judge imposed a sentence of 18 months of incarceration. A conditional sentence was not imposed because the judge felt that it would not serve the objectives of denunciation and deterrence. On appeal, the Manitoba Court of Appeal substituted a conditional sentence. The Crown appealed that sentence to the Supreme Court of Canada. The Supreme Court attempted to clarify the *Criminal Code* criteria to be used in imposing a conditional sentence. First, conditional sentencing may not be considered as an option in cases where a mandatory minimum penalty is given. Second, conditional sentencing can only be used if the term of imprisonment imposed is for less than two years. Third, the court must also be satisfied that the offender serving the sentence in the community would not endanger the community. Lastly, the decision to serve the sentence in the community must take into consideration the purpose and principles of sentencing. After considering all of the criteria to be used in this case, the Supreme Court held that the trial judge was correct in her decision. The Supreme Court allowed the appeal and restored the original 18-month period of incarceration.

There are some who argue that conditional sentencing is a weak form of sentencing that should not be used in serious cases. However, others argue that as long as substantial conditions are attached, such as house arrests and curfews, then conditional sentencing can meet the objectives of denunciation and deterrence. The court must also emphasize the proportionality principle and consider the gravity of the offence

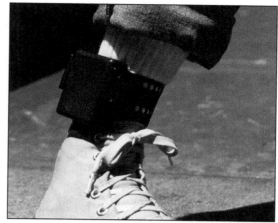

FIGURE 11.12 One of the conditions imposed on some parolees is the wearing of an ankle monitor that tracks their movements. The device lets authorities know immediately if the parolee breaks any travel restrictions, or goes into an off-limits area. What do you see as the pros and cons with using such a device?

before imposing a conditional sentence. The use of conditional sentencing allows the courts to reduce the emphasis on incarceration and to consider restorative justice goals.

Victims in Sentencing Hearings

The problem that arises in trying to determine whether a sentence is just is that various individuals affected by the crime may not share the same viewpoint. The perspectives of the victim, the accused, and society regarding a sentence may be different from that of the sentencing judge.

For years the focus of a sentencing hearing was on the offender, not the victim. The voice of the victim was often lost in the process. Beginning in the 1980s, however, more attention began to be focused on victims' rights. The Canadian Statement of Basic Principles of Justice for Victims of Crime was developed in 1988. (Federal, provincial, and territorial ministers of justice endorsed a new Canadian Statement of Basic Principles of Justice for Victims of Crime in October 2003. See Chapter 10, page 316.) The 1999 amendments to the *Criminal Code* gave victims a greater role in the sentencing process by codifying the right of a victim to prepare and read a victim impact statement in court. The amendments further require offenders to pay fines, in the form of a victim surcharge, in addition to the sentence imposed.

Victim Impact Statements

Section 722 (1) was added to the *Criminal Code* in 1999 to address the rights of victims. Under the law, a victim is entitled to prepare, in writing, a **victim impact statement** that details the harm or loss suffered as a result of the criminal offence. A victim must be notified of the opportunity to prepare a victim impact statement. The new amendments allow the victim to read the statement in court or present it in any manner that is considered appropriate by the court. If the victim died in the commission of the offence, is ill, or is not able to make a statement, the spouse, common-law partner, dependant, relative, or person who is responsible for the care of the victim would be permitted to write the statement.

The process of preparing and delivering victim impact statements may help in providing closure for the victims. It also allows the court to hear firsthand the impact of the crime and the offender's action on the victims' lives. The preparation and submission of a victim impact statement is a matter of choice for the victim. However, once it is submitted to the court, the judge must consider it in the sentencing process. As soon as the written victim impact statement is provided to the court, a copy must be provided to the offender, the defence lawyer, and the Crown prosecutor.

Victim Surcharge

In consideration of the harm or loss suffered by the victim, s. 737 of the *Criminal Code* authorizes the court to impose a **victim surcharge** in addition to the other sentence it imposes. A victim surcharge is imposed once an offender is convicted or given an absolute or conditional discharge for *Criminal Code* offences and those under the *Controlled Drugs and Substances Act.*

When a fine is imposed as part of the actual sentence, the offender is required to pay 15 percent of the fine as a victim surcharge. In cases that do not involve a fine as part of the actual sentence, the surcharge amounts to a minimum of $50 for a summary conviction offence and $100 for an indictable offence. The court is not held to these minimums, however, and could require the offender to pay more if the offender is able and it is appropriate in the circumstances.

Offenders may be exempted from paying the charge if they can establish that it would impose an undue hardship on themselves, dependants, or family. All money paid through the victim surcharge is distributed to victims' assistance programs in the province holding the sentencing hearing.

CONFIRM YOUR UNDERSTANDING

1. Explain the significance of an indeterminate sentence.
2. Distinguish between an absolute and a conditional discharge.
3. Explain the terms and conditions that may be attached to a probation order.
4. Outline the requirements that must be met before a conditional sentence can be imposed.
5. Explain the significance of a victim impact statement.
6. When may a judge impose a victim surcharge?

In Closing

In Canadian law, the accused is entitled to have his or her side of the argument heard. Defence lawyers will continue to suggest novel defences for their clients, and the Supreme Court and Parliament will have to determine the validity of their arguments.

Many of the defences you have read about in this chapter remain controversial. The courts and the public must continue to struggle with the idea that someone who kills or injures another person can be found not criminally responsible because he or she was sleepwalking, had a mental disorder, or was intoxicated. The courts and many lawyers have recognized the defence of self-defence as confusing and complex. Some women's groups have criticized the defence of provocation because they believe it offers offenders an excuse for violent behaviour toward women. The common-law defences of duress and necessity are becoming more available to accused persons because the Supreme Court has agreed that s. 17 of the *Criminal Code* can be used to convict a person who is morally blameless. Where defences fail, sentencing begins.

Throughout this chapter you have examined the complexities involved in determining an appropriate sentence. The judge, in exercising discretion, must weigh the seriousness of the offence, the blameworthiness of the offender, and the circumstances of the case against sentencing objectives such as denunciation, deterrence, separation, rehabilitation, reparations for harm, and the promotion of a sense of responsibility in offenders. Proportionality, parity, totality, and restraint are also considered in the sentencing process alongside aggravating and mitigating factors. Judges will continue to be challenged as they exercise their judicial discretion in an attempt to use both traditional sanctions and restorative justice models in the sentencing process.

Defence and sentencing will always be controversial topics in Canadian law. Due to the differing perspectives of the victim, offender, court, and general public, there may never be complete agreement on whether a particular defence is just or on what constitutes an appropriate sentence. Perhaps, through continued dialogue, our system will evolve and reforms will be made that will bring all parties closer to the best possible balance of interests.

CHAPTER ACTIVITIES

Extend Your Legal Knowledge

1. Prepare an organizational chart listing the various defences outlined in this chapter. Categorize the defences according to those that are based on an excuse and those that are considered justification in law. Create another category for those that do not fit into either category. Include cases that have successfully used each defence in your chart.

2. How did the decision in the Daviault case (p. 333) change the law? What amendments did the government make in response to the Daviault decision?

3. How does the defence of mental disorder distinguish moral from legal wrong?

4. Summarize the objectives of sentencing in chart form.

5. Describe the principle of proportionality and explain its importance in the sentencing process.

6. Distinguish between the various sentencing options available.

Think About the Law

7. Review the elements necessary to prove whether a person can be found not criminally

responsible by reason of a mental disorder (p. 334). Review the *Criminal Code* definition of mental disorder in s. 16 (1). For the following case, indicate what factors you would consider in determining whether the accused could be found not criminally responsible by reason of a mental disorder.

R. v. Spanos, 2001 B.C.C.A. 34

The appellant was convicted of various drug trafficking offences, including trafficking in heroin and cocaine. The facts are not in dispute. The appeal is based on the defence of mental disorder. The defence argued that the appellant should have been found not criminally responsible.

Spanos sold heroin to an undercover officer on numerous occasions. When he was arrested he was in possession of two pounds of heroin. The officer testified that the appellant was a "tough negotiator" in the drug business. According to the officer, the appellant did not demonstrate any characteristics that suggested he was of unsound mind. The appellant did tell the officer that he had been shot six times by the Mafia and the Saskatoon police, and that he had met Jesus and God and they told him he would return to earth to take control. He also said that cocaine is just a chemical, not real, and even if caught he would not be convicted. The officer testified that he believed Spanos made these strange statements because he was a heavy drug user and had made the statements when he was under the influence of drugs.

Following his arrest, two psychiatrists interviewed Spanos. Their evidence included the following information about the appellant. During examination, Spanos said, among other bizarre things, that he was holding a million-dollar lottery ticket that the government was trying to get from him; that he died and went to Heaven and talked to God (who was sitting on a burning throne); and that worms and spiders were sucking his blood.

The appellant's delusional beliefs had been consistent over many years and neither psychiatrist was of the opinion that Spanos was faking symptoms. The appellant had an IQ of approximately 70. His symptoms fluctuated depending on whether he was taking his proper medication and whether he was using drugs such as heroin.

8. Research the following cases of automatism on the Internet and briefly explain the *ratio decidendi* in each case:
   a) *R. v. Stone*, [1999] 2 S.C.R. 290
   b) *R. v. Parks*, [1992] 2 S.C.R. 871
   c) *R. v. Rabey*, [1980] 2 S.C.R. 513

9. Discuss the advantages and disadvantages of restorative justice models for sentencing.

10. Outline the advantages and disadvantages of including victims in the sentencing process by allowing them to express their sentiments through the use of the victim impact statement.

Communicate About the Law

11. Prepare a debate arguing either for or against the following statement:
    The concept of *mens rea* is central to our principle of justice. A person who commits a crime while intoxicated cannot form the *mens rea* and must be acquitted regardless of how unpopular such a decision may be.

LEGAL *p. 33* *HANDBOOK*

12. Comment on the sentencing objectives and principles that could be considered in each of the following scenarios. Be sure to refer to the *Criminal Code* for mandatory minimum or maximum sentence restrictions.
    a) An offender is charged with his or her second impaired driving offence.
    b) A first-time offender with an alcohol abuse problem is charged with assault causing bodily harm.
    c) An offender is charged with robbery with a weapon.
    d) A father ends the suffering of his severely disabled child and is convicted of second-degree murder.

e) An offender is charged with importing narcotics into Canada.

13. Prepare an argument in support of or against the use of mandatory minimum sentences.

14. An offender who is declared a dangerous offender may receive an indefinite sentence, even if the crime for which he or she was convicted does not carry a severe penalty. Some argue that an indefinite sentence violates an accused's *Charter* right to liberty. Do you agree or disagree? Prepare an argument supporting your position.

Apply the Law

15. Read the facts presented in the following case in which the accused used the defence of necessity. Considering the elements provided below and Justice Dickson's other comments in *R. v. Perka*, would you acquit or convict the accused? Prepare a *ratio decidendi* on your position.

R. v. Vandenelsen, ONSC, 2001

The accused, Carline Vandenelsen, was charged with abducting her eight-year-old triplets in October 2000. She fled Canada with the children, believing she was acting in the best interests of the children. The abduction began when Vandenelsen took the three children during a supervised day visit. They had been in the primary custody of their father for six years.

One of the children gave evidence at the trial. He described how he and his brother and sister were smuggled across the borders of the United States and Mexico in the trunk of a car. From there they fled to Panama, where they were refused entry because they had no proper identification papers. More than three months later, police arrested Vandenelsen in Acapulco, Mexico. The defence argued the common-law defence of necessity. There was no other legal defence. The Crown argued that the jury should not be allowed to consider necessity, but the trial judge allowed it.

16. Read the following case and write an argument explaining whether the jury should or should not be allowed to consider the defences of duress or necessity. Keep in mind that the defence of duress requires that a person act by reason of a threat of death or serious physical injury. Fear alone does not constitute duress in the absence of a threat. For comparison refer to the cases of *R. v. Ruzic* (p. 342) and *R. v. Perka* (p. 341).

R. v. Maragh, ONSC, 2003

The accused, Maragh, and two friends, R. and T., attended a high school basketball game in Pickering, Ontario. During an argument at the game R. pulled out a gun and shot someone. Maragh did not witness the shooting. When Maragh returned to his car, R. and T. were waiting for him. R. told the accused that he had shot someone and told Maragh to drive away from the school. After 15 minutes, a police car began following the accused's car. They were forced to stop at a train crossing. The police officer exited his vehicle and shouted to the occupants of the car to get out. All three occupants ignored his demand. Once the train passed, Maragh drove off at a fast speed and eventually collided with another car.

Maragh was charged with various offences, including accessory after the fact. He was tried separately from the other two offenders. At trial the defence asked the trial judge to instruct the jury on the defences of duress and necessity. The defence claimed that R. had a gun and ordered Maragh to drive fast and not stop for the police. Maragh said he continued to drive and did not surrender to police because he was afraid that R. would shoot him. The accused also said he was concerned that R. would shoot at the police officer, and if a police officer were killed or wounded he would be implicated. He was also afraid that the police officer would return fire and he, the accused, would be killed or wounded.

The Crown argued that Maragh voluntarily drove R. from the scene of the crime knowing what had taken place. There was no evidence that R. threatened Maragh and no evidence that Maragh ever told R. he did not wish to be involved in the crime.

17. Prepare a sentencing decision for the Court of Appeal decision in the case below. Consider whether a conditional sentence is appropriate. Include the rationale for the sentence imposed, including:
a) the sentencing objectives considered;
b) aggravating and mitigating factors;
c) the principle of proportionality; and
d) the principle of parity.

R. v. Elliott, 2001 SKCA 19

In June 1999, Kent Elliott began a night of drinking with his friends. He consumed two bottles of beer in the early evening and one more at a university pub later in the evening. Elliott agreed to be the designated driver. He drove himself and two friends to a sports bar where they stayed until the early hours of the morning. Elliott admitted to consuming three or four more bottles of beer. When it came time to drive everyone home in his friend's truck, he lost control of the vehicle. One of his friends died a few weeks later due to injuries sustained in the crash.

Elliott pleaded guilty to a charge of impaired driving causing death contrary to s. 255 (3) of the *Criminal Code*. He was convicted at trial and the judge imposed a conditional sentence of 18 months to be served in the community. He was also fined $1800, given a victim surcharge of $250, and prohibited from driving for three years.

A reconstruction expert who testified at the trial put forth evidence that Elliott was speeding.

When tested with a Breathalyzer, Elliott's samples measured .12. The legal limit under the *Criminal Code* is .08.

At the time of the offence, Elliott was 25 years of age, had no previous criminal record, and was employed. Subsequent to the tragedy, he expressed remorse for his actions. He stopped drinking and made efforts to continue his education. The family of the victim and Elliott remain in contact and they expressed a desire that Elliott not be given a **custodial sentence**, meaning one for which a period of incarceration has been ordered.

The trial judge accepted that the conditions for a conditional sentence were met; that is, the offence was one for which a sentence, if imposed, would be less than two years. Also the offender was not considered a danger to the community, and the sentencing decision was consistent with sentencing principles under the *Criminal Code*. Further, the trial judge imposed conditions on the offender, which included keeping the peace, being of good behaviour, appearing before the court when requested, remaining within the jurisdiction unless approval is granted otherwise, and refraining from purchasing, possessing, or consuming alcohol.

The Crown appealed the sentence arguing that the conditional sentence of 18 months was insufficient. The Crown submitted that the conditional sentence did not properly consider denunciation, deterrence, separation, and the promotion of a sense of responsibility. It further argued that the sentence was not proportional to the gravity of the offence and did not consider parity in sentencing. The Crown particularly emphasized that denunciation and deterrence were not adequately addressed by the sentence in the community.

BIBLIOGRAPHY

Barnhorst, Sherrie, and Richard Barnhorst. *Criminal Law and the Canadian Criminal Code.* Toronto: McGraw-Hill Ryerson Limited, 1996.

Canadian Legal Information Institute. Accessed 2 Feb. 2004 <www.canlii.org>.

Department of Justice Canada. Accessed 2 Feb. 2004 <www.canada.justice.gc.ca>.

Manson, Allan. *The Law of Sentencing.* Essentials of Canadian Law Series. Irwin Law Inc.: Toronto, 2001.

Martin, John C. *Martin's Annual Criminal Code 2003.* Aurora, ON: Canada Law Book Inc., 2003.

Native Law Centre of Canada, University of Saskatchewan. "Sentencing Circle: A General Overview and Guidelines." Accessed 31 Jan. 2004 <www.usask.ca/nativelaw/publications/jah/circle.html>.

Roach, Kent. *Criminal Law.* 2nd ed. Essentials of Canadian Law Series. Toronto: Irwin Law Inc., 2000.

Skurka, Steven. "Defending a Monster." *Toronto Star* 14 June 1999.

UNIT THREE CULMINATING ACTIVITY

Criminal Case Creation and Sentencing

Introduction

In 1996 amendments to the *Criminal Code* codified the purpose and principles of sentencing. Now that you have completed Unit 3, your challenge is to illustrate your understanding of criminal law, defences, and sentencing by creating a fictional criminal case for which a guilty verdict has been rendered. You will be asked to outline the factors to be considered by both the Crown and the defence at the sentencing hearing. Assuming the role of judge, you will then prepare a sentencing judgment providing the option for sentencing with a rationale for your choice.

In addition to addressing the Overall Learning Expectations outlined at the beginning of this unit, this culminating activity requires you to use a number of legal inquiry skills. You may want to consult Chapter 1 "The Legal Handbook" (on the pages indicated by the icons) to review each of these skills.

Your Task

1. Write a clear, concise criminal case scenario. Make sure the facts are such that a guilty verdict would be rendered. Outline the facts of the case including:

    a) The particulars of the offence
    b) The charge under the *Criminal Code* or related federal statute
    c) Evidence related to the background and character of the accused
    d) The circumstances surrounding the commission of the offence
    e) The harm caused to the victim
    f) Whether the offender is a repeat offender
    g) Any other relevant circumstances (e.g., whether the use of a sentencing circle is a possible option)

    (You may want to review "The Case Study Method" and "Creating Case Briefs" in the Legal Handbook.)

2. Prepare a written sentencing judgment for the criminal case you created. Justify your choice by outlining the following sentencing considerations:

    a) Indicate any mandatory minimum and mandatory maximum sentences given for the offence under the *Criminal Code*
    b) State the chosen sentencing option
    c) Justify your sentencing choice by referring to the specific principles and objectives of sentencing under the *Criminal Code* that the sentence is designed to address
    d) Identify specific aggravating or mitigating factors

    (You may want to review "Analyzing Court Decisions" and "Tips for Writing an Argumentative Essay" in the Legal Handbook.)

UNIT 4

REGULATIONS AND DISPUTE RESOLUTION

OVERALL LEARNING EXPECTATIONS

By the end of this unit, you will be able to:

- demonstrate an understanding of the role of governments, the courts, and individual and collective action in protecting the environment
- demonstrate an understanding of the legal process, of legal systems, and of sanctions used to protect the rights of the employer and the employee in the workplace
- demonstrate an understanding of the major concepts, principles, and purposes of international law
- evaluate the effectiveness of international law, treaties, and agreements in resolving conflicts of a global nature
- demonstrate an understanding of the complexity of making, interpreting, and enforcing law on a global scale

TABLE OF CONTENTS

Chapter 12

LABOUR LAW

LEARNING EXPECTATIONS

After reading this chapter, you will be able to:

- explain the roles of governments in developing labour and workplace law

- explain why unions were formed

- explain the purpose of key labour legislation (e.g., *Canada Labour Code, Trade Unions Act 1872, Labour Relations Act,* and provincial employment standards acts)

- investigate the major differences in employer–employee negotiations in unionized and non-unionized workplaces

- assess the usefulness of collective bargaining

- analyze the future impact of free trade, globalization, and changing technology on collective bargaining and workplace regulation

FIGURE 12.1 Labour Day, a holiday celebrated across Canada, is a tribute to Canada's workers and to the labour movement, begun in the nineteenth century. How do you think the workplace can be regulated so that it is fair to both workers and businesses?

> *Work is not just a paycheque. It is of sociological and psychological importance. Employment law rules deal with the imbalance between employers and employees and represent the court's desire to assist in developing a level playing field.*
>
> —Mr. Justice Peter Cory, Supreme Court of Canada, 1994

■ I N T R O D U C T I O N ■

Like thousands of other teenagers, Sarah Inglis worked part-time at a local outlet of a multinational fast-food chain. When new management took over, her hours and working conditions changed. Sarah felt some of the changes were unfair, but management insisted they were necessary. Instead of quitting, Sarah did some research and tried to organize a union to bargain with the employer for better conditions. There was a problem: Not one of the chain's 700 Canadian outlets was unionized. The company didn't want that situation to change.

Sarah's union drive made headlines in her hometown of Orangeville, Ontario, and across North America. Although a majority of her fellow employees eventually voted against unionizing, the experience was a valuable one for Sarah—she gained rare insights into labour relations. In 1994, the Canadian Auto Workers (CAW), the largest non-government union in Canada, asked her to address a conference on labour and youth. While Sarah spoke well of high school, she did have a criticism: Nothing she had been taught prepared her to do anything about achieving improved conditions in the workplace. Before her union drive, Sarah had no knowledge of workers' rights, no understanding of how to form a union, no knowledge of collective bargaining, and little experience with negotiation.

In the following pages, you will explore employment law and labour issues. You will learn how governments and courts regulate the workplace and how and why unions are formed. You will consider the advantages and disadvantages of different methods of bargaining for wages and benefits. As an informed future worker, employer, and/or business person, you will be in a better position to speculate on the future of the labour movement and on employment legislation in the global economy.

Bargaining and Employment

The world of work is a marketplace. If and when you sell your labour and skills, you must negotiate a contract with a buyer—your potential employer. In many respects, the principles of supply and demand apply. You attempt to negotiate a fair price for your labour, and the employer considers your qualifications, such as education, as well as the demand for your skills. Obviously, the more skills you have and the greater the demand for those skills, the more the employer will be willing to pay. Coming to an agreement on what your labour and skills are worth, however, is much more complex than agreeing on a price for a pair of jeans or a car. The most typical methods of bargaining an employment contract or **compensation package**—the total value of your wages and benefits—are individual bargaining, bargaining collectively, and bargaining though an agent. In negotiating an employment contract, there is often more to consider than straight monetary compensation. As Justice Cory says in the chapter's opening quote, work "is of sociological and psychological importance."

Individual Bargaining

Many workers in Canada enter into individual contracts with their employers. Each side negotiates to reach a fair compensation package and the terms of the agreement last until the contract ends. Such contracts are often standardized. To work as an entry-level sales clerk for a large retail chain, for example, you would probably sign a standard employment contract that sets out employer and employee rights and responsibilities. If you have years of experience and many loyal customers, you could possibly negotiate a contract that includes anything from the use of a company car to compensation if you are terminated.

Federal and provincial employment legislation, as well as contract law, applies to any individually negotiated employment contract. There are advantages and disadvantages to individual bargaining. It can work well for highly skilled, motivated, and mobile employees who are in demand and who have good negotiating skills. For less skilled workers and for people who are not good negotiators, individual bargaining can be a disadvantage.

Bargaining Through an Agent

Famous sports figures, media personalities, musicians, and actors are often too busy to negotiate contracts. Besides, they can afford to hire skilled negotiators, or agents, to negotiate on their behalf. Actors and sports figures will usually have many different contracts during their careers, so agents meet a practical need. Increasingly, top business executives are also using agents. They recognize the benefits of hiring an agent. Agents are often lawyers who understand contracts and bargaining. They generally receive a percentage of the value of the contracts they negotiate for their clients as payment.

Most employees will never use the services of an agent. However, as more people who work in industries such as the computer industry come to be hired on a contract basis, it is likely that bargaining through an agent will become more widespread.

Bargaining Collectively

A group of workers may choose to elect a representative or association to bargain with an

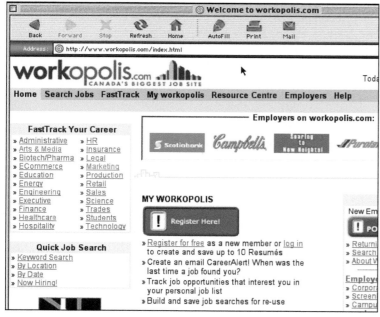

FIGURE 12.2   The job marketplace is vast and competitive. To gain an edge, some people post their résumé on sites such as this. How can you best sell yourself and protect yourself from exploitation?

employer on its behalf. This is known as **collective bargaining**. Unionized collective bargaining is the process by which a union represents employees in relations with their employer. (In Canada, the term "labour law" is often used to refer specifically to laws governing unions and collective bargaining.)

Workers with collective representation, however, are not necessarily unionized. Managers and professionals often form associations, rather than unions, to negotiate on their behalf. Doctors and dentists, for example, establish fee schedules for their services through their associations. Usually these are provincial bodies, such as the Ontario Medical Association and the Ontario Dental Association. Such associations also negotiate with government bodies, insurance agencies, and so on, on behalf of their members. Sports figures may also bargain collectively. The National Hockey League Players' Association, for example, bargains collectively for players with team owners.

Many people see collective bargaining as the best way to improve wages and benefits. Other people believe that individual skills and attributes improve their bargaining power. Regardless of how an employee bargains with his or her

FIGURE 12.3   A New York reporter questions a baseball players' union negotiator about contract talks with team owners, in August 2002. A strike was narrowly averted in this dispute, but if the two sides had not reached an agreement, the Major League Baseball season would have been cancelled. What does this say about the power of collective bargaining?

employer, both sides remain subject to federal and provincial employment laws governing the workplace and the employer–employee relationship.

CONFIRM YOUR UNDERSTANDING

1. Do you agree that bargaining with an employer for wages is psychologically different from negotiating the price of a new computer or car? Explain.
2. Assume that you are negotiating an individual employment contract with a potential employer. Besides wages, what would you try to include in your compensation package?
3. Although many workers in the fast-food restaurant where Sarah Inglis was employed were interested in joining a union, others were not. What problems would union organizers face in trying to organize a union in the fast-food industry?
4. Professional hockey players and baseball players are highly skilled and in great demand, yet many of them negotiate their wages collectively rather than individually or through an agent. Why do you think this is so?
5. Why do you think more chief executive officers and technical workers are using agents to negotiate their contracts? What disadvantages do you see in using an agent to negotiate an employment contract?

Governments and the Workplace

It certainly would be easier if laws relating to employment were the same across Canada, but as you learned in Chapter 5, the *BNA Act* divided powers between the federal and provincial levels of government. As a result, laws affecting the workplace today vary across the provinces and territories. Minimum wages, for example, are not uniform, and while some provinces and territories allow replacement workers during a **strike** (a group of workers withhold their labour during contract negotiations), others do not. Not only do laws and regulations differ from province to province, there are often power struggles between the federal and provincial levels of government. Although approximately 90 percent of employees in Canada are subject to provincial employment laws, the federal government controls certain types of workplaces that are national in nature or that operate in more than one province, such as airlines, railways, and broadcasting networks. Federal labour legislation also applies to all federal and Crown corporations and to federal civil servants.

Federal Legislation

Since Confederation, the federal government has passed laws regulating workers, the workplace, and labour–management relations for areas under its jurisdiction. The attitude of society and the government toward employer–employee relations has changed significantly over the past century, as is reflected in changes to the labour law. In 1872, the *Trade Unions Act* made it legal for workers in Canada to organize and form unions, under defined conditions, for the first time. However, workers could still be fired, even imprisoned for the crime of conspiracy, for trying to organize a union.

In 1907, in response to widespread strikes in vital industries such as mining and railroads, the federal government passed the *Industrial Disputes Investigations Act*. The most important feature of this act was the creation of a conciliation board, which would act as a neutral third party in labour disputes. In order for a strike to be legal, the two parties (workers and management) first had to meet with the board, which would investigate the dispute and issue a public report. The principle of third-party intervention in industrial disputes has since become a recognized method of dispute resolution in Canadian labour law. Most labour-relations statutes today include some kind of conciliation process.

Labour Milestones

As the twentieth century began, Canadian workers continued to fight for better working conditions, but with only modest success. Labour unrest came to a head in the Winnipeg General Strike of 1919, when thousands of workers brought the city to a halt by walking off the job over their right to bargain collectively for fair wages. Working with the Manitoba government, the federal government sent in troops to restore order and end the strike. Before it was over, two people were killed and hundreds of protestors were injured. Some concessions were eventually made to the striking workers, such as union recognition and, eventually, an eight-hour workday. Several organizers of the strike, who were jailed for their role, became prominent politicians who worked at the provincial and federal levels to change labour law. One such organizer, J.S. Woodsworth, went on to become a member of Parliament, continuing the fight for the right to strike as well as working to create social legislation that would benefit Canada's labour force. In general, however, governments continued to favour business, and labour reforms came slowly.

In 1927, the federal government passed its first *Old Age Pensions Act*, a social benefit that allowed workers to retire with a small measure of financial security. In 1929, however, the Great Depression began, and massive unemployment persisted throughout the 1930s. Workers struggled to get by. In the United States, the federal government responded to the Depression with a

FIGURE 12.4 During the Winnipeg General Strike tensions boiled over as thousands of workers flooded the streets. The group pictured clashed with armed police before the strikers attempted to upset a streetcar. Did this strike have any effect on government policy?

"New Deal," a series of economic initiatives intended to stimulate the economy and bring social relief. The centrepiece of the New Deal was the *National Labour Relations Act* or *Wagner Act* of 1935. The *Wagner Act* not only fully legalized union representation for workers in the United States, but it also obligated employers to recognize and negotiate with democratically elected unions. This legislation would have a major impact in Canada, but not for another decade, when World War II (1939–1945) made the demand for labour extremely high.

In 1941, the *Unemployment Insurance Act* came into effect, offering financial support to laid-off workers, but it wasn't until 1944 that key components of the *Wagner Act* were enacted into Canadian law, with the passage of *PC 1003* (*Wartime Labour Relations Regulations*). This legislation was a watershed for Canadian labour. For the first time, it was fully legal for Canadian workers to organize and form unions. Furthermore, employers were legally obligated to negotiate with union representatives. No longer could a worker in Canada be charged with conspiracy for trying to form a union.

PC 1003 adapted key elements of the *Wagner Act* to oversee the formation of unions in Canada. Later, in 1948, the *Industrial Relations and Disputes Investigation Act* embedded these elements in Canadian labour law by establishing

- the Canada Labour Relations Board to administer the collective bargaining system and the process of establishing a union
- a secret-ballot system to enable workers to freely exercise their choice of whether to join a union
- a code of unfair labour practices, which made it illegal for either the union or management to use coercion or intimidation in union drives or during negotiations; in other words, both sides must act and **bargain in good faith** (negotiate honestly and openly)

Similar labour-relations legislation was later passed by all 10 provinces. Although Canadian workers could now exercise free choice about union representation, many battles lay ahead for the labour movement. For example, postal workers had to strike illegally in 1965 before the *Public Service Staff Relations Act, 1967* gave them and other federal employees (except for members of the RCMP and the army) the same union rights as private-sector employees, including the right to strike.

Canada Labour Code

In 1967, many of the federal laws dealing with labour–management relations, including the *Industrial Relations and Disputes Investigation Act,* were consolidated into the *Canada Labour Code* (CLC). Today the CLC is part of the Labour Program of the federal Department of Human Resources and Skills Development. The Canada Industrial Relations Board (formerly called the Canada Labour Relations Board) is a quasi-judicial tribunal consisting of representatives of government, labour, and business that is responsible for interpreting and administering Part I (Industrial Relations) and certain provisions of Part II (Occupational Health and Safety) of the CLC. Similar boards in each province are responsible for overseeing collective bargaining in their jurisdiction.

Provincial Legislation

Provincial employment legislation covers everything from workplace safety and minimum wages to compensation for work-related illness and injury (see Figure 12.5). A cornerstone of provincial legislation is employment standards acts (ESA). Each province has it own ESA, and the legislation differs somewhat from province to province, but for most non-unionized workers in Canada the provincial ESA lays out the basic rights and responsibilities of employees and employers and establishes minimum workplace standards. The standards set for wages and benefits are just that—minimums. Many employers may offer employees better wages and benefits than are required under the ESA. Employees who work in industries under federal jurisdiction, such as banks, airlines, and the federal civil service, are not covered by the ESA, nor are students who work in work-experience programs or as community volunteers. Only parts of the ESA may apply to certain employees, such as agricultural and domestic workers.

Employment standards legislation is often amended by successive governments in response to public pressures. Such changes also reflect the governing party's political views and ideologies. For example, in 2000, Ontario's Progressive Conservative government overturned Bill 40, which the earlier New Democratic Party government had enacted to prohibit the use of replacement workers during a strike. The Conservative change was seen as a move favouring business rather than workers. The Conservatives also amended Ontario's *Employment Standards Act* to allow employers to have employees work a 60-hour workweek without paying overtime. In

Employment Area	Provincial Legislation
Occupational Health and Safety	Ontario *Occupational Health and Safety Act* • regulates health and safety in workplace • deals with issues such as dust, heat, noise, chemicals • entitles workers to refuse unsafe work
Employment Standards	Ontario *Employment Standards Act* • establishes minimum employer–employee obligations • sets minimum wages, vacation time, work hours, etc. • provides basic protections for non-unionized workers
Workers' Compensation	Ontario *Workplace Safety and Insurance Act* • provides compensation to workers disabled by work-related injury or illness • removes the right of employee claiming compensation to sue the employer
Human Rights	Ontario *Human Rights Code* • prohibits discrimination on the grounds of sex, race, age, handicap, colour, religion, ethnic origin, marital status, and sexual orientation

FIGURE 12.5 Provincial employment legislation.

2004, the new Liberal government of Ontario moved quickly to increase the minimum wage and also introduced amendments to reduce the 60-hour workweek. The key components of employment standards legislation are laid out in chart form in Figure 12.6.

Component	Employment Standards Acts
Minimum Wage	• set a minimum hourly wage for all employees • may set separate minimums for certain types of jobs and for younger workers
Termination and Severance	• set a minimum termination notice for both employer and employee • define terms for and amount of severance pay • establish special provisions to protect employees if a large number of workers are being laid off at the same time
Hours and Overtime	• define maximum daily and weekly hours that can be worked before overtime must be paid • set rate of overtime pay • set time periods and frequency for lunch, coffee breaks, etc.
Sick and Bereavement Leave	• provide protections that include entitlement to paid or unpaid leave for a specific time because of personal sickness or the death of a member of the family
Holidays and Vacation	• establish statutory holidays (Christmas Day, Labour Day, etc.) • may require employees to have worked a set number of workdays prior to the holiday in order to be paid • require the employer to pay the employee a set percentage of earned wages for annual vacation
Pregnancy and Emergency Leave	• establish the right to paid or unpaid time off for a specific period of time during pregnancy, after the birth of a child, or after adoption • in some jurisdictions, provide for time off for family emergencies, such as caring for a sick relative or family member

FIGURE 12.6   Each province and territory in Canada has its own employment standards act covering areas listed in this chart.

SHIFTING PERSPECTIVES: Child Labour

Throughout the nineteenth century, it was commonplace for Canadian children to work on Canada's farms and in its growing industries, including its factories and coalmines, to help support their families. Many children were also abandoned by parents who could not support them and were forced to live on the street as a result. The first significant child welfare legislation was passed in Ontario, in 1893. Known as the *Act for the Prevention of Cruelty to and Better Protection of Children*, it created the very first Children's Aid Society in Canada and paved the way for future child welfare legislation. More than 100 years later, it is surprising to hear that child labour has not been totally eradicated in Canada, as this report by Gwendolyn Richards in *The Globe and Mail* reveals:

> Thirteen-year-old Tim tries to do his homework before heading to the convenience store for the start of an eight-hour night shift. After stocking shelves and helping customers into the early morning, he tries to snatch some sleep before classes start.
> Not in Canada, you say. Think again, argue critics of new legislation tabled by the Liberal government in British Columbia.

Changes to the BC *Employment Standards Act*, which could go into effect this fall, will allow employers to hire children between the ages of 12 and 15 with parental consent alone, dropping the requirement for permission from a school counsellor and the director of the Employment Standards Branch.

The government says that it's simply cutting through red tape and argues that no one followed the old rules anyway, and that increased fines for not getting parental consent will keep employers in line.

But critics counter that the BC government is leaving children open to abuse and instead of easing the rules should have strengthened them.

Indeed, in BC, there are no restrictions on the types of jobs a child can do, how many hours the child can work nor any limitations on what the child can work—except that under the *School Act,* no child can miss school for work and under the *Occupational Safety Act,* a child can't work with toxic pesticides.

The proposed change "positions BC as an embarrassment, in terms of protecting our children's rights in the workplace," says Helesia Luke, who is leading the charge against the bill, along with FirstCall: BC Child & Youth Advocacy Coalition and the BC Teachers' Federation….

"…The notion that kids just need their parents' consent is very naïve," says Luke. "It assumes that parents have an equal footing with employers and can advocate for their child in those positions and be confident and effective. Certainly that wouldn't be the case in many situations."….

BC Teachers' Federation President Neil Worboys says that "Childhood is a time for learning and play, not jobs." … Currently, the Employment Standards Branch can set conditions of work and compel the employer to respect those conditions, says Mr. Worboys. With the proposed changes in place, the ESB would no longer have the ability to monitor workplaces.

Source: Richards, Gwendolyn. "Child Labour." *The Globe and Mail* 6 Aug. 2003:C1.

FIGURE 12.7   A young coal miner at the end of the nineteenth century. How have working conditions for young people improved? How have they not improved?

Your Perspective

1. Imagine that Bill 37, an act to amend the British Columbia *Employment Standards Act* to allow employers to hire children between the ages of 12 and 15 with only parental consent, is before that province's legislature. Choose one of the following roles and write an argument to present to the legislature either supporting or opposing the bill:
   a) a representative for small business
   b) a member of the BC Child and Youth Advocacy Coalition
   c) a representative of the BC Teachers' Federation

2. Research what happened to Bill 37 and then research another province's laws regarding child labour. Present a report comparing labour laws in the two provinces.

3. Research and write an article comparing the labour laws and working conditions for Canadian children today to those of 100 years ago. If possible, include photographic images.

Labour Boards and Tribunals

One interesting aspect of labour law in Canada is that workplace disputes can be resolved outside the court system. To enforce labour law, federal and provincial jurisdictions have established a system of boards and tribunals, based on the belief that specialized boards would be more expert in labour relations, less intimidating to workers, and less costly and time-consuming than the regular court system. Individuals appointed to labour boards generally must have experience and education in law, industrial relations, or human resources. Boards are appointed for specific terms on the recommendation of labour and management groups.

Labour relations boards are expected to adjudicate labour disputes fairly, impartially, and in accordance with legislation. Their job is to determine whether individuals and groups have been denied their rights under the relevant legislation and, if so, to provide a remedy. Boards have significant power to enforce their findings. For example, in the *United Steelworkers of America v. Radio Shack* case described in the following activities, the board held that Radio Shack had violated the *Labour Relations Act* and ordered the company to post a notice that they would not interfere with the efforts of workers to form a union.

CONFIRM YOUR UNDERSTANDING

1. What historical reasons are there for Canada having many different jurisdictions responsible for labour legislation?

2. The *Trade Unions Act 1872* made it legal for workers to join a union. Why was it still so difficult for workers to unionize?

3. Describe the impact of the Winnipeg General Strike on the labour movement in Canada.

4. What elements of the US *Wagner Act, 1935* were later adapted and enacted in the Canadian federal legislation *Industrial Relations and Disputes Investigation Act*?

5. Why is a province's employment standards act one of the most significant pieces of its employment legislation?

6. Describe how the views and ideology of the political party in power influence employee rights under a province's employment standards act.

7. Read the facts of the following case that was brought before the Labour Relations Board by the United Steelworkers of America, and then answer the questions that follow.

United Steelworkers of America v. Radio Shack, [1979] 2 C.L.R.B.R. 281.

Facts: The United Steelworkers of America applied for certification (to form a union) of the part-time employees of Radio Shack at the company's Barrie, Ontario, location. Full-time workers had already formed a union.

Evidence presented to the Labour Relations Board indicated that

- two employees were fired because of their union-organizing activities
- the company posted a notice forbidding union organization during working hours, which was legal within the act, but then the company allowed an anti-union petition to be circulated during working hours
- a foreman told workers that "if the union gets in the company will pack up and move west." He also told them that a scheduled seven percent raise would not be paid if the union got in
- Radio Shack management supplied between 20 and 30 of the employees with red t-shirts carrying the slogan "I'm a company fink" on the front and "I'm proud of it" on the back.

The part-time workers voted against joining the union and the United Steelworkers took their case to the Labour Relations Board, arguing the vote was not genuine.

Unions: Past and Present

For many of you, Labour Day simply marks the end of summer holidays, but to the union movement, it is a celebration of the courage and value of the ordinary working person in Canada. The world's first Labour Day parade took place in Toronto in 1872. The parade was not a celebration, however, but rather a protest against the imprisonment of 24 members of the Toronto Typographical Union who had been jailed for leading a strike in demand of a nine-hour workday. They were imprisoned for organizing a strike, which would interrupt trade, and that was a criminal offence at the time in Canada.

By the end of the nineteenth century, the Industrial Revolution had created huge factories and mines—dark, impersonal, dangerous places in which to work. Accidents were common and injured workers were dismissed with no access to medical care, workers' compensation, or any form of employment insurance. Even young children worked in mines and factories, where a workweek of 80 hours was not uncommon. The poet William Blake described the workplaces of nineteenth-century England as "dark, satanic mills," a description that applied equally well to industrialized Canada.

Early union leaders organized in order to fight the exploitation of workers, and to establish more humane working conditions and a living wage. They faced horrendous obstacles, including punishments such as beatings, imprisonment, and even death. Their actions were seen by employers and governments as a threat to public order, capitalism and, of course, profits. Early leaders were hampered not only by the legislation of the time, but also by attitudes regarding the relationship between an employer and employee. Until the *Trade Unions Act 1872* was passed, the *Master and Servant Act* was Canada's only existing employment contract. Under this law, servants were legally obliged to stay with their masters, no matter how poorly they were treated. Servants who ran away would be jailed if captured. The attitudes reflected in this legislation remained intact throughout much of the nineteenth century, and changing them required an enormous shift in the public's thinking.

Even today, the idea of workers forming unions to protect their interests is viewed with suspicion by some employers and governments in Canada. There is no question that labour unrest and strikes have an enormous economic impact, which is why unions use them as negotiating tools. The legal history of the union movement in Canada is a history of how these tensions between labour and business, with the government in between, are continually shifting in search of new resolutions.

Why Join a Union?

Employees have many reasons for joining a union. For most workers, economic factors rank

Men who are compelled to sell their labour very naturally desire to sell the smallest portion of their time for the largest possible price. They are merchants of their time. It is their only available capital.

—George McNeil, American labour reformer, 1890

high. They want their unions to negotiate for them such things as a living wage, increased equity in the workplace, and what they consider to be a fair share of the profits created in part by their work. However, there are other reasons to bargain collectively rather than through other methods. Through a union, workers may gain more influence over the terms and conditions of their workplace and employment and will probably have access to a grievance, or formal complaint procedure, to resolve conflicts with management. Many unions also provide a wide range of services for members, including access to legal support, counselling, professional development, and educational services. Some members also strongly support their union's involvement in political action and its position on social issues for all people—not just union members. Unions have taken positions favouring pay equity, worker safety, and environmental issues, and they offer support, including financial contributions, to political parties that share their goals and objectives.

Union Structure

Union structure in Canada is complex. Most unionized workplaces have what is called a union local. The local includes a number of union representatives who deal with local grievances and health and safety issues, and who inform local members on union issues. A union local can comprise workers from various workplaces or just one store, plant, or school.

Union locals may be quite autonomous, with their own policies, election procedures, bylaws, and so on. Some locals, such as the Toronto Police Association, are totally independent, with no outside union affiliation, but in most cases, a local is part of a larger national or international union structure. For example, workers at the Ford auto plant in Windsor, Ontario, have local union representatives and are affiliated with the Canadian Auto Workers (CAW). Workers at Stelco, a steel company in Hamilton, Ontario, are members of the United Steelworkers (USW). Both the CAW and USW, which are private-sector unions, are part of the Canadian Labour Congress, a national labour organization. The largest union in Canada, the Canadian Union of Public Employees (CUPE), and the Public Service Alliance of Canada (PSAC) are, as their names suggest, public-sector unions. They are also affiliated with the CLC.

The CLC, in turn, is affiliated with international labour associations such as the International Confederation of Free Trade Unions (ICFTU). International labour associations have become increasingly important as unions forge links and find support in dealing with issues that cross borders, such as child labour.

...To recognize the importance of economic growth as the foundation for mutually beneficial relations among employers, employees and trade unions.

Section 2 (5), "Purposes and Application of the Act," Ontario *Labour Relations Act, 1995*

Canada's Five Largest Unions in 2003	Membership
Canadian Union of Public Employees (CUPE)	521 600
National Union of Public and General Employees (NUPGE)	325 000
National Automobile, Aerospace, Transportation and General Workers Union of Canada (Canadian Auto Workers)	268 000
United Food and Commercial Workers International Union	220 000
United Steelworkers of America	180 000

SOURCE: Human Resources Development Canada. "Union Membership in Canada–2003." *Workplace Gazette,* Vol. 6, No. 3, p. 41.

FIGURE 12.8 What do these figures indicate about unionization in the public and private sectors?

CONFIRM YOUR UNDERSTANDING

1. What did the *Master and Servant Act* do?
2. Why do you think some employers would be opposed to their employees forming a union?
3. What was the main focus of early union organizers in Canada?
4. Identify five reasons why employees may choose to join a union.
5. A union local has been described as being autonomous. What does this mean?
6. Create an organizational chart showing the hierarchy and affiliations of the CAW and the USW.
7. Why are international labour links important for local and national unions?
8. Other than bargaining for better compensation packages for members, what other activities are unions involved in?

Types of Unionized Workplace

There are three types of unionized workplace in Canada: closed shop, union shop, and agency shop. In a **closed shop**, the employer agrees to hire only workers who are already members of a specific union; certain trade and construction unions operate in this way. This is the strongest, most secure workplace from the point of view of the union. In a **union shop,** which is more common than closed shops, employees must join the union after being hired. Public school teachers are an example of union shop workers. In an **agency shop**, which is a modification of the union shop, employees do not have to join the union, but they must still pay union dues.

The agency shop may seem like an odd arrangement, but it came about as the result of a Supreme Court of Canada decision in 1946. The case involved a tense labour dispute, which had started in 1945, between the United Auto Workers and the Ford Motor Company in Windsor, Ontario. The union demanded a full union shop, but management refused, so the union called a strike. When the long, bitter strike threatened to spread, the federal government appointed Supreme Court Justice Ivan Rand to settle the dispute. Rand came up with a compromise: Workers would not have to join the union, but they would have to pay union dues, which would be deducted automatically from their paycheques (which is called "check off"). This gave the union full security, but in return it had to represent all workers at the plant, not just union members. The Rand Formula, as it became known, was soon used in labour negotiations across Canada and in the United States. It is now included in most collective agreements. The case below, *Lavigne v. Ontario Public Service Employees Union*, challenged the Rand Formula on the grounds that it violates the *Charter* rights of employees who do not want to associate with or support a union.

Landmark CASE

Lavigne v. Ontario Public Service Employees Union, [1991] 2 S.C.R. 211

Read the following case analysis. The facts, issue, decision, and *ratio* have been provided for you.

The judge decided that the automatic deduction of union dues from an employee's paycheque does not violate that individual's *Charter* right to freedom of association. Assume that you disagree with the decision. Write a possible dissent for this case.

Facts: The appellant, Mr. Lavigne, has been a

teacher at the Haileybury School of Mines since 1974. As a staff member, he is represented by the respondent union, OPSEU. Lavigne has never been a member of the union nor has he been required to become a member. Union dues have, however, been deducted from his paycheque, as required under the terms of the collective agreement between the school and the union. Article 4 of the union's constitution sets out such general objectives as the advancement of the "common interests, economic, social, political, of all the members and of all public employees, wherever possible, by all appropriate means."

Lavigne is opposed to his dues being used to support causes that come within the broader aims of the union's constitution. He says the union has contributed to political parties such as the NDP, which passed a resolution supporting free choice with respect to abortion. Mr. Lavigne argues he should not be forced to pay dues and that his freedom of association should include the freedom not to associate in any way with the union, including the payment of dues.

Issue: Is the requirement that the appellant pay union dues an infringement of his rights and freedoms under the *Charter*?

Held: Appeal dismissed.

Ratio Decidendi: (Wilson, La Forest, L'Heureux-Dubé, Sopinka, Gonthier, Cory, and McLachlin JJ.) The Ontario Court of Appeal correctly held that the *Canadian Charter of Rights and Freedoms* does not apply in the circumstances of this case on the basis that the substance of the application concerns the expenditure of the funds and not the requirement that the appellant pay union dues.

On the larger issue of whether the appellant's rights have been violated under s. 2(b) of the *Charter* because he is compelled to pay union dues the answer is in the negative.

The Unionization Process

Today, the biggest hurdle organizers must overcome in unionizing a workplace is convincing employees to bring in a union. Union drives in local outlets of multinational fast-food chains and big-box stores have been notoriously unsuccessful, as you saw in the introduction to this chapter. The law no longer prevents unions from organizing, and employers can no longer fire or discriminate against employees who support and try to organize unions. Provincial labour relations acts have created labour relations boards to oversee the collective bargaining process and enforce rules that make it unlawful for management to obstruct workers' attempts to unionize. These acts also include legislation that regulates the process of forming a union as well as union **certification**. A union becomes certified when it receives the labour board order that grants it the authority to negotiate with the employer on behalf of employees.

The Certification Process

In order to form a union in a workplace in Canada, organizers must collect evidence that a majority of workers support the union, and then submit this evidence to the provincial labour relations board. Those who support the union drive must therefore convince enough employees that they will be better served by bargaining collectively for wages and benefits through a union. Some provinces permit employees to sign a membership card indicating their consent to be represented by a union, but other provinces, such as Nova Scotia, Ontario, and Alberta, require that a vote be held by secret ballot. If the union wins a majority vote, it becomes certified. The workers give up their right to bargain individually with their employer and accept that they will be represented in bargaining by the union negotiating team. The union now has the right to be the sole representative for all employees within the bargaining unit. The union, in return, must fairly represent all workers, including those who did not vote to certify or who are not members of the union. Employees who are union members can vote to elect representatives for union positions. These elected positions generally last one year, and any member is free to run for election.

Legal Protection During Organizing

Labour boards protect the right of employees to organize and forbid activities that would interfere with an open, democratic process during a union drive. During the certification process, management must not alter the conditions of work to influence workers' decisions. Management cannot offer bribes to workers in an effort to stop them from certifying, nor can it threaten to close down the plant or store if employees certify. Union organizers are also not permitted to intimidate or coerce workers into certifying.

The Bargaining Unit

The bargaining unit is the particular group of workers the union is expected to represent, such as plant workers, a particular trade, clerical staff, or a combination of these. In a large workplace, such as a hospital, different unions may represent specific bargaining groups, such as nurses, pharmacists, and custodial staff.

Decertification

Members who become dissatisfied with their union can take action to remove it through a process called **decertification**. To decertify, a majority of the union members must vote to remove the union. Generally, this process is overseen by the labour board. In Ontario, the *Labour Relations Amendment Act, 2000* (known as the *Workplace Democracy Act*) requires would-be union organizers to observe a one-year "cooling off" period between attempts to certify a union. The act also makes it easier for members to decertify a union if it fails to negotiate its first collective agreement within its first year. At the time that the legislation was enacted, the government announced that one of its goals was to make unions and union leadership more accountable to members.

CONFIRM YOUR UNDERSTANDING

1. Explain the difference between the following workplaces: closed shop, union shop, and agency shop.
2. What was the significance of the Rand Formula for unions?
3. Critics argue that the Rand Formula should be abolished because it forces workers to pay dues whether they want to belong to a union or not. Create a chart showing the pros and cons of the Rand Formula.
4. Why was the Supreme Court of Canada

decision in *Lavigne v. Ontario Public Service Employees Union* so important for the union involved?
5. What is the purpose of the labour relations boards?
6. Describe the process employees must follow to certify and to decertify a union.
7. Why do you think many union organizers were opposed to the *Workplace Democracy Act*?

Collective Bargaining

Once a bargaining unit has been established and the union certified, union representatives are

expected to bargain for a **collective agreement**, which is a contract that sets out the terms and conditions of employment between the employees it represents and the employer. To determine its goals, the union usually requires members to prioritize a list of demands, such as increased pension benefits, job security, and so on. The union must then give management notice of intent to bargain and time to prepare its position. Both sides elect spokespersons and then management and union representatives begin the negotiation process. As with Canada's courts, the collective bargaining system is adversarial. Initially, the two sides may be far apart when issues and objectives are brought to the table. Generally one side presents an offer; management may, for example, offer a wage increase of 2 percent. Union representatives will then analyze, evaluate, and debate this offer before accepting it or making a counter-offer.

Collective bargaining is complex and difficult because it involves so many economic, social, political, and legal issues. The bargaining power of both sides is shaped by factors such as the state of the economy, the demand for workers, company profits, new technologies, government policies, and the global economy. The process is highly regulated, and the union, employees, and management must follow strict procedures to make sure everyone plays by the rules. As in any democratic election, the minority must accept the majority position. Because the process is now so complex, negotiators must have excellent communication, strategic, and tactical skills, not to mention energy and stamina. Both sides are expected to return to their respective stakeholders with a reasonable settlement. The union must bring any negotiated contract back to the union membership for **ratification** (approval) and, of course, the workers must be convinced that they got a better deal than if there had been no union representation. Similarly, management negotiators must return with a contract that will satisfy both employers and shareholders.

As in all negotiations, the process does not always go smoothly. If both sides cannot come to an agreement, certain procedures allow the parties to resolve their differences. In most provinces, arbitration is compulsory to prevent

The following key areas are negotiated during the collective bargaining process:
- wages, salaries, and other forms of compensation
- employee security (seniority rules, lay-offs)
- grievance and arbitration policies and procedures
- hours and days of work (length of shifts and workweek)
- overtime (rate of overtime pay, when overtime applies)
- vacation and leave (vacation pay; type, duration, and payment of leaves)
- health and safety issues (workplace dangers, equipment problems, stress)
- benefits (pensions, health insurance, dental insurance)
- allowances (clothing, car, moving expenses)

FIGURE 12.9 Contract negotiations can break down in any of these areas. Which areas would you rank as the most important for (a) employers, (b) employees, (c) investors, and (d) consumers?

negotiations from breaking down and workers from walking off the job. Sometimes a third party is all that is needed to resolve a deadlock. Arbitration allows both sides to cool off, express their preferences, and suggest trade-offs. However, if both sides are still at an impasse after arbitration, other dispute resolution mechanisms can be put in place.

Alternative Dispute Resolutions

A mediator is a neutral third party, usually a professional, who provides both sides with information and suggests a possible compromise or other ways to settle the dispute. In **mediation**, both sides must agree on the choice of mediator and both sides are also free to ignore the mediator's recommendations. If mediation fails, the next step may be arbitration.

In **binding arbitration**, both sides must find the arbitrator acceptable. Unlike mediation, however, the decision of the arbitrator is binding.

One version of binding arbitration involves **final-offer-selection**. In this process, both parties present their bottom lines to the arbitrator and the arbitrator picks one only. Final-offer-selection is meant to force both sides to come together as close as possible on disputed issues. If union demands are too outrageous or management offers are too aggressive, one side will lose considerably.

Binding arbitration can be beneficial in that it settles the dispute without the disruption of a strike, but it has critics. Some people argue that arbitration discourages serious negotiation because both sides believe the arbitrator will "split the difference" in any event. For example, if the union is asking for a 10 percent wage hike and management refuses to offer more than 2 percent, the arbitrator may impose a 5 percent wage settlement.

Strikes and Lockouts

If mediation fails and there is no provision for compulsory arbitration, the last resort is either a strike or a **lockout**. In a strike, employees withdraw their labour to back up their contract demands. In a lockout, management locks workers out of the workplace. In either case, employees receive no pay from the business. Because the media gives labour unrest intense coverage, many people have the impression that strikes and lockouts are much more common-place than they actually are. Normally, negotiations do not end in strikes our lockouts. Most workers and businesses realize that strikes and lockouts can create lasting conflicts and hardship—not only for workers and the businesses involved, but also for the economy in general.

When union leaders feel that members strongly support a strike, however, they may call for a strike vote, which is held through secret ballot. If enough members vote in support of a strike, for example 80 percent, union leaders have a very strong mandate to call a strike. Union leaders can use such a vote as a bargaining tool to convince management to accept their demands without actually calling a strike. On the other hand, a strike vote of 51 percent puts the union in a vulnerable position. Management is not likely to settle if 49 percent of the employees do not support a strike, since the lack of support would probably translate into a strike of short duration. If management imposes a lockout and can keep the business running, it puts pressure on striking workers to accept management's terms.

During a strike, members of large unions such as the Canadian Auto Workers (CAW) may receive strike pay from the union in return for **picket duty**, or carrying picket signs and walking outside their place of employment. Generally, strike pay is hardly enough to cover basic expenses such as rent or car payments. Unions therefore try to use other tactics to pressure employers into settling a contract. In **work-to-rule**, for instance, workers follow the terms of the existing contract to the letter and do absolutely nothing more. For example, teachers have used this tactic during contract negotiations by withdrawing from volunteering for extracurricular activities and other extra services to pressure school boards to either return to the bargaining table or to agree to contract demands.

As with all aspects of the collective bargaining process, strikes and lockouts are governed by law. In some provinces, such as Québec, the employer cannot hire replacement workers, who are sometimes referred to as "scabs" by union members. In other provinces, such as Ontario, employers can hire replacement workers during a strike. Striking workers are legally free to picket outside their place of employment, which serves a two-fold purpose: It publicizes the strike and discourages the flow of other workers, products, and anything else that might support the employer in continuing to do business. Picketers, however, must not prevent non-union members or members from another union from crossing the picket line. For example, in the case of a custodial strike, teachers would still be permitted to enter the school to teach if they belong to a different union that is not on strike. As well, union picketers cannot stop management from entering the premises or from doing union jobs once they are inside. The law also prevents picketers from picketing on the employer's property or from threatening anyone entering the premises. However, judges take equally seriously the *Charter* right of free expression.

In *R.W.D.S.U. Local 558 v. Pepsi-Cola Canada Beverages (West) Ltd.*, a case involving a strike and lockout, the Supreme Court of Canada ruled that strikers not only have the right to picket outside the primary business (in this case, a plant producing bottled soft drinks), they also have the right to picket outside secondary locations—in this case, retail outlets that sold Pepsi products. Secondary picketing is lawful, then, unless it involves criminal conduct or the tort of nuisance or defamation. The court found that the commercial interests of the companies being picketed should not be more important than the value of free expression. Writing for the majority in 2002, Justice Binnie found that "both primary and secondary picketing engage freedom of expression, a value enshrined in the *Charter*." In another aspect of the case, picketing union members had chanted slogans and hurled insults outside the homes of Pepsi management employees. The court upheld an order prohibiting this activity.

Some workers whose services are considered essential to society are prohibited from striking. For example, in most provinces firefighters and

FIGURE 12.10 A striking postal worker's daughter pets a police horse in Toronto in August 1997. The federal government passed a bill ordering 45 000 Canada Post employees back to work. Should the government be able to order workers back to work?

police officers cannot go on strike, and some levels of government workers are also restricted from striking. Governments also have the power to end a strike by passing back-to-work legislation. Both provincial and federal governments have ordered striking teachers, nurses, postal workers, garbage collectors, and other public employees back to work. Back-to-work legislation is controversial because it interferes with the democratic rights of individuals. On the other hand, governments face public pressure to bring an end to prolonged strikes by groups whose work stoppages can have a severe impact on the economy and the well-being of citizens.

VIEWPOINTS: Labour Day is Propaganda for Unions

(editorial in the *Toronto Star*, Labour Day, 2003)

On September 1, almost every Canadian and American town will be occupied with parades, picnics, and other community festivities honouring labour. These events should focus on celebrating the fruits of our labour, namely higher living standards; instead they have been turned into marketing and propaganda tools for unions.

Unions, however, are about the last thing that ought to be celebrated on Labour Day.

The net economic effects of high unionization rates are clear. Unionized firms perform worse than non-unionized firms on productivity growth, investment growth, employment creation and profitability.

Professor Barry Hirsch, in a major review of research on unionization, concluded that unions tend to decrease profitability, [and] reduce investment in physical capital and research and development.... It's clear that unions also generally reduce labour market flexibility and adversely affect the overall efficiency of labour markets.

Unfortunately, Canada is a much more unionized country than our southern counterpart. Last year, more than 30% of Canadian employees were unionized while only 14.6% were unionized in the United States. The fact that Canada underperforms the U.S. on investment, profitability and average personal incomes shouldn't be a surprise given this self-imposed differential....

Canada's current labour laws protect what is called closed-shop unionism....They require workers to join and/or financially support a single union as a condition of employment. In the U.S., 22 states have worker protection laws, known as right-to-work laws, that provide workers with a choice. They are not required to join a union or support it through union dues. Tellingly, when workers are given the choice of whether or not to join a union, they join unions in much lower numbers than when they have no alternative....

There are substantial costs being imposed on our country because of unionization. Canada and its provinces should begin to address this problem by providing Canadians with more choice regarding union membership.

SOURCE: Clemens, Jason, Mark Mullins, and Niels Veldhuis. "Let's Celebrate the High Living Standards Resulting from the Fruits of Our Labour, Not Union Marketing and Propaganda." *Toronto Star* 1 Sept. 2003: A19.

Up for Debate

The original version of the above article was written by staff members of the Fraser Institute, an economic policy institute, or "think tank," based in Vancouver. This edited version appeared in the *Toronto Star* on Labour Day in 2003. Read this article as well as one expressing a contrary view, and write a persuasive, properly researched argumentative essay in opposition to this article. Use both articles to form your debate points.

LEGAL
p. 29
HANDBOOK

CONFIRM YOUR UNDERSTANDING

1. What outside influences could (a) strengthen and (b) weaken the bargaining power of a union negotiating team attempting to arrive at a collective agreement?

2. Who controls and regulates the collective bargaining process?

3. Why is it important that both sides appear to have won in negotiating a successful agreement?

4. Explain the difference between arbitration and mediation.

5. Why is final-offer-selection such a stressful strategy for both parties?

6. If 55 percent of the members of a union vote to strike, union representatives would be very concerned. Explain why.

7. Why is work-to-rule a useful strategy to force both sides back to the bargaining table?

8. Under what conditions would governments legislate striking workers back to work?

9. Assume you have been asked to advise government on whether to permit replacement workers in its employment legislation. Write a brief report outlining your position.

10. Assume the role of lawyer for a store whose business has dropped because of the picketers mentioned in *R.W.D.S.U. Local 558 v. Pepsi-Cola Canada Beverages (West) Ltd.*, above. Make an argument that secondary picketing should be prohibited.

The Collective Agreement

For unionized workers and businesses, the collective agreement is the key factor shaping work and the workplace. A collective agreement functions in the same way as any other contract—terms and conditions must be clearly defined. If a benefit is not included in the contract, there is no entitlement. If a dispute arises between employer and employee about when overtime is to be paid, for example, or if an employee is fired, the first step in resolving the dispute is to examine the contract. Union representatives and business managers spend much time making sure the other side lives up to its part of the bargain, and labour arbitrators will settle grievances according to their interpretation of provisions in the agreement.

Collective agreements exist in the context of other legal developments and must accord with human rights legislation, occupational health and safety acts, and employment standard laws (see the case of Tawney Meiorin in Chapter 6, p. 181). For example, any clause that excludes potential employees on the basis of sex, race, or disability would be unenforceable and open to legal action. At one time, collective agreements were relatively simple documents that set out hours of work and wages. Today's collective agreement is a complex legal document that includes clauses, sub-clauses, appendices, schedules, and so on. In many cases, collective agreements are so complex that the average worker barely understands them.

In Canada, there are thousands of collective agreements involving many types of businesses and occupations, but all share a similar structure and some common features. Almost every collective agreement begins with a preamble explaining its purpose. Most agreements also include clauses defining and regulating the relationship between the union and the employer; setting out the definition of the bargaining unit; outlining management and employee rights and responsibilities; and establishing grievance and arbitration procedures. Most collective agreements include a management rights clause that acknowledges management's right to manage the company. For employees, probably the most important articles of the agreement are those that specify working hours and details of compensation. Collective agreements may also include rules on how promotions are to be made and how layoffs are to be handled.

Union versus Non-Union

As you learned earlier, most employees in Canada negotiate with their employer individually rather than through union representation.

Landmark CASE

Parry Sound (District) Social Services Administration Board v. O.P.S.E.U., Local 324, 2003 S.C.C. 42

Read the following case analysis, which illustrates the conflict between a collective agreement and human rights legislation. The facts, issue, decision, and *ratio* have been provided. The court found that human rights legislation must take priority in a collective agreement, even if the employee is probationary. Assume that you disagree with the decision. Write a possible dissent for this case.

Facts: Joanne O'Brien was employed by the Parry Sound Social Services Administration Board on a probationary contract. Before the end of her probationary period, she took maternity leave and when she returned to work she was dismissed with no reason given. O'Brien filed a grievance through the Ontario Public Service Employees Union claiming discrimination on the basis of family status: "I have been discharged from my position without justification…this decision was arbitrary, discriminatory, in bad faith and unfair."

O'Brien's employer argued that the terms of the collective agreement stated that a probationary employee may be discharged at the sole discretion of the employer for any reason and that such action is not subject to the grievance and arbitration procedure. The Ontario Labour Relations Board found for O'Brien, arguing that she had been discriminated against according to the Ontario *Human Rights Code* and that the collective agreement had to

be interpreted in a manner consistent with the *Code*. The Divisional Court held that the Board had no authority to ignore the terms of the collective agreement and the case was appealed. The Ontario Court of Appeal ruled that tribunals do have the authority to apply human rights laws to collective agreements. The case was appealed to the Supreme Court of Canada.

Issue: Do human rights laws override the terms of a collective agreement?

Held: The appeal should be dismissed and the original decision of the Board accepted.

Ratio Decidendi: (Iacobucci J.) Speaking for the majority, Justice Iacobucci argued that while courts should not interfere unduly with collective agreements, the law must sometimes take priority. Substantive rights and obligations of human rights codes must be incorporated into each collective agreement over which an arbitrator has jurisdiction. Human rights and other statutes related to employment establish a floor beneath which an employer and union cannot contract. "Every person has a right to equal treatment in employment. This is implicit in the collective agreement, making the discriminatory discharge of a probationary employee arbitrable."

Therefore, although probationary employees may be discharged or not granted permanent status at the employer's discretion, labour tribunals and arbitrators must consider whether human rights laws have been violated. This means the substantive rights and obligations of employment-related statutes are implicit in each collective agreement over which an arbitrator has jurisdiction.

Employees not governed by a collective agreement must rely on their contracts and on employment legislation to protect their interests. Non-unionized workers have many of the same concerns as unionized workers. They want decent wages and benefits and to be treated fairly in the workplace. Non-unionized employees are protected by legislation such as their province's employment standards act, human rights code, health and safety act, and the *Canadian Charter of Rights and Freedoms*. In addition, in the absence of a collective agreement, employers and employees can turn to the courts for dispute resolution. Courts have ruled on how much severance pay long-term employees must receive if they are dismissed, for example. If an employer changes the conditions of the workplace significantly, thereby forcing an employee to resign, the courts may conclude that the action constitutes **constructive dismissal**, that is, the employee had no choice but to resign. In this situation, the court would award the employee compensation for lost wages.

For non-unionized employees, the employment contract is extremely important. For example, unless the contract stipulates paid sick leave, there is no entitlement, nor is there entitlement to overtime pay unless the employee works beyond the hours covered in the relevant province's employment standards act. Employers can dismiss a non-union employee for any reason or no reason. The only issue is how much severance pay the employee must receive according to the employment contract. On the other hand, a unionized worker who is dismissed has the benefit of union representation and can take steps to fight the dismissal and be reinstated. In the case of a non-union contract dispute between employee and employer, the employee who feels wronged must either sue in court or file a claim under the basic employment standards legislation. Generally, employees in supervisory or management positions must sue if a dispute cannot be resolved, while lower-level employees must file a claim under the basic employment standards legislation. In the unionized work-

place, the employee can file a grievance, or allegation of misapplication or misinterpretation of the collective agreement, and have the matter resolved by the union or by an arbitrator appointed by the department of labour.

Many workers in Canada prefer not to be unionized because they feel they can freely negotiate their own worth in the workplace. They point out that they are not bound by an agreement that imposes the same wage structures on all employees, and they have more flexibility in the workplace to pursue promotion without such restrictions as the seniority clauses and narrowly defined job descriptions common to collective agreements. Of course, they also do not have to pay union dues and are protected in the workplace by employment legislation.

The Global Economy and Labour

"Globalization" refers to the convergence of companies into massive multinational businesses, the expansion of free trade agreements, and the increased interdependence of national

FIGURE 12.11   Protestors attending the Summit of the Americas in Québec City (2001) flash the peace sign at police. Why do you think so many people protest free trade agreements and globalization?

economies around the globe. As it has on almost every aspect of life in the past two decades, globalization has had a major impact on labour. Unions in Canada have struggled to maintain wage and benefit levels for their members in a competitive environment where countries with lower labour standards can offer businesses lower production costs and other economic advantages.

Other factors have also affected the labour market and the bargaining power of the unions. Corporate mergers and technological automation have led to widespread industrial layoffs of many unionized workers, thus reducing levels of union membership and strength. Canada's economy continues to change, moving away from manufacturing and primary industries to service industries. Jobs in service industries are often lower paid and harder to unionize. Decades of cutbacks in government spending have also meant that there are fewer workers in the public sector, which has traditionally been a union stronghold.

The ease with which multinational businesses can move offices, production facilities, and service centres from country to country to keep down costs has contributed to the breakdown of prospects for secure, long-term employment. This reality has also tended to weaken the labour movement in Canada and elsewhere. It has meant that unions cannot always negotiate job security or rely on secure union membership and dues.

As free trade agreements such as the North American Free Trade Agreement (NAFTA) continue to facilitate the flow of capital, goods, and service across national borders, it is unlikely that this competitive environment will change. Canada was a founding member of the World Trade Organization (WTO), which promotes international trade by setting policies and settling trade disputes between nations. WTO rulings are binding on the more than 140 member nations. However, the WTO does not impose labour standards in its rulings. Critics say that by not setting core labour standards, the WTO is ignoring labour abuses in developing countries that have little or no labour law to protect workers. This, they say, makes it much easier for multinational businesses to exploit workers in those countries. The WTO's position is that freer trade will lead to economic growth, which in turn will create better labour conditions in the developing world. Imposing labour standards would impede that process. The 1996 Singapore ministerial declaration makes the WTO's official position clear: "We [the WTO] reject the use of labour standards for protectionist purposes, and agree that the comparative advantage of countries, particularly low-wage developing countries, must in no way be put into question."

The Future of Collective Bargaining

The rate of union membership in Canada has declined steadily for two decades. According to Statistics Canada, the rate of union membership (as a percentage of non-agricultural, paid employment) for the year 2003 was 30.4 percent. In 1983, the rate reached its peak of 40 percent. In other developed countries, the rate of union membership has declined even more dramatically.

All working people, both unionized and non-unionized, face serious obstacles moving into the twenty-first century. As businesses strive to be

FIGURE 12.12 The next time you phone for tech support, the friendly voice you get may be speaking to you from India. How may this development affect your work future and the future of labour law in Canada?

more flexible and cut costs, they hire fewer permanent employees. The worker of the twenty-first century is more likely to be self-employed or a temporary, part-time, or contract employee. This situation will make it more difficult, if not impossible, for workers to organize and become union members. In addition, new immigrants, who are playing an ever greater role in the Canadian labour force, are often more concerned with gaining Canadian experience than with joining a union. Ironically, it is workers such as these—those with low pay and little or no job security—who might benefit most from union protection. At the same time, the global economy is forcing employers to push for union concessions, arguing that Canada's highly paid workforce cannot compete with the low wages paid in developing nations. The declining bargaining power of unions in the domestic workplace has

also weakened the ability of unions to make much progress internationally. Unions have been largely unsuccessful in trying to unionize workers in Mexico and South America, for example.

Organized labour has traditionally opposed concessions and wage rollbacks, but it may no longer be in a position to do so. Even a union as powerful as the Canadian Auto Workers (CAW) had to accept wage rollbacks when it negotiated on behalf of Air Canada employees in 2003, and the United Food and Commercial Workers, the union representing workers at Loblaws Superstores, also accepted cuts to wages and benefits and fewer union jobs in its collective agreement in the same period. Employees who see wages and benefits reduced in collective agreements are likely to blame their unions and question why they should continue paying union dues.

Confirm Your Understanding

1. Outline some of the factors common to most collective agreements.
2. Harold Banjac, Aiden Lowell, and Kenneth Ghuri are all employees of a large corporation. Harold is a manager, Aiden works as a clerk, and Kenneth works on the assembly line making auto parts. All three employees were wrongfully accused of stealing from the company and then fired. Kenneth is the only union member, in this case the CAW. Prepare a chart indicating the procedure each employee would likely follow in attempting to fight the accusations and their dismissals.
3. Why is the increasing use of temporary, part-time, and contract workers making it more difficult for unions to increase their membership?
4. What global factors are influencing the bargaining power of the union movement?

In Closing

In Canada's early years as a nation, workers—including children—worked 60- and even 80-hour weeks in factories, mines, and other harsh environments. Although conditions have improved dramatically for most workers in Canada, problems still persist. Thousands of homeworkers, many of them illegal immigrants and many of them children, work 60-hour weeks sewing garments at home. In some developing countries, young girls work 60- to 80-

hour weeks assembling running shoes or computer boards in crowded unhealthy workplaces. It sometimes seems that nothing much has changed in the battle of workers to receive decent wages and safe working conditions. Jobs tend to go where inexpensive labour is found. As businesses outsource production and services, the "dark, satanic" factories of the nineteenth-century Industrial Revolution have reappeared in the twenty-first century, sometimes in Asia,

Africa, Mexico, or in crowded basement apartments in Toronto that no labour officials will ever inspect.

Labour laws have set standards and improved working conditions in Canada. *PC 100, the Canada Labour Code,* and provincial employment standards acts set minimum standards to protect workers and provide regulations to make labour–management relations more equitable and peaceful. Canada's courts have acknowledged the special relationship between employer and employee and have set precedents that established rights and responsibilities for both labour and management.

The union movement has been a driving force in obtaining fairer wages and more humane working conditions not only for the approximately 4 million union members in Canada but for all workers. Unions have also exerted their influence by taking action on social issues such as pay equity and child labour. They have brought unfair labour practices to light and fought to improve the safety of workers. Although there is much room for improvement, the workplace in twenty-first–century Canada is a better place because of those efforts.

As you enter the workforce, you will be feeling your way in a world of multiple careers and part-time jobs where nothing is constant but change. Will the changing workplace of the twenty-first century fulfill your needs and dreams? Will it fulfill the dream of Samuel Gompers, the first president of the American Federation of Labour who, when asked in Chicago in 1893 what does labour want, replied, "…more constant work and less greed, more justice and less revenge; in fact, more opportunities to cultivate our better natures."

CHAPTER ACTIVITIES

Extend Your Legal Knowledge

1. Examine the following six social and economic trends since the 1980s and choose two that you believe will have the most significance for the labour movement in the years ahead. Explain your answers:
   a) the movement from an economy based on manufacturing to a service-based economy
   b) the movement from permanent employment to temporary, part-time, and self-employment
   c) an increase in the number of women entering the workforce
   d) the movement from low unemployment rates to high unemployment rates
   e) the growth of multinational businesses
   f) the expansion of free trade agreements

2. Obtain a copy of a collective agreement and outline its key components in chart form.

3. Examine your province's employment standards act and answer the following questions:
   a) What is the minimum wage?
   b) What classes of employees does the act not cover?
   c) What are the maximum daily and weekly hours an employee must work before being paid overtime?
   d) What statutory holidays are mandatory and paid?
   e) What does the act say about sick leave, parental leave, vacation pay, and breaks?
   f) What are the most recent amendments to the act?
   g) Indicate two amendments you would make to the act.

4. Research and explain what is meant by the following terms:
   a) Constructive dismissal
   b) Just cause
   c) Wrongful dismissal
   d) Severance
   e) Wild-cat strike

5. What are some of the monetary and non-monetary gains that workers wish to achieve when they join a union?

6. Examine the Web site of the USW, OPSEU, OSSTF, CAW, or another union of your choice. Based on what you find there, create a chart that shows

the services the union offers its members that are not related to collective bargaining.

7. Trace the roots of selected social legislation such as the *Unemployment Insurance Act, Old Age Pensions Act, Canada Health Act,* and *Canada Welfare Act.* Identify political parties and organizations responsible for this legislation.

Think About the Law

8. How does mediation help to reduce the likelihood of a strike or lockout?

9. Of the three types of bargaining—individual, agent, or collective—which would you prefer to use at the beginning of your career? Explain your answer.

10. Read the following edited article and answer the questions below:

Ed Broadbent will launch his campaign to return to national politics armed with a hefty war chest, if he, as is widely expected, wins the NDP (New Democratic Party) nomination for an Ottawa riding tonight.

"We're confident of victory," Victoria Smallman, co-chair of his campaign in the riding of Ottawa Centre, said yesterday. Broadbent, who is coming back to the federal political scene after stepping down as leader in 1989, attracted roughly $36,000 in unsolicited donations in only forty-eight hours after announcing his intention to run in the next election.

Smallman said most of the money came from unions, who beat an end-of-the-year change in the law that now blocks them and corporations from making political donations.

The party is holding these funds in trust for Broadbent pending the nomination vote. (Lawton 2004)

a) Why would unions be willing to invest money in supporting a political party?

b) Do you agree with the new law forbidding donations to political parties from unions and corporations? Explain your answer.

c) What problems do you foresee with such a law?

d) Why do you think the writer used the term "war chest" to describe this donation? Do you think such a term reflects bias? Explain.

11. Many US states have what are called right-to-work laws, which state that workers cannot be forced to join a union or to pay union dues in order to work. In other words, there are no union shop or closed shop workplaces in these states. Would you support such legislation in Canada? Explain your answer.

12. The following poll was done by the *National Post* to find out how Canadian employees feel about unionization:

Would you like to be unionized? (Asked of non-unionized respondents)

Yes 13%   No 81%   Don't know/refused 6%

If you were given the choice in your current job between remaining unionized or not being a member of a union, which would you choose? (Asked of unionized respondents)

Remain Unionized 81%

Not be unionized 13%

Don't know/refused 6%

Source: *National Post*/Global National Poll. "State of the Unions." *Financial Post* 2 Sept. 2003: FP4.

a) How would you interpret this poll if you were a union organizer?

b) How would you interpret this poll if you were anti-union?

c) What do you think accounts for the results in this poll? You may want to consider the political bias of the newspaper.

Communicate About the Law

13. Research and prepare a debate arguing either for or against the following statement:

"Unions are the best hope for ensuring a fair distribution of income to the broadest reaches of our society"—Hassan Yussuff, Secretary-Treasurer, Canadian Labour Congress (Swartz 2003).

14. Read the following article and prepare a research paper, video, or PowerPoint presentation examining the role of government legislation and involvement in workplace safety.

Last year in Ontario, 14 young workers died from work-related injuries, according to the Workplace Safety and Insurance Board. More than 14 000 others between the ages of 15 and 24 were seriously enough injured to take time off work. Labour leaders argue the government has failed in its responsibility to ensure workplaces are safe by reducing the number of inspectors and allowing inspectors to investigate complaints about unsafe conditions on the phone rather than in person. Labour leaders argue that the government has shifted the burden of workplace safety to young workers.
(Perry 2003)

Apply the Law

15. Read the facts presented below. Using the precedent set in *R.W.D.S.U. Local 558 v. Pepsi-Cola Canada Beverages (West) Ltd.*, on page 383, what do you think the decision would be in this strike–lockout situation? Prepare a short *ratio decidendi*.

United Food and Commercial Workers Local 1518 v. KMart Canada, [1999] 2 S.C.R. 1083

Facts: The respondent, Kmart Canada Ltd., operated several stores in British Columbia, seven of them in the Lower Mainland, two in Victoria, one in Campbell River, and one in Port Alberni. The appellant was the union certified to represent employees at the Campbell River and Port Alberni stores only, which were the primary employer. During a labour dispute with the primary employer, groups of 2–12 of the two stores' unionized employees peacefully distributed leaflets to prospective Kmart customers at the secondary sites. The majority of the individuals stood between six to eight feet from the doors. They handed out two types of leaflets, describing the respondent's alleged unfair practices and urging customers to shop elsewhere.

In December 1992, pursuant to the *Industrial Relations Act*, RSBC 1979, c. 212, the respondent asked the province's Industrial Relations Council to restrain the leafleting

activity at the secondary sites. The case was appealed to the Labour Board, which argued that leafleting should be restricted. The union appealed to the Supreme Court of Canada, arguing that leafleting constituted lawful expression and that there was no basis to restrict it in a free and democratic society. The relevant parts of the leaflets read as follows:

ATTENTION K-MART SHOPPERS!!!

DID YOU KNOW THAT

K-mart locked out over 140 employees, preventing them from working in their K-MART stores in Campbell River and Port Alberni in an attempt to stop the employees from attaining the basic needs within a first collective agreement.

Please do not spend your Christmas $$$ at K-mart.

We are asking for your assistance by boycotting this giant multinational corporation called K-Mart. By doing so, we hope to move one step closer to eliminating the exploitation of employees who work for K-Mart and return our striking workers back to work with dignity, respect and a fair collective agreement.

16. Read the following case dealing with the issue of wrongful dismissal. Assume that you are one of the judges on the Ontario Court of Appeal, and write a decision on this case.

Bannister v. General Motors of Canada Ltd. (1998-08-27) ONCA Docket C20511

Facts: Alan Bannister was an employee of General Motors with 23 years' seniority. He had a good work record in the security department at the automaker's factory in St. Catharines, Ontario. One of Bannister's jobs was to supervise the work of female summer students. According to the evidence submitted, Bannister harassed some of these students, attempted to kiss them, and used inappropriate language in their presence. Although General Motors did have a sexual harassment policy in place, it was not strictly enforced. The work atmosphere was considered to be "rough" and workers believed that any women working in the plant would simply have to deal with the tough language and behaviour.

Bannister became the subject of many complaints of sexual harassment and eventually General Motors investigated the allegations against him. Bannister denied them all. General Motors fired Bannister and he sued for wrongful dismissal. The trial judge held that Bannister had been wrongfully dismissed because his actions were no worse than that of many employees in his department. The trial judge also accepted evidence from Bannister that not all of the women appeared to be particularly upset by his conduct. The judge said, "Some of them gave as good as they got," and "it takes two to tango," suggesting the women were quite capable of taking care of themselves in a sexist environment. The company appealed to the Ontario Court of Appeal.

17. The employer and employee in the following case have agreed to arbitration. Read the facts of the case and, assuming the role of arbitrator, determine an appropriate outcome. Indicate your decision and your reasons in a brief report.
Facts: Kurt Schwartz was employed as a set designer with a local television company. As part

of his job he was given a company credit card to buy props as needed. Schwartz got into trouble over a gambling debt and used the company credit card to purchase an expensive guitar that he later pawned for money to pay off his debt. Schwartz intended to make money by gambling the following week, and he would then buy back the guitar and return it to the store where he purchased it before the end of the month, when his employer would find out. Schwartz, however, did not make money gambling, and his supervisor discovered the guitar purchase.

Initially the supervisor did not question the purchase, assuming it was part of a set, and Schwartz managed to buy back the guitar and get the purchase price refunded on the credit card. In the meantime, however, the supervisor had realized that the guitar was not needed for any set and confronted Schwartz. Schwartz admitted that he had misused the card but argued that he had no intention of stealing the money, and that the money had been repaid. The supervisor told Schwartz he could either quit or the company would press charges against him for fraud. Schwartz agreed to quit, but after consulting with his union representative, withdrew his offer to quit. Both sides have agreed to accept the decision of an arbitrator.

BIBLIOGRAPHY

Baruth-Walsh, Mary E. *Strike!: 99 Days on the Line: The Workers' Own Story of the 1945 Windsor Ford Strike*. Manotick, ON: Penumbra Press, 1995.

Clemens, Jason, Mark Mullins, and Niels Veldhuis. "Let's Celebrate the High Living Standards Resulting from the Fruits of Our Labour, Not Union Marketing and Propaganda." *Toronto Star* 1 Sept. 2003: A19.

Gunderson, Morley, et al. *Union-Management Relations in Canada*. Toronto: Pearson Education Canada Inc., 2001.

Lawton, Valerie. "Unions Boost Broadbent's War Chest." *Toronto Star* 20 June 2004.

Perry, Ann. "Teaching Young Workers How to Just Say No." *Toronto Star* 28 June 2003: F1.

Richards, Gwendolyn. "Child Labour." *The Globe and Mail* 6 Aug. 2003: C1.

Springer, Jane. *Listen to Us: The World's Working Children*. Toronto: Douglas & McIntyre, 1997.

Swartz, Mark. "Labouring Over the State of the Unions." *Toronto Star* 23 Aug. 2003.

World Trade Organization. *Understanding the WTO*, Chapter 4. p. 74. Accessed 16 Feb. 2004 <www.wto.org/english/thewto_e/whatis_e/tif_e/utw_chap4_e.pdf>

ENVIRONMENTAL LAW

LEARNING EXPECTATIONS

After reading this chapter, you will be able to:

- explain the role of government and the courts in developing and enforcing environmental laws
- analyze the effectiveness of the major environmental statutes in Ontario and Canada
- evaluate the role of individuals or organizations in lobbying for laws that protect the environment
- evaluate the effectiveness of international treaties in the protection of the environment

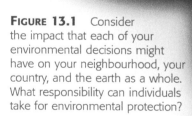

FIGURE 13.1 Consider the impact that each of your environmental decisions might have on your neighbourhood, your country, and the earth as a whole. What responsibility can individuals take for environmental protection?

Environment.... Seen from far away, we must take care of it. Now!

—Marc Garneau (1949–), Canadian astronaut

■ I N T R O D U C T I O N ■

Environmental law is an emerging and evolving area of law. Since the early 1970s, several factors have influenced the development of environmental laws, two of which are key. The first factor is the public's increasing awareness of the benefits of a clean environment, together with a better understanding of the undesirable and costly consequences of living on a polluted planet. The second factor is the sheer increase in the world's population, especially its urban population. In North America, this increase in urban population has, in turn, coincided with a rising standard of living and greater consumption of the earth's resources.

This combination of increased awareness and a larger population has caused a double effect on the environment. The first effect is that population increases cause more urban sprawl, which is poorly planned and uncontrolled development, where residents are dependent on cars to get to workplaces, stores, and services. Population increases also result in the depletion of forests, farmland, and natural resources such as fish stocks. The second effect is how the predominance of a higher standard of living causes environmental degradation. For example, bigger homes use more energy, and bigger vehicles, like SUVs, cause more air pollution.

Environmental concerns over such issues as chemical waste dumps, industrial toxins in the watershed, motor-vehicle pollution, species at risk, and resource depletion are all subject to regulation in Canada. As concerns about our environment grow, governments in Canada are being called on to address issues through environmental protection legislation. In this chapter, you will be introduced to key environmental laws in Canada as a whole and in Ontario, such as environmental protection and environmental assessment acts. You will also consider the extent to which these laws are effective in addressing environmental concerns. You will explore how legislation cannot always provide a remedy for alleged environmental harm, and how a remedy in such a case may be available in a civil action under tort law.

In cases where environmental laws are perceived to be inadequate, individuals and groups often play an active role in **lobbying** the government for change. Lobbying refers to actions that people take to try to influence legislation. When it comes to conflict resolution, the balance between environmental and economic interests often becomes a focal point. Are the two interests mutually exclusive?

We regard all created beings as sacred and important, for everything has a wochangi, or influence.

—Black Elk, Lakota Sioux Nation, 1986

Can you have economic prosperity while protecting the natural environment? As our concerns as global citizens increase, we become more aware of the complexity of balancing economic and environmental interests. And as it becomes increasingly clear that air and water pollution do not respect national boundaries, countries must now consider the impact of their actions in a global context. It is essential for countries to develop international agreements that demonstrate a commitment to environmental protection.

The Role of Government in Environmental Protection

Neither the federal nor provincial governments have complete jurisdiction over environmental protection in Canada. Both levels of government have been given the constitutional authority to establish environmental legislation that can be either general or specific. First, let's consider federal legislation. Under federal jurisdiction, legislation such as the *Canadian Environmental Protection Act* is used to broadly cover environmental issues. Conversely, federal legislation such as the *Fisheries Act* is resource-specific.

Now compare this federal scenario with a provincial one, looking specifically at Ontario. The provincial government of Ontario assumes primary jurisdiction over environmental protection through an extensive regulatory framework. In Ontario, provincial environmental protection legislation can be resource-specific, such as the *Safe Drinking Water Act*. However, provincial legislation can also broadly encompass resources and environmental issues under such mandates as the *Environmental Protection Act* and the *Environmental Assessment Act*. Furthermore, some provinces have also passed municipal acts to provide municipal governments with specific decision-making powers. Municipalities may pass environmental bylaws that regulate specific practices, such as land use, recycling, and the use of pesticides. All three levels of government have enacted laws relating to the environment and are involved in enforcing the provisions of the legislation. In this chapter, selected environmental protection statutes are highlighted in order to examine how federal and provincial governments have responded to the issue of environmental protection.

Federal Environmental Laws

Three main federal statutes that deal with environmental protection are the *Canadian Environmental Protection Act, 1999,* the *Fisheries Act,* and the *Species at Risk Act.* Each of these acts will be analyzed in terms of their scope and their effectiveness in regulating environmental concerns. These three statutes and other key federal environmental legislation are listed in Figure 13.2.

Canadian Environmental Protection Act, 1999

The *Canadian Environmental Protection Act,* often referred to as CEPA, was introduced in 1988. It is the main federal environmental statute in Canada. The law was reviewed in 1995 and subsequently amended in 1999 in order to make improvements to the following areas: prevention of pollution, the control of toxic substances, the control of waste management, and the protection of the environment and human health in Canada. Included in the act's preamble is the following:

> The Government of Canada seeks to achieve sustainable development that is based on an ecologically efficient use of natural, social and economic resources and acknowledges the

Major Federal Environmental Legislation

- *Arctic Waters Pollution Prevention Act*
- *Canada Shipping Act*
- *Canada Water Act*
- *Canadian Environmental Assessment Act*
- *Canadian Environmental Protection Act, 1999*
- *Fisheries Act*
- *Migratory Birds Convention Act, 1994*
- *Northwest Territories Waters Act*
- *Nuclear Safety and Control Act*
- *Pest Control Products Act*
- *Species at Risk Act*
- *Transportation of Dangerous Goods Act, 1992*

FIGURE 13.2   This chart lists Canada's key environmental statutes. The scope of this legislation ranges from such activities as regulating the transport of dangerous goods to protecting migratory birds and fisheries. Do you think environmental protection should be high on the federal government's priority list?

need to integrate environmental, economic and social factors in the making of all decisions by government and private entities....[The] Government of Canada recognizes the importance of an ecosystem approach [i.e., the maintenance of a natural, self-contained system of plants, animals, and micro-organisms that functions with the non-living components of its environment].

It is evident in the preamble of CEPA that the federal government has responded to environmental concerns by incorporating key environmental principles, such as sustainable development and pollution prevention, in the scope of its legislation. According to the legislation, the government is committed to **sustainable development**, which is defined under the legislation as "development that meets the needs of the present without compromising the ability of future generations to meet their own needs." The federal government also acknowledges pollution prevention as a goal. CEPA defines **pollution prevention** as "the use of

processes, practices, materials, products, substances or energy that avoid or minimize the creation of pollutants and waste and reduce the overall risk to the environment or human health."

In order to effectively manage issues such as pollution prevention, the minister of the environment, under s. 56 (1) of CEPA, may issue a notice requiring a person or class of persons to prepare and implement a pollution prevention plan regarding a substance listed as toxic under the act. The federal government has also established an "Environmental Registry" under CEPA. Through the registry, citizens are provided with access to information such as environmental policies and regulations. The registry also posts notices, approvals, objections to approvals, and other documents relating to issues addressed under the act. For example, if there has been a toxic spill and an environmental action is taken, documents submitted by the ministry to the court would be made publicly available through this registry. The legislation also gives citizens the right to sue if an action has resulted in significant environmental harm. Any action taken under this legislation must be initiated within a two-year limitation period. This period runs either from the time a plaintiff becomes aware of the alleged conduct or from the time it is deemed that he or she *should* have become aware of it. In an environmental action where significant harm is alleged, the plaintiff must prove his or her case on the **balance of probabilities**, meaning the standard of proof required for the believability of an argument.

In its commitment to environmental protection, CEPA embraces two progressive environmental principles: the precautionary principle and the polluter-pays principle. Under the **precautionary principle**, full scientific proof of harm does not have to be established before environmental action is taken. The threat of serious harm or irreversible damage may be enough to warrant action to protect the environment. The preamble of CEPA embraces the precautionary principle: "Whereas the Government of Canada is committed to implementing the precautionary principle that, where there are threats of serious or irreversible damage, lack of full scientific certainty shall not be used as a reason for postponing cost-effective measures to prevent environmental degradation." The government's endorsement of the precautionary principle is a significant step in addressing environmental concerns, but it remains to be seen how judges will apply this principle in the courts.

The **polluter-pays principle** requires that the users and producers of toxic substances and pollutants be held responsible for costs associated with the regulation of these substances, such as the cleanup of a toxic waste site. (Refer to the Legal Handbook for an article citing the use of the polluter-pays principle in the case of *Imperial Oil Ltd. v. Québec [Minister of the Environment]*, 2003 S.C.C. 58.)

CEPA is also committed to respecting biological diversity, (also known as biodiversity),

which can be defined as full genetic variety within and among species. CEPA regulates actions that would threaten this diversity. Under CEPA, toxic substances are specifically regulated. Health and environment ministries first scrutinize substances in question in order to assess the risk to human health or to the environment. The legislation defines a toxic substance under s. 64 as one that enters the environment or may enter the environment under conditions that

(a) have or may have an immediate or long-term harmful effect on the environment or its biological diversity;

(b) constitutes or may constitute a danger to the environment on which life depends; or

(c) constitutes or may constitute a danger in Canada to human life or health.

If a substance is designated as toxic under CEPA, then the federal government can regulate all aspects of dealing with the substance, from safe storage to safe disposal. Substances such as DDT (used as a pesticide), PCBs (used as heat-exchange fluids and in a variety of products, including some plastics and paints), and dioxins (used to bleach paper products and in such materials as rayon) are currently targeted for virtual elimination under the act. Under s. 65 (1) of CEPA, **virtual elimination** requires "the ultimate reduction of the quantity or concentration of [a toxic] substance [released into the environment to be] below the level of quantification specified."

The CEPA legislation has been criticized. For example, by January 2004, CEPA had listed 56 substances as toxic under Schedule I of the act. David R. Boyd, an environmental lawyer, professor, and author of the book *Unnatural Law*, questions CEPA's slow screening process for designating toxic substances as well as the limited number of substances that have been listed. Furthermore, Boyd acknowledges that, when the law is enforced, regulations can produce a reduction in point-source pollution (pollution that can be identified as originating from one specific, identifiable source), yet

FIGURE 13.3 Joe Blondin, Jr., a representative of the Dene Nation, appeared before the Commons Environmental and Sustainable Development Committee in June 1998. The committee was studying the health effects of uranium contamination in the Great Bear Lake District of the Northwest Territories. How does the concept of sustainable development relate to environmental concerns?

current approaches to environmental regulation are relatively ineffective in addressing the growing problems from non-point sources (pollution that originates from many different sources). For example, if an industry dumps waste material into a water system through one pipe, the source of the pollution is identifiable; therefore, action can be taken. However, if a chemical is introduced into the water system through runoff from chemically sprayed fields or through urban runoff, it is more difficult to trace the source.

Boyd recognizes the difficulty in regulating non-point sources of pollution: "Non-point source pollution is like the Internet: widely dispersed, international in scope, and difficult to regulate using conventional thinking." Boyd is also critical of the way in which the legislation allows Canadian companies to pollute as long as they have a permit and act within the limits of the permit. He also condemns the way in which water pollution legislation ties permissible levels of water pollution to production volumes. For example, the more pulp that is produced by a pulp mill, the greater the amount of effluent (waste product) that is allowed to be released into the water. The government, however, takes the position that a compromise must take place, so that the objectives both of economic growth and of pollution prevention are balanced. The preamble of CEPA reflects this compromise: it suggests that where you cannot eliminate pollutants and wastes, you can control and manage them. Hence, it expresses the idea of paying for the right to pollute in order to achieve pollution reduction over time.

CEPA designates the use of enforcement officers to control toxic substances. These enforcement officers are given the authority to investigate matters under the act and to make inspections. For example, they may search for a toxic substance or enforce emission requirements for vehicles, engines, or equipment. When an enforcement officer discovers that certain parties are not complying with the act or regulations, the officer may make an order for the parties to refrain from carrying out the particular activity, such as ceasing to dump a particular substance. The enforcement officer even has the authority to order that the particular work or activity be stopped or shut down for a specified period of time.

Enforcement provisions under CEPA carry strong penalties, including maximum penalties of a $1-million fine or five years in jail for specific indictable offences. One criticism of these penalty provisions, however, is that the courts do not typically impose fines of such magnitude or jail terms.

The legislation allows defendants to put forth a defence. One of the main defences allowed under CEPA is the defence of **due diligence**. If a defendant can show that he or she took all reasonable care to comply with regulations under the act, the defendant may be absolved from liability in an environmental protection action. The defence of due diligence is not allowed, however, if the offence knowingly involved, or if the offender negligently provided, false or misleading information.

In his book *Environmental Law*, Jamie Benidickson outlines a number of factors that the courts must weigh in considering the defence of due diligence. Such factors include the following:

> …nature and gravity of the adverse effect; forseeability of the effect, including abnormal sensitivities; alternative solutions available; legislative or regulatory compliance; industry standards; character of the neighbourhood; efforts (if any) made to address the problem; period of time over which such efforts were made, and promptness of response; matters beyond the control of the accused, including technological limitations; skill level expected of the accused; complexities involved; preventive systems; economic considerations; and actions of officials.

Fisheries Act

Although it may appear that the regulation of fisheries could fall under the protection of species legislation, fisheries have been given special protection in Canada. Given that fish is consumed throughout Canada and the world on such a grand scale and that fishing is a major source of income in Canada, much attention is focused on preventing the destruction of fish habitats and the depletion of fish stocks.

Federal fisheries officers are given the authority to make inspections and to ensure compliance under the act. Section 36 of the act makes it an offence to throw a prohibited substance, such as coal ashes, overboard, and it also makes it an offence to deposit or permit the deposit of a deleterious (i.e., harmful) substance into water inhabited by fish.

Under the legislation, there is no requirement for actual proof of harm to the fish. The act simply regulates the substances that can be deposited into water frequented by fish. The meaning of "deleterious substance" under s. 34 of the act includes any substance that would degrade or alter the quality of the water and render it harmful to fish.

The *Fisheries Act* has established penalties for violations. The maximum penalty for an indictable offence is $1 million for the first offence, and for subsequent offences the penalty includes a fine of $1 million and/or imprisonment for a term not exceeding three years. If a violation involves a summary conviction (less serious) offence, the maximum fine is reduced to $300 000 for the first offence, and for subsequent offences the penalty is a fine of $300 000 and/or a term of imprisonment not exceeding six months.

Under s. 35 (1) of the act, "No person shall carry on any work or undertaking that results in the harmful alteration, disruption or destruction of fish habitat." That is, any undertaking, such as the construction of a road, should not harm, alter, disrupt, or destroy fish habitat. Section 35 (1) is critically important to Canada's regulation of water pollution. The Department of Fisheries and Oceans (DFO) administers the *Fisheries Act*. DFO inspectors can investigate undertakings, such as the construction of a road, and require that those people who conduct the activity take reasonable measures consistent with the conservation of fish habitat.

The penalties for harmfully altering a fish habitat are the same as the penalties for depositing a deleterious substance. Under the *Fisheries Act*, penalties also exist for failing to provide requested information, to make a required report, to take reasonable measures required by the act, and to comply with a direction under the act. The first offence merits a penalty of $200 000. For subsequent offences, the penalty is a fine and/or a term of imprisonment not exceeding six months.

The legislation does authorize the deposit of certain substances by specific industries, as long as they meet regulated levels under the act. For

FIGURE 13.4 A Department of Fisheries and Oceans sign in White Rock, British Columbia, warns of contaminated shellfish and expressly forbids their harvesting. What laws are in place to protect Canada's fisheries?

example, pulp and paper mills are allowed to deposit substances, provided they meet the effluent regulations under the act. The pulp industry, however, must conduct studies on the effects of their actions.

In the case of *R. v. Imperial Oil*, (2000-10-13) B.C.C.A. Docket CA022519, Imperial Oil was charged with one environmental offence, under the *Fisheries Act,* for permitting a deleterious substance to be deposited into waters frequented by fish. The company was also charged under British Columbia's *Waste Management Act*, both

for allowing waste to be introduced into the environment and for non-compliance with its waste management permit.

Imperial Oil admitted to discharging a toxic effluent into Burrard Inlet, British Columbia, in February 1995. The effluent was found to contain the toxic compound MMT (a chemical that is added to gasoline in order to improve its octane level). Imperial Oil's effluent discharge permit required that the effluent pass a toxicity test before being discharged. The test required that at least 50 percent of the tested fish should be able to survive for a period of 96 hours while immersed in a 100 percent concentration of the particular effluent. Imperial Oil was able to verify that it had followed procedures for testing and had conducted these tests more often than was required by the terms of the permit. Results of tests performed by experts in February 1995 indicated that Imperial Oil had exceeded the permissible level of toxicity. It turns out that a relatively small amount of a chemical compound had escaped from a storage container, and the industry's separator did not remove the toxic compound from the effluent. The company had an environmental risk assessment program in place to identify and assess the potential risks; however, the program had not been fully implemented, such that not all of the risks had been identified. Imperial Oil argued that its program would have eventually identified the risk. Defence counsel for Imperial Oil argued that the company believed that a chemical separator would remove the compound from the effluent. They further argued at trial that the lack of toxicity warnings from the supplier about the toxic compound, MMT, and the lack of available data on the compound prevented them from knowing it would be dangerous to fish. Imperial Oil stated that the company thought it was using pure MMT, but in fact it was using a compound known as LP46, which its separator could not remove from the effluent.

Imperial Oil advanced the defence of due diligence—that it had taken reasonable care under the circumstances. The trial judge accepted the company's arguments and acquitted Imperial Oil. On appeal to the Summary-Conviction Appeal Court, a conviction was entered. The court rejected the defence of due diligence and concluded that Imperial Oil failed in exercising the required care both in determining the risks associated with the chemical and in determining whether the separator could remove it from the effluent.

Imperial Oil appealed the case to the Court of Appeal for British Columbia, arguing that the judge had wrongly interpreted the defence of due diligence and that the company should be acquitted. The majority of the court disagreed. The Honourable Justice Finch reasoned:

> Given the nature and size of the defendant, the sensitivity of the local environment, the information that the defendant possessed concerning the risks of MMT, the simplicity of testing to determine toxicity, and the defendant's broad range of expert advice, the learned trial judge did not, in my view, err in finding that the defendant had failed in its obligation to exercise reasonable care when it failed to obtain and to act upon information that it reasonably ought to have known.

In the dissenting opinion, Justice Newbury concluded that Imperial Oil had met the standard of due diligence by implementing its Haz-Ops environmental assessment program, by checking the separator and cleaning it regularly, and by using a Material Safety Data Sheet to report on all materials used in the plant and any irregularities in equipment. The majority of the court dismissed the appeal and affirmed the conviction.

Species at Risk Act

According to the Canadian environmentalist David Suzuki:

> Although extinction is as necessary to the evolutionary process as species formation, it has accelerated at an unprecedented rate as a

FIGURE 13.5   The *Species at Risk Act* protects biological diversity in Canada. One of the many species identified as endangered under the legislation is the Northern Spotted Owl. What other species are you aware of that have been identified and protected under the *Species at Risk Act*?

result of human degradation. There are many reasons to be alarmed by the loss of species, all of them completely selfish. Perhaps the shallowest is regret for loss of species whose potential utility for humankind is yet to be discovered. Another is that species such as spotted owls or marbled murrelets serve as "indicator species" of the state of the planet, just as canaries did for the state of air in coal mines. In other words, when such species disappear, they indicate that the planet as a whole may have become less habitable in a way that may be relevant to humanity. (1997)

As industries expand and urban centres develop and spread, an increasing number of wildlife habitats are being threatened. And when habitats are threatened, so are the animal and plant species contained within them. In December 2002, the federal government passed the *Species at Risk Act*, which protects 233 endangered species. The minister of the environment, the minister of fisheries and oceans, and the minister of Canadian heritage (responsible for national parks) administer the act.

The act has three specific purposes. First, it is meant to prevent Canadian wildlife species at risk from becoming extinct (i.e., no longer existing) or from being extirpated (i.e., destroyed in a particular place, in this case Canada, though it still exists elsewhere in the world). Second, it is meant to provide recovery for species at risk. Third, it is meant to encourage the management of species in order to keep them from becoming at risk. In order to ensure that documents relating to the act are more accessible to the public, a *Species at Risk Act* Public Registry was created. This registry provides greater public accessibility to information; it includes such items as listings of species at risk, proposed recovery strategies, and action plans.

The *Species at Risk Act* encourages species protection through voluntary action and **stewardship** programs. Stewardship can be defined as the activities that are necessary to maintain long-term protection of the environment from hazards. The *Species at Risk Act* provides for the creation of recovery programs and management plans to protect wildlife species. Under the act, anyone who harms or threatens animals that are considered endangered under this legislation, or damages their residence, can be prosecuted. The offence and enforcement provisions came into effect on June 4, 2004. Under the act, it is an offence to

kill, harm, harass, capture or take an individual of a wildlife species that is listed as an extirpated species, an endangered species or a threatened species, or a listed extirpated species if a recovery strategy has recommended its reintroduction into the wild in Canada.

The penalty structure for a summary conviction offence includes a fine of up to $300 000 for a for-profit corporation, a fine of up to $50 000 for a non-profit corporation, and/or a prison term of up to one year for each offence. If the offence is more serious, the penalties correspondingly increase. For an indictable offence, the penalty includes a fine of up to $1 million for a for-profit corporation, a fine of up to $250 000 for a non-profit corporation, a fine of up to $250 000 for an individual, and /or a jail term of up to five years.

In order to give the government time to put policies and programs into place, the act was phased in. Once the act came into full force, individuals being prosecuted were allowed to use the defence of due diligence.

Prior to 2002, when the proposed act was being debated, one of the strongest criticisms was that the act applied only to species on federal land. This would leave the provinces to deal with endangered species on provincial land under their own species protection legislation. Although Ontario, Manitoba, New Brunswick, and Manitoba have endangered species acts, not every province has enacted legislation in this area. A further criticism was that the act provided protection only to the residence of a species rather than to its **critical habitat** (i.e., the place where the species collects its food, breeds, and cares for its young). The concept of "residence" does not cover as broad an area as the concept of "critical habitat." Critics also expressed concern about the extent to which the Committee on the Status of Endangered Wildlife in Canada (COSEWIC) could play an unbiased role in identifying the species needing protection and in determining whether each species should be classified as endangered, threatened, extirpated, or of special concern. This concern arose because COSEWIC had already been assessing and classifying wildlife species in Canada since 1975, and critics wondered whether a fresh start was needed.

Under this legislation, COSEWIC's existing procedures would now be legally authorized. Under the act, after COSEWIC has assessed and analyzed a species, it sends a report to the

FIGURE 13.6   The *Species at Risk Act* protects both plant and animal wildlife species. Pictured here are four species on the endangered list: the wood poppy, the pink coreopsis, the leatherback turtle, and the North Atlantic right whale. Consider the whale. Due to hunting, a population of tens of thousands of North Atlantic right whales has been reduced to only a few hundred, making it one of the most endangered whales in the world. In July 2003, in the Bay of Fundy between Nova Scotia and New Brunswick, international shipping lanes were shifted in order to reduce the number of collisions between ships and these whales. Think of, or do research on, another endangered species in Canada. What measures can be taken to protect this species?

Ministry of the Environment and newly formed Canadian Endangered Species Conservation Council. The assessment is posted on the *Species at Risk Act* Public Registry Environmental Registry. The ministry has 90 days within which to respond regarding any concerns. Within nine months after the assessment is received by the government, the Governor-General-in-Council makes a decision about whether to add the species to the endangered list.

Under the act, once a species is added to the list of Wildlife Species at Risk, the federal government must provide immediate protection for this species on all federal lands. More specifically, listed aquatic species and migratory birds are protected irrespective of their being found on federal, provincial, or territorial lands.

For the listed species, the act outlines recovery strategies and management plans, and it specifies timelines for their completion. For species listed before June 2003, a recovery strategy must be prepared within three years if the species is identified as endangered and within four years if the species is threatened or extirpated. Should a species be denoted of special concern, a management plan must be prepared within five years. For all species listed after June 2003, the timelines for recovery plans have been reduced: a management plan must occur within one year for endangered species and within two years for threatened or extirpated species. For species of special concern, a management plan must be prepared within three years.

Confirm Your Understanding

1. Do offences under the *Fisheries Act* require proof of harm to fish? Explain.

2. Create a chart that summarizes the offences and penalties under the *Fisheries Act.*

3. How might a defendant charged with an environmental offence argue the defence of due diligence?

4. Summarize the purpose of the *Species at Risk Act*, and outline the benefits and drawbacks to this legislation.

5. Explain the process of protecting species under the *Species at Risk Act.*

Provincial Environmental Laws

This chapter examines four Ontario statutes that deal with environmental protection: the *Environmental Protection Act*; the *Environmental Bill of Rights, 1993* (EBR); the *Environmental Assessment Act*; and the *Safe Drinking Water Act, 2002.* Exploring these statutes helps to highlight the scope of provincial regulatory legislation dealing with environmental protection. (See Figure 13.7 for a list of these and other major environmental statutes in Ontario.)

Environmental Protection Act

The main environmental legislation in Ontario is the *Environmental Protection Act* (EPA). Some of the areas covered under the act work to protect and conserve the environment by prohibiting the discharge of contaminants, regulating waste management, controlling vehicle emissions, and regulating ozone-depleting substances. Section 14 (1) of the EPA states that "no person shall discharge a contaminant or cause or permit the discharge of a contaminant into the natural environment that causes or is likely to cause an adverse effect." The key to understanding this section of the act is the meaning of the phrase "adverse effect." It is defined under s. 1 of the act to include one or more of the following:

(a) impairment of the quality of the natural environment for any use that can be made of it,

Major Environmental Legislation in Ontario

- Conservation Authorities Act
- Dangerous Goods Transportation Act
- Environmental Assessment Act
- Environmental Bill of Rights, 1993
- Environmental Protection Act
- Municipal Act, 2001
- Nutrient Management Act
- Ontario Water Resources Act
- Pesticides Act
- Planning Act
- Safe Drinking Water Act, 2002

FIGURE 13.7   The provincial government of Ontario regulates environmental protection through an extensive regulatory framework. Which environmental issues are addressed through provincial legislation?

(b) injury or damage to property or to plant or animal life,

(c) harm or material discomfort to any person,

(d) an adverse effect on the health of any person,

(e) impairment of the safety of any person,

(f) rendering any property or plant or animal life unfit for human use,

(g) loss of enjoyment of normal use of property, and

(h) interference with the normal conduct of business

The definition of "adverse effect" covers a wide range of activities not limited to situations in which direct harm or injury result. For example, the legislation could apply to an unlawful discharge into the atmosphere that interferes with the use and enjoyment of your property. It could also apply to spills of industrial or hazardous waste that directly contaminate your water supply.

The *Environmental Protection Act* specifically addresses the cleanup of spills. The legislation places two key duties on those who cause the spill (or, when circumstances dictate it, on those who own or have control over the pollutant):

the duty to report and the duty to act. Essentially, under s. 92 (1), it requires that any person who has control over a spill or who has caused or permitted a spill (that has caused or is likely to cause an adverse effect) must notify the Ministry of the Environment, the municipality, the owner of the pollutant, or the person having control over the pollutant. This notice also must include information about the action that was taken or that is intended to be taken regarding the spill.

In essence, the act requires that there be a specific focus on cleanup and that the person or group responsible for paying the cleanup costs be notified. Next, the act requires that the owner of the spilled pollutant, together with the person having control of the pollutant that spilled, has a duty to mitigate (that is, to lessen the losses) and to restore the environment. Section 93 of the act states, "The owner of a pollutant and the person having control of a pollutant that is spilled and that causes or is likely to cause an adverse effect shall forthwith do everything practicable to prevent, eliminate and ameliorate the adverse effect and to restore the natural environment."

The owner of the pollutant, or the person having control over it, may not be held liable for the spill if it can be established either that he or she took all reasonable steps to prevent the spill or that the spill was caused by an external event such as a war, an act of terrorism, or an intention to cause harm by a third party.

In Ontario, regulation 346 of the *Environmental Protection Act* also controls air pollution. This regulation sets numerical limits on emissions of specific contaminants into the atmosphere and it creates an air quality index for monitoring air pollution levels. Furthermore, the act regulates waste management by requiring certificates of approval for the operation of waste management systems and waste disposal sites.

If investigators become aware of violations of the act, they have the authority to lay charges. Penalties are outlined in s. 187 of the EPA and are highlighted in Figure 13.8.

Under the EPA, directors and officers of a corporation have a duty of care and can be held liable. Section 194 (1) of the act states, "Every director or officer of a corporation that engages in an activity that may result in the discharge of a contaminant into the natural environment contrary to this Act or the regulations has a duty to take all reasonable care to prevent the corporation from causing or permitting such unlawful discharge." This liability provision ensures that corporate directors (those who are considered to be "the directing minds" of corporations) monitor the activities conducted by their businesses.

Environmental Assessment Act

Due to concern about the impact on the environment of many construction projects, legislation

Penalties Under the Ontario *Environmental Protection Act*

Offence	Occurrence	Maximum Daily Penalty for an Individual	Maximum Daily Penalty for a Corporation
contravene any part of the act or regulations	First	$20 000	$100 000
	Subsequent	$50 000 and/or up to one year's imprisonment	$200 000
contravene the act in a way that poses a risk of an adverse effect OR fail to comply with an order or Certificate of Approval OR obstruct a provincial officer	First	$50 000	$250 000
	Second	$100 000 and/or up to one year's imprisonment	$500 000
contravene the act in a way that causes an adverse effect OR haul liquid industrial waste or hazardous waste in a way that may cause an adverse effect OR fail to comply with a stop order	First	$4 000 000	$6 000 000
	Second	$6 000 000 and/or up to five year's imprisonment	$10 000 000

Notes

For some violations, additional terms can include:
- penalties equal to the monetary benefit accrued due to the violation
- an action ordered by the court to prevent or eliminate effects on the environment
- any other conditions that the court considers appropriate
- any changes to conditions that the court sees fit
- compliance even if the individual is in jail
- suspension of one or more existing or pending licences if fines are not paid

FIGURE 13.8   Penalties under Ontario's *Environmental Protection Act* vary according to the seriousness of the offence. Do you think these penalties are fair and reasonable?

has been developed, both at the federal and provincial levels, to deal with environmental assessment. Essentially, **environmental assessment** requires that proposed activities be studied before they are initiated in order to determine the possible consequences that might result from them. All proposed activities must be studied, regardless of whether they are being contemplated by a private corporation, a Crown corporation, a municipality, or even a branch of the federal or provincial governments, such as Transport Canada or the Ontario Ministry of Transportation. All these activities are subject to legislation pertaining to environmental assessment.

The federal government regulates environmental assessment under the *Canadian Environmental Assessment Act*. However, each province has its own provincial environmental assessment legislation in order to address activities under its authority. In most instances, Ontario's *Environmental Assessment Act* has authority over public activities and major municipal undertakings. This act stipulates that environmental assessments must take place for projects such as waterfront improvements, road building, bridge construction, industry expansion, hydro-line placement, and the development of landfill and waste disposal sites. Generally, projects undertaken by non-governmental organizations (NGOs), private companies, or individuals are exempt under the act. Furthermore, some events are exempt under this act because they take place on federal land or else receive federal funds, thereby falling under the authority of the *Canadian Environmental Assessment Act*.

The environmental assessment process requires that any person or group considering a project must include the following components in their analysis of the activity:

- a description of purpose and a rationale for the proposed undertaking
- a description of alternative methods of carrying out the undertaking
- a description of completely different alternatives to the undertaking
- an evaluation of these alternatives

The assessment must also describe how the environment will be affected. Furthermore, it must identify the effects that will be caused or that might reasonably be expected to be caused. For example, could areas be exposed to adverse smells or does the potential exist for chemicals to be released into the environment? Finally, the assessment must consider the actions that are required to prevent those effects from occurring.

Because undertaking a valid environmental assessment is complex, it generally takes a long time to prepare and complete one. It is also a costly endeavour. For example, it may require hiring an engineering consulting firm to conduct the assessment. Some people have criticized the fact that the process slows down development, particularly when approvals are not granted or when more assessment work is required. On the other hand, the process has been praised by those who maintain that environmental implications should always be considered before a project can be approved.

One of the main strengths of Ontario's environmental assessment legislation is that projects must be identified as necessary and that alternatives to the proposed methods must be explored. As discussed, the assessment must provide a rationale for the project. The assessment must also include an indication of its scope and an evaluation of alternative courses of action. Major construction projects require an environmental assessment study in order to determine the project's potential impact on the environment. The plan or proposal must be sent to the Ministry of the Environment for approval. The public is then given an opportunity to comment. Municipalities in which the activity is to be carried out must be notified of the project, at which point public objections can be made. In Ontario, an Environmental Review Tribunal may conduct hearings and make recommendations, but the minister of the environment has the ultimate decision-making power to accept or reject a project.

One challenge within the area of environmental assessment is the balancing of economic costs, such as assessment costs, costs of project delays, and project cancellations, with the costs of environmental degradation. This challenge is addressed by requiring those who undertake a project to consider several factors: the necessity of undertaking the project, the alternatives, and the environmental consequences.

Environmental Bill of Rights

Ontario's *Environmental Bill of Rights, 1993* (known as EBR) actually came into effect in February 1994. The EBR recognizes that Ontario residents should have the right to participate in the government's environmental decision making and should be able to hold the government accountable for its actions. Its preamble states, "The people of Ontario have a right to a healthful environment." The goals of the EBR are outlined in Figure 13.9.

In order to allow greater participation by the public in the decision-making process, an Environmental Registry was established. This registry provides information regarding laws, regulations, proposed acts, and policies. For example, the Ministry of the Environment may post an environmental proposal on the Environmental Registry, providing citizens with an opportunity to make public comments. Notices of appeals, appeal decisions, court actions, and court results are posted as well.

The EBR includes some substantive rights, such as the right to request an investigation and the right to seek leave to appeal from a decision to approve or not approve such instruments as a permit or proposal. The *Environmental Bill of Rights* allows any two people to request jointly that an alleged violation of environmental legislation be investigated. For example, if you discovered a strange chemical substance at a waterfront area or were nauseated by a foul chemical smell coming from an industry and wanted to investigate the legality of its presence, you could submit an application for an investigation to the Office of the Environmental

---

Goals of the *Environmental Bill of Rights, 1993*

- Protect, conserve, and restore the integrity of the environment.
- Provide environmental sustainability.
- Protect the right of Ontario citizens to a healthful environment.
- Prevent, reduce, and eliminate the use, generation, and release of pollutants that unreasonably threaten the integrity of the environment.
- Protect and conserve biological, ecological, and genetic diversity.
- Protect and conserve natural resources, including plant life, animal life, and ecological systems.
- Encourage the wise management of our natural resources, including plant life, animal life, and ecological systems.
- Identify, protect, and conserve ecologically sensitive areas or processes.
- Provide ways for Ontario residents to participate in environmental decision making.
- Increase the government's accountability for its environmental decision making.
- Increase access to the courts for Ontario residents who want to protect the environment.
- Improve protection for employees who take action against their employers for harming the environment.

SOURCE: Adapted from Environmental Commissioner of Ontario. *The Environmental Bill of Rights and You.* Toronto: Environment Canada, Mar. 1996, pp. 4–5.

FIGURE 13.9 The *Environmental Bill of Rights, 1993* describes fundamental environmental goals. Which goal do you think is the most important?

Commissioner. This office sends your application to the minister responsible for the area in which the alleged violation is said to have been committed. For example, if the alleged offence involves air pollution, the application for investigation would be sent to the minister of the environment, who regulates air pollution under the *Environmental Protection Act.* The minister of the environment would first review the application to consider whether an investigation was warranted. If the minister proceeded with the investigation, then the applicants would be notified of information regarding the outcome within 30 days of completing an investigation.

The EBR also contains an appeals process, so that a person can appeal such decisions as permit approvals. For example, a resident of Ontario may not agree with a water discharge permit or an operating permit for a company, and she or he may wish to appeal the approval of the permit. Furthermore, the EBR provides protection for employees who report on an employer's unlawful environmental practice. An employee who has made a complaint is protected against employer reprisals, such as dismissal or discipline.

While the aims of the legislation appear commendable, the EBR has been criticized. In a workshop entitled "Environmental Law: Why Doesn't It Work?" at the People and the Planet Conference in Kingston, Ontario, in June 2002, Bruce Pardy, a law professor at Queen's University, was critical of the EBR. While the preamble of Ontario's EBR sets out the purpose of the law and acknowledges the right of Ontario citizens to a healthful environment, this preamble has no legislative effect. Pardy states

There are no rights actually specified in the Ontario *Environmental Bill of Rights*. If a person were to approach the court to demand cleaner tap water as his/her right to a "healthful environment," the judge would throw the case out of court, because there is no specific rule in the statute that applies to this situation.

CONNECTIONS: Law and Smog

It is a brilliant, hot, humid summer day in Southern Ontario. You want to experience the natural world, so you go for a leisurely stroll through your favourite park. As you are walking, your eyes become irritated and your nose and throat begin to hurt. Obviously, your symptoms tell you that the air quality is poor. You have just become the victim of smog.

The air we breathe can be contaminated with pollutants that cause environmental and health problems. Motor vehicle emissions and chemical discharges into the air from industrial plants all contribute to air pollution. What is being done to address air pollution?

In Ontario, clean air is regulated under the *Environmental Protection Act*, especially under regulation 346. However, federal legislation such as the *Canadian Environmental Protection Act* (CEPA) also plays a role in this issue. Air pollution is defined under s. 3.1 of CEPA as:

a condition of the air, arising wholly or partly from the presence in the air of any substance, that directly or indirectly

(a) endangers the health, safety or welfare of humans;

(b) interferes with the normal enjoyment of life or property;

(c) endangers the health of animal life;

(d) causes damage to plant life or to property; or

(e) degrades or alters, or forms part of a process of degradation or alteration of, an ecosystem to an extent that is detrimental to its use by humans, animals or plants.

Certainly, if toxic substances are released into the air, they eventually damage the health of living beings and the ecosystem. More specifically, in many urban settings, the biggest threat to air quality is smog.

As society becomes more aware of the implications of poor air quality, governments are pressured to enact legislation that requires emission reduction guidelines. As a result of concerns over industrial pollutants and motor vehicle emissions, the province of Ontario developed an Anti-Smog Action Plan. As part of the plan, from May to September, Air Quality Index levels are calculated several times a day and reported through the media. The Ontario government sets out an Air Quality Index, available online, based on an air quality scale with ratings from very good to poor. Smog Alerts are issued if high levels of ozone (O_3) and fine particulate matter (i.e., dust, smoke), called a poor level index, are expected within 24 hours. A Smog Watch will be issued if there is a 50-percent chance of smog conditions occurring within the next three days.

One non-profit organization that focuses on air quality is Pollution Probe. Pollution Probe has emphasized that transportation contributes substantially to smog. In acknowledging that individual choices affect air quality, it recommends that people consider doing some of the following: use public transportation, walk, ride a bike, drive less often, carpool to work, use alternative fuels, avoid idling their vehicles, properly maintain their vehicles, properly inflate their tires, and purchase fuel-efficient vehicles.

Ontario has developed a mandatory vehicle-emissions testing program called Drive Clean. Under the Drive Clean program, light-duty trucks and cars in Southern Ontario smog zones must pass an emissions test every two years in order to receive vehicle registration renewal stickers for their licence plates. A vehicle must be inspected at an accredited Drive Clean test facility. If the vehicle does not pass the test because the emissions for the vehicle type and model year do not compare to the emissions standards required, the vehicle must be repaired to enable it to meet these standards. The Drive Clean program applies to cars that are more than three years old and less than 20 years old, because these are the vehicles that are likely to have greater emission problems.

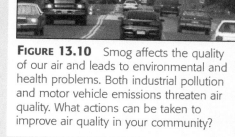

FIGURE 13.10   Smog affects the quality of our air and leads to environmental and health problems. Both industrial pollution and motor vehicle emissions threaten air quality. What actions can be taken to improve air quality in your community?

SOURCES: *Air Quality Ontario*. Government of Ontario, Ministry of the Environment. Accessed 14 Jan. 2004 <www.airqualityontario.com>;

Ontario's Drive Clean. Accessed 14 Jan. 2004 <www.driveclean.com>;

Pollution Probe. *The Smog Primer*. Toronto: June 2002. Accessed 14 Jan. 2004 <www.pollutionprobe.org/Publications/Air.htm>.

Questions

1. What causes air pollution in your community?
2. What are some of the choices that individuals make that affect air quality?
3. Explain how the Drive Clean program works to reduce pollution-causing emissions.
4. What other types of government programs could be introduced to improve air quality?

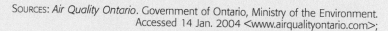

There is a public right to sue for harm under ss. 82–102 of the EBR. In order to launch an environmental claim, however, you need a cause of action. According to the Environmental Registry, "Any resident of Ontario may bring an action in court where it can be established that some person has or is about to imminently contravene a prescribed regulation or instrument, and that the contravention has or imminently will cause significant harm to a public resource in Ontario." Before the right to sue can be exercised, several preconditions must be met. First, an investigation into the incident must occur. Next, the action must be brought within the two-year limitation period. Notification of the lawsuit must be placed on the Environmental Registry, and the Attorney General of Ontario must be notified. If a cause of action is made available under common law, case law, or statute law, legal proceedings can begin. As with other environmental statutory proceedings, the accused is entitled to a defence. Such defences include the defence of due diligence, as well as the defence of statutory authority, which means that the action in question was authorized by law.

Safe Drinking Water Act, 2002

The *Safe Drinking Water Act* was passed in December 2002. The act was a result of both the concerns and the recommendations that emerged from the tragedy that occurred in Walkerton, Ontario, in 2000. (See Shifting Perspectives: Drinking-Water Safety, below, for more information on the Walkerton incident and inquiry.) The purposes of the Ontario *Safe Drinking Water Act, 2002* are described in s. 1 (1) as follows:

1. To recognize that the people of Ontario are entitled to expect their drinking water to be safe.
2. To provide for the protection of human health and the prevention of drinking-water health hazards through the control and regulation of drinking-water systems and drinking-water testing.

The act has set out the law for a required **standard of care** (i.e., the required degree of care) for the owner and those that oversee municipal drinking-water systems. Under s. 19, these individuals must "exercise the level of care, diligence and skill in respect of a municipal drinking-water system that a reasonably prudent person would be expected to exercise in a similar situation." Furthermore, the person or persons must "act honestly, competently and with integrity, with a view to ensuring the protection and safety of the users of the municipal drinking-water system." In cases in which the drinking-water system is owned by a corporation, the directors and officers of the corporation must be held to the standard of care. While much of the *Safe Drinking Water Act* came into effect on June 1, 2003, some sections, including the standard of care sections, were delayed to give municipalities time to ensure that all legislative requirements were met.

SHIFTING PERSPECTIVES: Drinking-Water Safety

Historically, Canada has been viewed as a country with an abundant supply of fresh water. Today, the public is becoming increasingly aware of and concerned about the conservation and use of water, the bulk export of water, and water pollution.

In the past, residents living in municipalities in Ontario had rarely questioned the safety of drinking water that came out of their taps. However, the water contamination that faced the town of Walkerton, Ontario, in the spring of 2000, brought the issue of safe drinking water to the forefront of the minds of citizens right across the country.

In May 2000, deadly E. coli bacteria contaminated the water supply in Walkerton. As a result, more than 2300 people became ill and seven people died. A commission of inquiry was struck to investigate and report on the incident. The Honourable Justice Dennis O'Connor delivered the *Report of the Walkerton Inquiry* in two stages. Part One of the report summarized the causes of the Walkerton tragedy; Part Two made recommendations for actions to prevent such incidents from occurring again. The Walkerton Inquiry concluded that manure, which had been spread on a farm near a town well, had entered the water system and contaminated the supply. The inquiry cited many causes for the incident, including the failure to properly monitor wells, improper operating practices by Public Utilities Commission (PUC) operators, and inadequate notification of adverse test results from private laboratories to government authorities. Furthermore, in Part One of the inquiry, Commissioner O'Connor indicated that at the time of privatization of laboratory water testing in 1996, the government knew that it was important to have labs directly notify the Ministry of the Environment (MOE) and the local medical health officer if there was an adverse test result. However, after this testing was privatized, no program was put into place to determine if notification procedures were being followed correctly. Commissioner O'Connor concluded, "The government should have enacted a regulation in 1996 to mandate direct reporting by testing laboratories of adverse test results to the MOE and to local Medical Officers of Health. Instead, it enacted such a regulation only after the Walkerton tragedy" (Ontario Ministry of the Attorney General, "Report...Part Two" 2002). Commissioner O'Connor made 93 recommendations in Part Two of the *Report of the Walkerton Inquiry*. Recommendations included the following:

- Plans for the protection of water sources should be developed for all watersheds in Ontario.
- Drinking-water standards, if met, should allow a reasonably informed person to feel safe about drinking the water.
- The establishment of standards should be based on the precautionary principle for contaminants with unknown effects.
- The provincial government should be responsible for setting legally binding standards for drinking-water safety.
- Environmental labs that test drinking water should be licensed and inspected; water treatment operations require continued accreditation.
- Those who oversee the safety of drinking water in a municipality should be held to a statutory standard of care.
- A safe drinking-water act should be enacted.
- Increased enforcement of regulations relating to drinking-water safety under the Ministry of the Environment should occur.
- The provincial government should ensure adequate funding of programs related to drinking-water safety.

FIGURE 13.11 In May 2000, a deadly E. coli outbreak contaminated the water supply in the town of Walkerton, Ontario. A sign on a drinking fountain in the Walkerton Hospital at that time warns people not to drink the water. What recommendations were made as part of the Walkerton Inquiry?

In Part Two of the *Report of the Walkerton Inquiry*, Commissioner O'Connor did not declare the right to safe drinking water as a substantive right (i.e., an actual right) that could be protected under law. He recognized that "the public is entitled to expect that the drinking water coming out of their taps is safe." Commissioner O'Connor wanted to ensure that the money used to secure drinking-water safety was spent responsibly, not through new rights for suing or for other expensive legal action, but through the proper management and regulation of water resources and water systems.

Commissioner O'Connor did not want to rule out any possibility for civil law actions in courts. In Part Two of the report, O'Connor comments: "I am satisfied that the existing causes of action, such as negligence, nuisance and breach of statutory duty, provide sufficient access to the courts to compensate those who suffer damages from consuming unsafe drinking water."

The *Safe Drinking Water Act* introduced in 2002 sets out standards to ensure drinking-water safety. It does not create a right to safe drinking water, but it establishes a series of regulations that must be met in order to effectively deal with municipal drinking-water safety. Drinking-water system regulations include frequent sampling and testing of drinking water, the use of licensed labs for drinking-water testing services, the use of certified operators or trained persons to work with the municipal drinking-water system, and the preparation of an annual report on the status of drinking water in every municipality.

According to environmental lawyer and author David Boyd:

> Acute drinking water problems affect only a small minority of Canadians—most notably Aboriginal people, a few small municipalities, and some rural populations. For these people, whose drinking water is currently unsafe, immediate remedial action is required and should be a national priority. (2003)

Boyd recommends that there be improvements in water resource protection through adequate water treatment, effective infrastructures, and rigorous testing. The public must be informed during each of these processes. Also, greater financial, technical, and political resources are needed to maintain and improve drinking-water systems.

SOURCES: Boyd, David R. *Unnatural Law.* Vancouver: UBC Press, 2003;

Ontario Ministry of the Attorney General. *Report of the Walkerton Inquiry. Part One and Part Two.* Toronto: Queen's Printer for Ontario, 2002.

Your Perspective

1. Explain how views about drinking-water safety have shifted since the Walkerton tragedy.
2. What problems might be associated with the implementation of the Walkerton Commission recommendations?
3. Explain why Commissioner O'Connor did not want to declare safe drinking water to be a protected right.
4. What follow-up has the provincial government undertaken with respect to the commission's recommendations?

Issues Facing Municipalities

Municipalities have authority over activities within their jurisdiction, such as waste management and the regulation of sewer treatment facilities. They can pass bylaws that deal with such environmental concerns as noise and recycling. An environmental issue that has attracted increasing attention in the twenty-first century is the regulation of pesticide use by municipalities. When the municipality of Hudson, Québec, passed a bylaw restricting the use of pesticides, businesses that depended on pesticide spraying for their livelihood, such as lawn-care companies, opposed it. In 2001, the Supreme Court of Canada upheld the authority of the municipality to pass the bylaw.

The Landmark Case below addresses the issue of municipal regulation of pesticide use. (Before beginning your analysis of the Landmark Case, consider referring to the Legal Handbook to familiarize yourself with Case Law and Precedent-setting Cases.)

LEGAL HANDBOOK pp. 7–8

Landmark CASE

114957 Canada Ltée (Spraytech, Société d'arrosage) v. Hudson (Town), [2001] 2 S.C.R. 241

Read the case analysis that follows. Show that you understand the nature of the ruling by applying the precedent to a case scenario that you create involving a similar situation (e.g., a case requiring the approval of a pesticide bylaw in your community). Clearly outline your rationale for justifying the bylaw. Identify any environmental concerns you have.

Facts: In 1992, the appellant lawn-care and landscaping companies from the Montréal area were charged with violating a municipal bylaw in the town of Hudson that regulated pesticide use. The companies used pesticides that were approved under the *Pesticides Control Products Act* and were licensed under the *Québec Pesticides Act* to carry out their operations. The companies appealed to the Superior Court of Québec, arguing that it was *ultra vires* (outside) the town's authority to regulate and restrict pesticide use. The Superior Court of Québec denied the motion and so did the Court of Appeal, citing that the town had a public interest in passing the bylaw, which was created in response to health concerns raised by the community's residents. The municipality had not passed a total ban, but had restricted the spread and use of pesticides within the community. The case was appealed to the Supreme Court of Canada.

Issues: Did the town of Hudson have the legislative authority to enact a bylaw regulating pesticide use? Was the bylaw in conflict with other federal or provincial legislation?

Held: Appeal dismissed.

Ratio Decidendi: In the ruling, the justices held that it was within the authority of the jurisdiction of Hudson to create bylaws for the "general welfare" within their territory. Section 410 (1) of the *Cities and Towns Act, R.S.Q. C-19* allows municipalities to create bylaws "to secure peace, order, good government, health and general welfare in the territory of the municipality, provided such bylaws are not contrary to the laws of Canada, or of Québec, nor inconsistent with any special provision of this Act or of the charter." Under s. 1 of the Hudson bylaw, a pesticide is referred to as "any substance,

FIGURE 13.12 In Canada, many communities are voting to not allow pesticides to be used for cosmetic purposes. How much input on environmental issues should residents of a community be allowed to have?

matter or micro-organism intended to control, destroy, reduce, attract or repel, directly or indirectly, an organism which is noxious, harmful or annoying for a human being, fauna, vegetation, crops or other goods or intended to regulate the growth of vegetation, excluding medicine or vaccine." The spread and use of a pesticide is restricted under s. 2 of the bylaw. Section 3 of the Hudson bylaw allows pesticide use in some specific situations, including public and private swimming pools, and for some specific purposes, including to control or destroy animals that constitute a danger to human beings, and to control or destroy plants that constitute a danger for people who are allergic to them. Section 6 of the bylaw allows the use of biological pesticides to control or destroy insects that constitute a

danger to human beings. Pesticides can also be used by farmers to protect crops. The Hudson bylaw, adopted in 1991, restricts the use of pesticides, primarily where the use is for appearance purposes. The bylaw is aimed at furthering goals, such as public health and safety, raised by concerned citizens. In upholding the municipality's authority to pass the bylaw, the Supreme Court respected the precautionary principle: "In the context of the precautionary principle's tenets, the Town's concerns about pesticides fit well under their rubric of preventative action." The court further held that the bylaw did not conflict with relevant provincial and federal legislation on the use and control of pesticides, such as the *Québec Pesticides Act* and the federal government's *Pest Control Products Act* and *Pest Control Products Regulations*, respectively.

CONFIRM YOUR UNDERSTANDING

1. In your own words, explain the meaning of the term "adverse effect" as used in Ontario's *Environmental Protection Act*.

2. Describe the components of an environmental assessment analysis under Ontario's *Environmental Assessment Act*.

3. a) Summarize the scope of Ontario's *Environmental Bill of Rights*.
   b) Outline the benefits and criticisms of the act.

4. a) Outline the purpose of Ontario's *Safe Drinking Water Act*.
   b) Identify the mechanisms that have been put into place to improve drinking-water safety in Ontario.

5. Should municipalities have control over pesticide use? Justify your opinion.

The Role of the Courts

Courts in Canada are involved in environmental disputes in a variety of capacities. They may become involved in settling a jurisdictional issue. For example, if an industry dumped PCBs, both federal and provincial governments could claim authority over regulating the activity through their environmental protection legislation. The courts would consider such factors as the

purpose of the legislation and the scope of the activity in order to determine if the alleged violation of the law fell under one jurisdictional area or another. Furthermore, the courts would play a role in interpreting legislation and applying the law to the environmental dispute. Additionally, environmental issues can be challenged in the courts under tort law, more specifically by launching a civil action in nuisance, negligence, and strict liability. The courts adjudicate the action and determine if a remedy is available. The plaintiff in a civil action is entitled to seek damages for harm done and may also seek additional remedies such as an **injunction**, which is a court order requiring a defendant to act or refrain from acting in a given situation.

Nuisance

A civil law action in **nuisance** allows a plaintiff to sue if there has been an unreasonable interference with use or enjoyment of property. For example, if toxic sludge were seeping from a business into an adjacent land, or if excessive noise were being made by equipment or machinery, a civil action could be taken in nuisance. In law, there are two types of nuisance: private nuisance and public nuisance. Private nuisance occurs when an individual's right to use and enjoy property has been unreasonably interfered with. A public nuisance occurs when a group as a whole is affected by an action, such as pollution being dumped in a water system that affects all neighbouring properties.

Trespass

In Canada, an action in trespass may enable a defendant to take his or her case to a civil court. A **trespass** occurs when someone intentionally enters onto another person's property or allows some material to be placed on the property. As a defence, the defendant may argue that he or she had a licence or was authorized under a law to carry out the activity. Furthermore, if it can be established that the plaintiff consented to the activity, then the action in trespass may fail.

Negligence

An action in **negligence** allows a plaintiff to address actual harm that was caused by a defendant who did not live up to a required standard of care. For example, if a defendant stored chemicals in his or her business and placed them too close to a heat source, causing them to explode and resulting in the injury of an employee, an action could be taken in negligence. A negligence case requires a plaintiff to suffer physical harm or property damage. The plaintiff must show that the defendant owed him or her a **duty of care** (a responsibility of care), that the defendant did not live up to the standard of care, and that the action was **foreseeable** (reasonably expected to occur). The plaintiff must also establish physical harm or loss and show that the defendant's actions caused the injuries or loss. Negligence law uses the neighbour principle, which requires defendants to consider those whom they could reasonably forsee might be injured by their actions. The plaintiff must prove his or her cause of action, and this burden of proof can be difficult to establish in an environmental case. For example, if a chemical toxin were discovered in a concealed landfill adjacent to your property, how would you prove harm? You would first have to consider who had control of the property and whether the person or company owed you a duty of care and lived up to the requisite standard of care. If you developed symptoms of illness, you would have to substantiate your claim by establishing that the toxins released caused your illness. Proving it may be difficult because health effects such as cancer may develop from exposure to toxins, but these effects may not be apparent for years.

Strict Liability

Under common law, an action is available using the principle established in the case of *Rylands v. Fletcher* (1868), L.R. 3 H.L. 330. The defendant built a reservoir of water on his property. Water escaped through an abandoned mine shaft located under the reservoir and subsequently flooded the neighbouring coal mine. When an action was brought for damages, the House of Lords in England ruled that those who, for their own purposes, bring anything onto their property that is liable to do mischief, if it escapes, are liable for all the consequences of the escape. The plaintiff had to prove only that a non-natural use of the land had occurred and that damage was

Figure 13.13 In September 2001, this backhoe was used in a cleanup operation in Port Colborne, Ontario, after dangerously high levels of nickel from the INCO mines were found to be contaminating the soil. How should the responsibility for cleanup costs be determined?

caused. The defendant was held accountable regardless of whether or not he or she acted negligently, hence the term "strict liability." For example, if someone discharged a pollutant or caused a chemical to spill onto another's property, he or she could be held liable under the common law principle of *Rylands v. Fletcher* for all the consequences of its escape.

Remedies in Tort Law

Under common law, tort actions provide an opportunity for a plaintiff to seek redress in the form of damages, or compensation. The difficulty arises in trying to establish that a right has been violated and that the plaintiff is entitled to a remedy. Furthermore, it is often difficult to determine the proper monetary compensation for damages in an environmental lawsuit because it is difficult to assess the extent of the damage.

A common remedy in environmental lawsuits is an injunction. This order of the court requires a party to either do or not do a certain action. For example, an injunction could be issued against a company ordering that it stop dumping a particular substance into a water system. Injunctions have also been granted in favour of defendants in environmental disputes. For

example, when environmentalists were protesting the logging of old-growth forests in Clayoquot Sound, British Columbia, the logging company MacMillan Bloedel obtained injunctions to stop protesters from blocking the roads and disrupting access to the routes used by the logging trucks. MacMillan Bloedel was pursuing its economic interests by logging the forests, and it did not want work to be disrupted by the actions of protesters. Failure to comply with a court-ordered injunction can result in criminal charges for contempt of court and the possibility of a jail sentence. Following the protests over the logging of Clayoquot Sound in British Columbia in 1993, many protesters were arrested and jailed for refusing to follow the terms of injunctions.

By 2004, environmental protests against logging policies were still taking place in the form of blockades of logging roads. Betty Krawczyk, a 75-year-old grandmother, who in 1993 had protested at Clayoquot Sound, continued her strong opposition to British Columbia logging policies and was arrested in May 2003 for blocking logging roads in the Walbran Valley on Vancouver Island. She was charged with contempt and spent four months in custody prior to her trial. She was not released initially because she refused to sign a statement agreeing not to return to the blockades.

Approximately three weeks after being placed in custody, another judge agreed to release Krawczyk on a promise to appear. In June 2004, she breached the terms of her release agreement when she returned to the blockade, where she acted as spokesperson for her group, Women in the Woods. She was brought back into custody, where she remained until the trial.

In considering sentencing for contempt, the judge noted that Krawczyk had a history of disobedience toward court orders, citing two previous convictions of contempt for refusal to obey court-ordered injunctions. Justice Harvey, in imposing a six-month imprisonment for criminal contempt, stated, "The defendant here, a member of society, cannot, with impunity, be permitted to choose which law she will obey and

FIGURE 13.14 Here, Betty Krawczyk is being arrested for criminal contempt for her continued anti-logging protest actions. How severe do you think penalties for criminal contempt should be?

conditions. In rejecting the consideration of time served, Judge Harvey stated, "Her confinement is entirely the result of her refusal on two occasions to agree to conditions of release which have been shown to be reasonable and necessary. In this regard I consider her confinement to be comparable to a self-inflicted wound." The judge sentenced Krawczyk to imprisonment for six months. He did not grant a probation order because he felt that Krawczyk made it clear by her actions that she would not follow the terms of such an order.

There are other constraints and drawbacks to civil litigation in environmental law. Court actions are both costly and lengthy and often require hiring expert witnesses to testify. Civil actions also require that the plaintiff or plaintiffs have **standing** in law, that is, the right to prosecute a claim or seek legal redress. The issue of standing is particularly problematic when a group of citizens wants to launch a class-action lawsuit. For example, if thousands of citizens develop breathing problems after an industrial fire spews toxic fumes, they may want to take legal action against the business that created the fumes. The legal standing of all plaintiffs must be determined by the courts before the action can proceed. In Ontario, the *Class Action Proceedings Act* regulates the certification of a class proceeding. The cause of action must be launched by an identifiable group of people who have common issues to resolve.

> *Sign[ing] a promise not to go back into the forest...would be a tacit admission that perhaps I had been doing something I should not have been doing.*
> —Betty Krawczyk, environmental activist

which she will defy and disobey" (*Hayes Forest Services Ltd. v. Forest Action Network*). The defendant argued that her four-month custody prior to trial should be considered in determining an appropriate sentence for the case. Typically, the time-served argument is used by defendants who have been refused bail or who cannot meet bail

CONFIRM YOUR UNDERSTANDING

1. Explain the jurisdictional issue that often arises in court actions involving an environmental dispute.
2. Differentiate between nuisance and negligence in a civil environmental action. Provide examples to illustrate your understanding.
3. Examine the drawbacks to a court action in negligence.
4. a) Explain the principle used in *Rylands v. Fletcher.*
   b) How could this principle be used today in an environmental action?
5. Explain the major remedies available in civil environmental actions. Outline the advantages and disadvantages of each.
6. a) Explain the concept of "standing" in a civil case.
   b) How does it apply to a class-action lawsuit?

Advocates for Environmental Protection

No longer can society watch complacently as the environment is threatened by pollution, resource depletion, and species extinction. Our current actions will affect future generations. Various individuals and groups in Canada work toward raising the profile of environmental issues, and they lobby industries and the government to take action when they perceive that not enough is being done to protect the environment. In this section, specific individuals and groups are profiled in order to further your understanding of their role in developing environmental awareness. Their efforts are often required in order to convince government bodies to take action and deal with environmental concerns. Some non-governmental organizations (NGOs), such as the Sierra Club of Canada, the David Suzuki Foundation, and Pollution Probe, keep the public informed of key environmental concerns affecting Canadians. Some of the groups also promote an awareness of environmental degradation worldwide. Other groups consist of paid lobbyists who influence the government decision-making process. Individual and group action does promote change and influence the development of environmental laws in Canada.

Two individuals who are particularly representative of their environmental organizations and who are considered influential in promoting environmental protection in Canada are Elizabeth May and David Suzuki.

Elizabeth May, one of Canada's top environmental activists, first came to prominence in the 1970s when she represented Cape Breton landowners in their fight against the forestry industry's spruce budworm spray program. She later held several government positions and became senior policy advisor to the federal environment minister in 1986. Since 1989, May has been the Executive Director of the Sierra Club of Canada, an organization committed to highlighting environmental concerns in Canada and the world.

Sierra Club campaigns address international issues, such as global climate change, and national issues, such as pesticide use and unrestricted clear-cut logging. Toxic waste is a central focus for the Sierra Club of Canada. Since 1986, Elizabeth May has been fighting a battle with provincial and federal governments over the issue of the cleanup of the Sydney Tar Ponds. Residents living in Nova Scotia near the old Sydney Steel coke ovens, which were used to burn coal in the steelmaking process, claim that there are many contaminated hot spots and that their health is suffering from exposure to contaminants. The by-products of burning coal in the ovens included the release of toxic wastes into the stream nearby. According to an article on *CBC*

Figure 13.15 Elizabeth May, a leading Canadian environmentalist, was instrumental in focusing government attention on the Sydney Tar Ponds toxic waste site. The February 2004 Throne Speech announced a statement of intention to allocate funds toward the cleanup of the Sydney Tar Ponds. How have individuals such as Elizabeth May helped bring about beneficial environmental changes in Canada?

News Online, "More than 80 years of this type of coke-oven operation left the ground water and surface water in the area seriously contaminated with arsenic, lead and other toxins. It also led to the accumulation of some 700,000 tonnes of chemical waste and raw sewage, 40,000 tonnes of which are PCBs (Polychlorinated Biphenyls)" (Tailleur and Sellinger 2001). Elizabeth May claims that the Sydney Tar Ponds constitute the worst hazardous waste site in Canada that is located in the middle of a city.

In May 2001, Elizabeth May staged a hunger strike on Parliament Hill to focus attention on the issues facing the Sydney Tar Ponds toxic waste site. In February 2003, the federal government announced in its budget that it would allocate $340 million over a two-year time period toward environmental cleanups in Canada. None of the money was specifically earmarked for Sydney. On February 24, 2003, residents of Sydney were presented with 10 options regarding the cleanup of the area. In March 2003, the Sierra Club forwarded a petition signed by 3000 residents of the local area urging a full-panel environmental assessment to examine the scope of the contamination and options for safe and effective cleanup. By May 2003, the Sydney residents had chosen two of the cleanup methods, including washing the soil and burning it, which could cost up to $450 million and take seven years to complete.

In its February 2004 Throne Speech, the federal government announced a statement of intention to clean up contaminated sites in Canada. A $3.5-billion, 10-year program will address cleanup of toxic waste sites for which the government is responsible. The environmental plan also included a $500-million, 10-year commitment to the cleanup of the Sydney Tar Ponds and other sites. Through the time and efforts of individuals, such as Elizabeth May, and organizations, such as the Sierra Club of Canada, environmental issues remain a focus of public attention, which can bring about change.

David Suzuki is another well-known environmentalist. He is also a geneticist, educator, author, and broadcaster. Suzuki was a professor at the University of British Columbia for 32 years and has been the host of the CBC television series *The Nature of Things.* In 1990, he founded the David Suzuki Foundation. The mission of the foundation states, "The David Suzuki Foundation works through science and education to protect the balance of nature and our quality of life, now and for future generations." The foundation focuses on four main areas: (1) oceans and sustainable fishing, particularly issues of overfishing, pollution, and habitat loss; (2) forests and sustainable wild lands, particularly logging and land-use practices in British Columbia; (3) clean energy, concentrating on such issues as recycling programs and energy conservation; and (4) climate change, promoting programs that provide sustainable climate-change solutions, such as solar energy and wind power.

As chair of the David Suzuki Foundation, Suzuki has been involved in many environmental issues of concern in British Columbia,

FIGURE 13.16 Through such activities as writing books and hosting television shows, environmentalist David Suzuki has been a prominent educator. Why is education a key means of making progress on environmental protection?

such as the fishing issues related to Pacific Coast salmon and the forestry issues related to logging of old-growth forests. The foundation has taken a strong stance in favour of the implementation of the *Kyoto Protocol* (an international agreement on climate change). The February 2004 Throne Speech reiterated the federal government's pledge to honour its commitments to the *Kyoto Protocol*.

In addition to the Sierra Cub of Canada and the David Suzuki Foundation, there are many other organizations in Canada that are committed to environmental initiatives. Pollution Probe is a non-profit organization committed to promoting clean air and water. Formed in 1969, its mandate includes researching environmental problems, promoting education about environmental issues, and seeking practical solutions through advocacy. Pollution Probe was involved in pressuring the government to ban DDT. In 2004, some of its programs encouraged the development of recycling and promoted air quality initiatives, such as smog-reduction programs.

Sometimes help is needed to pressure the government to focus its attention on a particular environmental issue. NGOs or industry may hire individuals and groups to lobby the government when there are perceived inadequacies in environmental laws or their enforcement. They may need someone who knows the inner workings of the political process. There are hundreds of such paid lobbyists in Canada. For example, former cabinet ministers and provincial premiers are sometimes hired to lobby the government. These individuals or groups may then be able to exert influence on the government decision-making process.

ASKING KEY QUESTIONS

Lobbying for Change

Individuals often join non-governmental organizations (NGOs) because they hope to focus public attention on issues such as environmental protection, social justice, or globalization and trade. As members of NGOs, they try to raise awareness of these issues and attempt to influence the government to make changes.

John Ralston Saul, a Canadian writer and philosopher, poses some interesting questions related to the relationship of NGOs to our democratic structure of government. In his book *On Equilibrium*, Saul writes:

What has been exciting for democracies over the last decade has been to see tens of thousands of mainly younger citizens engaging themselves in public debate through these voluntary groups. This is their way of saying that they will not submit to what much of the official political, administrative, economic and intellectual structures insist are inevitable forces. By refusing this ideology of inevitability, they are asserting the idea of individual responsibility.

Saul highlights the presence of these NGOs and indicates their importance in the debate of key issues such as the environment, biotechnology, and global markets. However, he reveals that a fundamental problem such groups face is that they do not have political decision-making power.

Saul highlights a dilemma faced by those who advocate change through advocacy groups or NGOs: they are not inside of government acting as representatives in the political process. He claims that some use the argument that they do not want to become politically active because they feel that politicians have no power. He is critical of such a stance and suggests that people should consider the value of being elected in a democracy. He asks those same people to reflect on whether or not they can recommend a system that would be better than a democracy. Saul then makes the following point:

> Let me come back to a central confusion which surrounds the use of public-interest groups. Why is it that they can capture the news and block policies, yet can't set new policies? Isn't it because in democracies policies are decided in assemblies, in legislative committees, in party caucuses, in offices, in endless discussion between a multitude of elected groups, one-on-one, in small groups, formally and informally, in ministerial jockeying and arguments, in the endless debate and pressuring between the elected, the ministers and the civil service?
>
> The levers of power are inside. If you're not there—elected and present—your only hope is to influence those who are. Suddenly your role is not that of a public person, but of a courtier—a lobbyist. You are on the outside, lobbying for change. Even if the cause is good, a lobbyist is a lobbyist is a lobbyist.

Source: Saul, John Ralston. *On Equilibrium*. Toronto: Penguin Books Canada Limited, 2001.

Form Your Questions

The excerpts from John Ralston Saul's book raise many questions about the role of NGOs and lobby groups in a democratic society. Develop three possible questions that you would ask to further clarify the issue. Share your questions with the rest of the class, and discuss possible answers.

The influence of individual and group action on the government's environmental decision making cannot be underestimated. Through the diligence and hard work of many people, environmental issues remain a focus of continued media attention. The more that citizens become active and vocal about their concerns for the protection of the environment, the more that governments will be pressured to account for their actions regarding environmental responsibility.

CONFIRM YOUR UNDERSTANDING

1. Explain the role of NGOs and lobby groups in environmental protection.
2. How have the actions of Elizabeth May and David Suzuki contributed to the environmental movement in Canada?
3. Should civil disobedience be used to protest laws that are perceived to be unfair? Justify your opinion.
4. Complete a comparison chart showing similarities and differences among the various environmental protection groups highlighted in the text, including the Sierra Club of Canada, the Suzuki Foundation, and Pollution Probe.

International Environmental Protection Agreements

For the first time in my life, I saw the horizon as a curved line. It was accentuated by the thin seam of dark blue light—our atmosphere. Obviously, this was not the ocean of air I had been told it was so many times in my life. I was terrified by its fragile appearance.

—Ulf Merbold (1941–), a German space-shuttle astronaut

Many environmental issues are global in nature, such as climate change, transboundary air and water pollution, and threats to biological diversity. As the global community becomes more concerned about environmental degradation, there will be more pressure on countries to commit to international environmental agreements. (The evolution of international environmental law is summarized in Chapter 14, beginning on p. 452.) Some people believe that Canada has shown leadership on international environmental issues. This has been specifically evident through Canada's contributions to such agreements as the *Convention on Long-Range Transboundary Air Pollution* in 1979, the *Montréal Protocol on Substances That Deplete the Ozone Layer* in 1987, the United Nations' *Convention on Biological Diversity* in 1992, and the *Stockholm Convention on Persistent Organic Pollutants* in 2001.

In many circumstances, Canada has signed an international agreement and then strengthened its own domestic laws on related concerns. In 1987, world environmental leaders met in Montréal and discussed the implications of chlorofluorocarbons (CFCs), which contribute to the deterioration of the ozone layer, a protective layer of gases surrounding the earth. The *Montréal Protocol on Substances That Deplete the Ozone Layer* was drafted, and countries worldwide signed on to reduce their CFC emissions. Effective results were achieved by changing domestic laws. For example, federal legislation was changed to prevent the import of ozone-depleting substances. Should a company import a refrigerator containing a substance known to deplete the ozone layer, it could be fined for violating the agreement. Within 10 years of passing the *Montréal Protocol*, Canada had reduced its production of ozone-depleting substances by 95 percent.

In 1992, Canada signed the United Nations' *Convention on Biological Diversity*. The previous year, Environment Canada had established the Biodiversity Convention Office in an effort to coordinate Canada's preparatory work leading up to negotiations for the convention. Once Canada signed the agreement, the office turned its attention to coordinating the development of a Canadian Biodiversity Strategy. Ten years after signing the convention, Canada put into place its own laws in order to uphold its commitment to the protection of endangered species. In 2002, Canada passed the *Species at Risk Act*, fulfilling its commitment to the UN convention and signalling its goal to protect Canada's biological diversity.

Canada has developed initiatives in the area of climate change. In 1992, Canada signed the *United Nations Framework Convention on Climate Change*. This agreement laid the framework for discussing actions and processes that could deal with the issue of global climate change. When research established that the burning of fossil fuels (i.e., oil, gas, and coal) produced greenhouse gas emissions and that global warming was a serious consequence, the world community began to consider what action could be taken to reduce the threat of environmental harm. Global warming results from gases such as carbon dioxide, nitrous oxide, and methane combining and then accumulating in the atmosphere. In 1997, countries from around the world met in Kyoto, Japan, and signed the *Kyoto Protocol*. The main aim of this agreement was to cut greenhouse gas emissions by five percent worldwide. Under the conditions set forth in the protocol, the signatory countries agreed to reduce their emissions by selected target dates from 2008 to 2012. Canada ratified the agreement in December 2002 and made a commitment to a six-percent reduction in emissions by 2012. In order for the agreement to come into force, 55 specific countries, which in 1990 produced 55 percent of the world's greenhouse gases, must ratify the agreement. By early 2004, the agreement still had not been ratified.

Whether environmental laws are developed domestically or internationally, there are often economic implications to their implementation. Some countries may not want to sign international conventions or protocols because they feel it may result in disastrous economic consequences. For example, the United States did not sign the *Kyoto Protocol* because it felt the agreement would impede its economic growth. Countries that do ratify agreements have to bear the costs associated with these initiatives. Some countries believe that the overall environmental interests outweigh the economic costs.

Another circumstance in which environmental and economic interests can be at odds is when a resource is involved in an international trade dispute. For example, the bulk sale of water from Canada to other countries has become a hot topic in both international trade and environmental discussions. (See Viewpoints, below, which explores the bulk sale of water.)

One of the greatest challenges to the strength of international law is the fact that the agreements are non-binding on their parties. Since there is no enforcement mechanism in place, countries that agree to comply with the terms of an agreement do so voluntarily. International pressure may be the only way to encourage countries reluctant to sign such international conventions and protocols to do so. A country may be influenced to sign an international agreement because it does not want its reputation tarnished in the international community. Fortunately,

FIGURE 13.17 Here, ice blocks are cut from McKinley Bay to study pollution after a controlled oil spill in the Beaufort Sea, Northwest Territories. What role does scientific testing play in environmental protection?

Canada takes pride in its international reputation and continues to sign international agreements that recognize the importance of global environmental concerns.

Unlike criminal law, environmental law is in its infancy. Furthermore, its extension into the international arena through agreements is even more recent. Although there is no international enforcer or binding structure for agreements at this time, these will likely come in the future as each country develops and strengthens its own environmental protection laws. Eventually, it may become internationally unacceptable not to participate in global environmental efforts.

VIEWPOINTS: The Bulk Sale of Water

The privatization of the water industry and the increased use of water as a commodity are considered by authors Maude Barlow and Tony Clarke in a book entitled *Blue Gold*. They examine how water is viewed by some to be the new gold, a commodity to be bought and sold in the open marketplace. Should water be considered a commodity? In this book Barlow and Clarke examine the use of water as a commodity:

When water was defined as a commodity at the second World Water Forum at The Hague in March 2000, government representatives at a parallel meeting did nothing to effectively counteract the statement. Instead, governments have helped pave the way for private corporations to sell water, for profit, to the thirsty citizens of the world. So a handful of transnational corporations, backed by the World Bank and the International Monetary Fund, are now aggressively taking over the management of public water services, dramatically raising the price of water to local residents, and profiting, especially from the Third World's desperate search for solutions to its water crisis. Some are startlingly open about their motives; the decline in freshwater supplies and standards has created a wonderful venture opportunity for water corporations and their investors, they boast. The agenda is clear: water should be treated like any other tradable good, its use and distribution determined by the principles of profit.

> *In an age when man has forgotten his origins and is blind even to his most essential needs for survival, water along with other resources has become the victim of indifference.*
> —Rachel Carson
> (1907–1964),
> American author

Maude Barlow and Tony Clarke expressed a contrary view:

We believe that fresh water belongs to the earth and all species and that no one has the right to appropriate it for personal profit. Water is part of the world's heritage and must be preserved in the public domain for all time and protected by strong local, national, and international law. At stake is the whole notion of the "commons," the idea that through our public institutions we recognize shared humanity and natural resources to be preserved for future generations. We believe that access to clean water for basic needs is a fundamental human right; this vital resource cannot become a commodity sold to the highest bidder. Each generation must ensure that the abundance and quality of water is not diminished as a result of its activities. Great efforts must be made to restore the health of aquatic ecosystems that have already been degraded and to protect others from harm. Local and regional communities must be the watchdogs of our waterways and must establish principles that oversee the use of this precious resource.

Above all, we need to radically restructure our societies and lifestyles in order to reverse the drying of the earth's surface; we must learn to live within the watershed ecosystems that were created to sustain life. And we must abandon the special notion that we can carelessly abuse the world's precious water resource because, somehow "technology" will come to the rescue. There is no technological "fix" for a planet that has run out of water.

Source: Barlow, Maude, and Tony Clarke. *Blue Gold*. Toronto: McClelland & Stewart Ltd., 2002.

Up for Debate

After studying the viewpoint of Maude Barlow and Tony Clarke, carefully conduct your own research on the issue. Then prepare a debate on the following resolution: Be it resolved that water is a commodity to be bought and sold in the open market.

CONFIRM YOUR UNDERSTANDING

1. Provide examples of areas where international agreements have focused on environmental concerns.

2. Summarize three examples of situations where Canada has demonstrated its commitment to international agreements.

3. a) Explain the advantage of international agreements on environmental issues.
   b) Describe one major drawback to the enforcement of international agreements.

In Closing

Environmental laws will continue to evolve as societies struggle with issues of environmental degradation. Environmental law in Canada has developed primarily since the 1970s and therefore is not able to rely on an immense collection of precedent-setting environmental case law. The federal and provincial governments have taken steps to develop laws that deal with environmental issues. However, economic concerns often influence the actions taken by government, industry, or citizens with respect to environmental issues.

Civil actions in environmental law bring their own challenges. In environmental law, it is very difficult to establish proof of actual harm because the consequences may be not be apparent until far into the future. Does that mean no action should be taken? On the contrary, new principles in environmental law, such as the precautionary principle, allow for action to be taken before the "perceived harm" and all the associated consequences manifest themselves. Should the precautionary principle gain a strong foothold, new environmental laws may eventually be passed in

FIGURE 13.18   In the twenty-first century, every level of community is responsible for environmental protection: the individual, the municipality, the region, the country, and the world. Here, a high-school student learns about tree regeneration by participating in an Ontario "Envirothon" competition. Which level of community do you think is most influential in protecting the environment?

order to address concerns about potential threats of harm.

As society becomes more aware of environmental degradation and as the population increases, the need to address environmental concerns will continue to grow. Over-consumption of resources and environmental pollution exist as we move into the twenty-first century. The following question remains: Can these trends be reversed?

As society adopts new values, public opinion changes. Will changing attitudes lead to more environmental protection legislation or less? Will international pressure be placed on countries to commit to more global environmental protective measures? Citizens and law-makers in the twenty-first century will have to consider the weight to be placed on environmental concerns. In their book *You Are the Earth*, David Suzuki and Kathy Vanderlinden put it this way:

> The problem with so many battles about the environment is that we get caught up in debates that force us to choose between two valuable things—spotted owls or jobs, logging or parks, people or wildlife. When problems are put that way, no matter what happens someone or something will lose. But if we care about a future for coming generations, we can't have any losers. We have to decide what is really important.

CHAPTER ACTIVITIES

Extend Your Legal Knowledge

1. Who has constitutional jurisdiction over environmental legislation in Canada?
2. Distinguish between the precautionary principle and the polluter-pays principle regarding environmental protection. Describe the difficulties in enforcing these principles.
3. Explain the concept of biological diversity. Provide three examples of legislation dealing with this concept.
4. Identify the various avenues available in tort law for launching an environmental action.
5. Explain the significance of the *Kyoto Protocol*.
6. Distinguish between the polluter-pays principle and the defence of due diligence. How can the two principles be reconciled? Explain.

Think About the Law

7. "Many Canadians believe, incorrectly, that they have a right to clean, safe water. While this right may exist at a philosophical level, it does not exist under Canadian law. There is no such right provided in Canada's Constitution, the *Charter of Rights and Freedoms*, or in the common law" (Boyd 2003).

Should access to clean water be included as a human right? Support your opinion.

8. "This new bottom line will not abandon the component of the old single bottom line, that of profit, but it will integrate with it the protection of the environment, concern for maintaining a sense of community and social cohesion, and ethics" (Sommerville 2000). Explain, in your own words, what is meant by the statement.
9. Should directors and officers of a corporation be held liable for environmental harm caused by that corporation? Explain.

Communicate About the Law

10. Read the following excerpt, and then answer the questions below it.

> Corporate attitudes and expectations are changing. It is not important to determine which came first: the awakening of environmental awareness or environmental policy making. What is important is that they support one another. In response to growing concern about the environment, the increased costs of non-compliance and the increased liabilities, growing numbers of

companies are seeing a "greening" of the boardroom. Many companies are realizing that pollution is bad for business and that sound environmental management can protect and enhance the value of physical assets as well as corporate reputations. In some cases, a product that is certified as environmentally responsible can be a marketing advantage or even a requirement for sales to some customers. (Phyper and Ibbotson 2003)

a) Explain what you think is meant by the term "greening" of the corporate boardroom.
b) Research a company, and highlight corporate actions taken by that company that are considered environmentally responsible.
c) Comment on whether you think that business is doing enough to address environmental concerns.

11. Research one of the following environmental organizations. Highlight the mandate of the organization, and describe the scope of its work. Summarize a current issue that the organization is addressing. Refer to the Legal Handbook for tips on conducting research over the Internet.

LEGAL HANDBOOK p. 23

a) Sierra Club of Canada
b) David Suzuki Foundation
c) Canadian Environmental Law Association
d) Greenpeace International
e) Friends of the Earth
f) World Wildlife Fund

12. Conduct research on one of the federal environmental statutes listed below. Briefly summarize the main purpose of the legislation, and outline the major activities that are regulated. Highlight a current issue relating to the act you have chosen.

a) *Transportation of Dangerous Goods Act, 1992*
b) *Canadian Environmental Assessment Act*
c) *Canada Shipping Act*
d) *Pest Control Products Act*

13. Read the following excerpt from *Environmental Law* by Jamie Benidickson:

Not long ago, the agility of such pre-robotic and pre-mutant cartoon characters as rabbits and road-runners was always being tested at the brink of disaster, notably in proximity to terrifying cliffs. As they approached the edge of a daunting precipice, some of these creatures would attempt—often with limited success—to screech to a halt; others seemed capable of launching themselves into the air and then, with an incredible reversal of spinning feet, defying gravity to return to the edge of the ledge. An assessment of the adequacy and prospects for the contemporary environmental protection regime is likely to be influenced by metaphor: do we still have a little traction to work with on the ledge, or have we already gone over the brink?

Prepare a response to the last question in the above quotation, which refers to Canada's environmental protection regime. Do we still have a little traction to work on the ledge, or have we already gone over the brink? Support your opinion with examples.

14. Using the Legal Quest Research Model, prepare a two-page summary of a current legal environmental issue.

LEGAL HANDBOOK p. 21

Apply the Law

15. Prepare a public education campaign that addresses pollution prevention in your community.

a) Identify the pollution prevention issue to be addressed.
b) What legislation currently addresses this issue in your community? Discuss the effectiveness of the legislation.
c) How could awareness of the issue be increased within your community?

16. In February and November 2002, two ships, the *MV Baltic Confidence* and the *CSL Atlas*, respectively, were charged under the *Canada Shipping Act* with spilling an oily substance into the Atlantic Ocean off the coast of Halifax, the *CSL Atlas* with 92 L and the *MV Baltic*

Confidence with 850 L. Each of these polluters was prosecuted under the *Canada Shipping Act* and issued the highest fine to marine polluters— $125 000.

Previously, such pollution incidents could be discovered by National Defence or the Coast Guard when conducting aerial surveillance. There is, however, a new participant in the fight against marine pollution, and it is located in the skies above you. RADARSAT, a remote sensing satellite system 800 km above the planet, operated by the Canadian Space Agency, employs radar images that can help determine if marine pollution violations are occurring. This satellite aids in the identification of oil slicks. According to Canadian government officials, it is thought that approximately 300 000 birds die from offshore oil dumping each year. The original six-month project was launched in September 2002. During that same month, an oil slick was tracked off Cape St. Mary's Ecological Reserve bird sanctuary in Newfoundland. Aerial surveillance was then used to locate ships nearby. The *Tecam Sea*, the only ship in the area at that time, was charged under the *Migratory Birds Convention Act, 1994*. In April 2003, the charges were dropped because federal prosecutors were not convinced they could successfully prosecute the owners of the vessels for intentional dumping.

a) Prepare an argument in favour of the use of the RADARSAT images in the fight against marine pollution.

b) Prepare an argument that condemns the use of RADARSAT imaging in the prosecution of a marine pollution offence.

c) Speculate as to other uses of RADARSAT imaging in the detection of environmental harm.

BIBLIOGRAPHY

Auld, Alison. "Oil Dumping Charges Dropped." *Canoe.* 17 Apr. 2003. Accessed 19 Aug. 2003 <www.argonauts.on.ca/CNEWS/Law/2003/04/17/67693-cp.html>.

Barlow, Maude, and Tony Clarke. *Blue Gold.* Toronto: McClelland & Stewart Ltd., 2002.

Benidickson, Jamie. *Environmental Law,* 2nd ed. Essentials of Canadian Law Series. Toronto: Irwin Law Inc., 2002.

Boyd, David R. *Unnatural Law.* Vancouver: UBC Press, 2003.

Canadian Legal Information Institute. Accessed Oct.–Dec. 2003 <www.canlii.org>.

David Suzuki Foundation. Accessed 10 Jan. 2004 <www.davidsuzuki.org/About_us/Our_Mission.asp>.

"Enforcement Offenders: Marine Pollution Prosecutions (2002–2003)." *Government of Canada.* Accessed 10 Jan. 2004 <www.marinepollution.gc.ca/en/enforcement/prosecutions.htm>.

Environmental Commissioner of Ontario. *The Environmental Bill of Rights and You.* Mar. 1996.

Government of Canada. *Species at Risk Act: A Guide.* Accessed Jan. 2004 <www.sararegistry.gc.ca/the_act/HTML/22>.

Government of Ontario. *Safe Drinking-Water Act, 2002.* Accessed 28 Dec. 2003 <www.e-laws.gov.on.ca/DBLaws/Statutes/English/02s32_e.htm>.

———. *Environmental Bill of Rights.* Accessed 28 Dec. 2003 <http://192.75.156.68/DBLaws/Statutes/English/93e28_e.htm#P301_5166>.

———. *Environmental Protection Act.* Accessed 28 Dec. 2003 <http://www.e-laws.gov.on.ca/DBLaws/Statutes/English/ 90e19_e.htm#P727_31900>.

————. Environmental Registry. Accessed 5 Jan. 2004 <www.ene.gov.on.ca/envision/env_reg/ebr/english/ebr_info/Right_to_sue.htm>.

Nugent, Olivia. "The Smog Primer." *Pollution Probe.* June 2002. Accessed 14 June 2004 <www.pollutionprobe.org/Publications/Air.htm>.

Ontario Ministry of the Attorney General. *Report of the Walkerton Inquiry. Part One and Part Two.* Toronto: Queen's Printer for Ontario, 2002.

"People and the Planet: Changing Values for a Sustainable Future." Conference Proceedings. *Sierra Club of Canada.* June 2002. Queen's University, Kingston, Ontario.

Phyper, John-David, and Brett Ibbotson. *The Handbook of Environmental Compliance in Ontario.* Toronto: McGraw-Hill Ryerson, 2003.

Raven, Peter H., Linda R. Berg, and George Johnson. *Environment.* (Includes *Canadian Environmental Issues Supplement*). Orlando, FLA: Saunders College Publishing, Harcourt Brace College Publishers, 1998.

Saul, John Ralston. *On Equilibrium.* Toronto: Penguin Books Canada Limited, 2001.

Sommerville, Margaret. *The Ethical Canary.* Toronto: Penguin Books Canada Ltd., 2000.

Suzuki, David. *The Sacred Balance.* Vancouver: Greystone Books, 1997.

Suzuki, David, and Kathy Vanderlinden. *You Are the Earth.* Vancouver: Douglas & McIntyre, 1999.

Tailleur, Terra, and Andrea Sellinger. "Tracking the Tar Ponds." *CBC News Online.* Accessed 11 Jan. 2004 <www.cbc.ca/news/indepth/background/tar_ponds.html>.

INTERNATIONAL LAW:
Concepts and Issues

LEARNING EXPECTATIONS

After reading this chapter, you will be able to:

- explain the major concepts and principles of international law

- demonstrate an understanding of the sovereignty of nation-states

- identify global issues that may be governed by international law

- explain the impact of international trade agreements on sovereignty

- explain the purpose of international jurisdictional and boundary treaties

- evaluate the effectiveness of international treaties for the protection of the environment

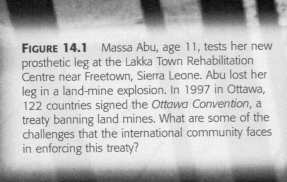

FIGURE 14.1   Massa Abu, age 11, tests her new prosthetic leg at the Lakka Town Rehabilitation Centre near Freetown, Sierra Leone. Abu lost her leg in a land-mine explosion. In 1997 in Ottawa, 122 countries signed the *Ottawa Convention*, a treaty banning land mines. What are some of the challenges that the international community faces in enforcing this treaty?

Of Law there can be no less acknowledged than that…her voice [is] the harmony of the world.

—Richard Hooker (1554–1600), English cleric and theologian

■ I N T R O D U C T I O N ■

In learning about Canadian law, you have seen just how difficult it is both to create and to enforce laws that can be applied to all Canadians. Imagine the challenge, then, of trying to create and enforce one legal code for the entire world in order to promote good relations among nations and protect mutual interests. In considering this idea, start with the broad question: How is the nature of laws by which people should live or be ruled determined? And once it is determined and laws are created, how should they be enforced and revised? Some international laws might be created because they would provide nations with mutual benefit. Other international laws might be created because they would be considered ethically correct by some powerful nations. In determining the substance of these laws, enforcing them, and revising them, however, it is essential to consider diversity. Diversity refers to differences among people in terms of their political systems, religion, culture, traditions, belief systems, and geography. As well, the concept of **sovereignty** (the right of nations to make and enforce laws within their own boundaries) affects the realization of international law. Considering all these differences that exist among the world's countries, can any consensus on laws ever be reached, or do the self-interest and competing goals of these countries make any form of international law unrealistic?

Defining International Law

Is International Law Real Law?

Given the degree to which countries differ on their approaches to law, can international law be considered real law as we have come to define and understand it? Do long-standing practices or agreements that exist among countries constitute actual law in some form, or are they more like rules of etiquette? We can approach these questions by examining the differences between the concept of **domestic law** (laws specific to one

state or nation) and practices that have occurred among countries, commonly called "international law."

In order for any domestic law to be effective, it must contain three parts. First, the law must specify the behaviour that people or parties must follow. Second, the law must specify what the penalties are for people or parties who fail to comply with it. Third, the law must specify how the ongoing enforcement of it will be achieved. Those who suggest that international law is not

FIGURE 14.2   A seven-year-old Iraqi boy, Sari Ali, working in a blacksmith shop in Baghdad in 2001. Many Iraqi children work hard to improve their family's standard of living. After the Persian Gulf War in 1991, a trade embargo was imposed on Iraq. In what ways do long-term trade embargoes affect average citizens?

real law point out the lack of a universal governing or legislative body to make laws, of a single court to determine penalties, and of a global police force to enforce penalties.

Consider how realistic it might be in a global context to establish such governing bodies, determine penalties, and then enforce these penalties. How willing would nations be to surrender sovereignty to some higher authority such as a world government? Then there is the matter of **adjudication**, which is a judgment made by a third party that was not determined through negotiation. With this type of judgment, one side wins and the other loses. In creating a system of adjudication, it would be an ambitious task to create a court that has jurisdiction over all issues, something comparable to the Supreme Court of Canada.

Regarding the penalties themselves, consider this extreme example. A country that does not agree with the laws of another country would never attempt to arrest, let alone imprison, all of its citizens. So what type of governing body would enforce penalties throughout the entire world? To address this question thoughtfully, it is important to accept that international law, by definition, is quite different from the domestic legislation of individual countries.

Current laws among countries were neither formulated nor passed by a supreme legislative body. However, there is an international agency that has facilitated solutions—the United Nations (UN). While it would be misleading to characterize the United Nations as any type of world government, it has certainly aided nations in reaching common goals and in settling disputes.

The international community has met with varying degrees of success when it comes to punishing nations in breach of agreements or policies. When some nations consider the actions of another country to be offensive, they may turn a critical spotlight on that country in the hope that their criticism will shame or pressure the country into rethinking its policies or actions. **Economic sanctions**, which are any actions that either minimize or prevent economic activity that would otherwise occur, can be a particularly effective tool. One example of economic sanctions took place in August 1990, when the UN Security Council declared a **trade boycott** of Iraq because of Iraq's invasion of Kuwait. A trade boycott is a form of protest whereby people abstain from buying or using the goods or services of a particular country or organization in order to pressure it to change its behaviour.

Wealthier countries may withhold foreign aid or they may limit or cease humanitarian programs in offending countries. These wealthier countries may also extend their sanctions to other nations that trade with the offenders. Some countries have also chosen to impose **trade embargoes** on offending nations. Trade embargoes are laws or policies that countries initiate to prohibit or restrict the import or export of goods. These countries may also follow sanctions with military actions, such as naval blockades, to force a country to comply with previous agreements or a request by the United Nations. For example, in 1963, during the Cuban Missile Crisis between the United States and the Soviet Union, an

American blockade successfully stopped Soviet ships from carrying missiles to Cuba.

At other times, countries will sever diplomatic ties with an offending country. By withholding co-operation and communication from the offender, they hope to change the offending country's policy. Some countries may choose the extreme measure of using military action to force a country into submission.

Over the past 60 years, international courts and tribunals have been established. A **tribunal** refers to any governmental body or official group of people engaged in resolving a dispute. The International Court of Justice was formed in 1946 at The Hague in the Netherlands and still exists today. In 2002, the International Criminal Court came into being. During these 60 years, temporary courts known as "ad hoc tribunals" were established. In the Nuremberg Trials, for example, 22 Nazi leaders were tried for crimes against humanity and violations of the rules of war. At the International Criminal Tribunal for the former Yugoslavia, former leaders were tried for war crimes and **genocide**, the systematic killing of an entire group of human beings based on their ethnicity or religion. These courts and tribunals demonstrate some type of collective will among nations to, if not actually solve disputes, at least offer informed opinions that may lead to dispute resolution. Although critics suggest that, in some cases, these courts' **rulings**, or decisions, are not carried out, this does not mean that these courts have no merit.

In our own courts, if contracts are broken or an offender continues committing crimes in violation of a court order, we do not point to this as evidence that the law is not real. Similarly, we must accept that the difficulty in creating and enforcing international law does not necessarily make it worthless. Surely there is enough evidence of its existence around us to conclude that international law is indeed real law. The commonly accepted definition of **international law** is the customs, rules, and agreements that govern relations between sovereign states.

The History of International Law

The concept of international law was not developed recently; attempts to solve international problems date back thousands of years. Many earlier civilizations, such as those of ancient Greece and Rome, and Aboriginal and Indigenous nations around the world, had concerns and solutions similar to ones we have today. One of those concerns is the manner in which war is waged. Some solutions include the creation of treaties and the use of **arbitration**, which is an alternative, private process for resolving a dispute that does not resort to litigation. But the roots of modern international law are often traced to the rise after the Middle Ages of **nation-states**, which were societies with defined borders and laws and a centralized government. This era experienced increasing use of the seas and the exchange among countries of **diplomats**, who are official representatives engaged in international activities or negotiations. From these events arose customary rules and practices to govern the use of the seas, as well as rules for diplomats. Rules and practices affecting other interactions among countries soon followed.

The Dutch lawyer and scholar Hugo Grotius, writing in 1625 CE, is considered by many historians to be the founder of international law. His opinions on such subjects as war, sovereignty, and legal equality were widely read and consulted for guidance in settling international disputes. In that same century, a series of treaties known as the *Peace of Westphalia* was signed in Germany, ending the Thirty Years War. In some European countries, numerous peace congresses resulted in the recognition of both internal sovereignty and external sovereignty (to be explored in detail in this chapter) among these nations. Indeed, the seventeenth century heralded a new era in international law—an era in which independent states formalized economic, political, and cultural relationships.

In subsequent centuries, European leaders continued to meet to explore the concepts of international law. The *Congress of Vienna* (1814–1815) reaffirmed certain principles of international law and added new practices, including the treatment of diplomats. The *Declaration of Paris* (1856) outlined rules for blockades, and the *Geneva Convention* (1864) stipulated that humane treatment must be given to people wounded during conflicts. The end of the nineteenth century brought with it conventions dealing with such issues as protections for prisoners of war, protection of sea and bird life, and the suppression of prostitution. Possibly the most important development in international law prior to World War I was a series of meetings known as The Hague Conferences, held at The Hague in the Netherlands in 1899 and 1907. Although the stated purpose of these conferences was to promote arms limitation, no agreement was reached. One great accomplishment of these conferences, however, was the establishment of The Hague Tribunal—the first attempt at an international court.

The twentieth century was witness to two world wars, which resulted in many new international concerns. Territories were redrawn, millions of refugees were displaced, and the genocide that occurred during World War II gave rise to a new perspective on war crimes. An international organization known as the League of Nations was created after World War I to seek solutions to international conflict (see Chapter 15). Although the League of Nations was disbanded at the onset of World War II, it laid the groundwork for the United Nations.

The tension known as the Cold War between the two superpowers, the United States and the Soviet Union, dominated the world from 1945 until the Soviet Union was dismantled between 1989 and 1991. The end to this tension raised hopes of a new world order, in which all nations

FIGURE 14.3 In 1899, The Hague Peace Conference was called by Nicholas II, Czar of Russia. Of 14 draft conventions, 12 specified rules relating to war. Procedures were developed for the peaceful settlement of disputes through mediation and arbitration.

would co-operate to form a new type of international law.

More recently, the United Nations has struggled with questions of when to use military force, when to send peacekeepers, and when to bend to the will of individual nations. The United Nations succeeded in establishing the first International Criminal Court in 2002. Since the early 1990s, despite ongoing international conflicts, various nations have signed agreements on such topics as environmental protection, trade promotion, and regulation of outer space. In a world made larger by population and smaller by telecommunications and transportation, there is no doubt that international law will grow in complexity and importance throughout the twenty-first century.

CONFIRM YOUR UNDERSTANDING

1. What is generally required of laws in order for them to be effective?

2. Why do some legal scholars suggest that international law is not real law? What arguments against this view could you offer?

3. Describe the options available for countries that wish to encourage or force other countries to comply with international obligations.

4. Construct a timeline that indicates key events and dates in the development of international law.

5. What was the significance of The Hague Conferences?

6. The dismantling of the Soviet Union between 1989 and 1991 left only one country in the world—the United States—with superpower status. Could this fact alter the way international problems are tackled or solved? Explain your answer.

Sources of International Law

Just as the law in general has been derived from various sources, so too has international law. These sources include, but are not restricted to, the following four areas: formal agreements, such as treaties and conventions; customary practices; general principles of law; and judicial decisions and teachings.

Formal Agreements

The most common means of establishing rules internationally is through formal agreements. These agreements might be called **treaties**, **conventions**, **protocols**, **covenants**, or **acts**. Although the terminology used for these agreements varies, the basic substance is the same: they contain the rules that all **signatories** (signers) of the agreement will follow for their mutual benefit. Treaties typically deal with the obligations that will be imposed on the signing nations. A treaty is considered to be **bilateral** if it

has been established between two nations; it is **multilateral** if three or more nations have agreed to it. Two examples of bilateral treaties that Canada has entered into with the United States are the *Pacific Salmon Treaty* (1985) and the *Agreement on Air Quality* (1991). Examples of multilateral treaties are the *North American Free Trade Agreement* (1994) and the *Kyoto Protocol* (1994). Treaties might deal with political actions such as declarations of war, declarations of peace, or the creation of formal alliances. Other types of treaties govern such areas as trade, commerce, and natural resources. Some treaties, such as the treaty to ban land mines, capture public interest and receive international attention, while other treaties go largely unnoticed by the public. Treaties can do one of two things. They can **codify** existing laws and practices, meaning that the laws are organized and assembled in one document, such as the *Convention on the Law of* _the Sea_ (1994). Treaties can also introduce new legislation, such as in the case of the _Outer Space Treaty of 1967_.

Treaties are negotiated by government representatives who have the necessary expertise in the required subject matter. After a treaty is drafted and signed, it is **ratified**, or formally approved and authorized, by each nation according to a procedure set by its government. In Canada, once a treaty is signed, it might be necessary to actually revise some aspect of domestic law in order to carry out the treaty's obligations. As with any contract, a treaty can be designed to end on a certain date. The treaty might specify that it can be terminated by mutual consent. If there is a disagreement between two nations regarding the interpretation of a treaty between them, or if one of the parties fails to measure up to its obligations, either nation can request that the International Court at The Hague act as an intermediary. However, unlike the judgments of a domestic court, those of the International Court at The Hague do not have the weight of enforcement behind them.

Treaties in Action: Antarctica

Antarctica is a cold, windy continent that covers nearly a fifth of the world's surface. It has no native population. Most of the land is covered with ice, under which lay mineral deposits, including coal and gas, and perhaps oil and precious metals as well. As a "sovereignless land," Antarctica has been the subject of disputes among numerous nations, each of which has claimed some interest in the region. Beyond these nations, some other groups in society have

FIGURE 14.4 Although many countries would like to claim all or part of Antarctica as their own, this continent is not governed or possessed by anyone. Since 1959, treaties have attempted to promote co-operation and conservation in Antarctica.

claimed interest as well. These groups can be divided into four categories: companies that have a commercial interest in minerals, the fishing and tourism industries, scientists who wish to study the landform and its plant and animal life, and conservationists interested in protecting what has been called the "last frontier."

By the 1950s, it was increasingly clear to many nations that it was time to take international action on the issue of ownership. In 1959, 11 countries signed the *Antarctic Treaty*. These countries—Argentina, Australia, Belgium, Chile, France, Japan, New Zealand, Norway, the Soviet Union, Great Britain, and the United States—saw the treaty come into being two years later. The *Antarctic Treaty* provides for usage consistent with peaceful purposes, bans nuclear waste and the disposal of radioactive waste, and promotes co-operation in scientific investigations. The treaty calls for regular meetings to take place among participants. At these meetings, binding recommendations are established. Today more than 40 countries are signatories of the *Antarctic Treaty*.

Since 1961, further agreements have been signed that protect plant life, animals such as seals, and mineral resources. Agreements such as the *Madrid Protocol* of 1991 underscore the importance of preserving the ecosystem. This protocol was a broad agreement that combined existing international agreements related to the environmental protection of the Antarctic, such as the *Agreed Measures for the Conservation of Flora and Fauna*. The *Madrid Protocol* established Antarctica as a "natural reserve, devoted to peace and science," and it prohibited mining for commercial purposes. In 1996, the United States Congress passed a legislative act known as the *Antarctic Science, Tourism and Conservation Act of 1996*, which dictates which environmental regulations American tour operators must follow.

Treaties in Action: The Seas

By 1400 CE, a distinction had been made between the so-called "high seas," which are the open seas at a distance from shorelines, and coastal waters, such as ports, harbours, and closed-in bays. As countries became more concerned about defending themselves and as their trade with other nations increased, their interest in dominating the high seas rose. At the end of the fifteenth century, some countries began claiming sovereignty over the high seas. In 1609 CE, the Dutch lawyer and scholar Hugo Grotius wrote that the high seas should be free of sovereignty. His views took hold, partly due to the impracticality of having nations police disputed territorial waters. By the early nineteenth century, customary rules in international law recognized two points regarding sovereignty of the seas. On the one hand, a nation could claim that "a belt of land" fell under its jurisdiction; some sovereign states, including Great Britain, suggested defining "a belt of land" as the water that extends three nautical miles (5.6 km) outward from the shoreline. On the other hand, no state could claim jurisdiction over the high seas.

By the early twentieth century, an increasing number of nations began actively claiming

FIGURE 14.5 In March 1995, Canadian authorities boarded a Spanish fishing trawler and brought it to the port in St. John's, Newfoundland. They charged the captain with using illegal fishing nets and violating rules on fish quotas, contravening the 1994 Northwest Atlantic Fisheries Organization's limits on turbot. Some European countries considered these quotas unfair. Spain, believing that Canada had no right to interfere with fishing outside Canada's coastal waters, complained to the International Court of Justice (ICJ). The ICJ ruled that Canada's actions were reasonable.

jurisdiction over their coastal waters. In 1958, the first UN Conference on the Law of the Sea was convened, followed by a second conference in 1960 and a third in 1973. In 1994, 20 nations ratified and enacted the *Convention on the Law of the Sea*. An increasing number of nations came on board until, by 2003, 138 nations, including every country in the European Union, had become signatories. Today, territorial waters are limited to 12 nautical miles (22.2 km). Every nation has exclusive rights to oil and gas contained within 200 nautical miles (370.4 km) offshore, as well as to the fish and other marine life in these waters. Perhaps the largest stumbling block to ratification of the agreement was the topic of mining rights on the ocean floor. Developing nations argued that the wealth of the deep seabed should be shared. Wealthy mining countries, such as the United States, argued that sharing the resources would deter exploration and the discovery of minerals. Compromises were made by the opposing sides, and the agreement was signed.

Treaties in Action: The Stars

Just as no country can claim sovereignty over the high seas, no country can claim ownership of outer space. Nevertheless, both territories require protection and regulation. **Space law** can be defined as the body of law that applies to outer space and governs space-related activities. The United Nations Office for Outer Space Affairs says that space law addresses a variety of diverse matters, such as "military activities in outer space, preservation of the space and earth environment, liability for damages caused by space objects, settlement of disputes, protection of national interests, rescue of astronauts, sharing of information about potential dangers in outer space, use of space-related technologies and international co-operation."

The launching of satellites and the beginning of the space age in 1957 led to the *Outer Space Treaty of 1967*. One urgent concern among many nations was the need for co-operation in ensuring that space was used for peaceful purposes. This treaty stated that no nation could make claims of sovereignty over outer space, the moon, or other celestial bodies. Further treaties dealt with the rescue and return of astronauts, liability for damages to earth caused by objects launched into outer space, and the regulation of activities on the moon and other celestial bodies. (As with the *Convention on the Law of the Sea*, commercial mining rights became a controversial issue in the *Moon Treaty* of 1979, because minerals are a potential source of great wealth.) One stipulation of the treaty was that every nation was to bear responsibility for actions carried out within its borders by governmental agencies, non-governmental agencies, and individuals. By 2003, space law included the following: five international treaties; five sets of principles; national laws, rules, and regulations; executive and administrative orders; and judicial decisions.

To this day, some individuals choose to ignore the terms of space treaties. Dennis Hope, an American who claims to represent the "Lunar Embassy," is the self-described "leader in extraterrestrial real estate," having sold parcels of the moon to thousands of people worldwide. He has chosen to interpret the silence of the United Nations as acceptance of his claim. A Scot named Virgiliu Pop claimed ownership of the sun when he was a Ph.D. candidate at Glasgow University, in an attempt to poke fun at the claims of those who register property claims to the sun, the moon, or the stars.

Customary Practices

Countries may choose, in the absence of any formal written agreements, to engage in practices that they feel ethically bound to follow. For example, nations extended **diplomatic immunity**, which is the right to be shielded from being charged with a crime or sued, to the members of embassy staff long before this practice was codified in the *Vienna Convention*. Nations may also engage with other nations in practices that they feel legally bound to follow based on their domestic laws. The most challenging question that springs from these types of scenarios is the following: When does a practice between nations occur for long enough and with such consistency that it becomes law? Some legal scholars suggest that there is a distinction to be made between practices that are followed as a courtesy and those that are followed with the intent to create legally binding obligations. The United States Supreme Court stated in 1900 that "...what originally may have rested in custom, courtesy or concession may grow, by the general assent of civilized nations, into a settled rule of law."

General Principles of Law

Article 38 of the Statute of the International Court of Justice lists "general principles of law" recognized by "civilized nations" as a third source of international law. However, it is very difficult to achieve international consensus on either the interpretation of the term "civilized" or the scope of these general principles. Would these principles be derived from domestic or international law? Would they include principles of justice or natural law or equity or all of these?

Judicial Decisions and Teachings

Decisions made by the International Court of Justice and domestic courts are considered to be of **persuasive value**, which means that, while these decisions can be consulted, they have no binding force. These decisions are not used to influence or determine outcomes in the same way that precedent is used in common law. While these decisions may help shape international custom and practice, they are not legally binding.

The teachings and writings of legal scholars are also sources of international law. The analysis and interpretation provided by learned legal experts can contribute to the understanding of current practices. They can also pinpoint or highlight new approaches to, or principles of, international law.

CONFIRM YOUR UNDERSTANDING

1. Identify four groups that have an interest in Antarctica. How might a series of treaties help to reconcile the interests of these four groups?

2. Explain the advantages and disadvantages of having a territory governed by a series of treaties rather than by one nation.

3. Prior to the signing of the *Antarctic Treaty* in 1959, sovereignty over the region was claimed by seven countries: Argentina, Australia, Chile, France, New Zealand, Norway, and Great Britain. Why do you think that the international community rejected plans by specific countries that would split the continent into sectors and award each sector to a different nation?

4. Thousands of tourists now visit Antarctica each year, the majority arriving by ship. Some

of the consequences of increased tourism include an increased need for airstrips and tourist accommodations, trails of garbage and graffiti, and accidental oil spills that kill sea life.

a) **Ecotourism** can be defined as travel to a relatively undisturbed natural area for the purpose of understanding its natural history and culture without altering its ecosystem. Research ecotourism. Explain some of the risks associated with ecotourism.

b) What laws are necessary to protect the continent of Antarctica? What laws provide environmental safeguards for the continent? Identify some of the problems associated with enforcing these laws.

5. How do you think the international community would respond if valuable resources

CONFIRM YOUR UNDERSTANDING (continued)

were discovered under the sea or on the moon? What new agreements would be needed?

6. Nations have rights to natural resources up to 200 nautical miles (370.4 km) from their shoreline. What difficulties might this practice cause among nations?

7. What factors have led to the growth of space law?

8. Imagine you are a lawyer hired by Dennis

Hope or Virgiliu Pop. What historical and legal arguments could you make to defend your client's claims?

9. Identify and explain four different sources of international law.

10. For individual countries, what would be the advantage of taking existing customs and formalizing them in a treaty or agreement?

11. Explain the significance of judicial decisions and teachings to international law.

Concepts in International Law

Sovereignty

There is no concept more important to our understanding of international law than sovereignty. The origins of the term and of the concept itself lie within the notion of a sovereign or ruler—a king, queen, or prince—exercising power over his or her subjects. Originally, a ruling sovereign had supreme power over subjects living within his or her state. This power, which includes the right to make laws, is often referred to as **internal sovereignty**. A result of this power is the right, again unhampered by outside influences, to engage in relationships with foreign states. This right or power can be exercised by forging a trade agreement with another state or sharing responsibility, such as joint jurisdiction over a shared waterway. This type of sovereignty has been called **external sovereignty,** and it recognizes that, in theory, independent states are free to either enter or not enter into relationships with other states.

The concept of sovereignty has been well ingrained across cultures for centuries. However, since World War II, there has been a definite shift away from the notion that individual states should be free from external interference in their internal matters. Globally, there has been an increasing awareness of the ways in which countries' inter-

dependence requires international co-operation. Legal writers now discuss the erosion of sovereignty, suggesting that initiatives in international law will increasingly affect our traditional view of sovereignty. Politics, economics, and technology have caused this **globalization**, which can be defined as the increase in worldwide social interconnectedness, in which local happenings are shaped by events occurring far away.

An excellent example of the need for global co-operation is the need to safeguard the environment. Pollution does not respect political boundaries. This means that effective and reasonable management of resources must involve all nations that either use these resources or are affected by them.

The protection of human rights raises a second challenge to traditional ideas of sovereignty. The *Universal Declaration of Human Rights* (1948) codified a number of human rights that, according to the declaration, should be considered universal. Such a declaration raises the following questions: Are these universally recognized human rights so important that one nation or one organization has the right to interfere in the internal affairs of another nation? Are these rights reflective of the diversity of values we see around the world? Do some countries' rights

If we cannot end our differences, at least we can make the world safe for diversity.

–John F. Kennedy (1917–1963), former president of the United States carry more weight in the international community? As we wrestle with emerging concerns, it is likely that the world community will be forced to re-examine its long-cherished sense of entitlement regarding sovereignty.

SHIFTING PERSPECTIVES: Sovereignty versus Globalization

Historically, human beings have considered marine life and the oceans to be a limitless resource. In the last century, the global community became aware that certain species were endangered. It took steps to remedy some species' endangerment. An interesting example is the practice of whaling. The Japanese have eaten whale meat for hundreds of years. Commercial whaling was the mainstay of some of Japan's coastal villages. Should Japan be allowed to continue with whaling in some limited form? Do global agencies and treaties overrule Japan's right to pursue economic activity as it sees fit?

A hundred years ago, whale hunting was a major commercial industry. In the mid-twentieth century, protection and conservation of whales became a focal point of international concern. Whale hunting practices became increasingly controversial. Whaling nations recognized the importance of international cooperation, and, in 1946, 14 countries signed the *Whaling Convention*. The intent of the convention was to regulate the whaling industry in order to ensure the "proper and effective conservation and development of whale stocks." In 1986, it became clear that some species of whales were on the brink of extinction. The convention therefore issued a **moratorium** on commercial whaling, meaning that it decreed a total ban on all whaling until such time as it was considered safe. At such a point, the convention would lift the moratorium, meaning that they would reverse the ban.

A controversy surrounding whaling practices, however, arose because one article of the *Whaling Convention* does permit whaling for the "purposes of scientific research." This controversy continues to this day. Many conservationists throughout the world, as well as a number of countries including the United States and Australia, allege that Japan is violating international whaling regulations and environmental norms. Since 1994, Japan has conducted a research whaling program, which it maintains is consistent with provisions of the *Whaling Convention* that allow for research. Japan claims that the consumption of fish by whales has led to an imbalance in the marine ecosystem and that this concern provides grounds for expanding its research program.

FIGURE 14.6   Japanese whalers hoisting a whale head near the Japanese coastline. When this photo was taken, around 1902, whale hunting was a major commercial activity. Today the protection and conservation of whales is a major international concern.

Critics of Japan's whale research say that whales are, in fact, being killed for parts to be sold as food in restaurants and as jewellery in boutiques. The Japanese Whaling Association argues that the ban on commercial whaling deprives Japan of an important part of its culture and tradition, because whale meat is a prized delicacy. Any trade sanctions imposed by the United States could then be called an example of **cultural imperialism**, a complex concept meaning the imposition of one society's values, behaviours, institutions, and identity onto another society. Japan could view any restrictions on its whaling as an attack on its sovereignty.

Source: Ackerman, Reuben. "Japanese Whaling in the Pacific Ocean: Defiance of International Whaling Norms in the Name of 'Scientific Research,' Culture, and Tradition." *Boston College International Law Journal* 25.2 (2002): 323–342.

Your Perspective

1. In chart form, list both sides of the argument for whether or not the international community should exert pressure on Japan to change its whaling practices. Which side do you feel is more compelling? Support your opinion.
2. Japan maintains that if the United States imposed trade sanctions, the United States would in fact be in breach of existing trade agreements. Should the need to uphold trade agreements supersede the concerns of conservationists? Explain.
3. Research the term "cultural imperialism." Apply the concept of cultural imperialism to an issue other than whaling practices that arises in international law.
4. Explain the conflict between the principles of sovereignty and globalization.

Extradition

When a crime is committed in Canada and the suspect is captured and detained in Canada, Canada clearly has the jurisdiction to investigate the crime, arrest and charge the suspect, and commit him or her to trial in a Canadian courtroom. If convicted, the accused would serve the sentence in Canada. The accused need not be a Canadian citizen or what is known legally as an "ordinary resident" in order for this criminal process to occur. However, this process is hampered if the suspect flees to another country. If the suspect is apprehended, the country of flight has no jurisdiction to prosecute the suspect. At the same time, Canada has no jurisdiction to send law enforcement agents into another country to bring the suspect back to Canada. Unless a suspect willingly returns to Canada, the only solution is **extradition**, which is the legal surrender or delivery of a fugitive to the jurisdiction of another state, country, or government to face trial. The term "extradition"

comes from Latin, with *ex* meaning "out" and *traditio* meaning "handing over."

Most extradition treaties contain principles and rules that must be complied with in order for an extradition to occur. First, the **double-criminality rule** states that a crime must be a crime in both nations. Second, the principle of **reciprocity** suggests that if Country A extradites a person to Country B, then Country B will reciprocate in the future. Third, it is not enough that a country requests extradition; evidence of guilt must be provided. Fourth, the principle of **speciality** suggests that an accused will be charged only with the crime that is specified in the request for extradition. This principle stops a country from engaging in **subterfuge**, or deception, by providing one crime as a reason for extradition when its intent is, in fact, to prosecute a different one.

There are many reasons why an extradition request might be denied. Some countries will refuse to extradite a "national," meaning one of their own citizens. Historically, Canada has generally been willing to extradite Canadian citizens who have committed crimes in other countries to those countries. Extradition could be denied if the accused has already been convicted and served a penalty, if the accused has been acquitted, or if there is a concern about the fairness of the trial that the accused would face. Countries may distinguish between criminal offences and political offences. An example of a criminal offence would be the charge of murder or of trafficking in narcotics. A political offence could include criticizing the existing government in a newspaper editorial or practising a religion that has been outlawed by the state. Humanitarian grounds may be taken into account; for example, the health or age of the accused may make extradition seem unreasonable and uncompassionate. Sometimes, the controversial issue of the death penalty affects the decision. Some countries will not extradite if the death penalty might be used in sentencing. This issue may be avoided if the requesting country gives assurances that the death penalty will not be sought. Canada's Supreme Court was forced to rule on this issue in the case of Charles Ng in 1991 (see p. 464) and, more recently, in the case of Burns and Rafay in 2000 (see p. 446).

It is well established within international law that no right to extradition exists without a treaty. The first recorded extradition treaties date back to ancient Egypt, suggesting that respect for jurisdiction has existed for thousands of years. By 2003, Canada was a party to 49 bilateral treaties and 8 multilateral conventions that contain extradition provisions with other countries. In 1999,

Canada had created the *Extradition Act*, replacing two earlier acts that were each over a hundred years old. The new legislation works hand in hand with amendments to other acts in order to streamline the extradition process and bring Canada closer in line with its international obligations.

These changes to legislation included the following:

- Allowances have been made for incorporating new extraditable offences, such as a computer crime or a **transnational crime** (a crime that crosses national boundaries).
- Allowances have been made for Canada to extradite people not just to other nations but to international criminal courts and tribunals as well.
- More flexibility exists around rules of evidence; no longer must evidence be admissible under Canadian rules of evidence.
- More flexibility exists around the practice of extraditing without a treaty.
- Provisions have been made for the temporary surrender of a person in a criminal case; for example, a person imprisoned in Canada can temporarily return to a foreign country for prosecution, then be sent back to Canada to finish his or her sentence.
- Once a fugitive is informed of his or her rights, the fugitive may waive the right to an extradition hearing, reducing the legal system's workload and cost.
- Provisions have been made for changes to other Canadian statutes, including allowing, for the first time, the use of video- and audio-link technology to gather evidence.

CONFIRM YOUR UNDERSTANDING

1. Distinguish between internal and external sovereignty.
2. What international forces are contributing to the erosion of sovereignty?
3. The European Union (EU) is an organization formed by numerous European countries in

1993; by the spring of 2004, it had 25 member countries. Its member states have set up common institutions to which they delegate some of their sovereignty, so that decisions on specific matters of interest can be made for Europe as a whole. Why do you

CONFIRM YOUR UNDERSTANDING (continued)

think these individual countries would surrender some sovereignty to a higher authority? What benefits would they hope to gain?

4. Explain some of the conditions that must be met before a person is extradited.

5. How could the use of the death penalty

complicate extradition proceedings?

6. Outline some of the changes made to the law in the _Extradition Act_ of 1999. How would these amendments improve the extradition process? Why might some of these changes have been necessary?

United States v. Burns, [2001] 1 S.C.R. 283, 2001 SCC 7

Read the following case analysis. The facts, issue, and _ratio decidendi_ have been provided for you. Write a possible dissenting opinion for this controversial case.

Facts: Glen Sebastian Burns and Atif Rafay were Canadian citizens who were each 18 years of age when the father, mother, and sister of Rafay were found murdered in their home in the state of Washington in the United States in 1994. Burns and Rafay are Canadian citizens who had been high-school friends in British Columbia. Both Burns and Rafay admitted that they were at the Rafay home on the night of the murders. They were arrested in British Columbia in July 1995. Authorities in the United States began extradition proceedings. The minister of justice for Canada, Alan Rock, considered their ages, their nationality, the nature of the alleged offences, and the structure of the US judicial system. He ordered their extradition without seeking assurances that the death penalty would not be imposed. The British Columbia Court of Appeal, in a majority decision, ruled that the unconditional extradition order would violate the mobility rights of the respondents under s. 6 (1) of the _Charter_. The Court of Appeal set aside Rock's decision and directed him to seek, as a condition of surrender, assurances that the death penalty would not be used. The justice minister appealed this decision to the Supreme Court of Canada.

FIGURE 14.7　Sebastian Burns, left, and co-defendant Atif Rafay, right, listened to proceedings on December 1, 2003, in King County Superior Court in Seattle, as their trial for the 1994 clubbing deaths of Rafay's parents and sister continued. Each of the two faced three counts of aggravated first-degree murder.

Issue: Is the government of Canada obligated to receive assurances that the death penalty will not be used before a suspect is extradited?

Held: Except in rare cases, such assurances should be received before extradition is ordered.

Ratio Decidendi: (McLachlin C.J. and L'Heureux-Dubé, Gonthier, Iacobucci, Major, Bastarache, Binnie, Arbour, and LeBel JJ.) Death penalty cases are uniquely bound up with basic constitutional values and the court is the guardian of the Constitution…. [While mobility rights are the] right of every Canadian citizen to "remain in" Canada, efforts to stretch mobility rights to cover the death penalty controversy are misplaced…. Nor is section 12 of the *Charter* ("cruel and unusual treatment or punishment") the most appropriate head of relief [that is, the means to remedy the situation]…. Section 7 ("fundamental justice") applies because the extradition order would, if implemented, deprive the respondents of their rights of liberty and security of the person since their lives are potentially at risk…. The "shocks the conscience" language signals the possibility that even though the rights of the fugitive are to be considered in the context of other applicable principles of fundamental justice, which are normally of sufficient importance to uphold the extradition, a particular treatment or punishment may sufficiently violate our sense of fundamental justice as to tilt the balance against extradition…. Countervailing factors favour extradition only with assurances. First, in Canada, the death penalty has been rejected as an acceptable element of criminal justice…. Second, at the international level, the abolition of the death penalty has emerged as a major Canadian initiative and reflects a concern increasingly shared by most of the world's democracies. Canada's support of international initiatives opposing extradition without assurances, combined with its international advocacy of the abolition of the death penalty itself, leads to the conclusion that in the Canadian view of fundamental justice, capital punishment is unjust and should be stopped…. Third, almost all jurisdictions treat some personal characteristics of the fugitive as mitigating factors in death penalty cases…. Even though the respondents were 18 at the time of the crime, their relative youth constitutes a mitigating circumstance in this case, albeit of limited weight. Fourth, the accelerating concern about potential wrongful convictions is a factor of increased weight since *Kindler* and *Ng* were decided…. Fifth, the "death row phenomenon" is another factor that weighs against extradition without assurances. The finality of the death penalty, combined with the determination of the criminal justice system to try to satisfy itself that the conviction is not wrongful, inevitably produces lengthy delays, and the associated psychological trauma to death row inhabitants, many of whom may ultimately be shown to be innocent…. A review of the factors for and against unconditional extradition therefore leads to the conclusion that assurances are constitutionally required in all but exceptional cases. This case does not present the exceptional circumstances that must be shown.

Diplomatic Immunity

The governments of most countries have a branch that provides foreign service, carried out by an entity that is often called a **diplomatic corps**. It consists of a staff of trained officials whose function is to assist in implementing their country's policy in foreign countries. They work at locations called embassies and consulates. In Canada, the federal Department of Foreign Affairs and International Trade (which was called the Department of External Affairs until 1993) oversees this role. Embassies in foreign countries are headed by **ambassadors**, who are either career civil servants or political appointees. In the case of Commonwealth countries, heads of embassies are called high commissioners. The ambassador is assisted by other diplomats and **attachés** who often carry out specific roles related to such areas as trade or the military. The Canadian embassy provides help to Canadians travelling or working abroad and to foreign nationals who wish to travel or work in Canada.

It has long been recognized that a diplomatic corps helps immensely with international affairs.

FIGURE 14.8 In 1979, Jean Casselman-Wadds, shown here in front of the Canadian Embassy in the Court of St. James, London, was the first Canadian woman to be appointed to the post of high commissioner. In 1961, she had been the first woman to be appointed by the Canadian government as a delegate to the United Nations.

Over 3000 years ago, Egypt engaged in diplomatic negotiations with its neighbours. Diplomacy became more formalized in the twelfth and thirteenth centuries, with Italian city-states taking the lead. These city-states developed rules to govern the appointment and conduct of ambassadors. In the sixteenth century, other European states followed the Italian example. During this era, it also became clear that diplomats working abroad needed protection, especially in hostile territories. The rules regarding the protection of diplomats became more specific in the late sixteenth and seventeenth centuries, and were codified in the _Congress of Vienna_ in 1815.

In 1961, the _Vienna Convention on Diplomatic Relations_ laid out the laws and the means by which specific people would be protected under the shield of diplomatic immunity. Diplomats in foreign countries are shielded from the laws of the host country in which they reside. The embassy and its grounds are treated as if they belong to the diplomat's home country. Therefore, the embassy staff cannot be charged with any crime nor sued, and the privacy of its correspondence must be protected. These rights, with some limitations, are also extended to the embassy staff's family members. If the host country is unhappy with a diplomat for any reason, the country can declare him or her a _persona non grata_, meaning a person who is undesirable and no longer able to stay in the county. This decision to send a diplomat home, called the **expulsion** of a diplomat, is not taken lightly because it could seriously jeopardize the relationship between the two nations. At times, countries will recall a diplomat because they anticipate that the diplomat is about to be expelled, and they wish to avoid embarrassment.

In dangerous or hostile circumstances, embassies may choose to send family members and non-essential staff home or to neighbouring countries; the embassies continue to operate with only a skeleton staff. Most countries want to do whatever it takes to avoid the drastic step of cutting off formal diplomatic relations, at which time the embassy is closed and the entire staff is recalled to the country of origin.

Over the last century, modern developments in communication and transportation have changed the role of diplomats in foreign countries. Government representatives can travel the world with relative ease in order to attend top-level meetings, rather than needing to be stationed in particular countries. As well, telecommunications and computers allow for the instant transfer of messages and documents, which facilitates long-distance communication. However, the embassy staff still provide the "eyes" and "ears" in a foreign country, as they influence decisions and promote and protect a country's image and best interests abroad.

The Case of Augusto Pinochet

In Chile in 1973, an army general named Augusto Pinochet came to power as president through a military coup d'état, that is, in a sudden, violent overthrow of the existing government. Pinochet's administration has been described as ruthless. For almost 20 years, thousands of Chileans fled the country for their own safety while dissidents at home were tortured. Other dissidents were "disappeared." This term refers to a particularly cruel form of murder in which victims, who are kidnapped, simply vanish; no bodies are found and no explanations are given, leaving families with few answers. Pinochet left the presidency in 1990 and, due to the provisions of the Chilean constitution, remained commander-in-chief of the army until 1998, when he took a senatorial position for life.

A Spanish judge issued a warrant for Pinochet's arrest for crimes against humanity in late 1998. Pinochet was arrested in London, England, by British police at a clinic where he had undergone back surgery. Spanish authorities requested his extradition to Spain in order to face trial for crimes that included torture, hostage taking, and murder.

London's High Court ruled that Pinochet was immune from arrest because he was the head of state at the time the alleged crimes were committed. Despite the favourable ruling, Pinochet was held in custody, pending an appeal. The Law Lords, members of the House of Lords qualified to perform its legal work, heard the appeal. In the United Kingdom, the House of Lords had the task of defining the conditions for immunity from arrest and extradition proceedings for a former head of state who committed a crime while in office. The British prosecution contended that a foreign head of state would be immune from arrest or trial regarding alleged charges only if he or she were still head of state. But once he or she ceased to be the head of state, the immunity ended and thus the person could be arrested and prosecuted for such crimes. Senator Pinochet alleged that his immunity came from acts committed while he was head of state and that his immunity should continue even after he ceased to be head of state.

Three groups of Chileans had differing views on the legal issues. One group believed that significant violations of human rights had taken place, and they wanted to see Pinochet prosecuted somewhere in the world. A second group consisted of supporters of Pinochet, who contended that he had saved Chile from the socialist government of Salvador Allende (1970–1973). A third group took the position that it was an internal matter for Chile to sort out and that no third-party interference should occur.

In November 1998, in a majority vote of 3 to 2, the Law Lords ruled that Pinochet was not entitled to immunity. According to this ruling, Pinochet would remain in England, where he would await the outcome of the extradition proceedings. At the conclusion of the hearing, rumours surfaced that one of the lords who ruled on the case was linked to the international human rights organization Amnesty International. The appearance of bias was enough for a second hearing. Again the lords ruled that Pinochet was not entitled to immunity. In October 1999, the British court ruled that Pinochet could be extradited to Spain in order to stand trial on torture charges. One month later, the Chilean government asked the British government

It's unbelievable that a criminal should escape justice because he is ill or in pain. The pain of my Chilean people is worse than what Pinochet is suffering.

—Carlos Reyes-Manzo, Chilean photojournalist imprisoned for two years during Pinochet's rule

Where law ends, tyranny begins.

—William Pitt (1708–1778), Earl of Chatham

FIGURE 14.9 Pinochet argued that he should be shielded from prosecution because he was the head of state when his alleged crimes were committed. Do you agree that heads of state should never face criminal prosecution? What are the potential implications of this diplomatic immunity?

to have Pinochet examined to see if he was medically fit to stand trial.

Doctors said Pinochet was in poor health, and, should he be extradited and ordered to stand trial, he would be unable to understand the specifics of the legal proceedings. On humanitarian grounds, the British government decided to allow Pinochet to return to Chile in March 2000.

In August 2000, the Chilean Supreme Court ruled that Pinochet should be stripped of his parliamentary immunity and stand trial. In December 2000, a Chilean judge, Juan Guzman Tapia, indicted Pinochet for crimes against humanity. The Court of Appeals of Santiago de Chile threw out the charges on the grounds that the judge had failed to question Pinochet, a requirement under Chilean law. The Supreme Court of Chile supported the ruling of the Court of Appeals. Next, Judge Guzman questioned Pinochet in January 2001 and re-indicted him.

In July 2002, Chile's highest court supported a lower-court decision, made in July 2001, which found that the 86-year-old general's dementia should halt his prosecution.

CONFIRM YOUR UNDERSTANDING

1. Why is there a need for countries to send diplomats to foreign countries?
2. In 1961, which document codified diplomatic immunity? Outline key aspects of diplomatic immunity.
3. In 1984, a demonstration took place against Libyan leader Colonel Gaddafi outside the Libyan embassy in London, England. Shots fired from inside the Libyan embassy killed British police officer Yvonne Fletcher. No one was arrested, and at no time did British authorities enter the embassy. Diplomatic ties between Libya and England were severed. Some days later, 30 diplomats left the embassy and were escorted to the airport in order to return to Libya. In 1999, Libya admitted general responsibility for the killing of the police officer and agreed to pay compensation to the family. Diplomatic relations were resumed later that year. British Home Secretary Leon Brittan said that the government would press for changes to the *Vienna Convention*.

   a) Why didn't the British authorities enter the Libyan embassy and make an arrest?
   b) What are the potential consequences when one country severs diplomatic ties with another?
   c) What changes could be made to the *Vienna Convention* to avoid a situation in which diplomats are shielded from what is referred to legally as "criminal responsibility"?

CONFIRM YOUR UNDERSTANDING (continued)

4. It is well established in customary international law that a serving head of state is entitled to immunity from criminal prosecution and civil court actions, such as lawsuits, with respect to his or her official acts. However, acts such as torture are against international law. Which of these two laws should take precedence? Justify your opinion.

5. Prepare a timeline of the judicial proceedings against Pinochet, and highlight the outcome at each stage of the process.

6. Explain the risks of waiving immunity for heads of state. How could this action limit the sovereignty of a state?

ASKING KEY QUESTIONS

Diplomatic Immunity and Justice

In New York City, there are thousands of unpaid parking tickets that will likely never be paid. That's because they belong to international diplomats working at UN headquarters. Diplomatic immunity, intended to prevent the arbitrary harassment of diplomats, shields them from their fines. Not all offences committed by diplomats or their families are so minor. In Canada, between 1996 and 2001, 76 foreign diplomats or their family members were accused of crimes such as attempted murder, child abuse, and sexual assault. Most of them used diplomatic immunity to escape prosecution. Is it really necessary to afford diplomats this degree of protection?

FIGURE 14.10   Andrei Knyazev, a former Russian diplomat to Canada, leaving a district court on March 15, 2002, after his trial in Moscow. After killing one woman and injuring another in a drunk-driving accident in Ottawa, he was extradited to Russia, where he was charged and convicted of involuntary manslaughter.

Russian heads home with diplomatic immunity following fatal accident

BRUCE CHEADLE
Canadian Press

OTTAWA (CP) A Russian diplomat accused of mowing down two Ottawa women in a drunken stupor headed home to Moscow on Monday and won't stand trial in Canada for criminal negligence causing death. A second diplomat, charged with drunk driving following a fender-bender nearby just minutes after the first accident, was also expelled from Canada.

Foreign Affairs Minister John Manley had asked that Russia waive diplomatic immunity for Andrei Knyazev, but Russia refused, promising instead to prosecute both the accused men in Moscow.

"The main issue here is that Canadian justice should be done," said Richard Kohler, chief of protocol for the Department of Foreign Affairs.

"We would prefer to have justice done in Canada, but if we cannot have justice done in Canada, we would want to see justice done in Russia."

Manley spoke by phone with his Russian counterpart, Igor Ivanov, on Monday and expressed his "regret" at Russia's refusal to let Canadian authorities prosecute Knyazev, said Manley's spokeswoman.

Jennifer Sloan said Ivanov promised Manley the case would be investigated thoroughly. Ivanov also offered his condolences and said he planned to write personally to the families of both women.

Knyazev, a mid-level political functionary, was returning from a day of ice fishing Saturday afternoon when he drove his car up on a sidewalk, running down Catherine MacLean, 50, and Catherine Doré, 56.

MacLean died at the scene, while Doré broke both legs and suffered severe facial injuries. MacLean's dog, which the two women were walking, had to be euthanized due to its injuries.

Police at the scene said Knyazev, who refused to take a Breathalyzer, was so impaired he could barely walk or speak.

Under the 1961 *Vienna Convention*, diplomats and their families can be charged with crimes but are immune from criminal prosecution. Once Russia refused to waive immunity, Canada had no choice but to expel Knyazev, said Kohler. "I do not at present see an indication where further intervention (by the Canadian government) [is] required," he said, calling the incident "a deeply troubling situation."

Canada has international obligations under the *Vienna Convention* and "we cannot abrogate our obligations because of sorrow."

Still, friends, neighbours and colleagues of MacLean—a labour lawyer and mother of two teenage sons—said they will not let the matter drop.

Under the *Vienna Convention on Diplomatic Relations*, there are three exceptions to the blanket immunity, all involving property or commercial crimes. Kohler said the *Vienna Convention* could be modified if enough countries can agree.

Canada has refused to waive immunity for its diplomats charged with crimes abroad, opting instead to bring the individuals home and try them under Canadian law. There have been many cases of foreign diplomats committing crimes in Canada.

Source: Cheadle, Bruce. "Russian Heads Home with Diplomatic Immunity Following Fatal Accident." Canadian Press. 29 Jan. 2001.

Form Your Questions

A controversial case such as this one raises complex issues. Suggest three questions that would lead to meaningful debate and discussion on the issue of diplomatic immunity and justice.

Issues in International Law

Environmental Protection

Two issues that have attracted considerable attention and activity since World War II are protection of the environment and the explosion in international trade. Both issues raise questions that extend far beyond the law since they are affected by political, economic, and moral considerations. Both issues contribute to the erosion of sovereignty, and both demand global concessions and co-operation. In fact, both issues generate controversy and, at times, even polarize the world community.

The Environment and the World Community

As you saw in Chapter 13, environmental concerns are essentially complex. Solutions, therefore, will be multifaceted. In Canada, governmental response requires co-operation at the municipal, provincial, and federal levels. Corporations, other organizations, and private citizens have a role to play in solving environmental problems. However, our understanding of interdependence makes it clear that solutions must also include all the nations of the world.

Why did environmental issues attract such attention in the second half of the last century? One reason is that scientific methods improved, allowing us to measure and predict damage to the environment and to the health of individuals. For centuries, natural resources were plentiful and were treated as if they would never run out. We now recognize that environmental damage is often irreversible; endangered species that become extinct and holes that appear in the ozone layer are only the more obvious examples. New technologies have been developed that enable industries to use production methods that are less damaging to the environment. Non-governmental organizations (NGOs), which are professional, non-profit, non-membership, community-based organizations that render services, solve problems, and communicate ideas, have encouraged the public to tackle environmental concerns. As well, the prevalence of the mass media has brought information, including disturbing facts about the environment, to a much wider population.

The Evolution of International Environmental Law

According to author John O'Brien in his book *International Law*, there are four distinct periods in the evolution of international environmental law. The first period began in Europe in the eighteenth century during the Enlightenment, an era in which scientists tried to understand the nature and history of the physical world. This first period extended right up to the mid-twentieth century. In the eighteenth century, there had been little international interest in the protection of the environment. By the nineteenth century, industrialization led to some concerns about public health and housing within countries. On the international front, the *International Convention for the High Seas Fisheries of the North*, designed to prevent overfishing, was signed in 1882, and, in 1916, the United States and Canada signed a convention to protect migratory birds in their two countries.

The second period began with the signing of the *United Nations Charter* in 1945. That same year, the first use of nuclear weapons raised new and alarming concerns about both the environment and humanity. Also in 1945, the *Truman Declaration on the Continental Shelf* was signed to ensure conservation of fish stocks and mineral resources. Over the next several years, the United Nations became involved in matters related to conservation and development when the General Assembly began discussing issues such as atmospheric nuclear testing and oil pollution. Then, in the 1950s, work began on codification of the law of the sea. The *Antarctic Treaty* of 1959 (see p. 439) contained provisions designed to prevent environmental damage through the disposal of radioactive waste. A conference held in 1968 by the **United Nations Educational, Scientific, and Cultural Organization (UNESCO)** made it clear that, while more nations were expressing interest in environmental protection, virtually no progress had occurred at the international level.

The third period began with the United Nations Conference on the Human Environment held in Stockholm, Sweden, in 1972. This conference issued a document known as the *Stockholm Declaration of the United Nations Conference on the Human Environment,* which contained 26 principles. Some of these principles explored the following:

- the way in which the quality of the environment is linked with human rights
- the need to protect natural resources
- the documenting of particular environmental threats, such as the discharge of toxic substances and the pollution of the seas
- the relationship between development and environmental protection
- demographic policies and population growth

The *Stockholm Declaration* was not intended to impose legal obligations but to provide a frame of reference for future discussions and proposals. The conclusions of the conference were endorsed by the United Nations and were in fact followed by further conventions, including the *Montréal Protocol on Substances that Deplete the Ozone Layer* (1987).

In 1987, a report called *Our Common Future*, referred to unofficially as the *Brundtland Report*, was issued by the new World Commission on Environment and Development. This report focused on four areas: it called for more public education; recognized that international law had not developed at a pace necessary to safeguard the environment; highlighted the need to break from traditional environmental categories and deal with these issues in a more general way; and endorsed the principle of sustainable development, which is development that meets the needs of the present without compromising the ability of future generations to meet their own needs (see Chapter 13).

The fourth period, 1992 to the present, began with the United Nations Conference on Environment and Development (known as the Earth Summit), held in Rio de Janeiro, Brazil, in 1992. Three non-binding agreements were adopted, and two treaties were opened for signature. One treaty dealt with climate change and the other with biological diversity. Just as in the *Stockholm Declaration* two decades earlier, principles of co-operation and sustainable development were endorsed.

The *Nairobi Declaration* of 1997 stated that the United Nations Environment Programme (UNEP) should be the principal United Nations

body in the field of the environment and should "set the global environmental agenda and serve as an advocate for the environment." Environmental ministers from around the world met in Malmö, Sweden, in 2000. Emerging concerns listed in the *Malmö Ministerial Declaration* included the discrepancy between commitments and action, the need to pay close attention to consumption patterns in richer nations, the increase in urbanization, the risk of climate change, and the need for "food security." Food security is defined as access by all people at all times to enough nutritious food for them to be able to lead an active, healthy life.

In 2002, a world summit on sustainable development was held in Johannesburg, South Africa. The *Johannesburg Declaration* underscored the "collective responsibility to advance and strengthen…the pillars of sustainable development—economic development, social development and environmental protection." Challenges that were identified included the gap both between the rich and people living with poverty and between developed and developing countries. Mounting environmental crises were listed, including the following challenges: depleted fish stocks; air, lake, and sea pollution; and desertification, which is the degradation of drylands through variations in climate and unsustainable human activities such as overcultivation, overgrazing, deforestation, and poor irrigation practices. The declaration, however, concluded on a positive note, stating that sustainable development could be achieved with effective and accountable institutions and the support of the United Nations.

The United Nations has increased its profile on environmental issues through two agencies: the permanent United Nations Environment Programme (UNEP) and the United Nations Division for Sustainable Development. In addition, in 2000, the Economic and Social Committee of the United Nations (ECOSOC) established the United Nations Forum on Forests (UNFF), an organization with the objective of

FIGURE 14.11   South African President Thabo Mbeki and a child celebrating the opening ceremony of the 10-day World Summit on Sustainable Development in Johannesburg, South Africa, in August 2002.

promoting the management, conservation, and sustainable development of forests.

One principle found in customary law is that a state should never do environmental harm to another state. Decisions by the International Court of Justice suggest that a state must act responsibly or else be prepared to pay damages if arbitration rules against it.

A modern principle known as the "**precautionary principle**" may reflect a new direction in policy and actions that protect the environment. This principle suggests that "damage to the environment can be irreversible or [else] remediable only at a considerable cost and over long periods of time...[therefore] we must not wait for proof of harmful effect before taking action." It may become increasingly advisable that proof of an economic activity's environmental soundness be supplied before the activity is undertaken. The following excerpt is the conclusion of the *Malmö Ministerial Declaration*:

> At the dawn of this new century, we have at our disposal the human and material resources to achieve sustainable development, not as an abstract concept but as a concrete reality. We can decrease poverty by half by 2015 without degrading the environment, we can ensure environmental security through early warning, we can better integrate environmental consideration in economic policy, we can better coordinate legal instruments and we can realize a vision of a world without slums. We commit ourselves to realizing this common vision.

Confirm Your Understanding

1. Create a timeline indicating the four periods in the evolution of environmental law.
2. Describe the substance of each of the following:
  a) *Stockholm Declaration*
  b) *Montréal Protocol on Substances That Deplete the Ozone Layer*
  c) *Brundtland Report*
  d) *Nairobi Declaration*
  e) *Johannesburg Declaration*
3. What are some of the most pressing environmental issues facing the world community?
4. How does the increase in international laws relating to the environment contribute to the erosion of sovereignty?

International Trade

International trade can be defined as the exchange of goods and services among countries. The theory behind international trade is that every country can specialize solely in the goods and services that it is able to produce most efficiently. Each country can purchase all other goods and services from other countries. According to this theory, consumers benefit from increased choice, since there is a wider, more diverse range of goods available to them than there would be without specialization.

Historically, the search for new, unusual goods led people of the ancient world to journey far from home. At different times, world trade was dominated by the Egyptians, the Greeks, the Spanish, the Dutch, and the British. In North America, the exchange of goods between different nations rather than individuals dates back to Aboriginal groups long before contact with Europeans. In Europe, the practice of international trade dates back to the rise of the nation-states at the end of the Middle Ages. The predominant economic school of thought in the sixteenth and seventeenth centuries was **mercantilism**. The policy of mercantilism promoted the acquisition of wealth, particularly in the form of gold, as the prime objective of nations. Exports, predominantly to the colonies, were encouraged, while imports were discouraged. This policy was consistent with the focus on finding new markets. The Industrial Revolution in the nineteenth century placed greater emphasis on free trade. Later, new technologies, larger corporations, and mass production increased world trade.

Figure 14.12   This fifteenth-century fabric market is in Ravenna Gate, Bologna, Italy, one of the many European city-states that thrived during the Renaissance era (1300–1600). During this era, European interior cities became wealthy through agriculture and commerce, while maritime cities gained control of the trade in spice and other Asian products.

World trade was interrupted in the twentieth century by two world wars. As well, the Great Depression of the 1930s led to high unemployment and a decline in national income. During this period, many countries implemented **protectionist policies**—policies that shielded domestic products from international competition and inhibited the growth of international trade. In 1944, the Bretton Woods Conference was held in the United States in order to launch a post-war plan for the start-up of global commerce.

In 1945, the International Monetary Fund and the World Bank were born, signalling a major development in international trade. The World Bank, a UN affiliate, was set up to make loans available for the reconstruction of Europe. When this goal was accomplished, the priorities of the World Bank shifted from focusing on Europe to concentrating on developing countries.

Since the inception of the World Bank, those nations wishing to be members must first join the International Monetary Fund. In 2003, the World Bank had 184 member countries. Member countries agree not to alter the exchange value of their currency without the consent of the World Bank. Every member country pledges to "endeavor to direct its economic and financial policies toward the objective of fostering orderly economic growth with price stability." Members may borrow from the fund to cover emergencies; they must then meet strict conditions that may dictate domestic policies, such as limiting their government spending.

Developing countries that receive loans are encouraged to pursue a Western, democratic, capitalist model of enterprise. The stated purpose of this requirement is that this type of enterprise will bring growth and prosperity. These loans are not without controversy. Critics argue that interest payments are too costly for developing nations and that far too many economic and political strings are attached, leading to a new form of colonialism. Recently, for example, Argentina had to limit government spending in order to be eligible to obtain World Bank funding.

In its defence, the World Bank says that it invests money in projects that it thinks will lead developing countries "onto a path of stable, sustainable and equitable growth." The World Bank acknowledges that it must continue to evolve in order to fulfill its goal of finding increasingly better ways to aid the most economically disadvantaged nations.

The second major development in international trade that occurred at the end of World War II was the establishment of the **General Agreement on Tariffs and Trade** (**GATT**). This multinational treaty to facilitate world trade came into effect in 1948 in Geneva, Switzerland. Originally, 23 countries signed the GATT, which had an impact on four-fifths of world trade at that time. Three key principles of this agreement were as follows:

- It contained a commitment to consult other nations in order to overcome trade problems.
- It called for the reduction of **tariffs**, which are taxes that countries impose on incoming goods to protect domestic industries.
- It called for the elimination of discriminatory trade practices.

By 1993, 106 countries had signed the GATT, tariffs had been cut, and problems surrounding disagreements on duties and the types of products that would be covered had been addressed at a series of three negotiations or rounds, labelled the Kennedy Round, the Tokyo Round, and the Uruguay Round. In 1994, 117 countries signed the Uruguay Round, and the GATT was replaced by the **World Trade Organization** (**WTO**).

By 2003, the World Trade Organization had 146 member countries. The WTO describes itself as "the only global international organization dealing with the rules of trade between nations." Agreements are negotiated and signed by the majority of the world's trading nations and ratified by their governments. The goal of the WTO is to help the producers of goods and services, the exporters, and the importers conduct their business. The functions of the WTO are:

- to administer trade agreements that fall under the WTO umbrella,
- to provide a forum for trade negotiations,
- to handle trade disputes,
- to monitor national trade policies,
- to offer technical assistance to developing countries,
- to co-operate with other international organizations.

Since its inception, this institution has been rocked by criticism. Protests and violence marked the 1999 World Trade Organization conference in Seattle. The most common criticism of the WTO has been that the liberalization of world trade is, in fact, an undesirable goal. Many poorer countries believe that negotiations are biased in favour of industrialized countries and that "the globalization of trade" in reality means that government policies are superseded by corporate agendas.

Aid and debt relief can only go so far. We are asking for the opportunity to compete, to sell our goods in Western markets. In short, we want to trade our way out of poverty.

—President Yoweri Kaguta Museveni of Uganda (2003)

Canada and International Trade

Canada's first prime minister, Sir John A. Macdonald, established the **National Policy** in 1879. The cornerstone of the National Policy was a tariff wall that was set up against American goods. According to this policy, if the United

FIGURE 14.13 A woman holds a candle as she participates in a celebration of the collapse of talks at the September 2003 Cancún World Trade Organization ministerial meeting. Talks collapsed after delegates were unable to bridge differences on agriculture and investment between developed and developing nations.

States wanted market access to Canada, then American companies had to establish branch plants in Canada. Over the next 100 years, the conflict between the liberalization of trade and the policy of protectionism became a recurring theme in Canadian election campaigns.

In 1984, after Conservative Prime Minister Brian Mulroney was elected, negotiations began in earnest to develop a free trade agreement between the two countries. The bilateral *Canada–United States Free Trade Agreement* was signed in 1988. Free trade polarized Canadians into either harsh critics or staunch supporters; it became the key election issue in 1988. Critics of free trade said that it would threaten Canadian institutions such as education and health care, damage domestic industries, and allow the United States to take advantage of Canada's natural resources. Supporters of free trade believed that it would provide Canadians with better prices on goods and services and a greater array of choices. These supporters believed that employment opportunities would expand as trade contributed to economic growth and prosperity. Skeptics, on the other hand, wondered if Canada could possibly benefit from an agreement with a superpower 10 times its size.

The Progressive Conservative Party won the election in 1988 and moved toward the signing of the expanded **North American Free Trade Agreement (NAFTA)** in 1993, an agreement that included Mexico as well as the United States and Canada. Although the Liberals had opposed the first free trade agreement, after coming to power in 1993, they completed the negotiations on NAFTA.

When launched in 1994, NAFTA formed the world's largest free trade area. Over the next four years, Canada–US trade became tariff-free, with some exceptions. Duties on farm products and American-made cars would be eliminated over a 10- to 15-year period. Agreement was also reached on the regulation of such areas as investment, services, **intellectual property** (ideas that are owned or at least claimed by their originators), competition, and the temporary entry of businesspeople into each country. Further tariff reductions between Canada and Mexico were implemented by 2001, followed by another reduction in 2003.

Critics of NAFTA raised many concerns, including a fear of environmental damage and job losses. Further concerns were that NAFTA would not raise the standard of living for people living with poverty in Mexico and that Canada's culture would be at risk.

In promoting NAFTA, in 2002, the Department of Foreign Affairs and International Trade released a list of what it claimed were the benefits that NAFTA had extended to Canada: an economy growing at an annual rate of 3.8 percent, the creation of almost 2.1 million jobs, and an increase in trade and foreign investment. The ministry wrote, "Consumers benefit from this heightened competition and integrated marketplace with better prices, greater choices of

FIGURE 14.14   Consider trade agreements that are intended for both wealthy industrialized nations and developing nations. Can agreements be drafted that benefit all parties equally?

Imports and Exports of Canadian Goods on a Balance-of-Payments Basis ($ millions)

	1997	1998	1999	2000	2001	2002
Exports from Canada	**303 378.2**	**327 161.5**	**369 034.9**	**430 033.1**	**421 518.8**	**414 305.1**
United States[1]	242 542.3	269 318.9	309 116.8	359 000.9	352 081.7	346 990.6
Japan	11 925.5	9 745.8	10 125.9	11 386.0	10 227.9	10 291.6
United Kingdom	4 689.5	5 323.3	6 002.9	7 326.3	6 984.7	6 239.4
Other European Economic Community countries	13 260.4	14 000.5	14 383.8	16 982.2	16 887.5	16 496.4
Other OECD[2]	8 849.0	9 120.9	9 947.2	12 246.4	12 369.2	12 341.9
Other countries[3]	22 111.6	19 652.2	19 458.4	23 091.4	22 967.8	21 945.3
Imports to Canada	**277 726.5**	**303 398.6**	**327 026.0**	**362 206.5**	**350 631.9**	**356 459.3**
United States[1]	211 450.8	233 777.6	249 485.3	266 514.5	254 952.6	254 929.0
Japan	8 711.0	9 671.8	10 592.2	11 729.3	10 571.7	11 732.2
United Kingdom	6 126.5	6 083.1	7 685.4	12 289.7	11 947.9	10 312.4
Other European Economic Community countries	18 112.9	19 141.2	20 765.8	21 178.9	23 218.0	25 863.3
Other OECD[2]	11 376.7	11 398.8	13 257.2	18 945.0	18 636.7	19 670.3
Other countries[3]	21 948.7	23 326.1	25 240.1	31 549.0	31 305.0	33 952.1
Balance	**25 651.7**	**23 762.9**	**42 008.9**	**67 826.6**	**70 886.9**	**57 845.8**
United States[1]	31 091.5	35 541.3	59 631.5	92 486.4	97 129.1	92 061.6
Japan	3 214.5	74.0	-466.3	-343.3	-343.8	-1 440.6
United Kingdom	-1 437.0	-759.8	-1 682.5	-4 963.4	-4 963.2	-4 073.0
Other European Economic Community countries	-4 852.5	-5 140.7	-6 382.0	-4 196.7	-6 330.5	-9 366.9
Other OECD[2]	-2 527.7	-2 277.9	-3 310.0	-6 698.6	-6 267.5	-7 328.4
Other countries[3]	162.9	-3 673.9	-5 781.7	-8 457.6	-8 337.2	-12 006.8

[1]Includes also Puerto Rico and Virgin Islands

[2]Organization for Economic Co-operation and Development excluding the United States, Japan, United Kingdom and the other European Economic Community

[3]Countries not included in the European Economic Community or the OECD

Source: Statistics Canada, CANSIM, tables 228-0001, 228-0002 and 228-0003.
Last modified: 2003-11-13.

Figure 14.15   What factors might account for the growth in trade between Canada and other countries from 1997 to 2000?

products and higher-quality goods and services. In terms of Canada's total merchandise export, 86.6 percent goes to our NAFTA partners."

Labour unions point to the loss of thousands of well-paying manufacturing jobs. They also claim that NAFTA's stipulations for protecting the environment are ineffective. In general, critics of NAFTA suggest that it has ultimately been beneficial only for investors and financiers.

Canada continued to expand trade relations by signing agreements such as the *Canada–Chile Free Trade Agreement* in 1997 and the *Canada–Costa Rica Free Trade Agreement* in 2001. As well, Canada is a member of multilateral trade structures, including the World Trade Organization (WTO) and the Free Trade Area of the Americas (FTAA).

Creating the FTAA has been an ambitious undertaking, enveloping nearly 800 million people and a $13 trillion market. Negotiations on the creation of the FTAA began in 1994, when the heads of 34 governments in the Western Hemisphere met and agreed to construct a trade zone where barriers to trade and investment would be slowly eliminated. The end date for negotiations was set at 2005. A number of principles guided the negotiations, including the following:

- Decisions would be made by consensus.
- Negotiations would be conducted in a transparent manner.
- The FTAA would be consistent with WTO rules and disciplines.
- Special attention would be given to the needs of the smaller economies.

The government of Québec City was so concerned about opposition to the increasing liberalization of trade law that, in 2001, it built barricades to keep protesters away from the Summit of the Americas conference. Protestors believed that the FTAA would harm developing countries, undermine democratic principles, and pose a threat to environmental protection and social programs.

In representing the other side of this debate, US Trade Representative Robert B. Zoellick declared his support for the FTAA: "It is our shared hemispheric vision that free trade and openness benefit everyone and provide opportunity, prosperity and hope to all our peoples...we've put all our tariffs on the table because free trade benefits all and brings us closer together as neighbors."

CONNECTIONS: Law and Science

In the 1970s, scientists discovered new technology that would allow specific genes to be inserted into plants and animals. This technology has been used to genetically modify particular foods. This procedure has led to enormous controversy over the benefits and risks of the consumption of these genetically modified food products.

Supporters of genetically modified food suggest that the technology could lead to improved nutritional and health benefits for humanity. For example, food could be engineered to contain more vitamins and minerals and less fat. Crops could be grown that are resistant to drought and insects. Higher-quality food, produced more efficiently and more quickly, could help eradicate world poverty and hunger.

Critics of genetically altered food believe that the new technology was introduced too quickly and without adequate research. Detractors include Prince Charles of England, who has said, "We simply do not know the long-term consequences for human health and for the wider environment of releasing plants bred in this way." Specifically, concerns have been raised about whether the consumption of genetically modified foods might compromise the immune system, leading to an increase in diseases such as celiac disease and Crohn's disease.

In 2003, the European Union ended its five-year moratorium on genetically modified food but said that each product must undergo a scientific risk assessment and include special labelling. US producers and sellers say that labelling the food is unnecessary, that it would frighten consumers, and that it would violate international trade agreements. The United States, Canada, and Argentina have asked the World Trade Organization to force the European Union to approve genetically modified food without any attached conditions.

In 2000, most of the world's governments agreed to the *UN Biosafety Protocol.* It allows bans in any countries in which governments fear genetically modified food would have an adverse effect on human health. The United States is not a party to the protocol, and it called the European Union ban an "illegal infringement of trade."

Another opponent of the American position is Tewolde Egziabher, who in 2003 was the general manager of Ethiopia's Environmental Protection Authority. He has argued that the US action is designed to intimidate African nations by not allowing them to determine their own systems for regulating genetically modified food. Should countries be forced to conform to international trading agreements, or instead should they be allowed to dictate their own policies within their own countries, providing they don't export these products?

FIGURE 14.16   In January 2000, a protestor dressed as a mutant tomato led other demonstrators on Parliament Hill in Ottawa. They were calling on the federal government to enact legislation requiring all genetically modified foods to be identified as such with labels.

SOURCES: "Lift Rules on Biotech Crops: U.S. Tells WTO." *Toronto Star* 19 Aug. 2003;

Dyer, Gwynne. "Frankenstein Foods." *The Globe and Mail* 20 Feb. 1999;

Mitchell, Paul, and Keith Lee. "Concern grows over genetically modified food." *World Socialist Web Site* 21 Nov. 1998;

"GMO Import Ban Caught in Crossfire." *New Scientist Online News* 10 Sept. 2003.

Questions

1. What is the purpose of listing all of the ingredients on food labels?
2. Do you agree or disagree that labelling genetically modified foods as such would scare off consumers? Explain your answer.
3. Assume that you are a Canadian government official who has been directed to investigate the advantages and risks of genetically modified foods. Where would you find the research required to present a complete picture of the issue? What biases would you expect to encounter?

CONFIRM YOUR UNDERSTANDING

1. What is the definition of mercantilism? How has mercantilism contributed to the development of trade?

2. Explain what is meant by a protectionist trade policy.

3. What were some of the initiatives undertaken immediately after World War II to aid in the world's economic recovery and growth?

4. What is NAFTA? Chart the positions of its supporters and its detractors. Then prepare arguments in favour of and against NAFTA.

5. Why do you think the FTAA negotiations that took place in 2001 in Québec City and in 2003 in Miami, Florida, were met with large-scale protests?

In Closing

Throughout this chapter, we have defined the nature of international law by examining its history and its sources. Unlike domestic law, international law is not dictated by a central system of government but rather by international customs, agreements, and organizations such as the United Nations. The forces of globalization and shifting values often infringe on the traditional sovereignty of nations. Long-standing practices such as diplomatic immunity and extradition have evolved to accommodate current conditions and needs. Such political events as the last century's two world wars have shaped inter-national law, as has a desire by the world's citizens to protect the environment through an increasing number of treaties and agreements. As all nations strive to improve their standards of living, more formal agreements are made, which facilitate a global economy; these agreements also create controversy surrounding the benefits and drawbacks of globalization. The coming decades will undoubtedly see an increasing number of challenges that will demand the co-operation of the world community. These challenges will increase both the complexity and the importance of international law.

CHAPTER ACTIVITIES

Extend Your Legal Knowledge

1. Create a chart that outlines the sources of international law, and provide an example for each source.

2. Explain the significance of sovereignty to the study of international law.

3. Outline the controversies surrounding the concepts of extradition and diplomatic immunity.

4. Explain the purpose of international treaties relating to the protection of the environment.

Think About the Law

5. **Ethnocentrism** is the belief that one's own culture is best and most natural. In what way might this concept have an impact on the development of international law?

6. Cornelius Vanderbilt, a wealthy American industrialist (1794–1877) once said, "Law! What do I care about the law? Ain't I got all the money?" Although he was undoubtedly referring to domestic law, could the same philosophy apply to international law? Explain.

7. Find an editorial in a newspaper on an international issue. Using the Legal Quest Research Model in the Legal Handbook, prepare a two-page analysis of the international legal issue.

8. The first multilateral treaty that Canada signed was the *Treaty of Versailles* in 1919. The first bilateral treaty negotiated and signed by Canada and the United States was the *Convention for the Preservation of the Halibut Fishery*.

a) Why did Canada not enter into any treaties from the time it became a country in 1867 until it signed the *Treaty of Versailles*?

b) What was the subject matter of these two treaties?

c) In what ways is each of these treaties an example of external sovereignty?

9. In 1963, a train in England was robbed of more than £2.5 million (C$5.9 million) by a gang of 15 men. One of the robbers, Ronnie Biggs, was sentenced to 30 years for his part in the crime. After 15 months in jail, he escaped, fleeing first to Australia and then to Brazil. In 1997, Great Britain and Brazil ratified an extradition treaty. The Brazilian court in Rio de Janeiro ruled that because the crime was more than 20 years old, Biggs could not be extradited under Brazilian law. In 2001, Biggs returned to Great Britain of his own free will so he could receive medical treatment. Despite his plea for leniency, he was arrested and returned to prison.

a) Do you agree with Brazil's refusal to extradite Biggs? Based on the principle of reciprocity, how could Brazil's refusal to extradite Biggs affect future cases involving Brazil and Great Britain?

b) Biggs, following a series of strokes, was left partially paralyzed and unable to speak. To what extent do you agree or disagree with the decision of the British authorities to return Biggs to prison? Support your opinion.

Communicate About the Law

10. Research one of the following blockades. Explain the purpose of the blockade, and justify the extent to which you believe the blockade was either a reasonable use or an abuse of power.

- In 1902, Germany, Great Britain, and Italy used a naval blockade against Venezuela because Venezuela had defaulted on its debts to these three countries.

- The United States used a naval blockade in 1962 to prevent Soviet vessels from carrying missiles to Cuba.

- The United States and its allies blockaded Iraq in 1990 in order to enforce a United Nations trade embargo. Iraq had invaded Kuwait, and the embargo was intended to force Iraq to withdraw from Kuwait.

11. Select one of the debate topics below. Research the issue within international law. Prepare arguments that support the resolution and counter-arguments that dispute it. (You may wish to refer to the Legal Handbook to review the section on Detecting Bias.)

- Diplomatic immunity should be suspended if a diplomat is suspected of committing a serious criminal offence.

- International law operates primarily as a tool to protect and maintain the interests of Western capitalist nations.

- Environmental treaties have little value without international police to enforce them.

12. It is estimated that there are millions of land mines all over the globe. Human costs when people are killed or maimed are staggering. According to the *Ottawa Convention*, an anti-personnel mine is "a mine designed to be exploded by the presence, proximity or contact of a person and that will incapacitate, injure or kill one or more persons." Governments and NGOs worked together to spur the political will to create a treaty to ban mines. The negotiations began in Ottawa in 1996 and concluded with 122 countries signing on in Ottawa in 1997. The *Ottawa Convention* was enacted on March 1, 1999. Research one of the following topics, and write a paragraph that outlines its significance to the banning of land mines.

- the role of non-governmental organizations (NGOs) in promoting this treaty
- the refusal of the United States to sign this treaty
- the procedure for removing or disarming existing land mines
- the role played by Diana, Princess of Wales (1961–1997), in promoting the ban

13. Tony Juniper, the policy director for the Friends of the Earth in 2003, said, "The West has preached free trade, while keeping the barriers to its markets high for the most important third world goods—textiles and agriculture."

a) Do research into an organization that opposes globalization. Present its criticisms of world trade.

b) Locate the Web site for the World Trade Organization. Explain the way in which the organization uses its Web site to respond to its critics.

14. Refer to the section of the Legal Handbook on Discovering Legal Vocabulary. Prepare a glossary of terms in your notebook for all bolded terms in this chapter.

15. What are the stated goals of the World Bank and the World Trade Organization? Research an example in which the real outcome does not live up to a stated goal, and present it to the class.

Apply the Law

16. In 1985, Charles Ng was arrested in Calgary during a bungled shoplifting attempt in which a security guard was shot. Canadian authorities soon discovered that Ng was wanted for the torture and murder of 12 people in California. Ng retained legal counsel and fought the extradition on a number of grounds, including the fact that California had the death penalty (see *Reference Re Ng Extradition (Can.)*, [1991] 2 S.C.R. 858). The extradition judge allowed the United States' application for his extradition and put him in custody. The minister of justice of Canada then ordered his extradition pursuant to s. 25 of the *Extradition Act* without seeking assurances from the United States, under Article 6 of the *Extradition Treaty* between the two countries, that the death penalty would not be imposed nor, if imposed, carried out. The Governor-General-in-Council, in accordance with s. 53 of the *Supreme Court Act*, later referred a key question to the court. The question raised the same issues considered in *Kindler v. Canada (Minister of Justice)*, [1991] 2 S.C.R. 779. The court had to determine whether the extradition of a fugitive who might face the death penalty to the United States constituted a breach of the fugitive's rights under the *Canadian Charter of Rights and Freedoms*. The majority of the court ruled that it would not; three judges dissented, believing it would.

Mr. Justice La Forest wrote for the majority in the Supreme Court. His comments included the following:

> The minister's actions do not constitute cruel and unusual punishment. The execution, if it takes place, will be in the United States under American law against an American citizen, in respect of an offence that took place in the United States. It does not result from any initiative taken by the Canadian government...There can be no doubt that the appellant's right to liberty and security of the person is very seriously affected because he may face the death penalty following his return....This court has held that extradition must be refused if surrender would place the fugitive in a position that is so unacceptable as to "shock the conscience."...But I do not think that the surrender of fugitives who may ultimately face the death penalty abroad would in all cases shock the conscience of Canadians....The government has the right and duty to keep out and to expel aliens from this country if it considers it advisable to do so....If it were otherwise, Canada could become a haven for criminals and others whom we legitimately do not wish to have

among us. The possible significance of the temptation of an accused to escape to Canada should not be overlooked...the two countries have a long, relatively open border and similar cultures, which makes the possibility of an escape over the border much more likely. The fact that Ng was found in Canada only because he had been committing crimes here is indicative of the danger we are opening ourselves up to if we allow Canada to become a "safe haven" for murder suspects...Therefore, the decision to extradite the appellant without restrictions...was made in pursuit of a legitimate and compelling social goal...surrendering the appellant with the restriction that the death penalty would not be imposed would completely undermine the deterrent effect the government is seeking to achieve.

Mr. Justice Peter Cory gave the dissenting opinion:

In my view, since the death penalty is a cruel punishment, the argument that the *Charter* would not apply is an indefensible abdication of moral responsibility. Canada has the obligation not to extradite a person to face a cruel and unusual treatment or punishment. To surrender a fugitive who may be subject to the death penalty violates section 12 of the *Charter* just as surely as would the execution of the fugitive in Canada....The only remaining question is whether this violation can be justified under section 1 of the *Charter*. The primary section 1 justification put forth by the respondent was the so-called "safe haven" argument. It is not an unreasonable supposition that people facing criminal charges may flee. But in Europe the decision not to extradite without death penalty assurances has not led to any known exodus of violent criminals from one state to another....Article 6 has been in existence since 1976, yet only two instances are

known of American murderers or alleged murderers fleeing to Canada: Kindler and Ng. Canada has committed itself in the international community to the recognition and support of human dignity and to the abolition of the death penalty. These commitments reflect Canadian values and principles. Canada cannot, on the one hand, give an international commitment to support the abolition of the death penalty and at the same time extradite a fugitive without seeking the very assurance contemplated by the treaty.

a) Outline the three *Charter* sections used in this decision. (You may wish to refer to the Legal Handbook to review the section on The Case Study Method.)

b) Explain the "safe haven" argument.

c) To what "deterrent effect" is the court referring?

d) What does the phrase "an indefensible abdication of moral responsibility" mean?

e) Compare this case to the more recent case of *United States v. Burns*, [2001] 1 S.C.R. 283, 2001 SCC 7, on page 446. Which judgment do you prefer? Explain.

17. In 1994, the Ng case was submitted to the United Nations Human Rights Committee. The committee found that Canada had not breached its international obligation "to protect life" but had failed in its obligation to protect individuals from cruel and inhuman treatment. California used the gas chamber, and evidence suggested that gas asphyxiation was cruel and inhuman treatment.

a) What weight or authority does this opinion carry?

b) Do you agree or disagree with this ruling? Explain.

18. In 1989, the *Convention on International Trade in Endangered Species* put elephants on its most endangered list. The ban was considered one of the biggest conservation success stories of the 1990s. Poaching, in this case of elephants, decreased in the early 1990s, only to increase later in that decade. Today reports from India, Cambodia, Kenya, and the Congo suggest that poaching is on the rise. Park rangers in Africa report that the illegal killing of elephants has increased. Since 1997, several African nations have successfully lobbied to be allowed to make sales of stockpiled legal ivory to foreign countries. Legal ivory is from elephants that have died naturally or were killed for conservation purposes. Critics of these limited sales suggest that they fuel tourist demands, especially in the tourist markets of Southeast Asia. Some African nations say that their customs and wildlife agencies are too weak to counter the demand. Other countries claim that they should have the right to sell ivory in order to raise cash for conservation purposes.

a) There is no proper system in place to monitor elephants and the number poached. How does this hamper conservation efforts?

b) Once a treaty is in place, what type of enforcement is necessary for the treaty to be effective?

c) Research the topic of poaching and endangered species. What other types of wildlife are at risk?

19. In 1990, Mexican citizens acting on behalf of the American Drug Enforcement Administration (DEA) kidnapped Alvarez Machain from his office in Mexico for his alleged involvement in the kidnapping and murder of an American DEA agent in Mexico. The arrest of Machain took place without an extradition request by the United States, without the involvement of the Mexican judiciary or law enforcement, and under protest by Mexico. Machain was brought to the United States, stood trial on criminal charges, and was acquitted. He then sued his former captors, the United States, and the DEA agents for his abduction.

In 1992, in *United States v. Alvarez Machain* 504 U.S. 655 (1992), the Supreme Court of the United States ruled that Machain's abduction did not prohibit his trial in a United States court. The 1978 *United States–Mexico Extradition Treaty* does not prohibit abduction: it says nothing about either country refraining from forcibly abducting people from the other's territory, nor does it discuss the consequences if an abduction should occur.

a) How do the principles of sovereignty and jurisdiction apply to this case?

b) Was the United States justified legally or morally in its actions?

c) Should there be a clause in extradition treaties expressly forbidding forcible abductions? Explain.

d) Why could this case be considered to set a dangerous precedent?

BIBLIOGRAPHY

Ackerman, Reuben. "Japanese Whaling in the Pacific Ocean: Defiance of International Whaling Norms in the Name of 'Scientific Research,' Culture, and Tradition." *Boston College International Law Journal* 25.2 (2002): 323–342.

The American Society of International Law. Accessed July–Sept. 2003 <www.asil.org>.

Bresler, Fenton. *Interpol.* Toronto: Penguin Books Canada Ltd., 1992.

Britannica Encyclopedia. 2002 edition.

Canadian Legal Information Institute. Accessed July–Sept. 2003 <www.canlii.org>.

Castel, Jean Gabriel. *International Law Chiefly as Interpreted and Applied in Canada.* Toronto: University of Toronto Press, 1965.

The Canadian Encyclopedia. Toronto: McClelland & Stewart Inc., 2000.

"The Charter: The Death Penalty and Beyond." *Just in Time* 19.3 (2001).

Cheadle, Bruce. "Russian Heads Home with Diplomatic Immunity Following Fatal Accident." Canadian Press. 29 Jan. 2001.

Delupis, Ingrid Detter. *International Law and the Independent State.* New York: Crane, Russak & Company, Inc., 1974.

Department of Foreign Affairs and International Trade. Accessed July–Sept. 2003 <www.dfait-maeci.gc.ca/menu-en.asp>.

Department of Justice Canada. Accessed July–Sept. 2003 <http://canada.justice.gc.ca>.

Dyer, Gwynne. "Frankenstein Foods." *The Globe and Mail* 20 Feb. 1999.

"GMO Import Ban Caught in Crossfire." *New Scientist Online News.* 10 Sept. 2003. Accessed Oct. 2003 <www.newscientist.com>.

Grewe, Wilhelm G. *The Epochs of International Law.* Translated by Michael Byers. Berlin, New York: Walter de Gruyter, 2000.

Grolier Encyclopedia. 1997 edition.

Janis, Mark, and John Noyes. *Cases and Commentary on International Law.* 2nd ed. St. Paul, MN: West Group, a Thomson Company, 2001.

Larson, Arthur. *When Nations Disagree.* Baton Rouge, LA: Louisiana State University Press, 1961.

"Lift Rules on Biotech Crops: U.S. Tells WTO." *Toronto Star* 19 Aug. 2003.

Malmö Ministerial Declaration. First Global Ministerial Environment Forum, 29–31 May 2000, Malmö, Sweden.

Mitchell, Paul, and Keith Lee. "Concern Grows Over Genetically Modified Food." *World Socialist Web Site.* 21 Nov. 1998. Accessed Jan. 2004 <www.wsws.org/news/ 1998/nov1998/gen-n21.shtml>.

Moore, Emily. "Sad Tails." *Guardian Unlimited* 25 Jan. 2000.

Moynihan, Daniel Patrick. *On the Laws of Nations.* Cambridge, MA: Harvard University Press, 1990.

Nussbaum, Arthur. *A Concise History of the Law of Nations.* New York: The Macmillan Company, 1947.

O'Brien, John. *International Law.* London: Cavendish Publishing Company, 2001.

Soros, George. *On Globalization.* New York: Public Affairs, 2002.

Staff of *Journal of International Law and Economics* (ed.). *Guide to International Legal Research.* 4th ed. Washington D.C.: George Washington University, 2002.

United Nations. Accessed July–Sept. 2003 <www.un.org>.

Wallace, Rebecca. *International Law.* 4th ed. London, Toronto: Sweet and Maxwell, 2002.

Chapter 15

CONFLICTS AND RESOLUTIONS IN THE GLOBAL CONTEXT

LEARNING EXPECTATIONS

After reading this chapter, you will be able to:

- explain the role of agencies that define, regulate, and enforce international law
- explain the role of the International Court of Justice in resolving issues
- explain the limits of the use of force to resolve conflicts in international law
- compare peaceful methods of resolving conflicts
- explore domestic laws that conflict with the principles of international law
- evaluate international intervention in conflicts between nations
- evaluate Canada's role as a member of NATO and NORAD
- evaluate Canada's role in international peacekeeping

FIGURE 15.1   In June 2004, Canadian Louise Arbour left the Supreme Court of Canada to become the United Nations High Commissioner of Human Rights. In 1996 she had been appointed by the UN's Security Council to be Chief Prosecutor for the International Criminal Tribunals for the Former Yugoslavia and for Rwanda. Here, in April 1998, Arbour tours a site in Bosnia where a forensic team had dug up a mass gravesite for evidence of ethnic cleansing of Bosnian Muslims by Serbian forces. What role do you think the international community should play in the investigation, arrest, and prosecution of individuals accused of war crimes?

> *It's co-existence...or no existence.*
>
> —Bertrand Russell (1872–1970), British author and Nobel Prize winner

∎ I N T R O D U C T I O N ∎

Conflict among nations and the human suffering that results can be traced back to ancient times. Peace and well-being for humans has always been an elusive if noble pursuit. However, each world war of the last century spurred the creation and development of global organizations that bring new rules and accountability to nations and their citizens. This chapter examines the origin and the dissolution of the League of Nations, as well as the origin, structure, and challenges faced by the United Nations. World War II not only inspired the founding of the United Nations but also made people aware that they should be individually accountable for their actions during times of conflict and war. This awareness led to a series of war-crimes tribunals. In addition, large-scale initiatives were undertaken to deal with millions of refugees, and both the United Nations and non-governmental agencies took huge strides to promote and safeguard human rights. Against the backdrop of collective security provided by the North Atlantic Treaty Organization (NATO) and the North American Aerospace Defence Command (NORAD), a new era in international law began in 2003 with the creation of the International Criminal Court. The world now faces the challenge of identifying the optimum conditions for peace, so that its citizens become not just peacekeepers but peacemakers.

The Road to the United Nations

Creating the League of Nations

In 1918, the victorious nations in World War I recognized the need to agree on the terms of peace. Several countries organized the Paris Peace Conference in early 1919, to which Germany and the other defeated powers were not invited. Great Britain, France, Italy, and the United States dominated the proceedings. Many of the 27 nations represented had competing agendas, which made consensus on treaties difficult to achieve. Much of the *Treaty of Versailles*, which emerged from this conference, dealt with economics, the establishment of territories, and **reparations**, which refer to the payments and actions that defeated countries must undertake to compensate for losses to victorious countries incurred during war.

This treaty, or covenant as it was known, outlined the details for forming a new international organization called the League of Nations.

The original League of Nations, with its headquarters in Geneva, had four permanent members: the United Kingdom, France, Italy, and Japan. Although President Woodrow Wilson of the United States was a strong advocate of the League of Nations, he was unable to convince the US Senate to ratify the *Treaty of Versailles*, a requirement for membership in the League of Nations. Consequently, the United States, by default, did not join the organization. While the original League of Nations had 44 members, 63 countries in total belonged to the league at some point during its history. As some countries were admitted, others withdrew or were expelled. For example, Germany was admitted in 1926 and withdrew in 1933, and the former Soviet Union joined in 1934, only to be expelled in 1939 when it invaded Finland.

Evaluating the League of Nations

If the primary goal of the League of Nations was to preserve peace and avoid another world war, it was a complete failure. In 1939, exactly 20 years after the league's creation, World War II began. What had gone wrong? Although the league had been successful in finding peaceful solutions to minor territorial disputes in the 1920s, historians point to two colossal failures in the 1930s.

In 1931, Japan invaded Manchuria, China; although the League of Nations formed a commission of inquiry, it did not rule that Japan must give back the conquered land. Japan soon left the league. If members of the league believed that they could maintain peace closer to Europe, they were wrong. Under dictator Benito Mussolini, Italy attacked Ethiopia in 1935. When Ethiopia's emperor, Haile Selassie, turned to the league for help, the league voted to impose economic sanctions against Italy. A **sanction** is any disciplinary action or restriction, limitation, suspension, or termination of normal privilege. This response was considered ineffectual; ultimately Italy withdrew from the league in 1937. Simultaneously, Hitler's rise to power in Germany had gone unchecked; by 1933, Germany was out

of the league. The most common criticism of the league during this period was that the aggression of both Hitler and Mussolini was allowed to run rampant while the remaining members of the league half-heartedly looked for compromises. The last significant act of the League of Nations took place in December 1939, when it expelled the Soviet Union for attacking Finland. Even though the League of Nations was unable to maintain peace, it heralded the way for the United Nations.

The drafters of the *Charter of the United Nations* believed that there was much to learn from the failure of the league. They adopted those parts of the league's structure that they believed were effective and then created new guidelines. The League of Nations included the Permanent Court of International Justice and the International Labour Organization; both of these organizations remain under the supervision of the United Nations today.

The Beginning of the United Nations

During the course of World War II (1939–1945), it became clear to the international community that a new global organization would be necessary. A series of conferences were held between 1944 and 1945, culminating in a meeting in San Francisco in 1945, at which 50 countries drew up the *Charter of the United Nations*.

Just as the victors of World War I were primarily responsible for the League of Nations, the victors of World War II, known as the Allies, together conceived of the United Nations. These Allies—the United States, Great Britain, the Soviet Union, and China—believed that their role would be to lead the United Nations, together with France, while less powerful nations would play a secondary role. Some of the controversies that arose included the following: the Soviet Union demanded that each of its constituent republics, such as Uzbekistan and Chechnya, receive a vote; Great Britain feared that the organization would undermine its influence over its colonies; and numerous countries were concerned about the veto power that the UN Security Council would wield. **Veto power** refers to the official privilege, given to a specific person or persons, to overrule a recommendation if desired.

By the fall of 1945, the *Charter of the United Nations* had been ratified by the United States, France, the United Kingdom, the Soviet Union, and China, as well as by the majority of the other participants. The United Nations came into existence in October 1945 and, by 2003, had 191 member countries.

The *Charter of the United Nations* states that the purposes of the United Nations are as follows:
- the maintenance of international peace and security
- the development of friendly relations among nations
- the facilitation of co-operative problem solving for social, economic, cultural, and humanitarian issues

The charter contains the following requirements:
- All members are equal.
- All members must fulfill their charter obligations.
- Disputes should be settled peacefully.
- The United Nations should not interfere in domestic affairs.

The Preamble to the *Charter of the United Nations* captures all the optimism that must have been felt in San Francisco in 1945:

We the peoples of the United Nations determined
- to save succeeding generations from the scourge of war, which twice in our lifetime has brought untold sorrow to mankind, and
- to re-affirm faith in fundamental human rights, in the dignity and worth of the human person, in the equal rights of men and women and of nations large and small, and
- to establish conditions under which justice and respect for the obligations arising from treaties and other sources of international law can be maintained, and
- to promote social progress and better standards of life in larger freedom....

By the beginning of the twenty-first century, had the United Nations fulfilled any of its early promise?

CONFIRM YOUR UNDERSTANDING

1. What was the origin of the League of Nations? How did the League of Nations develop?

2. Explain the reasons for the failure of the League of Nations.

3. What influence did the League of Nations have on the development of the United Nations?

4. Explain the origins of the United Nations.

The United Nations at Work

The Structure of the United Nations

The United Nations has six main branches, known as "organs":
- the General Assembly
- the Security Council
- the Secretariat
- the Economic and Social Council
- the Trusteeship Council
- the International Court of Justice

All organs are located at the United Nations headquarters in New York City except for the International Court of Justice, which is at The Hague in the Netherlands.

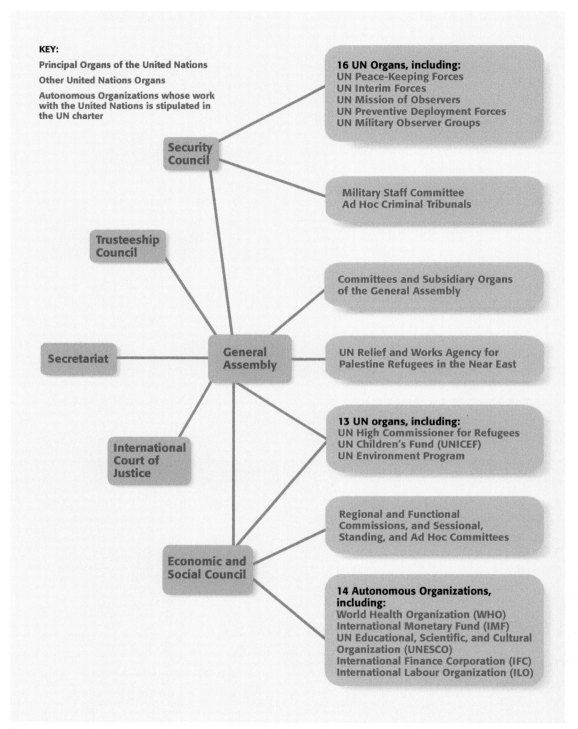

KEY:

Principal Organs of the United Nations

Other United Nations Organs

Autonomous Organizations whose work with the United Nations is stipulated in the UN charter

Security Council

16 UN Organs, including:
UN Peace-Keeping Forces
UN Interim Forces
UN Mission of Observers
UN Preventive Deployment Forces
UN Military Observer Groups

Military Staff Committee
Ad Hoc Criminal Tribunals

Trusteeship Council

Committees and Subsidiary Organs of the General Assembly

Secretariat

General Assembly

UN Relief and Works Agency for Palestine Refugees in the Near East

13 UN organs, including:
UN High Commissioner for Refugees
UN Children's Fund (UNICEF)
UN Environment Program

International Court of Justice

Regional and Functional Commissions, and Sessional, Standing, and Ad Hoc Committees

Economic and Social Council

14 Autonomous Organizations, including:
World Health Organization (WHO)
International Monetary Fund (IMF)
UN Educational, Scientific, and Cultural Organization (UNESCO)
International Finance Corporation (IFC)
International Labour Organization (ILO)

FIGURE 15.2 At its inauguration in 1945, the United Nations' primary goal was the preservation of peace. Over the years, some international observers have suggested that the United Nations has been more successful in its economic and social initiatives than in peacekeeping. In 2004, the majority of the United Nations' commissions and agencies reported to its Economic and Social Council.

The General Assembly

Every member state of the United Nations is represented in the General Assembly. Each member state has one vote. The General Assembly convenes for regularly scheduled meetings and for emergency sessions when issues are deemed urgent. In the General Assembly, some decisions pertaining to such issues as peace, security, the budget, and the admission of new members into the United Nations are considered so important as to require a two-thirds majority. Other issues are decided by a majority vote. The General Assembly cannot force nations to follow a particular course of action, but the recommendations of the group represent world opinion and carry moral weight.

The Security Council

The role of the Security Council of the United Nations is to maintain international peace and security. According to the *Charter of the United Nations*, the Security Council is made up of 15 member states: 5 are permanent members, and 10 are non-permanent members elected by the General Assembly to serve for two-year terms. The permanent members of the Security Council are France, Russia, Great Britain, the United States, and China—all the victors of World War II. This council meets whenever necessary in order to make critical decisions that the member states, as members of the United Nations, are sometimes compelled to uphold. At other times, the council makes recommendations. In the Security Council, nine affirmative votes are needed before a decision is made, and no decision can be made if a permanent member of the Security Council exercises its veto power by voting "no."

In the event of a threat to international peace, the Security Council can take several distinct courses of action. One course is to make recommendations regarding mediation or a settlement. The Security Council may recommend the use of peacekeeping missions. If fighting has already occurred, the council may recommend ceasefires.

> *Necessity knows no law except to conquer.*
>
> —Publius Syrus (born 42 BCE, death unknown), a Syrian brought to Italy as a slave but freed by his owner to become a writer

FIGURE 15.3   The United Nations General Assembly consists of every member nation of the United Nations. According to Article 18 of the *Charter of the United Nations*, decisions can be made by a two-thirds majority of the members who are present and voting. Each country, regardless of size, wealth, or power, is entitled to one vote.

In the strictest sense, **ceasefires** are agreements in which both sides in an armed conflict agree to no longer use arms or any other means of violence. Other recommendations might include economic sanctions, arms embargoes, and military action.

Since the creation of the United Nations, the Security Council has been involved with joint military action. Examples include the Korean War in 1950 and the Persian Gulf War in 1991, as well as military operations in Somalia from 1992 to 1993, in Uganda and Rwanda from 1993 to 1994, and in Haiti from 1993 to 1996. Although the Security Council approved each of these operations, each was conducted under the joint authority of the nations that launched them.

However, the creation of the United Nations in 1945 occurred at the same time as the beginning of the Cold War. The **Cold War** was the period between 1945 (the end of World War II) and 1990, during which tension and military rivalry characterized the relationship between the United States and the Soviet Union. During this period, the power of the veto in the Security Council essentially blocked decision making because either the United States or the Soviet Union repeatedly exercised its right in order to block the other's wishes.

With the end of the Cold War, the Security Council could finally act when faced with a crisis. When Iraq invaded Kuwait in 1990, the Security Council voted to use economic sanctions against Iraq and then to use "all means necessary" to restore peace and security to Kuwait. This time, the United States, Britain, France, and Russia were in agreement, while China abstained. The result was the Persian Gulf War, which ended after six weeks when Iraq withdrew from Kuwait. More recently, the composition of the Security Council has been examined and criticized. Since its origin, the Security Council has not changed in its membership. Today, Britain and France are no longer considered to be as powerful internationally as they once were, and the absence of permanent members from Africa and Latin America seems difficult to justify. One suggested

Nation shall not lift up sword against nation, neither shall they learn war anymore.
–Book of Isaiah, 2:4, Old Testament , *The Bible*

reform is to replace the two seats of Britain and France with one European Union seat. The **European Union (EU)** refers to more than twenty European member states joined in an organization with common economic and political interests. This change in seats would free a position for a representative from an African or Latin American country.

When economic sanctions and blockades ordered by the UN Security Council fail to bring countries into compliance with the aims of the United Nations, force may be used. The *Charter of the United Nations* allows a country to use force only in self-defence or when authorized by the Security Council. In 1950, the Security Council authorized member states to assist the South Koreans in warding off the aggression of North Korea; it designated the United States as the commander of this action. In 1990, when Iraq invaded Kuwait, the Security Council again authorized its members to use force to compel Iraq to leave Kuwait.

One of the acceptable uses of force outlined in the *Charter of the United Nations* is found in Article 39, which states that force may be used when there is a "threat to the peace, breach of the peace, or act of aggression." Historically, the Security Council has interpreted the definition of a "threat to the peace" to include a humanitarian crisis within one country. Consequently, it authorized operations in Somalia in 1992 and Rwanda in 1994, the goals of which were to protect civilians at risk and ensure the distribution of relief supplies. Conversely, when the United States declared war on Iraq in 2003, President George W. Bush said that it was a lawful war because Iraq possessed weapons of mass destruction. Critics of the American action claimed that the war was a breach of international law because the declaration did not receive the support of the Security Council, and deemed it a pre-emptive strike, meaning an action that is not directly provoked but is undertaken by one side because it believes that an attack from the other side is close at hand.

The Secretariat

The administrative organ of the United Nations is known as the Secretariat and is headed by a Secretary-General. Its staff of approximately 7500 people from 170 countries provides the daily services and programs that keep the United Nations running. The seventh UN Secretary-General, Kofi Annan of Ghana, began his first term of office in 1997. In 2001, the General Assembly appointed him to a second term in office. That year, the Nobel Peace Prize was awarded to Kofi Annan and the United Nations for "their work for a better organized and more peaceful world."

The Economic and Social Council

Under the authority of the General Assembly, the Economic and Social Council oversees the economic and social work of the United Nations; it also coordinates what is referred to as the United Nations' "family of organizations." This "family" refers to organizations that are not part of the key functioning of the United Nations but are affiliated with it. One example of a subsidiary organization is the Commission on Human Rights, an international monitoring organization. Other organizations are concerned with such diverse issues as the status of women, crime prevention, and environmental protection. The Economic and Social Council consults with non-governmental organizations (NGOs), which are voluntary, non-profit organizations that use research, communication, and service to foster community, national, and international political and economic co-operation. In 1948, a specialized agency of the United Nations known as the World Health Organization (WHO) was created. The mandate of WHO is threefold: to promote international technical co-operation in support of global health, to develop and manage programs for controlling and eliminating disease, and to work to improve the quality of life of people all over the world. The international goals of the WHO are ambitious: to provide world leadership in the field of health, to set world standards for health, to work in conjunction with individual countries to strengthen national health programs, and to develop and provide useful and appropriate technologies and information to countries around the world.

CONNECTIONS: Law and Health

In late February 2003, a flu-like illness hit Toronto, Canada's largest city. This illness appeared to be highly contagious, infecting people at an alarming pace. Then people started to die from it. It became clear that the point of origin of the illness was Guangdong Province, China; Canadian health officials determined that this illness had been carried to Toronto by a single traveller.

On April 23, 2003, the WHO issued the following travel advisory:

> As a result of ongoing assessments as to the nature of outbreaks of severe acute respiratory syndrome (SARS) in Beijing and Shanxi Province, China, and in Toronto, Canada, WHO is now recommending, as a measure of precaution, that persons planning to travel to these destinations consider postponing all but essential travel. Following global alerts about cases of SARS issued by WHO on 12 and 15 March, national authorities have heightened surveillance for suspect and probable cases. In many countries, prompt detection and isolation of initial cases have prevented further transmission. Using the same criteria, WHO has assessed the SARS situation in Toronto. The outbreak in this area has continued to grow in magnitude

FIGURE 15.4 During the outbreak of SARS in Toronto in early 2003, hospital workers heading home at the end of their shift were required to wash their hands, put on a new mask, and pick up a quarantine kit. Over 400 Canadians were infected with the disease, resulting in the death of more than 40 people, including health-care professionals.

and has affected groups outside the initial risk group of hospital workers and their families. The WHO travel advice is issued in order to protect public health and reduce opportunities for further international spread. The SARS situation is assessed on a daily basis (World Health Organization, "WHO Extends…").

More than 40 people in the Toronto region died from SARS in 2003. The travel advisory scared away tourists and stopped many local residents from frequenting public places, resulting in the cancellation of performing arts and sports events, as well as nearly empty restaurants and hotels. This crippled Toronto's economy. Canadian health officials and politicians campaigned to get the WHO to withdraw the warning. Although the WHO had said it would not revisit its policy for three weeks, it agreed to a meeting with Canadian officials by teleconference on April 23 and then lifted the travel advisory on April 30. Canadians were left to investigate the causes and treatment of the disease and to work to entice visitors back to Canada.

SOURCES: McIlroy, Anne. "On the Road to Recovery." *Guardian Unlimited* 28 April 2003 <www.guardian.co.uk>;

"WHO Travel Warning As SARS Death Toll Mounts." *Guardian Unlimited* 23 April 2003 <www.guardian.co.uk>;

World Health Organization. Accessed 29 Sept. 2003, 14 Dec. 2003 <www.who.int/csr/sars/archive>;

———. "WHO Extends Its SARS-related Travel Advice to Beijing and Shanxi Province in China and to Toronto, Canada." Accessed 29 Sept. 2003 <www.who.int/mediacentre/notes/2003/np7/en/>.

Questions

1. Why do you think that the WHO posts travel advisories?
2. At the time of the SARS advisory, there had been 15 deaths and 250 infected patients in Toronto. Do you think that the number of deaths and infected patients warranted a global travel advisory? Explain your answer.
3. One of the results of the SARS outbreak was that some members of the public began to discriminate both against people from Toronto and against those of Asian descent. For example, some international cruise ships did not allow residents of Toronto to travel aboard them. As well, many people avoided Asian restaurants in Toronto, including Japanese, Vietnamese, Korean, and Thai restaurants. Chinatown in Toronto was nearly empty for weeks. Some parents kept their children out of school if their children's classes included students of Asian descent. Discuss ways in which this type of discrimination can be reduced.

The WHO has dealt with numerous diseases, infections, viruses, and syndromes, such as smallpox, polio, and malaria. In an address to the UN General Assembly in September 2003, the WHO identified the failure of the international community to adequately deal with and treat HIV/AIDS as a global health emergency. In 2003, the WHO committed itself to providing life-saving treatments by the end of 2005 to the 3 million people who had AIDS in developing countries. Clearly, much more will need to be done in order to deal with this global crisis.

The Trusteeship Council

In 1945, the Trusteeship Council of the United Nations was established for a very specific reason: to supervise 11 territories placed under its jurisdiction by individual agreements with the states overseeing them. According to Article 77 of the *Charter of the United Nations*, the Trusteeship System applied to the following:

- Territories held under Mandates established by the League of Nations after the First World War
- Territories detached from "enemy states" as a result of the Second World War
- Territories voluntarily placed under the System by states responsible for their administration

The mandate of the Trusteeship Council was to help prepare these 11 territories to become independent countries. For example, Italy's Somaliland territory and Britain's Somaliland territory joined together in 1962, becoming the country of Somalia. Subsequently, other territories in the world achieved independence with the help of the council. For example, in 1994, Palau, an island group in the Pacific Ocean that had been administered by the United States, became independent; at the same time, Palau became the 185th member of the United Nations. After this occurred, the Trusteeship Council ceased being active within the United Nations. However, according to UN rules, the five permanent members of the Security Council can convene under the guise of the Trusteeship Council if the United Nations as a whole deems it necessary.

SHIFTING PERSPECTIVES: What Role Should Corporations Play in the Pursuit of UN Goals?

Thriving markets and human security go hand in hand. Global corporations can do more than simply endorse the virtues of the market....Their active support for better governance policies can help create environments in which both markets and human security flourish.

—Kofi Annan, UN Secretary-General, in an address to the World Economic Forum, 1998

Follow the trail of the money and you will find the criminals. If you stop the money then you stop the crime.

—Luis Moreno Ocampo, International Criminal Court Chief Prosecutor, in reference to blood diamonds bought from the Democratic Republic of the Congo, 2003

What we all want are prosperity diamonds: for Africa's people to experience the prosperity that diamonds can bring. But to do so, first we must block the conflict diamonds which fuel the suffering of people whose lives are being decimated by war.

—Peter Haines, British Minister of State, 2000

In September 2000, various heads of state and other government officials gathered at the United Nations headquarters in New York City in order to reaffirm their faith in the idea that the United Nations and its charter are "indispensable foundations of a more peaceful, prosperous and just world." At this meeting, the United Nations also adopted a *Millennium Declaration*, which established the United Nations' goals and priorities for the new century. One of the principles found in the declaration is "to give greater opportunities to the private sector, non-governmental organizations and civil society—in general to contribute to the realization of the organization's goals and programmes."

Certainly the business communities of many countries have played a role in the United Nations since its inception in 1945. Today, many in the international community view the United Nations as looking increasingly favourably on the ways in which business communities generate employment and wealth through finance, investment, and trade. Many UN member states stress the importance of private investment in development. According to the UN Office for the Co-ordination of Humanitarian Affairs, "Some multinational corporations now have market capitalizations [market values determined by share prices] that exceed the Gross National Product [the total market value of goods and services produced by a nation's economy in a year] of medium-sized countries."

Although many businesses support initiatives relating to human rights and environmental protection, some businesses are not socially responsible. A dramatic example of lack of social responsibility is the diamond trade in parts of Africa. In some places, such as parts of Sierra Leone, the Democratic Republic of the Congo, and Angola, diamonds are mined and then sold for the purpose of purchasing weapons used in civil wars. These actions intensify and prolong the fighting as well as the suffering of civilian populations in conflict areas.

These diamonds, called "conflict," "dirty," or "blood" diamonds, are sold to purchase small arms and light weapons. It is estimated that between 4 and 15 percent of all diamonds entering Europe are illicit gems that have been mined in Africa. Illicit gems are mined or stolen by governments or rebel military forces in order to finance civil conflict. The diamonds are traded for guns or for cash to pay and feed soldiers.

In 2000, Canada's ambassador to the United Nations, Robert Fowler, investigated this issue. His report outlined the way in which the United Nations had tried to cut off illicit mining activity in the conflict zones through condemnations and embargoes. However, diamond mining continued to flourish. Workers in some mines were literally forced to work at gunpoint. The diamonds were then moved into neighbouring countries such as Liberia and Gambia. From 1996 to 1997, Gambia exported over $100 million in raw diamonds even though it had no diamond-mining industry.

In May 2001, the United Nations announced sanctions against Liberia because of its diamond-mining practices. The sanctions included a ban on all rough diamonds, an **air embargo**, meaning the cancellation of all international flights into or out of the country, and a travel ban for senior government officials. Furthermore, the United Nations tightened an arms embargo against Liberia. An **arms embargo** is a particular type of sanction that prohibits the supply of arms or other military equipment to designated countries. By 2004, the arms embargo against Liberia had been in place for approximately a decade.

In 2000 in Belgium, an industry symposium known as the World Diamond Congress voted to develop strict guidelines that would prevent this trafficking in conflict diamonds. A key element was the plan to include tracking numbers in each lot of diamonds. These numbers would be entered into a database that would be updated with each transaction.

Although the United Nations and the Group of Eight (G8—Canada, France, Germany, Italy, Japan, Russia, the United Kingdom, and the United States, industrial countries that meet regularly to discuss economic and political issues) are ready to continue to intervene in the dirty diamond industry, the United Nations encourages the members of the industry to be "good corporate citizens" through self-regulation. When the International Diamond Manufacturers Association and an association known as the World Federation of Diamond Bourses passed a resolution establishing a system of certification that verifies diamonds' origins, the UN Security Council officially expressed its appreciation. By encouraging business to put pressure on illicit industries, the United Nations is expressing its vision of having private business encourage its own industries to act ethically.

Sources: Graves, Gary. "Dirty Diamonds." *CBC News Online*.
Accessed 17 Dec. 2000 <www.cbc.ca/national>;

Hooper, John. "Cook Urges End to Trade in Illicit Gems." *Guardian Unlimted* 18 Dec. 1999.
Accessed 17 Dec. 2003 <www.guardian.co.uk>;

United Nations Department of Public Information.
"Diamond Industry's Move on 'Conflict' Stones Welcomed at UN."
Press Release 21 July 2000. Accessed 17 Dec. 2003 <www.reliefweb.int/w/rwb.nsf/s>;

United Nations. "Guidelines on Co-operation Between the United Nations and the Business Community."
Issued by the Secretary-General 17 July 2000. Accessed 17 Dec. 2003
<www.un.org/partners/business/otherpages/guide.htm>;

United Nations Office for the Co-ordination of Humanitarian Affairs.
"Protection of Civilian in Armed Conflict—The Private Sector."
Accessed 17 Dec. 2003 <www.reliefweb.int/ocha_ol/civilians/private_sector/>;

Wilkinson, Bruce. "Dirty Diamonds." *Christian Science Monitor*
28 July 2000. Accessed 17 Dec. 2003 <www.csmonitorarchive.com>.

Your Perspective

1. Should the diamond industry be self-regulated, or is it necessary for organizations such as the United Nations to get involved? Explain.
2. Should goals of global peace and prosperity be pursued not only by the United Nations but also by NGOs and corporations? Explain.
3. In what ways do large and multinational corporations have the ability to influence global policy?
4. In the 1970s, an advertising campaign against the Canadian seal hunt caused a drop in consumer demand for sealskin. Do you think consumers would respond with the same degree of sensitivity to a public awareness campaign against the conflict diamond industry? Explain your answer.
5. Two of the goals of the United Nations' *Millennium Declaration* make specific reference to the private sector. One suggests that, "in co-operation with pharmaceutical companies, [we should] provide access to affordable essential drugs in developing countries." A second one says that, "in co-operation with the private sector, [we should] make available the benefits of new technologies—especially information and communications technologies." Are these goals reasonable and attainable? Explain potential roadblocks to the achievement of these goals by the United Nations.

The International Court of Justice

The International Court of Justice (ICJ) is the legal organ of the United Nations. It is situated at The Hague in the Netherlands. On the recommendation of the Security Council, the General Assembly elects 15 judges to this court. The function of the International Court of Justice is to settle disputes among member states, as well as to render opinions in the form of advisories on behalf of the United Nations and its agencies.

Participation by member states is voluntary. However, once a member agrees to participate, that member is obligated to comply with whatever decision is made by the ICJ. Since the court's beginnings in 1946, it has been called on to rule on diverse types of cases, such as fishing rights (e.g., *United Kingdom v. Iceland* [1974], *Spain v. Canada* [1998]); boundary disputes (e.g.,

FIGURE 15.5   Shown here are employees at the United Nations headquarters searching through the rubble after an explosion on August 19, 2003, in Baghdad, Iraq. Outside the Canal Hotel, which housed the UN headquarters, a suicide attacker set off a truck bomb, killing 22 people and wounding a further 100. One of the victims was the Secretary-General's Special Representative for Iraq, Sergio Vieira de Mello.

Cambodia v. Thailand [1962], *Cameroon v. Nigeria* [1994]); and reparations (e.g., *United Kingdom v. Albania* [1949]). The court does not hear cases relating to individual citizens.

Future Challenges for the United Nations

If you return to the Preamble of the *Charter of the United Nations* (on p. 471), written in 1945, you'll be reminded that the first goal of the United Nations' founding countries was to "save succeeding generations from the scourge of war." Although a tremendous amount of military aggression and armed combat has occurred since 1945, there has not been another world war. Does this mean that the United Nations has achieved its goal?

Over the years, the United Nations has been greatly criticized. Some observers believe that the United Nations has been much more successful in improving social conditions and addressing economic hardships than it has been in keeping the peace. Unquestionably, avoiding conflict and settling conflict within or between sovereign nations are extremely difficult tasks. However, the United Nations has been accused of being nothing more than an expensive debating club; of having an unwieldy, wasteful, and costly bureaucracy; and of practising ineffectual peacekeeping measures.

In 1997, Secretary-General Kofi Annan, sensitive to the need for reform, addressed some of these issues before the General Assembly. In his speech, he acknowledged that the United Nations must not only be responsive to the needs of its member states, but must also address and respond to criticisms: "We stand at the threshold of a new beginning for the United Nations. Our aspiration with this reform plan—simply and immediately—is to transform the conception, quality and delivery of the services we provide. That is what you and the world demand of us."

CONFIRM YOUR UNDERSTANDING

1. According to the Preamble of the *Charter of the United Nations*, what are the primary goals of the United Nations?

2. Identify the six organs of the United Nations, and briefly describe the role of each.

3. A former US senator, George Mitchell (b. 1933), once said, "The UN is an imperfect institution…and we should do all we can to improve it. But we ought to be much more supportive of it, because frankly, if it didn't exist, we'd [have to be] doing much more." In your own words, explain what you think Mitchell meant by his comments.

4. Outline the main limitations of the International Court of Justice.

Human Rights

Traditionally, international law has focused on relations among sovereign states. Accordingly, the way in which any particular state treated its citizens has been considered an internal matter, regulated by domestic law. Historically, any interference from outside of the sovereign state reflected a lack of respect for the state and was considered inappropriate. For centuries, various nations have raised humanitarian concerns over behaviours by other nations, such as the way in which prisoners of war are treated. However, the rapid development in human rights law has been relatively recent.

In fact, since 1945, one of the most significant developments in international law has been the evolution of human rights. A catalyst for this evolution was the disclosure of the abuses committed by the Nazis during World War II. Awareness of these abuses contributed to a greater recognition of the need to protect human rights. Numerous countries, including Canada, developed human rights legislation, and the United Nations made the issue a high priority. In 1948, the UN General Assembly adopted a covenant called the *Universal Declaration of Human Rights*. This declaration outlines the basic rights and freedoms that all human beings can claim. These rights and freedoms include the following:

- the right to life, liberty, and nationality
- freedom of opinion, conscience, and religion
- the right to work
- the right to an education
- the right to take part in the nation's public business

In 1966, two further international agreements were adopted: the *United Nations Convention on Economic, Social, and Cultural Rights*, and the *International Covenant on Civil and Political Rights*. Together, these three documents comprise the *International Charter of Human Rights*.

Since 1966, further conventions have been implemented. These include conventions to eliminate racial discrimination, to eliminate torture, and to promote the rights of children. Some examples are the *Convention on the Elimination of All Forms of Discrimination Against Women* (1984), the *Convention Against Torture and Other Cruel, Inhuman or Degrading Treatment or Punishment* (1986), and the *Convention on the Rights of the Child* (1989). United Nations' committees have been formed to implement the conventions. These committees meet regularly and issue reports on their activities.

Due to the large number of these conventions and initiatives, in 1993 the United Nations decided to create a new department called the Office of the United Nations High Commissioner for Human Rights (OHCHR). The role of the high commissioner is to co-ordinate all the activities of the UN agencies, to prevent violations of basic rights, to investigate violations, and to work with governments to assist them in solving problems.

Indigenous Peoples

At the end of the twentieth century, the OHCHR initiated the International Decade of the World's Indigenous People (1995–2004). The General Assembly declared this special decade in hopes of drawing attention to the needs of indigenous groups worldwide. **Indigenous peoples** in any country are defined as the original inhabitants of the land and their descendants. The United Nations elaborates on the term "indigenous" in this way:

> Indigenous communities, people and nations are those which, having a historical continuity with pre-invasion and pre-colonial societies that have developed on their territories, consider themselves distinct from other sectors of the societies now prevailing in those territories, or parts of them. They form at present non-dominant sectors of society and are determined to preserve, develop and transmit to future generations their ancestral territories, and their ethnic identity, as the basis of their continued existence as peoples, in accordance with their own cultural patterns, social institutions and legal systems." (www.unep.org/Biodiversity)

There are approximately 300 million indigenous people living in over 70 countries around the world. In Canada, the federal government has worked with Aboriginal organizations in order to develop an action plan for the decade.

A second major initiative was the creation of a new United Nations body, the Permanent Forum on Indigenous Issues. The 16-member body is composed of 8 government-nominated experts and 8 indigenous-nominated experts who report and make recommendations to the Economic and Social Council on "economic and social development, culture, the environment, education, health and human rights."

FIGURE 15.6   In Ottawa in 2001, Canadian Foreign Affairs Minister John Manley greeted 1992 Nobel Peace Prize winner and human rights crusader Rigoberta Menchú Tum, a representative of the Quiché Mayan culture in Guatemala, during the Indigenous Peoples Summit of the Americas. Menchú acted as a goodwill ambassador for the United Nations International Decade of the World's Indigenous People. Can you think of an event in which the united actions of several indigenous groups brought attention to their shared concerns?

The Role of NGOs

As you read earlier in the chapter, non-governmental organizations (NGOs) are non-profit organizations that work to foster political and economic co-operation. The emergence of NGOs has played a critical role in improving protections for human rights. The strength of NGOs lies in their ability to mobilize public opinion, spread information, and pressure governments to conform to international human rights standards.

NGOs are diverse in their goals and methods. Some NGOs, such as the International Federation for Human Rights, conduct surveys, publish newsletters, and distribute detailed reports. Others, such as Oxfam, work to relieve poverty through such actions as lobbying for policy changes at national and global levels and responding to humanitarian disasters with preventive measures, preparedness, and emergency relief.

The world's largest human rights organization is Amnesty International. In 2003, it had 1.2 million members in 160 countries. Amnesty International has been very successful in investigating human rights violations throughout the world. It has organized letter-writing campaigns in order to free people who have been imprisoned because of political or religious views or because of their ethnicity.

One of many issues investigated by and reported on by Amnesty International is the treatment of indigenous people in the Americas. In a report from 2001, the organization stated, "Intimidation, harassment and violent attacks against indigenous communities are frequent occurrences in countries including Honduras, Brazil, Colombia, Guatemala, Mexico and Venezuela." The report documents that in some countries, such as Venezuela and Brazil, members of indigenous communities face threats or actual violence from local landowners, government authorities, or corporate representatives because they oppose policies that threaten their land or natural resources.

Amnesty International's report also investigates challenges within the justice systems of Mexico and Guatemala, where native people are at a disadvantage in dealing with police and the courts because they do not speak Spanish. It focuses, too, on attacks on indigenous people in countries such as Honduras and Guatemala, where people who are believed to be responsible for the attacks often are not prosecuted. The report concludes, "Challenging impunity [freedom from punishment] is one of the crucial steps governments in the Americas must take if they want to show they are serious about their obligation to ensure the full protection of the human rights of indigenous people."

The largest human rights NGO in the United States is Human Rights Watch. This organization was originally set up in 1978 under the name Helsinki Watch; initially, its goal was to monitor Soviet bloc countries through the use of the human rights provisions of the landmark *Helsinki Accords*. In the 1980s, an organization called Americas Watch was set up to counter the notion that human rights abuses by one side in the war in Central America were somehow more tolerable than abuses by the other side. As these organizations grew, human rights advocates in various countries decided to unite various "Watch" committees into one organization in 1988.

The work by Human Rights Watch has included the following:

- collaborating to establish the International Campaign to Ban Landmines (ICBL), which shared the Nobel Peace Prize with activist Jody Williams in 1997
- leading an international coalition, or temporary political alliance, to lobby for the adoption of a treaty banning the use of child soldiers
- supporting the establishment of international war-crimes tribunals for the former Yugoslavia and Rwanda
- supporting legal action against former Chilean dictator Augusto Pinochet, which led to a principle known as the Pinochet Precedent. This principle states that even former heads of state can be responsible for human rights crimes, and if their prosecution at home is blocked, then they can be tried elsewhere.

Another prominent NGO is the Canadian Human Rights Foundation (CHRF), based in Montréal, Québec. The CHRF was established in 1967 by a group of Canadian jurists, scholars, and advocates, among them John P. Humphrey (1905-1995), one of the drafters of the *Universal Declaration of Human Rights*. Through education, the CHRF supports the creation and consolidation of human rights support networks in Canada and worldwide.

The Rights of Refugees

For centuries, people have fled their homes to seek refuge from conflict, social and religious persecution, and racial intolerance. **Refugees** are people who have escaped from their homeland due to persecution or justifiable fear of persecution there based on their race, religion, nationality, political opinion, or membership in a particular social group. In the twentieth century, international political upheavals have led to major changes in populations worldwide. For example, over a million refugees fled Communist Russia after the Russian Revolution of 1917. Between 1915 and 1923, approximately a million Armenians and hundreds of thousands of Greeks fled what was then known as Turkish Asia Minor to escape genocide by the Turks. **Genocide** can be defined as the act of killing, or causing serious harm with the intent to destroy, national, ethnic,

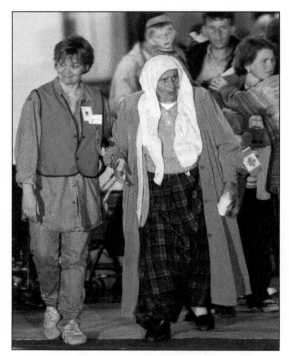

FIGURE 15.7   A Red Cross volunteer assists one of 267 Bosnian refugees who arrived at the Canadian Forces Base in Greenwood, Nova Scotia, in 1999 after fleeing Kosovo. The conflict in the former Yugoslavia led to the largest forced movement of a civilian population since World War II.

or religious groups. Prior to and during the building of the Berlin Wall between 1949 and 1961, approximately 2.5 million East Germans fled to West Germany. Between the construction of the Berlin Wall in 1961 and its dismantling in 1989, another 5000 East Germans fled to West Germany. There they sought **political asylum**, which is protection given by one country to refugees from another. During the 1990s, both the war in Yugoslavia and the flight by Rwandans to escape genocide created millions of refugees. Altogether, since the beginning of World War II, it is estimated that 100 million people have been uprooted from their homelands.

The first international response to the plight of refugees came in 1921. In that year, the League of Nations appointed a High Commissioner for Refugees, Fridtjof Nansen from Norway. The commissioner began the practice of issuing travel documents to refugees. This documentation provided them with some formal legal status so that they could cross borders more easily. Following World War II, the United Nations established various agencies in order to work with refugees. The largest of these was the UN High Commission for Refugees (UNHCR), which was established in December 1950.

In July 1951, the *Convention Relating to the Status of Refugees* was approved at a special UN conference. The convention defines who qualifies as a refugee and outlines the kind of legal protection and rights that refugees are entitled to in their host country. It also details the obligations that a refugee has to the host country. This document was created in response to the post-war refugee crisis in Europe. A protocol was added in 1967 that removed time constraints and expanded the mandate to include refugees anywhere in the world.

The convention outlines the main purpose and functions of the UNHCR. The UNHCR offers international protection to refugees, seeks lasting solutions to refugees' problems, and provides refugees with assistance in the form of food, shelter, medical aid, and other social services.

Sometimes it is possible for the UNHCR to help refugees return home and be reintegrated into their community once the danger has subsided. When this is not possible, the UNHCR helps people to resettle in new host countries. In 2003, the United Nations estimated that there were approximately 20 million refugees worldwide. Approximately 9 million of these were situated in Asia, 4 million in Europe, 4 million in Africa, 1 million in North America, and more than 1 million in both Latin America and the Caribbean.

In 1951, Canada signed the *Convention Relating to the Status of Refugees*; Canada then signed the follow-up protocol in 1967. According to these two documents, "convention refugees" are defined as persons who:

- have a well-founded fear of persecution based on their race, religion, nationality, political opinion, and/or membership in a particular social group;
- are outside the country of their nationality and are unable or unwilling to be protected by that country; and/or

ASKING KEY QUESTIONS

Palestinian Refugees and the Right of Return

Introduction

The establishment of the state of Israel in 1948 and the war that followed resulted in hundreds of thousands of Palestinians fleeing or being forced out of their homes in a region that had been called Palestine and was now called Israel.

Despite a UN resolution recognizing the Palestinians' right to return to their homes, Israeli law barred those Palestinians from re-entering Israel at the end of the war. The Palestinians became refugees, taken in by other Arab states.

The United Nations established the UN Relief and Works Agency for Palestinian Refugees in the Near East to help care for those Palestinians. More than 3.7 million Palestinians—the refugees and their descendants—are registered with the agency in Jordan, Syria, Lebanon, the West Bank, and Gaza.

More than one million of those refugees live in 59 UN-operated refugee camps—27 of them in the West Bank and Gaza. Almost half of the roughly three million Palestinians living in the West Bank and Gaza are refugees, and more

than 600 000 of them live in the camps. Gaza's population has particularly increased: UN figures indicate 824 000 out of 1.1 million are refugees.

Jordan hosts the most refugees—about 1.6 million, of which 280 000 live in 10 camps. Another 376 000 live in Lebanon, with 210 000 of those living in 12 camps. And in Syria, 112 000 of the country's 383 000 refugees live in 10 camps. Al-Awda—the Palestinian Right of Return Coalition—says there are an additional 2 million refugees unregistered and living in other neighboring countries, but those refugees are not directly covered by UN resolutions and programs.

The Israeli Viewpoint

Israeli leaders have held the position that the right of return is non-negotiable. It would create a demographic problem for Israel, making it unable to continue as a Jewish state. Israel has suggested it would accept a proposal for some 10 000 Palestinian refugees to rejoin their families inside Israel as a "humanitarian gesture" and financial compensation for refugees from Western donors.

The Palestinian Viewpoint

The displacement of Palestinians cuts to the core of Palestinian national identity. Many Palestinians say their right to return goes beyond the UN resolution, stemming from a right of a people to live in their homeland. For Palestinians, it's a matter of principle and historical redress, in which Israel acknowledges the wrongs it has caused to the Palestinian people.

SOURCE: Adapted from *CNN.com*. "Mideast: Land of Conflict." In-Depth Special, 2001. Accessed 10 Aug. 2003 <www.cnn.com/SPECIALS/2003/mideast/stories/issues.refugees/>.

Form Your Questions

The information above raises many questions. For example, what are the long-term costs to people permanently living in refugee camps? Does the international community have the legal or moral authority to resolve the status of the Palestinian refugees? What other questions might you ask regarding the competing claims of the state of Israel and the Palestinian refugees? Think of three key questions. Share your questions with the rest of the class, and discuss possible answers or solutions.

• do not have a country of nationality, are outside the country of their former habitual residence and are unable or, by reason of that fear, are unwilling to return to that country.

It is important to note that clauses in the *Convention Relating to the Status of Refugees* exclude from the definition of "refugee" those persons who have committed serious crimes, including in the extreme either war crimes or crimes against humanity. Article 147 of the fourth Geneva convention (to be discussed later in this chapter) defines **war crimes** as various acts that are "not justified by military necessity and [are] carried out unlawfully and wantonly." These include "torture, or inhuman treatment, including unlawful deportation or transfer or unlawful confinement of a protected person, compelling a protected person to serve in the forces of a hostile power, or wilfully depriving a protected person of the rights of fair and regular trial." A **crime against humanity** is generally defined as an act of violence that is committed as part of a full-scale or systematic attack on a civil population. Crimes against humanity can include torture, rape, and enslavement.

By 2003, Canada was accepting between 20 000 and 30 000 convention refugees annually. At that time, approximately half of these refugees were being selected from abroad for resettlement in Canada and the other half were claimants already in Canada who were seeking protection from their country of origin.

Landmark CASE

Suresh v. Canada (Minister of Citizenship and Immigration), [2002] 1 S.C.R. 3

Read the following case analysis. The facts, issue, and *ratio decidendi* have been provided for you. Assume, however, that you disagree with the decision. Write a possible dissent for this controversial case.

Facts: The appellant, Manickavasagam Suresh, is categorized as a convention refugee from Sri Lanka. He arrived in Canada in 1990 and was granted refugee status in 1991. In 1995, he applied for landed immigrant status in Canada. The Canadian government detained him and began deportation proceedings on the grounds that he posed a security threat to Canada. The Canadian Security Intelligence Service believed he was a member of the Tamil Tigers, a group allegedly engaged in terrorist activities in Sri Lanka. However, members of the Tamil Tigers are subject to torture in Sri Lanka by the police and security forces. The Federal Court upheld as reasonable the ruling of an adjudicator who believed the appellant was a danger to security in Canada. The appellant made a number of legal arguments, including that deportation under s. 7 of the *Canadian Charter or Rights and Freedoms* would be a violation of his rights. Section 7 ensures the "right to life, liberty and security."

Issue: Does the *Charter* prevent the deportation of a person who may pose a security threat to Canada if that person might face torture in the country to which he or she will be deported?

Held: The appeal should be allowed.

Ratio Decidendi: (McLachlin C.J. and L'Heureux-Dubé, Gonthier, Iacobucci, Major, Bastarache, Binnie, Arbour, and LeBel JJ.) "The appellant should be entitled to a new deportation hearing. The Minister must provide written reasons for her decision dealing with all relevant issues. These procedural protections apply where the refugee has met the threshold of establishing a *prima facie* case that there may be a risk of torture upon deportation. The appellant has met this threshold. Since he was denied the required procedural safeguards and the denial cannot be justified under s. 1 of the *Charter*, the case is remanded to the Minister for reconsideration.

"Canadian law and international law reject deportation to torture. Canadian law views torture inconsistent with fundamental justice. The Canadian rejection of torture is reflected in the international conventions, which Canada has ratified. Deportation to torture is prohibited by both the *International Covenant on Civil and Political Rights* and the *Convention Against Torture and Other Cruel, Inhuman or Degrading Treatment or Punishment*.

"In exercising the discretion found in s. 53 (1)(b) of the *Immigration Act*, the Minister of Citizenship and Immigration must conform to the principles of fundamental justice. The refugee is entitled to present evidence and make submissions on whether his or her continued presence in Canada will be detrimental to Canada, the risk of torture upon return, and the value of assurance of non-torture."

CONFIRM YOUR UNDERSTANDING

1. Why is the field of human rights a relatively new area of international law?

2. Identify some of the rights and freedoms found in the *Universal Declaration of Human Rights*.

3. How do NGOs improve international human rights protections?

4. Explain, in your own words, the term "convention refugee."

5. Describe the role of the UNHCR.

International Peace and Security

Diplomacy, Arbitration, and Mediation

As long as sovereign states have existed, there have been conflicts. Just as domestic laws contain various methods for resolving conflicts, nations experiment with various options in their attempts to resolve their differences. Traditionally, the goal of **diplomacy**, which often refers to peaceful negotiation between or among nations, was to safeguard and promote a nation's interests. These interests included safeguarding a nation's security. Although the term "diplomacy" once referred primarily to negotiations carried out by two sovereign states, increasingly diplomacy is being used to refer to negotiations among many nations represented at international conferences and summits.

A second way to resolve conflicts is through **mediation**, a process by which an appointed neutral party facilitates an agreement between two or more parties. Essentially, a mediator's role is to guide the two parties toward an agreement. In the nineteenth century, mediation was used in some conflicts. The *Declaration of Paris* (1856) and The Hague Conferences of 1899 and 1907 made attempts to formalize mediations. Both the League of Nations and the United Nations acknowledged the importance of mediation by including it in their charters. One example of the use of mediation was the UN General Assembly's appointment of a mediator to Palestine in May 1948. Folke Bernadotte, a Swede, was sent to the Middle East to try to obtain a settlement in the Arab–Jewish conflict over Palestine, which had escalated with the UN plan to partition Palestine. Bernadotte was assassinated the same year and replaced by Ralph Bunche, an American.

Another method of resolving conflicts is **arbitration**—an alternative, private process in which litigation is not pursued; rather, the dispute is referred to a third party, who will make a decision. Arbitration has a long history, beginning with its use among the ancient Greek city-states. One of the purposes of arbitration has been to settle boundary disputes. One example is the *Jay Treaty* (1794), in which arbitration commissions were established to settle boundary disputes between the United States and Great Britain, which arose out of the American War of Independence. Arbitration over the boundary dispute between New Brunswick and Maine was unsuccessful, and the dispute was not settled until 1842.

In 1899, a convention known as the *Convention for the Pacific Settlement of International Disputes*, signed at The Hague Peace Conference, created a permanent court of arbitration. However, this convention did not require the nations that signed it to submit disputes to arbitration, which limited the court's power. This court heard cases until 1922, when the League of Nations formed an independent court at The Hague. This court heard cases from 1922 until 1940, when World War II interrupted its functioning. After World War II, the *Charter of the United Nations* provided for the continuation of the court, which today is known as the International Court of Justice.

When the *Charter of the United Nations* was drafted, it was recognized that any or all means of conflict resolution should be employed to preserve peace and resolve differences without resorting to force. Article 33 of the charter states that nations should "seek a solution by negotiation, inquiry, mediations, conciliation, arbitration…or other peaceful means of their own choice." If diplomacy, mediation, and arbitration all fail, then the General Assembly of the United Nations can refer disputes to the Security Council.

Security

In the period immediately following World War II, Western European countries and their North American allies viewed with suspicion the expansionist policies of the Soviet Union. While Western governments were downsizing their military forces, it seemed that the Soviets were

FIGURE 15.8   This photo shows a US tactical action officer surveying the air and surface space around New York City in November 2001, from within the onboard Combat Direction Center aboard the American aircraft carrier *USS George Washington*. The ship was providing air defence to the city at the request of the North American Aerospace Defence Command (NORAD) after the terrorist attacks on the World Trade Center in New York City and on the Pentagon in Arlington, Virginia, on September 11, 2001.

intent on maintaining their armed forces. In general, Western countries believed that their democracies were vulnerable both to outside aggression and to internal revolt, representing a threat to their independence. The governments' curtailment of rights and freedoms and the repression of opposition in many Central and Eastern European countries added to these fears.

By 1948, two events had occurred in Europe that brought these matters to a head. In 1947, Czechoslovakia experienced a coup d'état, which is a violent overthrow of an existing government. As well, in March of 1948, the Soviet Union began a rail and road blockade of Berlin, hoping to force the Western Allies (France, the United States, and the United Kingdom) to leave their post–World War II position in West Berlin. The Soviets were able to do so without breaking any international laws on a technicality: the West and the Soviet

Union never made a written pact regarding the right of Western ground access to Berlin. The blockade was not lifted until May of 1949. These events directly led to the signing of the *Brussels Treaty* by France, Belgium, the Netherlands, the United Kingdom, and Luxembourg. In the treaty, these countries agreed to develop a common defence system and to strengthen ties that would enable them to resist all manner of threats to their security.

NATO

In April 1949, the *North Atlantic Treaty* was signed by 12 nations in Washington, DC. This treaty provided for mutual defence and collective security. The major concern of its signatories was the need to feel protected from the potentially aggressive Soviet Union. The 12 signatories were the United States, Great Britain, France, Canada,

Belgium, Holland, Luxembourg, Italy, Portugal, Norway, Denmark, and Iceland. In July of the same year, these signatories established the **North Atlantic Treaty Organization (NATO)**. More European countries gradually joined the alliance, and by 2003 it had 19 members. NATO's main interest is ensuring peace and security. In 2002, Canada's financial contribution to NATO reached $115 million, making it NATO's sixth largest contributor.

Members of NATO are committed to sharing the risks and responsibilities, as well as the benefits, of collective security. **Collective security** can be defined as a strategy whereby several nations are committed to defending one another against attacks. An attack on one country becomes an attack on the entire group. Critics of collective security suggest that countries will act on their promise to defend one another only if it is in their best interest at a particular time. A second criticism is that small conflicts can turn into large ones, and an alliance formed for purposes of security could also become an aggressor. Each country has agreed not to enter into other international treaties that would conflict with its obligations to NATO. Over the years, NATO has developed a broader mandate, becoming, according to its own definition, "a security and co-operation organization at the service of peace."

With the end of the Cold War came a need for NATO to transform itself into an organization with a new direction. NATO therefore redefined itself. One of its new objectives was to foster dialogue and co-operation with former adversaries from the **Warsaw Pact** (or **Warsaw Treaty Organization**), which was a military alliance of the Eastern European Soviet bloc countries intended to organize against the perceived threat from the NATO alliance. The pact was drafted by Soviet President Khrushchev in 1955 and signed in Warsaw in May 1955; its members were the Soviet Union, Albania, Bulgaria, Romania, East Germany, Hungary, Poland, and Czechoslovakia—all the Communist countries of Eastern Europe except Yugoslavia. The members of the *Warsaw Pact* pledged to defend one another if one or more of the members were attacked. The pact came to an end on March 31, 1991, when the threat of the Communist bloc countries had diminished, and was officially dissolved at a meeting in Prague in July 1999.

Another one of NATO's new objectives was to manage conflicts in areas on the European periphery, such as the Balkans. Consistent with its second goal, NATO used military force for the first time when it entered the war in Bosnia and Herzegovina in the Balkans in 1995. It did so by staging air strikes against Bosnian Serb positions around the capital city of Sarajevo. NATO was attempting to force Slobodan Milosevic, the Serb leader who in 1989 had become the president of what was then Yugoslavia, to agree to protect the Muslim Albanian population in the province of Kosovo.

At the end of the twentieth century, Russia and NATO got together to address such global concerns as terrorism and arms control.

On September 12, 2001, the day after terrorist attacks on the United States, NATO for the first time invoked Article 5 of the *North Atlantic Treaty*. Article 5 states:

> The parties agree that an armed attack against one or more of them in Europe or North America shall be considered an attack against them all, and consequently they agree that if such an armed attack occurs, each of them, in exercise of the right of individual or collective self-defence recognized by Article 51 [of the *Charter of the United Nations*], will assist the Party or Parties so attacked by taking forthwith, individually and in concert with the other Parties, such action as it deems necessary, including the use of armed force, to restore and maintain the security of the North Atlantic area. Any such armed attack and all measures taken as a result thereof shall immediately be reported to the Security Council. Such measures shall be terminated when the Security Council has taken the measures necessary to restore and maintain international peace and security.

By invoking Article 5, NATO interpreted the attacks on the United States to be an attack against all Allies. According to Canada's Department of Foreign Affairs and International Trade Web site, Canada is "a member of NATO because we have always believed that collective defence is the most effective and efficient way of protecting our democratic values and traditions."

NORAD

In 1958, Canada and the United States signed an agreement that established the North American Aerospace Defence Command (NORAD) to monitor and defend North American airspace. The NORAD agreement has been renewed eight times since 1958, with three revisions. NORAD's headquarters are in Colorado Springs, Colorado, and its commander-in-chief is appointed by and is responsible to both the prime minister of Canada and the president of the United States. Using data from satellites and ground-based radar, NORAD monitors the use of aircraft, missiles, and spacecraft. It then assesses the likelihood of an attack on North America.

Prior to the terrorist attacks of September 11, 2001, NORAD focused primarily on potential air threats that might originate in countries geographically distant from Canada and the United States. Subsequently, NORAD has focused on safeguarding Canadian and American airspace by increasing patrols and adjusting alert levels as necessary. By placing jetfighters on alert and using its radar and satellite capabilities, the organization scrambled fighters or diverted flights over 1500 times in the first two years following the terrorist attacks.

UN Peacekeeping

The term "peacekeeping" is not found in the *Charter of the United Nations*. However, in the early years of the United Nations, it became apparent that some type of peacekeeping role should be undertaken by the organization. The United Nations first backed this type of mission in 1948 in both Kashmir, a disputed territory between India and Pakistan, and in Palestine, a disputed territory in what is now Israel. Troops were called in to monitor ceasefires.

Currently, according to the United Nations, peacekeeping missions may be required for any of the following reasons:

- to deploy troops in order to prevent the outbreak of conflict or the spillover of conflict across borders
- to stabilize conflict situations after a ceasefire in order to create an environment in which the parties can reach a lasting peace agreement
- to assist in implementing comprehensive peace agreements
- to lead states or territories through a transition period to stable governments based on democratic principles, good governance, and economic development

Between 1948 and 1988, the United Nations undertook 13 peacekeeping missions. These missions used troops from countries that were not permanent members of the Security Council and were therefore perceived as neutral. Typically, these troops came from some of the following countries: Canada, Sweden, Finland, Norway, Ireland, India, and Italy. These troops, easily recognizable in their blue helmets, were only lightly armed and were allowed to use force only in self-defence. During this 40-year period, the peacekeepers were always deployed with the consent of all parties involved in the conflict. In 1956, Lester B. Pearson, Canada's Secretary of State for External Affairs (he later became the prime minister) suggested that the United Nations send peacekeeping forces into the Suez Canal region in order to keep the peace in a conflict between Israel and Egypt. Pearson later received a Nobel Peace Prize for his role in resolving the conflict. In 1987, the Nobel Peace Prize was awarded to the United Nations peacekeeping forces.

During the 1990s, UN peacekeepers were sent to Cambodia, Somalia, and the country then known as Yugoslavia. These troops consisted of armed forces personnel from permanent members of the Security Council, as

FIGURE 15.9 In 1956, Egypt nationalized the Suez Canal, converting it from private ownership to state ownership. The Israelis, who had been denied passage through the canal, attacked and invaded the canal zone. This was followed by an attack by Great Britain and France. The United Nations, concerned about an escalating crisis in the Middle East, dispatched the first armed UN peacekeepers to the region in 1957. Here, British scuba divers recover weapons hidden by Egyptian forces in the canal. What are some of the challenges faced by peacekeepers who have been deployed to conflict zones?

well as from some **developing countries** (130 countries in Asia, Africa, and Latin America that have yet to achieve the social, economic, and technical standards common in the "industrialized world," meaning Europe, Australia, Japan, and North America). At times, it became necessary to take sides in domestic disputes. In limited cases, the use of force was authorized. For example, peacekeepers were authorized to use force if necessary in the United Nations operation in the Congo from 1960 to 1964.

Since the end of the Cold War, the greatest change in the activities of NATO has been its increased involvement in peacekeeping. In 1995, a peace accord was signed in Dayton, Ohio, by Bosnia and Herzegovina, the Republic of Croatia, and the Federal Republic of Yugoslavia. Afterwards, NATO stationed its own peacekeeping forces in Bosnia and Herzegovina. By 2003, NATO had organized three "peace-support" operations in Bosnia-Herzogovina, Kosovo, and Afghanistan. Its involvement in and around Kabul, Afghanistan, marked the first time NATO moved outside of the Euro-Atlantic region.

In the early part of the twenty-first century, traditional military forces are still being used. While peacekeeping was initially developed to deal with conflict between and among independent states, known as **interstate** conflict, increasingly it has been applied to conflicts within states, known as **intrastate** conflicts. These intrastate conflicts may escalate into full-fledged civil wars.

In some instances, peacekeepers have found themselves in complex situations. Their presence may be treated with hostility, local order may be absent or broken down, and basic humanitarian norms may be ignored.

By 2003, the majority of peacekeeping missions were made up of more than just armed forces personnel. These missions also included civilian police officers, electoral experts and observers, human rights monitors, and other specialists. The work of this additional personnel ranges from delivering humanitarian assistance to monitoring the state of human rights to supervising elections. For example, since 1990, UN forces have distributed food in Somalia and supervised elections in Nicaragua and Cambodia.

Challenges to Peacekeeping

In March 2000, UN Secretary-General Kofi Annan appointed a panel of experts to study UN peace and peacekeeping operations. The panel's mandate was to investigate and report on the lapses in, and challenges to, UN peacekeeping. A number of serious incidents had triggered this investigation. One was the United Nations' slow response to genocide in Rwanda in 1994. A second episode was the killing of Bosnian Muslims by Serbs in 1995 in Srebrenica, which was supposed to have been a UN safe haven, meaning a neutral territory established to provide a particular group with a place in which it is guaranteed not to come under attack.

The results of the investigation, known as the *Brahimi Report*, were released in 2000. The report recommended the creation of a rapid deployment force, meaning squadrons of troops that could be quickly stationed at various posts. According to the report, this force would not simply monitor areas but would intervene in conflicts around the world. The report recom-

mended that the UN force not necessarily be neutral. The force should be allowed to use force to bring disputes to an end. The report stated, "In the worst case, [neutrality] may amount to complicity with evil."

The report documented other challenges facing UN peacekeeping troops. One is the cost to taxpayers, estimated to be in the billions of dollars (US) yearly. A second is that some troops have limited gear and weaponry and are poorly trained by their home countries, which places them at greater risk.

A number of initiatives have been undertaken since that report. The UN headquarters have more staff to support the UN mission, and ongoing training has been provided to ensure new rapid-response capacity. More financial,

Peace is not the absence of war.
—Baruch Spinoza (1632–1677), Portuguese Jewish philosopher

FIGURE 15.10 In 2003 in Afghanistan, Canada made up the largest contingent of NATO's peacekeeping force, known as the International Security Assistance Force. Between 1948 and 2003, there were 1865 UN peacekeepers killed in the line of duty. India (108 deaths) and Canada (106 deaths) suffered the most casualties of all the participating countries. In what way does this cartoon address attitudes toward peacekeepers?

political, and material support has been initiated by member states.

If UN peacekeeping operations are to be successful in the future, certain criteria must be met. The international community must be convinced that peacekeeping is necessary. A majority of or all parties must be willing to agree to a ceasefire, and key parties to the conflict must consent to UN intervention. The members of the UN Security Council must be in agreement that a peacekeeping operation is the best solution, and troops must be deployed quickly. Finally, there is a growing realization that, in order to successfully resolve a conflict, attention must be paid to political, economic, development, human rights, and humanitarian efforts that complement the quest for peace.

CONFIRM YOUR UNDERSTANDING

1. Explain the reasons for the formation of NATO.

2. Why did the end of the Cold War force NATO to change direction?

3. What role did NATO play in the Balkan wars?

4. What is Article 5 of the *North Atlantic Treaty*? Why was it invoked in 2001?

5. What role does NORAD play in safeguarding Canada's security?

6. Describe how UN peacekeeping has changed since 1948.

7. Explain the significance of the *Brahimi Report*.

8. Describe some ways in which the definition of "ceasefire" could be debated.

Resolving Conflicts

The Rules of War

Historically, concerns have been raised about how war should be waged and how soldiers and civilians should be treated. The concept of "war crimes" arose because actions that are viewed as necessary by one party in order to win a war may violate all standards and principles that another society considers to be humane. In ancient India's Hindu *Laws of Manu*, the issue of humaneness in war was raised and debated. In ancient Greece, Plato reported that Socrates proposed to limit the concept of war to fights with "barbarians." In ancient Rome, it was important that a war be declared only if it were considered to be "both just and pious," or in Latin, *bellum justum et pium*. During the Middle Ages, the Roman doctrine of "just war" was resurrected by theologians such as Saint Augustine (354–430 CE) and Thomas Aquinas (1227–1274 CE). Rules of chivalry prohibited attacks on the sick and the wounded or on women and children. The founder of international law, the Dutch lawyer, historian, theologian, and poet Hugo Grotius (1583–1645 CE), published the famous treatise *De Iure Belli ac Pacis* (*On the Law of War and Peace*) in 1625. This work was essentially an examination of the laws of war. Just as evidence of armed conflict goes back to the beginnings of recorded history, so too do concerns about fairness and humanity.

War Reporting

Author Phillip Knightly suggests that the emergence in the nineteenth century of war correspondents led to a more realistic picture of war. In the past, war reporting was based on heroic, biased stories of bravery that were communicated to the home front by commanding officers of the armed forces. War correspondents first emerged during the Crimean War (1854–1856) aided by a new invention, the telegraph, a machine by which a coded message was sent by electrical current along wires. These correspondents were newspaper reporters. For the first time, war correspondents put a human face on the suffering both of soldiers and of civilians.

The first war to be covered by a large number of correspondents was the American Civil War (1861–1865). The reports of suffering led President Abraham Lincoln to authorize the War Department to draft a code governing the conduct of the United States Army during the Civil War. This code served as a model for the creation of some other codes for some military forces in other countries.

The Geneva Conventions

The *Geneva Conventions* are a series of four international agreements—signed in Geneva, Switzerland—that govern the humane treatment of civilians and soldiers during war. The history of the *Geneva Conventions* is a complex one. The first Geneva convention, the *Convention for the Amelioration of the Condition of the Wounded in Armies in the Field*, was signed by 12 European governments in Geneva in 1864. It established an agreement stating that all armed forces must receive medical attention, regardless of their alliance. It also established the creation of the Red Cross.

In 1899, a second Geneva convention was drafted. This convention dealt with members of armed forces who are wounded at sea. In 1929, the third convention on the treatment of prisoners of war was ratified, followed in 1949 by the fourth convention, which dictated the treatment of civilians during a war. In 1949, all four conventions were revised by the Red Cross and signed to form the current *Geneva Conventions* that are referred to today. In 1977, protocols were added dealing further with the treatment of civilians and prisoners of war. By 2003, the conventions had 189 signatory countries.

The conventions are complex, but they are essentially a series of dos and don'ts to apply during conflict to protect vulnerable and defenceless individuals. Their underlying principles are based on the idea that the human dignity of individuals must be respected at all times. All

FIGURE 15.11   Ancient Roman philosophers believed that war should have a just and pious cause, be enacted in self-defence, or redress a wrong. Do we view war any differently today?

effort must be made, without discrimination, to reduce the suffering of people who have been put out of action by sickness, wounds, or captivity, regardless of whether or not they have taken part in the conflict.

The first protocol extends the conventions, taking into consideration modern means of warfare and transport, and it aims to give further protection to civilians. The second protocol provides a code of minimum protection for the combatants and the civilian population during civil wars.

War Crimes Since World War II

At the end of World War I, the British had supported the idea of establishing a tribunal in order to put the German kaiser and other German leaders on trial. The Americans had opposed the idea, believing that international law should not take precedence over domestic law. Although the *Treaty of Versailles* provided for international prosecution of those charged with "acts in violation of the laws and customs of war," ultimately the Allies left the Germans to prosecute their own war criminals. By the time World War II had broken out, however, further international agreements had been adopted at The Hague and in Geneva. These set the stage for the Nuremberg and Tokyo trials.

The Nuremberg and Tokyo Trials

At the end of World War II, both the British and the Soviets favoured the execution of top Nazis and some German armed forces officers. This time it was the Americans who advocated the use of trials. Between November 1945 and October 1946, war-crimes trials took place in the German city of Nuremberg. The tribunal was composed of judges from Great Britain, France, the Soviet Union, and the United States. The **indictments**, or criminal charges, against 22 Germans contained the following four counts:

- crimes against peace: the planning, initiating, and waging of wars of aggression in violation of international treaties and agreements
- crimes against humanity: deportations, exterminations, and genocide
- war crimes: violations of the laws of war
- a common plan or conspiracy to commit the criminal acts listed in the first three counts

The defence submitted key arguments for the court's consideration. First, the defendants contended that only states, not individuals, could be found guilty of war crimes. Second, the defence argued that the tribunal was prosecuting the accused for newly created crimes. The tribunal rejected this argument, stating that the acts had been criminal prior to the war. Altogether, 22 German Nazi leaders were tried: 12 were sentenced to death, 3 were given life sentences, 4 were sentenced to 20 years in prison, and 3 were acquitted.

With the conclusion of the Nuremberg trials, the Allied nations turned their attention to the prosecution of Japanese war criminals. Between 1946 and 1948, 28 Japanese were tried in Tokyo. All but two were found guilty. Seven of the defendants received death sentences after being found guilty of conventional war crimes and of conspiracy to wage aggressive war. One judge, Justice Radhabinod Pal of India, provided a dissenting opinion and suggested that aggressive war was not illegal under international law. He would have acquitted all the defendants. In fact, he stated, "When the conduct of nations is taken into account, the law will perhaps be found to be that only a lost war is a crime." He further questioned whether the Americans who made the decision to drop the atomic bombs should also be put on trial.

Internationally, these war tribunals were not universally applauded. The main criticism suggested that the war-crimes trials were "a victor's justice." The Allies had won the war, and this victory gave them the power to define the scope of the trials, to choose judges and prosecutors, and to place on trial only those people who had fought for the losing side. The entire process overlooked any wrongdoing on the part of the Allies, focusing on the conduct of only the Germans and the Japanese. Top Nazis were charged with a somewhat vague and new crime—"waging an aggressive war"—and they were charged retroactively, meaning that these actions were not considered to be crimes at the time they took place. The act of charging people retroactively was troubling to some critics. However, supporters of the war-crimes trials pointed to the many positive results of these trials, including the following:

- Military and civilian leaders were held responsible for crimes committed under their authority.
- Guilt for war crimes was attached to specific individuals, not to a country or an entire ethnic group.
- Atrocities that had been committed were documented and verified in a court of law.

FIGURE 15.12   On November 27, 1945, Nazi leader Hermann Goering pleaded guilty to war crimes at the International Military Tribunal at Nuremberg, Germany. The Nuremberg principles, formulated in 1950, included declarations that government officials or heads of state were responsible for their actions and not relieved of "responsibility under international law" because of their position. Individuals acting under government orders or orders of a superior were still responsible for their actions "provided a moral choice was possible." How might the phrase "moral choice" be interpreted?

- The trials demonstrated that international law could effectively and fairly deal with crimes that were complex and took place on a large scale.

Following the trials, the United Nations undertook several initiatives to create a permanent international criminal court; however, this notion was buried by the onset of the Cold War. Nevertheless, between the end of World War II and the 1990s, a number of relevant treaties were concluded that codified well-accepted international law and provided the basis for the definitions of crimes in the International Criminal Court statutes. These include, most notably, the *Geneva Conventions* and their protocols and the *Torture and Genocide Conventions*.

International Humanitarian Law (IHL)

According to the Red Cross, **international humanitarian law** can be defined as "the branch of international law that encompasses both humanitarian principles and international treaties that seek to save lives and alleviate suffering of both combatants and non-combatants during the Geneva convention of 1949."

The Geneva convention of 1949 explicitly designates certain acts as war crimes. In 1977, a further two conventions were added to the list of offences considered war crimes, and they expanded on rules governing internal conflicts, which are conflicts within one nation or state. The International Committee of the Red Cross has always been instrumental in enforcing the provisions of these conventions.

The end of the Cold War signified a new era for the Security Council of the United Nations because it was no longer repeatedly deadlocked by the veto powers of the United States and the Soviet Union. In 1993 and 1994, the Security Council was able to establish two international criminal tribunals, one for the former Yugoslavia and one for Rwanda.

War-Crimes Tribunals for the Former Yugoslavia

In 1946, the new constitution of the country known as the Socialist Federated Republic of Yugoslavia, situated in the Balkan peninsula in southeast Europe, established the six republics of Bosnia-Herzegovina, Croatia, Macedonia, Montenegro, Serbia, and Slovenia. This ethnically diverse region consisted of three main religious groups—the Eastern Orthodox Serbs, the Muslims, and the Roman Catholic Croats. Religious and ethnic nationalism had been a source of conflict in the region for years. With the death of the long-time president Marshall Tito in 1980, and the fall of Communism in Eastern Europe in 1989, ethnic tensions increased. It appeared that nationalism had replaced Communism as the dominant force in Yugoslavia.

The republics of Croatia and Slovenia declared independence in 1991. Slovenia was allowed to leave the Republic of Yugoslavia after a brief struggle. In Croatia, however, the Serb minority took up arms against the government and war broke out. The next year, Bosnia-Herzegovina jointly tried to gain independence from the Republic of Yugoslavia.

This led to further conflict, since the Serbs in Bosnia-Herzegovina wanted to remain in Yugoslavia and build a Greater Serbia. Bosnian Serb militias began a campaign against Croatian and Muslim villages. The United Nations intervened in conjunction with the European Union. Together, the United Nations and the EU imposed a trade embargo to try to force Serbian

President Slobodan Milosevic to end the fighting in Bosnia.

The continuing war in Bosnia and Herzegovina contributed a new term to the vocabulary of international relations—"ethnic cleansing." **Ethnic cleansing** is a literal translation of the Serbo-Croat expression "*etnicko ciscenje.*" It is a purposefully vague term that in fact refers to the systematic obliteration of an entire culture, and it includes genocide. The term was initially used by journalists and politicians who later applied it to other crisis situations, but it has also been used as part of the official vocabulary of UN Security Council documents and by other UN institutions, as well as by governmental and non-governmental international organizations.

The United Nations said that the Serbs were responsible for ethnic cleansing of Muslims from 1992 to 1995. In response to this concern, the Security Council passed a resolution in 1993 establishing the International Criminal Tribunal for the Former Yugoslavia (ICTY). The tribunal's authority was to prosecute four clusters of offences:

- grave breaches of the 1949 *Geneva Conventions*
- violations of the laws or customs of war
- genocide
- crimes against humanity

The jurisdiction of the court was restricted to include only the four types of war crimes committed in the former Yugoslavia since 1991, and it applied only to individuals, not organizations or political parties. The court was situated at The Hague. The maximum sentence was life imprisonment, which would be served in one of the states that had signed an agreement with the United Nations to accept prisoners. The death penalty was not an option.

It has been estimated that more than 250 000 people died between 1992 and 1995 in the Bosnian war, and a further 20 000 people are still missing. It is presumed that many of the missing are dead and buried in mass graves that have not all been uncovered. One of the largest mass graves was uncovered in Bosnia in July 2003. It

Between judgment at Nuremberg and the Balkans, tribunal at The Hague is a half-century struggle for accountability— imperfect, passionate, yet rooted in law and universal principles.

—Aryeh Neier (1937–), war-crimes prosecution expert

may hold the remains of 8000 Muslim men and boys who were executed near Srebrenica in July 1995.

Between 1993 and 2003, over 100 people were charged with war crimes that occurred during the war in the Balkans. Notable among them was Slobodan Milosevic, the first former head of state to ever face charges as a war criminal. Delivered to The Hague in 2001, Milosevic refused defence lawyers and did not acknowledge the court's jurisdiction. His trial was repeatedly delayed because of his ill health, and early estimates that his trial would conclude in 2003 were revised to 2006.

According to a European community fact-finding team, more than 20 000 Muslim girls and women were raped in Bosnia during the war in the Balkans. **Systemic rape**, meaning rape that is used deliberately as a weapon against the enemy, and forced pregnancies were alleged to be part of the ethnic cleansing that took place during the war. According to UNICEF, "in many societies women are viewed as repositories of a community's cultural and spiritual values," so the rape of a woman is also an attack on her culture. The decision of the war-crimes tribunal to classify these instances of rape as crimes against humanity was welcomed by such entities as Amnesty International, the US State Department, and many women's groups. Three Bosnian Serbs were tried and convicted in 2001 for the rape of women in the village of Faoca during the 1992–1995 war in Bosnia. Amnesty International commented, "This verdict is a significant step for women's human rights—sexual enslavement in armed conflict in now legally acknowledged as a crime against humanity, and perpetrators can and must be held to account."

The Case of Biljana Plavsic

In February 2003, Biljana Plavsic, known as the "Iron Lady of the Balkans," was sentenced to 11 years in prison for her part in war crimes during the Bosnian conflict. Plavsic was the former president of the Bosnian Serb republic and the most senior politician from the former Yugoslavia to be

FIGURE 15.13   Biljana Plavsic, the Bosnian Serb president, waved to her supporters as she arrived at a rally organized by Bosnian Serb opposition parties in July 1997 in Prijedor in northern Bosnia. Six years later, in 2003, she pleaded guilty at the International Criminal Tribunal for the former Yugoslavia to one count of persecution on political, racial, and religious grounds, a crime against humanity. Plavsic, nicknamed the "Iron Lady of the Balkans," was sentenced to 11 years in prison.

jailed by The Hague war-crimes tribunal. She had admitted to "publicly rationalizing and justifying the so-called ethnic cleansing of non-Serbs."

Although the British judge detailed the severity of the offences, which included mass killings, deportations, and cruel and inhumane treatment, he balanced it with the mitigating factors of her guilty plea, her remorse, and her subsequent contribution to peace by accepting the 1995 Dayton peace agreement. Her defence counsel made arguments that the sentence should not exceed eight years, because the 72-year-old would likely die in prison. The UN prosecutors had requested a sentence of 15 to 25 years, but the judges ruled that Plavsic should be given credit for voluntarily surrendering and pleading guilty. In June 2003, Plavsic was sent to Sweden to serve the remainder of her sentence. Sweden is one of the nine European countries that agreed to incarcerate convicted war criminals.

The Rwandan War-Crimes Tribunal

The country of Rwanda in Africa is predominantly composed of two tribes, the Hutus and the Tutsis. Although the Hutus formed the larger population group, hundreds of years ago the Tutsis became the rulers. Complicating politics in the region was a period of German colonial rule, which lasted from 1885 until the Belgians took over Rwanda at the end of World War I. As a result of the Belgians' encouragement of a more democratic rule in Rwanda and their support of increased status for the Hutus, the Hutus revolted in 1959, deposed the Tutsi king, and inaugurated a new Hutu political party. Many Tutsis fled during and after the 1959 rebellion, and a new political party was created. When the Belgian trusteeship ended in 1962, Rwanda was granted full independence. Tension and, at times, conflict between the two ethnic tribes continued over the next three decades. In 1990, exiled Tutsis banded together and invaded Rwanda, leading to escalating conflict that resulted in as many as 800 000 deaths.

FIGURE 15.14   In 1998 at the International Criminal Tribunal for Rwanda, a former Hutu militiaman, Omar Serushago, pleaded guilty to genocide and three counts of crimes against humanity—murder, extermination, and torture. During his pre-sentence hearing, he expressed his remorse for his crimes and asked for forgiveness from his victims. He was sentenced in February 1999 to 15 years of imprisonment. He appealed the sentence as being too harsh, but his appeal was denied in 2000.

The war continued over a two-year period until a ceasefire was agreed upon in July 1992. UN peacekeeping forces were sent to Rwanda and were present on April 6, 1994, when a plane carrying the president of Uganda was shot down by Hutu extremists, killing the president. The Canadian commander of the peacekeeping mission, General Roméo Dallaire, requested urgent and immediate support from the United Nations. With few troops at his disposal and no new forces arriving, Dallaire and his peacekeeping unit could do little to stop the coming massacre. Hutu soldiers and civilians began killing all Tutsis, as well as any Hutus seen as sympathetic to a plan in which Tutsis and Hutus would share power in Rwanda. It is estimated that as many as 1 million people were killed between April and July of 1994. A political group comprised of Tutsis, called the Rwanda Patriotic Front (RPF), undertook military action, gaining control of most of Rwanda by July 1994. Up to 2 million Hutu people fled to the neighbouring countries of Zaire and Tanzania in one of the greatest mass flights of refugees ever recorded.

In 1994, the RPF announced a "national unity government." On November 8 of that year, the UN Security Council voted to create an international tribunal to place people accused of war crimes on trial. The International Criminal Tribunal for Rwanda (ICTR) was established to prosecute people accused of committing genocide and other violations of international humanitarian law in Rwanda between January 1 and December 31 of 1994. In 1995, it was decided the tribunal would convene in Arusha in the United Republic of Tanzania. Through the creation of the ICTR, the United Nations hoped to demonstrate that the international community would not tolerate genocide.

Since 1995, the ICTR has arrested over 50 people and completed several trials, including that of Jean Kambanda, the former prime minister of Rwanda. The conviction and sentencing of Kambanda marked the first time someone had ever been convicted of genocide by an international court. Among other accomplishments and contributions to the growth of international law, the ICTR has pioneered victim-oriented **restitutive justice** by means of international criminal tribunals. The concept of restitutive justice suggests that true justice is concerned with more than simply the punishment of offenders. It's based on the notion that

victims' needs must be met, including assistance with medical care, counselling, rehabilitation, and, when necessary, reintegration into the community or relocation. The concept of restitutive justice is now included in the statute of the International Criminal Court.

CONFIRM YOUR UNDERSTANDING

1. What concerns did various ancient cultures raise about the treatment of people in times of war?
2. In what way did war correspondents contribute to an understanding of war?
3. Compare the Nuremberg and Tokyo trials with respect to the purpose of the trials, the outcomes, and the criticisms levelled against each.
4. Despite such perspectives as Justice Pal's at the Tokyo Trials, at the end of World War II, Americans were not prosecuted for war crimes. Suggest what factors might have led to this decision.

5. What mitigating factors were given as the reason for a relatively lenient sentence for Biljana Plavsic?
6. Do you think Plavsic's sentence might encourage other defendants to plead guilty? Explain.
7. Some Balkan observers said that the 11-year sentence was not long enough compared to other sentences passed by the tribunal. Would you agree? Justify your answer.

The International Criminal Court

Throughout the 1970s and 1980s, human rights groups lobbied for a permanent tribunal for the purpose of placing suspected war criminals on trial. Since World War II, the international community had witnessed a willingness by nations to strike **ad hoc tribunals**, which are courts set up according to an individual circumstance on an as-needed basis. Certainly the ad hoc tribunals in former Yugoslavia and Rwanda illustrated a world community committed to the punishment of war criminals. However, some human rights groups asserted that without the presence of a permanent tribunal, a large number of abuses would continue to occur internationally.

After years of preparatory work, the United Nations Diplomatic Conference on the Establishment of an International Criminal Court convened in Rome in 1998. With a stated purpose to "finalize and adopt a convention on the establishment of an international criminal court," 120 UN member states adopted a treaty

called the *Rome Statute of the International Criminal Court*. This treaty entered into force on July 1, 2002, two months after 60 states ratified the statute.

This new court has a mandate to place individuals, rather than states, on trial to prosecute such crimes as genocide, war crimes, and crimes against humanity. Crimes against humanity include torture, rape, enslavement, and forced disappearance, as well as persecution on political, racial, national, and ethnic grounds. To be categorized as such, these crimes would have to be committed on a significant scope, which implies that single or random acts of rape, murder, or torture may not qualify. War crimes include breaches of the *Geneva Conventions* and other violations of the laws and customs that can be applied in international armed conflict. While there was discussion in Rome about including terrorism and drug trafficking in the court's mandate, it was believed that these two crimes needed further review and research before they could be seriously considered for inclusion.

FIGURE 15.15   On March 11, 2003, UN Secretary-General Kofi Annan addressed the inaugural session of the International Criminal Court at The Hague. The court has jurisdiction to punish offenders of war crimes, including genocide, in any country that has ratified the *Rome Statute* if that country itself refuses to prosecute suspects. Non-participating states can ask the court to intervene, as can the UN Security Council. In 2003, the president of the International Criminal Court was Canadian Philippe Kirsch (seated fourth from the right).

This new court is situated at The Hague; a permanent building is scheduled to be ready between 2007 and 2009. The primary responsibility to try crimes will belong to member states, but the court will take action if national legal systems are unable or unwilling to act. Only crimes committed after July 1, 2002, will come under the jurisdiction of the court.

Of much interest to the world community were the circumstances under which the United States sided with China, Libya, and Saudi Arabia in voting against the *Rome Statute*. The United States was concerned about losing jurisdiction and sovereignty, and about the prospect of American soldiers or peacekeepers being unjustly prosecuted. In July 1998, at a press briefing, James Rubin, spokesperson for the US State Department from 1997 to 2000, said that the proposed international court would "...not [be] an effective instrument...it opens the possi-

bility of politically motivated and unjustified prosecution, which is unacceptable." President Bill Clinton also commented that the United States was hesitant to support a court that under certain circumstances claimed international jurisdiction over the US armed forces and US civilians. Nevertheless, President Clinton decided to compromise and sign the treaty. However, US involvement was revoked when President George W. Bush came to power. It remains to be seen whether lack of support from the United States will hamper the effectiveness of the International Criminal Court. By 2003, the United States had put pressure on more than 20 countries to sign bilateral treaties that would prevent them from turning American suspects over to the court. The United States had threatened to cut off humanitarian and military aid to countries that were unwilling to sign these treaties.

Conflict Prevention and Peacemaking

Given that peacekeeping is difficult, expensive, dangerous, and potentially ineffective, what can be said of initiatives that aim to prevent conflict before it starts and to build or make peace? Organizations that promote peace suggest that it is necessary to go beyond simply resolving conflicts that are already underway and to begin to build peace. What would constitute an appropriate "climate" for peace? Some authors writing about the peace movement suggest that a climate for peace in the world must include democratic governments for all countries and the socioeconomic factors that lead to an adequate income, health-care system, and education system for each of their citizens.

The United Nations has expanded its role to include peacemaking and peacebuilding. Since 1990, UN forces have undertaken such tasks as supervising elections and encouraging peace negotiations. Peacemaking includes the identification of potential crisis areas through early warning, the reporting of accurate information, mediation, and negotiation. Peacebuilding includes electoral assistance, the re-establishment of the rule of law, economic assistance, and the return of refugees to their homeland.

In 1997, the United Nations created the Department of Political Affairs (DPA). The role of this department is to provide advice and support to the Secretary-General on matters relating to the maintenance of peace and security. More specifically, the DPA is responsible for conflict prevention, peacebuilding, and peacemaking. According to the DPA, conflict prevention is a way to prevent "human suffering and act as an alternative to costly political-military operations

> *The law spoke too softly to be heard in such a noise of war.*
> —Plutarch
> (c. 47–120 CE),
> Greek historian

FIGURE 15.16   Peacemaking and peacebuilding include such activities as election supervision. The United Nations monitored elections in East Timor in August 2001. Here, UN International Electoral Commission employees are processing ballots in Dili, East Timor. After struggling under the rule of first Portugal and then Indonesia, East Timor became the independent country of Timor-Leste and a member of the United Nations on May 20, 2002.

to resolve conflicts after they have broken out." Although the DPA views diplomacy as the main method by which conflicts can be prevented or resolved, other methods are available as well. The DPA encourages "good governance, human rights, and economic and social development." It

is clear that the primary responsibility for conflict prevention still rests with national governments, but an important role is played by a global community, based on trust and social solidarity, in which people are willing to co-operate in joint ventures.

CONFIRM YOUR UNDERSTANDING

1. Briefly describe the conflict in the former Yugoslavia that led to the war in the Balkans.
2. Three Serbians were convicted in 2001 of the war crime of rape, in which rape is considered a weapon of war. Do you agree that rape should in some instances be treated as a war crime? Explain your answer.
3. What events led up to the massacre in Rwanda between April and July of 1994?

4. Explain the concept of restitutive justice.
5. What is the jurisdiction of the International Criminal Court? How is it different from the International Court of Justice?
6. Explain why the United States was unwilling to ratify the *Rome Statute*. Do you believe that its concerns were justified? Explain.

In Closing

In this chapter, you have examined the origins of the United Nations, from the formation of the League of Nations leading up to the inception of the United Nations in the dying days of World War II. The United Nations is made up of six organs, each with a very specific function and jurisdiction. After more than half a century of operation, the United Nations faces the new millennium with many initiatives and challenges. It has been able to solve some international conflicts through diplomacy, mediation, arbitration, and, on occasion, UN-sanctioned force. One initiative pursued in the post–World War II years was the prosecution of war criminals in Germany and Japan. More recently, tribunals have been set up to try war criminals following a war in the Balkans and a massacre in Rwanda. The *Universal Declaration of Human Rights* specifies human rights that should be available to all

citizens of the world. Not only have governments and the United Nations been proponents of human rights, but NGOs have played a role as well.

A second pressing global issue that needs to be addressed is aid for the millions of refugees worldwide. The United Nations appointed a High Commissioner for Refugees in order to oversee this concern. In a world bent on avoiding war, peace and security initiatives such as the UN peacekeeping forces and the work of NATO and NORAD take on ever-increasing importance. The concept of peacemaking, which deals not just with diplomacy but with socio-economic and political challenges within the countries in conflict, provides the hope that people can foster conditions internationally that are conducive to peace rather than conflict.

CHAPTER ACTIVITIES

Extend Your Legal Knowledge

1. Explain the role of the International Court of Justice in resolving international disputes.
2. Compare different peaceful methods of resolving conflicts.
3. Describe the positive and negative aspects, for Canada and for the international community, of Canada's involvement in international peace-keeping.

Think About the Law

4. Explain the meaning of the following quotation: "It is misleading to consider international law as a piece of reality cut off from its historical, political and ideological context" (Cassese 2001).
5. The International Criminal Police Organization, commonly referred to as Interpol, is an inter-governmental organization with headquarters in Lyon, France. In 1914, the First International Criminal Police Congress was held; police officers and legal experts from 14 countries participated. Although the workings of Interpol have been interrupted twice by world wars, the organization has continued to evolve. In 2003, it had 181 member states. Article 2 of Interpol's constitution lists these aims:

   - ensuring and promoting assistance between all criminal police authorities, within the limits of the laws existing in the different countries and in the spirit of the *Universal Declaration of Human Rights*
   - establishing and developing all institutions likely to contribute effectively to the prevention and suppression of ordinary law crimes

   Interpol is committed to respecting national sovereignty and recognizing the equality of member states, as well as recognizing universality—the principle that any member state may co-operate with any other state. Contrary to its glamorous portrayal in some movies, Interpol does not hire James Bond–like spies who travel the world, legally empowered to operate in many countries. Rather, the purpose of the organization is to share information with law enforcement agencies around the world and co-operate whenever possible in criminal investigations.

   a) List some of the reasons why it would be virtually impossible to have an international police force that would have all the powers of Western domestic-law enforcement agencies.
   b) In what way has the political landscape changed internationally in the last century to make an agency such as Interpol so important?
   c) Interpol maintains, "With the escalation of serious transnational crime, the need for a global police co-operation response has never been more acute." What types of crime do you think could be defined as "transnational"?

6. During the so-called "Dirty Wars" in Argentina (1976–1983), citizens who opposed the right-wing military regime sometimes disappeared, becoming *los desparecidos*, meaning "the disappeared ones." Between 13 000 and 15 000 people may have disappeared, often after being imprisoned and tortured. The attention of the international community was drawn to these human rights violations by the Mothers of the Plaza de Mayo, mothers whose children had disappeared. This group held weekly vigils in the Plaza de Mayo, in front of the presidential plaza in Buenos Aires. Human rights organizations now report on "disappeared" people worldwide. Explain how the practice of making people disappear is a means of oppressing dissenters.

7. Both Amnesty International and Human Rights Watch are against the death penalty. Of particular concern to them is the execution of what they call "juvenile offenders," that is, anyone under the age of 18. According to Human Rights Watch, between 2000 and 2003, only the

United States, the Democratic Republic of the Congo, Pakistan, and Iran have used the death penalty on juvenile offenders. The Democratic Republic of the Congo executed a 14-year-old in 2000. Pakistan executed a juvenile offender in 2001 for a crime he committed at the age of 13. Subsequently, Pakistan, Iran, and the Congo stopped the practice of putting juvenile offenders to death. In 2002, three juvenile executions were known to have taken place, all in the state of Texas. Since 1990, the United States has put 18 juvenile offenders to death. Human Rights Watch condemns the execution of juvenile offenders as a violation of human rights, and it urges those few countries that retain capital punishment for juvenile offenders to put an immediate end to the practice.

a) Do countries have a legal and moral right to implement the death penalty? Explain your views.

b) At what age do you believe that an offender should be sentenced to an adult penalty? Would your answer vary depending on the crime? Explain.

8. Apartheid was the social and political policy of racial segregation in South Africa that was enforced by its government from 1948 until 1994. The *Population Registration Act* of 1950 put all South Africans into one of three categories: Bantu (Black African), White, or Coloured (of mixed race). Asians were later added as a fourth category. During the 1950s, other laws were passed that did the following: segregated different races both in residential and business neighbourhoods; limited the rights of Black Africans to own land; prohibited most social contact among races; and enforced segregation in schools, in the workplace, and at public facilities.

Within the country, protests against apartheid took the form of strikes, demonstrations, sabotage, and violence. In 1961, South Africa was forced to withdraw from the British Commonwealth by member states that were critical of apartheid. In 1985, Great Britain and the United States imposed selective economic sanctions on South Africa to protest its segregation and discrimination policies. Other nations and the United Nations also imposed sanctions. These international economic sanctions affected the South African economy, raising the cost of necessities and cutting foreign investment. In 1990, the National Party government began the dismantling of apartheid, and in 1994, free elections were held, resulting in majority representation for the African National Congress, an organization founded in 1918 in South Africa with the goal of obtaining equality and civil rights for non-Whites through non-violent actions.

a) One legal scholar suggested that international economic sanctions were a more successful type of protest than internal unrest. Speculate on why that might be true.

b) Did the concept of sovereignty give the South African government the right to make and enforce any laws it wished? Comment on the legality and morality of the international community's actions.

Communicate About the Law

9. Many Canadians have played prominent roles in international affairs. Research each of the following people, and outline their contributions to the international community.

a) John Peters Humphrey
b) Lester B. Pearson
c) Justice Jules Deschênes
d) Major General Lewis MacKenzie
e) General Roméo Dallaire
f) Louise Frechette
g) Stephen Lewis

10. International political and economic affairs were heavily influenced by the Cold War, which lasted from approximately 1945 until 1990. Research and write a report on the Cold War.

11. Compile a list of Canada's various peacekeeping missions since 1948. Outline the details of the conflicts that necessitated the missions.

12. In March 2003, the United States, backed by Great Britain, went to war against Iraq. The American government said that Iraq had not co-operated with UN weapon inspectors and that attempts to rid Iraq of weapons of mass destruction had failed. The United States believed it was necessary for a coalition of willing countries to begin a military campaign. Countries that did not support the Americans included France, Germany, and Canada. The UN Security Council voted against military action. The *Charter of the United Nations* outlaws the use of force except in the following instances: it recognizes "the inherent right of individual or collective self-defence if an armed attack occurs against a Member of the United Nations" and also authorizes the Security Council to take measures when there is a "threat to peace, breach of the peace or act of aggression." Research the events leading up to the war against Iraq, and prepare to debate in class whether or not the war could be justified under international law. Consider referring to the Legal Handbook to review the section on Honing Your Debating Skills.

13. Research and report on some of the initiatives undertaken by both the United Nations and the Canadian government in support of the International Decade of the World's Indigenous People.

Apply the Law

14. On December 21, 1988, a Pan Am flight from London to New York exploded over Lockerbie, Scotland. All 259 people aboard were killed, as well as 11 people on the ground. After an investigation, it was concluded that the crash was a result of the detonation of an explosive device that was located in a baggage container. Two Libyans were charged in the United States and in Scotland with the bombing. The US, French, and British governments demanded that Libya surrender the suspects in order that they stand trial. Libya replied that it would try the two men in its own courts. The United Nations ordered the surrender of the men, and when Libya did not comply, the United Nations imposed sanctions on it. All air travel to and from Libya was banned. In 1993, sanctions were tightened: Libyan assets in foreign banks were frozen, and the import of spare parts for the Libyan oil industry was banned. The Libyan government then agreed to a trial for the men in Switzerland, but not in Scotland or the United States. In 1998, the International Court of Justice at The Hague ruled that it had the right to decide where the suspects should be tried. In 1998, Libyan leader Mu'ammer Gaddafi agreed to hand over the suspects to be tried in the Netherlands under Scottish law. In 1999, UN Secretary-General Kofi Annan, South African President Nelson Mandela, British Foreign Secretary Robin Cook, a Scottish law professor, and diplomats from Saudi Arabia and South Africa became involved in diplomacy and mediation. In February 1999, the UN Security Council extended sanctions for another four months. In April 1999, the two suspects were flown to The Hague and charged with the bombing. UN sanctions against Libya were suspended. Abdelbaset Ali Mohmed Al Megrahi was convicted in 2001 and his co-accused, Al Amin Khalifa Fhimah, was found not guilty. After losing an appeal in 2002, Al Megrahi was transferred to a Scottish prison to begin serving his life sentence.

a) Construct a timeline of the key events in the Lockerbie case.

b) What measures were taken by the UN Security Council to force Libya to surrender the accused?

c) In what ways was the trial the result of compromise and negotiation?

d) What precedent may have been set by the trial of the two accused? You may wish to refer to the Legal Handbook to review the section on Comparing and Contrasting Cases.

15. Following the terrorist attacks on the United States on September 11, 2001, the American government declared a "war on terrorism." American troops in Afghanistan arrested people whom they believed were fighting for the Taliban (a fundamentalist Sunni faction of Islam that formed the government of Afghanistan from 1996 to 2001) or were al-Qaeda operatives (members of an extremist, international, militant network). In 2003, suspects from Afghanistan were being held by the Americans at a high-security prison called Camp Delta, at Guantanamo Bay, an American naval base operating in Cuba since 1903. In the month of August alone, an additional 680 men were incarcerated.

In 2003, the United States maintained that the prisoners were being treated humanely. However, it stated that the men were not prisoners of war as dictated by the *Geneva Conventions*. The men had not been charged with crimes and might be subjected to indefinite detention without charges or trial. The United States claimed that the prisoners were not guaranteed the rights afforded to criminals under the *United States Constitution*, such as the presumption of innocence until proven guilty and a trial by jury. The United States said that these prisoners could, however, be tried by a military tribunal, with the possibility of the death penalty as a sentence. Although a prisoner of war is required to provide only his or her name, rank, and serial number according to the *Geneva Conventions*, these prisoners had been subjected to lengthy interrogations. The International Committee of the Red Cross visited prisoners and facilitated correspondence with their families. Neither families nor journalists were allowed to visit.

a) Outline the purpose of the *Geneva Conventions*.

b) Did the United States gain any advantage by holding these prisoners in Cuba rather than in another location?

c) Did the war on terrorism justify the treatment these prisoners received? Explain your answer.

d) What rights, if any, should these prisoners have been accorded?

e) Prepare a newspaper editorial in which you either criticize or support the imprisonment of the suspected terrorists at Guantanamo Bay.

16. In 1999 in Nigeria, 12 northern states adopted the concept of *sharia*, which is a strict interpretation of Islamic law. Under *sharia*, pregnancy outside of marriage is sufficient evidence for a woman to be convicted of adultery. In March 2002, a Nigerian woman, Amina Lawal, was convicted of having a child outside of marriage and was sentenced to death by stoning. In September 2003, an Islamic court overturned Lawal's conviction. A panel of five judges ruled in Lawal's favour, citing procedural error and noting that she had not had a lawyer and was not given the proper opportunity to defend herself. Lawyers hailed the ruling as a triumph for Islamic justice. "It's a big relief for all of us," defence lawyer Hauwa Ibrahim said. "Amina can have her life back and we are grateful to the court." At the same time, conservative Muslims in Nigeria's chiefly Islamic North said Amina Lawal should have been executed. Katherine Mabille, of Avocats sans Frontières (Lawyers Without Borders), applauded the ruling for Amina Lawal but said other cases are pending. International lawyers are assisting two Nigerians facing amputation of their hands for theft.

a) In your opinion, what role should the international press and international aid agencies play in cases such as this one?

b) How could international law be used to support Nigeria's use of *sharia*? How could international law be used to support the defence of someone such as Amina Lawal?

c) In what ways might some journalists in the Western press corps not exhibit enough of an understanding of Nigerian culture and law to form an unbiased opinion on this case? Explain. You may wish to refer to the section What Is Bias? in the Legal Handbook.

17. A number of German Nazis fled Germany at the end of World War II, taking up residence in places such as South America and Canada. Subsequently, critics of Canadian immigration policy at the time argued that an anti-Semitic Canadian federal government made it easier for Nazis and the members of Hitler's Secret Service (SS) to emigrate to Canada than for Jewish refugees to gain admittance. Canada decided to add a war-crimes section to its *Criminal Code* in 1987 after exhibiting reluctance to do so for decades. Between 1987 and 1994, Canada prosecuted alleged war criminals Imre Finta, Stephen Reistetter, Michael Pawlowski, and Radislav Grujicic, but it did not win any convictions. In practical terms, the trials were hampered by the age of the witnesses, language barriers, and old evidence. Legally, questions were raised about the fairness of retroactivity and the rationale for prosecuting crimes that were not committed on Canadian soil. Those people who supported the trials believed that justice must be served, claiming that these men should not escape prosecution. Those people who opposed the trials believed that it opened old wounds unnecessarily and that the chance for a conviction was too remote. Other opponents of the trials wondered whether it was necessary or desirable to prosecute men in their 70s, 80s, and 90s, some in fragile health, who posed no threat to Canadian society.

a) In chart form, list the arguments for and against prosecuting these crimes in Canada. State which arguments you find more compelling and why.

b) In 1992, Jac Luitjens was deported from Canada to Holland, where he received a jail sentence for helping Nazi forces capture Dutch resistance fighters. Since 1995, Canada's preferred strategy for dealing with war crimes has been to revoke citizenship and then deport the war criminal. Should Canada pursue this option (i.e., deportation) rather than attempting to prosecute war criminals in Canada? What would be the advantages and disadvantages of deportation?

c) In 2000, the Canadian government proclaimed the *Crimes Against Humanity and War Crimes Act*, which incorporated provisions of the *Rome Statute of the International Criminal Court*. This act requires the prosecution of any individual in Canada for any offence stated in the act, regardless of where the offence occurred. The act included the new offences of genocide, crimes against humanity, and war crimes. It also recognized the need to provide restitution to victims. Is it important that Canada's domestic legislation be compatible with the international agreement of the new International Criminal Court? Explain.

18. Read the summary of the case below.

a) Why did the court blame the Iranian government for the actions of the militant students?

b) What did the court order? Suggest methods for how the court could enforce the order.

c) Why did the court find it necessary to reaffirm principles regarding diplomatic relations?

United States Diplomatic and Consular Staff in Tehran (United States of America v. Iran), [1980] I.C.J. 3

In November 1979, Iranian student militants seized and occupied the American embassy in Tehran, Iran. Diplomatic and consular staff were held captive. After negotiations through diplomatic channels failed to obtain the release of the hostages, the United States went to the UN Security Council. The Security Council condemned the actions of Iran. The Security Council called upon the government of Iran to "immediately release the personnel of the

Embassy of the United States of America being held in Teheran, to provide them with protection, and to allow them to leave the country." When Iran failed to comply, the United States applied to the International Court of Justice. In May 1980, the court ruled that Iran had violated its obligations to the United States, and the Iranians should secure the release of the hostages, restore the embassy premises, and make reparation for any injuries caused to the United States government. Although the court recognized that the actions of the militant students could not be attributed to the Iranian government, it noted that the Iranian government had done nothing to prevent the attack or to force the militants to withdraw from the embassy and release all hostages. The court also reaffirmed the importance of laws governing diplomats and embassies.

BIBLIOGRAPHY

America's Defense Monitor (producer). *Ridding the World of Landmines.* Port Credit, ON: McNabb & Connolly Video Distributors, 1999.

Amnesty International. Accessed July–Aug. 2003 <www.amnesty.org>.

Black, Ian. "Ex-president of Bosnian Serbs Jailed." *Guardian Unlimited* 28 Feb. 2003. Accessed July 2003 <www.guardian.co.uk>.

Bresler, Fenton. *Interpol.* Toronto: Penguin Books Canada Ltd., 1992.

Britannica Encyclopedia. 2002 edition.

Canadian Legal Information Institute. Accessed Oct. 2003 <www.canlii.org>.

Cassese, Antonio. *International Law.* New York: Oxford University Press, 2001.

CNN.com. "Mideast: Land of Conflict." Accessed 10 Aug. 2003 <www.cnn.com/SPECIALS/2003/mideast/stories/issues.refugees/>.

Department of Foreign Affairs and International Trade. *The Canadian Reference Guide to the United Nations.* Ottawa: Minister of Public Works and Government Services, 1999.

Department of Foreign Affairs and International Trade. Accessed July–Nov. 2003 <www.dfait-maeci.gc.ca>.

Department of Justice Canada. Accessed July–Nov. 2003 <www.canada.justice.gc.ca>.

Department of National Defence and Canadian Forces. Accessed July–Nov. 2003 <www.dnd.ca>.

Graves, Gary. "Dirty Diamonds." *CBC News Online.* Accessed 17 Dec. 2000 <www.cbc.ca/national>.

Grolier Encyclopedia. 1998 edition.

Guardian Unlimited. Accessed July–Nov. 2003 <www.guardian.co.uk>.

———. "WHO Travel Warning As SARS Death Toll Mounts." Accessed 23 Apr. 2003.

Hooper, John. "Cook Urges End to Trade in Illicit Gems." *Guardian Unlimited* 18 Dec. 1999. Accessed 17 Dec. 2000 <www.guardian.co.uk>.

Human Rights Watch. Accessed 22 Oct. 2003 <www.hrw.org>.

International Committee of the Red Cross. Accessed Sep.–Nov. 2003 <www.icrc.org>.

Maga, Timothy P. *Judgment at Tokyo: The Japanese War Crimes Trials.* Lexington, KY: The University Press of Kentucky, 2001.

McIlroy, Anne. "On the Road to Recovery." *Guardian Unlimited* 28 April 2003.

Meisler, Stanley. *United Nations: The First Fifty Years.* New York: The Atlantic Monthly Press, 1995.

NATO. Accessed Sep.–Oct. 2003 <www.nato.int>.

Neier, Aryeh. *War Crimes: Brutality, Genocide, Terror and the Struggle for Justice.* New York: Random House, 1998.

NORAD. Accessed Aug. 2003 <www.norad.mil>.

Northedge, F.S. *The League of Nations: Its Life and Times, 1920–1946.* Leicester, Great Britain: Leicester University Press, 1986.

Off, Carol. *The Lion, the Fox and the Eagle: A Story of Generals and Justice in Rwanda and Yugoslavia.* Toronto: Random House, 2000.

Rosenne, Shabtai, and Terry Gill. *The World Court: What It Is and How It Works.* 4th ed. Leiden, Netherlands: Nijhoff Martinus, 1989.

Special Rapporteur of the UN Economic and Social Council Sub-Commission on Prevention of Discrimination and Protection of Minorities. *Cultural and Spiritual Values of Biodiversity.* New York: United Nations Environment Programme, 1999. Accessed 14 Jan. 2004 <www.unep.org/Biodiversity>.

United Nations. Accessed July–Nov. 2003 <www.un.org>.

———. "Diamond Industry's Move on 'Conflict' Stones Welcomed at UN." Department of Public Information Press Release. 21 July 2000. Accessed 17 Dec. 2003 <www.reliefweb.int/w/rwb/nsf/s>.

———. "Guidelines on Co-operation Between the United Nations and the Business Community." Issued by the Secretary-General. 17 July 2000. Accessed 17 Dec. 2003 <www.un.org/partners/business/otherpages/guide.htm>.

———. "Protection of Civilians in Armed Conflict— The Private Sector." United Nations Office for the Co-ordination of Humanitarian Affairs. Accessed 17 Dec. 2003 <www.reliefweb.int/ocha_ol/civilians/private_sector/>.

World Health Organization. Accessed Aug. 2003. <www.who.int/csr/sars/archive>.

———. "Who Extends Its SARS-related Travel Advice to Beijing and Shanxi Province In China and to Toronto, Canada." Accessed 29 Sept. 2003 <www.who.int/mediacentre/notes/2003/np7/en/>.

UNIT FOUR CULMINATING ACTIVITY

Investigative Reports

Introduction

This unit covered labour law, environmental law, and international law. Your task is to research and present to your class one of the challenges or controversies surrounding regulations and dispute settlement in one of these broad areas.

In addition to addressing the Overall Learning Expectations outlined at the beginning of this unit, this culminating activity requires you to use a number of legal inquiry skills. You may want to consult Chapter 1 "The Legal Handbook" (on the pages indicated by the icons) to review each of these skills.

Your Task

With a partner, assume the roles of an investigative reporting team for a current affairs program on television, radio, or a news magazine. You are to research one of the following topics and present your findings in the form of an informational report. Outline the parties involved in the issue, the legalities investigated, and the domestic or international laws that apply to the situation. Your goal is to find and present a fresh perspective on the topic or to focus on a particular aspect of interest to you. To do this:

1. Chose one of the following topic areas and then focus on one particular issue within it:
   - current labour issues in Canada
   - international environmental issues
   - the role of the United Nations in the twenty-first century
   - the viability of an International Criminal Court
   - human rights violations around the globe

2. The main challenge in this activity is to make connections between the legal issue presented and the methods of dispute resolution. You are to illustrate how different stakeholders may influence outcomes and help or hinder dispute resolution.

Research your topic using a variety of sources including, but not necessarily limited to, libraries, Web sites, magazines, newspapers, current affairs programs on television and the radio. Gather information that is relevant to your topic and write it into a comprehensive report in order to illustrate your understanding of the situation or issue. Ensure you present the topic from different perspectives and offer a variety of opinions. (Make sure you keep proper bibliographical references for all the sources you consult.)

In your report, clearly identify and explain:
- the issue
- the main players or parties and their differing perspectives on the issue
- the laws in question
- past events surrounding the issue, the current situation, and what could possibly happen in the future

3. Watch or listen to current affairs programs for ideas on how to structure and present your report. Determine which format you will use; for example, will you present your report as a radio piece, television piece, or news magazine article? (Make sure you are comfortable using the technical tools you may need for your report, such as video cameras, computer equipment, or tape recorders, etc., before you begin.)

4. You are to make informed judgments on what would be the best technological tools and enhancements needed to present your report. Your report should be informative, creative, entertaining, and focused on the legal aspects of the issue. The reports are to be presented to the class as segments in a current affairs program.

Present the information clearly and concisely with an appropriate introduction and conclusion. Consider your audience and use appropriate language levels and visual aids.

■ A P P E N D I X ■

Canadian Charter of Rights and Freedoms

Part I of the *Constitution Act, 1982*

Whereas Canada is founded upon principles that recognize the supremacy of God and the rule of law:

Guarantee of Rights and Freedoms

Rights and freedoms in Canada

1. The *Canadian Charter of Rights and Freedoms* guarantees the rights and freedoms set out in it subject only to such reasonable limits prescribed by law as can be demonstrably justified in a free and democratic society.

Fundamental Freedoms

Fundamental freedoms

2. Everyone has the following fundamental freedoms:

   (a) freedom of conscience and religion;

   (b) freedom of thought, belief, opinion and expression, including freedom of the press and other media of communication;

   (c) freedom of peaceful assembly; and

   (d) freedom of association.

Democratic Rights

Democratic rights of citizens

3. Every citizen of Canada has the right to vote in an election of members of the House of Commons or of a legislative assembly and to be qualified for membership therein.

Maximum duration of legislative bodies

4. (1) No House of Commons and no legislative assembly shall continue for longer than five years from the date fixed for the return of the writs of a general election of its members.

Continuation in special circumstances

(2) In time of real or apprehended war, invasion or insurrection, a House of Commons may be continued by Parliament and a legislative assembly may be continued by the legislature beyond five years if such continuation is not opposed by the votes of more than one-third of the members of the House of Commons or the legislative assembly, as the case may be.

Annual sitting of legislative bodies

5. There shall be a sitting of Parliament and of each legislature at least once every twelve months.

Mobility Rights

Mobility of citizens

6. (1) Every citizen of Canada has the right to enter, remain in and leave Canada.

Rights to move and gain livelihood

(2) Every citizen of Canada and every person who has the status of a permanent resident of Canada has the right

   (a) to move to and take up residence in any province; and

   (b) to pursue the gaining of a livelihood in any province.

Limitation

(3) The rights specified in subsection (2) are subject to

   (a) any laws or practices of general application in force in a province other than those that discriminate among persons primarily on the basis of province of present or previous residence; and

   (b) any laws providing for reasonable residency requirements as a qualification for the receipt of publicly provided social services.

Affirmative action programs

(4) Subsections (2) and (3) do not preclude any law, program or activity that has as its object the amelioration in a province of conditions of individuals in that province who are socially or economically disadvantaged if the rate of employment in that province is below the rate of employment in Canada.

Legal Rights

7. Everyone has the right to life, liberty and security of the person and the right not to be deprived thereof except in accordance with the principles of fundamental justice.

Life, liberty and security of person

8. Everyone has the right to be secure against unreasonable search or seizure.

Search or seizure

9. Everyone has the right not to be arbitrarily detained or imprisoned.

Detention or imprisonment

10. Everyone has the right on arrest or detention

Arrest or detention

   (a) to be informed promptly of the reasons therefor;

   (b) to retain and instruct counsel without delay and to be informed of that right; and

(c) to have the validity of the detention determined by way of *habeas corpus* and to be released if the detention is not lawful.

Proceedings in criminal and penal matters

11. Any person charged with an offence has the right

(a) to be informed without unreasonable delay of the specific offence;

(b) to be tried within a reasonable time;

(c) not to be compelled to be a witness in proceedings against that person in respect of the offence;

(d) to be presumed innocent until proven guilty according to law in a fair and public hearing by an independent and impartial tribunal;

(e) not to be denied reasonable bail without just cause;

(f) except in the case of an offence under military law tried before a military tribunal, to the benefit of trial by jury where the maximum punishment for the offence is imprisonment for five years or a more severe punishment;

(g) not to be found guilty on account of any act or omission unless, at the time of the act or omission, it constituted an offence under Canadian or international law or was criminal according to the general principles of law recognized by the community of nations;

(h) if finally acquitted of the offence, not to be tried for it again and, if finally found guilty and punished for the offence, not to be tried or punished for it again; and

(i) if found guilty of the offence and if the punishment for the offence has been varied between the time of commission and the time of sentencing, to the benefit of the lesser punishment.

Treatment or punishment

12. Everyone has the right not to be subjected to any cruel and unusual treatment or punishment.

Self-crimination

13. A witness who testifies in any proceedings has the right not to have any incriminating evidence so given used to incriminate that witness in any other proceedings, except in a prosecution for perjury or for the giving of contradictory evidence.

Interpreter

14. A party or witness in any proceedings who does not understand or speak the language in which the proceedings are conducted or who is deaf has the right to the assistance of an interpreter.

Equality Rights

Equality before and under law and equal protection and benefit of law

15. (1) Every individual is equal before and under the law and has the right to the equal protection and equal benefit of the law without discrimination and, in particular, without discrimination based on race, national or ethnic origin, colour, religion, sex, age or mental or physical disability.

Affirmative action programs

(2) Subsection (1) does not preclude any law, program or activity that has as its object the amelioration of conditions of disadvantaged individuals or groups including those that are disadvantaged because of race, national or ethnic origin, colour, religion, sex, age or mental or physical disability.

Official Languages of Canada

Official languages of Canada

16. (1) English and French are the official languages of Canada and have equality of status and equal rights and privileges as to their use in all institutions of the Parliament and government of Canada.

Official languages of New Brunswick

(2) English and French are the official languages of New Brunswick and have equality of status and equal rights and privileges as to their use in all institutions of the legislature and government of New Brunswick.

Advancement of status and use

(3) Nothing in this Charter limits the authority of Parliament or a legislature to advance the equality of status or use of English and French.

English and French linguistic communities in New Brunswick

16.1 (1) The English linguistic community and the French linguistic community in New Brunswick have equality of status and equal rights and privileges, including the right to distinct educational institutions and such distinct cultural institutions as are necessary for the preservation and promotion of those communities.

Role of the legislature and government of New Brunswick

(2) The role of the legislature and government of New Brunswick to preserve and promote the status, rights and privileges referred to in subsection (1) is affirmed.

Proceedings of Parliament

17. (1) Everyone has the right to use English or French in any debates and other proceedings of Parliament.

Proceedings of New Brunswick legislature

(2) Everyone has the right to use English or French in any debates and other proceedings of the legislature of New Brunswick.

Parliamentary statutes and records

18. (1) The statutes, records and journals of Parliament shall be printed and published in English and French and both language versions are equally authoritative.

New Brunswick statutes and records

(2) The statutes, records and journals of the legislature of New Brunswick shall be printed and published in English and French and both language versions are equally authoritative.

Proceedings in courts established by Parliament

19. (1) Either English or French may be used by any person in, or in any pleading in or process issuing from, any court established by Parliament.

Proceedings in New Brunswick courts

(2) Either English or French may be used by any person in, or in any pleading in or process issuing from, any court of New Brunswick.

Communications by public with federal institutions

20. (1) Any member of the public in Canada has the right to communicate with, and to receive available services from, any head or central office of an institution of the Parliament or government of Canada in English or French, and has the same right with respect to any other office of any such institution where

(a) there is a significant demand for communications with and services from that office in such language; or

(b) due to the nature of the office, it is reasonable that communications with and services from that office be available in both English and French.

Communications by public with New Brunswick institutions

(2) Any member of the public in New Brunswick has the right to communicate with, and to receive available services from, any office of an institution of the legislature or government of New Brunswick in English or French.

Continuation of existing constitutional provisions

21. Nothing in sections 16 to 20 abrogates or derogates from any right, privilege or obligation with respect to the English and French languages, or either of them, that exists or is continued by virtue of any other provision of the Constitution of Canada.

22. Nothing in sections 16 to 20 abrogates or derogates from any legal or customary right or privilege acquired or enjoyed either before or after the coming into force of this Charter with respect to any language that is not English or French.

Rights and privileges preserved

Minority Language Educational Rights

23. (1) Citizens of Canada

(a) whose first language learned and still understood is that of the English or French linguistic minority population of the province in which they reside, or

(b) who have received their primary school instruction in Canada in English or French and reside in a province where the language in which they received that instruction is the language of the English or French linguistic minority population of the province,

have the right to have their children receive primary and secondary school instruction in that language in that province.

Language of instruction

(2) Citizens of Canada of whom any child has received or is receiving primary or secondary school instruction in English or French in Canada, have the right to have all their children receive primary and secondary school instruction in the same language.

Continuity of language instruction

(3) The right of citizens of Canada under subsections (1) and (2) to have their children receive primary and secondary school instruction in the language of the English or French linguistic minority population of a province

(a) applies wherever in the province the number of children of citizens who have such a right is sufficient to warrant the provision to them out of public funds of minority language instruction; and

(b) includes, where the number of those children so warrants, the right to have them receive that instruction in minority language educational facilities provided out of public funds.

Application where numbers warrant

Enforcement

24. (1) Anyone whose rights or freedoms, as guaranteed by this Charter, have been

Enforcement of guaranteed rights and freedoms

infringed or denied may apply to a court of competent jurisdiction to obtain such remedy as the court considers appropriate and just in the circumstances.

Exclusion of evidence bringing administration of justice into disrepute

(2) Where, in proceedings under subsection (1), a court concludes that evidence was obtained in a manner that infringed or denied any rights or freedoms guaranteed by this Charter, the evidence shall be excluded if it is established that, having regard to all the circumstances, the admission of it in the proceedings would bring the administration of justice into disrepute.

General

Aboriginal rights and freedoms not affected by Charter

25. The guarantee in this Charter of certain rights and freedoms shall not be construed so as to abrogate or derogate from any aboriginal, treaty or other rights or freedoms that pertain to the aboriginal peoples of Canada including

(a) any rights or freedoms that have been recognized by the Royal Proclamation of October 7, 1763; and

(b) any rights or freedoms that now exist by way of land claims agreements or may be so acquired.

Other rights and freedoms not affected by Charter

26. The guarantee in this Charter of certain rights and freedoms shall not be construed as denying the existence of any other rights or freedoms that exist in Canada.

Multicultural heritage

27. This Charter shall be interpreted in a manner consistent with the preservation and enhancement of the multicultural heritage of Canadians.

Rights guaranteed equally to both sexes

28. Notwithstanding anything in this Charter, the rights and freedoms referred to in it are guaranteed equally to male and female persons.

Rights respecting certain schools preserved

29. Nothing in this Charter abrogates or derogates from any rights or privileges guaranteed by or under the Constitution of Canada in respect of denominational, separate or dissentient schools.

Application to territories and territorial authorities

30. A reference in this Charter to a province or to the legislative assembly or legislature of a province shall be deemed to include a reference to the Yukon Territory and the Northwest Territories, or to the appropriate legislative authority thereof, as the case may be.

Legislative powers not extended

31. Nothing in this Charter extends the legislative powers of any body or authority.

Application of Charter

Application of Charter

32. (1) This Charter applies

(a) to the Parliament and government of Canada in respect of all matters within the authority of Parliament including all matters relating to the Yukon Territory and Northwest Territories; and

(b) to the legislature and government of each province in respect of all matters within the authority of the legislature of each province.

Exception

(2) Notwithstanding subsection (1), section 15 shall not have effect until three years after this section comes into force.

Exception where express declaration

33. (1) Parliament or the legislature of a province may expressly declare in an Act of Parliament or of the legislature, as the case may be, that the Act or a provision thereof shall operate notwithstanding a provision included in section 2 or sections 7 to 15 of this Charter.

Operation of exception

(2) An Act or a provision of an Act in respect of which a declaration made under this section is in effect shall have such operation as it would have but for the provision of this Charter referred to in the declaration.

Five year limitation

(3) A declaration made under subsection (1) shall cease to have effect five years after it comes into force or on such earlier date as may be specified in the declaration.

Re-enactment

(4) Parliament or the legislature of a province may re-enact a declaration made under subsection (1).

Five year limitation

(5) Subsection (3) applies in respect of a re-enactment made under subsection (4).

Citation

Citation

34. This Part may be cited as the *Canadian Charter of Rights and Freedoms*.

Universal Declaration of Human Rights

Adopted and proclaimed by General Assembly Resolution 217 A (III) of 10 December 1948

Preamble

Whereas recognition of the inherent dignity and of the equal and inalienable rights of all members of the human family is the foundation of freedom, justice and peace in the world,

Whereas disregard and contempt for human rights have resulted in barbarous acts which have outraged the conscience of mankind, and the advent of a world in which human beings shall enjoy freedom of speech and belief and freedom from fear and want has been proclaimed as the highest aspiration of the common people,

Whereas it is essential, if man is not to be compelled to have recourse, as a last resort, to rebellion against tyranny and oppression, that human rights should be protected by the rule of law,

Whereas it is essential to promote the development of friendly relations between nations,

Whereas the peoples of the United Nations have in the Charter reaffirmed their faith in fundamental human rights, in the dignity and worth of the human person and in the equal rights of men and women and have determined to promote social progress and better standards of life in larger freedom,

Whereas Member States have pledged themselves to achieve, in cooperation with the United Nations, the promotion of universal respect for and observance of human rights and fundamental freedoms,

Whereas a common understanding of these rights and freedoms is of the greatest importance for the full realization of this pledge,

Now, therefore,

The General Assembly,

Proclaims this Universal Declaration of Human Rights as a common standard of achievement for all peoples and all nations, to the end that every individual and every organ of society, keeping this Declaration constantly in mind, shall strive by teaching and education to promote respect for these rights and freedoms and by progressive measures, national and international, to secure their universal and effective recognition and observance, both among the peoples of Member States themselves and among the peoples of territories under their jurisdiction.

Article 1

All human beings are born free and equal in dignity and rights. They are endowed with reason and conscience and should act towards one another in a spirit of brotherhood.

Article 2

Everyone is entitled to all the rights and freedoms set forth in this Declaration, without distinction of any kind, such as race, colour, sex, language, religion, political or other opinion, national or social origin, property, birth or other status.

Furthermore, no distinction shall be made on the basis of the political, jurisdictional or international status of the country or territory to which a person belongs, whether it be independent, trust, non-self-governing or under any other limitation of sovereignty.

Article 3

Everyone has the right to life, liberty and security of person.

Article 4

No one shall be held in slavery or servitude; slavery and the slave trade shall be prohibited in all their forms.

Article 5

No one shall be subjected to torture or to cruel, inhuman or degrading treatment or punishment.

Article 6

Everyone has the right to recognition everywhere as a person before the law.

Article 7

All are equal before the law and are entitled without any discrimination to equal protection of the law. All are entitled to equal protection against any discrimination in violation of this Declaration and against any incitement to such discrimination.

Article 8

Everyone has the right to an effective remedy by the competent national tribunals for acts violating the fundamental rights granted him by the constitution or by law.

Article 9

No one shall be subjected to arbitrary arrest, detention or exile.

Article 10

Everyone is entitled in full equality to a fair and public hearing by an independent and impartial tribunal, in the determination of his rights and obligations and of any criminal charge against him.

Article 11

1. Everyone charged with a penal offence has the right to be presumed innocent until proved guilty according to law in a public trial at which he has had all the guarantees necessary for his defence.
2. No one shall be held guilty of any penal offence on account of any act or omission which did not constitute a penal offence, under national or international law, at the time when it was committed. Nor shall a heavier penalty be imposed than the one that was applicable at the time the penal offence was committed.

Article 12

No one shall be subjected to arbitrary interference with his privacy, family, home or correspondence, nor to attacks upon his honour and reputation. Everyone has the right to the protection of the law against such interference or attacks.

Article 13

1. Everyone has the right to freedom of movement and residence within the borders of each State.
2. Everyone has the right to leave any country, including his own, and to return to his country.

Article 14

1. Everyone has the right to seek and to enjoy in other countries asylum from persecution.
2. This right may not be invoked in the case of prosecutions genuinely arising from non-political crimes or from acts contrary to the purposes and principles of the United Nations.

Article 15

1. Everyone has the right to a nationality.
2. No one shall be arbitrarily deprived of his nationality nor denied the right to change his nationality.

Article 16

1. Men and women of full age, without any limitation due to race, nationality or religion, have the right to marry and to found a family. They are entitled to equal rights as to marriage, during marriage and at its dissolution.
2. Marriage shall be entered into only with the free and full consent of the intending spouses.
3. The family is the natural and fundamental group unit of society and is entitled to protection by society and the State.

Article 17

1. Everyone has the right to own property alone as well as in association with others.
2. No one shall be arbitrarily deprived of his property.

Article 18

Everyone has the right to freedom of thought, conscience and religion; this right includes freedom to change his religion or belief, and freedom, either alone or in community with others and in public or private, to manifest his religion or belief in teaching, practice, worship and observance.

Article 19

Everyone has the right to freedom of opinion and expression; this right includes freedom to hold opinions without interference and to seek, receive and impart information and ideas through any media and regardless of frontiers.

Article 20

1. Everyone has the right to freedom of peaceful assembly and association.
2. No one may be compelled to belong to an association.

Article 21

1. Everyone has the right to take part in the government of his country, directly or through freely chosen representatives.
2. Everyone has the right to equal access to public service in his country.
3. The will of the people shall be the basis of the authority of government; this will shall be expressed in periodic and genuine elections which shall be by universal and equal suffrage and shall be held by secret vote or by equivalent free voting procedures.

Article 22

Everyone, as a member of society, has the right to social security and is entitled to realization, through national effort and international co-operation and in accordance with the organization and resources of each State, of the economic, social and cultural rights indispensable for his dignity and the free development of his personality.

Article 23

1. Everyone has the right to work, to free choice of employment, to just and favourable conditions of work and to protection against unemployment.
2. Everyone, without any discrimination, has the right to equal pay for equal work.
3. Everyone who works has the right to just and favourable remuneration ensuring for himself and his family an existence worthy of human dignity, and supplemented, if necessary, by other means of social protection.
4. Everyone has the right to form and to join trade unions for the protection of his interests.

Article 24

Everyone has the right to rest and leisure, including reasonable limitation of working hours and periodic holidays with pay.

Article 25

1. Everyone has the right to a standard of living adequate for the health and well-being of himself and of his family, including food, clothing, housing and medical care and necessary social services, and the right to security in the event of unemployment, sickness, disability, widowhood, old age or other lack of livelihood in circumstances beyond his control.
2. Motherhood and childhood are entitled to special care and assistance. All children, whether born in or out of wedlock, shall enjoy the same social protection.

Article 26

1. Everyone has the right to education. Education shall be free, at least in the elementary and fundamental stages. Elementary education shall be compulsory. Technical and professional education shall be made generally available and higher education shall be equally accessible to all on the basis of merit.
2. Education shall be directed to the full development of the human personality and to the strengthening of respect for human rights and fundamental freedoms. It shall promote understanding, tolerance and friendship among all nations, racial or religious groups, and shall further the activities of the United Nations for the maintenance of peace.
3. Parents have a prior right to choose the kind of education that shall be given to their children.

Article 27

1. Everyone has the right freely to participate in the cultural life of the community, to enjoy the arts and to share in scientific advancement and its benefits.
2. Everyone has the right to the protection of the moral and material interests resulting from any scientific, literary or artistic production of which he is the author.

Article 28

Everyone is entitled to a social and international order in which the rights and freedoms set forth in this Declaration can be fully realized.

Article 29

1. Everyone has duties to the community in which alone the free and full development of his personality is possible.
2. In the exercise of his rights and freedoms, everyone shall be subject only to such limitations as are determined by law solely for the purpose of securing due recognition and respect for the rights and freedoms of others and of meeting the just requirements of morality, public order and the general welfare in a democratic society.
3. These rights and freedoms may in no case be exercised contrary to the purposes and principles of the United Nations.

Article 30

Nothing in this Declaration may be interpreted as implying for any State, group or person any right to engage in any activity or to perform any act aimed at the destruction of any of the rights and freedoms set forth herein.

Glossary

A

Aboriginal title: a specific Aboriginal right referring to claims for land ownership

absolute discharge: a sentencing option used by a judge whereby no conviction is recorded and no conditions are attached

absolute liability: the concept that there is no defence, fault is not an issue, and the accused is convicted based on the guilty act

abstract: a summary of the essential components of a larger case

accommodation: the adaptation of an existing requirement or condition by an employer to enable an employee to carry out the essential aspects of a job (e.g., making a work environment accessible for people with disabilities)

acquitted: released after being declared not guilty

acts: formal agreements between two or more sovereign states; *see also* **conventions**, **covenants**, **protocols**, and **treaties**

actus reus: a Latin term meaning "guilty act" that refers to the physical aspects of a crime

ad hoc tribunals: courts set up to deal with individual circumstances on an as-needed basis (e.g., the Nuremberg tribunal at the end of World War II)

adjudication: a judicial decision; the act or process of arriving at a decision after considering the facts

administrative law: the law that governs the governmental agencies empowered by the legislature to make decisions on certain matters

adversarial trial system: the trial system, used in Canada, that seeks the truth by having two opposing parties, represented by lawyers, argue a case in front of an impartial judge who weighs the evidence presented

adverse-effect discrimination: a requirement or standard that may outwardly appear neutral but is, in fact, discriminatory in effect toward an individual or group (e.g., a height requirement for police officers)

adverse possession: a method of acquiring title to property or land if an occupant remains on the land for a lengthy period of time with the knowledge of the owner but without his or her permission

affirmative-action programs: plans designed to remedy disadvantages faced by four designated groups—women, Aboriginal peoples, visible minorities, and people with disabilities

agency shop: a workplace in which a new employee is not required to join the union but still must pay union dues; also called the "Rand formula" (introduced by Judge Rand)

aggravating factors: elements that increase an offender's responsibility for his or her actions and are considered by the judge in imposing a more severe sentence (e.g., evidence that the offender was motivated by ethnic prejudice)

air embargo: the cancellation of all international flights into or out of a country

ambassadors: heads of embassies in foreign countries, who are either career civil servants or political appointees

anomie theory: a sociological hypothesis arguing that criminal behaviour is more likely to thrive in an anonymous urban setting than in a more traditional rural setting

appeal allowed: overturning of a lower court's decision by a higher court and substitution with its own decision

appeal dismissed: acceptance by a higher court of the previous court's decision

appellant: the person launching an appeal to a higher court in a legal action

arbitrary: without reason or judgment

arbitration: a form of dispute resolution in which a neutral third party hears a dispute between two parties and then makes a decision, which both parties have agreed to follow

arms embargo: a particular type of sanction that prohibits the supply of arms or other military equipment to designated countries

assumption of sovereignty: for the purpose of defining Aboriginal rights, the requirement for proof of occupation of the land prior to the time of European contact and control

atheist: a person who does not believe in the existence of God or gods

attachés: technical experts on a diplomatic staff (e.g., military attaché)

authority: the legal power to command, act, implement, and enforce laws

automatism: the state in which a person has no conscious control over his or her actions; a defence used so that people in this state cannot be found criminally responsible

B

bail: (1) the judicial release of an accused pending trial; (2) the sum of money deposited with the courts to ensure that an accused will appear for trial

bail hearing: a court hearing to determine whether an accused should be released into the public until trial

balance of probabilities: the standard of proof required in a civil action showing that it is more likely than not that something occurred

bargain in good faith: to negotiate a collective agreement in an honest and open fashion

battered woman syndrome: a condition of fearfulness and hopelessness experienced by women who have been abused over a long period; used recently as a defence for abused women who have killed their abusers

bias: a preconceived opinion or state of mind about an issue often without any factual basis

bigamy: the criminal offence of wilfully and knowingly marrying a second person while still legally married to the first person

bilateral: regarding a treaty in international law, agreed to by two nations

bill: a document submitted to Parliament or a provincial legislature for consideration, which must pass by a majority vote to become law in the form of a statute

binding arbitration: a process of dispute resolution in which both sides must find the arbitrator acceptable and the decision of the arbitrator is binding

biological trait theory: the idea that individuals can be predisposed to criminal activity due to genetic factors

bona fide occupational requirement: a provision that is deemed necessary in order to perform a job safely and efficiently; in a discrimination complaint, it can be used to justify a particular job requirement that may otherwise be perceived as discriminatory

brief: a document containing a brief statement of the facts of the case, the issues, and the arguments

burden of proof: the responsibility to prove one's case

C

cabinet: the group of individuals who make the policy decisions and oversee the various departments of government; federally comprised of the prime minister and the cabinet ministers, provincially consists of the premier and the cabinet ministers

case: the written record of a legal dispute that has proceeded through the courts

case citation: the name of a case including the names of the parties involved, the place in which the case was heard, and the year of the trial

case law: a collection of judgments by judges on various cases

ceasefires: agreements whereby both sides in an armed conflict agree to no longer use arms or any other means of violence

certification: the process by which a union becomes the sole bargaining agent for a group of employees; usually requires a majority vote and is overseen by a labour board

challenge for cause: an objection made by a Crown or defence lawyer to remove a prospective juror from consideration because of his or her bias or knowledge about the facts of a case

challenged: made a formal objection to a prospective juror

charge the jury: to instruct the jury outlining the law that must be considered and applied to the facts in the case

circumstantial evidence: indirect evidence that allows an inference to be made about the guilt of the accused (e.g., something belonging to an accused at the crime scene)

civil actions: legal steps taken beginning when a plaintiff files a lawsuit against a defendant and ending when the court rules in favour of either the plaintiff or the defendant

civil law: (1) the branch of law that governs the relations between individuals, as opposed to criminal law, which governs relations between individuals and the state; (2) a system of law based on codified or statute law

civil liberties: actions or rights exercised without government interference (e.g., freedom of expression, freedom of religion)

civil rights movement: a body of people who organize to protest what they perceive as a violation of rights (e.g., in the United States during the 1960s, the civil rights movement protested the treatment of Black citizens)

civil service: the people hired to perform the various day-to-day functions of government and provide services to the public

closed shop: a type of workplace in which all new employees must already be members of a union

coalition: a temporary political alliance

codify: to collect or to arrange existing laws and practices in one document

Cold War: the period between 1945 and 1990 during which tension and military rivalry characterized the relationship between the United States and the Soviet Union

collective agreement: a contract that sets out the terms and conditions of employment between employees and employer

collective bargaining: the formal process of negotiating conditions of employment between organized employees and their employer; the contract produced through this process is a collective agreement

collective security: a strategy whereby several nations are committed to defending one another against attacks (e.g., NATO is an organization that provides collective security)

common law: (1) a system of legal principles based on custom and past legal decisions, also called "judge-made law" or "case law"; (2) the law that came to Canada from Britain; (3) the law that is common to all

communal court: an early English court system administered by the local inhabitants of a small community

community standards test: a test of tolerance used in law to determine whether something is obscene—not for oneself but for others in general

compensation package: a negotiated offer of payment for work that may include wages, benefits, and other items of value

conciliation: a voluntary method of settling disputes whereby a neutral third party assists the parties involved to identify and discuss the issues, and then to resolve the conflict

concurring: agreeing with the majority of the court

conditional discharge: a sentencing option used by a judge whereby no conviction is entered but conditions are attached to a probation order

conditional sentencing: a sentencing option whereby the offender serves the sentence in the community subject to certain conditions; only imposed for sentence terms under two years and when the public would not be put in danger

consecutive: used to describe a sentence that allows for one sentence term to follow another; may be imposed in circumstances where the offender has been charged and convicted of multiple offences

consensus theorists: people who assume there is a universal or communal definition of right and wrong and that our criminal law reflects that consensus

constitution: the legal framework outlining the operation of the government, its authority, the limitations of that authority, and (in a federal state) the division of powers between the federal and provincial/state governments

constitutional law: the law that concerns the principles, rules, regulations, and laws that establish and define the political, governmental, and legal structure of the state

constructive dismissal: a major change of workplace conditions that forces an employee to resign

consumer law: the law that regulates the purchase and safety of products and services

contract law: the branch of law that determines whether a promise to exchange or sell goods or services shall be legally binding

conventions: (1) rules of behaviour that are historically accepted, though not always legally enforced, and that often influence the content of treaties between nations; (2) formal agreements between two or more nations; *see also* **acts**, **covenants**, **protocols**, and **treaties**

corporal punishment defence: a defence permitting a parent, or one who acts in place of a parent, to physically discipline a child as long as the discipline is reasonable and falls within the Supreme Court's guidelines

corporate law: the law that governs the rules and regulations associated with public and private corporations

Court of Common Pleas: one of the court systems set up by the king of England to adjudicate civil law

Court of King's Bench: the grandest court in the royal court system made up of nobles appointed by the king to adjudicate criminal cases

Courts of Appeal: the highest courts in the provinces and territories, which have jurisdiction to hear cases from all lower courts; they can dismiss, uphold, or change a lower ruling, or order a new trial for a case

courts of first appearance: the courts in which an action is first brought against an individual and consideration for bail is reviewed

covenants: formal agreements between two or more sovereign states; *see also* **acts**, **conventions**, **protocols**, **treaties**

crime against humanity: an act of violence (e.g., torture, genocide) that is committed as part of a full-scale or systematic attack on a civil population, the punishment of which has international implications

criminal harassment: the persistent insulting, taunting, or challenging of a person, which is an offence under the *Criminal Code*; *see also* **stalking**

criminal law: the law that regulates conduct that may be harmful to another individual or society as a whole (i.e., an offence contrary to the *Criminal Code* and other federal statutes)

criminology: the study of the nature, causes, and means of dealing with crime

critical habitat: the specific area where a species lives, breeds, and cares for its young; the minimum area required to maintain a healthy population of a species

critical legal studies (CLS): a theory that argues that law is neither neutral nor value-free but is about value choices; the law exists to support the interests of the elite and can be a powerful instrument for injustice

cross-examination style debating: a type of debate format that follows the principles of a courtroom, whereby each person has a chance to speak and is subject to examination from his or her opponent

Crown attorney: the lawyer who, on behalf of the queen (state), files charges against and prosecutes someone who has allegedly committed a crime

culpability: that which renders an action criminal or deserving of moral blame or punishment

cultural imperialism: the imposing of one society's values, behaviours, institutions, and identity onto another society

custodial sentence: a penalty that requires a period of imprisonment for the offender

customs: unwritten laws that may become established by long practice

D

damages: money awarded by the court as compensation for loss or injury; such compensation may be given for actual losses and/or future losses

dangerous offender: a *Criminal Code* classification given to someone who has committed an offence for which there was serious personal injury and who continues to pose a threat to society

decertification: a process whereby employees who become dissatisfied with their union can take action to dissolve the union if, in a free vote, the majority of members agree

defamation: the act of making false statements that damage a person's reputation; "slander" is the oral form of defamation, "libel" is the written form

defame: to attack a person's reputation by making a false or malicious statement; to defame someone orally is called "slander," to defame someone in written form is called "libel"

defaults: does not live up to payment obligations under a court order

defendant: (1) in a civil proceeding, the party being sued; (2) in a criminal proceeding, the accused

deliberates: discusses and weighs the evidence in order to determine a verdict

democracy: a form of government in which citizens participate in the making of public decisions through a system of elected representation

denunciation: an objective of sentencing that allows a judge to consider society's revulsion for a particular crime or the character or actions of a particular accused

deterrence theory: the sociological hypothesis that if the risks outweigh the benefits and punishment is almost certain, most rational people will not knowingly break the law

developing countries: countries in Asia, Africa, and Latin America that are striving to achieve the social, economic, and technical standards common in the "industrialized world," meaning Europe, Australia, Japan, and North America

diplomacy: the peaceful negotiation between or among nations

diplomatic corps: government employees whose function is to assist in carrying out their country's policies in foreign countries

diplomatic immunity: the right of diplomats and their families while posted in foreign countries to be shielded from criminal prosecution and civil litigation

diplomats: officials involved in international activities or negotiations

direct discrimination: a practice or behaviour that is overt and clearly discriminatory (e.g., refusal to rent an apartment to someone on the basis of ethnicity)

direct evidence: witness testimony that is used to verify a fact (e.g., a statement heard by the witness, what the witness actually saw)

direct examination: the questioning by a lawyer of his or her own witness; also called an "examination in chief"

discharge: a sentencing option used by a judge whereby no conviction is entered and which may be absolute or conditional

disclosure: a requirement that all relevant information be made available (e.g., the Crown must provide the defence with all case-related information)

discussion style debating: a less formal type of debate that uses a discussion-type format and is regulated by a moderator

disenfranchisement: the depriving of a citizen of his or her right to vote

dissent: the decision(s) of the judge(s) who did not agree with the majority opinion

distributive justice: the idea that the state should ensure a fair distribution of advantages and burdens to subjects within the nation

divine law: moral principles that are ascribed to God and cannot be changed or overruled

divine right of kings: a theory that a sovereign or king ruled because he had the divine, or God-given, right to do so

doctrine of transferred intent: a principle of law whereby an illegal, unintended act resulting from an intent to commit a crime is also an offence (e.g., if a person intends to shoot one person but misses and kills another)

domestic law: the law that is enforceable within the defined territory or boundaries of a particular nation or state

double-criminality rule: a rule governing the process of extradition stating that an offence must be a crime in both nations before a fugitive is extradited from one nation to another

due diligence: the defence that a defendant acted as any reasonable person would under the circumstances

due process: the use of established rules and principles to properly carry out the administration of justice

duress: a defence arguing that an accused was forced to commit a criminal act under threat of personal injury or death

duty of care: in a civil action for negligence, a requirement of proof that the defendant owes the plaintiff a responsibility to avoid actions that might cause harm

E

ecological school: a sociological theory arguing that poor or transient communities are more likely to condone criminal activity than more affluent neighbourhoods

economic sanctions: economic penalties that can be imposed on a nation for a breach of international law

ecotourism: a type of travel to relatively undisturbed natural areas in order to understand and appreciate their natural history and culture without altering the environment

enemy aliens: citizens of a country at war with the country in which they are currently residing or travelling

entrapment: a defence arguing that an accused was induced by a government agent (e.g., police officer) into committing a crime he or she would not otherwise have committed

entrench: to codify rights so that they can be changed only by constitutional amendment, safeguarding them from political interference

environmental assessment: a study of the impact and potential consequences of a proposed activity on the environment and of possible alternative courses of action

equality: the concept of treating everyone in the same manner with the same rights, privileges, and duties

equity: the concept of administering justice according to fairness, that is, treating like cases alike and different cases differently

estate law: the law dealing with the degree, nature, and extent of an interest in ownership of land or property and how that property is to be divided after death; also called "succession law"

ethnic cleansing: the mass expulsion or extermination of people from opposing ethnic or religious groups within a certain area

ethnocentrism: the belief that one's own culture is best and most natural; a tendency of people to interpret or evaluate other cultures by referring to their own

European Union (EU): an association of over a dozen European countries with common economic and political interests

exigent circumstances: situations that allow for a search and/or seizure without a warrant if there is a danger that the evidence will be lost, removed, or destroyed

expulsion: (*v.* to expel) the decision to send a diplomat home

external sovereignty: the right or power of independent states to either enter or not enter into relationships with other states (e.g., to forge a trade agreement)

extinguished: cancelled

extradition: the legal surrender or delivery of a fugitive from one state, country, or government to the jurisdiction of another to face trial

F

family law: the law that governs the rights and obligations of family members toward one another relating to marriage, support, custody of children, separation, and divorce

federal courts: special courts, created by statute, that hear cases within specific areas of law, often because of the unique expertise required by the judges hearing the cases

feminist jurisprudence: a theory of law arguing that the legal system upholds and reinforces political, economic, and social inequality for women

fiduciary duty: an obligation that arises by nature of a confidence or trust relationship (e.g., between a lawyer and a client)

final-offer-selection: a process of arbitration in which both sides in a labour dispute present their bottom line to an arbitrator, who must then choose only one

foreign nationals: under the *Immigration and Refugee Protection Act*, people who are not Canadian citizens and/or permanent residents of Canada

foreseeable: reasonably anticipated

G

General Agreement on Tariffs and Trade (**GATT**): a multinational treaty to facilitate world trade, which came into effect in 1948 in Geneva, Switzerland

general deterrence: an objective of sentencing that aims to deter or discourage other members of society from committing the same crime

general intent: the goal of committing an illegal act, with no illegal purpose beyond that act

***Geneva Conventions*:** a series of four international agreements—signed in Geneva, Switzerland—that govern the humane treatment of civilians and soldiers during war

genocide: the planned killing of any group identifiable by colour, religion, nationality, or ethnic origin

globalization: (1) an integrated system of production, marketing, finance, and management, including free trade and the increased interdependence of national economies around the world; (2) an increase in worldwide social interconnectedness in which local happenings are shaped by events occurring far away

grounds for appeal: reasons for asking a higher court to review the decision from a lower court, which may include claims of an error of law or fact or both

H

habeas corpus: a court document, called a "writ," used to determine whether an accused can be legally detained; a *Charter* right that protects against unlawful arrest and detention

head tax: a tax paid by Chinese immigrants on admission to Canada between 1895 and 1923

hearsay evidence: testimony that comes from a third party and is not within the knowledge or personal experience of the witness (Opposing counsel may object to this.)

humanity: the concept of kindness and respect toward all people

hybrid offences: violations for which the prosecution has a choice to proceed by way of indictment or summary conviction offence; also called a "dual procedure offence"

I

impartial (impartiality): unbiased or unprejudiced

incriminating: tending to establish or infer guilt of the accused

indeterminate sentence: a penalty that has no fixed length but is subject to periodic review

indictable offences: more serious criminal violations (e.g., murder, arson, aggravated assault) as distinguished from summary conviction offences

indictments: criminal charges

indigenous peoples: the original inhabitants of the land and their descendants

injunction: a remedy granted by the court directing a party to continue or refrain from an action

inquisitorial trial system: a trial system, used in many parts of Europe, that seeks the truth through the questioning of witnesses, in which judges play a much greater role in the selection and questioning of witnesses than they do in the adversarial system

intellectual property: legally protected ownership of ideas and works of art including literature, through means of trademarks, patents, and copyright

intent: the state of mind in which a person seeks to accomplish an act or chooses not to accomplish an act

intermittent: serving a term on weekends or evenings, which is sometimes allowed in short-term sentences

internal sovereignty: the supreme power originally held by a ruler over subjects living within his or her state; includes the right to make laws

international humanitarian law: the law between countries that focuses on saving both military and non-military individuals

international law: the customs, rules, and agreements recognized as binding on sovereign (independent) states to ensure orderly conduct within the international community

interstate: between and among independent states

intoxication: being rendered incapable of forming criminal intent by alcohol or drugs; this condition may be used to disprove the existence of *mens rea* necessary for some crimes or as a mitigating factor in sentencing

intrastate: within states

intra vires: a Latin term meaning "within the powers" referring to a law that is within the jurisdiction of the government or the courts

J

judicial reasoning: a process used by judges in making decisions in which abstract legal concepts are applied to one another to form rules and systems

jurisdiction: the parameters within which power and authority may be exercised (e.g., a judge in small claims court would have no jurisdictional authority to render a decision in a criminal case)

jurisprudence: the science of law, sometimes referred to as the "philosophy of law"; the study of the structure of the legal system, one of whose functions is to determine how legal rules apply to new or doubtful cases

jury of peers: in criminal law, a group of 12 ordinary, reasonable people who decide on the guilt or innocence of the accused based on the evidence presented

jury panel: the group of individuals from which a jury is chosen; also known as a "jury array"

justice: a legal concept that is characterized by the fair distribution of advantages and burdens; in law, the concept of treating like cases alike and different cases differently

K

***Kyoto Protocol*:** an agreement that commits many industrialized nations to reducing their greenhouse gas emissions between 2008 and 2012 to a level 5.2 percent below 1990 levels

L

law: the set of rules, impartially applied, for regulating human behaviour and settling disputes

leading questions: questions that suggest the answer, which may not be asked on direct examination of a witness but may be allowed on cross-examination

leave to appeal denied: the application to hear the case at a higher level of court has been rejected

leave to appeal granted: permission has been given to hear the case at a higher level of court

legalese: the type of professional language used by lawyers that sometimes clouds the issues for the ordinary person

legal formalism: a theory arguing that law consists of a body of rules and nothing more, and that the role of a judge is to apply these rules

legal paternalism: the idea that the government, functioning as a father figure, takes responsibility for the welfare of citizens by enacting laws that prohibit people from harming themselves

legal realism: a theory that rejects the principles of legal formalism and argues that the law, itself, is often vague, uncertain, and frequently influenced by the views of judges

legislative supremacy: the principle that the ultimate authority to make and unmake laws in Canada is the federal or provincial parliament under whose jurisdiction the laws fall

legitimacy: (1) that which is lawful or recognized in law; (2) the right to inherit property or title

litigation: a legal action including all the proceedings (e.g., a lawsuit)

lobby group: a body of like-minded individuals who attempt to persuade legislators to vote a certain way or to change a particular law

lobbying: persuading legislators to vote a certain way or to change a particular law

lockout: a negotiating strategy used by management in a labour dispute in which the employer locks the premises so that the employees cannot enter

M

manorial tribunal: an early English court system used during the feudal period in which the lord of the manor would adjudicate criminal and civil cases

material facts: facts that are relevant to or have a bearing on the issues in question

mediation: a dispute resolution process whereby a neutral third party, called a "mediator," facilitates the settlement of an argument between two or more parties

***mens rea*:** the Latin word meaning "guilty mind" that refers to the mental element of a crime, which may be shown by intent, knowledge, recklessness, or wilful blindness

mental disorder defence: a defence that, in 1992, replaced the insanity defence, with the verdict changing from "not guilty by reason of insanity" to "not criminally responsible by reason of mental disorder"

mercantilism: the economic theory, popular in Europe from the sixteenth to eighteenth centuries, that trade generates wealth, is stimulated by the acquisition of gold, and should be encouraged by nations through promotion of exports and limiting of imports

meritocracy: the idea that individuals in a society should be rewarded based on their own merit and performance of civic duty rather than on family or other connections

minimal impairment: a part of the proportionality test to determine whether a law interferes with rights and freedoms as little as possible

mistake of fact: a legal defence that permits an accused to argue he or she may have misinterpreted the law and did not have the requisite *mens rea* necessary for the alleged offence

mistake of law: a defence sometimes used if an accused has made every effort to conform to the law and has been provided with professional, but incorrect, advice

mitigating factors: factors that decrease the offender's responsibility for his or her actions and are considered by the judge in imposing a less severe sentence (e.g., evidence that it was a first-time offence for the accused)

M'Naghten's rules: the test applied to the defence of insanity whereby an accused is not held criminally responsible if, at the time of committing the act, there was a disease of the mind that made him or her incapable of knowing the nature and quality of the act or that the act was wrong

monogamy: being married to only one person

morality: a concept that pertains to character, conduct, and the general principles of right conduct

moratorium: a suspension or deferment of an action

motions for adjournment: requests to carry over the trial to another time or date

motive: the reason why a person acts or fails to act

multilateral: regarding a treaty in international law, agreed to by three or more nations

N

National Policy: a plan of action established by Sir John A. Macdonald in 1879 to protect Canadian manufacturers through tariffs

nation-states: countries; territories with specific borders and laws and a centralized government

natural law: (1) unchanging moral principles common to all people, who strive to be good; (2) an observable law relating to things that occur in nature

necessity: a defence that may excuse a person from criminal liability if it can be shown that he or she acted to protect life or limb in a reasonable manner

negligence: a civil action in tort law requiring a plaintiff to establish that the defendant breached the standard of care, which resulted in foreseeable harm or loss to the plaintiff

neurophysiological theorists: people who subscribe to the view that certain neurological dysfunctions and genetic defects are connected to some types of criminal behaviour

non-governmental organizations (NGOs): non-profit organizations that are independent of governments and have specific goals (e.g., protecting the environment, safeguarding human rights)

North American Free Trade Agreement **(NAFTA):** a trade agreement among Canada, the United States, and Mexico, implemented in 1994, to promote trade among the three countries by lessening or abolishing tariffs and other trade barriers on many goods and services

North Atlantic Treaty Organization (NATO): an alliance providing for mutual defence and collective security involving the United States, Great Britain, France, Canada, Belgium, Holland, Luxembourg, Italy, Portugal, Norway, Denmark, and Iceland

nuisance: a civil action taken against a defendant when there has been an unreasonable interference with the use and enjoyment of property

O

obiter dictum: an opinion that is unnecessary for the decision of the case; a "by the way" statement made by the judge that may be introduced by way of illustration

objective standard: a measure of comparison with what a reasonable person would do, which is used to determine whether an accused ought to have been able to foresee the consequences of his or her actions

oligarchy: a government in which the authority to rule rests in the hands of a few individuals (Generally, it was assumed that only those born into the upper class were entitled to rule.)

orders-in-council: regulations or commands issued by the Cabinet that are broader in scope than statutes and whose details are often written in separate legal documents

ownership: the exclusive right of possession of a property, title, or thing

P

parity: a principle of sentencing that allows a judge to consider sentences imposed on similar offenders committing similar offences in similar circumstances

parliamentary style debating: a formal style of debating, similar to that used in the House of Commons, in which points of order, personal privilege, and heckling are allowed

parole: a form of release, subject to conditions, into the community for offenders after they have served part of their sentence

patent: a grant or right to exclude others from making, using, or selling one's invention

patriate: to bring legislation under the legal authority of the nation to which it applies (e.g., the Canadian Constitution was patriated from the United Kingdom to Canada)

pay equity: a program designed to remedy pay inequalities for women by allowing a comparison of the value of jobs traditionally done by women with jobs traditionally done by men

peremptory challenge: an objection made by a Crown or defence lawyer to remove a prospective juror without a specific reason being given

perjury: in criminal law, a formal charge laid against an individual for making a false statement under oath

persuasive value: a means of describing court decisions that are not legally binding but can be used for guidance or influence

physical evidence: material evidence used to prove facts relating to a crime (e.g., weapons, bodily fluids, fingerprint impressions)

picket duty: the process whereby strikers carry picket signs and walk outside their place of employment to publicize their strike and discourage others from entering

pith and substance: the overriding purpose or intent of the law, which must be determined when it covers two identifiable powers of a federal and provincial nature

plaintiff: (1) the person in a civil suit who initially brings the action before the court; (2) a defendant who brings a counterclaim

plea bargaining: the negotiation between the Crown and the defence whereby the Crown agrees to a lesser charge or to recommend a lighter penalty in return for a guilty plea by the accused; *see also* **resolution discussion**

political asylum: the protection given by one country to refugees from another country

polluter-pays principle: an environmental principle, contained in Canadian legislation, requiring that the costs of restoring the environment be directed toward those responsible for pollution

pollution prevention: an environmental principle requiring that actions be guided by the desire to avoid or minimize pollution, thus reducing health risks and harm to the environment

polygamy: the criminal offence of having several husbands or wives at the same time

positive law: laws that are enacted and adopted by government (Positive law supporters agree that positive law may or may not be based on the principles of natural law.)

positivist: focused on biological and psychological factors to explain criminal behaviour

power: the right, ability, or authority to do something, which may be achieved through legal or illegal means

precautionary principle: an environmental principle, often used in international law, that enables action to be taken to restrict or limit an activity prior to having actual proof of harm when a threat of serious harm or damage exists

precedent: a rule developed in one case and followed in subsequent similar cases

prima facie **case:** from a Latin term meaning "first face or impression," a case in which something is presumed to be true unless or until it is disproved by evidence

primary sources: original sources of law, such as customs and conventions, religious doctrines, and social and philosophical views, that have been influential in shaping substantive law

principles of fundamental justice: the freedoms and democratic rights guaranteed in the Canadian *Charter*

private law: the law that involves disputes between individual citizens and/or private entities such as corporations; *see also* **civil law**

probation: a sentencing option that allows offenders to live in the community subject to conditions (e.g., being of good behaviour)

procedural law: the process by which law is enforced, including the collection of evidence, the enforcement of rights, and the formal steps to be taken in any legal action

promise to appear: a judicial release procedure allowing an accused to sign a document guaranteeing he or she will show up in court

property law: the branch of law dealing with the rights or interest associated with the ownership of property such as a home, cottage, or car

proportionality: a fundamental principle of sentencing that allows the judge to weigh the seriousness of the offence when selecting an appropriate sentence

proportionality test: a test used to determine whether the limitation of rights under s. 1 of the *Charter* is justifiable

protectionist policies: courses of action that shield domestic products from international competition and inhibit the growth of international trade

protocols: formal agreements between two or more sovereign states; *see also* **acts**, **conventions**, **covenants**, and **treaties**

provocation: a defence that reduces the charge of murder to manslaughter if it can be proven that the accused acted in the heat of passion and was sufficiently provoked such that any reasonable person may have reacted

public law: the law that regulates the relationship between the state and the individual; constitutional, administrative and criminal law are all branches of public law

Q

quasi-criminal offences: violations that are enforced by the courts and may result in substantial penalties but are not "crimes" (e.g., failure to wear a seat belt, speeding, drinking under age)

R

rapid deployment force: squadrons of troops that can be quickly sent to areas of conflict anywhere in the world when needed

ratification: the act of officially approving and passing a bill, treaty, collective agreement, or other legal agreement in a formal legal or political process

ratified: regarding a contract, formally approved or authorized

ratio decidendi: a Latin term meaning "reason for the decision," referring to that part of the judges' decision that provides the legal reasoning for the judgment

rational choice theory: many criminals carefully calculate the costs and benefits of engaging in criminal activity

rational connection: a part of the proportionality test to determine whether there is a reasoned connection between the limitation of rights and the objective of the law

reading down: in constitutional law, narrowing the interpretation given to legislation in order to prevent it from being declared unconstitutional (done by a judge)

reading in: in constitutional law, inserting a term that had not been present in the actual legislation in order to prevent the legislation from being declared unconstitutional (done by a judge)

reasonable doubt: the level of uncertainty beyond which proof must be established in a criminal trial

reciprocity: the mutual exchange of privileges

recklessness: behaviour that is careless and without regard for the consequences

recognizance: a judicial release procedure allowing an accused to make a written promise to appear in court or pay a sum of money for failing to do so

redress: a remedy for injury or loss (e.g., damages for pain and suffering)

reference: the submission of a significant legal question (e.g., one relating to the constitutionality of a law) to the Supreme Court for consideration

referendum: the process of referring a political or policy question to the electorate for a direct vote

referendum process: the process of referring an issue to the electorate for approval or rejection (e.g., in Québec in 1980 and 1995, the process was used to consider the issue of Québec's sovereignty)

refugees: people who have escaped from their homeland due to persecution or justifiable fear of persecution based on their religion, nationality, political opinion, or membership in a particular social group

rehabilitation: an objective of sentencing that provides for the treatment or correction of the offender

relevance: the relation to the matter in question (Lawyers may object to questions that are irrelevant.)

religion: a belief system that ascribes to the existence of superior beings who exercise power and control over humans by imposing rules of conduct and future rewards and punishments

reparations: payments of money as compensation for harm or injury; compensations for war damage incurred during war paid by defeated countries to victorious countries

repealed: regarding an existing law, revoked or cancelled by the enactment of a statute that declares the former law to be no longer in force

res judicata: a Latin term meaning "the thing decided" referring to the fact that an issue in dispute that has previously been decided cannot be litigated again

residual power: the authority of the federal government to deal with any issue not specifically designated as being under the authority of a province or listed anywhere in ss. 91, 92, or 93 of the *Constitution Act, 1867*

resolution discussion: negotiation between the Crown and the defence whereby the Crown agrees to a lesser charge or to recommend a lighter penalty in exchange for a guilty plea by the accused; *see also* **plea bargaining**

respondent: the person (or the Crown in a criminal case) against whom an appeal is being launched

restitution: a sentencing option whereby a judge orders the offender to compensate the victim for loss or harm done

restitutive justice: the concept that true justice is concerned with more than simply the punishment of offenders; it strives to meet victims' needs (e.g., assistance with medical care, counselling, rehabilitation)

restorative justice: the concept that an offender is required to restore or re-establish justice by recognizing and accepting responsibility for his or her actions and by returning the victim or the community, as much as possible, to the original state prior to the offence

restraint: a principle of sentencing that allows judges to consider options other than imprisonment when imposing a sentence

retributive justice: the theory that every crime demands an equal payment or that the punishment should fit the crime

reverse onus provision: a shift of responsibility in a criminal case such that the defence must prove aspects of the case rather than the Crown

right: (1) justice; (2) a power, privilege, or demand that the state is obligated or has a duty to provide; (3) in constitutional law, can be classified as a natural, civil, or political right

royal court system: a court system set up by the king of England that was initially used to collect taxes and handle civil matters

rule of law: the principle that the government must follow the law that it makes, that no one is exempt from the law and that it applies equally to all, and that no action can be taken unless authorized by law or a legal principle

rule of precedent: the principle of following legal rules established in previous court cases if the case is the same or similar; *see also* **stare decisis**

rulings: court decisions

S

safe haven: a neutral territory established to provide protection for people

sanction: a disciplinary action imposed by a court (e.g., imprisonment, a fine, a conditional sentence), restriction, limitation, suspension, or termination of normal privilege; may be used in labour or international disputes and by the legal system

search warrant: a formal court document authorizing a person to enter a building or place to search for and seize evidence

secondary sources: laws that have been written down and are legally binding (e.g., our Constitution, legal statutes, common law)

secular: non-spiritual or non-religious

secured: closed off to ensure that unauthorized people cannot enter a crime scene and that evidence inside the scene is not tampered with

self-defence: a justification for an alleged criminal act whereby an accused had the necessary *mens rea* and was supposedly defending himself or herself, property, or others

sentencing circles: a system of restorative justice, rooted in Aboriginal cultures, whereby the community helps to determine an appropriate sentence for an offender who is willing to participate and accept responsibility for his or her actions

signatories: in international law, the parties or countries who have signed an agreement or treaty

social conflict theories: hypotheses arguing that criminal behaviour is more likely in a capitalist society because of increased competition for scarce resources and wealth

socialization theory: the idea that nurture is more influential in criminal behaviour than nature (genetics)

sovereignty: the supreme authority of a nation-state to impose its power on its subjects within its defined boundaries, including the drafting and enforcement of laws

sovereignty association: the mandate of the Parti Québécois advocating Québec's independence while maintaining political and economic ties with Canada

space law: the body of law that applies to outer space and governs space-related activities

speciality: the principle that an accused will be charged with only the crime that is specified in the request for extradition

specific deterrence: an objective of sentencing that aims to prevent an individual offender from committing a crime again

specific intent: the mental purpose to accomplish a specific act prohibited by law (e.g., murder); the defendant must intend not only to commit the act charged, but also to violate the law

stalking: following or pursuing a person persistently, which is an offence under the *Criminal Code*; *see also* **criminal harassment**

standard of care: in a civil action for negligence, a requirement of proof that the degree of care taken was that of any reasonable person

standing: the right to sue in a legal action

stare decisis: a Latin term meaning "to stand by what has been decided" that refers to the principle of following legal rules established in previous court cases if the case is the same or similar; *see also* **rule of precedent**

state: a nation

statute: a law that is enacted by a government

stay: to stop the proceedings in a trial

stay of proceedings: a judicial remedy used by the courts to stop the action against an accused if the continuance of the action would be considered prejudicial to the accused

stewardship: the responsibility for long-term protection of the environment; the prevention of degradation to the environment

strain theory: the idea that people commit criminal acts out of desperation or frustration at being unable to fulfill wants or needs legally

strict liability: the concept that there can be responsibility without fault; strict liability offences (e.g., illegal dumping of toxic waste) do not require intent and may endanger public welfare

strike: a negotiating strategy whereby employees stop working during contract negotiations with their employer

struck down: (*pres.* strike down) pertaining to a law, remove from the *Criminal Code* and no longer in effect

style of cause: the part of the title of a case referring to the parties involved in a legal action (R. v. the accused in a criminal case, the plaintiff v. the defendant in a civil action)

subjective standard: a measure of comparison whereby the Crown must prove that the accused actually knew the consequences of his or her actions

substantive law: the positive law enacted by government that creates, defines, and regulates the rights and obligations of citizens

subterfuge: a strategy to conceal information

summary conviction offences: criminal violations that are minor in nature (e.g., causing a disturbance), are tried by justices or provincial court judges, and have consequences much less severe than indictable offences

summonses: (*sing.* summons) a court order requiring an accused to appear in court to answer the allegation or to respond to an action against him or her

superior trial courts: the courts of highest jurisdiction in the provinces and territories, which hear virtually all civil law cases and the most serious of criminal offences

Supreme Court of Canada: the final Court of Appeal for all cases from the provincial and territorial courts and the federal courts

surety: an individual who takes the responsibility for ensuring that an accused appears in court and who agrees to pay a sum of money should the accused fail to do so

sustainable development: growth that meets current needs without compromising the ability of future generations to meet their own needs

systemic rape: forced sexual intercourse that is widely practised

T

tariffs: taxes that countries impose on incoming goods to protect domestic industries

tort law: a branch of civil law dealing with the right to compensation for damages resulting from another party's unlawful action or negligence

totality: a principle of sentencing allowing a judge to consider a sentence that is not excessively harsh or long when an offender is ordered to serve a consecutive sentence

trade boycott: a form of protest whereby people refrain from buying or using the goods or services of a particular country or organization in order to pressure it to change its behaviour

trade embargoes: (*sing.* trade embargo) a ban on the trade of all goods or certain goods to a particular nation or nations

transnational crimes: offences that involve more than one nation (e.g., acts of terrorism, hijacking, kidnapping, drug trafficking)

treaties: formal agreements between two or more sovereign states; *see also* **conventions**, **protocols**, **covenants**, and **acts**

trespass: to intentionally enter onto property without legal authority or consent; this action is prosecuted in a civil court

tribunals: any governmental bodies or official groups involved in dispute resolution, possibly using a court-like structure (e.g., a human rights tribunal dealing with discrimination complaints)

trier of law: the person who rules on how the law is applied to the facts; in an adversarial system, the judge

Twinkie defence: a defence used by the lawyers of Dan White who allegedly suffered from depression as a result of eating junk food, such as Twinkies, causing him to murder his employer and colleague

U

ultra vires: a Latin term meaning "beyond or outside the power" referring to a law that may exceed the power of the courts or the government

undertaking: a judicial release procedure allowing an accused to be released from custody as long as he or she agrees to abide by specified conditions (e.g., not contacting certain people)

undue hardship: in a discrimination case, the negative effect on a business, which the employer must prove, of accommodating the needs of a person by being too costly or producing health or safety risks

uniformity: consistent decisions in similar cases

union shop: a type of workplace in which the employer is free to hire anyone he or she chooses, but the employee must join the union shortly after being hired

unitary state: a country having only one parliament or legislature with the authority to make and pass laws

United Nations: an international organization set up in 1948 to promote peace, in part, by limiting the sovereignty of those nation-states that agreed to membership

United Nations Educational, Scientific, and Cultural Organization (UNESCO): a specialized UN agency that "promotes international co-operation among its…member states and six associated members in the fields of education, science, culture and communication" (UNESCO.org)

utilitarianism: a philosophical theory stating that laws should be based on what is practical and realistic rather than on an idealistic moral view

V

validity: government action that is exercised properly

veto power: the official privilege, given to a specific person or people, to overrule a recommendation if desired

victim impact statement: a declaration made by the victim or the victim's family detailing the harm done to them and the effect of the crime on their life

victim surcharge: a percentage of the fine that an offender is required to pay to the court, which is used for victim services in the province or territory

vigilantism: a system whereby individuals take the law into their own hands and engage in acts of personal revenge for perceived injuries

virtual elimination: the reduction of a substance being released into the environment such that it is hardly measurable

voir dire: the exclusion of the jury from the courtroom while the admissibility of evidence is discussed; often referred to as a "trial within a trial"

W

war crimes: offences that take place during an armed conflict that violate international laws of war

Warsaw Pact: (1) a military alliance of the Eastern European Soviet bloc countries to protect against the perceived threat from the NATO alliance; (2) a treaty of mutual defence and military aid signed by Eastern European Soviet bloc countries; *see also* Warsaw Treaty Organization

Warsaw Treaty Organization: a military alliance of the Eastern European Soviet bloc countries to protect against the perceived threat from the NATO alliance; *see also* Warsaw Pact

wilful blindness: a situation in which the accused suspects a harmful or criminal outcome but chooses to avoid considering the consequences

work-to-rule: a negotiation strategy in which workers follow to the letter the terms of the existing contract

World Trade Organization (WTO): a global organization established in 1995 to supervise and liberalize world trade

writs: written commands or formal orders in the name of the sovereign (e.g., a writ of summons compels a defendant to appear in court to answer charges)

Index

Legal Abbreviations

Case Reporting Series Citations

Courts

C.A.	Court of Appeal
C.Q.	Court of Québec
Ct. J. (Gen. Div.)	Court of Justice General Division
Dist. Ct.	District Court
Div. Ct.	Divisional Court
F.C.A.	Federal Court of Appeal
F.C.T.D.	Federal Court, Trial Division
Gen. Div.	General Division
H.L. (Eng.)	House of Lords (England)
J.C.P.C.	Judicial Committee of the Privy Council (UK)
Ont. CA	Ontario Court of Appeal
Ont. Ct. Gen. Div.	Ontario Court General Division
Prov. Div.	Provincial Division
Q.B.	Court of Queen's Bench
Sup. Ct.	Superior Court
S.C.C.	Supreme Court of Canada
Sup. Ct.	Superior Court
T.C.C.	Tax Court of Canada
Terr. Ct.	Territorial Court

Case Reporting Series

A.C.	Law Reports, Appeal Cases (UK)
Alta. L.R.	Alberta Law Reports
C.C.C.	Canadian Criminal Cases
C.H.R.R.	Canadian Human Rights Reporter
C.L.R.B.R.	Canadian Labour Relations Board Reports
C.R.	Criminal Reports
D.L.R.	Dominion Law Reports
E.R.	English Reports (UK)
ICJ Rep.	International Court of Justice: Reports of Judgments, Advisory Opinions and Orders
L.R.H.L.	Law Reports, English and Irish Appeal Cases
M.V.R.	Motor Vehicle Reports
Nfld. & P.E.I.R.	Newfoundland and Prince Edward Island Reports
O.L.R.	Ontario Law Reports
Q.B.	Queen's Bench Reports (UK)
Q.B.D.	Law Reports, Queen's Bench Division (UK)
S.C.R.	Supreme Court Reports

Jurisdictions

Alta.	Alberta
BC	British Columbia
Can.	Canada
Man.	Manitoba
NB	New Brunswick
NL	Newfoundland and Labrador
NS	Nova Scotia
NU	Nunavut
NWT	Northwest Territories
Ont.	Ontario
PEI	Prince Edward Island
Que.	Québec
Sask.	Saskatchewan
Yuk.	Yukon

Neutral Citation Courts and Tribunals
(a new method of on-line citation)

ABCA	Alberta Court of Appeal
ABPC	Alberta Provincial Court
ABQB	Alberta Court of Queen's Bench
BCCA	British Columbia Court of Appeal
BCPC	Provincial Court of British Columbia
BCSC	Supreme Court of British Columbia
EAB	Environmental Appeal Board
LRB	Labour Relations Board
MBCA	Manitoba Court of Appeal
NBCA	New Brunswick Court of Appeal
NLPC	Newfoundland and Labrador Provincial Court
NSSC	Supreme Court of Nova Scotia
NUCJ	Nunavut Court of Justice
ONCA	Ontario Court of Appeal
ONLRB	Ontario Labour Relations Board
ONSC	Ontario Superior Court of Justice
ONSCDC	Ontario Divisional Court
PESCTD	Supreme Court of Prince Edward Island Trial Division
QCCA	Québec Court of Appeal
QCCS	Québec Superior Court
QCCQ	Court of Québec
SKCA	Saskatchewan Court of Appeal

Case Index

(Landmark Cases in bold)

Photo Credits

t=top; b=bottom; c=centre; l=left; r=right